Sustainability

Business and Investment Implications

World Scientific Series in Health Investment and Financing

Print ISSN: 2591-7315
Online ISSN: 2591-7323

Series Editor: Alexander S. Preker *(Columbia University, USA and Health Investment & Financing Corp, USA)*

Most western developed countries offer universal access to healthcare through mechanisms that provide financial protection against its high cost, either through insurance or government subsidy programs.

In most middle- and low-income countries, financing is often at the center of reforms in the healthcare sector. Success or failure of these reforms can have major impact on the political survival of governments that get involved, and major implications for the dynamics of the healthcare industry and overall economy.

With this series, World Scientific will contribute knowledge about a policy area which is still poorly-understood. The series merges policy and practice, exploring the economic underpinnings of real trends in health investment and financing.

The series will appeal and be accessible to investors, the health insurance industry, healthcare actuaries, business schools with healthcare tracts, healthcare management programs, researchers, graduate students, policy makers and practitioners working in the health sector worldwide.

Vol. 6   *Global Health in Practice: Investing Amidst Pandemics,*
          Denial of Evidence, and Neo-dependency
          by Olusoji Adeyi

Vol. 5   *Sustainability: Business and Investment Implications*
          edited by Diane-Charlotte Simon, Alexander S. Preker and Susan C. Hulton

Vol. 4   *Health Microinsurance: Implementing Universal Health Coverage in*
          the Informal Sector
          by David M. Dror

Vol. 3   *Financing the Education of Health Workers: Gaining A Competitive Edge*
          edited by Alexander S. Preker, Hortenzia Beciu and Eric L. Keuffel

Vol. 2   *Financing Micro Health Insurance: Theory, Methods and Evidence*
          by David M. Dror

Vol. 1   *Financing Universal Access to Healthcare: A Comparative Review of*
          Landmark Legislative Health Reforms in the OECD
          by Alexander S. Preker

More information on this series can also be found at https://www.worldscientific.com/series/wsshif

(Continued at end of book)

World Scientific Series in Health Investment and Financing – Vol. 5

Sustainability

Business and Investment Implications

Diane-Charlotte Simon
Credit Agricole Corporate & Investment Bank, USA

Alexander S. Preker
Columbia University, USA
Commission on Pollution, Health and Development, USA

Susan C. Hulton
SCH Legal Adviser, USA

World Scientific

EW JERSEY · LONDON · SINGAPORE · BEIJING · SHANGHAI · HONG KONG · TAIPEI · CHENNAI · TOKYO

Published by

World Scientific Publishing Co. Pte. Ltd.

5 Toh Tuck Link, Singapore 596224

USA office: 27 Warren Street, Suite 401-402, Hackensack, NJ 07601

UK office: 57 Shelton Street, Covent Garden, London WC2H 9HE

Library of Congress Cataloging-in-Publication Data
Names: Simon, Diane-Charlotte, editor.
Title: Sustainability : business and investment implications /
    Diane-Charlotte Simon, Credit Agricole Corporate & Investment Bank, USA,
    Alexander S. Preker, Columbia University, USA & Commission on Pollution,
    Health Development, USA, Susan C. Hulton, SCH Legal Adviser, USA.
Description: New Jersey : World Scientific, [2024] | Series: World scientific series in health
    investment and financing, 2591-7315 ; volume 5 | Includes bibliographical references and index.
Identifiers: LCCN 2023015057 | ISBN 9789811240911 (hardcover) |
    ISBN 9789811240928 (ebook for institutions) | ISBN 9789811240935 (ebook for individuals)
Subjects: LCSH: Economic development. | Sustainability--Economic aspects. | Investments.
Classification: LCC HD82 .S873 2024 | DDC 338.9--dc23/eng/20230628
LC record available at https://lccn.loc.gov/2023015057

British Library Cataloguing-in-Publication Data
A catalogue record for this book is available from the British Library.

For any available supplementary material, please visit
https://www.worldscientific.com/worldscibooks/10.1142/12385#t=suppl

Desk Editors: Aanand Jayaraman/Geysilla Jean

Typeset by Stallion Press
Email: enquiries@stallionpress.com

Preface

This book provides an overview of the business and investment implications of sustainability. Over the past few decades, the world has witnessed significant improvements in economic development that meet a wide range of human needs. Ensuring that such development takes place in a "sustainable" way is the central focus of many recent social movements and industrial policies.

These trends have created a business environment and investment climate in which there is strong consumer demand for sustainable solutions. And they have led to trillions of dollars in both private investments and public subsidies to providers of solutions that address some of the most pressing negative consequences of unbridled economic development: climate change caused by fossil fuel consumption, loss of access to water, uncontrolled population growth, depletion of both non-renewable resources and renewable resources, pollution, loss of biodiversity, etc. Not surprisingly, many private businesses and investors are attracted to what they perceive as a potentially lucrative and high impact area of the economy, while others see their contributions to sustainability as a social and corporate responsibility.

Economic development with sustainable solutions is, however, a complex field. Both businesses and investors that venture into this area will immediately face a myriad of challenges. These range from dealing with market distortions from government industrial policies, regulations, and subsidies, to pressure from conflicting ideologies, activists, social networks, and powerful industry lobbies on both sides of the ideological divide.

Businesses and financial institutions must first and foremost be "financially sustainable" themselves to survive and to be able to contribute to a more sustainable future. When this is lost sight of, there is a risk of not safeguarding the "bottom line" and bankruptcy. This can have a devastating impact not only on the business and financial institutions themselves but also on the overall economy, pensioners and working-class families who lose their jobs.

Fostering competitive business and investment entities that are not reliant on subsidies, tax credits or distorting legislation for their survival beyond an initial transition period, will ensure that they become and remain financially viable.

The book provides insights for businesses and investors on how to navigate this complex landscape. It describes both opportunities and risks of engagement in the field of sustainability. It is intended as a primer for university business schools and schools of public policy and administration where there has been recent increased interest in the topic but a dearth of comprehensive synthesis. The book is also intended for a broader readership, including thought-leaders, policymakers, regulators, technical specialists, professionals, entrepreneurs, businesses, investors, the press, social media, and the public at large.

The reader is cautioned that there are differing and conflicting opinions and ideologies, and often a paucity of evidence on how best to address the many topics related to sustainability. There is a broad consensus on the "why" — importance of addressing the challenges of sustainable development (ranging from a measured concern to extreme depictions of systemic collapse). There is less consensus on the "what" — prioritization of the issues (ranging from a focus on several pressing concerns to a central focus on the fossil fuel industry and global warming). There is even less consensus on the "how" — the approaches used (ranging from market-driven solutions to more interventionist industrial policies, bias by rating agencies, and pressure on corporate boards by special interest groups using proxy votes). There is little agreement on the "when" — starting-point and timeframe (ranging from gradual transformation to an immediate "call to action"). And there is a lack of consensus on the "to what effect" — does it make any difference (ranging from a focus on clear measurable results to "leaps of faith").

The editors and chapter authors of the book, guided by the lead technical expert and initiator of this volume, Diane-Charlotte Simon, reflect this diversity of views. They all support sustainable solutions to development. Not all, however, support an industrial policy approach and narrow focus on the energy transition rather than an open competitive market-based approach to achieve broader sustainable development.

The specific views that are expressed in the various chapters are the personal views of each of the chapter authors. They do not represent the views of the organizations for which the chapter authors work or that of the individual editors of the book. This range of perspectives adds strength to the volume and avoids dogma.

Alexander S. Preker
Series Editor-in-Chief
World Scientific Series in
Health Investment and Financing

Acknowledgments

The Editors would like to thank the following chapter authors for their contributions to the volume: Robert L. Berridge, Karl Boyd Brooks, R. Daniel Bressler, James Gifford, Peter S. Heller, Laurie Lane-Zucker, Andrea E. McGrath, Alan Miller, Robert Pojasek, Ingmar Schumacher, Jerome Tagger, and Tensie Whelan. Their intellectual input and long experience working in the field were invaluable in writing the book.

The Editors also thank a number of other experts who provided inspiration, advice, support, or peer reviews of various drafts: Nicholas Barr, Alexander Bassen, Philip Clayton, Robert Eccles, Cecile Fruman, Richard Fuller, the late Ralph Warner Harbison, Tessa Hebb, Bruce Kahn, Michael Klein, Cary Krosinsky, Philip J. Landrigan, Oliver Laasch, Florian Lüdeke-Freund, Gina McCarthy, Katherine Ng, Charlotte Peyraud, Asheen Phansey, Matthew Phillip Johnson, Janez Potonick, Eva Primmer, Mary Therese Winifred Robinson, Marcelo Selowsky, Mathy Stanislaus, Stacy Swann, Stephen Viederman, and Aaron Yoon.

The Editors of this volume would like to thank Nisha Das and Ranjana Rajan for the opportunity to publish this volume with World Scientific Publishing. They also thank Aanand Jayaraman and Nandha Kumar Krishnan on the production team, Lee Hooi Yean with the marketing team, and Geysilla Jean T. Ortiz, the Desk Editor, for their support in producing the volume.

The support of spouses, family, and friends was greatly appreciated during the long process of writing, editing, and publishing the volume.

The book is dedicated to the memory of the late Ali Iz and the late Carter Bales, Founding Partners at NewWorld Capital.

Contents

Preface		v
Acknowledgments		ix
List of Figures		xv
List of Tables		xvii
Abbreviations and Acronyms		xix
Summary of Chapter Abstracts		xxv
About the Editors		xliii
About the Contributors		li
Chapter 1	Background and Context *Diane-Charlotte Simon*	1
Chapter 2	Science and Challenges of Sustainability *R. Daniel Bressler*	9
Part I	**Business Implications**	**39**
Chapter 3	Business and Sustainability *Diane-Charlotte Simon and Laurie Lane-Zucker*	41

Chapter 4   Entrepreneurship and Sustainability   81
             Andrea E. McGrath and Laurie Lane-Zucker

Chapter 5   Corporate Sustainability and Financial Performance   113
             Diane-Charlotte Simon

Chapter 6   The Financial Case for Embedding Sustainability
             Core into Business Strategy   155
             Tensie Whelan

Chapter 7   Risk Management and Sustainability   171
             Robert Pojasek

Part II   Investment Implications   **193**

Chapter 8   Introduction to Sustainable Finance & Investing   195
             Diane-Charlotte Simon

Chapter 9   Building a Sustainable Portfolio   241
             Diane-Charlotte Simon

Chapter 10   Impact Investing   265
             James Gifford and Jerome Tagger

Chapter 11   Shareholder Engagement   287
             James Gifford and Robert L. Berridge

Part III   Environmental Implications   **303**

Chapter 12   Environmentally Sustainable Businesses,
             Energy Transition, and Climate Finance   305
             Diane-Charlotte Simon

Chapter 13   Business and Financial Implications of
             Climate Change   335
             Alan S. Miller

Part IV   Policy Implications   **385**

Chapter 14   Market Imperfections: Internalizing the Externalities   387
             Ingmar Schumacher

Chapter 15   Environmental Policies, Laws, and Regulations   411
             Karl Boyd Brooks and Diane-Charlotte Simon

Chapter 16   Climate Change Adaptation, the Role of the State,
             and Fiscality   439
             Peter S. Heller

Chapter 17   Macro-economic Implications of Sustainability   481
             Alexander S. Preker and Susan C. Hulton

Afterword: Pitfalls of Industrial Policy   521

Glossary A: Sustainability Terms   533

Glossary B: Business and Investment Terms   549

Index   571

List of Figures

Figure 2.1.	The Depletion of the Aral Sea	19
Figure 2.2.	The Depletion of Lake Mead	20
Figure 2.3.	The United Nations' 17 Sustainable Development Goals	29
Figure 3.1.	Double Materiality	52
Figure 3.2.	Materialities	53
Figure 3.3.	Main Financial and Sustainability Disclosure Frameworks	54
Figure 3.4.	Growth in Global Sustainability Reporting Rates	56
Figure 3.5.	Sustainability Reporting Rates by Region	57
Figure 3.6.	Sustainability Reporting Rates by Subregion	57
Figure 3.7.	The Three Layers of CSR	64
Figure 3.8.	The Stakeholders	67
Figure 3.9.	Stakeholder Theory vs. CSR	68
Figure 5.1.	The Value Driver Model	146
Figure 6.1.	Components of S&P 500 Market Value	159
Figure 6.2.	Sustainability Drivers of Financial Performance and Competitive Advantage	163
Figure 7.1.	The Three Pillars of ISO 31000 Risk Management	177
Figure 7.2.	ISO Harmonized High-Level Structure Clauses	178
Figure 7.3.	Some ISO Documents Involving Sustainability and CSR	181

Figure 8.1.   Assets Employing Sustainable Investment
               Strategies 2012–2020 (in Billion USD)   214
Figure 8.2.   Assets Employing Sustainable Investment
               Strategies by Region in 2020 (in %)   215
Figure 8.3.   Global Assets Allocation per Sustainable Strategy
               in 2020   218
Figure 8.4.   Sustainable Investment Strategies by Region
               in 2020 (in %)   219
Figure 9.1.   The Sustainable Debt Market Issuance Volume
               Over the 2008–2021 Period (in %)   250
Figure 10.1.   Impact of Enterprises   279
Figure 10.2.   Investor Contribution   282
Figure 12.1.   The Circular Economy   310
Figure 12.2.   Overview of GHG Protocol Scopes and Emissions
               across the Value Chain   318
Figure 12.3.   Global Investment in the Deployment of Existing
               Energy Transition Technologies   328
Figure 12.4.   Global Investment in Energy Transition by Region   329
Figure 13.1.   World CO_2 Emissions from Fossil Fuel
               Combustion and Global Atmospheric
               Concentrations CO_2 (1751–2018)   339
Figure 13.2.   Global GHG Emissions by Sector, End Use,
               and Gas in 2019   340
Figure 13.3.   GHG Emissions by Country and Sector in 2019   343
Figure 13.4. CO_2 Emissions by Capita in 2018   343
Figure 17.1.   Interaction between Macro-Economic/Financial
               Factors and Sustainability   486
Figure 17.2.   Total Value of Natural Resources in Top 10
               Countries (in Billion USD, 2021)   487
Figure 17.3.   Role of Biodiversity in Providing Critical Resource
               for Industries   489
Figure 17.4.   Physical and Transition Risks with Related
               Macro-economic Linkages   491

List of Tables

Table 3.1.	Selected ESG Issues	62
Table 4.1.	Types of Sustainability-Oriented Entrepreneurship	97
Table 5.1.	Moderators to Sustainability Impact on Financial Performance	136
Table 5.2.	SASB Materiality Map	137
Table 5.3.	The Financial Impact of Sustainability Initiatives Over Time	142
Table 5.4.	Moderators at the Initiatives Level	144
Table 8.1.	Assets Considering Sustainability Relative to Total Managed Assets Over 2012–2020 Period (in Billion USD)	215
Table 8.2.	Assets Considering Sustainability by Region Over 2012–2020 Period (in Billion USD)	216
Table 8.3.	Assets Allocation per Sustainable Strategy Across Regions 2012–2020 (in Billion USD)	219
Table 9.1.	Sustainable Products across Asset Classes	244
Table 9.2.	Eligible Projects and Categories, and Examples of Applications under the Green, Social, and Sustainable Bond ICMA Frameworks	251
Table 12.1.	Major GHG, Impact, and Sources	314
Table 12.2.	Global GHG Emissions and Sector Contribution	316

Table 12.3.   Energy Transition Investments by Subsectors
              and Stage (in Billion USD)   324
Table 15.1.   Global Environmental Agreements   421
Table 15.2.   Uses of Economic Incentives   434
Table 17.1.   Linkages between Macro-economic Risks
              and Sustainability   494
Table 17.2.   Effects of Competition on Macro-economic
              Performance and Sustainability   510

Abbreviations and Acronyms

ABCP	Asset-Backed Commercial Paper
AIGCC	Asia Investor Group on Climate Change
APLMA	Asia Pacific Loan Market Association
AUM	Assets Under Management
BCG	Boston Consulting Group
BMC	Business Model Canvas
BNEF	Bloomberg New Energy Finance
CAGR	Compound Annual Growth Rate
CAPM	Capital Asset Pricing Model
CDP	Carbon Disclosure Project
CDSB	Climate Disclosure Standard Board
CED	Committee for Economic Development
CEO	Chief Executive Officer
CFP	Corporate Financial Performance
COP	Conference of the Parties
CRO	Chief Risk Officers
CSP	Corporate Sustainability Performance
CSR	Corporate Social Responsibility
CSRD	Corporate Sustainability Reporting Directive
DJSI	Dow Jones Sustainability Index
DNSH	Do No Significant Harm
EDGAR	Electronic Data Gathering, Analysis, and Retrieval
EFRAG	European Financial Reporting Advisory Group

EPA	Environmental Protection Agency
ERISA	Employee Retirement Income Security Act of 1974
ERM	Enterprise Risk Management
ESG	Environmental, Social, and Governance (also Environmental, Social, and Corporate Governance)
€STR	Euro Short-Term Rate
EU	European Union
EUROSIF	European Sustainable Investment Forum
ETF	Exchange-Traded Funds
DFI	Development Finance Institutions
GAAP	Generally Accepted Accounting Principles
GBP	Green Bonds Principles
GEM	Global Entrepreneurship Monitor
GHG	Greenhouse Gases
GIIN	Global Impact Investor Network
GLP	Green Loan Principles
GMO	Genetically Modified Organism
GSIA	Global Sustainable Investment Alliance
GSIR	Global Sustainable Investment Review
GRI	Global Reporting Initiative
GW	Gigawatt
HR	Human Resources
ICE	Intercontinental Exchange
ICMA	International Capital Market Association
IEA	International Energy Association
IEC	International Electrotechnical Commission
IFC	International Finance Corporation
IFRS	International Financial Reporting Standards
IGCC	Investor Group on Climate Change
IIRC	International Integrated Reporting Council
IMF	International Monetary Fund
IPO	Initial Public Offering
IPPC	International Panel on Climate Change
IRIS	Impact Reporting Investment Standards
IRR	Internal Rate of Return

IRS	Internal Revenue Service
ISO	International Organization for Standardization
ISS	Institutional Shareholder Services
ISSB	International Sustainability Standards Board
JOBS	Jumpstart Our Business Startups Act
KPI(s)	Key Performance Indicator(s)
LCOE	Leveraged Cost of Electricity
LIBOR	London Interbank Offered Rate
LLC(s)	Limited Liability Companies
LMA	Loan Market Association
LSTA	Loan Syndications & Trading Association
MBS	Mortgage-Backed Securities
MDGs	Millennium Development Goals
MVP	Minimum Viable Product
NAV	Net Asset Value
NFRD	Non-Financial Reporting Directive
NGO(s)	Non-Governmental Organizations
NPV	Net Present Value
NYSE	New York Stock Exchange
OECD	The Organization for Economic Cooperation and Development
OMS	Operating Management Systems
PBC	Public Benefit Corporation
PDCA	Plan-Do-Check-Act
PE	Private Equity
PESTEL	Political, Environmental, Social, Technological, Environmental, and Legal
PRI	Principles for Responsible Investment
PV	Photovoltaic
REIS	Real Estate Investment Trusts
ROI	Return on Investment
ROSI	Return on Sustainable Investment
SASB	Sustainable Accounting Standards Board
SBP	Social Bonds Principles
SDGs	Sustainable Development Goals

SEA	Sustainable Entrepreneurship Awards
SEC	United States Securities and Exchange Commission
SFDR	Sustainable Finance Disclosure Regulation
SIFMA	Securities Industry and Financial Markets Association
SLBP	Sustainability-Linked Bond Principles
SLLP	Sustainability-Linked Loan Principles
SLP	Social Loan Principles
SME(s)	Small and Medium-Sized Enterprises
SOFR	Secured Overnight Financing Rate
SPAC	Special Purpose Acquisition Company
SRI	Socially Responsible Investing
SROI	Social Return on Investment
SSA	Supra-nationals and Agencies
SSB	Sustainability Standards Board
SSE	Sustainable Stock Exchanges
TCFD	Taskforce on Climate-related Financial Disclosure
TECOP	Technological, Economic, Cultural, Organizational, and Political
TW	Terrawatt
UK	United Kingdom
UN	United Nations
UNCTAD	United Nations Conference on Trade and Development
UNEP	United Nations Environment Programme
UNEPFI	United Nations Environment Programme Finance Initiative
UNFCCC	United Nations Framework Convention on Climate Change
UN PRI	United Nations-supported Principles for Responsible Investment
US	United States
USD	United States Dollars
USSIF	Forum for Sustainable and Responsible Investment
VC	Venture Capital

WBCSD	World Business Council for Sustainable Development
WRI	World Resources Institute
WMO	World Meteorological Organization

Summary of Chapter Abstracts

The following Summary of Chapter Abstracts provides a brief overview of the key messages and conclusions from each chapter in the book.

The abstracts follow the chapter order in the book and are organized in the following way:

Introductory Section
Part I - Business Implications
Part II - Investment Implications
PART III - Environmental Implications
PART IV - Policy Implications

The Chapter Abstract for Chapter 1 provides an overview and a road map on how the volume is organized. The Chapter Abstract for Chapter 2 sets out the underlying scientific basis for the rest of the volume.

The Chapter Abstracts under Part I on Business Implications (Chapters 3–7) include brief summaries of the business landscape, the main elements of entrepreneurship, the links between the financial performance of a company and its commitment to a corporate sustainability agenda, how to embed sustainability in a company's business strategy, and monitoring corporate sustainability.

The Chapter Abstracts under Part II of the book on Investment Implications (Chapters 8–11) include brief summaries of the meaning of sustainable finance and investing, a range of implementation strategies across different investment instruments, the meaning of impact investing, and stakeholder engagement.

The Chapter Abstracts under Part III of the book on Environmental Implications (Chapters 12–13) include brief summaries of the financing of environmental sustainability and action to address climate change.

The Chapter Abstracts under Part IV of the book on Policy Implications (Chapters 14–17) include brief summaries of public policy responses to market failure, such as information asymmetry or externalities; environmental policies, laws, and regulations; fiscal implications; and macroeconomic implications.

The Afterword highlights some of the pitfalls of using industrial policy to address the various sustainability challenges discussed in the book.

Chapter 1. Background and Context — Diane-Charlotte Simon

This book explores the business and investment implications of sustainability. The heightened attention to sustainability presents both opportunities and risks for companies and investors. There are immense opportunities for companies that understand how to identify, measure, manage and mitigate accompanying risks. New regulations, subsidies and other environmentally friendly policies provide an opportunity for companies that are skilled at taking advantage of such conditions. Smart managers understand that a company's financial success is influenced by sustainability. If this additional information is considered when making investment and resource allocation decisions it can result in enhanced resilience and long-term profitability of the company. Ultimately it is the long-lasting, value creating, and lucrative business practices that transform a company into a market leader which transforms the business and investment environment overtime. One hundred years ago the Model T Ford became the market leader for consumer affordable cars. Today Tesla has become the leader in the transition from gasoline and diesel to electric cars. At the same time, there is a significant material risk to inexperienced business and investors that get involved in this highly regulated and politically charged area of the economy but are not skilled in navigating this complex landscape. The authors demonstrate that companies and investors can successfully navigate the challenges of sustainability, mitigating risks and seizing opportunities.

Chapter 2. Science and Challenges of Sustainability — R. Daniel Bressler

This chapter sets the scene for the rest of the volume by providing the scientific basis for the business and investment implications of sustainability. The chapter describes how over the past few hundred years, and especially over the past few decades, the world has witnessed significant economic development and made great progress in meeting human needs. Unfortunately, this economic development has come with significant consequences in terms of climate change, access to water, population growth, depletion of resources, pollution, loss of biodiversity, poverty, inequity, and diseases. Continuation of current trends has been deemed by many as unsustainable. The chapter defines *"sustainable development"* as the study of how to eliminate and mitigate these challenges so that the progress enjoyed by many parts of the world can be extended to all parts of the world and sustained far into the future. Finally, it presents the UN Sustainable Development Goals, which have been widely adopted by the international community and the public sector. More recently, many private businesses and investors have also started to embrace *"sustainability"* in their underlying business models. The chapter concludes that without significant changes, the ecological, environmental, and climatic resilience that have supported economic development in the past may not hold up into the future.

Part I. Business Implications

Chapter 3. Business and Sustainability — Diane-Charlotte Simon and Laurie Lane-Zucker

This chapter provides a framework for Part I on the Business Implications of sustainability. First, the chapter reviews the business landscape of sustainability and how various business models of different companies impact the broad concept of sustainability as discussed in this book. Second, it presents the two main schools of thought around the notion of *materiality* which determine the scope of sustainability disclosure. One perspective focuses on the "outside-in": how sustainability impacts a business and its financial performance (*financial materiality*). A second perspective focuses on the "inside-out": how a business impacts the environment, people, and society (*sustainability impacts* also called *impact materiality*). Combined, they form what is referred to as the *double materiality* of sustainability. The chapter explores the broad spectrum of conceptual frameworks at the intersection of sustainability and business. These concepts can range from *Corporate Social Responsibility (CSR)* to *Environmental, Social, and Governance (ESG)*. The latter, after becoming investors' main sustainable investing strategy (see Chapter 8), has become the primary approach to corporate sustainability. The chapter discusses ESG data and presents the main sustainability disclosure frameworks which are critical to investors to assess risks, opportunities, and sustainability impacts so as to price financial instruments. Lastly, the chapter introduces the concept of an *impact economy* and concludes with a discussion on the changes that could be made to address sustainability. The chapter concludes that to become truly sustainable, businesses must consider their 360° impact on society — from their business model to the human and environmental impacts of their products and services.

Chapter 4. Entrepreneurship and Sustainability — Andrea E. McGrath and Laurie Lane-Zucker

This chapter defines the main elements of entrepreneurship — stages of development, sources of funding, and approaches of launch and development. It explores the emergence and expansion of entrepreneurs that are tackling a diversity of environmental, social, and governance challenges and some of their differentiating characteristics. While companies of all sizes have been addressing numerous sustainability challenges for years, the adoption of the Sustainable Development Goals (SDGs) by 193 countries in 2015 sparked a global call to action for all stakeholders to work toward achieving the 17 ambitious targets by 2030. Limited progress and wide funding gaps now highlight the need for innovative business models, investing strategies, and even — as some might argue — a completely new way of doing business. While much of this book focuses on how mainstream businesses and investors are adapting to the challenges and opportunities presented by the sustainability agenda, the authors argue that entrepreneurs are also playing a critical role. While tackling sustainable development, entrepreneurs are creating new products and services, identifying and capturing new customers and markets, creating and demonstrating new business models, and helping to move toward a more sustainable economy. The chapter highlights how key global developments are helping to support the market demand for these entrepreneurs. It concludes that a supportive ecosystem, informed by systems thinking, is increasingly critical to launch and develop these entrepreneurs and the economy that holds and fosters them.

Chapter 5. Corporate Sustainability and Financial Performance — Diane-Charlotte Simon

This chapter looks at the links between financial performance of companies and their commitment to a corporate sustainability agenda. The chapter challenges the traditional view that there is a trade-off between environmental concerns and financial performance, and that corporate sustainability conflicts with shareholder wealth maximization. Instead, the chapter highlights a body of research that suggests companies with strong sustainability focus can outperform comparable companies with poor sustainability performance. The chapter once again explores the impacts (*materiality)* of corporate sustainability and the ESG factors, first introduced in Chapter 3, with a particular focus on the environment. The chapter also provides an overview of sustainability-related risks and opportunities for business and investment. The chapter then analyzes the impact that sustainability can have on companies' financial performance, considering both profitability and market valuation indicators. It reviews key methodological indicators of financial performance and highlights how sustainability can have an impact on each of them. These indicators involve revenues (demand, innovation, etc.), costs (risks, productivity, savings, cost of capital, etc.), and market performance (share price, market risk, impact on investors, and access to investors) as well as competitiveness, intangible assets, and reputation. Finally, the chapter investigates how a company can improve its positive financial outcomes from sustainability initiatives. In this respect, the chapter concludes that the financial stakes of corporate sustainability are rising and that there is growing evidence of links to a company's financial performance and investment returns. These links are observed both at the profitability level, with growing demand for sustainable products, and at the market valuation level.

Chapter 6. The Financial Case for Embedding Sustainability Core into Business Strategy —
Tensie Whelan

This chapter makes a financial case for embedding sustainability central to a company's business strategy. A growing number of studies are finding a strong correlation between positive ESG performance and better stock and operational performance as well as lower cost of capital. However, it is challenging to demonstrate causality, partially because most firms do not have metrics and accounting systems in place to assess the comprehensive return on sustainability investment (ROSI). The chapter notes that most of the Fortune 500 firms have sustainability strategies and report on ESG issues. Corporate managers across many industries — from manufacturing to mining, from apparel to electronics — are facing a wide range of ESG issues. These issues are highlighted by the radical transparency that social media provides, the growing expectation by Millennials across the world that corporations be good citizens, and the abdication by government of their responsibility of taking care of societal goods. The chapter presents various initiatives, which have begun to tackle this problem. Some have found that cost savings, revenue enhancement, and risk reduction accompany positive ESG/sustainability performance. This chapter more closely examines the methodology developed by the NYU Stern Center for Sustainable Business, along with its first case study. The chapter concludes that corporate commitments to sustainable policies and practices have outstripped their ability to track the financial impact of those practices. In some cases, establishing the financial case may not be necessary or may even be unnecessarily complex. Markets increasingly force corporate managers to increase margins by reducing costs. Companies need to be better able to demonstrate the financial case for sustainability.

Chapter 7. Risk Management and Sustainability — Robert Pojasek

This chapter proposes different approaches to monitor corporate sustainability, which go beyond unstructured standalone CSR and sustainability programs. Historically, corporate sustainability has largely consisted in "stand-alone" sustainability programs that use publicly stated sustainability goals, independent sustainability initiatives, and sustainability reports. There has been little effort on the part of large corporations to stray from this model. The chapter focuses on companies' integration of sustainability through the lens of risk management with the support of standards and operating management systems (OMS). First, the chapter examines the foundations of risk management and a systematic method to handle sustainability risks through the International Organization for Standardization (ISO) guidelines. It then explores the principles, framework, and processes to implement a risk management practice in accordance with the ISO 31000:2018 standard. It demonstrates how to integrate all the management systems that contribute to sustainable development into a single sustainable organizational model through the high-level structure of ISO management system standards presented in this chapter. After introducing the fundamentals of ISO standards and how they function, the chapter focuses on the standards dedicated to Sustainability and CSR. The chapter presents a "plan–do–check–act" (PDCA) model, which is used for the control and continuous improvement of processes and products within an organization and can be employed for corporate sustainability. The chapter concludes that a key to success is to replace old unstructured sustainability programs with a new unique structured sustainability program that works best for each organization.

Part II. Investment Implications

Chapter 8. Introduction to Sustainable Finance and Investing — Diane-Charlotte Simon

This chapter introduces Part II on Investment Implications of sustainability and other topics of sustainable finance. The chapter begins with an introduction to finance and investing. In layman's terms, finance is defined as an instrument to support the payment of everyday expenses for individuals (personal finance), companies (corporate finance), or governments (public/government finance). From this perspective, finance provides access to things that could not otherwise be purchased with cash at hand. Personal finance can assist an individual through a student loan, a consumer loan, or a mortgage to buy a house. Corporate finance can provide a company with resources for its operations or its growth to develop new products or acquire new equipment and other companies. The financial instruments used will depend on the company's needs and the stage of its life cycle. Public/government finance can provide government resources to pay sovereign debt, country budgets (for education, social security, public health, national defense, etc.), and public servants' salaries and pensions. The chapter then presents a brief history of the field of sustainable finance and describes various sustainable investment strategies ranging from risk management to mission-driven investments. It tries to bring clarity to what some call an "alphabet soup" of acronyms (MDGs, SDGs, SRIs, ESGs, etc.). The chapter notes several important challenges in sustainable finance that still need to be addressed such as the lack of a shared language and rigor in the use of terminology as well as the risk of "greenwashing" and mislabeling that fails to capture sustainability impact. The chapter concludes with a discussion on investor profiles and the relationship between sustainable investment strategies, risk, return, and impacts.

Chapter 9. Building a Sustainable Portfolio —
Diane-Charlotte Simon

This chapter complements the previous chapter on sustainable finance and investing, by looking in more detail at a range of implementation strategies across the main financial instruments. The chapter begins with an introduction to the main asset classes present in the financial market (bonds, loans, equity, mutual funds, and exchange-traded-funds (ETFs)). The chapter distinguishes between debt and equity instruments. Since their creation in 2007, more than $4 trillion of sustainable debt instruments have been issued. This estimate does not capture several sustainability-related areas that are not specifically classified as sustainable such as renewable energy financing, project finance, capital markets for infrastructure, etc. The chapter highlights the fact that it is now possible to employ investing strategies considering sustainability across nearly all financial products, which in turn makes it possible to build a sustainable portfolio. The chapter also introduces the popular Green, Social, and Sustainable bonds, and loans (sustainable debt with the *Use-of-Proceeds* approach) as well as the Sustainability-linked debt instruments (sustainable debt with the *Objectives* approach). Portfolios can be built either by investors themselves, or with the support of financial advisors. Investors can also purchase diversified pre-built portfolios like ETFs or mutual funds following sustainable investment strategies. However, while the proportion of sustainable products has dramatically increased, it still does not represent most financial assets. Strikingly, in certain regions such as Europe, considering sustainability risks is now mandatory for all financial products. The chapter concludes with an example of a climate change portfolio.

Chapter 10. Impact Investing — James Gifford and Jerome Tagger

This chapter introduces the key concepts, opportunities, and challenges of impact investing, a subset of sustainable finance characterized by the *"intentionality"* of an investment. Impact investing is a term coined by the Rockefeller Foundation in 2007 to describe investments that generate a social and/or environmental impact alongside a financial return. Different organizations use the term "impact investing" to describe different practices. Some investors retain a strict definition, that is, investments that themselves create impact. Other investors use the term interchangeably with sustainable and ESG investing. Yet others define impact investing as investing in companies whose intent is to have impactful products and services — whether or not the investor and their capital contributed to that impact. For the purposes of this chapter, impact investing is defined as an investment strategy that can deliver both financial returns and positive social and environmental outcomes — beyond what would otherwise have occurred had the investment not been made. The chapter lays out why impact investing matters and what sets it apart from other sustainable finance strategies. This type of investment considers factors beyond financial return and includes the double/triple bottom line without necessarily impairing the traditional *"alpha"*, as illustrated in the section on returns-on-investment. Finally, the chapter explores how to report on the impact. The chapter concludes that only a fraction of total investment happening globally qualifies as impact investment. It often excludes the bulk of the development finance, renewable energy, clean tech, sustainable forestry, and the healthcare, education, and other social sectors, where the impact qualification remains inconsistent, either because of lack of intentionality or because of labeling concerns by the investors.

Chapter 11. Shareholder Engagement — James Gifford and Robert L. Berridge

This chapter focuses on shareholder engagement, a subset of sustainable finance dedicated to the unique role that investors can play in influencing a company's strategy in areas of sustainability. Pension funds, mutual funds, foundations, wealth managers, insurance companies, and other institutional investors control most of the capital invested into listed equities globally. Shareholder engagement by US and European pension funds on environmental and social issues is increasing rapidly. The chapter describes a broadening of the mainstream shareholder engagement agenda, from traditional governance and strategic financial issues, to include environmental and social drivers. This is potentially one of the most profound shifts in institutional investment over many years and may significantly increase the role of investors in moving the corporate sector, and ultimately society, toward a more sustainable future. While traditional shareholder activists focus exclusively on the financial performance of individual firms, ESG engagement can also address economywide and systemic sustainability issues. The chapter traces the origins of shareholder engagement and explores its primary strategies and tools. It raises the critical question of whether shareholder engagement works. One convenient mechanism (primarily relevant in the US) that indicates whether shareholder activism has been effective in changing corporate behavior is the number of resolutions withdrawn after successful negotiation in advance of going to a vote. The chapter concludes by emphasizing that although shareholder engagement may not be the highest profile strategy within the sustainable investing space, given recent evidence of its efficacy, its scalability, and its potential for delivering financial returns, its importance should be elevated in the future.

Part III. Environmental Implications

Chapter 12. Environmentally Sustainable Businesses, Energy Transition, and Climate Finance — Diane-Charlotte Simon

This chapter introduces the Environmental Implications of sustainability. It discusses how environmental sustainability has become a critical matter for stakeholders, and also provides a unique opportunity for businesses to enter a potentially lucrative and high impact area of the economy. While presenting risks for businesses and investors, environmental sustainability also presents an opportunity amounting to trillions of dollars for those developing and scaling successful solutions. The chapter highlights how in the past few decades, there have been increased stakeholder expectations for corporate environmental responsibility, which has transformed the business landscape. Consumers, investors, NGOs, and regulators are now pressing companies to account for their environmental impact. The chapter introduces the European Union (EU) Taxonomy for sustainable activities. It presents the concept of a *"circular economy"*, which aims to reduce waste and improve product design to optimize recycling. It explores climate change mitigation for companies, touching on greenhouse gases, net-zero targets, the energy transition, and the critical importance of carbon removal solutions. It then covers adaptation strategies. The chapter concludes by calling attention to the need to develop and scale economically viable carbon capture technologies. It emphasizes that, while necessary, the energy transition alone may not be sufficient to tackle climate change given the long lifespan of carbon dioxide in the atmosphere. Carbon capture and transformation technologies following the *"circular economy"* model, such as mineral carbonation, are particularly promising as they would transform carbon dioxide, a threat, into a valuable resource.

Chapter 13. Business and Financial Implications of Climate Change — Alan S. Miller

This chapter draws attention to the fact that, as temperatures and sea levels rise and extreme weather events become more frequent and intense, climate change has begun to impact business and investments in increasingly diverse ways. Science is also making it possible to attribute these events to climate change and to predict the timing and severity of future events with greater precision and confidence. The magnitude of financial impacts from climate extremes is already becoming significant and much larger damages are on the way. Based on this background, the chapter introduces readers to the many implications of climate change for business and investment, ranging from the direct physical impacts of higher temperatures, sea-level rise, and more intense storms to more indirect risks and opportunities resulting from climate policies, litigation, and good and bad reputational benefits/damages. The chapter highlights new business opportunities for clean energy, climate-resilient infrastructure, and new means of transport requiring investments in the many trillions of dollars, but cautions that the transformation of the global energy system is an enormous challenge that will not be accomplished quickly. The chapter underlines that corporate management must internalize an understanding of climate risks and opportunities to make timely decisions; waiting until after its impacts are realized or certain will often cost much more and limit the range of options. Investors and the financial community, particularly those with long-term obligations and perspectives like pension funds and insurance companies, are beginning to appreciate climate risks and demand greater transparency from their investments, potentially impacting risk calculations among companies. The chapter concludes that the tools to develop business-specific climate change strategies are improving rapidly and becoming widely available.

Part IV. Policy Implications

Chapter 14. Market Imperfections: Internalizing the Externalities — Ingmar Schumacher

This chapter introduces Part IV on Policy Implications of sustainability. It introduces the concept of market imperfections and externalities. It reviews the theoretical economic background and some empirical evidence on the concept of *externalities,* which is key to understanding market imperfections related to sustainability issues (one entity pays while others get the benefit or bear the burden). It highlights the fact that market prices rarely factor in these externalities and that actors producing negative externalities do not always pay for them and that other actors bear the negative consequences (i.e., end up paying for them). The chapter highlights the trend that consumers, producers, and governments are starting to take production and market externalities much more seriously. Consumers more and more buy only products that are labeled organic, as they know that these products contain fewer pesticides that harm them and those that produce these products. Producers and investors understand that corporate social responsibility is not simply a buzzword that attracts consumers but that it does provide a value-added for the company. Employees are more motivated to work if they feel that they are needed and welcomed, and supply chains work more efficiently if every company down the chain gets a fair share. Products produced by motivated employees and manufactured with high-quality materials tend to last longer and are more appealing to consumers. Governments are understanding that they need to be careful in the way they introduce new policies, and they are starting to introduce these in a more subtle way. Some environmentally harmful industries, energy sources, technologies, or processes may become obsolete. The chapter concludes that although corporate social responsibility is the right way, it needs to be supplemented with more consumers who are less price-oriented in their purchase decisions, and it needs to be induced by governments that understand that maximizing the pie also requires dealing with these externalities.

Chapter 15. Environmental Policies, Laws, and Regulations — Karl Boyd Brooks and Diane-Charlotte Simon

This chapter introduces the history and basics of environmental policies, laws, and regulations. It explains why governments regulate actions that affect the environment. While policies outline the intention to act on a topic to achieve certain objectives, they do not carry legal force. Environmental law therefore includes a combination of rulemaking, interpretation, and enforcement. The chapter expands on the concept that rulemaking and law enforcement can take place at different levels which can be driven by geographical scope (international, multi-country, country, state, etc.) or by subject matter (e.g., agricultural, industrial, etc.). It stresses that a hierarchy of laws exists and determines which law has ultimate control or primacy. Given the complexity of environmental issues and the range of adverse impacts, the reader is reminded of the importance of understanding what laws govern and identifying which one has primacy, especially if there is a conflict of laws whereby different laws coexist but are contradictory. The chapter also stresses the importance of understanding in which jurisdiction a law applies and determining which court or institution has the power, right, or authority to interpret and apply the law. The chapter also reviews the forces that shape regulations. Unlike most other types of law that shape business and finance — contract law, labor law, corporate law, etc. — environmental law arouses intense political passions and commands vibrant (though not always accurate) news coverage. The chapter describes how the rules governing air, water, or land pollution, typically include not only a mix of considerations of science, technical feasibility, and economics, but also both explicit and hidden political agendas. The chapter concludes by presenting the main tools of economic regulations ranging from traditional command-and-control approaches to market-based instruments that policymakers can employ.

Chapter 16. Climate Change Adaptation, Role of the State, and Fiscality — Peter S. Heller

This chapter summarizes some of the main fiscal challenges to sustainability arising out of the use of fossil fuels as a predominant source of energy and the related environmental damage from climate change. The chapter argues that countries need to be actively engaged in considering the fiscal and macro-economic implications of the climate change hazards they will confront. The phenomenon of climate change poses significant challenges for analysts seeking to assess a government's long-run financial condition. Looking forward, climate change hazards are likely to increasingly threaten multiple aspects of a country's environment. Governments will necessarily be challenged to support private sector agents in adapting to these hazards. While for most countries the effects of climate change are an exogenous policy threat, considerable uncertainty exists as to the nature and magnitude of the adaptation burdens that will be faced, in part because the trajectory of climate change that will be experienced will to some extent depend on whether global mitigation efforts succeed. The chapter emphasizes that most developing and many emerging market countries will face serious limits in their fiscal capacity to confront these adaptation challenges. The chapter highlights differences in the two main approaches for addressing climate change: *mitigation,* which focuses on reducing greenhouse emissions; and *adaptation,* which focuses on reducing the vulnerability of economic agents to the negative effects of climate change. Existing development strategies now tend to silo the challenge of climate change, only adding to the prospective burdens that will be experienced. The chapter highlights recent initiatives by the International Monetary Fund (IMF) to strengthen its economic policy surveillance in support of member countries' climate change adaptation policies (complementing its support for aggressive mitigation efforts). The chapter concludes that to wait for a decade on this issue until we are clearer on the success of mitigation efforts is to delay policy development and implementation on adaptation that could reduce serious economic and social losses looking forward.

Chapter 17. Macro-economic Implications of Sustainability — Alexander S. Preker and Susan C. Hulton

This chapter demonstrates strong links between the sustainable use of non-renewable and renewable resources, and macro-economic performance. The chapter goes beyond the earlier discussion of factors that contribute to climate change and the narrow focus on the fossil fuel industry to include consideration of a broader range of non-renewable and renewable resources that are an integral part of a sustainable environment. The chapter describes both physical and transition risks. And it highlights relevant linkages that exist between mitigation and/or adaptation strategies and macro-economic performance in terms of gross domestic product (GDP), national wealth, economic growth, inflation, stagnation, deflation, consumer spending, borrowing, employment, unemployment, monetary policy, and fiscal policy. The review indicates that well-planned and well-executed sustainability policies and action plans can confer significant macro-economic benefits. At the same time, it reveals that overzealous and poorly executed mitigation strategies as well as failure to pursue adaptation can damage industrial performance and lead to significant negative macro-economic outcomes in terms of slowing growth, damaging supply chains, contributing to inflation, increasing unemployment, and reducing sectoral competitiveness. The chapter warns about the potentially damaging effect of expanding the environmental (E) sustainability agenda to the social (S) and governance (G) spheres. And it raises doubts about the use of industrial policy to achieve durable industrial transformation. The chapter presents cautionary remarks about several hidden threats to macro-economic performance from overambitious, poorly designed, and badly executed sustainability policies. These threats include pitfalls associated with lack of realism, mission creep in corporate governance, single issue capture, hidden political agendas, greenwashing, whitewashing, and loss of competitiveness. The chapter concludes that if these threats are addressed effectively, "doing business" in this area could possibly provide an attractive commercial opportunity for businesses and investors, while at the same time it might advance the sustainability agenda and contribute to macro-economic performance.

Afterword: Pitfalls of Industrial Policy —
Alexander S. Preker and Susan C. Hulton

The Afterword provides a minority opinion, among the authors that contributed to this book, on the use of industrial policy as a public policy tool for influencing businesses and investors to engage in the sustainable use of non-renewable and renewable resources. The section defines "industrial policy" or "industrial strategy" as any intervention by governments that encourages the growth or strengthening of the economy in general or that causes a shift from one industry to another, by deliberate policies that influence supply, demand, price equilibrium, or the competitive environment of those industries. The section describes how industrial policies are often used to achieve economic objectives such as growth, competitiveness, and strengthening a particular sector. They can also be used to achieve political, security, ideological, and social objectives through sanctions, trade embargoes, and import or export restrictions that favor a specific sector (agriculture, steel, fossil fuels, alternative energy, etc.). The section also describes how industrial policy has had some notable successes in the past when used in large public infrastructure and civic works projects. But it distorts markets, often leads to poor economic outcomes, and rewards companies for their lobbying skills rather than maximizing economic value and return on investment for shareholders. It has had mixed results when used for strategic purposes like sanctions, trade barriers, and other areas where the negative economic impact on the countries imposing such measures can be significant. Examples are provided of spectacular failures in industrial policy when used for restructuring manufacturing industries and when used for the purpose of social engineering. The Afterword concludes that, given the checkered history and lack of broad consensus on the use of industrial policy in the manufacturing sectors, the increased reliance on such policy interventions in many areas of sustainability, like the energy sector and other areas, carries significant medium- and long-term risks. Some of these risks can be mitigated by fostering truly competitive businesses and investment opportunities that have high financial performance on their own without being reliant on subsidies, tax credits, or distorting legislation for their survival. The guiding principle for any policy intervention — regulatory intervention, government funding, or public production — should always be *primum non nocere* (first, do no harm).

https://doi.org/10.1142/9789811240928_fmatter

About the Editors

Diane-Charlotte Simon is one of the three co-editors, a chapter author, and the lead technical expert of this volume. She is a finance professional committed to sustainability and the energy transition. She has dedicated her career to the financing of business solutions fostering sustainability and addressing environmental issues such as climate change. Ms. Simon has participated in transactions worth more than $10 billion dollars in the renewable energy sector. She has financed organizations of all sizes from start-ups to mature public companies with both equity investments (private equity and venture capital) and debt instruments under various structures and maturities.

Ms. Simon is currently a Vice President and Sustainable Banking Coordinator at Credit Agricole Corporate & Investment Bank, where she has contributed to the execution of debt transactions including green-labeled structures. She currently focuses on project finance and corporate bank loans in the US power sector. In her previous role, she focused on bonds and debt capital market solutions for the power and infrastructure sectors in the US and Latin America. She also worked on warehouse facilities, securitizations, and asset-backed securities (ABS) for residential solar and energy efficiency assets. She co-authored several articles on project finance bonds and contributed to the launch of a new Environment, Social, and Governance (ESG) product: the green asset-backed commercial paper (ABCP).

Previously, she worked as a Research Analyst at NewWorld Capital, a private equity firm providing growth capital and business assistance to companies generating environmental co-benefits in clean energy, energy efficiency, water, environmental products and services, food and agriculture, and recycling.

Ms. Simon began her work in sustainable finance writing her thesis on the financial opportunities and threats linked to the environmental dimension of ESG. In this capacity, she interviewed sustainability experts from around the world about the financial impacts of sustainability and performed an extensive literature review. She further developed her credentials by obtaining a certification on the Fundamentals of Sustainability Accounting (FSA Level 1) developed by the Sustainable Accounting Standards Board (SASB). Ms. Simon graduated summa cum laude with a Master's in Business Management from City University of New York (CUNY), New York, USA and a Master's in Business Management from the Institut de Préparation à l'Administration Générale (IPAG) Business School in Paris, France.

Alexander S. Preker is one of the co-editors and chapter authors of this volume. He is also the Editor-in-Chief for the World Scientific Series on Health Investment and Financing.

Professor Preker was one of the Commissioners on the Commission on Pollution, Health, and Development. He is a globally recognized expert on financing, capital investment, private sector development, and market-based solutions to public policy challenges. Professor Preker is active as an early-stage investor and business development advisor. He is a Founding Member of the New York Chapter of the Keiretsu Forum, a Limited Liability Partner with the Keiretsu Capital Fund, an active investor with OurCrowd and other investment vehicles that focus on early-stage companies that have a high potential for impact including in the environmental sector. He is President and CEO of the Health Investment & Financing Corporation and a member of the board of several companies and organizations, including the USA HealthCare Alliance (USAHA) that works closely with the US Department of Commerce and the Export-Import Bank of the USA (EXIM).

Prior to his current work, Professor Preker had a distinguished career, working at different times for the World Bank Group (WBG), including the International Bank of Reconstruction and Development (IBRD), the International Development Association (IDA), and the International Finance Corporation (IFC). And at various times he was on external assignment with the World Health Organization (WHO) and International Labour Organization (ILO). From 2007 to 2012, Professor Preker was Head of the Health Industry Group and Investment Policy for the Investment Climate Department of the World Bank/IFC. The Department was a leader in investing in the new solutions to the threats of climate change, infrastructure, public-private-partnerships, health and education, e-Government solutions, and competition. He and his team set up a US$1 billion Investment Facility to improve the market environment for private sector participation and expand small and medium-sized businesses in the Africa Region, and did the preparatory work to set up a similar facility for Asia.

Earlier in his World Bank career, as Chief Economist for the health sector, he was responsible for oversight over an annual lending pipeline of about US$3 billion with a total portfolio value in the range of US$15 billion. During this period, he had the privilege of working with both Lawrence Summers (former Director of the National Economic Council in the Obama Administration) and Joseph Stiglitz (recipient of the Nobel Memorial Prize in Economic Sciences) during their respective tenures as Chief Economist for the World Bank Group (WBG), as well as many ministers, other senior officials, and private businesses and investors. It was in the 1990s, during Mr. Summers's tenure at the Bank, that the organization largely abandoned industrial policy in favor of more market-based approaches to industrial development. Notably, during the 1990s, Professor Preker was involved in the transformation of the moribund planned economies and the failed socialist industrial policy of Central and Eastern European countries to more dynamic market-based economies following the collapse of the former Soviet Union. He and others from his team were also involved in providing technical inputs into and compliance monitoring of several of the Millennium Development Goals (MDGs) as well as the later Sustainable Development Goals (SDGs).

Professor Preker has published extensively, having written many scientific articles and authored over 20 books. Previously, he was the Chair of the Editorial Board for the *World Hospitals and Health Services* journal of the International Hospital Federation (IHF) and is now an Honorary Member of the Governing Council of the Federation. During his tenure at the World Bank, he was a member of the Editorial Board for the World Bank's External Operations Publication Department and Editor-in-Chief of the Bank's Health, Nutrition, and Population Series.

Professor Preker holds several academic appointments. He is an Adjunct Associate Professor of Health Policy and Management at Columbia University, an Executive Scholar at the Icahn School of Medicine at Mount Sinai in New York and a Lecturer with the joint École des Hautes études commerciales de Paris (HEC) — Weill Cornell Medicine-Qatar Leadership Program. His education includes a PhD in Economics from the London School of Economics and Political Science, an MD from the University of British Columbia/McGill, and a Diploma in Medical Law and Ethics from Kings College, London.

Susan C. Hulton is one of the co-editors and chapter authors of this volume. She is an international lawyer and legal adviser specializing in public international law. She has extensive experience advising governments, and a record of leadership and innovation as a senior manager working with the United Nations, an international criminal tribunal, and an international nongovernmental organization (NGO). She is active in advocacy work in New York City and State in support of environmental justice, leading, for example, to the enactment of legislation establishing a moratorium on carbon-intensive cryptocurrency mining; and in human rights, in support of the International Rescue Committee, a global humanitarian aid, relief, and development NGO.

From 2001 to 2018, Ms. Hulton served as a senior official with the United Nations Department of Political Affairs, advising chiefly on Security Council matters, preventive diplomacy, and peacemaking initiatives. She helped to establish an interagency rule of law unit, which recognized that the rule of law and human rights are imperative to achieving and sustaining peace. This was a precursor to the vision now set forth in the Sustainable Development Goals (SDGs), Goal 16 of which calls for "Peace, Justice, and Strong Institutions". During this period, Ms. Hulton was privileged to work with Edward C Luck, a special advisor to the UN Secretary-General, who was instrumental in codifying when and how the UN and its member states were obliged to intervene to prevent genocide and fulfill their "responsibility to protect". She also played a leading role, as co-editor and one of the authors of the *Repertoire of the Practice of the Security Council,* in bringing this important annual publication up-to-date and paving the way for a digital version. In 2008, she was seconded to serve on mission to Beirut, Lebanon, as Special Assistant to the Commissioner of the UN International Independent Investigation Commission, investigating the assassination of former Prime Minister Rafik Hariri of Lebanon. From 2009 to 2018, she served as Special Assistant and Acting Chief of Staff to the Prosecutor of the Special Tribunal for Lebanon (STL), based in The Hague, the first tribunal of international character to prosecute terrorist offences. Ms. Hulton was privileged to work in this capacity with two eminent Prosecutors: Daniel Bellemare, who launched the work of the Office of the Prosecutor (OTP), and Norman Farrell, who successfully conducted the trial leading to the conviction of the four accused. In addition to conducting legal diplomacy with partner States, and mobilizing and overseeing resources for the OTP, Ms. Hulton was responsible for preparing numerous legal submissions and writing the external reports of the OTP to render its complex work comprehensible to all stakeholders.

Prior to joining the United Nations, Ms. Hulton served as a Legal Adviser with the UK Foreign and Commonwealth Office (FCO) in London between 1994 and 2000. She dealt chiefly with UN matters, including the negotiations for the International Criminal Court and the work of the International Law Commission on State Responsibility. She was also involved in international human rights issues, including humanitarian intervention; and international environmental issues, including State responsibility for phosphate mining despoiling the environment. Ms. Hulton is grateful to FCO Legal Advisers Sir Frank Berman KC and Sir Michael Wood KC for the opportunity to serve in this capacity. Ms. Hulton worked in the early 1990s as a Legal Adviser on territorial sovereignty disputes; boundary issues (land and sea); and international environmental and natural resources law. During this period, she was also a part-time Lecturer in International Law at University College London and contributed with Maurice Mendelson KC to the work of the International Law Association, British Branch, on the formation of customary international law. Ms. Hulton formerly served as the founding Legal Director of the influential human rights NGO, the International Centre for the Legal Protection of Human Rights (*Interights*), established by Anthony P. Lester QC, one of Britain's leading human rights lawyers. Based in London and working in Europe and the Commonwealth with an international network of lawyers, *Interights* focused on the practical application of international and comparative human rights law in national, regional, and international, courts and tribunals. In addition to her legal advisory role, Ms. Hulton was the Editor of the quarterly *Interights Bulletin* on significant developments in international human rights law and practice, and published with Anthony Lester QC on freedom of expression under the European Convention on Human Rights.

Ms. Hulton holds a BA in History and International Relations from the University of British Columbia, a Bachelor of Laws (LLB) from Osgoode Hall Law School, Toronto, and a Master of Laws (LLM) specializing in International Law from the London School of Economics.

About the Contributors

Robert L. Berridge is an Environmental, Social, and Governance (ESG) Investing Practitioner currently Director of Shareholder Engagement at Ceres. In this role, he coordinates and provides strategic advice to the nation's leading ESG shareholder activists, including several of the largest US public pension funds as well as leading social, labor, and religious investors. Ceres focuses primarily on encouraging companies to address the profound risks and opportunities of climate change, including a wide variety of ESG issues such as investing in renewable energy, reducing deforestation, and issuing annual sustainability reports including goals for managing material ESG issues. The primary goal of this work is to protect long-term shareholder value at the company and portfolio levels. Mr. Berridge has been with Ceres since 2006.

Previously, he worked for Green Century where he designed models for environmental equity indexes and developed active management strategies, focusing on best-in-class ESG strategies combined with a selective screening of extractive industries such as the fossil fuel companies. Prior to that, he worked at the EPA's Energy Star Program, where he helped to launch the Energy Star Lighting and Buildings Programs to assist S&P500 companies and others in achieving project ROIs that regularly topped 15 percent annually.

Mr. Berridge received a Bachelor in Environmental Studies from Brown University and an MBA from the Kellogg School of Management.

R. Daniel (Danny) Bressler is a researcher who served in the Biden Administration as a Climate Staff Economist at the Council of Economic Advisers from 2021–2022. His research focuses on climate change economics as well as other global risks, especially nuclear proliferation, biosecurity, and war. His research has been cited by the Supreme Court and covered in outlets such as the *New York Times*, NPR, *Scientific American*, and Vox.

He is a Global Priorities Fellow and a 2020 Nuclear Scholar at the Center for Strategic and International Studies (CSIS). He is a 5th-year PhD candidate in Sustainable Development at Columbia University, where he was trained in economics with additional social and natural sciences' training.

Before his PhD studies, Mr. Bressler worked for the Institute for Strategy and Competitiveness at Harvard Business School with Michael Porter and as a management consultant for Altman Vilandrie & Company. He holds a BA in Economics and History from Brown University.

Karl Boyd Brooks is a former EPA Regional and Assistant Administrator (acting). In 2018, he began serving the New Mexico Supreme Court as deputy director. Prior to that, in 2016, Karl Boyd Brooks started directing the Lyndon B. Johnson School's public leadership program of the University of Texas, Austin, and taught as Clinical Professor of Public Leadership. After practicing law for a dozen years, Brooks was named EPA Regional Administrator for the American Heartland by President Obama in 2010. He served in that post for 5 years, and then worked in the agency Headquarters in Washington for 2 years after the President nominated him EPA Assistant Administrator for Administration.

In the earlier stages of his career, he practiced in Boise, Idaho, first as a litigator with an international wood and paper firm, then as a trial and appellate attorney with the Mountain West's premier law firm. During his legal practice, he served as a three-term Idaho State Senator, which involved him in a wide range of issues mixing law, politics, justice, and public policy. An Idaho native, he began his career working for Idaho US Senator Frank Church, in Washington and Boise. Mr. Brooks holds a Bachelor's degree in History from Yale University, after earning his MSc from the London School of Economics, as a Marshall Scholar, he attended

Harvard Law School. He entered the field of environmental history while earning a History PhD from the University of Kansas, where he joined the faculty and taught, studied, and wrote about the interaction of law and government administration for a decade.

James Gifford is Head of Sustainable and Impact Investing Advisory for Credit Suisse, working with the bank's clients, advisors, and product specialists to mobilize capital into impact investing. He is a Senior Fellow at the Center for Sustainable Finance and Private Wealth at the University of Zurich and teaches a program at the Harvard Kennedy School on impact investing for the next generation of ultra-high-net-worth family members.

He was the founding Executive Director of the UN Principles for Responsible Investment and built the organization from its inception in 2003 over the following 10 years into the pre-eminent global initiative on responsible investment with 1200 signatories representing $40 trillion in assets. Previous roles include Head of Impact Investing at UBS and Director of Impact at Tau Investment Management: a supply chain impact fund focused on sustainable apparel. He has published numerous articles and book chapters on sustainable investment.

Dr. Gifford has a PhD from the University of Sydney on the effectiveness of shareholder engagement in improving corporate environmental, social, and governance performance, degrees in Commerce and Law, and a Master's in Environment Management. He was named by the World Economic Forum in 2010 as one of 200 Young Global Leaders.

Peter S. Heller worked at the International Monetary Fund (IMF) for almost 30 years, where he wrote extensively on issues of economic development and poverty reduction, macro fiscal policy, aging populations, public expenditure policy, healthcare reforms in developing countries, pension and civil service reform, climate change, privatization, and globalization. At the IMF, he was the Deputy Director of the Fiscal Affairs Department of the International Monetary Fund. He has had extensive experience in Asia, working on China, India, Indonesia, Japan, Korea, Malaysia, and Thailand, Africa (where he worked on Somalia, Kenya, and Ethiopia), and Europe (where he worked on Bosnia). While working at

IMF, he was involved intensively with the WHO's Commission on Macro-economics and Health as well as the United Nations' Millennium Development Plan. He also was a member of an advisory committee to the Director General of the World Health Organization on tobacco policies.

His book, *Who Will Pay? Coping with Ageing Societies, Climate Change, and other Long-Term Fiscal Challenges*, was published by the IMF in 2003. The book emphasized the challenges posed by climate change and the need for governments to begin planning on budgeting for the adaptation efforts that would be increasingly required as the century developed.

During his career, he was an Assistant Professor of Economics at the University of Michigan, and after leaving the IMF, he taught several years at the School of Advanced International Studies of the Johns Hopkins University. During the last decade, he taught in the Master's Program of Williams College in the Center for Development Economics. Dr. Heller received his PhD in Economics from Harvard University and his BA from Trinity College (Hartford).

Laurie Lane-Zucker is the Founder and CEO of Impact Entrepreneur Center and sits on the Advisory Board of the University of Vermont's Sustainable Innovation MBA program. His Impact Entrepreneur Center, based in the Berkshires of Massachusetts, does on-site and online programming, collaborative think-tanking, and business incubation. It serves both a growing global network as well as a regional audience, developing and advancing models of "impact economy" as well as a set of mechanisms/instruments for influencing economic transformation, such as public benefit enterprise zones and integrated impact finance vehicles.

In the mid-2000s, a digital media project he began incubating in the Triad Institute, Hotfrog, introduced him to B Corps and Impact Investing, which were just then launching out of think tanks. He changed course and entered the world of sustainable business, with Hotfrog becoming one of the first "Founding" B Corps and the first company to have an equity transaction on an impact investing exchange (Mission Markets).

Earlier, frustrated by the fact that as a "social entrepreneur" he was impeded by a single bottom line-dominated business paradigm, in 2011 he coined the term "impact entrepreneur", defining it as "social entrepreneurship 2.0" and as a "systems-minded" approach to social and environmental innovation. Using the young LinkedIn platform to locate like-minded entrepreneurs, investors, scholars, and students around the world, he created a global network (now with 20,000+ members) of systems change agents.

He spent the first half of his 30-year professional career — all in the field of sustainability — working for international NGOs, as the founding Executive Director of The Orion Society, which publishes *Orion* magazine, called by some the "philosophic voice of the environmental movement", and as the founder of the Triad Institute, a sustainability think tank that advocated for a new form of citizenship whose sensibility is at once deeply local, national, and global. Having had the honor to work with and be mentored by many leading environmental minds, such as Wendell Berry, E.O. Wilson, Barry Lopez, Jane Goodall, and Bill McKibben, he came to understand and champion the importance of the sustainability context in all human endeavors, including education and business.

In the early to mid-1990s, while at Orion, Mr. Lane-Zucker led an effort to create a new pedagogy that put the study of place at the center of an interdisciplinary curriculum. Along with Dr. John Elder of his alma mater Middlebury College, he coined this pedagogy place-based education, and seeded its principles into educational institutions, nature centers, and the culture more broadly.

Mr. Lane-Zucker's educational qualifications include a BA and an MA, Middlebury College/Edinburgh University; MFA, Columbia University.

Andrea E. McGrath is a strategic and entrepreneurial leader with deep experience helping individuals and organizations across sectors, ranging from start-ups to the Fortune 500 companies, to catalyze ideas into action. As founder of Amplified Impact, a boutique advisory and research firm, Andrea has worked at the epicenter of game-changing ideas and solutions in social enterprise, civic innovation, venture philanthropy, and impact investing over the past decade, collaborating with executives, entrepreneurs, educators, accelerators, funders, and field builders. Andrea's career is defined by her curiosity to solve problems that matter and her keen ability to quickly move from systems thinking and big-picture insights to the details and "connecting the dots" between strategy and execution.

Prior to her work in social impact, Andrea was a strategist with a Fortune 500 financial services organization, a research director at a Wall Street executive search firm, and a fundraiser with a national health organization.

Ms. McGrath earned her AB in Political Science at Boston College, MBA in Management and Finance at the University of Connecticut, and MPA in Leadership and Social Change at the Harvard Kennedy School.

Alan S. Miller retired from the International Finance Corporation (IFC), the private sector arm of the WBG, in January 2014 after working on climate change and development issues for 16 years. His career began as an environmental lawyer including six years at the Natural Resources Defense Council (NRDC) working on ozone depletion and energy efficiency standards for appliances. From 1989 to 1997, he directed the Center for Global Change at the University of Maryland. In 1997, he joined the Global Environment Facility (GEF) as manager of climate change projects for developing countries overseeing approval of more than $1 billion in funding for climate projects in more than 70 countries. At the World Bank, his responsibilities included representing the Global Environment Facility and WBG in international forums focused on climate change and green growth. He continues to do independent consulting; recent clients include UNDP, US AID, Sustainable Energy For All, the UNEP Finance Initiative, and the World Bank Group. His recent work includes projects on climate risks for the financial system and the need for sustainable cooling to address climate change and achieve the Sustainable Development Goals.

Mr. Miller has taught courses on global environmental issues at 10 universities in four disciplines and is currently an adjunct professor at the University of Michigan School of Environment and Sustainability. He was twice a Fulbright Scholar, in Australia in 1977 and Japan in 1987. He is co-author of a leading environmental law textbook and of the book *Cut Super Climate Pollutants, Now!* published in April 2021 by Changemakers Books. A full list of his many publications is available at his author website, AlanSMiller.com.

Mr. Miller's training includes an AB, in government, Cornell University, a JD in law, University of Michigan Law School, and a Master's in Public Policy, University of Michigan.

Robert Pojasek has been teaching pollution prevention, process improvement, management systems, risk management, and sustainability at the Master's degree level and through open enrollment arrangements at Harvard University and Tufts University since 1987. He was presented the Petra T. Shattuck Excellence in Teaching Award at Harvard University. Dr. Pojasek is a certified "Competency-Based Trainer". This credential enables him to conduct classes involving approximately 40 international standards, including environment, health & safety, quality, business continuity, sustainable procurement, sustainable supply chains, community sustainable development, sustainability, social responsibility, energy management, and resilience. It is now possible to integrate all of the management systems that contribute to sustainable development in to a single sustainable organizational business model. His chapter in this book provides an overview of this model.

After reading Dr. E.O. Wilson's book on consilience, Dr. Pojasek has spent his career searching for a way to organize all business activities so that they can contribute to sustainable development. This led to the publication of *Organizational Risk Management and Sustainability: A Practical Step-by-Step Guide* (CRC Press — Taylor & Francis Publishers, 2017). This book (available on Amazon) has helped his clients through his sole proprietorship, Pojasek & Associates, LLC. He is currently writing a book (Business Expert Press) on the use of ISO 31000:2018 risk management in sustainability programs to help end the practice of "stand-alone sustainability".

Pojasek obtained his AB/BS in Chemistry from Rutgers University in New Brunswick, New Jersey, and attended the first Earth Day celebration. He earned a PhD in Chemistry from the University of Massachusetts in Amherst, Massachusetts.

Ingmar Schumacher is a professor of Environmental Economics at IPAG Business School in Paris. His research focuses on environmental economics, with particular emphasis on climate change, migration, and endogenous preferences. Prior to his position at IPAG Business School, he worked as an economist for the Central Bank of Luxembourg and held a post-doctoral position at Ecole Polytechnique in Paris.

He is the Managing Editor of *Environmental & Resource Economics.* His research has been published in peer-reviewed journals such as *European Economic Review, Journal of Environmental Economics and Management, American Journal of Agricultural Economics, Journal of Economic Dynamics and Control, Oxford Economic Papers,* and with the Sustainable Future Policy Lab. He also contributes to newspapers and magazines, and he gives public talks and courses as well as provides consulting or policy advice. He also writes a regular blog at www.ingmar-schumacher.com.

Professor Schumacher obtained an MSc in Economics from the London School of Economics and a PhD from the Université Catholique de Louvain in Belgium.

Jerome Tagger is an executive and entrepreneur with a focus on the Responsible and Impact Finance sectors. He is currently the CEO of Preventable surprises, a New York-based "think-do" tank that seeks to drive behavior change within the investment sector to help prevent major market dysfunctions. Their major program focuses on climate-related systemic risk. They also work in ESG leadership, sell-side research, and investment scenarios.

Mr. Tagger has spent his career working with early-stage start-up organizations and projects, setting them on a course to success by building trusted relationships, bringing an open, creative, and resilient mind, and focusing relentlessly on execution. He has worked as an advisor to UNEP FI and World Benchmarking Alliance. Some of his other former roles include Advisory Board Member at Suguba, Chief Revenue Officer at ImpactAlpha, Director at the Global Impact Investor Network (GIIN), and COO of the Principles for Responsible Investment (PRI).

Mr. Tagger received a Master's in Business and Economics from ESSEC Business School.

Tensie Whelan is the Director of NYU Stern Center for Sustainable Business and a Clinical Professor for Business and Society where she brings her 25 years of experience working on local, national, and international environmental and sustainability issues to engage businesses in proactive and innovative mainstreaming of sustainability. She launched the Center for Sustainable Business in 2016 with the mission to ensure current and future business leaders develop the knowledge and skills needed to embed sustainability in core business strategy to reduce risk, create competitive advantage, develop innovative services, products, and processes, all while building value for society and protecting the planet. The center's current research examines how corporate sustainability improves financial performance.

As President of the Rainforest Alliance, she built the organization from a $4.5 million to a $50 million budget, transforming the engagement of business with sustainability, and recruiting 5,000 companies in more than 60 countries. She transformed Rainforest Alliance into an internationally recognized and credible brand.

Her previous work includes serving as Executive Director of the New York League of Conservation Voters, Vice President of the National Audubon Society, Managing Editor of *Ambio*, a journal of the Swedish Academy of Sciences, Vice President for Communications at the National Audubon Society, and a journalist in Latin America.

Ms. Whelan has been recognized by Ethisphere as one of the 100 Most Influential People in Business Ethics. She was the Citi Fellow in Leadership and Ethics at NYU Stern in 2015 and was awarded the Stern Faculty Excellence award in 2020. She has served on numerous non-profit boards and corporate advisory boards such as the Unilever Sustainable Sourcing Advisory Board and the Nespresso Innovation Fund Advisory Board and is a member of the Board of Directors for Aston Martin and GlobeScan. She is also an Advisor to the Future Economy Project for *Harvard Business Review*.

Ms. Whelan holds a BA from New York University, an MA from American University, and is a graduate of the Harvard Business School Owner President Management (OPM) Program.

Chapter 1

Background and Context

Diane-Charlotte Simon

Learning Objectives

- Lay the groundwork for understanding and working in the field of sustainability
- Discuss major business, investment and other implications
- Describe opportunities and risks for companies and investors
- Present the main paradigms in this evolving field
- Provide an overview and a road map on how the volume is organized

---

Abstract

This book explores the business and investment implications of sustainability. The heightened attention to sustainability presents both opportunities and risks for companies and investors. There are immense opportunities for companies that understand how to identify, measure, manage, and mitigate accompanying risks. New regulations, subsidies, and other environmentally friendly policies provide an opportunity for companies that are skilled at taking advantage of such conditions. Smart managers understand that a company's financial success is influenced by sustainability. If this additional information is considered when making investment and resource allocation decisions, it can result in enhanced resilience and long-term profitability of the company. Ultimately, it is the long-lasting, value creating, and lucrative business practices that transform a company into a market leader which transforms the business and investment environment over time. One hundred years ago, the Model T Ford became the market leader for consumer affordable cars. Today, Tesla has become the leader in the transition from gasoline and diesel to electric cars. At the same time, there is a significant material risk to inexperienced business and investors who get involved in this highly regulated and politically charged area of the economy but are not skilled in navigating this complex landscape. The authors demonstrate that companies and investors can successfully navigate the challenges of sustainability, mitigating risks, and seizing opportunities.

I. Introduction

The concepts of corporate sustainability and sustainable finance are evolving so quickly that it can be difficult to keep up with it all. This volume lays the groundwork for understanding and working within this flourishing context. It provides a solid foundation, presenting the main paradigms on which greater expertise can be built. The book distinguishes two opposing blueprints: **value-first,** which focuses on the financial materiality of sustainability and is employed by most investors and companies, and **valueS-first,** which prioritizes the positive or "do no harm" impacts on society and the environment, sometimes over financial gain, mainly employed by foundations and high-net-worth individuals. It is however important to stress that businesses and financial institutions must be "financially sustainable" to survive. The volume tries to disentangle the multiplicity of frameworks, regulations, and a confusing "alphabet soup" of acronyms (ESG, SRI, etc.) that has emerged over time.

The volume is organized in the following way:

Introductory Section
Part I - Business Implications
Part II - Investment Implications
PART III - Environmental Implications
PART IV - Policy Implications

The Introductory Section includes this introductory Chapter 1 which provides an overview and Chapter 2 which presents the fundamentals of sustainability science and the main sustainability challenges. These chapters convey the importance of the topic before the following sections delve into the implications for private sector businesses and investors, the environment, and public policy.

Part I explores the business implications of sustainability. Chapter 3 introduces key concepts related to corporate sustainability and examines the critical topic of **materiality**: both the **"outside-in"** (how sustainability impacts business and financial performance) and the **"inside-out"** (how a business impacts the environment and society). It also highlights the limitations of siloed approaches to sustainability. Chapter 4 offers an alternative approach, investigating the integration of sustainability from a company's very inception by looking at sustainability considerations for entrepreneurship and startups. Chapter 5 explores the financial implications of sustainability, analyzing both profitability and market valuation indicators, while Chapter 6 presents the financial case for embedding sustainability core into business strategy. The section closes by examining the intersection of sustainability and risk management in Chapter 7.

Part II transitions to the investment implications of sustainability and the perspectives of investors and financial institutions. Chapter 8 introduces sustainable finance and investing with its various strategies. Chapter 9 puts these strategies into practice by exploring how to build a sustainable portfolio using financial products that can span across all asset classes from green bonds to sustainable exchange traded funds (ETFs). The section also examines two specific sustainable investment strategies: impact investing (Chapter 10) and shareholder engagement (Chapter 11).

Part III then focuses on the environmental dimension of sustainability. Chapter 12 broadly explores environmental sustainability, the energy transition, and climate finance while Chapter 13 focuses on the business and financial implications of climate change.

The final section, Part IV, moves beyond the private sector to look at public policy implications. Chapter 14 investigates the field of economics and brings to light market imperfections that materialize through the concept of externalities. Chapter 15 explores how policymaking can address these externalities through environmental policy and regulations, while Chapter 16 focuses on the role of the State and fiscal policy in tackling the challenges of climate change adaptation. Chapter 17 highlights the macro-economic implications of sustainability and makes some cautionary remarks about some hidden threats to the sustainability agenda.

The Afterword discusses the pitfalls of using industrial policy in the area of sustainability.

Chapter 1 is organized as per the following sections:

    I. Introduction
   II. Why does sustainability matter to society
  III. Why does sustainability matter for business and investment?
  IV. Conclusion: Why this volume?

Why does sustainability matter to society?

As described in detail in Chapter 2, over the past 250 years, which have witnessed the spread of capitalism, the world has witnessed significant economic development and made great progress in meeting human needs. For example, human living standards have never been as high as in our current time, as illustrated by per capita food consumption, reduction of extreme poverty, violence reduction, as well as massive improvements in health, which have increased life expectancy from the 30s to over 70. Unfortunately, this economic development has come with significant con-sequences such as climate change, access to water, resources use, pollu-tion, and biodiversity loss. The impact of these issues is so great that they have been qualified as potentially "compromising the ability of future generations to meet their own needs". An alternative development model that makes it possible to preserve sufficient resources for the next genera-tion to meet their needs is defined as "sustainable development".

Human industrial activity and consumption patterns have produced effects on the environment called "externalities" (see Chapter 14). Historically, governments have played the leading role in addressing sus-tainability issues and externalities, mainly through environmental poli-cies, laws, and regulations (see Chapter 15). They still have a major part to play, particularly with respect to climate change adaptation (see Chapter 16). Though governments have recently demonstrated their ability to provide large amounts of capital to support the economy amidst the

COVID-19 pandemic, their high level of debt and fiscal constraints have led many to question their ability to tackle sustainability issues on their own. The private sector is well-positioned to fill the gap.

Why does sustainability matter for business and investment? What are its implications for both?

As used in the business and investment world, sustainability encompasses all topics related to sustainable development but tends to look at sustainability more broadly than environmental sustainability alone. Corporate Social Responsibility (CSR) or Corporate Sustainability (see Chapter 3) are terms referring to the business perspective, while Sustainable Finance and Investing (see Chapter 8) considers the perspectives of investors and financial institutions. The Environmental, Social, and Governance (ESG) sustainable strategy incorporates social and governance considerations in addition to environmental factors.

Ultimately, sustainability is important for both businesses and investors because it can have a material impact on a company's fundamentals including revenues, costs, profitability, valuation, etc. (see Chapters 5 and 6) — in some cases, a very significant financial impact. This is why several of the authors recommend that the private sector broaden its traditional parameters, both in scope, to include sustainability considerations, and in timeframe, to factor in long-term performance and impacts. The impact materializes first through risks and their related costs. Environmental incidents can be extremely costly for companies, both in terms of the damage incurred and in potential fines. Their reputations can also be damaged, along with their market valuation. Poor governance can also lead to steep fines or bankruptcy as seen in both the 2008 Financial Crisis and 2023 Banking Crisis. The macro sustainability issues discussed earlier also pose risks for companies. For example, climate change impacts sectors with different levels of severity. Infrastructure and physical assets are at risk from flooding and extreme weather events. The heat alone can impact human health, the overall productivity of employees, companies' ability to operate, and even disrupt transportation and supply chains. In the summer of 2022, China had to close factories across the country due to record heat waves. Finally, sustainability management itself presents pitfalls for companies and investors: greenwashing, the lack of skilled sustainability professionals, and regulatory risks.

Sustainability does not only present risks. The challenges discussed above also present business and investment opportunities to develop solutions in every sector, from energy to agriculture, industry to fashion, building to tech, transportation to healthcare. When there is an unmet need, there is a potential new market. Companies can choose to address specific sustainability issues as part of the product or service they offer. They can develop and scale new technologies with the support of investors and policies, which can open new markets, create new jobs, and lead to successful economic outcomes. Considerable business opportunities also arise from consumers' growing preferences for environmentally friendly or healthy alternatives. It is strategic for companies to attract these customers especially as younger generations gain importance and financial assets in the overall market.

The degree to which an organization considers sustainability in its strategy and operation varies greatly from company to company. Too often sustainability is handled in a silo while companies incorporating sustainability into their business model actually tend to perform better. Entrepreneurs can develop companies for which sustainability functions as a foundation (see Chapter 4). In addition, considering sustainability has become a requirement in many jurisdictions around the globe, particularly in the European Union, sustainability can also be fully embedded into a company's risk management (see Chapter 7).

By nature, sustainability is complex; it requires us to rethink paradigms, overcome silos, and emphasize collaboration. This volume highlights the importance of considering sustainability as core to business strategy. This can be accomplished by adopting sustainable business models, supply chains, and resource use following the concept of the "circular economy," which aims to reduce the amount of waste and improve resource productivity throughout the overall product's life cycle, from its sourcing to its customer uses to its end-of-life.

Turning to the investor perspective, sustainable portfolios can now be built whereby a sustainable finance strategy is implemented across all asset classes from equities to bonds and beyond (see Chapter 9). And there are numerous strategies to choose from (see Chapter 8). The main sustainable investing strategy, typically adopted by investors following a "value-driven" approach, is the integration of Environmental, Social, and Governance (ESG) factors. The first wave of sustainable finance, called Socially Responsible Investing (SRI), was "valueS-driven" and characterized by the use of screenings. Foremost among them are "negative screenings" which exclude from an investment portfolio companies that deal in weapons, alcohol, gambling, and, more recently, fossil fuels. Another strategy is shareholder engagement (see Chapter 11), whereby investors attempt to drive change in company management by raising sustainability issues via the use of proxy voting. Impact investing (see Chapter 10) is a growing area of sustainable finance that emphasizes the purpose and impact of an investment, paying close attention to the impact strategy and its monitoring. ESG and sustainable investing have recently come under sharp criticism for greenwashing, insufficiency, and pushing a political agenda in the US. Critics often target the "valueS-driven" approach, but overlook the financial materiality of sustainability.

With respect to environmental sustainability, this book underscores the significant opportunities presented by the energy transition away from fossil fuels, while cautioning against the potential pitfalls of ignoring their harmful effects (see Chapter 12). This transition will impact most sectors including transportation, and must occur as fast as possible to keep global warming from reaching an irremediable tipping point. The authors acknowledge that this must be a pragmatic transition to maintain reliable access to energy and will vary from region to region based on their energy mix. The transition will require the phasing out of the most polluting energy sources such as coal plants, while preserving gas-fired plants and nuclear facilities that complement renewable energy sources and batteries, in the short- to medium-term. Viable climate change solutions exist and make sense from a bottom-line perspective. Renewable energy is now cheaper than fossil fuels in most parts of the world. Other solutions like green hydrogen, or nuclear fission, have great potential but are still early stage. They require further innovation, research and development, and could also benefit from policy support and venture capital investments. Developing and scaling economically viable carbon capture technologies presents a huge business opportunity and may also play a critical role in mitigating climate change.

This volume also highlights the impact of climate change for companies and the financial sector (see Chapter 13). The risks of climate change can be divided into two categories: physical (resulting from weather events) and transition (resulting from enacted policies). Transition risks are significant for the fossil fuel industry. The value of fossil fuel assets may change because of policies requiring them to remain underground to prevent further warming of our planet, thereby leading to their devaluation (the "stranded asset phenomenon"). This impact could be accentuated if carbon tax mechanisms are put in place on a global scale and at a sufficiently high price. If such mechanisms are spread across sectors and countries, the effect could be systemic. Financial institutions including banks, insurance companies, and asset owners would be particularly vulnerable if their portfolios were exposed to many of these stranded assets. This is why financial regulators consider climate risk seriously and, in some cases, require disclosures.

Conclusion: Why this volume?

To conclude, for centuries, competitive markets have been drivers for growth and improvement of quality of life. It is paramount to ensure these markets are compatible with sustainability and can adequately mitigate and adapt to climate change. These changes require a significant amount of capital, and knowledgeable investment and business professionals to deploy it. But while the awareness of sustainability has significantly increased over the past decade, there are still major gaps in both investments and skilled professionals who understand sustainability-related opportunities and threats. These factors led to the development of this handbook.

The editors and chapter authors of the volume invite readers to be part of the solution — whether they work for a large company or a not-for-profit, build their own business, become an investor, a banker, an engineer, a researcher, or a policymaker. Sustainability is multi-faceted and requires the involvement of professionals of all kinds. We hope that readers will be inspired by this book so that they can tackle the challenges and seize the opportunities that lie ahead.

Chapter 2

Science and Challenges of Sustainability

R. Daniel Bressler

Learning Objectives

- Describe the history of and define the concept of sustainable development
- Understand the science and major challenges related to sustainable development
- Discuss the damage done to the environment by unsustainable economic development
- Present the UN Sustainable Development Goals
- Provide a vision for a more sustainable economic development

Abstract

This chapter sets the scene for the rest of the volume by providing the scientific basis for the business and investment implications of sustainability. The chapter describes how over the past few hundred years, and especially over the past few decades, the world has witnessed significant economic development and made great progress in meeting human needs. Unfortunately, this economic development has come with significant consequences in terms of climate change, access to water, population growth, depletion of resources, pollution, loss of biodiversity,

9

poverty, inequity, and diseases. Continuation of current trends has been deemed by many as unsustainable. The chapter defines *"sustainable development"* as the study of how to eliminate and mitigate these challenges so that the progress enjoyed by many parts of the world can be extended to all parts of the world and sustained far into the future. Finally, it presents the UN Sustainable Development Goals, which have been widely adopted by the international community and the public sector. More recently, many private businesses and investors have also started to embrace *"sustainability"* in their underlying business models. The chapter concludes that without significant change, the ecological, environmental, and climatic resilience that have supported economic development in the past may not hold up into the future.

I. Introduction

The last 250 years have been extremely atypical compared to the previous 99.9% of human history. Anatomically, modern humans arose around 200,000–300,000 years ago (Brown *et al.*, 2012; McDougall *et al.*, 2008; Richter *et al.*, 2017). For over 95% of this history, humans hunted and foraged for their own food in small hunter-gatherer bands that numbered a few hundred people (Dunbar, 1993). The total world population during the hunter-gatherer period was likely no more than 10 million (Burger and Fristoe, 2018).

It was only around 10,000 years ago that humans began farming. Instead of spending their days hunting and foraging, agricultural humans spent long days manipulating the lives of a few species of domesticated plants and animals to provide for their subsistence. It was during this time that key aspects of modern human society, such as cities, buildings, writing, and most modern diseases — many of which developed due to the close proximity between humans and farm animals — came into existence (Quammen, 2012).

While agricultural society was profoundly different from hunter-gatherer societies, the last 250′ years of human history have marked an even greater change.

With the advent of the industrial revolution around 250 years ago, fossil fuel-powered machines replaced human and animal muscle power.

The adoption of industrial machines allowed for the first period of sustained and consistent growth in living standards in human history (Galor and Weil, 2000). As the industrial revolution spread throughout the world, economic growth accelerated. Since then, gross world product has grown at an increasing rate from 0.3% annually in the 18th century to 1.0% in the 19th century to 2.4% in the first 60 years of the 20th century and to 3.7% since 1960 (Bolt *et al.*, 2018; Lucas, 2002; Roser, 2013a).[1]

Meanwhile, the global human population has expanded by an order of magnitude since the industrial revolution. In 1750, the world population numbered 700 million people. In 2019, over 7.7 billion people inhabited the planet.

During this 0.1% of human history, it is undeniable that significant progress has been made in meeting human needs:

- *Living Standards*: Despite the increase in population, the average worldwide standard of living is an order of magnitude higher than in 1750 (Roser, 2013a).[2]
- *Food Security*: During the early industrial revolution, there was concern that agriculture would not be able to keep up with the large increase in human population (Malthus, 1817). Food production has more than grown to keep pace with the population growth. Per capita, worldwide food consumption is now higher than at any other time in human history (Fogel, 2004, p. 9).
- *Life Expectancy*: The average life expectancy in developed countries has increased from the mid-30s in the mid-18th century to the mid-80s today, and is quickly catching up in developing countries (Roser, 2013b).
- *Poverty*: A billion people were lifted out of extreme poverty from 1990 to 2015 (United Nations Millennium Development Goals: Poverty, 2019). In developed countries, the rate of extreme poverty[3] is now nearing 0% (Ravillion, 2014; Roser and Ortiz-Ospina, 2013).

---

[1] Data from cited sources and analysis from author's calculations.

[2] Data from cited source, analysis from author's calculations.

[3] Extreme poverty is a condition characterized by extreme deprivation, and it is measured as lacking resources below some absolute level. This is different from relative poverty, which is low income relative to other citizens of a country.

- *__Violence Reduction__*: Violence has significantly decreased — today, ~7 people per 100,000 die violent deaths per year compared to ~50 in the Middle Ages and ~500 in pre-state societies (Pinker, 2012).

In short, the 99% of human history before the industrial revolution was defined by *scarcity*, whereas the last few centuries have increasingly been defined by *abundance*. *Development* is the process by which human societies have advanced from a condition of scarcity to a condition of abundance.

This increasing abundance, however, has not come without significant consequences. Humans have come to so dominate the planet that some scientists have argued that we have already entered an entirely new epoch in geological history: *the Anthropocene* (Subramanian, 2019). This term derives from the Greek word *Anthropo*, meaning human. More than anything, human activity is the driving force in altering the Earth's conditions in the Anthropocene (Cooper *et al.*, 2018).

Since the agricultural revolution, human societies have developed under the relatively stable set of conditions provided by the 11,700-year Holocene epoch (Steffen *et al.*, 2015). In the Anthropocene, this is changing. Human-driven change to natural systems poses a significant risk not just for future human prosperity, but it is already having significant impacts today.

In 1987, the United Nations Commission for Society and the Environment, commonly called the Brundtland Commission, produced a report called *Our Common Future*, where they coined the term "sustainable development". The report defined sustainable development as follows: "development that meets the needs of the present without compromising the ability of future generations to meet their own needs" (Brundtland *et al.*, 1987).

In sustainable development thinking, protecting the environment is not just a moral imperative to protect the environment for its own sake. It views the preservation of ecological systems as a critical asset in promoting prosperity for current and future generations of humans. In essence, the concept of sustainable development celebrates the progress that has occurred since the industrial revolution in meeting human needs, but it is wary that the ecological and environmental systems that support humanity may not hold up into the future. In addition to the profound environmental changes already underway, post-industrial human society has created or exacerbated a new set of risks that also may get in the way of meeting human needs in the future, such as the risk from pandemics.

The related concept of *sustainability* is a broader term than sustainable development, but it captures the same zeitgeist. It alludes to actions that can be taken by any institution that works to achieve progress that can be sustained for future generations. In the context of business, sustainability is often associated with actions that create shared value for society and consider environmental, social, and governance objectives in addition to private objectives.

Chapter 2 is organized as per the following sections:

   I. Introduction
  II. Challenges of Sustainable Development
 III. The 17 Sustainable Development Goals
 IV. Conclusion

II. Challenges of Sustainable Development

The rest of this chapter discusses some of the major challenges of sustainable development. Or, said another way, issues that may make it difficult to meet the needs of today as well as the needs of the future. For clarity, these challenges are discussed in turn, but it is critical to emphasize that none of them can be fully understood as separate phenomena. Each of these phenomena involves complex and coupled interactions between human systems and natural systems. The climate system, for instance, affects all aspects of society, often in profound ways, and in ways that we are discovering increasingly. Climate change is a major driver of biodiversity loss, it contributes to water scarcity in many regions, and the coal fire plants and internal combustion engines that are responsible for increasing the concentration of carbon dioxide in the atmosphere are also the major drivers in increasing the concentration of local particulate matter, which is now one of the largest health risk factors in the world. Identifying such feedback loops in these complex systems is difficult, but this is part of the challenge of sustainable development, and necessary to ensure that current and future human needs will be met.

1. Climate Change

As of 2019, carbon dioxide levels have increased over 25% from preindustrial times and global land temperatures have risen by over 1°C over preindustrial temperatures. Although geophysical processes including the El Niño-Southern Oscillation and volcanic activity produce climatic variations on yearly time scales, the increased concentration of greenhouse gases (GHG) in the atmosphere is causing the long-term trend of increased warming at a pace that is unprecedented in recorded human history. The last 7 years have been the warmest 7 years on record, and 2020 is the warmest single year on record (Brown, 2021). If the world continues on its current trajectory, global average temperatures are expected to increase by 2–4°C above preindustrial by 2100. Roughly 25% of greenhouse gas emissions come from deforestation, while 75% come from the burning of fossil fuels. Of the GHG emissions that come from fossil fuel burning, roughly 33% of these come from electricity production and heating, 28% from industry, and 19% from transportation (Pachauri *et al.*, 2015). The effect that climate change is already having on society is well-documented. Climate change warms the oceans, providing more energy, and thus causing more intense tropical cyclones that cause billions of dollars of damages every year (Walsh *et al.*, 2019). Climate change is contributing toward creating the drier and hotter conditions that make forest fires more likely in California and Australia (Alejandra Borunda, 2020).

Over the last decade, there has been an explosion of new empirical research that explores the impact of the climate on society. This includes the effects of climate on economic performance, agriculture, violence, health, trade, and migration. A common finding in these studies is that the negative effects associated with warmer temperatures are convex — i.e. damages increase with increase in temperatures at an increasing rate. The result is that especially hot days (e.g. over 35°C or 95°F) are especially harmful. As the climate warms, the frequency of these very hot days is expected to increase substantially, and much of the expected damages from climate change are forecasted to come from these especially hot days.

Climate damages are expected to be significant in agriculture. Yields for corn, soybeans, and cotton fall substantially when temperatures exceed around 30°C (86°F), and the frequency of days with these temperatures is expected to rise significantly in high emissions scenarios. One study projected that yields of major crops are projected to fall by roughly 20% in Sub-Saharan Africa in 2050 (Schlenker and Lobell, 2010).[4] Another study projected that corn yields are projected to fall by 63–83% in the Eastern United States in 2100 (Schlenker and Roberts, 2009).[5]

Likewise, the effect of very hot days on human health is expected to be significant. Just one additional day over 32°C (90°F) in the United States relative to a 10–15°C (50–60°F) day causes nearly one additional death per 100,000 people (Deschênes and Greenstone, 2011). As the frequency of these hot days is expected to increase significantly into the future in business-as-usual emissions scenarios, the increase in the global mortality rate due to climate change-induced temperature changes in 2100 is expected to be larger than the current mortality rate due to all infectious diseases (Carleton *et al.*, 2020; Greenstone, 2019). Recent research has shown that today's emissions will have large effects on human mortality over the course of the 21st century. The emissions of an incremental 4,434 metric tons of carbon dioxide emissions in 2020 — equivalent to the lifetime emissions of 3.5 Americans — causes one excess death in expectation between 2020 and 2100 (Bressler, 2021). Only considering the effect of climate change on human mortality is enough reason to take significant action on climate change (Bressler, 2021; Carleton *et al.*, 2020). People will take measures to mitigate the impact of climate change, such as installing air conditioning (Barreca *et al.*, 2016), but these adaptive measures are often costly. The poor will be especially vulnerable as they will find it more difficult to adapt (Bressler *et al.*, 2021), and climate change is projected to widen existing inequality (Hsiang, 2019).

Climate change is also expected to have significant damages on economic production. Estimates for how damaging vary widely. If little is done to address climate change and the world warms by 5°C by the end of the century, estimates for the loss in GDP vary from single-digit estimates of ~3–8% of GDP (Diaz and Moore, 2017; Nordhaus and Moffat, 2017) to over 20% of GDP (Burke *et al.*, 2015).

---

[4] In the A1B emissions scenario.
[5] In the A1F1 emissions scenario.

Statistical evidence has also suggested that climate change is likely to increase the frequency of violence between individuals and between groups (Hsiang *et al.*, 2013; Mach *et al.*, 2019; Ranson, 2014), including civil wars (Burke *et al.*, 2009). Climate change is also expected to cause increased migration pressure (Missirian and Schlenker, 2017).

Climate change will lead to sea-level rise and is expected to cause significant flooding in coastal areas. There is a good deal of uncertainty as to how much sea levels will rise as the earth warms, but there is a high level of confidence that sea levels will continue to rise for centuries even if drastic measures are taken to reach zero net emissions over the next few decades (Intergovernmental Panel on Climate Change, 2018). In 2009, a paper published in the journal *Nature* found evidence from the past that painted an ominous picture. In the last interglacial stage 125,000 years ago, global temperatures were 3–5°C warmer than they are today. The authors found that global sea levels at that time were likely 26–31 feet (8–9.5 m) higher than they are today (Kopp *et al.*, 2009). This would be enough sea-level rise to swallow the homes of roughly 10% of the world's current population, or 725 million people.[6] Fortunately, it is believed that it would take many centuries for the ice sheets near the Earth's poles to melt, giving humanity time to adapt and relocate as the seas slowly rose. However, a 2016 paper in *Nature* found that ice sheets may melt much faster than previously thought. In particular, the West Antarctic Ice Sheet, roughly the size of Saudi Arabia, could start breaking apart around 2050. Combined with ice melting in other regions, this could lead to a sea-level rise of 5–6 feet by 2100 (DeConto and Pollard, 2016). This would be enough sea-level rise to put New Orleans and Miami Beach underwater (Copel *et al.*, 2016).

Climate change affects all aspects of society and businesses will not be spared (see Chapters 12 and 13). The labor force will be adversely affected by higher food prices and health consequences of climate change. Businesses will need to adapt to climate change; energy spending will go up

---

[6]Author's calculations using data from: Center for International Earth Science Information Network — CIESIN — Columbia University. 2013. Low Elevation Coastal Zone (LECZ) Urban–Rural Population and Land Area Estimates, Version 2. Palisades, NY: NASA Socioeconomic Data and Applications Center (SEDAC) (McGranahan *et al.*, 2013).

significantly as spending on air conditioning will be necessary to maintain a productive work environment. Businesses in low sea-level areas will be disrupted by sea-level rise, and supply chains will be compromised by flooding of ports and more intense cyclones.

Some businesses will be more disrupted than others. Businesses that rely heavily on the physical environment to produce their product, such as agriculture, will find it harder to adapt to climate change and are likely to be more disrupted. On the other hand, businesses that can better shield their operations from climate damages, such as service-based businesses operating in modern office buildings in developed countries, will generally find it easier to adapt (Nordhaus, 2013).

Businesses that have to operate outdoors, such as construction, will be especially affected as the productivity of workers goes down significantly during very hot days. In business-as-usual climate scenarios by the end of the century, some parts of the world may be uninhabitable as the humidity-adjusted temperature makes it impossible to dissipate metabolic heat that is generated by the human body (Raymond *et al.*, 2020; Sherwood and Huber, 2010). Any business that must operate outdoors will find it very hard to be productive in these conditions.

On the flip side, the ominous projections described above are not set in stone. If aggressive action is taken to address climate change, then much of the climate impacts described above in high emissions scenarios can be avoided. Business, in addition to policy that creates the right incentives (see Chapter 15), must play a crucial role in transitioning toward a low-carbon economy. The cost of renewable energy has gone down significantly over the last decade due in large part to private-sector innovation. Solar and wind electricity generation is now the lowest-cost electricity in many markets. Further innovation in energy storage is needed to match increasingly cheap renewable generation with energy demand at the right time. Private sector innovation is needed to decarbonize the economy in other ways, especially in transportation and heavy industry. Innovations in carbon capture solutions are also imperative given the lifespan of carbon dioxide in the atmosphere which can remain long after emissions drop, up to 1000 years.

Providing goods and services to meet the new demands of a low-carbon economy is a large opportunity for business, but the specter of future regulations that correct the greenhouse gas externality poses a significant risk to businesses that continue to operate in carbon-intensive industries (see Chapter 13). The Obama administration Interagency Working Group on the social cost of carbon convened by the US government has suggested that the social cost of carbon is in the $40 per ton range (Interagency Working Group, 2013). To achieve economic efficiency, the social cost of carbon estimated along the optimal emissions path is equal to the global Pigouvian tax that should be placed on carbon.[7] A ton of carbon dioxide is roughly equal to the emissions from a roundtrip economy-class flight from New York to Los Angeles. However, recent literature has suggested that this ~$40 social cost of carbon estimate is too low (Bressler, 2021; Cai and Lontzek, 2019; Carleton *et al.*, 2020; Daniel *et al.*, 2019; Greenstone, 2019; Hänsel *et al.*, 2020; Howard, 2014; Howard and Sterner, 2017; Moore *et al.*, 2017; Scovronick *et al.*, 2019). Many of these recent papers have projected that a more accurate social cost of carbon is in the hundreds of dollars per ton. While the Interagency Working Group was disbanded by the Trump administration, President Biden reconvened the Interagency Working Group on day 1 of his presidency (Kavi, 2021). If a future carbon tax were to be implemented in the range of hundreds of dollars, carbon-intensive industries would see their tax base go up significantly. In addition, if companies hold fossil fuel assets that they intend to sell in the future, a large carbon tax or a broader shift toward a low-carbon economy would cause such assets to lose a significant portion of their value. This concept is known as *stranded assets*. Companies might see their enterprise value fall significantly in the future if they hold a large amount of these stranded assets.

2. Access to Water

Many people in many parts of the world are already facing significant water stress (Mekonnen and Hoekstra, 2016). Irrigation for agriculture is often a driving cause behind water scarcity. In the United States, for

---

[7]A Pigouvian tax, named after 1920 British economist Arthur C. Pigou, is a tax on a market transaction that creates a negative externality, or an additional cost, borne by individuals not directly involved in the transaction. Examples include tobacco taxes, sugar taxes, and carbon taxes.

instance, around 80% of the extracted water is used for irrigation (Aillery, 2019). One of the most dramatic environmental catastrophes in human history involved injudicious use of water: the draining of the Aral Sea. The Aral Sea was located in the former Soviet Union in modern-day Uzbekistan and Kazakhstan. It was the 4th largest freshwater body in the world. To support local agriculture, Soviet engineers diverted the rivers that recharged the Aral Sea to croplands in massive irrigation projects in the 1970s. The engineers extracted water much faster than could be replenished. Within a few decades, the sea had shrunk drastically. Hundreds of square miles that had once been sea turned into desert. By the 1990s, authorities had realized their mistake and attempted to redirect water to the sea, but it was too late. Today, over 90% of what was the Aral Sea has been drained, and the area has been economically devastated (Dunbar, 2012) (see Figure 2.1).

In arid regions, most of the water used for agriculture comes from wells. Water in wells is often called fossil water because it is typically not replenished on any human timescale. As humans have drained fossil water for agriculture, particularly in arid regions, water tables have dropped and

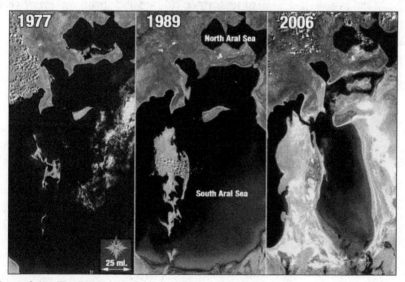

Figure 2.1. The Depletion of the Aral Sea

Source: http://www.columbia.edu/~tmt2120/introduction.htm.

in some areas, such as in agricultural regions of Syria, have completely dried up (Schwartzstein, 2016).

Even in the United States, water shortages are a major issue, especially in the West. Much of the water used in the western states including California, Utah, Nevada, and Arizona is supplied by the Colorado River. The river relies on melting snowpack from the Sierra Nevada and Rocky Mountains to recharge. Climate change is causing lower levels of snowpack in the mountains, leading to less available water to recharge the river. When combined with over-extraction, particularly for agricultural projects, the river continues to shrink every year. Before widespread extraction and significant climate change, the Colorado River poured over 22,000 cubic feet per second into its delta in the Gulf of California. Now, the river seldom even reaches the Gulf of California (Nowak, 2011).

Perhaps the most striking example of water overuse in the American West is Lake Mead. Lake Mead was created by damming the Colorado River with the 726-foot Hoover Dam as part of Franklin Roosevelt's New Deal public works projects in the 1930s. Lake Mead covers 250 square miles and it currently supplies water to 25 million Americans, including those living in Las Vegas. Due to shrinking flows from the Colorado River, Lake Mead is now just 37% of its former volume and shrinking every year (Stone, 2016) (see Figure 2.2.).

Figure 2.2.   The Depletion of Lake Mead
Source: NASA.

While water scarcity is a threat to regions around the globe, it is inherently a regional issue. The world as a whole is unlikely to run out of freshwater, but water scarcity poses a significant risk to societies. To overcome water challenges, developing a method of cheap desalinization is key. Water covers 71% of the Earth's surface, but only 1.7% of it is liquid freshwater (Perlman, 2019). Desalinization is currently highly energy-intensive and too expensive for most purposes in most regions. In the future, a breakthrough in desalinization technology would go a long way in overcoming the world's biggest water challenges.

3. Population and Resource Use

In the 1960s and 1970s, concern grew that overpopulation and overuse of finite resources was a significant threat to future prosperity. Some reputable scientists, such as Stanford Biology Professor Paul Ehrlich, raised the public alarm. As Paul Ehrlich said in the first sentence of his 1968 book *The Population Bomb*: "The battle to feed humanity is over. In the 1970s and 1980s hundreds of millions of people will starve to death..." (Ehrlich, 1968). Thanks to a demographic transition and continued improvements in agricultural technology, Ehrlich's dire prediction did not come to pass and we largely avoided the worst predictions of overpopulation. As people lived longer and became healthier and wealthier, they voluntarily decided to have fewer children. World population growth peaked at 2.1% in the 1960s. Now, the world population growth rate is down to 1.2% and dropping (Roser *et al.*, 2013). Today, population growth rates are even negative in many developed countries including Japan and much of Europe. Demographers predict that the Earth's population will continue to grow, but at a decreasing rate. Barring some catastrophe, world population is likely to plateau at 9.5–12 billion in the year 2100 (United Nations, 2015a).

Instead of just focusing on population like it has been done in the past (Ehrlich, 1968), modern analysis thinks of human impacts on natural systems more holistically. Impact is a function of not just population but also affluence and technology. This is represented by the well-known IPAT equation (Ehrlich and Holdren, 1972; Raskin, 1995; York *et al.*, 2002):

$$I = PAT$$

which stands for

$$Impact = Population \times Affluence \times Technology$$

What the IPAT equation implies is that it is not a world population of 10 billion people that we should fear, but a world population of 10 billion people that all live high-impact lifestyles. More people living higher impact lifestyles — such as greater meat consumption, use of fossil fuels, and consumption of goods and services that are resource-intensive — leads to greater human impact on natural systems. Businesses can play a large role in addressing this challenge by innovating new technologies — such as low-carbon technologies and tasty meat-alternatives — that allow people to live affluent yet low-impact lives.

4. Pollution

Pollution is one of the leading health risk factors in the world. Diseases caused by pollution are responsible for 16% of all premature deaths in the world in 2015. That is three times as many deaths as malaria, AIDS, and tuberculosis combined and 15 times as many deaths as all forms of violence. Low- and middle-income people are disproportionally affected by pollution: 92% of pollution-related deaths occur in low and middle-income countries (Landrigan *et al.*, 2018).

Air pollution is a particularly large problem. It leads to a loss of 1.8 years of life expectancy on average (Greenstone and Fan, 2018). A variety of airborne pollutants have adverse consequences on human health including surface ozone and nitrogen dioxide, but the largest killer is particulate matter: fine particles that lodge themselves deep in human lungs and the bloodstream. Particulate pollution comes from a number of sources, 82% of which are caused by humans. A large portion of particulate matter production comes from the burning of fossil fuels, but in developing countries, the burning of biomass is also a significant source of pollution. Some of the worst air pollution in the world is occurring around expanding megalopolises in China and India. In Delhi, the average person loses about a decade of life due to a perfect storm of pollution from dirty industries, electricity production from coal-fired power plants, vehicle engines, and the burning of biomass in the surrounding areas (Berkowitz *et al.*, 2018).

Since the activities that produce air pollution are often the same activities that produce greenhouse gases, abating emissions to limit climate change has a co-benefit of improving health by lowering air pollution. This co-benefit provides an even stronger incentive to pursue climate mitigation policies (Scovronick *et al.*, 2019). On the flip side, human-produced particulate matter has a significant cooling effect on surface temperatures by absorbing some of the sun's energy, and this partially offsets the increases in surface temperatures from greenhouse gas emissions that exacerbate the greenhouse effect. If global carbon emissions were to continue unabated, but effective policy was made to eliminate particulate matter pollution on a global scale, this would quicken the pace of global warming. Optimal climate and pollution policy require a reduction in both particulate matter production and carbon emissions, which suggests that a move toward low-carbon and low-particulate pollution technologies such as wind, solar, and nuclear power generation will play an important role in reducing both global warming and air pollution.

From the perspective of business, pollution imposes significant costs, but also opportunities to innovate solutions. Health problems caused by pollution have significant adverse effects on worker productivity. In low- and middle-income countries, pollution is estimated to cause a 2% reduction in GDP annually in low- and middle-income countries (Landrigan *et al.*, 2018). Businesses, particularly those operating in developing countries, could see significant improvements in worker productivity if regulations are undertaken to reduce pollution levels.

Clean technologies are a significant business opportunity because they will be crucial to addressing climate change, but they are also crucial to reducing air pollution. Carbon dioxide and particulate matter are causing two of the largest externalities affecting countries around the world: climate change and air pollution. Both of these pollutants are largely derived from the burning of fossil fuels. If governments take action to correct these externalities (see Chapters 14 and 15), investment in fossil fuels pose a regulatory risk not only just from potential future regulation on greenhouse gases, but also increased regulation on particulate matter.

5. Biodiversity Loss

There have been five great mass extinctions in the ~3.8-billion-year history of life on earth. These include the Ordovician-Silurian mass extinction ~443 million years ago, the late Devonian mass extinction ~359 million years ago, the Permian mass extinction 251 million years ago, the Triassic–Jurassic mass extinction 201 million years ago, and the cretaceous–tertiary mass extinction 66 million years ago (Baez, 2006; Brannen, 2017; Brenchley, 2001; Jablonski, 1994). These extinction events killed off on average 75% of the world's species.[8] Importantly, changes to the carbon cycle and the subsequent changes in temperature patterns may have played a role in causing all five of these great mass extinctions (Brannen, 2017).[9] The largest mass extinction in history — The End-Permian Mass extinction that is nicknamed "The Great Dying" — was likely caused by an intense burst of greenhouse gases from the Siberian Traps lava flow ~251 million years ago that may have increased ocean temperatures in the tropics to over 40°C (104°F) and to 60°C (140°F) on land (Brannen, 2017; Sun *et al.*, 2012). Some scientists have argued the sixth mass extinction is currently underway, primarily driven by human activity (Ceballos *et al.*, 2015; Kolbert, 2014).

Today, human activities including habitat destruction (Newbold *et al.*, 2015) and climate change (Peterson *et al.*, 2004) are causing species extinction at a rate hundreds to thousands of times above the baseline level (Wake and Vredenburg, 2008). Around 25% of the world's species are

---

[8] Author's calculations with extinction percentages for each mass extinction gathered from cited sources.

[9] Scientific debate continues to rage over the cause of the 5th great mass extinction, the most well-known of the mass extinctions that led to the extinction of dinosaurs. (Alvarez *et al.*, 1981) provided strong evidence that the mass extinction was caused by the Chicxulub asteroid impact in modern day Mexico, but recent evidence (Schoene *et al.*, 2015) has also suggested that lava flows in the Deccan traps in India may have also contributed toward the mass extinction by releasing greenhouse gases and increasing global temperatures, similar to the mechanisms that caused the Permian and Triassic mass extinctions. There is speculation that the events may not be independent and may have both contributed toward the mass extinction, as the Chicxulub impact may have increased the flow-rate of the Deccan traps (Richards *et al.*, 2015).

currently threatened with extinction. Since prehistory, the global biomass of wild mammals has fallen by 82% (Fischer *et al.*, 2018).

If human activity continues along the current trajectory, humans could end up causing an extinction event on par with the five great extinction events. A mass extinction would be not just a tragedy for nature, but a tragedy for businesses and society broadly, since these institutions rely heavily on ecosystem services. The destruction of biodiversity erodes the foundations on which society and business depends. It may be possible for future generations to continue to thrive and produce the food required to feed billions of mouths despite the drastic number of species extinctions that humans are causing. However, humans may be offsetting the delicate ecological balance in ways that we are not fully aware of, which could seriously compromise future generations. We are changing the climate, we are clearing vast tracts of land for agriculture, we are overfishing many species of fish into extinction, we are polluting the air and water with toxic chemicals that we do not fully understand, we are causing eutrophication[10] of lakes and estuaries through agricultural run-off, our modern transportation networks are introducing new invasive species all over the globe, and much more.

As of 2019, scientific evidence has shown that humans are having profound and mostly negative impacts on biodiversity (Fischer *et al.*, 2018), but literature on the effect that biodiversity loss is likely to have on human societies is nascent, and similar to where the climate change impacts literature was in the 1990s. Scientists are recognizing that humans are causing drastic changes in biodiversity, but there has so far been little work that has been able to reliably quantify these costs using statistical and econometric methods. Hopefully, over the next few decades, researchers will be able to fill in this gap.

6. Global Poverty and Inequality

While much of the world has benefited from economic development, much of the world remains left behind. Roughly 1 billion people still live

---

[10]Harmful algal blooms, dead zones, and fish kills are the results of a process called eutrophication — which occurs when the environment becomes enriched with nutrients, increasing the amount of plant and algae growth to estuaries and coastal waters.

in extreme poverty, primarily in sub-Saharan Africa and South Asia (Sachs, 2015). In their definition of the needs that sustainable development seeks to meet, the Brundtland Commission especially emphasized the "essential needs of the world's poor, to which overriding priority should be given".

While much progress has been made over the last few decades in bringing people out of extreme poverty, bringing this bottom billion out of extreme poverty has been especially challenging (Roser, 2019). The first UN Sustainable Development Goal is "eradication of extreme poverty for all people everywhere" (United Nations, 2015b). Yet, a recent World Bank report has projected that if past trends continue, almost 500 million people will remain in poverty by 2030 (World Bank Group, 2018).

Another headwind facing the bottom billion is that they are especially vulnerable to climate change. They are concentrated in parts of the world that are closer to the equator and are most likely to bear the brunt of climate damages. In addition, the investments that will be required to adapt to climate change — such as sea walls, air conditioning, and relocation from especially vulnerable areas — are costly. The poorest people in the world will find it very difficult to make these investments, and climate change is therefore expected to be especially damaging to these people (Bressler *et al.*, 2021; Carleton *et al.*, 2020; Hsiang, 2019).

For these reasons, it is crucial for institutions, especially businesses, to make investments in the developing world. Many businesses have found profitable investment opportunities that are often overlooked by investing in the developing world (Porter and Kramer, 2011).

In addition, aggressive climate policy may be among the best ways to help the world's poorest over the long run. When developed countries consider their climate policy, they must consider the full consequences of their emissions on the world's poor. The poor are often heavily discounted in economic analyses of climate change because their willingness to pay to avoid climate harm is lower than the willingness to pay in developed countries, because willingness to pay scales with ability to pay. Economic analysis can offset the discounting of the world's poor through a process called weighting, which accounts for diminishing marginal utility, i.e. an extra dollar in the hands of someone living on a subsistence income is worth much more to that person than a dollar in the hands of a billionaire.

Weighting thus counts money in the hands of poorer individuals higher than money in the hands of richer individuals so that the world's poorest are not heavily discounted due to their low ability — and thus willingness — to pay to avoid climate damages (Carleton and Greenstone, 2021; Fleurbaey *et al.*, 2019; IPCC, 2018).

7. Infectious Diseases

In the globalized 21st century, millions freely travel from every corner of the globe to every other corner of the globe through air travel every day, and contagious diseases can spread all over the world over the course of a few days as seen during the COVID-19 pandemic. The potential for a contagious and deadly disease to cause mass death now poses a serious global risk. The direct effects of pandemics on human health are serious, but experts project that the indirect economic effects may be of similar magnitude. The COVID-19 pandemic has caused millions of deaths globally and has raised unprecedented health challenges. It also produced major economic impacts across the world leading the global economy to shrink by over 3% in 2020 (IMF, 2022). A major pandemic like COVID-19 can wreak havoc on commerce globally. Many countries introduced extensive lockdown measures, school closures, and disruption to large segments of the economy. The way of working has also been deeply reshaped with the spread of remote work. Following lockdowns, there was an economic rebound, supply chain disruption, and continued tax-funded pandemic relief. However, past pandemics like the 14th Century Black Death and the 1918 Influenza were deadlier than COVID-19, and the future pandemics may be even more disruptive. A tabletop exercise conducted by the Johns Hopkins Center for Health Security in 2018 projected the impact of a deadlier pathogen that caused a worldwide death toll of over 150 million, and they projected that this would cause the Dow Jones Industrial Average to fall by 90%, with a mass exodus from cities amid famine and unrest (Watson *et al.*, 2019).

Although globalization has created new pathways for disease transmission, modern science and sanitation has given humans greater defense mechanisms against disease than ever before. We have antibiotics that fight bacterial infections and vaccines that protect against some of the worst viral diseases like smallpox and the flu. We saw with COVID-19 that vaccines could be developed and massively produced in a very short timeline (Sanders and Ponzio, 2017).

Pandemic diseases are often zoonotic, meaning they jump from animals to humans. Recent epidemics such as Ebola, Zika, SARS-CoV-1, and HIV are all zoonotic. The emergence of such diseases depends a great deal on the chance meeting of different animal species and mutation-triggering circumstantial factors. However, possible future pandemics may not depend on such circumstantial factors, but may be deliberately designed. New tools from the field of synthetic biology are increasingly endowing scientists with the ability to design and manufacture maximally dangerous pathogens, leapfrogging natural selection (Bressler and Bakerlee, 2018). Even with current capabilities, an engineered pandemic may be possible. Sufficiently capable actors could resurrect the deadliest pathogens of the past, like smallpox or Spanish flu, or modify existing pathogens such as bird flu to be more contagious and lethal. Genome engineering technologies are becoming more powerful and ubiquitous, and the tools necessary for making these modifications are becoming increasingly accessible. This leads to the specter of independent actors intentionally or unintentionally engineering pathogens with the potential to cause more damage than history's deadliest pandemics. Unfortunately, no obvious physical or biological constraints preclude the construction of such potent biological weapons.

Fortunately, there is important work that business can do to address the problem. Companies working in the biotechnology space should comply with current best practices to reduce the risk. For instance, the International Gene Synthesis Consortium proposed guidelines for how gene synthesis companies should screen customers' orders for potentially dangerous chunks of DNA, such as those found in harmful viruses. Most companies voluntarily follow these guidelines, and they represent 80% of the global market (DiEuliis *et al.*, 2017). Adequate screening of all synthesized DNA could eliminate the most serious foreseeable hazards of biotech misuse by nonstate actors (Esvelt, 2018). In addition, innovations made in biotechnology could mitigate pandemic risks. Better diagnostics based on better genome sequencing methods are improving detection of emerging pathogens. Broad-spectrum antivirals may be effective in defending against a pandemic before a pathogen-specific treatment is developed.

III. The 17 Sustainable Development Goals

At the Millennium Summit in 2000, world leaders set forth a series of UN Millennium Development Goals (MDGs) around global poverty, health, education, gender equality, and environmental sustainability that they hoped to achieve by 2015. The MDGs related to poverty and health mostly exceeded expectations. Target #1a of MDG #1, which called for halving the proportion of people living in extreme poverty, was met seven years ahead of the target in 2008. Progress on MDG #7 (ensuring environmental sustainability) was less successful in large part because of disappointing progress on climate change and biodiversity loss.

In 2015, the UN Sustainable Development Goals (SDGs) were launched as a successor to the MDGs (United Nations, 2015b). They placed a larger emphasis on environmental issues compared to the MDGs (Sachs, 2012). The SDGs presented a series of targets to be met by 2030. The SDGs attempted to continue the strong momentum on poverty alleviation. SDG #1 is to "end poverty in all forms everywhere". MDG #1

Figure 2.3. The United Nations' 17 Sustainable Development Goals
Source: United Nations (2015b).

was successful largely due to strong economic performance in China and India, but to achieve the end of poverty worldwide will require significant structural change in countries that have had poor institutions and little economic development.

Although the SDGs are intended in large part to drive the priorities of policymakers, SDG #17 emphasizes the role of public–private partnerships to make the investments required to achieve the goals and SDG #5 emphasizes the role of the private sector in promoting gender equality. In addition, the SDGs are useful as a set of goals that businesses can use to help them decide which social needs they might be able to address with their business model (see Figure 2.3).

IV. Conclusion

Over the last few hundred years and especially over the last few decades, humanity has made tremendous progress in meeting human needs. With this progress has come significant consequences: ecological, environmental, and climatic systems that have supported this progress may not hold up into the future. This progress has also caused externalities that negatively affect health and exacerbate inequality. In addition, our globalized modern world has created or exacerbated a new set of risks that also may get in the way of meeting human needs in the future, such as the risk from pandemics. Sustainable development is the study of how to eliminate and mitigate these challenges so that the progress enjoyed by many parts of the world can be extended to all parts of the world and sustained far into the future.

References

Aillery, M. (2019). "Irrigation & water use", *USDA Economic Research Service*, https://www.ers.usda.gov/topics/farm-practices-management/irrigation-water-use.aspx. Accessed August 28, 2019.

Alejandra, B. (2020). "The science connecting wildfires to climate change", *National Geographic*, https://www.nationalgeographic.com/science/2020/09/climate-change-increases-risk-fires-western-us/. Accessed January 31, 2021.

Alvarez, L. W., Alvarez, W., Asaro, F., and Michel, H. V. (1981). Extraterrestrial cause for the cretaceous-tertiary extinction: Experiment and theory, *Applications of Space Developments*, Elsevier, pp. 241–271.

Baez, J. (2006). "Extinction". University of California Riverside, http://math.ucr.edu/home/baez/extinction/. Accessed August 28, 2019.

Barreca, A. *et al.* (2016). "Adapting to climate change: The remarkable decline in the US temperature-mortality relationship over the twentieth century". *Journal of Political Economy*, 124(1), pp. 105–159.

Berkowitz, B., Muyskens, J., Sharma, M., and Ulmanu, M. (2018). "How many years do we lose to the air we breathe?" *Washington Post*, https://www.washingtonpost.com/graphics/2018/national/health-science/lost-years/. Accessed March 9, 2019.

Bolt, J., Inklaar, R., de Jong, H., and van Zanden, J. L. (2018). "Rebasing 'Maddison': New income comparisons and the shape of long-run economic development". *GGDC Research Memorandum*, p. 174. https://cepr.org/voxeu/columns/rebasing-maddison-shape-long-run-economic-development.

Brannen, P. (2017). *The Ends of the World: Volcanic Apocalypses, Lethal Oceans, and Our Quest to Understand Earth's Past Mass Extinctions*, HarperCollins, New York.

Brenchley, P. J. (2001). "2.4. 2 Late ordovician extinction", *Palaeobiology II*, 2, p. 220.

Bressler, R. D. (2021). "The mortality cost of carbon", *Nature Communications*, 12(1), p. 4467, https://doi.org/10.1038/s41467-021-24487-w. Accessed July 29, 2021.

Bressler, R. D., Moore, F. C., Rennert, K., and Anthoff, D. (December 2021). "Estimates of country level temperature-related mortality damage functions", *Scientific Reports*, 11(1), 20282. https://doi.org/10.1038/s41598-021-99156-5.

Bressler, R. D., and Bakerlee, C. (2018). "'Designer bugs': How the next pandemic might come from a lab", *Vox*, https://www.vox.com/future-perfect/2018/12/6/18127430/superbugs-biotech-pathogens-biological-warfare-pandemic. Accessed December 28, 2018.

Brown, F. H., McDougall, I., and Fleagle, J. G. (2012). "Correlation of the KHS tuff of the Kibish formation to volcanic ash layers at other sites, and the age of early homo sapiens (Omo I and Omo II)", *Journal of Human Evolution*, 63(4), pp. 577–85.

Brown, K. (2021). "2020 tied for warmest year on record, NASA analysis shows", *NASA*, http://www.nasa.gov/press-release/2020-tied-for-warmest-year-on-record-nasa-analysis-shows. Accessed January 31, 2021.

Brundtland, G. H. *et al.* (1987). *Our Common Future.* World Commission on Environment and Development, New York.

Burger, J. R., and Fristoe, T. S. (2018). "Hunter-gatherer populations inform modern ecology", *Proceedings of the National Academy of Sciences*, 115(6), pp. 1137–1139.

Burke, M. B. *et al.* (2009). "Warming increases the risk of civil war in Africa", *Proceedings of the National Academy of Sciences*, 106(49), pp. 20670–20674.

Burke, M., Hsiang, S. M., and Miguel, E. (2015). "Global non-linear effect of temperature on economic production", *Nature*, 527(7577), pp. 235–239.

Cai, Y. and Lontzek, T. (2019). "The social cost of carbon with economic and climate risks", *Journal of Political Economy*, 127(6), 701890.

Carleton, T. *et al.* (2020). "Valuing the global mortality consequences of climate change accounting for adaptation costs and benefits", *NBER Working Paper.* https://www.ssrn.com/abstract=3224365. Accessed August 3, 2020.

Carleton, T., and Greenstone, M. (2021). "Updating the United States Government's social cost of carbon", *SSRN Electronic Journal*, https://www.ssrn.com/abstract=3764255. Accessed January 30, 2021.

Ceballos, G. *et al.* (2015). "Accelerated modern human–induced species losses: Entering the sixth mass extinction", *Science Advances*, 1(5), p. e1400253.

Cooper, A. H. *et al.* (2018). "Humans are the most significant global geomorphological driving force of the 21st century", *Anthropocene Review*, 5, pp. 222–229.

Copel, B., Keller, J., and Marsh, B. (2016). "What could disappear", https://www.nytimes.com/interactive/2012/11/24/opinion/sunday/what-could-disappear.html. Accessed August 27, 2019.

Daniel, K. D., Litterman, R. B., and Wagner, G. (2019). "Declining CO_2 price paths", *Proceedings of the National Academy of Sciences*, 116(42), pp. 20886–20891.

DeConto, R. M. and Pollard, D. (2016). "Contribution of Antarctica to past and future sea-level rise", *Nature*, 531(7596), p. 591.

Deschênes, O., and Greenstone, M. (2011). "Climate change, mortality, and adaptation: Evidence from annual fluctuations in weather in the US", *American Economic Journal: Applied Economics*, 3(4), pp. 152–85.

Diaz, D., and Moore, F. (2017). "Quantifying the economic risks of climate change", *Nature Climate Change*, 7(11), pp. 774–782.

DiEuliis, D., Carter, S. R., and Gronvall, G. K. (2017). "Options for synthetic DNA order screening, revisited", *mSphere*, 2(4), mSphere.00319-17, p. e00319–17.

Dunbar, B. (2012). "Landsat top ten — A shrinking sea, Aral sea", *NASA*, https://www.nasa.gov/mission_pages/landsat/news/40th-top10-aralsea.html. Accessed August 28, 2019.

Dunbar, R. I. M. (1993). "Coevolution of neocortical size, group size and language in humans", *Behavioral and Brain Sciences*, 16(4), pp. 681–694.

Ehrlich, P. R. (1968). *The Population Bomb*. Sierra Club/Ballantine Books, San Francisco.

Ehrlich, P. R., and Holdren, J. P. (1972). "Critique", *Bulletin of the Atomic Scientists*, 28(5), pp. 16–27.

Esvelt, K. M. (2018). "Inoculating science against potential pandemics and information hazards", *PLoS Pathogens*, 14(10), https://www.ncbi.nlm.nih.gov/pmc/articles/PMC6171951/. Accessed June 12, 2019.

Fischer, M. *et al.* (2018). "Summary for policymakers of the regional assessment report on biodiversity and ecosystem services for Europe and Central Asia of the intergovernmental science-policy platform on biodiversity and ecosystem services". https://www.ipbes.net/assessment-reports/eca.

Fleurbaey, M. *et al.* (2019). "The social cost of carbon: Valuing inequality, risk, and population for climate policy", *The Monist*, 102(1), pp. 84–109.

Fogel, R. W. (2004). *The Escape from Hunger and Premature Death, 1700–100: Europe, America, and the Third World*, Cambridge University Press, Cambridge/New York.

Galor, O., and Weil, D. N. (2000). "Population, technology, and growth: From Malthusian stagnation to the demographic transition and beyond", *American Economic Review*, 90(4), pp. 806–828.

Greenstone, M. (2019). *Statement of Michael Greenstone*. Washington, D.C. https://epic.uchicago.edu/wp-content/uploads/2019/12/Greenstone-Testimony-12192019-FINAL.pdf. Accessed December 30, 2019.

Greenstone, M., and Fan, C. Q. (2018). "Introducing the air quality life index". https://aqli.epic.uchicago.edu/wp-content/uploads/2018/11/AQLI-Intro-Report.pdf.

Hänsel, M. C. *et al.* (2020). "Climate economics support for the UN climate targets", *Nature Climate Change*, http://www.nature.com/articles/s41558-020-0833-x. Accessed July 21, 2020.

Howard, P. (2014). "Omitted damages: What's missing from the social cost of carbon", Electronic copy, http://costofcarbon.org/files/Omitted_Damages_Whats_Missing_From_the_Social_Cost_of_Carbon.pdf.

Howard, P. H., and Sterner, T. (2017). "Few and not so far between: A meta-analysis of climate damage estimates", *Environmental and Resource Economics*, 68(1), pp. 197–225.

Hsiang, S. (2019). "Statement of Solomon Hsiang", https://budget.house.gov/sites/democrats.budget.house.gov/files/documents/House_Testimony_Hsiang_6_10_19_final.pdf. Accessed August 27, 2019.

Hsiang, S. M., Burke, M., and Miguel, E. (2013). "Quantifying the influence of climate on human conflict", *Science*, 341(6151), pp. 1235367.

IMF. (2022). "World Economic Outlook Database". https://www.imf.org/en/Publications/WEO/weo-database/2022/April.

Interagency Working Group. (2013). "Technical update on the social cost of carbon for regulatory impact analysis-under executive order 12866", *Interagency Working Group on Social Cost of Carbon, United States Government.*

Intergovernmental Panel on Climate Change (IPPC). (2018). *Global Warming of 1.5°C*, http://www.ipcc.ch/report/sr15/. Accessed May 28, 2019.

Jablonski, D. (1994). "Extinctions in the fossil record", *Philosophical Transactions of the Royal Society of London. Series B: Biological Sciences*, 344(1307), pp. 11–17.

Kavi, A. (2021). "Biden's 17 executive orders and other directives in detail", *The New York Times*, https://www.nytimes.com/2021/01/20/us/biden-executive-orders.html. Accessed January 30, 2021.

Kolbert, E. (2014). *The Sixth Extinction: An Unnatural History*, A&C Black, London.

Kolstad, C., Urama, K., Broome, J., Bruvoll, A., Cariño-Olvera, M., Fullerton, D., Gollier, C., Hanemann, W. M., Hassan, R., and Jotzo, F. "Social, economic and ethical concepts and methods", *IPCC AR5 Climate Change 2014: Mitigation of Climate Change*: 2014. https://www.ipcc.ch/report/ar5/wg3/social-economic-and-ethical-concepts-and-methods/.

Kopp, R. E. *et al.* (2009). "Probabilistic assessment of sea level during the last interglacial stage", *Nature*, 462(7275), pp. 863–867.

Landrigan, P. J. *et al.* (2018). "The lancet commission on pollution and health", *The Lancet*, 391(10119), pp. 462–512.

Lucas, R. E. (2002). "The industrial revolution: Past and future", *Lectures on Economic Growth*, 44(8), pp. 109–188. American Institute for Economic Research.

Mach, K. J. *et al.* (2019). "Climate as a risk factor for armed conflict", *Nature*, http://www.nature.com/articles/s41586-019-1300-6. Accessed June 14, 2019.

Malthus, T. R. (1817). *An Essay on the Principle of Population, as It Affects the Future Improvement of Society. With Remarks on the Speculations of Mr. Godwin, M. Condorcet, and Other Writers. Encyclopedia Britanica Online* https://www.britannica.com/topic/An-Essay-on-the-Principle-of-

Population-as-It-Affects-the-Future-Improvement-of-Society-with-Remarks-on-the-Speculations-of-Mr-Godwin-M-Condorcet-and-Other-Writers.

McDougall, I., Brown, F. H., and Fleagle, J. G. (2008). "Sapropels and the age of hominins Omo I and II, Kibish, Ethiopia", *Journal of Human Evolution*, 55(3), pp. 409–420.

McGranahan, G., Balk, D., and Anderson, B. (2013). "Low Elevation Coastal Zone (LECZ) Urban-Rural Population Estimates, Global Rural-Urban Mapping Project (GRUMP), Alpha Version. Palisades, NY: NASA Socioeconomic Data and Applications Center (SEDAC)", NASA Socioeconomic Data and Applications Center (SEDAC), Palisades, NY.

Mekonnen, M. M., and Hoekstra, A. Y. (2016). "Four billion people facing severe water scarcity", *Science Advances*, 2(2), p. e1500323.

Missirian, A., and Schlenker, W. (2017). "Asylum applications respond to temperature fluctuations", *Science*, 358(6370), pp. 1610–1614.

Moore, F. C., Baldos, U. Hertel, T., and Diaz, D. (2017). "New science of climate change impacts on agriculture implies higher social cost of carbon", *Nature Communications*, 8(1), p. 1607.

Newbold, T. *et al.* (2015). "Global effects of land use on local terrestrial biodiversity", *Nature; London*, 520(7545), pp. 45–50S.

Nordhaus, W. D. (2013). *The Climate Casino: Risk, Uncertainty, and Economics for a Warming World*, Yale University Press, New Haven.

Nordhaus, W. D., and Moffat, A. (2017). *A Survey of Global Impacts of Climate Change: Replication, Survey Methods, and a Statistical Analysis*. Cambridge: National Bureau of Economic Research.

Nowak, K. C. (2011). "Stochastic streamflow simulation at interdecadal times scales and implications for water resources management in the Colorado River Basin".

Pachauri, R. K., Mayer, L., and Intergovernmental Panel on Climate Change (eds.). (2015). *Climate Change 2014: Synthesis Report*, Intergovernmental Panel on Climate Change, Geneva, Switzerland.

Perlman, H. (2019). "How much water is there on Earth?" *US Geological Survey*, https://www.usgs.gov/special-topic/water-science-school/science/how-much-water-there-earth?qt-science_center_objects=0#qt-science_center_objects. Accessed August 29, 2019.

Peterson, A. T. *et al.* (2004). "Extinction risk from climate change", *Nature*, 427(6970), p. 145.

Pinker, S. (2012). *The Better Angels of Our Nature: Why Violence Has Declined*, New York: Penguin Books.

Porter, M. E., and Kramer, M. R. (2011). "The big idea: Creating shared value". Harvard: Harvard Business Review.

Quammen, D. (2012). *Spillover: Animal Infections and the Next Human Pandemic*, W.W. Norton & Company.

Ranson, M. (2014). "Crime, weather, and climate change", *Journal of Environmental Economics and Management*, 67(3), pp. 274–302.

Raskin, P. D. (1995). "Methods for estimating the population contribution to environmental change", *Ecological Economics*, 15(3), pp. 225–233.

Ravillion, M. (2014). "Poverty in the rich world when it was not nearly so rich", Center for Global Development, https://www.cgdev.org/blog/poverty-rich-world-when-it-was-not-nearly-so-rich. Accessed August 26, 2019.

Raymond, C., Matthews, T., and Horton, R. M. (2020). "The emergence of heat and humidity too severe for human tolerance", *Science Advances*, 6(19), p. eaaw1838.

Richards, M. A. *et al.* (2015). "Triggering of the largest deccan eruptions by the Chicxulub impact", *Geological Society of America Bulletin*, 127(11–12), pp. 1507–1520.

Richter, D. *et al.* (2017). "The age of the Hominin Fossils from Jebel Irhoud, Morocco, and the origins of the middle stone age", *Nature* 546(7657), pp. 293–296.

Roser, M. (2013a). "Economic growth", *Our World in Data*, https://ourworldindata.org/economic-growth. Accessed August 26, 2019.

Roser, M. (2013b). "Life expectancy", *Our World in Data*, https://ourworldindata.org/life-expectancy. Accessed August 26, 2019.

Roser, M. (2019). "As the world's poorest economies are stagnating half a billion are expected to be in extreme poverty in 2030", *Our World in Data*, https://ourworldindata.org/extreme-poverty-projections. Accessed December 21, 2019.

Roser, M., and Ortiz-Ospina, E. (2013). "Global extreme poverty", *Our World in Data*, https://ourworldindata.org/extreme-poverty. Accessed August 26, 2019.

Roser, M., Ritchie, H., and Ortiz-Ospina, E. (2013). "World population growth", *Our World in Data*, https://ourworldindata.org/world-population-growth. Accessed August 27, 2019.

Sachs, J. D. (2012). "From millennium development goals to sustainable development goals", *The Lancet*, 379(9832), pp. 2206–2211.

Sachs, J. D. (2015). *The Age of Sustainable Development*, Columbia University Press, New York.

Sanders, J. W., and Ponzio, T. A. (2017). "Vectored immunoprophylaxis: An emerging adjunct to traditional vaccination", *Tropical Diseases, Travel Medicine and Vaccines*, 3(1), p. 3.

Schlenker, W., and Lobell, D. B. (2010). "Robust negative impacts of climate change on African agriculture", *Environmental Research Letters*, 5(1), p. 014010.

Schlenker, W. and Roberts, M. J. (2009). "Nonlinear temperature effects indicate severe damages to US crop yields under climate change", *Proceedings of the National Academy of Sciences*, 106(37), pp. 15594–15598.

Schoene, B. *et al.* (2015). "U-Pb Geochronology of the deccan traps and relation to the end-cretaceous mass extinction", *Science*, 347(6218), pp. 182–184.

Schwartzstein, P. (2016). "Inside the Syrian dust bowl", *Foreign Policy*, https://foreignpolicy.com/2016/09/05/inside-the-syrian-dust-bowl-icarda-assad-food-security-war/. Accessed August 28, 2019.

Scovronick, N. *et al.* (2019). "The impact of human health co-benefits on evaluations of global climate policy", *Nature Communications*, 10(1), p. 2095.

Sherwood, S. C., and Huber, M. (2010). "An adaptability limit to climate change due to heat stress", *Proceedings of the National Academy of Sciences*, 107(21), pp. 9552–9555.

Steffen, W. *et al.* (2015). "Planetary boundaries: Guiding human development on a changing planet", *Science*, 347(6223), pp. 1259855.

Stone, W. (2016). "Lake mead at lowest level on record, 37% capacity", *Arizona Public Media*, https://www.azpm.org/s/39254-lake-mead-at-lowest-level-on-record-37-capacity/. Accessed August 28, 2019.

Subramanian, M. (2019). "Anthropocene now: Influential panel votes to recognize Earth's New Epoch", *Nature*, http://www.nature.com/articles/d41586-019-01641-5. Accessed August 26, 2019.

Sun, Y. *et al.* (2012). "Lethally hot temperatures during the early Triassic greenhouse", *Science*, 338(6105), pp. 366–370.

United Nations. (2015a). "World population prospects: The 2015 revision", *United Nations Economics and Social Affairs*, 33(2), pp. 1–66.

United Nations. (2015b). "Sustainable Development Goals". (*SDGs), Transforming Our World: The* 2030 (General Assembly).

United Nations Millennium Development Goals: Poverty. (2019). https://www.un.org/millenniumgoals/poverty.shtml. Accessed August 26, 2019.

Wake, D. B., and Vredenburg, V. T. (2008). "Are we in the midst of the sixth mass extinction? A view from the world of amphibians", *Proceedings of the National Academy of Sciences*, 105(Supplement 1), pp. 11466–11473.

Walsh, K. J. E. *et al.* (2019). "Tropical cyclones and climate change", *Tropical Cyclone Research and Review*, 8(4), pp. 240–250.

Watson, C. *et al.* (2019). *Clade X: A Pandemic Exercise*, Mary Ann Liebert, Inc., New Rochelle.

World Bank Group. (2018). "Poverty and shared prosperity 2018: Piecing together the poverty puzzle". Washington, DC: World Bank, https://documents.worldbank.org/en/publication/documents-reports/documentdetail/104451542202552048/poverty-and-shared-prosperity-2018-piecingtogether-the-poverty-puzzle.

York, R., Rosa, E. A., and Dietz, T. (2002). "Bridging environmental science with environmental policy: Plasticity of population, affluence, and technology", *Social Science Quarterly*, 83(1), 18–34.

Part I

Business Implications

Chapter 3

Business and Sustainability

Diane-Charlotte Simon and Laurie Lane-Zucker

Learning Objectives

- Present the foundational concepts
- Describe the intersection between sustainability, business, and investment
- Define financial "materiality", sustainability impact, and double materiality
- Understand the difference between "value-first" and "valueS-first"
- Introduce the concept of sustainability reporting and the ESGs
- Highlight the limitations of siloed sustainability initiatives
- Discuss the concept of an "impact economy" and the transformation of systems

Abstract

This chapter provides a framework for Part I on the Business Implications of sustainability. First, the chapter reviews the business landscape of sustainability and how various business models of different companies impact on the broad concept of sustainability as discussed in this book. Second, it presents the two main schools of thought around the notion of *materiality* which determine the scope of sustainability disclosure. One perspective focuses on the "outside-in": how sustainability impacts a business and its financial performance (*financial materiality*). A second perspective focuses on the "inside-out": how a business impacts the environment, people, and society (*sustainability impacts* also called *impact materiality*). Combined, they form what is referred to as the *double materiality* of sustainability. The chapter explores the broad spectrum of conceptual frameworks at the intersection of sustainability and business. These concepts can range from *Corporate Social Responsibility* (*CSR*) to *Environmental, Social, and Governance* (*ESG*). The latter, after becoming investors' main sustainable investing strategy (see Chapter 8), has become the primary approach to corporate sustainability. The chapter discusses ESG data and presents the main sustainability disclosure frameworks which are critical to investors to assess risks, opportunities, and sustainability impacts so as to price financial instruments (Carroll, 1999). Lastly, the chapter introduces the concept of an *impact economy* and concludes with a discussion of the changes that could be made to address sustainability. The chapter concludes that to become truly sustainable, businesses must consider their 360° impact on society — from their business model to the human and environmental impacts of their products and services.

I. Introduction

Sustainability provides a unique opportunity for businesses to better manage their risks and also enter potentially lucrative and high-impact areas of the economy. The behavior of businesses and individuals as consumers typically lie at the root of the sustainability issues discussed in Chapter 2. As such, they are particularly well-positioned to seed the solutions.

In this first chapter of the Business Implications section, we introduce the two primary approaches to sustainability. One approach focuses on the *single materiality* of the financial impacts of sustainability on business (*financial materiality*, further explored in Chapters 5 and 6). The other approach, *double materiality*, broadens the focus to also consider how business impacts the environment, people, and society (*sustainability impacts* or *impact materiality*). Along these lines we explore another important dichotomy of vision: *value-first* which prioritizes financially material sustainability opportunities and risks and *valueS-first* which privileges/upholds ethical values and proposes a reimagining of the role of business within society (Krosinsky and Purdom, 2017).

But first, we step back to review the fundamentals of business and discuss how a company's structure and size influence its approach to sustainability. Second, we cover the concepts of governance and materiality. Third, the chapter examines ESG data and the main sustainability disclosure frameworks — critical areas for investors — and explores their current limitations. Next, the chapter presents foundational concepts of corporate sustainability including ESG factors, CSR, Stakeholder Theory, and Conscious Capitalism. In this way, the chapter offers a map of the main paths corporate sustainability can take.

The chapter then describes the various degrees to which sustainability can be integrated into business. Many companies still too often approach sustainability as siloed initiatives, while sustainable businesses adopt a fully integrated approach, impacting the entire product life cycle and supply chain. This leads us to our final area of inquiry: the concept of *impact economy* and the changes that could be made to truly address sustainability.

Chapter 3 is organized as per the following sections:

I. Introduction
II. Business Fundamentals and Societal Trends
III. Sustainability Reporting and Data
IV. Foundational Concepts of Corporate Sustainability
V. From Siloed Sustainability Initiatives to Sustainable Business
VI. Impact Economy and the Transformation of Systems
VII. Conclusion

II. Business Fundamentals and Societal Trends

1. Business Landscape

Before delving into the concepts at the intersection of sustainability and business, it is important to revisit the basics of business and the business landscape in terms of structure and size, as these will influence how an organization approaches sustainability.

A. *What is a Business?*

A *business* is typically defined as an organization that provides goods and/or services meeting a particular need of society in exchange for money, with the goal of becoming profitable. A business distinguishes itself from non-profits and charities which also provide goods and/or services meeting a particular need of society but do not seek profits in return.

B. *Business Sizes*

Much of the discussion on corporate sustainability tends to focus on the role and response of large companies whose scale and impact can be felt across the globe. But the business implications of sustainability are relevant for businesses of all sizes and all through their life from inception to maturity.

Small and Medium-Sized Enterprises (SMEs). According to the OECD, small and medium-sized enterprises (SMEs) are independent firms (as opposed to subsidiaries) with a workforce below a certain threshold, which varies across countries (OECD, 2005). The most common upper limit of employees is 250, but it is 500 in the US. They are also defined by thresholds of revenue and sometimes balance sheet. Small firms and micro-enterprises are subsets of SMEs with up to 50 and 10 employees, respectively.

As of 2021, there were approximately 333 million SMEs worldwide (Statista, 2022). SMEs account for close to 90% of businesses and more than 50% of employment globally (World Bank, 2022). Given their contribution to job creation and global economic development, SMEs play a critical role in most economies, particularly in developing countries (World Bank, 2022). Access to finance is a major constraint to SME growth, particularly in emerging markets and developing countries (World Bank, 2022). While often overlooked, the success and growth of the SME sector is key to creating a sustainable economy. Where climate change is concerned, large organizations have typically faced most of the public pressure. Yet, for most large organizations (excluding those in the energy business), the vast majority of their greenhouse gas emissions actually come from their supply chain, typically comprising SMEs. For large companies, supply chain emissions are more than 11 times higher than operational emissions, and up to 25 times higher in the retail industry (CDP, 2021; *BBC*, 2022).

Startups. Startups are young SMEs founded to develop new products or services which typically differ from existing alternatives, involve innovation, and open new markets. Startups are often considered disruptive. In 2020, the US boasted the most startups in the world with about 70,000 startups. India ranks second with around 12,500, and the UK ranks third with 6,000. Around 20% of startups fail in their first year, with only 10% surviving in the long term (US Bureau of Labor Statistics, 2021).

Successful startups are a vital part of efforts to make the economy more sustainable. New businesses can be launched with sustainability as part of their DNA, using sustainability-embedded business models across their value chain. It is much harder to transform existing organizations to new ways of doing business than to grow an already environmentally friendly business.

Unicorns. A Unicorn is a startup or SME that reaches an estimated value of over $1 billion. A decade ago, unicorns were rare. Very few startups "strike it lucky" to become unicorns. Most startups would take their companies public after two or three rounds of venture capital funding by selling shares to raise capital for growth. During 2021, despite the pandemic, 519 new unicorns were created, bringing the total number worldwide to over 1,000 by early 2022.

Large Enterprises. The rest of the business landscape is made up of large enterprises. A large enterprise in the US typically refers to a business with more than 500 employees, and more than 250 in most other countries. In the US, large businesses are also characterized by a minimum threshold in federal taxable income which must exceed $1 million across three taxable years. Despite rising inflation, supply chain crises, and the unstable global business environment, Fortune 500 corporations recently generated a record $16.1 trillion in revenue and $1.8 trillion in profits (Fortune 500, 2022).

***Company Size, Approaches to Sustainability, and Investor Sustainability
Strategy***. The way a startup, an SME or a unicorn approaches sustainability differs from the way a large organization does. Since startups
have less resources, when they consider sustainability, they tend to focus
on business solutions addressing sustainability issues which have material financial impacts for them. Typically, these solutions pertain to their
products which can be environmentally friendly, address health issues,
or focus on education or under-served communities. They may attract
venture capital or private equity investors with a focus on impact investing or sustainability themes (see Chapters 8, 9 and 10). As of October
2022, there were 180 impact unicorns globally, representing 18% of
total unicorns, which were valued at $443 billion in aggregate (HolonIQ,
2022a). These included 97 health tech unicorns, 36 edtech unicorns, and
49 climate tech unicorns (HolonIQ, 2022a). Climate tech unicorns
collectively raised over $46 billion over the past decade and were col-
lectively valued at $109 billion as of October 2022 (HolonIQ, 2022b).
But the reality is that for many SMEs which do not embed sustainability
at the core of their value proposition, sustainability is a luxury they
cannot afford as they often struggle for their very survival and lack
knowledge, funding, and time (*BBC*, 2022).

Larger companies' approaches to sustainability can take more shapes
and forms. Larger corporations tend to emphasize ESG risks while also
looking at business opportunities related to sustainability, but typically to
a lesser extent. Acquiring "pure play" sustainable businesses (startups or
SMEs) can be part of an established business's strategy to improve its
overall sustainability. It is important to note that large companies' sustainability management tends to be more swayed by outside forces such as
consumer demand and institutional investors, for whom ESG has become
mainstream with the growth of the United Nations-supported Principles
for Responsible Investment (UN PRI) whose signatories represented $121
trillion as of March 2022 (see Chapter 8 — Introduction to Sustainable
Finance and Investing). Given their size and potential impacts on society
and the environment, there is also a greater emphasis on large companies'
Corporate Social Responsibility (CSR) toward the environment and society as a whole (see section on CSR below). Indeed, large companies
require a tacit "license to operate" from Society which typically involves

some form of philanthropic efforts to benefit communities and sustainability initiatives. While the focus of the rest of this chapter applies particularly to large organizations, the following chapter (Chapter 4 — Entrepreneurship and Sustainability) focuses on sustainability for smaller organizations.

C. *Business Structures*

The allocation of legal liabilities and taxes between an organization and its owner(s) is determined by its legal structure. There are some correlations between company size and business structure. For example, by nature large businesses are typically corporations, and sole proprietorships are small businesses. The name of the structures and their characteristics vary by country, but are modeled after the five main structures present in the US which are presented in what follows. It is interesting to note that a business's structure and ownership influence how an organization considers sustainability beyond regulatory requirements and the dynamics which shape its strategy.

Sole Proprietorships: In a sole proprietorship, which is owned and operated by a single person, there is no legal distinction between the business and its owner. As such, the tax and legal liabilities of the business are the responsibility of its owner. Sole proprietorships are small businesses by definition, but it is easy to change the structure as they grow. As of 2015, the vast majority of businesses in the US were sole proprietorships, representing 70% of total businesses (IRS, 2022). More than in any other structures, the decision of a sole proprietorship to consider sustainability concerns will be driven by the owner's own beliefs and its customers.

Partnerships: A partnership comprises several partners who contribute resources and money to the business. The business's profits and losses are shared by the partners and recorded on each partner's tax returns. Partners are jointly and severally liable for the company's debts. Law firms and tax equity firms are typically structured as partnerships. This type of structure ensures that the partners have "skin in the game". While the costs to set up a partnership are lower than those to create a corporation or a limited liability company, it is typically more difficult for a partnership to scale and have access to external capital from banks. As of 2015, partnerships represented 11% of US businesses (IRS, 2022).

A partnership's decision to pursue sustainability will typically be driven by its partners. In the case of private equity funds structured as partnerships, limited partners who invest in these funds (and act as customers as a result) can also drive their momentum. They do this influencing the way funds are invested and the management of their portfolio companies.

Corporations: Contrary to sole proprietorships and partnerships, corporations have a legal entity distinct from the owners of the business. In sight of the law, a corporation is considered as a legal "person" which can enter contracts, incur debts, sue and be sued, and pay taxes apart from its owners. Because of this, incorporating a business releases owners from personal liability. Corporations are run by a board of directors and the owners of a corporation's common stock are commonly referred to as shareholders. It is easier for corporations to transfer business ownership relative to other business structures. As of 2015, corporations were the second largest type of business in the US representing 17% of US businesses (IRS, 2022). Large companies and tech start-ups hoping to become large businesses are typically set up as corporations. Venture-backed companies tend to be registered as a corporation because investors typically dislike the "pass-through" tax status of Limited Liability Company (LLC), which requires each owner to file a separate tax form that documents the company's income.

Corporations' approach to sustainability is driven by their management, but also guided by their customers' preferences. Sometimes the campaigns of non-governmental organizations (NGOs) will target large companies for their poor sustainability performance or alleged greenwashing, indirectly impacting their sustainability strategies. The sustainability strategies of publicly traded corporations are particularly influenced by their shareholders. Shareholder engagement is in fact one of the foremost sustainable investing strategies (see Chapters 8 and 11).

Limited Liability Companies (LLCs): A limited liability company combines the limited liability benefits of a corporation with the pass-through taxation benefits of a partnership. As of 2015, LLCs represented 7% of US businesses (IRS, 2022). How a limited liability company will consider sustainability will be influenced by its owners, its management, and its customers.

Public Benefit Corporations (PBCs): Public benefit corporations are a form of business structure launched in 2010 whose governance is accountable not just to shareholders, but to all stakeholders (see Sect. III.4 Stakeholder Theory) including employees, customers, local communities, wider society, and the environment (B Lab, 2022). "A public benefit corporation is a corporation created to generate social and public good, and to operate in a responsible and sustainable manner" (Cornell Law School, 2020). PBCs represent a small portion of US businesses, but their numbers are growing and include some publicly traded companies such as Coursera and Warby Parker. By nature, PBCs are accountable for their sustainability performance and impact on all their stakeholders.

2. The Rise of Corporate Sustainability

Surging interest in corporate sustainability in the demands of shareholders, employees, and consumers alike has been observed for decades (Hoffman, 1999; King and Lenox, 2000). Gen Zs and millennials especially are concerned about the state of the world and aim to drive societal change in everything they do from their work to what they consume to their investments (Deloitte, 2022). Nowadays, successful companies are being defined and judged by how fully sustainability is integrated into their business models. This includes environmental management but also management quality, corporate ethics and talent management (Lopez *et al.*, 2007). Sustainability is a firm reality in a growing number of organizations, as evidenced by the increase of Chief Sustainability Officers, a relatively new executive-level position (Choi *et al.*, 2010). In the US, we see a clear reflection of the rise of corporate sustainability in the updated 2019 Business Roundtable Statement on the Purpose of a Corporation. 181 CEOs signed the statement, committing to lead their companies for the benefit of all stakeholders: customers, employees, suppliers, communities, and shareholders, moving away from shareholder primacy (Business Roundtable, 2019).

Since 2009, MIT Sloan Management Review and The Boston Consulting Group (BCG) have studied how corporations address sustainability, surveying tens of thousands of managers and interviewing more than 150 executives and thought leaders. According to their 2017 report, 60% of managers indicated that their organization employs some form of sustainability strategy, and 90% of all managers reported that sustainability strategy is critical to their business, even if it was not currently in place (Kiron *et al.*, 2017). Even in the aftermath of the 2008 financial crisis, this issue remained prominent. A 2011 study conducted by Ernst and Young (2013) revealed that of the 300 directors of global companies interviewed, 44% reported that their company had increased its sustainability expenses since the financial crisis and just as many reported their expenses remained stable.

3. Governance

Corporate governance is the set of resolutions, policies, rules, practices, processes, and controls by which large firms are directed and controlled (Bloomfield, 2022). Corporate governance involves balancing the interests of a company's many stakeholders, such as shareholders, executives, customers, and financiers, and compliance with government regulations and tax laws. Governance is also one of the pillars of ESG, which has become the main approach to corporate sustainability. This is discussed further in the section on the foundational concepts of corporate sustainability.

More recently, large companies have come under pressure to consider a "double bottom line" that goes beyond financial optimization to also consider sustainability. This is driven partly by regulators, especially in Europe, by consumers, civil society, and by shareholder resolutions. Boards of directors nevertheless have a responsibility to ensure that a company's core corporate governance policies still include fiduciary responsibility, risk management, accountability, transparency, and return on investment for its shareholders.

4. Materiality

Much research has focused on the relationship between sustainability and companies' financial performance and reveals a relationship that tends to be positive, with the *financial materiality* of sustainability (Whelan *et al.*, 2022; Khan *et al.*, 2016). Chapters 5 and 6 of the volume focus more closely on the topic. The financial materiality of sustainability is a key driver for companies to embed it in their business models and their risk management frameworks. It is also a key justification for investors to include it in the scope of their fiduciary duties. This is the reason why the US Department of Labor is allowing consideration of ESG factors by fiduciaries of employee benefit plans that are subject to the Employee Retirement Income Security Act of 1974 (ERISA) (Federal Register, 2022).

But it is important to understand that "materiality" does not always refer to the same thing. Two schools of thought exist around the materiality of sustainability and why it should be taken into consideration by business and financial institutions. One is dedicated to the financial impacts, and one to the impacts on environment and society. In its Non-Financial Reporting Directive (NFRD) adopted in 2014, the European Union (EU) defined the *double materiality* **of sustainability** (see Figure 3.1) which consists of the following:

- *Financial Materiality* or "outside-in" perspective of how sustainability issues affect companies' financial performance, position, and development, and
- *Sustainability Impacts*, also called *Impact Materiality* or the "inside-out" perspective of a company's impact on the environment, people, and society as a whole.

There is much debate around which type of materiality should be considered and disclosed. Financial materiality is the more prevalent approach in the US, while double materiality is a regulatory requirement in Europe (Schumacher *et al.*, 2022). Some argue that the concept of materiality is complex and includes nuances beyond the main concepts described above. *Dynamic materiality* is a common concept borne from

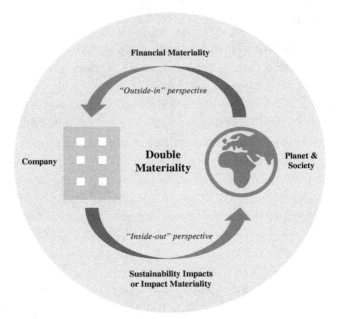

Figure 3.1.   Double Materiality

Source: Authors

the claim that some sustainability information now material only for society and the planet may also become financially material over the medium or longer term (World Economic Forum, 2020). Others argue that building bridges between financial and impact materiality is unnecessary and needlessly complicates the concept of materiality (GRI, 2022a).

Financial materiality and the greater good for society and the environment may be pursued simultaneously; returns need not necessarily be sacrificed for impact. But the distinction is clear, and some investors may prioritize one type of materiality over the other (Figure 3.2).

III. Sustainability Reporting and Data

Classical economic theories assert that transparency and availability of information are both necessary for financial markets to operate efficiently and for market players to accurately price financial instruments and assess their risk. Granting these assertions, both financial and sustainability

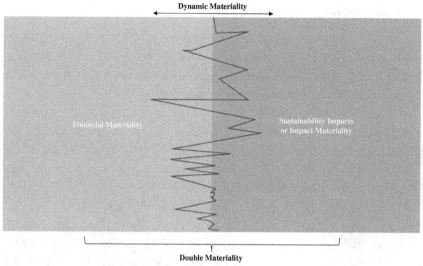

Figure 3.2. Materialities

Source: Authors

disclosures are critical. Sustainability-related data are certainly necessary to implement sustainable investment strategies and to develop sustainable finance products. But ESG data often highlight financially material information and can be decision-useful even for investors indifferent to sustainable concerns.

Companies' sustainability and ESG performance has historically been assessed using data from voluntary disclosures in sustainability reports and publicly available information. With the advent of sustainability reporting regulations, mandatory disclosures are becoming increasingly available as a source of data. Data on companies' sustainability and ESG performance are critical for economic actors like consumers and investors to make purchasing and investment decisions. It's another page from market economics 101: market efficiency requires transparency enabled by information availability, quality, comparability, and relevance. While companies' sustainability data and ratings are often criticized, efforts driven by both regulators and non-profit standard-setters are underway, including consolidation in disclosure frameworks, to improve sustainability disclosures and their comparability.

1. Sustainability Disclosure Frameworks

The two schools of thought around the materiality discussed above (single financial materiality and double materiality, which surveys the materiality of sustainability beyond its financial implications) are also reflected in sustainability disclosure frameworks (see Figure 3.3).

On the one hand, the International Financial Reporting Standards (IFRS) Sustainability Disclosure Standards within the IFRS Foundation follow a financial materiality approach which focuses on information relevant to investors such as sustainability-related risks and opportunities (see Figure 3.3). The IFRS Sustainability Disclosure Standards are currently being developed by the International Sustainability Standards Board (ISSB), which consolidated most sustainability disclosure frameworks in 2022, excluding the Global Reporting Initiative (GRI, 2022a, 2022b) with the hope to improve the field consistency. The IFRS Foundation also produces the widely accepted IFRS Accounting Standards, which are required to be used by publicly listed companies in 167 jurisdictions globally. While the General Accepted Accounting Principles (GAAP) are the accounting standards in the US, more than 500 foreign SEC registrants, representing an aggregated capitalization of $7 trillion, use the IFRS Standards in their filings (IFRS Foundation, 2022a).

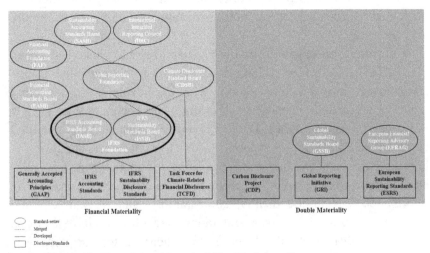

Figure 3.3. Main Financial and Sustainability Disclosure Frameworks

Source: Authors

The Sustainability Accounting Standard Board (SASB), which spearheaded the use of investor-focused material information and identified the subset of environmental, social, and governance issues most relevant to financial performance for 77 industries, was merged with the International Integrated Reporting Council in 2021 to form the Value Reporting Foundation (IFRS Foundation, 2022b). The Value Reporting Foundation was later consolidated with the Climate Disclosure Standard Board (CDSB), which developed a framework for companies to disclose specifically on their climate-related risks called the Taskforce on Climate-Related Financial Disclosure (TCFD), to form the ISSB within the IFRS Foundation in 2022 (IFRS Foundation, 2022b).

On the other hand, the Global Reporting Initiative (GRI), the first and currently the most widely adopted sustainability disclosure and reporting framework, follows a double materiality approach which considers the interests of various stakeholders (see Figure 3.3). In 2000, GRI launched the first version of the Sustainability Reporting Guidelines, which calls for organizations to voluntarily disclose their actions on Corporate Social Responsibility and on sustainability as a whole.

In November 2022, the European Parliament adopted the Corporate Sustainability Reporting Directive (CSRD) which requires companies to report on the "double materiality" of sustainability and complements the Non-Financial Reporting Directive The CSRD was approved by the EU council and entered into force in January 2023. The scope of reporting should not only include data necessary to assess the company's financial performance, but also information on the impact of its "activities on environmental, social and employee matters, respect for human rights, anti-corruption and bribery matters". Provided that no existing standard or framework satisfies the EU's needs for sustainability reporting by itself, the European Financial Reporting Advisory Group (EFRAG) has been tasked with the endorsement of international financial reporting standards.

2. The State of Sustainability Disclosure

The major audit and consulting firm KPMG has tracked the evolution of sustainability disclosure and conducted sustainability reporting surveys

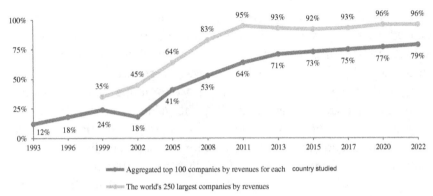

Figure 3.4. Growth in Global Sustainability Reporting Rates

Source: KPMG (2022).

since 1993, when sustainability was in its infancy. In 2022, of the 5,800 companies interviewed by KPMG representing the largest 100 companies across 58 countries, close to 80% were reporting on sustainability, up from 12% in 1993, and 64% in 2011. This was even higher among the world's largest 250 companies by revenues according to the *2021 Fortune 500 ranking* at a rate of 96% (see Figure 3.4).

Notable regional discrepancies remained in 2022. While 89% of companies in Asia Pacific disclosed on sustainability matters, 82% disclosed in Europe (85% in Western Europe vs. 72% in Eastern Europe), 74% in the Americas (97% in North America vs. 69% in Latin America), and 56% in the Middle East and Africa (see Figures 3.5 and 3.6). The increase in corporate sustainability reporting has been driven by governments, regulators, stock exchanges, and investors.

Across these regions, corporate sustainability reporting is moving from voluntary to mandatory, dictated by either regulations or stock exchanges. In 2014, the European Union established a landmark directive on non-financial reporting, requiring companies of more than 250 employees to report on environmental, social, and board diversity information. In the United States, companies are required to include climate change-related disclosures in their filings with the Securities Exchange Commission, as per Regulation S-K. Trends are also emerging in corporate sustainability reporting, such as reporting on climate-related financial

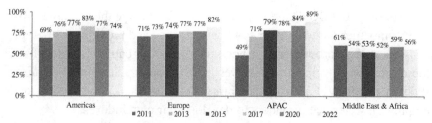

Figure 3.5. Sustainability Reporting Rates by Region
Source: KPMG (2022).

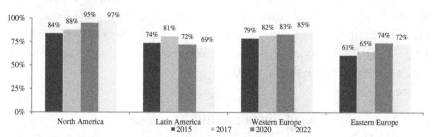

Figure 3.6. Sustainability Reporting Rates by Subregion
Source: KPMG (2022, 2017).

risk, the UN Sustainable Development Goals (SDGs), carbon reduction targets, and human rights.

3. ESG Data Providers

The sustainability data presented in companies' voluntary disclosures, their financial reports, and the media are then collected and analyzed by ESG data providers. Third-party organizations gather additional data by conducting detailed surveys on companies. Other sources of information include mandatory disclosures (e.g. Management and Disclosure Discussion section in companies' public filing in the United States), news, and relevant information published by NGOs. According to The Global Initiative for Sustainability Ratings, there were more than 125 ESG data providers as of 2016. Reputable organizations in the field include ISS ESG, Morningstar Sustainalytics and Moody's V.E (F.K.A. Vigeo Eiris), MSCI, RepRisk, S&P's Trucost, and Bloomberg. Certain providers such as S&P Global Trucost and CDP focus solely on environmental data.

Not only do ESG data providers gather and analyze the data, they also rank companies based on their ESG performance and provide scores, typically using their proprietary methodology. Investors can use the data from these providers to support their investment decisions. Sustainable indexes such as the Dow Jones Sustainability Index or the UK's FTSE4Good employ these service providers to develop their own indexes.

Similar to the other areas of sustainable finance, mainstream financial data providers such as MSCI or Bloomberg have entered the space more recently to develop a wide range of ESG data offerings. In addition, mainstream financial service firms have begun to acquire pioneer firms: S&P Dow Jones Indices acquired Trucost in 2016, Moody's acquired Vigeo Eiris in 2019 (rebranded as V.E since the acquisition), and Morningstar, Inc. bought Sustainalytics in 2020.

4. The Limitations of Sustainability Disclosure and ESG Data

Corporations widening their scope of reporting to include ESG criteria is certainly progress, but it falls short of fully and accurately reflecting the extent and scale of their environmental impacts and risks. It also largely fails to place a company's performance within the context of the limits of and demands on environmental or social resources (also called the "sustainability context" principle), according to the United Nations Environment Program (UNEP, 2015). Sustainability disclosure is also criticized for neglecting material information that is industry-specific and decision-useful to investors (i.e. affecting company financial performance). Another pitfall of reporting is that the information companies communicate is difficult to compare. For instance, while many use the same GRI framework, they lack a standardized reporting methodology and scoring, and do not always disclose on the same key performance indicators. This can complicate the benchmarking process for investors. But recent efforts in the space, including the consolidation of many standard setters under the IFRS Foundation, are expected to improve the status quo and provide clarity in key areas like materiality reporting (KPMG, 2022). Several organizations dealing with sustainability-related disclosure frameworks themselves, including CDP and GRI, recently acknowledged the need for a more standardized set of reporting standards and called for further cooperation to establish a comprehensive reporting system in partnership with the IFRS Foundation

The voluntary nature of sustainability reporting and companies largely disclosing their own ESG data arouses caution from investors. As with financial disclosures, third-party warranties or audits are recommended to verify the accuracy and integrity of sustainability disclosures. ESG data audits have become a more common activity and a regularly provided service by mainstream audit companies (KPMG, 2020). Indeed, more and more investors are requesting these third-party reviews. And some regulatory bodies around the globe are attempting to oversee and standardize ESG ratings.

These limitations have prompted countries, governmental agencies, and exchanges to develop their own frameworks and regulations for companies to disclose on ESG, while providing guidance on methodologies and setting legal ground for enforcement. More and more, sustainability is being driven by regulatory concerns rather than voluntary initiatives.

5. Credit Agencies Are Now Factoring ESG in Their Ratings

A recent development illustrates the materiality of ESG criteria: rating agencies such as Moody's, Standards & Poor's, Fitch and Kroll have included ESG considerations in their traditional credit rating reports. These agencies devised internal frameworks and mapping specifically for ESG criteria. Many published their first ESG methodologies in 2019 and 2020. Rating agencies are traditional institutions providing material credit analysis to investors, and this move reinforces the non-equivocal financial implications of sustainability. It also addresses investors' growing interest in ESG and sustainability.

IV. Foundational Concepts of Corporate Sustainability

The scope of corporate sustainability goes well beyond environmental sustainability. It is a broad topic encompassing many concepts discussed in the following paragraphs. These range from good management practices to redefining the role of business in society.

The most common approaches place the company and its shareholders at the center and assess how sustainability affects their performance; in this case, financial materiality prevails. The focus of this approach seeks to understand sustainability-related risks and opportunities. Sustainability approaches that prioritize financial materiality can be called *value-first* (Krosinsky and Purdom, 2017) or *value-driven*.

The alternative prioritizes moral or ethical values and seeks the greater good of society and the environment; in this case the materiality of the effects on the planet and communities are the focus. This approach is intended to redefine the purpose business in society and can be called *valueS-first* (Krosinsky and Purdom, 2017) or *valueS-driven*. As with the different types of materiality they consider, these approaches may be taken in tandem.

1. Environmental, Social, and Governance (ESG)

ESG falls under the *value-first* category most of the time, though not all ESG topics have material impact on companies' financial performance (cf. Chapter 5).

Corporate sustainability can be examined both from a company and investor perspective. ESG is an analysis conducted by investors to assess a company's sustainability performance by examining its environmental, social, and governance performance. This approach to sustainable investing emerged in the early 2000s (Fulton *et al.*, 2012) and has become a leading sustainable strategy globally. Representing over $16.6 trillion in US assets at the beginning of 2020, or one out of three dollars professionally managed with ESG considerations, it is the main sustainable investing strategy in the US (USSIF, 2020). Key topics assessed include climate change (e.g. renewable energy, mitigation and adaptation strategies, etc.), sustainable natural resources, agriculture (e.g. organic food, Non-GMO, etc.) and commerce (e.g. fair trade, etc.), labor conditions, board diversity, executive pay, corruption, conflict risk (terrorist or repressive regimes), or tobacco (USSIF, 2020).

ESG criteria present not only financial and reputational risks but also opportunities for companies, their shareholders, and creditors (cf. Chapters 5 and 6). ESG management can therefore be considered good management practice. More and more financial institutions are considering ESG factors when making financing and investing decisions (cf. Chapter 8). Monitoring ESG factors is becoming the new normal; they can be seen as just another set of performance parameters for executives and board members to manage. The analysis can be conducted both on a company's historical performance and forward looking, considering its objectives and goals. In places like Europe, this practice goes beyond a voluntary approach — it is required by regulation. Table 3.1 presents some typical ESG issues and parameters.

2. The Purpose of Business

The concept of "sustainable development" was first defined in 1987 by the United Nations Brundtland Commission as "development that meets the needs of the present without compromising the ability of future generations to meet their own needs" (Brundtland *et al.*, 1987). In 2015, the United Nations drew up 17 Sustainable Development Goals (SDGs), each of which aims to tackle its own sustainability issue. These issues present threats for businesses, but also opportunities. And in the midst of it all lies the question: what is the role of business?

Since the dawn of industrialization, the role of business in society has been debated. While improving living conditions for most of the industrialized world, the diverging interests of enterprises, employees, consumers, and governments have also led to social tensions and at times, social conflicts. The various interests of stakeholders may converge over the long term, but conflict in the short term. Historically, these conflicts have been resolved through social movements followed by governmental interventions. Governments and the public sector have been responsible for mitigating negative externalities through regulations (see Chapters 14 and 15). But in recent years, as colossal government debt has slashed public budgets, and a public torn between competing political agendas has lost faith in the welfare state, the role of the private sector has become critical.

To begin exploring valueS-driven approaches, we need to go back to the basics. From a traditional capitalist point of view, the purpose of business is to increase profits, commonly referred to as the "bottom line" because of how net income appears on a company's financial statements

Table 3.1. Selected ESG Issues

Key Pillars	Key Themes	Key Parameters	Key Issues
Environment	Climate change	Carbon footprint	Vulnerabilities from extreme weather events
	Natural resources	Energy efficiency Sourcing of raw materials	Water efficiency Usage of land
	Pollution and waste	Toxic emissions Wastewater management Hazardous materials management	Air quality Electronic waste management
	Opportunities and policy	Renewable energy Clean technology	Green buildings Environmental and biodiversity targets and investment
Social	Human capital	Workplace health and safety Development opportunities	Employee engagement, diversity, and inclusion Labor practices (e.g., wages, working conditions)
	Product responsibility	Product safety and quality Selling practices and product labeling	Customer privacy and data security Access to products
	Relations	Community Government	Civil society
Governance	Corporate governance	Board structure and accountability Accounting and disclosure practices	Executive compensation and management effectiveness Ownership and shareholder rights
	Corporate behavior	Management of corruption Systemic risk management Earnings quality	Competitive behavior Management of business environment (e.g., legal, regulations) Transparency on tax and related-party transactions

Source: IMF (2019).

(at the bottom). Some neoliberals like Professor Milton Friedman of the University of Chicago (1970) vouch that this is the sole social responsibility of business. Along these lines, it is commonly accepted that the primary function of business is "to improve shareholder's value, which is determined by return (profit) and risk" (Movassaghi and Bramhandkar, 2012).

However, the role of business can include broader societal considerations. For many entrepreneurs, the purpose of business is to solve problems and answer the unmet needs of consumers, the very raison d'être of the endeavor. Business creates jobs which allow people to earn a living and, in the best cases, enjoy meaningful and fulfilling careers. In his 2019 Letter to CEOs, the CEO of BlackRock stressed that "Purpose is (…) a company's fundamental reason for being (…)" while clarifying that "Purpose is not the sole pursuit of profits but the animating force for achieving them" and adding that "Profits are in no way inconsistent with purpose — in fact, profits and purpose are inextricably linked" (Fink, 2019).

Several concepts, such as Stakeholder Theory and Corporate Social Responsibility, highlight the importance of integrating societal interests into business and argue that its role goes far beyond making a profit. According to Aflac 2020 CSR Survey, 86% of executives interviewed and 80% of consumers interviewed think that large companies have either a very important or somewhat important responsibility to make the world a better place.

The following pages outline the main concepts which place moral values first and comprise the field of corporate sustainability. While they all share a values-driven approach, they differ in approach, focus, and how deeply they integrate the sustainability components into the business model.

3. Corporate Social Responsibility

The concept of CSR is not new. References to it can be found in documents from almost a century ago. Oliver Sheldon (1924) laid out the principles of CSR, claiming that the foremost responsibility of a company's management was social and communal. He stressed that management efficiency had to be assessed "not only by scientific standards, but also by the supreme standard of communal well-being". Howard Bowen (1953) published Social Responsibilities of the Businessman in 1953 and is today considered another father of CSR. In his book, he claims the duty of businessmen is to make decisions which are "desirable in terms of the objectives and values of our society".

CSR was defined in greater detail by Clarence Cyril Walton (1967) as the acknowledgment of the intimate relationship between corporations and society. He urged top managers to keep this in mind while pursuing goals. Already in 1971, the Committee for Economic Development (CED) observed that the social contract between business and society was shifting and that companies were being asked to assume broader societal responsibilities than ever before. They developed a conceptual circular model for CSR, built of three layers of business responsibility (see Figure 3.7):

- The *Inner Circle* focuses on the effectiveness of a business's core economic function. This includes the development and

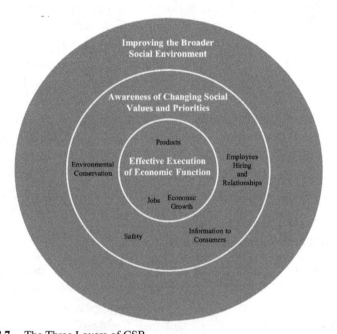

Figure 3.7.   The Three Layers of CSR

Source: Based on the Committee for Economic Development (1971).

commercialization of quality products and services, job creation, and the contribution to economic growth.

- The *Intermediate Circle* extends to problems that can arise directly from a company's economic activity, considered its "direct responsibility". This level considers a company's awareness of society's shifting social values and priorities and its own impacts on them. This includes hiring and employee relationships, fair treatment and worker safety, transparency with customers and shareholders, as well as environmental conservation.
- The *Outer Circle* points to broader responsibilities considered to be "moral responsibilities". This layer goes beyond the direct impacts of a business's economic activity. It recognizes that large corporations have access to considerable resources and skills that could be leveraged for the public good, complementing the activity of public institutions and non-profits. It highlights the role that business can play to improve the social environment and tackle issues such as urban blight or poverty. This includes corporate philanthropy.

More recently, another three-dimensional definition of CSR has been developed. This framework acknowledges that CSR involves the generation of profit and also a responsibility toward the planet and the people (Elkington, 1998). Here, profit alludes to "economic prosperity", planet, to "environmental quality", and people, to "social justice". Elkington argues that companies should be held accountable for all three dimensions and not only the "bottom line", hence the creation of the term "triple bottom line". In assessing a company's CSR performance, its complete three-layer impact on profit, planet, and people should be considered.

The Global Reporting Initiative (GRI) identifies these three dimensions as economic, environmental, and social. The economic dimension considers the main economic impacts of the organization throughout society, the environmental dimension assesses the organization's impact on living and non-living natural systems (e.g. land, air, water, ecosystems, etc.), and the social dimension encompasses labor practices, human rights, product responsibility, and impact on society as indicated in the Sustainability Reporting Guideline G4 of 2013.

Whether labeled as "planet, people, and profit" (Elkington, 1998) or "environmental, social, and economic" (GRI), most CSR frameworks rethink the role of business from an ethical perspective and demand the implementation of certain policies to improve companies' impacts on society and the environment. Yet, for those like Milton Friedman, CSR is an immoral concept that infringes on the rights of business owners. This school of thought argues that by engaging in non-business "social" activities, executives are hijacking shareholders' dues. It claims that if shareholders intend to address these issues, they can use their own resources in the form of donations to foundations or non-profits (Friedman, 1970). This argument rejects the idea of business's moral responsibility conceptualized in the *Outer Circle* of the CED model discussed above.

4. Stakeholder Theory

The Stakeholder Theory, another pillar of corporate sustainability, can be seen as the business application of Kant's dictum "treat persons as ends unto themselves". According to this theory, companies must be accountable not only to their shareholders but also to their employees, customers, suppliers, and local communities as they all have a stake in the firm (Evan and Freeman, 1988). Figure 3.8 places these stakeholders in the inner circle and creates a second circle for other stakeholders: society, consumer advocate groups, special interest groups, media, competitors, and government. This concept, attributed to Edward Freeman, posits that business's responsibility is to operate in the interest of all its stakeholders (Freeman, 1984).

This theory asserts that stakeholders are interdependent and that creating value for one stakeholder benefits the others as well (Freeman *et al.*, 2010). Stakeholder Theory reimagines the role of business as building relationships and creating value for all its stakeholders, as they are all crucial to its success. For this reason, companies must consider both their own perspective and those of its immediate stakeholders to develop strategies, operate the organization, and solve problems in general (Freeman and Dmytriyev, 2017). Stakeholder Theory emphasizes the importance of putting purpose in the driver's seat. Purpose should influence an organization's direction and thereby its vision, mission, strategy, and its corporate responsibilities (Freeman and Dmytriyev, 2017). In 2010, B-Lab created

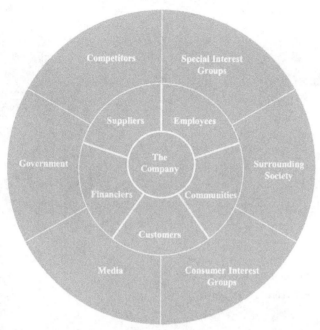

Figure 3.8. The Stakeholders

Source: Based on Freeman and Dmytriyev (2017).

a new legal structure called the Public Benefit Corporation (PBC) founded on stakeholder governance which enables a company's governance structure to be accountable to all stakeholders, not just shareholders. In 2021, the largest asset manager in the world, Blackrock, provided more legitimacy to the legal structure by supporting companies in their portfolio that want to convert to benefit corporations.

Stakeholder Theory and CSR differ primarily in scope, as illustrated in Figure 3.9. Stakeholder Theory focuses on the interactions and needs of many parties with a stake in the firm while CSR extends to areas not directly impacted by a firm's activity.

The 2019 statement by the Business Roundtable, backed by CEOs representing nearly 30% of total US market capitalization, explicitly counters Milton Friedman's view that profit is the only purpose of business and proclaims their adherence to a stakeholder-focused capitalism already prevalent in Europe (Gartenberg and Serafeim, 2019).

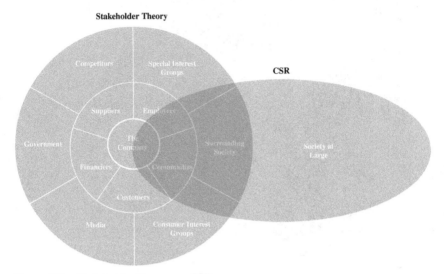

Figure 3.9.   Stakeholder Theory vs. CSR

Source: Based on Freeman and Dmytriyev (2017).

5. Conscious Capitalism

The Conscious Capitalism philosophy was developed following the Stakeholder Theory by Raj Sisodia, Professor of Global Business at Babson College and John Mackey, the co-founder of Whole Foods. Conscious Capitalism provides a blueprint for a new system of doing business in which a business incorporates four tenets to become a conscious company: Higher Purpose, Stakeholder Orientation, Conscious Leadership, and Conscious Culture (Mackey and Sisodia, 2013).

Higher Purpose: Businesses should exist for reasons beyond profit. For conscious businesses, profit is the means, and the end is the company's purpose. Profit enables a company to sustainably accomplish its purpose.

According to Blackrock CEO, "when a company truly understands and expresses its purpose, it functions with the focus and strategic discipline that drive long-term profitability. Purpose unifies management, employees, and communities. It drives ethical behavior and creates an essential check on actions that go against the best interests of stakeholders. Purpose guides culture, provides a framework for consistent decision-making, and, ultimately, helps sustain long-term financial returns for the shareholders (…)" (Fink, 2019).

Stakeholder Orientation: Conscious businesses value and consider every stakeholder in their ecosystem. By seeking win–win solutions that benefit all stakeholders, they provide sustainable, long-term motivation for their stakeholders.

Conscious Leadership: Conscious leaders are characterized by their focus on the common interest of stakeholders, rather than their own personal benefits. Their leadership inspires positive transformation and brings out the best in those around them. They focus the organization on its higher purpose, implement stakeholder orientation, and foster a culture that supports these pillars.

Conscious Culture: This principle emphasizes the critical importance of a business culture to enable its success. Culture is considered the "heartbeat" that acts as an energizing and unifying force that "brings a conscious business to life". Culture translates to values, principles, and practices aimed at fostering care and trust between employees and stakeholders. A conscious culture is embedded with accountability, transparency, and integrity. It promotes loyalty and fairness, and facilitates and values employees' personal growth.

Conscious Capitalism differs from CSR in its orientation toward society. Whereas CSR is a laudable step toward sustainability, Conscious Capitalism is a fully integrated form of a sustainable business. For conscious businesses, socially responsibility is part of their DNA (Sisodia, 2009).

6. Philanthropy

Of all the concepts discussed in this chapter, philanthropy is probably the most familiar and the one with the deepest roots. The word "philanthropy" comes from Ancient Greek and literally means love of humanity.

Philanthropy consists of private initiatives for the common good focusing on quality of life (McCully, 2009). A philanthropist is a person who contributes with her money, time, skills, or talent to help create a better world. Famous philanthropists stepping up include successful businessmen like Carnegie, Rockefeller, or Ford in the 20th century or Bill Gates, Warren Buffet, and Jeff Besos more recently. Celebrity philanthropy has also become a phenomenon since the 1990s with figures like Bono, Angelina Jolie, or Leonardo Dicaprio.

Philanthropy is closely related to the concept of charity, but the two should not be confused. While both are driven by altruism, generosity, and helpfulness, charity tends to provide immediate relief especially toward the needy or suffering, while philanthropy focuses on addressing a broader range of issues (health, environment, development, science, culture, etc.) over the longer term.

Historically, philanthropy and business have often been considered opposites, with business focusing on material gain, typically for a small group of people, and philanthropy focusing on positive impacts for the public good. But with the spread of concepts such as corporate social responsibility, the Stakeholder Theory, social entrepreneurship (cf. Chapter 4), and more recently impact investing (cf. Chapter 10), the common ground between business and philanthropy broadened to the extent that some think that the boundaries between both are blurring. Philanthropy can actually include market-driven initiatives. Indeed, philanthropists are now increasingly active in sustainable investing, and especially via impact investing, in parallel to their traditional donations and grants.

Yet, the fundamental difference between the two is that a business is constrained by its economic sustainability; it needs to at least breakeven and preferably generate profits. But not all issues can be solved by profitable business solutions and sometimes market-based solutions are not applicable (e.g. food access and shelters for the homeless, etc.). And this is why non-profits' role remains critical to the society and the public good, but also for their role complementing market-based and government led solutions. Indeed, concessional capital is a needed tool to address sustainability issues in parallel to public funds and profit-seeking finance and business.

V. From Siloed Sustainability Initiatives to Sustainable Business

1. The Limits of Siloed Initiatives

Many organizations still handle their corporate sustainability in a silo. And it often amounts to a public relations exercise or a sporadic corporate philanthropy initiative, rather than a strategic top management consideration impacting the whole organization. Still today, in too many cases, corporate sustainability remains disconnected from the business itself. You can expect to see a lot of messaging about green initiatives to celebrate Earth Day with employees sporting green t-shirts and tote bags... but this display is somewhat undermined when you realize the company's products cannot be recycled while their production is outsourced in a location where the workers' basic human rights are not respected and that involves a lot of pollution. This focus on the reputational aspect of CSR, striving to improve environmental image without rethinking how products are made and how they are consumed, can lead to a practice known as "greenwashing". This can easily backfire and have the adverse effect. Moreover, the direct value from isolated sustainability initiatives is difficult to assess, while integrating sustainability into business increases an organization's chance of profiting from its sustainability activities (Kiron *et al.*, 2017).

2. Implementing Successful Sustainability Practices

As per the 2017 MIT BCG study, 90% of executives saw the clear importance of sustainability, but only 60% had a sustainability strategy in place and only 25% had developed a clear business case for their sustainability efforts (Kiron *et al.*, 2017). Yet, as leadership struggles to adapt, evidence continues to show that organizations integrating sustainability in their business models, using cross-functional teams, setting up clear targets and key performance indicators (KPIs), are more likely to generate profits from sustainability. Support from top management is critical in establishing effective sustainability practices, yet less than half of the respondents in the 2017 MIT BCG study indicated that their CEOs were engaged, and less than a third witnessed strong board-level oversight (Kiron *et al.*, 2017). Sustainability implementation also demands cultural and behavioral change, making employee engagement key to its success (Eccles *et al.*, 2012). Moreover, the environmental impact of any capital expenditure program should be assessed to mitigate risks related to the location of their facilities or the products.

3. What Is a Sustainable Business?

A sustainable business is a business which incorporates sustainability in its business model and adopts a holistic approach to sustainability across its product life cycle, from its development through its supply chain to its recycling. It also imbues environmental sustainability (see Chapter 12) into its operations, and strives to reduce its negative impact on its community and the environment. And importantly, it responsibly manages its greenhouse gases emissions with the goal of reducing them to a minimum.

VI. Impact Economy and the Transformation of Systems

1. Impact Economy

In this final section, we investigate perhaps the purest values-driven approach to corporate sustainability. So, again, let's take a moment to return to basics. Merriam-Webster defines a system as "a regularly interacting or interdependent group of items forming a unified whole". Earth is one the best examples of a system, with ecosystems as its networks of natural subsystems. Human civilization can also be viewed as a system, which can vary in form and function, much like natural ecosystems. It is striking that our current civilization has taken a shape so at odds with the Earth's ecosystems. This profound misalignment has led to climate change, mass biological extinctions, toxic releases, polluted oceans, and depleted topsoil.

Some scientists argue that the gravity of these consequences calls for a deep transformation of our societies. They stress that quick fixes will not be sufficient to address these serious environmental issues; institutions and individuals should work toward "systems alignment", shifting from a human-centric model to an Earth-centered system. This would involve both deep reflection on the purpose of the system and the intention to renegotiate power dynamics as a means for re-envisioning the system itself (Waddell, 2018). Transformational change can happen in different ways and on many timelines, but given the findings in reports such as the 2018 IPCC which calls for drastic greenhouse emissions cuts to avoid the worst impacts of climate change, there is reason to shift to a sustainable system as quickly as possible.

The *impact economy* is an economic system geared toward this transformational change, driven by the intention to transform society toward sustainable economic development that is regenerative, resilient, circular (see Chapter 12), and just. Its primary goal is the transformation of systems to achieve these goals. An impact economy fosters economic growth and wealth creation, while also addressing global, social, and environmental challenges with the same importance (McKinsey, 2018).

2. The Challenges to the Development of the Impact Economy

A. *The Scale of the Changes Necessary*

One of the major challenges to building an impact economy lies within the beliefs of its opponents: defenders of the status quo who maintain that incremental changes to the existing economy will suffice. Many corporations, investors, and policymakers prefer to mitigate sustainability risks with small adjustments to current systems, rather than embrace transformational change. From an Impact Economy perspective, a company's overall business strategy and operation needs to be rethought to comply with sustainable considerations. Realizing that the goodwill of companies and investors alone may not be enough to tackle the issues at stake, policymakers in certain parts of the world have begun to implement regulations to accelerate the transformation to a clean economy.

B. *The Threat of Greenwashing*

The flourishing interest of consumers and investors alike has attracted more players in the space. Pure play pioneering leaders have been joined by mainstream companies and investors to seize the business opportunity presented by sustainability and sustainable finance. The threat of greenwashing has grown out of this expansion, with new players surfing on the trend to reap its benefits, without the same integrity and intension to generate tangible positive impacts. In some cases, firms use sustainability strictly for its reputational benefits, promising bogus environmental or social impacts. They see it as a marketing tool or a public relations spin. Regulation is increasingly used to answer the greenwashing threat. For example, in March 2021 greenwashing was criminalized in France and can now lead to fines and a mandatory 30-day disclosure of the offense on the organization's website. Regulations like the EU Taxonomy Climate Delegated Act, adopted in May 2021, can guard against greenwashing by targeting ESG disclosures and specifying what can be defined as green or sustainable.

C. *The Terminology Challenges*

Another obstacle to building an impact economy comes from the rapid and chaotic evolution of its key concepts, structure, and language. The fields of corporate sustainability and sustainable finance are filled with acronyms and terms used interchangeably but with different meanings. The viability of this approach depends on developing a common language, guiding principles, and best practices. This volume seeks to clarify the meaning of these key terms.

D. *Unlocking the Private Sector's Impact with Effective Risk Allocations, Funding Sources, Regulations, and Incentives*

Addressing sustainability issues effectively and at scale demands an understanding of the various stakeholders at play and their drivers and paradigms. It is critical to determine limitations of each stakeholder and leverage the areas where they can have the greatest impact. For instance, while business and finance possess enormous power to scale sustainability solutions and mitigate negative impacts, they are constrained by their need to be profitable for their own survival. It is important to identify the areas where the private sector can act, and the areas where it will tend to fall short. In some of these areas, public and concessional philanthropic funds can be deployed to fill the gap to get the job done. Allocating risks to different stakeholders in the most effective way can increase the chances of fixing the sustainability issues at stake.

Public and philanthropic efforts are key in areas of research and development of new technology, science, and education. But these efforts can also be applied to financing solutions for early-stage businesses when angel investors are insufficient and venture capital, or other sources of capital, may not be employable yet. Financing the "valley of death" for business (see Chapter 4) is another critical area.

The brunt of sustainability issues is felt in developing countries. Yet those markets do not often fit in the traditional paradigm of large businesses or financial institutions. Accessing them will present financial and political risks, for which these businesses may need additional support. Multilateral agencies have historically provided guarantees to limit risks, much like insurance companies. This approach could also be applied to address sustainability issues and complement existing initiatives. Such mechanisms would catalyze the scarce public sector funds to areas that business and traditional finance cannot undertake on their own, unlocking the private sector's full potential for impact.

While this volume mainly focuses on the private sector and the implications of sustainability for business (in Part I) and investment (in Part II), it also considers the mechanisms that could support the private sector's actions. Further attention is paid to the role of stakeholders beyond the private sector in Part IV, and the roles of government policies, regulations, and incentives in Chapter 15.

VII. Conclusion

The role of business in society is clearly changing, and this change is only accelerating with escalating sustainability issues. The corporate sustainability concepts introduced and examined in the previous pages have been developed and refined in recent years in an effort to redefine this shifting role. Terms such as CSR, Stakeholder Theory, Impact Economy, and ESG have been widely embraced by large organizations and adopted into their corporate vocabulary. In too many cases, however, the corporate sustainability team operates in a silo with isolated, extraneous initiatives that are negligible to the business. They often end up in the public relations sphere which leans toward greenwashing and seldom impacts the bottom line.

To become truly sustainable, businesses must consider their 360° impact on society — from their business model to the human and environmental impacts of their products and services, all while operating in a transparent, accountable, and fair manner. The reputational benefits of sustainability for customers and investors are huge, but unless it is supported by tangible and relevant data, it can backfire. Financial performance remains a pillar for the sustainability of a business and its investors, even for businesses with a sustainability focus, and sustainability-driven initiatives undertaken by companies too often neglect a strong business case.

As for sustainable disclosure, this historically voluntary practice is shifting to either a regulatory or exchange requirement. Financial and sustainable/ESG data alike are critical to efficient markets, especially so in a world where the intangible value of shares is mainly driven by intangible assets. The lack of objective data from companies and the absence of a consistent framework present considerable barriers to generating any representative benchmarks. Third-party service providers can help address the first issue by assessing the quality of the data, and the second issue by promoting more precise international regulations.

A wide spectrum of strategies exists to improve a company's sustainability performance, from the incremental to the transformational. Each presents its own set of challenges and opportunities. But with the right approach, these strategies can be leveraged by businesses to ensure their own longevity in a rapidly changing system.

References

Aflac (2020). "2020 Aflac CSR survey", p. 13. https://www.aflac.com/docs/about-aflac/csr-survey-assets/2020-aflac-csr-infographic-and-survey.pdf.

BBC. (2022). "Small firms have a big role fighting climate change", https://www.bbc.com/news/business-63460919.

B Lab. (2022). "Benefit corporations". Consulted in October 2022, https://usca.bcorporation.net/benefit-corporation/.

Bloomfield, S. (2022). *Absolute Essentials of Corporate Governance*, Routledge, Milton Park, https://www.routledge.com/Absolute-Essentials-of-Corporate-Governance/Bloomfield/p/book/9780367557850.

Bowen, H. (1953). *Social Responsibilities of the Businessman*, Harper & Row, New York, p. 6.

Brundtland, G. H. *et al.* (1987). *Our Common Future,* World Commission on Environment and Development, New York.

Business Roundtable. (2019). "Business roundtable redefines the purpose of a corporation to promote an economy that serves all Americans." Published on August 19, 2020. Consulted in December 2020, https://www.businessround table.org/business-roundtable-redefines-the-purpose-of-a-corporation-to-promote-an-economy-that-serves-all-americans.

Carroll, A. (September 1999). "Corporate social responsibility: Evolution of a definitional construct", *Business & Society*, 38(3), pp. 268–295.

CDP. (2021). "SMEs equipped to join race to net-zero with dedicated climate disclosure framework", https://www.cdp.net/en/articles/companies/smes-equipped-to-join-race-to-net-zero-with-dedicated-climate-disclosure-frame work.

Committee for Economic Development of The Conference Board (CED). (1971). *Social Responsibilities of Business Corporations*, CED, New York.

Choi, J. S., Kwak, Y. M., and Choe, C. (2010). "Corporate social responsibility and corporate financial performance: Evidence from Korea", *Australian Journal of Management*, 35(3), pp. 291–311.

Cornell Law School. (2020). "Public benefit corporation", https://www.law.cornell.edu/wex/public_benefit_corporation#:~:text=A%20public%20benefit%20corporation%20created,or%20benefits%20for%20the%20public.

Deloitte. (2022). "The Deloitte global 2022 Gen Z & Millennial survey", https://www2.deloitte.com/content/dam/Deloitte/global/Documents/deloitte-2022-genz-millennial-survey.pdf.

Eccles, R. G., Miller Perkins, K., and Serafeim G. (2012). "How to become a sustainable company", *MIT Sloan Management Review*, Summer, 53(4), pp. 43–50.

Elkington, J. (1998). *Cannibals with Forks: The Triple Bottom Line of 21st Century Business*, Capstone Publishing Ltd., Oxford.

Ernst and Young (2013). "2013 Six growing trends in corporate sustainability" GreenBiz group. https://www.fm-house.com/wp-content/uploads/2015/01/Six_growing_trends_in_corporate_sustainability_2013.pdf.

Evan, V. M., and Freeman, R. E. (1988). "Stakeholder theory of the modern corporation: Kantian Capitalism", in T. L. Beauchamp, and N. E. Bowie (eds.),

Ethical Theory and Business, Prentice Hall, Englewood Cliffs, NJ, pp. 97–106.

Federal Register. (2022). "Prudence and loyalty in selecting plan investments and exercising shareholder rights", https://www.federalregister.gov/documents/2022/12/01/2022-25783/prudence-and-loyalty-in-selecting-plan-investments-and-exercising-shareholder-rights.

Fink, L. (2019). "Larry Fink's 2019 letter to CEOs — Purpose & profit", https://www.blackrock.com/corporate/investor-relations/2019-larry-fink-ceo-letter.

Fortune 500. (2022). 68th edition of fortune 500 largest companies, https://fortune.com/fortune500/2022/search.

Freeman, R. E. (1984). *Strategic Management: A Stakeholder Approach*, Pitman Publishing.

Freeman, R. E., and Dmytriyev, S. (2017). "Corporate social responsibility and stakeholder theory: Learning from each other", *Symphonya Emerging Issues in Management*, 1.

Freeman, R. E., Harrison, J. S., Wicks, A. C., Parmar, B. L., and De Colle, S. (2010). *Stakeholder Theory. The State of the Art,* Cambridge University Press, New York.

Friedman, M. (1970). "The social responsibility of business is to increase its profits", *The New York Times Magazine,* September 13.

Fulton, M., Kahn, B. M., and Sharples, C. (2012). *Sustainable Investing: Establishing Long-term Value and Performance*, SSRN Papers. https://papers.ssrn.com/sol3/papers.cfm?abstract_id=2222740

Gartenberg, C., and Serafeim, G. (2019). "181 top CEOs have realized companies need a purpose beyond profit", *Harvard Business Review*. Published on August 20, 2019, https://hbr.org/2019/08/181-top-ceos-have-realized-companies-need-a-purpose-beyond-profit. Accessed March 2021.

Global Reporting Initiative (GRI). (2022a). "The materiality madness: Why definitions matter", https://www.globalreporting.org/media/r2oojx53/gri-perspective-the-materiality-madness.pdf.

Global Reporting Initiative (GRI). (2022b). "Standards", https://www.globalreporting.org/how-to-use-the-gri-standards/gri-standards-english-language/.

HolonIQ. (2022a). "Global impact unicorns", https://www.holoniq.com/impact-unicorns.

HolonIQ. (2022b). "Global climate tech unicorns", https://www.holoniq.com/climatetech-unicorns.

International Monetary Fund (IMF). (2019). "Global financial stability report", 2019, Chapter 6 Sustainable Finance.

IFRS Foundation. (2022a). "Who uses IFRS accounting standards?" https://www.ifrs.org/use-around-the-world/use-of-ifrs-standards-by-jurisdiction/#analysis-of-use-of-ifrs-standards-around-the-world.

IFRS Foundation. (2022b). "Consolidated Organisations (CDSB & VRF)", https://www.ifrs.org/about-us/consolidated-organisations/.

Internal Revenue Service (IRS). (2022). "SOI tax stats — Integrated business data". Consulted in October 2022, https://www.irs.gov/statistics/soi-tax-stats-integrated-business-data.

Khan, M., Serafeim, G., and Yoon, A. (2016), "Corporate sustainability: First evidence on materiality", *The Accounting Review*, 91(6), pp. 1697–1724, http://www.aaajournals.org/doi/abs/10.2308/accr-51383.

Kiron, D., Unruh, G., Kruschwitz, N., Reeves, M., Rubel, H., and Meyer Zum Felde, A. (2017). "Corporate sustainability at a crossroad: Progress toward our common future in uncertain times", *MIT Sloan Management Review*, https://sloanreview.mit.edu/projects/corporate-sustainability-at-a-crossroads/. Accessed May 23, 2017.

KPMG. (2017). "The road ahead — The KPMG survey of corporate responsibility reporting 2017". https://www.integratedreporting.org/resource/kpmg-the-road-ahead-the-kpmg-survey-of-corporate-responsibility-reporting-2017/.

KPMG. (2022). "Big shifts, small steps — Survey of sustainability reporting 2022". https://kpmg.com/dk/en/home/insights/2022/10/key-global-trends-in-sustainability-reporting.html.

Krosinsky, C., and Purdom, S. (2017). *Sustainable Investing: Revolutions in Theory and Practice*, Routledge, London.

Lopez, M. V., Garcia, A., and Rodriguez, L. (2007). "Sustainable development and corporate performance: A study based on the Dow Jones sustainability index", *Journal of Business Ethics*, 75, pp. 285–300.

Mackey, J., and Sisodia, R. (2013). *Conscious Capitalism: Liberating the Heroic Spirit of Business*, Harvard Business Review Press, Boston, MA.

McCully, R. (2009). *Philanthropy Reconsidered*, Bloomington, Indiana, p. 13.

McKinsey Report By Fine, D., Pandit, V., Hickson, H., and Tuinenburg, P. (2018). "Catalyzing the Growth of the Impact Economy". New York. https://www.mckinsey.com/~/media/McKinsey/Industries/Private%20Equity%20and%20Principal%20Investors/Our%20Insights/Catalyzing%20the%20growth%20of%20the%20impact%20economy/Catalyzing-the-growth-of-the-impact-economy.pdf.

Movassaghi, H., and Bramhandkar, A. (2012). "Sustainability strategies of leading global firms and their financial performance: A comparative case based analysis", *Journal of Applied Business and Economics*, 13(5), pp. 21–34.

OECD (2005). *OECD SME and Entrepreneurship Outlook: 2005*, OECD, Paris, pp. 17, https://stats.oecd.org/glossary/detail.asp?ID=3123.

Schumacher, K., Baek, Y. J., In, S. Y., and Nishikizawa, S. (2022). "Sustainability reporting in Asia: Are the EU's initiatives a benchmark for ESG disclosure in the region?" Tokyo Tech Research Report, Tokyo, Japan.

Sheldon, O. (1924). *The Philosophy of Management*, Pitman Publishing Corp., London.

Sisodia, R. (2009). "Doing business in the age of conscious capitalism", *Journal of Indian Business Research*, 1(2/3), 2009, pp. 188–192.

Statista. (2022). "Estimated number of small and medium sized enterprises (SMEs) worldwide from 2000 to 2021", https://www.statista.com/statistics/1261592/global-smes/.

UNEP. (2015). "Raising the bar — Advancing environmental disclosure in sustainability reporting", Report of The United Nations Environment Program. https://www.unep.org/resources/report/raising-bar-advancing-environmental-disclosure-sustainability-reporting. United National Environmental Program, New York.

US Bureau of Labor Statistics. (2021). "Survival of private sector establishments by opening year". https://www.bls.gov/bdm/bdmage.htm.

USSIF. (2020). "Report on US sustainable and impact investing trends 2020", https://www.ussif.org/files/US%20SIF%20Trends%20Report%202020%20Executive%20Summary.pdf.

Waddell, S. (Spring 2018). "Four strategies for large systems change". *Stanford Social Innovation Review*. https://ssir.org/articles/entry/four_strategies_for_large_systems_change.

Walton, C. C. (1967). *Corporate Social Responsibilities*, Wadsworth, Belmont, CA, p. 18.

Whelan, T., Atz, U., Van Holt, T., and Clark, C. (2022). "ESG and financial performance: Uncovering the relationship by aggregating evidence from 1,000 plus studies published between 2015–2020", https://www.stern.nyu.edu/experience-stern/about/departments-centers-initiatives/centers-of-research/center-sustainable-business/research/research-initiatives/esg-and-financial-performance.

World Bank. (2022). "Small and Medium Enterprises (SMEs) finance". Consulted in November 2022, https://www.worldbank.org/en/topic/smefinance.

World Economic Forum. (2020). "Measuring stakeholder capitalism towards common metrics and consistent reporting of sustainable value creation", https://www3.weforum.org/docs/WEF_IBC_Measuring_Stakeholder_Capitalism_Report_2020.pdf.

Chapter 4

Entrepreneurship and Sustainability

Andrea E. McGrath and Laurie Lane-Zucker

Learning Objectives

- Understand the fundamentals of entrepreneurship
- Describe the role of entrepreneurs in social and sustainable development
- Define and discuss the concept of an "impact economy"
- Introduce new sustainable business models
- Summarize key global developments in expanding sustainable businesses

---

Abstract

This chapter defines the main elements of entrepreneurship — stages of development, sources of funding, and approaches of launch and development. It explores the emergence and expansion of entrepreneurs that are tackling a diversity of environmental, social, and governance challenges and some of their differentiating characteristics. While companies of all sizes have been addressing numerous sustainability challenges for years, the adoption of the Sustainable Development Goals (SDGs) by 193 countries in 2015 sparked a global call to action for all stakeholders to work toward achieving the 17 ambitious targets by 2030.

Limited progress and wide funding gaps now highlight the need for innovative business models, investing strategies, and even — as some might argue — a completely new way of doing business. While much of this book focuses on how mainstream businesses and investors are adapting to the challenges and opportunities presented by the sustainability agenda, the authors argue that entrepreneurs are also playing a critical role. While tackling sustainable development, entrepreneurs are creating new products and services, identifying, and capturing new customers and markets, creating and demonstrating new business models and helping to move toward a more sustainable economy. The chapter highlights how key global developments are helping to support the market demand for these entrepreneurs. It concludes that a supportive ecosystem, informed by systems thinking, is increasingly critical to launch and develop these entrepreneurs and the economy that holds and fosters them.

I. Introduction

The concept of sustainability is becoming mainstream in our economy today, attracting increasing attention not only from businesses of all sizes but also importantly from their key stakeholders, including investors, employees, and consumers. As this book highlights, businesses are also developing the financial case, new business and operational models, and improved management practices in support of sustainability. Innovative companies are also starting to redefine the role of business in society.

While large corporations and investors often attract much of the public and media attention on the actions they take (or don't take) toward sustainability — it is important to note that entrepreneurs are also playing an increasingly important role in developing innovative solutions and enterprises that seek to tackle some of these same challenges to sustainable development.

Indeed, globally, it is the micro, small, and medium-sized enterprises (defined as organizations with less than 250 employees) that actually make up over 90% of all businesses, account for 60–70% of the world's total employment, and contribute to half of global GDP (International Council of Small Businesses Conference, 2018). Thus, similar to larger businesses, these enterprises can also play an enormously important role in achieving more sustainable development. As evidence, in recognition of their critical role, the UN hosted in June 2018 its first Global Symposium to discuss the Role of Micro-, Small- and Medium-Enterprises (MSMEs) in the achievement of the Sustainable Development Goals (SDGs) and develop strategic recommendations on the best ways to help maximize the potentials of MSMEs in more sustainable development. Within this MSME community, entrepreneurship is increasing in both developed and developing economies globally. The 2017/2018 Global Entrepreneurship Monitor report found that over 43% of the global population sees themselves as starting a business within the next 6 months (Global Entrepreneurship Monitor (GEM), 2017, 2018).

Entrepreneurs, as natural innovators and disruptors, are playing a key role in helping to identify new approaches to many of the critical threats to sustainable development — including climate change, food waste, supply chain transparency, access to clean water, and more. These entrepreneurs are applying the approaches and solutions as diverse as the range of issues on which they focus. While some are working on a specific sustainability challenge (or opportunity), others are increasingly working to embrace and embed sustainability more *holistically* — applying this lens to their operations, supply chains, funding sources, energy uses, human capital strategies, and more as they can. Collectively, these entrepreneurs are also helping to demonstrate a new business paradigm, inspired and directed by a "triple bottom line" approach and informed by systems thinking, to move us toward a more sustainable, impact economy. We call these "impact entrepreneurs".

To be sure, mainstream businesses are also applying entrepreneurial approaches in similar areas — such as supply chain transparency, product design, sourcing, energy use, and waste (just to name a few). While these innovative approaches are certainly important, we would like to distinguish here between these innovators working within larger organizations (often called intrapreneurs) and those who are working to launch and grow *new enterprises* that can solve social, economic, and environmental challenges. This chapter focuses on the latter.

We would like to clarify an important term before moving forward. The term "sustainable" can often refer to specific operations or outcomes that can be "sustained" (i.e. supported, maintained, or repeated at a certain level or rate by fundraising levels, customer growth, or product revenues).

These goals can be particularly important to early-stage ventures trying to demonstrate to investors and customers their ability to scale. In this chapter, we are focusing on entrepreneurs who incorporate the concept of "sustainability" defined as "meeting the needs of the present without compromising the ability of future generations to meet theirs" (United Nations World Commission on Environment and Development, 1987 and further anchored and detailed by the United Nations Environment Programme, 2015). These entrepreneurs are focusing on economic, environmental, or social challenges — often referred to as "profits, planet, and people" — and adapting a "triple bottom line" approach to their business models, in contrast to the more traditional "bottom line" approach, which accounts for purely financial results.

This chapter first describes entrepreneurship, highlighting typical life cycles and funding sources and exploring more traditional and emerging approaches to venture development. It then focuses on the types of entrepreneurs who are tackling social and sustainable development challenges, and some of the key differences among them. It highlights important developments catalyzing and supporting the growth of these entrepreneurs, including recent global trends, important shifts in public demands, and concludes by describing the critical role of an emerging, supportive ecosystem to help support their launch, growth, and expansion.

Chapter 4 is organized as per the following sections:

I. Introduction
II. Entrepreneurship
III. Entrepreneurship and Sustainability
IV. Supporting Global Trends
V. Supportive Ecosystem
VI. Conclusion

II. Entrepreneurship

1. Definition

While the term entrepreneur can in some ways seem like one of those business identities (like "manager" or "technologist") that people instinctively feel they understand, we would like to offer here a brief history of the more significant developments over time that have helped define what we know today about an entrepreneur.

The literal translation of entrepreneur comes from the French (*entreprendre*), which means "one who undertakes". In the early 18th century, French economist Jean-Baptiste Say built on that understanding, defining entrepreneurs as "adventurers" who "shift economic resources out of an area of lower and into an area of higher productivity and greater yield" (Say, 1803). Say's definition thus expanded from the literal to add the pursuit of an opportunity to "shift" resources and create value.

In the 20th century, political scientist and economist Joseph Schumpeter (often called the "father of entrepreneurship") built on Say's definition and added in the concept of "innovation". Known for coining the term "creative destruction" to describe the constant product and process innovations (in manufacturing), he noted the importance of entrepreneurs as "innovators driving the "creative destruction" process of capitalism" (Schumpeter, 1942). Forty years later, management guru Peter Drucker made the case that innovation required "purposeful and systematic effort", and that entrepreneurs (as innovators) needed discipline and diligence, always "searching for change, responding to it, and exploiting it as an opportunity" (Drucker, 2006).

Building from this brief history of its theoretical bases, we see that some definitions can focus on the mindset or personal attributes of entrepreneurs or *who they are* (i.e. visionary, opportunity-obsessed, risk taking) — while other definitions can focus on *what they do* (i.e. disrupting markets, creating value, exploiting changes, etc.). Building from the key concepts of the definitions above (i.e. enterprising, innovative, and always searching for, responding to, and exploiting an opportunity), and with a lens toward entrepreneurs tackling critical social and sustainable challenges, we define these entrepreneurs utilizing the words of a pioneering leader in the field of social entrepreneurship, Professor J. Gregory Dees:

"Entrepreneurs are "change agents" in the economy... By serving new markets or creating new ways of doing things, they help to move the economy forward" (Dees, 2001).

Building from this working definition, we would also like to share some reflections from our work regarding the education, backgrounds, and characteristics of entrepreneurs:

- *First*, entrepreneurs can start their journey at any age — from grade school to senior citizens. Organizations like *Student Inc*, the first K-12 public-school entrepreneurship program and *Do Something*, which encourages young people to create or join a social change, civic action campaign are just two examples of numerous programs supporting the entrepreneurial spirit and ventures of young people. At the other end of the spectrum, the award-winning Encore.org started the Purpose Prize in 2005 to recognize entrepreneurs over 60 who were launching social ventures globally. After recognizing more than 500 people and awarding over $5 million in prizes during its first decade, the Purpose Prize has now become a key program of the AARP (formerly the American Association of Retired Persons).

- *Second*, while some believe that entrepreneurs must come from a business school or background, we regularly meet and work with entrepreneurs from a wide diversity of backgrounds, education, and experiences. We see students (and graduates) with studies in urban design, global health, pre-K education, public policy, and marketing all develop and pursue entrepreneurial ventures. A quick review of the current and alumni fellows with Ashoka, Echoing Green, Skoll Foundation, Schwab Foundation, Acumen and other leading champions of "social" entrepreneurs demonstrates this diversity. Of course, understanding basic concepts of business, marketing, markets, and operations can indeed be helpful. We have seen entrepreneurs develop those skills and/or bring on the talent and skills they need to help them develop and scale their ideas and organizations.

While embracing the diversities above, there is some consensus on the key qualities of entrepreneurs — tenacity, adaptability, curiosity, passion, confidence — that can strengthen their chances for success. As investors (and philanthropists) often state — they invest in leaders, they invest in the team. The qualities of "founders" and their early teams play an important role in a venture's journey to success.

There is also some consensus on common challenges that can hinder or ultimately end the journey of an entrepreneurial venture. These can include a lack of knowledge or experience, the inability to develop customers or a market, or the inability to attract the right talent. Financial challenges can include inadequate cash flow and what is commonly known as "the valley of death" — that is, the challenge to cover the negative cash flow in the early stages before the product or service brings in revenue from real customers. The hope is to move out of the "valley" toward positive cash flow (from revenues and investments), but ventures can often get stuck and eventually close down. Finally, more personal challenges to success can include an entrepreneur's ability to prioritize, manage time, or even manage the loneliness that can come from solo ventures.

It is interesting to note that even when successful — and ventures have grown to become household names — founders often remain known as entrepreneurs. Founders such as Mark Zuckerberg (Facebook) and Jeff Bezos (Amazon) are just two examples of numerous famous successful entrepreneurs. Successful founders of "triple bottom line" ventures include Yvon Chouinard of Patagonia (1973) and Ben Cohen and Jerry Greenfield of Ben and Jerry's (1978). Award-winning founders of game-changing social ventures include Wendy Kopp of Teach for America (1989), and Muhammad Yunus, who founded the pioneering microfinance provider Grameen Bank in 1983 and later won a Nobel Peace Prize for his efforts in 2006. All of these founders remain known as successful entrepreneurs.

Despite the many differences in these ventures, in terms of their structures, business models, funding sources, and more — most entrepreneurial ventures share similar "stages" of development and funding. These are detailed in the following section.

2. Stages and Life Cycles

While entrepreneurship can be exciting, it is important to note that it is also inherently risky. While statistics can vary, depending on the study or source, failure rates remain high. The US Bureau of Labor Statistics states that the failure rate of all US companies was over 50% after

5 years and over 70% after 10 years as of the end of 2015. Survival is hard. To be successful requires constant adaptation and innovation — figuring out new ways to service customer needs in cheaper, faster, better ways. As a famous American inventor, Thomas Edison, once stated: "genius is 1% inspiration and 99% perspiration". The same holds for entrepreneurship.

For any founder, the entrepreneurial journey begins with an idea. From there, any entrepreneur continues through several stages of growth and development until maturity — and possible exit. Regardless of the idea pursued, most entrepreneurs go through similar "stages" or life cycles and are supported (financed) by similar sources at various stages. Each stage can bring a unique set of challenges to manage (and overcome) and each can require different approaches. While descriptions can vary on the exact number of "stages" or life cycles, highlighted in the following are what we view as six key stages.

A. *Ideation*

The entrepreneurial journey begins here, when an entrepreneur identifies a need or an opportunity and pushes forward to develop a solution through brainstorming and advice from others. Sometimes an entrepreneur may lead with his or her ideas on a "solution", in which case the ideation phase helps to further understand the problem (or opportunity) they are targeting.

B. *Seed Stage*

This stage is the true beginning of a venture's life cycle. After clearly identifying the problem (or opportunity) and proposed solution, the entrepreneur begins to test and develop the idea to see just how viable it may be. This stage can include: creating a "minimal viable product" (discussed more later), product/service testing and iteration, market research/testing assumptions, and gathering advice from multiple sources — mentors, friends, colleagues, business associates, etc. Ventures in this stage are typical "pre" revenue and viewed as rather risky.

C. *Early Stage*

At this stage, entrepreneurs have tested their solutions, begun operations, and are bringing on early customers and revenues (although they may not yet be profitable). Much of their time is spent on the following: product/ service testing and iterations, gathering feedback from customers, experimenting with pricing, improving/increasing sales and marketing, and (possibly) hiring new team members. This is a critical stage for entrepreneurs: decisions or actions here can determine how long the venture may last. Many entrepreneurs must also overcome what is known as the "valley of death" — that is, the challenge of covering negative cash flow before their new product or service begins to bring in steady revenues.

D. *Growth Stage*

At this stage, ventures are now generating more consistent revenues, regularly bringing in new customers, and becoming more established in their industry. Cash flows and profits should begin to improve. Ventures also debate how best to expand, through new offerings or entering new regions (or both). Some of the biggest challenges in this stage are navigating the increasing demands from customers and investors, dealing with competitors, and managing organizational growth (people, systems, structures). For founders, the shift to now become "leaders" of a growing organization (rather than innovators of a fragile startup) can be a significant one. While growth in revenues and profits are good signs here, there is a risk in getting too comfortable with the status quo — or taking on too much, or too much risk — in growth plans (new markets, new products) that don't succeed. The challenges for the venture in this stage are "smart growth" and risk management, as well as increasing market competition.

E. *Maturity + Exit*

At this final stage, organizations have successfully navigated growth and expansion, and have earned an established (or even dominant) position in the marketplace. As the business has matured, the question for founders can often be — should we continue to push for growth or should we consider an "exit" (typically a full or partial sale). Challenges may include increasing competition, growth plans (new markets, new products), and deciding on the best exit strategy. Leadership can often change at this stage, too, where the founder(s) may decide it is time to move on to another challenge or idea.

Most entrepreneurs go through the "stages" or life cycles described above and are financed by similar sources at various stages, as outlined in the following section.

3. Funding Sources and Stages

While the entrepreneurial journey begins with an idea, the funding to pursue that idea often comes from the entrepreneur herself. Self-funding through personal savings or credit cards (often called *bootstrapping*) is the most common way many entrepreneurs support their ventures in their early days. Indeed, according to the 2017/2018 Global Entrepreneurship Monitor Report, 57% of entrepreneurs supplied all of the required funding themselves. Beyond self-funding, typical sources of early-stage funding for entrepreneurs include the following:

- Friends and family
- Grants/donations
- Accelerators
- Competitions
- Crowdfunding (debt and equity)
- Small business loans (or grants)
- Government funds (grants and loans)
- Angel investors
- Early-stage venture capital

After gaining some "traction" (i.e. number of users, revenue, views, or other key performance indicators (KPIs)), enterprises are ready to raise a Series A round from venture capitalists. Venture Capital (VC) focuses on early-stage, high-potential growth enterprises, and includes the following: early-stage financing, expansion financing, and acquisition or buyout financing. Typical rounds include seed, angel round, and then a series of rounds (Series A, Series B, Series C), that may eventually lead to an Initial Public Offering (IPO) or sale. That said, making it through the various rounds is incredibly challenging. According to 2018 CB Insights, nearly 67% of startups stall at some point in the VC process and fail to exit or raise follow-on funding (CB Insights, 2018). Entrepreneurship is inherently risky, and those challenges are evidenced in the funding data.

4. Developing and Launching New Ventures

For many years, entrepreneurs championing a new idea followed a "fairly" standard approach to develop and execute their ideas: develop a business plan, seek out funders or in-house support, and then sell (sell, sell) your product or service based on your plan. Whether pursuing an innovative idea, either in-house within larger enterprises, or as part of various universities, accelerators, competitions, or other programs, crafting a business plan has been a priority of venture development. A typical business plan would include the following:

- Executive summary
- Business description
- Team overview
- Market analysis
- Competitive analysis
- Products/services
- Marketing and sales
- Financials/budget
- Risks

While much of this "conventional" approach remains in place today, some important "innovations" in how to approach venture development emerged over the past decade that helped launch what many view as a new "movement" in entrepreneurship.

In 2005, entrepreneur, investor, and educator Steve Blank wrote *Four Steps to the Epiphany: Successful Strategies for Products that Win*, making the argument that rather than focus on "selling" something (as above), startups should focus on what he called "customer development" — that is, learning about customers and their problems as early in the development process as possible (Blank, 2005). His argument that entrepreneurs should focus first on customer discovery and validation (*search*) — rather than sales and execution (of a business plan) — was viewed as game-changing when it was published. Over the next few years, Blank's ideas would be further developed by two colleagues, helping to solidify a new approach to venture development.

- In 2010, business theorist and entrepreneur Alexander Osterwalder developed a strategic management template (called the *Business Model Canvas*) to help capture the series of hypotheses that founders would be testing in the customer discovery and validation approach championed by Blank. The BMC is a one-page visual chart highlighting key elements of product/service development, including the value proposition, infrastructure, customers, and finances (Osterwalder and Pigneur, 2010).
- In 2011, Eric Reis, an entrepreneur and former student of Steve Blank, combined Blank's insights on customer development with his own insights on "agile development" (that is, building products iteratively) and wrote the *Lean Startup*, which emphasizes the core principles of developing a minimum viable product (MVP), focusing on actionable metrics, and learning when to "pivot" (Reis, 2011).

These three core key concepts from Blank, Osterwalder, and Reis helped launch what we know today as the *Lean Startup* method (or movement), which includes the following:

1. *Business Model Canvas*, which helps ventures to frame all of their key hypotheses (Alexander Osterwalder).
2. *Customer Development*, which encourages ventures to test their key hypotheses with customers (Steve Blank).
3. *Agile Engineering*, which advises ventures to build an MVP in order to test and pivot rapidly (Eric Reis).

The Lean Startup movement has increasingly helped inform how entrepreneurs develop and launch their ventures today. Many accelerators, schools, competitions, and other supporters of early-stage ideas — as well as corporations and government agencies — teach, advise, or otherwise include key, lean concepts: an MVP, prototyping and rapid testing, and customer development. Frameworks such as the Business Model Canvas (or Lean Canvas) are increasingly replacing the traditional business plan. The concepts of Lean Startup are also being improved and expanded upon in various ways across sectors, such as the following:

- Variations on the *Business Model Canvas*, including the Lean Canvas model (2012) designed by Ash Maurya and the Mission Model Canvas (2016), developed by Alexander Osterwalder and Steve Blank as they prepared for their first "Hacking for Defense" class at Stanford, which focused on utilizing "lean" methods to develop innovative ideas within the Department of Defense and the Intelligence Community (Stanford). The Mission Model canvas is increasingly used today with nonprofits and government ventures.
- Various extensions of the term "lean" to describe tools and ideas in a way that reflect their embodiment of the key concepts continue to develop. For example, Acumen (a leading social venture funder) developed a new method of data collection known as "Lean Data" as a way for ventures in their portfolio to quickly and efficiently "capture data on customer feedback, behavior, and social performance" (Acumen). In another example, Anne Mei Chang, former head of the Global Development Lan at USAID wrote "Lean Impact: How to Innovate for Radically Greater Social Good" which "builds on the best practices of innovation outlined in Lean Startup (Reis) and adapts them for the unique challenges of doing social good" (Nauffs, 2018).

While business plans, executive summaries, and "pitch decks" are still very much valued elements in venture development, the lean approach and methodology has become increasingly mainstream, particularly in venture development environments like schools and accelerators. The work of Blank, Osterwalder, Reis plays an important role in how entrepreneurial ventures are developed and launched today.

Now that we've covered the basics of entrepreneurship — definitions, life cycles, funding, and venture development — we want to explore more deeply entrepreneurship that specifically focuses on the critical social and sustainable development challenges of our world.

III. Entrepreneurship and Sustainability

Although entrepreneurship has long been associated with private sector innovators, entrepreneurial approaches to tackle social challenges have existed across sectors for years. In the late 1980s, these innovators (dubbed social entrepreneurs) were first championed by Ashoka, an accelerator and advocacy group, which helped to identify and promote a broader understanding of their important work in the field of social change. Thought leaders like Professor J. Gregory Dees, often referred to as the "father" of social entrepreneurship after launching programs at Yale, Harvard, Stanford, and then Duke universities, began to demonstrate how the "theories and practices of entrepreneurship combined with a social mission could be employed to tackle the major societal challenges in the world" (Duke University, 2013).

In the 1990s, more funders and advocates for social entrepreneurs developed, including Echoing Green, Omidyar, Skoll, the Schwab Foundation, and others. Knowledge development and sharing increased and social entrepreneurs began to gain recognition in both private and public sectors. David Bornstein (2003) wrote *How to Change the World: Social Entrepreneurs and the Power of New Ideas*, which brought international recognition and attention to pioneering social entrepreneurs like Mohammed Yunus (Grameen Bank) and Wendy Kopp (Teach for America) — and helped to inform a diverse, global audience in this emerging field. By the 2000s — reflecting both the mainstreaming of the social entrepreneur movement and the lessons learned about "impact" from its own community — early pioneer Ashoka expanded its focus on championing the individual social entrepreneur to advocating the idea of "Everyone is a Changemaker". Mainstream media ran stories highlighting these ventures, Fast Company honored these entrepreneurs in their annual Social Capital Awards, universities developed programs and courses, and governments at all levels looked at how they could partner with or support these innovators.

Becoming more broadly known, the challenges that social entrepreneurs were addressing expanded from more traditional human service issues (such as education, workforce development, adult literacy, and college access, among others) to include critical environmental and sustainability challenges, including renewable energy, clean water, sustainable agriculture, repurposing materials, and many other issues. Social entrepreneurs were also recognized across sectors — private, public, nonprofit — as models emerged that blended profit and purpose, and entrepreneurs focused on "public" systems increasingly emerged.

Although entrepreneurs focusing on the diverse array of social, environmental, economic, and sustainable development challenges have become more generally known as "social" entrepreneurs, there are actually distinguishing characteristics among these models, and different names for several types of entrepreneurs working on these challenges, which have been well documented and explored by academic thought leaders globally. Indeed, the term "sustainable" entrepreneur and the study of related forms of entrepreneurship have been recognized for over two decades (Johnson and Schaltegger, 2019). While there are multiple references and definitions for each (similar to the definitions of entrepreneurship), we highlight here the names and working definitions for the following most common types of entrepreneurs relevant to sustainability:

- *Social Entrepreneurs*: As defined by Ashoka, social entrepreneurs are individuals with innovative solutions to society's most pressing social, cultural, and environmental challenges. They are ambitious and persistent, tackling major issues and offering new ideas for systems-level change. Social entrepreneurs can also play a key role in creating new markets and market niches, such as fair trade and microfinance.
- *Environmental Entrepreneurs* (also referred to as eco or green): These entrepreneurs differ from traditional, economic, or social entrepreneurs in that they "place the principle of environmental protection and/or restoration at the center of their organization" (Gutterman).

While some describe eco-entrepreneurs as a "subclass" of sustainable entrepreneurs, it is clear that the challenges from environmental degradation and climate change represent important opportunities for entrepreneurial action, so it is somewhat unsurprising that there is an entire category of entrepreneurs focused specifically on these issues. These models are not only ameliorating problems, but are also designing new processes, approaches, and designs that are working toward "more efficient uses of natural resources, and a more ecologically sustainable economy" (Dean and McMullen, 2007).

- *Sustainable Entrepreneurs*: These entrepreneurs contribute to the sustainable development of the social–ecological system and are guided and measured by the three pillars of the triple bottom line: economy, society, and the environment (commonly known as "profit, people, and planet"). Sustainable entrepreneurs are also noted as playing a lead role in the emerging shifts in capitalism that look to address environmental and sustainable challenges, with some arguing that they may be the "true wealth generators of the future".
- *Institutional Entrepreneurs*: these entrepreneurs are interested "in particular institutional arrangements and leverage resources to create new institutions or to transform existing ones". They focus beyond the market change and seek to contribute to regulatory, societal, and market institutions (Schaltegger and Wagner, 2010).

In their paper on sustainable entrepreneurship and sustainability innovation, thought leaders Schaltegger and Wagner propose a comparison of the characteristics of the different types of sustainability-oriented entrepreneurship that, while not fully inclusive, provides a helpful snapshot, as follows (see Table 4.1).

Building on the models above, we propose an additional type of entrepreneur-tackling sustainability challenge that includes several of the characteristics above, but goes even further in their work on systems change as follows:

- *Impact Entrepreneurs ¾ Transforming the Economy*: These pioneers are "systems-minded" and strive not only to "bake" sustainability into their organizational DNA (i.e. through their sourcing, energy

Table 4.1. Types of Sustainability-Oriented Entrepreneurship

	Social Entrepreneurship	Eco-Entrepreneurship	Sustainable Entrepreneurship	Institutional Entrepreneurship
Core Motivation	Contribute to solving societal problems and create value for society	Contribute to solving environmental problems and create economic value	Contribute to solving societal and environmental problems through the realization of a successful business	Contribute to changing regulatory, societal, and market institutions
Main Goal	Achieve societal goal and secure funding to achieve this	Earn money by solving environmental problems	Create sustainable development through entrepreneurial corporate activities	Change institutions as a direct goal
Role of Economic Goals	Means	Ends	Means and Ends	Means or Ends
Role of Non-Market Goals	Societal goals as ends	Environmental issues as integrated core element	Core element of integrated end to contribute to sustainable development	Changing institutions as core element
Organizational Development Challenge	From focus on societal issues to integrating economic issues	From focus on environmental issues to integrating economic issues	From small contributions to large contributions to sustainable development	From changing institutions to integrating sustainability

Source: Schaltegger and Wagner (2010).

use, diversity, waste, etc.), but also to collaborate with funders, legal and policy experts, and others to create an "impact affirmative" eco-system that can more comfortably hold and affirm mission-driven companies. They are also working to stretch more traditional meth-ods, structures, and funding models to successfully implement their solutions, while helping to lay the groundwork for a new, transforma-tional "impact economy".

Regardless of the diversity of challenges, sectors, structures, or inten-tionality, these entrepreneurs are identifying and developing solutions to some of our most critical social, environmental, and sustainable chal-lenges. In pursuit of their solutions, these entrepreneurs are also creating new products and services, identifying (and capturing) new customers and markets, creating or demonstrating new business models, and playing an important role in helping to build a more sustainable economy. The growth of these types of entrepreneurs is being dramatically impacted by a number of important developments — including global trends with sus-tainability, important shifts in attitudes and behaviors among key stake-holders, and an increasingly supportive ecosystem. We explore these further in the following section.

IV. Supporting Global Trends

Over the past few years, we have seen important "shifts" in how global populations view the increasing threats to sustainable development — and responses to those shifts — all of which are catalyzing and supporting the development of innovative solutions to these challenges. Three of the more significant "shifts" are outlined in the following sections.

1. The Sustainable Development Goals (SDGs)

In September 2015, the 193-member countries of the United Nations adopted the 2030 Agenda for Sustainable Development. Among other things, the SDGs focus on inequalities, economic growth, decent jobs, cities and human settlements, industrialization, oceans, ecosystems, energy, climate change, sustainable consumption and production, peace, and justice. The SDGs came into force on January 1, 2016, projecting a 15-year time frame for achievement. All global stakeholders — including governments, civil society (nonprofits, global development organizations), and the private sector — are expected to contribute toward reaching these goals.

Since their approval, the SDGs have become a widely accepted framework for enterprises across sectors (as well as investors and consumers) to identify and measure how their actions and investments "map" toward specific challenges or goals. The increased awareness and concern about sustainable development challenges resulting from the SDGs — as well as the important global "call to action" they represent — is not only inspiring entrepreneurs globally to focus on solutions to these challenges, but it is also encouraging their development and growth, given how broadly this framework is understood among all of the key stakeholders.

2. The Business Case for Sustainability

Businesses globally have become increasingly aware of the critical threats posed by sustainability challenges and are taking actions (and applying innovative approaches) to address those threats. Identifying solutions to these challenges have moved beyond a "risk management" lens, as it becomes increasingly acknowledged (and demonstrated) that products, services, processes, and operations that improve sustainability can also improve the "bottom line".

Further, businesses are increasingly seeing the market opportunity in sustainability, as data continue to emerge that demonstrate the opportunities. For example, according to the Business and Sustainable Development Commission, sustainability-driven business could unlock at least US $12 trillion in new market value by 2030 and grow employment by up to 380 million jobs (Business and Sustainable Development Commission, 2017). Paul Polman, CEO of Unilever and a leading champion of sustainable innovation, noted at the release of this report that there are "enormous opportunities" for "enlightened businesses" to make the markets work for a sustainable and inclusive future (Polman, 2018). He has also called finding solutions to the SDGs "the greatest economic opportunity of a lifetime". As the business case for sustainability and its connection with financial performances continues to be studied and understood, increasing numbers of CEOs are agreeing that solving sustainable problems is the future of business.

3. Demands from Key Stakeholders

In addition to the powerful developments above, we are seeing important "shifts" in the behaviors and attitudes of individuals globally — as they increasingly seek to invest in, buy from, and work for "values-aligned" businesses.

A. *Investors*

Demand from individual and institutional investors for companies that integrate environmental, social, and corporate governance (ESG) practices into their long-term strategies is growing rapidly. Although these types of investments have existed for years, building on the long-standing responsible investment movement, the total amount of funds in these types of investments has remained relatively small. However, the growth in ESG investments in the past decade has been substantial, as demand has evolved from smaller groups of socially conscious investors to more "mainstream" investors. As of January 2018, $1 of every $4 invested in the United States was under ESG investment strategies, amounting to $11.6 trillion overall, up to $3 trillion in 2010 (The Forum for Sustainable and Responsible Investment (US SIF), 2018).

Demonstrating how mainstream this shift in attitude has become, Larry Fink, Chairman and CEO of Blackrock, sent "shock waves" throughout the investment world in 2018 when he sent a letter to the CEOs of their portfolio companies stressing the importance of focusing on their social purpose as part of their long-term growth strategy (Fink, 2018).

A company's ability to manage ESG matters demonstrates the leadership and good governance that is so essential to sustainable growth, which is why we are increasingly integrating these issues into our investment process.

Building on this history of responsible investing, sustainable finance investing, and mission/program-related investing, the concept of "impact investing" emerged in the early 2000s after an important convening hosted by the Rockefeller Foundation on "Evolving Social Capital Markets" (Bellagio Social Investing meeting October 2007). On September 2009, former President Clinton announced, at the Clinton Global Initiative, the launch of a new "industry group" — the Global Impact Investing Network (the GIIN). This new movement has been gathering speed.

"Impact investments" are companies, organizations, and funds that have the intention to generate social and environmental impact alongside a financial return (GIIN, 2018). As of 2018, just a decade later, there were $228 billion in assets under management globally, with JP Morgan predicting that impact investments could grow to $400 billion to $1 trillion in the next decade (impact investing will be discussed in more detail further in this book).

While terms like responsible, sustainable, ESG, and impact investing are often used interchangeably (and can sometimes be confusing), the overall trends show that the demand from investors for opportunities that blend financial returns and impact (environmental, social) is rapidly increasing. Supporting this demand is increasing data proving that sustainable investment strategies are the "smart" strategies in terms of performance and returns. Together, this increasing investor demand is energizing entrepreneurs who are keen to develop new ventures blending financial and "social" value.

B. *Consumers*

Consumer demands are also playing an important role in how companies are responding to sustainability challenges and opportunities. For example, global research by PwC in 2015 found that 78% of customers stated that they are more likely to buy the goods and services of companies that had signed up to the SDGs (PwC, 2015). Consumers are also increasingly indicating their willingness to pay a premium for more sustainable products. A Nielsen survey in 2015 found that 66% of respondents would pay more for a product or service if the company was committed to positive social and environmental change (up from 50% in the same survey in 2013) (Nielsen, 2015). Another study in 2015 found that consumers were willing to pay, on average, 30% more for ethically produced goods, compared to their conventionally produced counterparts (Bizzozero, 2018). These consumer trends are incentivizing a growing group of entrepreneurs to develop new products and services that meet these demands. They are also highlighting new market opportunities and gaps in the competitive landscape.

C. *Workers*

The shifting attitudes of today's workers are having a dramatic impact on businesses, as they increasingly demand that the companies for whom they work have a "social" or positive impact in the world in which we live. Deloitte's Annual Millennial Survey (2018) noted that "the role business plays in society has been an increasingly prominent concern for millennials. Respondents indicate businesses' priorities should be job creation, innovation, enhancing employees' lives and careers, and making a positive impact on society and the environment". A 2018 Fast Company survey showed that 70% of millennials said that they were more likely to choose to work at a company with a strong environmental agenda (compared to less than 25% of Gen X respondents and only 17% of Baby Boomers).

These dramatic shifts in the attitudes and demands from today's workforce are not only playing an important role in business operations, communications, recruitment, and leadership — but also helping to support a new group of entrepreneurs focused on solving social and sustainable development challenges. In an increasingly competitive marketplace for talent and skills, those ventures who are aligned with the values of the workforce will find themselves with the competitive advantage to attract the "best and brightest".

Taken together, these global developments and the shifting behaviors and attitudes of investors, consumers, and "workers" are all helping entrepreneurs and businesses targeting "sustainable" challenges to launch, grow, survive, and thrive. In addition to the macro trends described above, there is also an increasingly robust ecosystem helping entrepreneurs tackling social and sustainable development challenges to launch, grow, and thrive, which we explore further in the following section.

V. Supportive Ecosystem

While "social" entrepreneurship was gaining recognition as a practice in the early 2000s, it was not yet widely understood, and some felt the field was actually at quite a "fragile" point. Professor J. Gregory Dees published "Developing the Field of Social Entrepreneurship" in 2008, recognizing that social entrepreneurship was at a critical point of development and emphasizing the need for a "healthy institutional and social environment" (or ecosystem) for social entrepreneurship to thrive moving forward. This included both resources (financial, human, social/political, and intellectual capital) and environmental conditions (public policy and politics, media, economic and social conditions, and related fields) that could support or undermine the practice of social entrepreneurship.

Dees and Professor Paul Bloom (Duke University) continued to push forward their ideas on the importance of an ecosystem approach, for both supporters and for social entrepreneurs themselves, who should both identify and "cultivate" their own ecosystem in order to grow their ventures more effectively and sustainably (Bloom and Gregory Dees, 2008).

In the past decade, the consensus among supporters of "social" entrepreneurs that a healthy ecosystem can play a critical role in their creation, launch, and expansion has become even stronger. Building on the earlier suggestions that entrepreneurs learn to "cultivate" an ecosystem, lessons learned from early supporters and funders of social entrepreneurs (New Profit and Draper Richards Kaplan Foundation) highlighted that adapting a "systems" approach was actually a key strategy for increasing impact. Another important lesson is that any changes in key elements of an ecosystem can play an important role in the development and success (or failure to launch) for these social entrepreneurs.

The importance of developing a healthy ecosystem and adapting a systems lens are both critical for any entrepreneur tackling social, environmental, or sustainability challenges if they are to have lasting, positive social impact. We have seen in recent years the emergence (or growth) of several developments in the broader "ecosystem" surrounding these entrepreneurs that are playing an increasingly critical role in helping to support their launch, growth, and expansion. The following sections highlight a few of these key developments.

1. Financial Capital

A. *Crowdfunding*

An important development in early-stage funding for entrepreneurs has been the growth of "crowdfunding", which in essence refers to website platforms that allow for large numbers of supporters (donors, lenders, and equity investors) to provide funds in small(er) increments to a project or venture. The steady growth and increasing popularity of these platforms is catalyzing critical, early capital and providing improved visibility and "recognition" to entrepreneurs tackling social and sustainable development challenges — helping their launch, development, and expansion.

That said, equity investments in emerging ventures were restricted to accredited investors only (defined as anyone whose earned income exceeds $200,000 or who has a net worth over $1 million (excluding the value of the person's primary residence)) (US Securities and Exchange Commission). This restriction was substantially changed in 2012, when Congress passed important legislation (Jumpstart Our Business Startups (JOBS) Act), containing important provisions to help make more capital available to entrepreneurs, including Title III (Regulation Crowdfunding), which allows startups and small businesses to now raise up to $1,070,000 per year from both retail and accredited investors (removing the requirement that all investors be "accredited"). The JOBS Act is helping to propel crowdfunding platforms as increasingly important sources of capital for early-stage ventures tackling critical social and sustainable challenges. It is also helping to connect emerging investors (and consumers) who value the solutions they are championing.

B. *Impact Investing*

As mentioned above, the demand for investments that seek both financial and "social" returns is rapidly increasing, particularly among younger generations of investors and philanthropists. Impact investing is discussed in much more detail later in this book, so this highlight is purposely brief — but it is important to note the importance to entrepreneurs focusing on social and sustainable development challenges of the steadily increasing demand from investors and philanthropists.

C. *Integrated Finance*

One of the more important recent developments in impact investing, and one that provides powerful fuel for transformational change, is the development of integrated financial strategies (also known as "blended finance" strategies). Integrated finance helps to activate the full range of philanthropic funding (grants, program-related investments, and mission-related investments) and combine these with public and private sector investments (with different levels of risk) "to catalyze risk-adjusted, market-rate seeking capital into impact investments" (Global Impact Investing Network, 2018). The hope is that this more patient and sophisticated funding, increasingly called "catalytic capital" (Tideline *et al.*, 2019), will help to transform some of the "single strategy" practices of philanthropists and investors and help support the increasing growth of impact businesses. Some good examples of pioneers in the integrated finance space are RSF Finance and Boston Impact Initiative, both of whom utilize grants, loans, and equity investments to support impact ventures.

2. Structures and Regulations

Many enterprises targeting social and sustainable issues are increasingly challenging "traditional" sectors and legal structures — adopting more hybrid models to pursue their dual purposes of profit and impact. In response, legislation and regulations continue to evolve to help these ventures launch and grow. The JOBS Act (discussed above) is an example of one that is dramatically impacting early-stage funding. While not covering the full range of updates, we highlight in the following sections some recent developments in US policy and regulations impacting how these ventures are structured.

A. *New Legal Structures: Benefit Corps*

Public Benefit Corporations (PBC) launched in 2010 as a new legal structure for businesses (like an LLC or S-Corp) that legally empowered businesses to consider multiple stakeholder interests, not just shareholder interests (B Corporation). The launch of the PBC was helped enormously by previous efforts, including legal structures like the L3C (low profit limited liability company) — as well as the branding, advocacy, and movement-building efforts from the B-Lab community, who created the B-Corp certification in 2007 for companies that "do well and do good" (see more in the following). As of 2021, Benefit Corporation legislations were adopted in more than 50 jurisdictions comprising mainly US states but also Italy and Columbia (B-Lab, 2022).

B. *New Certifications*

In 2006, three colleagues collaborated to launch the nonprofit B-Lab (B for "beneficial") with a mission to help for-profit organizations pursuing profit and purpose to "protect and improve their impact" (B Corporation). The team created and popularized an assessment tool (called B Impact Assessment) that helps organizations analyze and score their operations through numerous lenses of impact. Those achieving high enough scores earned a "B-Corp" certification — similar to fair trade and other popular certification — demonstrating that they meet certain standards of sustainability, diversity, good governance, community, and more. In their first full year (2007), there were 19 certified "B-Corps". As of 2021, there were more than 4,300 certified "B-Corps" in 77 countries including 30 public companies (B-Lab).

The B-Lab team played a critical role advocating for the creation and adoption of the "benefit corporation" legal status (see above). They also continue to improve the B Certification tool. In 2019, B-Lab announced that it would develop a new tool (leveraging its B Impact Assessment) for companies to assess, compare, and improve their performance against the SDGs. The B-Lab team is working closely with the UN Global Compact and the Leeds School of Business at the University of Colorado on this effort.

C. *New Rules for Ownership: Newman's Own Exemption*

In February 2018, the Philanthropic Enterprise Act of 2017 was signed into law, allowing private foundations to own for-profit companies without needing to pay taxes on the revenue they generate — provided that all the revenue goes toward the foundation's mission (Congress.gov and

BNY Mellon Wealth Management). This is also known as the "Newman's Own Exception", referencing the issue that arose from Paul Newman Foundation's ownership of Newman's Own Corporation. Previously, the IRS did not allow private foundations to own more than 20% of any for-profit business. Many are hoping that this new ruling may open the door to more foundations considering ownership of mission-aligned, for-profit businesses.

3. Educational Institutions

In addition to developments in funding and legal/regulatory environments, another important development in the ecosystem surrounding social and sustainable entrepreneurs is among educational institutions. In 1993, Harvard Business School was the first business school to launch a program on "social enterprise" (Professor J. Gregory Dees played a founding role here). In the 26 years since that first program launched, numerous classes, programs, centers, and even degrees focusing on social enterprise, social innovation, sustainable development (or other similar topics) have flourished at universities globally. Today, it is hard to find a graduate or undergraduate program that doesn't have at least one course focused on these topics. Universities are also becoming "hosts" or sponsors of many accelerator and competition programs, which can be open to students, alumni, and even community entrants from the field at large. This tremendous growth in the creation of classes, initiatives, centers, and degrees at universities across the globe — as well as the evolution of more "traditional" classes and degrees to embody elements of social impact or sustainability — is playing an important role in educating, training, and supporting students of all ages who are keen to develop sustainable solutions to today's critical challenges.

4. Supporting Networks

Finally, in addition to some of the important changes in the ecosystem outlined above, mirroring the tremendous growth in educational opportunities is the similar growth in critical "supporting networks" (including accelerators, competitions, and awards/fellowships). Together, they are helping to launch a new generation of students and entrepreneurs who are focused on solving social and sustainable development challenges — and helping to catalyze their launch, growth, and expansion. The following are some brief highlights on each of these key supportive networks.

A. *Accelerators*

Hundreds of accelerators for entrepreneurs focusing on a broad range of social and sustainable challenges in both developed and emerging markets have launched around the world in just the past decade. These programs are playing a critical role in providing early-stage support — such as mentors, advisers, connections, space, and even some early-stage funding — that are helping many entrepreneurs make it to the next stages of development.

B. *Competitions and Awards*

Similar to accelerators, the number of competitions and challenges for students and entrepreneurs focusing on social and sustainable development challenges has exploded in the last decade, providing critical early-stage support. These are sponsored by a wide range of sources, including universities, funders, corporations, multinational or development agencies, governments, and select partnerships.

It is also interesting to note how several global awards and challenges have given rise to communities of social change agents globally. As an example, Ashoka launched its first social entrepreneur award in the 1980s, which then helped to seed an emerging field, influence others to replicate and grow, inspire the public and private sectors to learn and engage, and today host a global community of alumni who continue to engage and support each other. In another example, several partners in Europe launched the International Sustainable Entrepreneurship Awards (SEA) in 2012, recognizing companies combining economic and sustainable excellence. Three members of the awards organization (including the founder) went on to write one of the first books dedicated to the topic of entrepreneurship and sustainability: *Sustainable Entrepreneurship: Business Success through Sustainability* (2013). SEA later evolved from its annual award to become a new organization, future4you Gmbh, whose mission is to identify, fund, and support sustainable entrepreneurship. It will be interesting to watch how this organization helps to develop and push forward the concepts of sustainable entrepreneurship (possibly viewing Ashoka's work with social entrepreneurship as a model).

The increasing strength and growth of a supporting ecosystem is playing an incredibly important role in helping to launch, support, and scale an emerging class of entrepreneurs targeting social and sustainable development challenges.

VI. Conclusion

This chapter argues that entrepreneurs working on sustainability challenges have a key role to play in not only alleviating the problems and developing innovation solutions, but in helping to build a more sustainable (impact) economy. It also makes the case for changes happening globally — including heightened awareness of climate change and the importance of progress towards the SDGs, significant changes in investor, consumer, and "worker" demands, evolutions in "traditional" sectors and structures tackling "social" challenges, and an increasingly supportive ecosystem and infrastructure. Together, they are helping to catalyze the emergence and development of entrepreneurs targeting sustainability challenges, as well as laying the groundwork for building a more sustainable economy. As they create new products and services, identify (and capture) new customers and markets, and create or demonstrate new business models, these entrepreneurs are indeed the beating heart of transformational change toward an impact economy. Moving forward, these innovators — together with a growing community of investors, scholars, policymakers, intermediaries, advocates, and others across the broader ecosystem who understand the critical importance of collaboration — will help to transform our "traditional" business paradigms and move us toward a more sustainable and just world.

References

B-Lab. (2022). 2021 "Annual report", https://www.bcorporation.net/en-us/news/blog/b-lab-global-2021-annual-report.

Bizzozero, J. (2018). "Demand for sustainable products transforming the supply chain". Last Modified September 14, 2018, https://www.naturalproduct sinsider.com/supply-chain/demand-sustainable-products-transforming-supply-chain.

Blank, S. (2005). *Four Steps to the Epiphany: Successful Strategies for Products that Win*, Wikey, New Jersey.

Bloom, P. N., and Gregory Dees, J. (2008). "Cultivate your ecosystem", *Stanford Social Innovation Review*. https://ssir.org/articles/entry/cultivate_your_ecosystem#.

Bornstein, D. (2003). *How to Change the World: Social Entrepreneurs and the Power of New Ideas*, Oxford University Press, Oxford.

Business and Sustainable Development Commission (the Commission). (2017). "Better Business, Better World". New York: UN Department of Economic and Social Affairs. https://sustainabledevelopment.un.org/index.php?page=v iew&type=400&nr=2399&menu=35.

CB Insights. (2018). "Venture capital funnel shows odds of becoming a unicorn are about 1%". September 6, 2018.

Dean, T. J. and McMullen, J. S. (2007). "Toward a theory of sustainable entrepreneurship: Reducing environmental degradation through entrepreneurial action", *Journal of Business Venturing*, 22(1), pp. 50–76. https://doi.org/10.1016/j.jbusvent.2005.09.003.

Dees, J. G. (1998, Revised 2001). *The Meaning of Social Entrepreneurship*, Fuqua School of Business, Durham, NC: Duke University. https://centers.fuqua.duke.edu/case/wp-content/uploads/sites/7/2015/03/Article_Dees_MeaningofSocialEntrepreneurship_2001.pdf.

Deloitte's Annual Millennial Survey. (2018). https://www2.deloitte.com/global/en/pages/about-deloitte/articles/millennialsurvey.html.

Drucker, P. (2006). *Innovation and Entrepreneurship*, Harper Business, New York.

Duke University. (2013). "Greg Dees memorial, published in academics and CASE website", https://today.duke.edu/2013/12/gregdees. Accessed December 21, 2013.

Fink, L. (2018). "A sense of purpose" Note to CEOs, https://www.blackrock.com/corporate/investor-relations/larry-fink-ceo-letter.

Fontaine, A. T. (2018). "From philanthropy to social investing: A new way of giving", *BNY Mellon Wealth Management.* https://www.ropesgray.com/-/media/Files/articles/2018/10/Thought_From-Philanthropy-to-Social-Investment.pdf.

Forum for Sustainable and Responsible Investment (US SIF). (2018). "Trends report", https://www.ussif.org/files/2018%20_Trends_OnePager_Overview (2).pdf.

Global Entrepreneurship Monitor (GEM). (2017). Report. https://www.gem consortium.org/report/gem-2017-2018-global-report.

Global Entrepreneurship Monitor (GEM). (2018). Report. https://www.gem consortium.org/report/gem-2017-2018-global-report.

Global Impact Investing Network (GIIN). (2018). Annual impact investment survey. https://thegiin.org/research/publication/annualsurvey2018/.

Hedstrom, G., Poltorzycki, S., and Stroh, P. (1998). "Sustainable development: The next generation of business opportunity", *Arthur D. Little*. https://www. adlittle.com/sites/default/files/prism/1998_q4_01-07.pdf.

Johnson, M. P., and Schaltegger, S. (2019). "Entrepreneurship for sustainable development: A review and multilevel causal mechanism framework", *Entrepreneurship Theory and Practice*, 44(6). https://doi.org/10.1177/ 1042258719885368.

Nauffs, M. (2018) "A conversation with Ann Mei Chang, author, lean impact: How to innovate for radically greater social good", *Philanthropy News Digest*, November 18.

Nielsen. (2015) "Green generation: Millennials say sustainability is a shopping priority". Last Modified November 11, 2015, http://www.nielsen.com/us/en/ insights/news/2015/green-generation-millennials-say-sustainability-is-a- shopping-priority.html. Accessed November 2018.

Osterwalder, A., and Pigneur, Y. (2010). *Business Model Generation: A Handbook for Visionaries, Game Changers, and Challengers*, 1st edn. Wiley, New Jersey.

Polman, P. (2018). "Why sustainable development makes good business sense", *Business Commission Blog Post*, Accessed December 2018, http://business commission.org/our-work/sustainable-development-isnt-just-doing-the-right- thing-its-good-business-sense.

PwC. (2015). "Make it your business: Engaging with the sustainable development goals", https://www.pwc.com/gx/en/sustainability/SDG/SDG%20Research_ FINAL.pdf.

Reis, E. (2011). *The Lean Startup: How Today's Entrepreneurs Use Continuous Innovation to Create Radically Successful Businesses*. Random House, New York.

Say, J. B. (1803). *A Treatise on Political Economy, or the Production, Distribution, and Consumption of Wealth*. Taylor and Francis, New York.

Schaltegger, S., and Wagner, M. (2010). "Sustainable entrepreneurship and sustainability innovation: Categories and interactions", *Business Strategy and the Environment.* 20(4), pp. 222–237.

Schumpeter, J. (1942). *Capitalism, Socialism and Democracy,* Harper, New York.

Tideline, J. D., Catherine, T., and MacArthur Foundation. (2019). "Catalytic capital: Unlocking more investment and impact". Klimate KC, EU. https://www.transformation.capital/assets/uploads/Transformation-Capital-Systemic-Investing-for-Sustainability-1-1_2021-06-25-114435.pdf.

United Nations Environment Programme. (2015). "Raising the bar — Advancing environmental disclosure in sustainability reporting". UN Environment Report, New York.https://www.unep.org/resources/report/raising-bar-advancing-environmental-disclosure-sustainability-reporting.

Chapter 5

Corporate Sustainability and Financial Performance

Diane-Charlotte Simon

Learning Objectives

- Understand the background of financial materiality of sustainability
- Become familiar with the impact of corporate sustainability on companies
- Present key indicators for profitability and performance of shares
- Understand sustainability-related risks and opportunities for businesses and investors
- Identify the relationship between corporate sustainability and financial performance
- Discuss the challenges in measuring ESG performance
- Review factors that lead to positive financial outcomes from sustainability initiatives

---

Abstract

This chapter looks at the links between financial performance of companies and their commitment to a corporate sustainability agenda. The chapter challenges the traditional view that there is a trade-off between environmental and financial performance, that corporate sustainability conflicts with shareholder wealth maximization. Instead, the chapter highlights a body of research that suggests companies with strong sustainability focus can outperform comparable companies with poor sustainability performance. The chapter once again explores the impacts (*materiality*) of corporate sustainability and the environmental, social, and governance (ESG) factors, first introduced in Chapter 3, with a particular focus on the environmental. The chapter also provides an overview of sustainability-related risks and opportunities for business and investment. The chapter then analyzes the impact that sustainability can have on companies' financial performance, considering both profitability and market valuation indicators. It reviews key methodological indicators of financial performance and highlights how sustainability can have an impact on each of them. These indicators involve revenues (demand, innovation, etc.), costs (risks, productivity, savings, cost of capital, etc.), and market performance (share price, market risk, impact on investors, and access to investors) but also competitiveness, intangible assets, and reputation. Finally, the chapter investigates how a company can improve its positive financial outcomes from sustainability initiatives. In this respect, the chapter concludes that the financial stakes of corporate sustainability are rising and that there is growing evidence of links to a company's financial performance and investment returns. These links are observed both at the profitability level, with growing demand for sustainable products, and at the market valuation level.

I. Introduction

It has been demonstrated that sustainability can have material financial impacts for companies — in some cases, they are significant. ESG risks materialize first through cost. Environmental incidents in particular can be extremely costly for companies, both in terms of damage incurred and potential fines. When a company is implicated in an ESG-related incident, its reputation can also be damaged, along with its market valuation.

Poor governance can also lead to steep fines, as those borne by the banks deemed at fault during the financial crisis. Macro sustainability issues also present risks for companies. For example, climate change impacts almost every sector with different levels of severity. The heat alone can impact human health, the overall productivity of employees, companies' ability to operate, and even disrupt transportation and supply chains.

But sustainability not only involves risks. It also present business and investment opportunities to develop solutions in every sector from energy to agriculture, industry to fashion, building to tech, transportation to healthcare, etc. When there is an unmet need, there is a potential new market. Companies can intentionally choose to address specific sustainability issues as part of the product or service they offer. It also represents considerable business opportunities, especially as the millennial population gains importance and financial assets in the overall market. As consumers, millennials care deeply about the environmental impact of the products they buy and value businesses that operate with purpose. Companies that are able to recognize and adapt to those customers' preferences may maximize revenues from them. Furthermore, it has been demonstrated that diversity in organizations and greener business operations tend to improve productivity and employee retention, which can be critical for business financial performance (Whelan, Holt, and Clark, 2021).

Many studies have examined the financial impacts of corporate sustainability. The traditional belief is that there is a trade-off between corporate environmental and financial performance and that corporate sustainability conflicts with shareholder wealth maximization (Friedman, 1970; Levitt, 1958). However, a growing body of research suggests that companies with a strong sustainability focus financially outperform comparable companies with poor sustainability performance (Eccles *et al.*, 2014; Morgan Stanley Institute for Sustainable Investing, 2015) and investing in sustainability can create long-term value (Sage, 1999; Bebbington, 2001). Furthermore, it has been demonstrated that certain ESG factors can have material financial impacts on companies and in some cases, with high importance. The impact of ESG dimensions on companies' financial performance is so critical that credit rating agencies have now developed their own ESG methodologies which are integrated into their overall rating systems. Some argue that integrating ESG factors are part of investors' fiduciary duty (The Generation Foundation, UNEP FI and the PRI, 2019). In Europe, large companies are now required by law to include sustainability and ESG considerations in their disclosures, given their financial materiality.

A company's financial performance can be assessed in two ways: the first is to analyze its profitability, which involves revenues and costs; and the second is to analyze market-based performance, including company share price. Orlitzky *et al.* (2003) conducted a meta-analysis based on 52 studies, yielding a total sample size of 33,878 observations from 1972 to 1997. Their analysis demonstrates that corporate social responsibility, and to a lesser extent environmental responsibility, has a positive impact on corporate financial performance (CFP) across industries and across various contexts. They found that the relationship is both immediate and bidirectional, creating a virtuous cycle. Their findings suggest that corporate sustainability is more highly correlated with accounting-based measures of CFP than with market-based indicators. This may be due to the fact that the latter are considered noisier as not based solely on actual performance (Lopez *et al.*, 2007). Fulton *et al.* (2012) performed one of the most comprehensive literature reviews to date on the financial implications of sustainable strategies. They reviewed more than 100 academic studies, 56 research studies, two literature reviews, and four meta-analyses. They considered conjointly and separately overlapping sustainable finance concepts such as Corporate Social Responsibility (CSR), Socially Responsible Investing (SRI), and Environmental, Social, and Governance (ESG) factors. Their analysis exposed both higher accounting-based performance as well as higher market-based performance for sustainable strategies. However, it is worth noting that many authors suggest a time lag between the implementation of sustainability initiatives and the positive repercussions on financial performance, using both accounting-based and market-based indicators (Eccles *et al.*, 2014; Kim, 2010; Lopez *et al.*, 2007; Movassaghi and Bramhandkar, 2012; Hart and Ahuja, 1996; Guenster *et al.*, 2011).

Yet, the nature of this relationship between corporate sustainability and financial performance is not straightforward. First, there is "no single concept of sustainability nor is there a commonly accepted way of measuring it" (Lopez *et al.*, 2007). Challenges lie in the fact that corporate sustainability is a multifaceted concept encompassing environmental, social, and governance factors (Lopez *et al.*, 2007; Waddock and Graves, 1997) and includes a myriad of key performance indicators (KPI). This renders corporate sustainability's assessment complex and subject to the interpretation of investors and ESG rating firms such as MSCI, ISS ESG, Sustainalytics, or Bloomberg. This is illustrated by the fact that it is not uncommon to see the same company rated differently by organizations providing ESG scores and ratings as they use different methodologies. Some even caution on the reliability of ESG ratings on which investors rely (Larcker *et al.*, 2022). Other impediments to the ability of investors to properly integrate ESG in their investment decisions include the lack of reporting standards as well as the associated lack of comparability, reliability, quantifiability, and timeliness (Amel-Zadeh and Serafeim, 2018). In addition, ESG KPI do not have the same impacts either on accounting-based or on market-based performance indicators. The relationship is further complicated by an array of uneven sustainability initiatives and several moderators such as the sector in which a company operates.

Another element to keep in mind is that corporate sustainability and sustainable investing have a large scope which ranges from "value-first" initiatives which focus on maximizing financial value to "values-first" initiatives which put emphasis on sustainability objectives prior to financial considerations. Indeed, not all sustainable initiatives are financially material for companies and investors. But some efforts such as the Sustainability Accounting Standards Board (SASB) Standards (soon to be replaced by IFRS Sustainability Disclosure Standards) have been developed to identify financially material industry-specific sustainability items to be reported on in order to provide financially relevant comparable sustainability disclosures to investors.

This chapter elaborates on the topics covered in a previous chapter. It will methodically examine the financial impacts that corporate sustainability can have on profitability and market-based indicators, and provide examples so that the reader can grasp them in a tangible way. It will consider both direct and indirect effects. The analysis will look at the different ESG factors with an emphasis on the environmental factor.

Chapter 5 is organized as per the following sections:

  I. Introduction
 II. Impact of Corporate Sustainability on Profitability
III. Indirect Impact of Corporate Sustainability
IV. Impact of Corporate Sustainability on Market Performance
 V. Challenges to Assessing Sustainability Impact on Financial Performance
VI. How to increase chances for Positive Financial Outcomes
VII. Conclusion

II. Impact of Corporate Sustainability on Profitability

1. Impact on Costs

Costs are the most obvious financial impacts of ESG, whether voluntary, as when a firm takes on an initiative like developing a new product, or unintentional, as when an accident occurs or when a regulation is implemented. Tracking the impact on costs seems easier than analyzing other financial indicators, but it is deceptively complex. Costs, as with savings, can be direct or indirect and can be affected differently over time. The impact can take place in the short term or the long term, and can be isolated or recurring. In addition, "identifying cost savings in operations may sound easy, but it often means adopting an entirely new perspective that requires time and money" (Kiron *et al.*, 2012). The impact on costs and savings will be analyzed in the following paragraphs while differentiating the various types of costs.

A. *Risk-Related Costs*

The first ESG impact that a company can experience is when it has no sustainable practices in place. ESG issues can have a material impact on firms' risk profiles (IMF, 2019), and failure to effectively manage ESG risks can lead to significant costs. Indeed, poor ESG practices increase the risk of incidents, which can lead to potential sanctions or lawsuit costs, but also interrupt the flow of business and reduce revenues (Setó Pamies and Angla, 2011; Perrow, 1984; Rees, 1994; Reinhardt, 1999). US banks paid $100 billion in legal settlements for their governance failures during the 2008 financial crisis. The ten largest fines and settlements in corporate history exceed $45 billion. Global pharmaceutical firms incurred over $30 billion in fines since 1991 (University of Oxford and Arabesque Partners, 2015). Environmental incidents such as corporate liabilities related to asbestos, toxic spills in the mining industry, and chemical plant explosions have also led to dramatic costs losses and bankruptcies (IMF, 2019). In some cases, the environmental risk liability costs can be so extreme that management teams may be tempted to file for bankruptcy to avoid them (Bauer and Hann, 2010).

Low ESG performance results in higher risk in terms of damage to reputation, lower intangible assets value, and intangible liabilities (Konar and Cohen, 2001; Reinhardt, 1999). It also yields risk related to compliance with future legislation. But by effectively managing their stakeholders' relationships, organizations can mitigate negative regulatory and fiscal risks (Freeman, 1984; Berman *et al.*, 1999; Hillman and Keim, 2001).

Some risk management professionals argue that one of the most effective ways to decrease an organization's environmental risk is to implement ISO 14,001, an Environmental Management System standard (see Chapter 7). ISO 14,001 requires companies to identify every element in their operations impacting the environment, determine which represent the most significant risk, and address them. The efficacy of the standard depends on the company's measures being systematic and known to every single one of its employees, thus enabling it to overcome the silos prevalent in the organization structure.

Some experts stress that certain environmental risks are not properly provisioned in companies' financial statements and could lead to high insolvency in the case of an incident, especially for companies in high environmental risk sectors (such as the fossil fuel sector). They warn that the magnitude of these risks could very well trigger financial crisis.

The Stranded Assets Programme at the University of Oxford's Smith School of Enterprise and the Environment was established in 2012 to understand the environment-related risks that could lead to unanticipated or premature write-downs, devaluations, or conversion to liabilities of assets, a phenomenon commonly referred as "stranded assets" (University of Oxford, 2014). According to their findings, environmental risks are impacting the value of assets but are not properly understood, assessed, and priced in a way that leads to an "overexposure to such risks". They go on to stress that, more and more, these risk factors are "stranding assets and this trend is accelerating, potentially representing a discontinuity able to profoundly alter asset values across a wide range of sectors". They identify some of these risk factors:

- "Environmental challenges (e.g. climate change, natural capital degradation).
- Changing resource landscapes (e.g. shale gas abundance, phosphate scarcity).
- New government regulations (e.g. carbon pricing, air pollution regulation).
- Falling clean technology costs (e.g. solar Photo Voltaic (PV), onshore wind, electric vehicles).
- Evolving social norms (e.g. fossil fuel divestment campaign) and consumer behavior (e.g. certification schemes).
- Litigation (carbon liability) and changing statutory interpretations (fiduciary duty, disclosure requirements)".

Climate change is a major ESG risk, which may result in large losses for firms across sectors. The span of its effect would also include impact on banks, insurers, financial institutions, and asset owners, amplifying systemic risks and threatening financial stability (IMF, 2019). Climate risk reveals itself in two main forms:

- **Physical risks**, which include damage to property, land, and infrastructure caused by severe weather, sea-level rise, fire, and other climate change-related events.
- **Transition risks** include those due to economic disruption during a period of adjustment to a lower-carbon economy that may arise from new climate policy (e.g. carbon tax), technology, market sentiment as well as potential premature write-downs, devaluations, or conversion to liabilities of fossil fuel assets as per the stranded asset phenomenon (IMF, 2019).

Transition risks can be huge; in 2020, two major European oil companies, BP and Shell, wrote off around $40 billion in aggregate to account for stranded assets (Kusnetz, 2020). Of note, the world's oil and gas companies would need to cut their combined production by 35% from 2019 to 2040 to meet the greenhouse gas emission reduction targets set during the 2015 Paris Agreement (Carbon Tracker Initiative, 2019). In addition, the implementation of a carbon tax could deeply affect the profitability of the oil and gas sector.

Risk management requires taking on some costs to avoid potentially greater costs. However, its benefits are not easily measurable as the savings from the incident reduction are difficult to assess and predict. But it is enough for investors to factor into their investment decisions, and weighty enough to affect a company's valuation and its share price.

B. *Costs and Savings of Corporate Sustainability Initiatives*

Some researchers argue that implementing sustainable practices may lead to increased operating costs at the expense of shareholders' wealth (Walley and Whitehead, 1994). Others flag that "the introduction of the philosophy of sustainability involves a cost or reallocation of resources that negatively affects the firm performance", at least in the short term, as with any investment (Lopez *et al.*, 2007). Implementing sustainability initiatives can bring expenses in research and development, product safety and quality as well as training in risk prevention. Moreover the benefits of these investments tend to take time to materialize into savings or reputational benefits which may then translate to increased sales and stock price. Yet, the benefits related to operating costs are internal drivers for sustainability within organizations (Kiron *et al.*, 2012).

An important element to keep in mind is that the company sector and its business model are key moderating factors for financial impacts (Dixon-Fowler *et al.*, 2013; Russo and Fouts, 1997). Environmental preparedness and performance can improve operating performance in low-risk industries, but operational costs may offset reputational benefits in high environmental risk industries where firms face burdensome environmental standards (Semenova and Hassel, 2008).

The reality is that not all sustainable initiatives produce the same financial impacts over time. Take, for example, the following initiatives:

- Resource efficiency initiatives, pertaining to the circular economy concept, tend to have a positive impact on profitability (Guenster *et al.*, 2011) with a high degree of predictability, thanks to the savings they enable both in the short and long term. In addition, they can benefit companies irrespective of sector. Product innovation to improve environmental impacts often leads to lower production costs through material substitution or by using less packaging (Porter and Van der Linde, 1995). Closed-loop systems, waste reduction, disposal or recycling initiatives, pollution prevention or total quality program can lead to decreased operating costs and higher resource productivity (Porter and Van der Linde, 1995). Waste management initiatives can lead to savings and potential revenues if the wastes are sold at a sufficient price. Recycling initiatives, however, tend to be less predictable than resource efficiency initiatives and their effect tends to unfold in the long term.
- Energy efficiency initiatives tend to generate savings that are easily measurable and are usually quite predictable, barring potential variation in the payback period (Christoffersen *et al.*, 2013). This type of initiative can benefit industries subject to high environmental risk such as chemical, transportation, or the oil and gas sectors. However, energy efficient products can clash with the business models of energy producers; they certainly don't benefit from reduced energy demand and consumption.
- Adopting renewable energy sources like solar can enable energy savings over time and when using off grid solutions, it can also provide energy independence. The financial returns of solar investment depend on the location of the solar panels given that they depend on the availability of the solar resources, but also on the characteristics of the energy market in which the solar system is installed and the incentives in place.
- CDP (previously Carbon Disclosure Project) is an initiative focusing on tracking companies' actions toward carbon emission reduction. In 2013, it reported $459,000 annual savings for the 300 companies in

heavy emitting industries, and a median internal rate of return of 33.6% for the 471 emissions projects with a median initial investment of $1 million. This means that it took these projects an average of three years to break even.

- Initiatives in emissions reduction and discharges can lead to potential cost reduction in the long term as they mitigate risks.
- Carbon capture and storage initiatives could generate revenues and be profitable if the price of carbon becomes sufficiently high to payback the initial investment, but it is typically not the case for the moment.
- Biodiversity initiatives mainly increase costs, but can also serve as an "entrance fee" to operate in certain places, and can therefore generate some indirect positive impacts on financial performance, in addition to serving offset purposes.
- Regulations are costly by nature. But opportunities exist to decrease these costs. Whether by taking a step to stay ahead of potential new regulations, or by proactively trying to solve the issues or in contributing in the structuring of the regulation, companies can prevent costlier options imposed by the regulatory body without their inputs.

C. *Impact on Productivity*

The benefits arising from the implementation of sustainability practices exemplify the old adage "what gets measured gets managed" (KPMG, 2013a, 2013b). Indeed, the development of corporate sustainability disclosures may bring "better internal systems and control leading to better decision-making and cost savings" (Adams, 2002). Many studies have evidenced that corporate sustainability increases managerial competencies and contributes to organizational efficiency (Orlitzky *et al.*, 2003).

The reputational gains that come with strong ESG performance have a positive impact on recruiting as they tend to attract better workers (Reinhardt, 1999; Turban and Greening, 1997) and improve employees' engagement (Kiron *et al.*, 2012) that, in turn, improves companies' productivity.

Moreover, process innovations to address environmental impacts can result in "higher resource productivity such as higher process yields, less downtime through more careful monitoring and maintenance, material savings (due to substitution, reuse, or recycling of production inputs), better utilization of by-products, lower energy consumption during the production process, reduced material storage and handling costs, conversion of waste into valuable forms, reduced waste disposal costs or safer workplace conditions" (Porter and Van der Linde, 1995).

D. *Impact on Cost of Capital*

Companies with better sustainability performance can enjoy better and cheaper access to finance (Cheng *et al.*, 2014; El Ghoul *et al.*, 2011). Regarding the environmental component of ESG, Fulton *et al.* (2012) found that strong performance leads to a lower cost of capital. They observed that companies with poor environmental practices tend to pay a premium on their cost of debt financing and are assigned lower credit ratings, while companies with proactive environmental engagement tend to benefit from a lower cost of debt (Bauer and Hann, 2010).

Investors in polluting companies are exposed to greater risk and therefore will expect to be compensated in consequence. They will expect a higher return to account for the higher risk, thereby penalizing these companies by increasing their cost of capital (Konar and Cohen, 2001). The incentive for polluting companies to become cleaner will increase as the proportion of sustainable investors grows.

2. Impact on Revenues

A. *Consumer Demand*

It is undeniable: consumers' interest in sustainable products is increasing (Kiron *et al.*, 2012). More and more, they expect brands to deliver sustainable products, from sourcing to production to packaging, while remaining competitively priced. It has been demonstrated that better sustainability performance may increase overall demand for products and services (Sen and Bhattacharya, 2001; Milgrom and Roberts, 1986). The business-to-business segment is particularly active as companies attempt to improve their own sustainability performance. In addition, product sustainability is a key driver for companies seeking to expand in the developing world. Reducing pollution may increase demand from environmentally sensitive consumers (King and Lenox, 2002). However, in most cases, scandals of poor ethical behavior slash sales faster than introducing green products enhances them (Lopez *et al.*, 2007).

B. *Revenues*

Companies can differentiate themselves and their products by implementing sustainability initiatives (Lopez *et al.*, 2007). Products that meet higher environmental standards can generate very positive and measurable impact on sales. However, it is not an easy task to track the impact of sustainability performance on non-differentiated products in contrast to organic food or environmentally friendly products. But thanks to reputational gains, companies can depend on environmental initiatives to boost sales in the long term. In addition, companies can generate additional revenues by acquiring companies in green sectors while benefiting from increased diversification.

Sustainability initiatives can also produce critical *indirect* impacts on sales not easily measurable in monetary terms. For example, sustainability initiatives can give license to operate in sectors subject to high environmental risks. Companies can obtain this license to operate formally by meeting regulations, or informally by serving the community where they operate by, for example, initiating local social initiatives. Sustainability initiatives can be considered an "entrance fee" or as a "cost to stay in business" in some cases. Sustainability initiatives can also allow companies to renew their rights to explore and produce. It can increase the chances of companies to win tenders in the oil and gas industry because their environmental and overall corporate responsibility is taken into account during the tender process to obtain exploration rights with governments and it can also facilitate negotiations.

C. *Product Innovation and Increased Value Added*

The development of products that meet higher environmental standards is one of the most profitable sustainable initiatives. Companies generating revenues from sustainable products are actually more likely to see positive financial impacts from their ESG endeavors (UN Global Compact and UNPRI, 2013). While the outcomes of product development initiatives and sustainability-driven innovation are less predictable than those related to resources efficiency, they tend to generate profitability over a longer period (Kiron *et al.*, 2012). Indeed, product innovation to address environmental issues presents opportunities for long-term revenues by opening new markets or expanding existing ones (Kiron *et al.*, 2012). It can also improve a company's offer by proposing "better performing, higher quality or safer products" (Porter and Van der Linde, 1995). Greater product "recyclability" or ease of disassembly leads to higher resale or scrap value, while also potentially lowering the costs of product disposal for users. As obvious as it may be, the product quality and how it compares with traditional alternatives will be critical in its success. All these aspects might justify a price premium which could also contribute to increased revenues and gross margins (Reinhardt, 1999). The impact on sales will be affected by several moderators such as the demand, the product/service, and its price.

Pricing strategy is another key factor of success. While some studies have demonstrated that better sustainability performance may reduce consumer price sensitivity (Sen and Bhattacharya, 2001; Milgrom and Roberts, 1986), the incremental increase in price should be limited. A fundamental challenge lies in the fact that people tend to buy the cheapest products and that the price lever to cover potential higher production costs is limited. Producing cleaner, greener products may be more costly, but adding a premium to cover the margin loss does not always work. Aiming for price parity and focusing on a greater volume of production allowing economies of scale may be a better strategy enabling to reduce costs in a longer term. Only if the performance is higher can the price be higher. Increasing price is viable only in certain cases, for products with overtly higher performance or organic products, and only incrementally. They may claim otherwise, but in reality, most consumers are unwilling to pay more for products with higher environmental performance because they do not want an environmentally damaging product in the first place.

III. Indirect Impacts of Corporate Sustainability

One of the challenges of corporate sustainability initiatives is that beside their costs, most of the time their financial impact is indirect and dependent on many factors.

1. Impact on Reputation

We have already established the reputational benefits of undertaking corporate sustainability initiatives, but as they are perhaps the primary motivation for companies, they warrant further discussion. By managing their sustainability performance, most companies are attempting to reduce their reputational risks and react to pressure or threat from their stakeholders. As shown by multiple studies (Fombrun and Shanley, 1990; Freeman *et al.*, 2014), effective management of stakeholder relationships may protect and enhance corporate reputation. The positive impact on reputation is perceived by all stakeholders including customers, suppliers, collaborators, employees, investors, and society as a whole, producing a "virtuous circle". Existing empirical research shows a positive relationship between reputation and financial performance. These reputational gains tend to translate to an increase in sales, competitiveness, and stock price. Furthermore, the intangible nature of reputation makes replication by competing firms challenging, which proves that companies with "good reputations are better able to sustain superior profit outcomes over time" (Roberts and Dowling, 2002).

Companies can improve their reputation by earning strong ESG ratings. They can go further by winning sustainability awards and a place in rankings, publications in the press, or sustainability indexes such as the Dow Jones Sustainability Index (DJSI). All of these can generate positive reputation outcomes. In addition, evidence suggests that "public sentiment influences investor views about the value of corporate sustainability activities and thereby both the price paid for corporate sustainability and the investment returns of portfolios that consider ESG data" (Serafeim, 2020).

Environmental initiatives have a positive impact on reputation provided the organization is handling its costs strategically, as these will affect investor perception. Indeed, being *too good* environmentally may *damage* a company's reputation, if investors believe the company is reckless in its cost management.

The potential reputational benefits are many, but are however limited by a company's business model and industry-specific risks. And the reputational damages incurred from incidents are higher and more likely in high-risk industries such as the oil and gas sector. For this reason, the positive impact of environmental initiatives can be limited in high-risk industries. For instance, it is difficult to improve the image of an oil producer, as the sector has an overall negative image. However, ESG performance can improve the acceptability and the company image to a certain extent. The impact of the company's business model is even more determining than the industry. ESG management and performance will be well-perceived when companies incorporate business models which allow them to benefit from the initiatives they implement.

It is worth stressing that in some industries, such as oil and gas or soft drinks, companies transitioning to more sustainable practices or business lines may receive some pushback from investors who dismiss ESG factors, or consider that the company is changing its strategy too radically. Investors can apply pressure to sustain the business lines which traditionally generate revenues. To the extent that environmental performance is associated with the core business, it will be looked upon favorably, as it promotes longevity or helps the company be in compliance, or a little ahead of it. But when it appears to distract from the core business, it starts to look unfavorable by traditional investors. In addition, the efficiency of communication is a moderator in the impact on reputation (see Section VI.4).

2. Impact on Intangible Assets

The growing impact of intangible assets on companies' market valuation can be observed by the declining ratio of company net assets to enterprise value ratio (Ocean Tomo, 2020). One of the key financial impacts of sustainability is its effect on intangible assets which include non-exhaustively the quality of management, branding power, human capital development, and intellectual capital (RobecoSam, 2014). These increasingly contribute to a firm's ability to generate earnings, and investment professionals can no longer afford to underestimate them. Company sustainability management acts as a proxy for assessing a company's intangible assets. It is a new dimension of the fundamental analysis that provides a more comprehensive view to assess a company's potential to create value. The magnitude of the losses of intangible assets value in case of poor environmental performance is larger for traditionally polluting industries (Konar and Cohen, 2001).

3. Impact on Competitiveness

Historically, it was believed that responsible companies were subject to a competitive disadvantage due to a supposed increase in operating costs (Aupperle *et al.*, 1985). After two decades of analysis, most authors now believe the contrary: implementing sustainable strategies should confer competitive advantages on the companies, which implement them compared to those who do not (King and Lenox, 2002). They argue that companies can differentiate their products, processes, and overall organization with sustainability practices (Lopez *et al.*, 2007). Contrarily, based on the stakeholder analysis, firms that lower their costs by being "socially irresponsible" are likely to incur even higher costs, resulting in a competitive disadvantage (Waddock and Graves, 1997).

Innovation is a road to competitiveness, and companies seeking to address environmental issues while improving products or processes can benefit from it (Porter and Van der Linde, 1995). Indeed, a product's environmental performance and the company's posture toward sustainability have become a basis for competitiveness (Prahalad and Hamel, 1994). Companies with higher ESG performance are better managed. And it has been established that better sustainability management helps to attract and retain employees, both imperative to a company's success.

In 2011, two-thirds of the 2,874 managers interviewed around the world by Kiron *et al.* (2012) acknowledged that sustainability was critical to being competitive compared to 55% in 2010. At the same time, 22% of respondents said that it was not critical then, but anticipated it would be in the future. Some argue that sustainability strategy has already become a competitive necessity and highlight that the "competitive differentiation or reputational advantage may wear-out as green products become more and more the norm" (Christoffersen *et al.*, 2013).

IV. Impact of Corporate Sustainability on Market Performance

1. Impact on Investors and Access to Investors

Firms with better corporate sustainability performance, better stakeholder engagement, and better transparency on ESG issues tend to enjoy greater access to finance and lower capital constraints (Cheng *et al.*, 2014). Investors are becoming increasingly sensitive to corporate sustainability strategy and aware that sustainability is an imperative value for success (Lopez *et al.*, 2007; Eccles and Klimenko, 2019). Mounting inquiries from investors and shareholders is one of the six growing trends in corporate sustainability (Ernst and Young, 2013). This suggests that by proactively engaging action on ESG, firms are more likely to satisfy their shareholders. Therefore, not only are socially responsible investors taking notice, traditional investors are also examining areas such as risk management, resource efficiency, and employee retention and treating sustainability performance as an overall business indicator to predict future profitability (Kiron *et al.*, 2012).

Furthermore, by having a sustainability strategy, a company management appears to contribute to the image of management which seems to be more enlightened and disciplined, which is one of the most important features investors look for when buying stock (Knoepfel, 2001). Managers of sustainable companies are expected "to anticipate market opportunities for sustainable products and services while mitigating risks and reducing sustainability costs to create shareholder value" (Knoepfel, 2001). Having a sustainable strategy and being recognized as a sustainable company in a sustainable index such as the DJSI Index are affecting investors' investment decisions.

2. Impact on Stock Price

Many factors influence the effect of ESG on stock price, and measuring it is not easy (see section below on Measurability). Sustainable investing is growing, but it still represents only a minority of investors. Most investors have their set ways of building their models. They are accustomed to reading indicators such as the operating income, capital expenditures, and the multiple of earnings-to-share price. But many investors still disregard ESG performance and sustainability considerations in general, when making an investment. Investors do however consider intangible assets which are affected by ESG as discussed above. But their assessments are mainly based on opinion and expertise rather than on objective ratios and measurement (Vilanova *et al.*, 2009), as there are currently no indicators of ESG performance accepted by all financial analysts even though ESG ratings have recently gained popularity among investors. These elements weaken the ability to measure the relationship between ESG performance and stock price.

It is more straightforward to observe the negative effects arising from an incident than the positive ones, which are diluted by many other elements including competitiveness and product demand. Yet, companies that effectively manage long-term sustainability risks and opportunities such as climate change, resource scarcity, or demographic change tend to "exhibit a superior capacity to prosper over the long run" (RobecoSam A. G., 2014). This may translate into a company's financial market valuation as it is tied to its capacity to create value against its competitors. If we accept that a company's market valuation represents how market currently measures its competitiveness, robust ESG performance should strengthen market valuation (Copeland *et al.*, 2000).

Firms with a better ESG record than their peers tend to encounter higher three-year returns, are more likely to become high-quality stocks, less likely to have large price declines, and less likely to go bankrupt (Eccles and Klimenko, 2019). A study by Nordea Equity Research focusing on the 2012–2015 period revealed that "the companies with the highest ESG ratings outperformed the lowest rated firms by as much as 40%" (Eccles and Klimenko, 2019). In addition, a study suggests that ESG ratings impact future market expectations and stock price (Serafeim and Yoon, 2020). A paper by Eccles *et al.* (2014) studied 180 US companies and found that corporations that had voluntarily adopted sustainability policies significantly outperformed those that did not, with significantly higher stock returns over the long term. This research supports the argument that the integration of ESG considerations into a company's business model and strategy will be a competitive advantage in the long term. Other research by Fulton *et al.* (2012) examined a number of studies, isolating the environmental factor of ESG, and found that three out of the five suggest a positive correlation between market-based performance and the environmental factor. They hypothesize that investors' growing interest in ESG may increase stock returns. They go so far as to claim that this might lead to a "first mover advantage" and to companies being able to anticipate future regulations related to climate change, carbon emissions, or energy efficiency. A study found that "the valuation premium paid for companies with strong sustainability performance has increased over time and that the premium is increasing as a function of positive public sentiment momentum" (Serafeim, 2020).

However, those positive results are not systematic. Christoffersen *et al.* (2013) studied the influence of environmental issues on financial performance in the healthcare sector. They hypothesized that, if being a good steward for the environment reflects enlightened leadership, then financial markets should find these stocks attractive. They expected a positive impact on prices, driving up both the numerator (earning per share: EPS) and denominator (share price: P) of the EPS/P variable. Yet they did not find the anticipated correlation while examining the price-to-earnings ratio (P/E) and stressed that stock price was affected by many other factors.

One of those factors is the company industry. Some studies have in fact demonstrated that the environmental risk of an industry stifles the impact of environmental initiatives on market value. Whereas the positive effect of environmental performance on market value is stronger in low-risk industries (Semenoval and Hassel, 2008), environmental preparedness offers "reputational benefits to market value in both low and high-risk industries" (Semenoval and Hassel, 2008). Anticipation of environmental regulation can contribute to higher market-based performance (Fulton *et al.*, 2012). Companies can not only protect but enhance their reputation by taking a proactive approach to regulation, as it allows them to structure the regulation in a more cost-effective way than if regulatory bodies did so on their own.

On the other hand, poor environmental performance is linked to a decrease in market valuation, due to the loss of intangible asset value.

The magnitude of this adverse effect varies across industries, but hits in traditionally polluting industries (Konar and Cohen, 2001). ESG-related costs and associated reputational damages can also impact a company's stock price. Following the Deepwater Horizon oil spill in the Gulf of Mexico in 2015, BP's share more than halved. Following the Brumadinho mine disaster in 2019, the Vale S.A. share price fell by close to a quarter. After recognizing that their cars included a system to cheat on air pollution test results in the United States for years, Volkswagen was exposed in 2015, and lost almost a quarter of its market value (The Generation Foundation, UNEP FI and the PRI, 2019).

Another important element to consider is the type of ESG initiative taken, as they can have different impacts on market value. Some are considered financially material and others are not (see Section below on concept of materiality). Some initiatives such as resource efficiency have positive impacts irrespective of sector (Guenster *et al.*, 2011), but others are more relevant to certain sectors and not always financially material. Research has found evidence of a positive impact of eco-efficiency on stock price and confirmed that the cost reduction through resource efficiency initiatives is favored by all investors (Guenster *et al.*, 2011).

Some investors recognize that companies reducing their ESG risks may ultimately yield better returns to shareholders than businesses who do not. From an investor perspective, ESG management can be seen as a proxy attesting that the company is responsible, anticipates the forthcoming challenges, and is able to adapt to a changing environment. Socially responsible investors which follow a "values-first" investing approach are the most swayed by sustainability considerations as this factor alone determines their choice to own a company's stocks and keep the investment over time not just the financial performance of a company or sector. "Values-first" investing may exclude polluting companies and leads to fewer investors holding polluting firms' stocks which may penalize polluting firms by decreasing their market value (Konar and Cohen, 2001).

Yet, the incentive for polluting companies to become cleaner will depend on the proportion of sustainable investors (Konar and Cohen, 2001). More broadly, some argue that sustainability is not yet appropriately valued by the market, and especially by traditional investors. This presents an opportunity for investors who seize this market mis-pricing.

3. Impact on Market Risks

Environmental performance minimizes uncertainty in the long term once a company is deemed "ethical" (Kim, 2010). Two main market risks exist in finance: the systematic risk and the unsystematic risk. The systematic risk measures the volatility of a stock compared to the rest of the stock market and is captured by an indicator called the Beta. The unsystematic risk, on the other hand, involves a company- or industry-specific hazard inherent to each investment that can be mitigated through portfolio diversification. It has been shown that environmental practices may reduce both systematic risk and unsystematic risk (Christoffersen *et al.*, 2013).

V. Challenges to Assessing Impact of Sustainability on Financial Performance

The relationship between corporate sustainability and financial performance is complex and it is important to understand that moderators exist such as the sector in which a company operates. In addition, corporate sustainability not only involves "value-first" sustainable initiatives which focus on maximizing financial value and fit with investors' fiduciary duty, it also includes "valueS-first" sustainable initiatives which may produce some positive social, environmental, or governance impact while putting financial considerations second and sometimes do not perform as well. Indeed, not all sustainable initiatives are financially material for companies and investors. But some efforts such as the SASB Standards (soon to be replaced by IFRS Sustainability Disclosure Standards) have been developed to identify financially material industry-specific sustainability items to be reported on in order to provide financially relevant comparable sustainability disclosures to investors. Lastly, measurability remains challenging.

1. Moderators

Many factors influence the financial impacts of a company's sustainability performance. A study conducted by Hoepner and Yu identified five such moderators: type of sustainability approach and initiatives, firm character-istics, time, national framework, and industrial characteristics (Hoepner and Yu, 2010). Other moderators include the sector, the business model, the location, and the management's philosophy. In some high environ-mental risk sectors, such as the oil and gas industry, there is a very high risk of not doing the right thing, which may affect the company's very survival. The efficacy of environmental initiatives depends on how the company's products and services respond to environmental issues, and how they integrate them. For example, companies in the recycling or water treatment industry, will greatly benefit from such initiatives. Environmental initiatives will facilitate more sales and allow them to become leaders of environmental stewardship. On the other hand, there are companies with business models completely incompatible with envi-ronmental issues, and they will suffer. Geographic considerations are also significant as regulations and tax incentives vary from place to place. Location also impacts sales because of varying tastes and demands. In addition, initiatives will perform differently according to the level of maturity of the sustainability integration in business practices in each country and region. Table 5.1 lists internal and external moderators that affect the impact of environmental sustainability initiatives on financial performance.

2. Materiality

Not all ESG topics and initiatives are financially material for companies and investors (Khan, Serafeim, & Yoon, 2016). Companies focusing on "material issues report up to 50% added profit from sustainability", while those who don't "struggle to add value from their sustainability activities" (Kiron *et al.*, 2017). It has been evidenced that firms with high ratings in material sustainability issues significantly outperform those without, while high ratings in immaterial sustainability issues do not bring signifi-cant impact (Khan *et al.*, 2016). In addition, considering the financial materiality in ESG ratings may improve their accuracy for forecasting returns (Khan, 2019).

Material ESG dimensions tend to be sector- and industry-specific. The Sustainability Accounting Standards Board (SASB 2018), now part of the

Table 5.1. Moderators to Sustainability Impact on Financial Performance

Internal Factors	External Factors
• Sustainability initiatives • Firm characteristics • Sector • Business model • Level of environmental risk • Resource availability • Managerial support • Time allocated • Internal willingness • Attitude toward change • Systemic approach • Employee awareness and involvement • Collaboration with other stakeholders • Anticipation of regulation, and active participation in its establishment	• Investor awareness and fluency in evaluating ESG • Availability and quality of a global set of metrics for both sustainability performance and its value creation • Attitude toward change • Competition • Stakeholder willingness • Quality of communication among stakeholders • Infrastructure • Government support • Regulatory framework • Natural disasters and environmental hazards • Time • National Framework

Source: Based on Simon (2015) and Hoepner and Yu (2010).

IFRS, has identified material ESG topics by industry. As of 2022, SASB Standards (soon to be replaced by IFRS Sustainability Disclosure Standards) have identified in excess of 26 environmental, social, and governance issues most relevant to financial performance and enterprise value for 77 industries accessible on their website.

The Materiality Map on the next page lists some of the major material sustainability topics by main industry groups (SASB, 2018 — see Table 5.2). While selling practices and labeling management will be common material sustainability issues for financial institutions and food and beverage companies, other issues will be industry specific. For example, systemic risk and business ethics will be critical for financial firms, but not as relevant for companies in the food and beverage sector. Alternatively, water and waste water management will be material for companies in the food and beverage sector, but not for companies in the financial sector (see Table 5.2).

Table 5.2. SASB Materiality Map

Legend:
- ■ Issue is likely to be material for more than 50% of industries in sector
- ■ Issue is likely to be material for fewer than 50% of industries in sector
- □ Issue is not likely to be material for any of the industries in sector

Dimension	General Issue Category	Consumer Goods	Extractives & Minerals Processing	Financials	Food & Beverage	Health Care	Infrastructure	Renewable Resources & Alternative Energy	Resource Transformation	Services	Technology & Communications	Transportation
Environment	GHG Emissions											
	Air Quality											
	Energy Management											
	Water & Wastewater Management											
	Waste & Hazardous Materials Management											
	Ecological Impacts											
Social Capital	Human Rights & Community Relations											
	Customer Privacy											
	Data Security											
	Access & Affordability											
	Product Quality & Safety											
	Customer Welfare											
	Selling Practices & Product Labeling											
Human Capital	Labor Practices											
	Employee Health & Safety											
	Employee Engagement, Diversity & Inclusion											
Business Model & Innovation	Product Design & Lifecycle Management											
	Business Model Resilience											
	Supply Chain Management											
	Materials Sourcing & Efficiency											
	Physical Impacts of Climate Change											
Leadership & Governance	Business Ethics											
	Competitive Behavior											
	Management of the Legal & Regulatory Environment											
	Critical Incident Risk Management											
	Systemic Risk Management											

Source: Based on SASB (2018).

3. Measurability

Some methodologies have been developed to tackle the measurability issue and are discussed in earlier chapter. Measuring the impact of sustainability on financial performance can be challenging, especially when examining stock price and sales unrelated to high environmental performance products. The complexity of the profitability measurement stems from the profusion of moderators involved, the timespan of the effects of initiatives on revenues, costs, and savings and their traceability to the initiatives taken. It is sometimes difficult to assess the benefits of sustainability initiatives in monetary terms, particularly because the impact of reputational gains on sales and the costs saved through risk management are difficult to measure and not always perceived by investors. But it also relates to the fact that the "true" value assigned to sustainability performance is not always tangibly measurable in a company's financial statements.

Another factor explaining the imperfect relationship of ESG and financial performance relates to the fact that many companies implement non-material ESG initiatives and have been considering sustainability as a siloed effort. We now know that companies integrating material ESG in their business models are more likely to generate positive financial outcomes (Kiron *et al.*, 2012).

In addition, methodological shortcomings to measure corporate sustainability performance (Salzmann *et al.*, 2005; Movassaghi and Bramhandkar, 2012) impair investors' understanding of ESG. It can be difficult for investors to compare sustainability performance among companies and find relevant benchmarks. A common set of metrics would significantly help them understand key indicators of performance and facilitate the process of assessing value and risks. In addition, the current practice of voluntary disclosure and the resulting subjectivity can be overcome through sustainability audit (Christoffersen *et al.*, 2013).

Another measurability challenge is linked to the economists problem of negative externalities. Environmental impacts and externalities are neither appropriately measured nor monetized while natural resources like water, land, and clean air are critical to any business. Most profit-seeking organizations would understand the benefit of reducing the environmental impact of financial performance if the total impact, including all externalities, was measured. But at present, they are not. This constitutes a considerable market imperfection. Only recently, as we begin to pay for the consequences of decades of poor resource management, have people started to take notice. Understanding the true costs of being in business is a key step to long-term financial success. It is not easy to put a price on natural resources. But there is a need to appropriately value nature and understand the risks of undervaluing it. Carbon dioxide (CO_2) is one environmental impact that has begun to be widely adopted, but is not yet monetized. The greenhouse gas (GHG) protocol is a measurement system encompassing the whole value chain, which was developed by a large coalition of stakeholders including companies, governments, and non-profits such as the World Resource Institute (WRI) and the World Business Council for Sustainable Development (WBCSD). If a price on carbon was to be agreed upon (and sufficiently high) it could internalize the negative externalities of CO_2 on climate change. It would shift the profitability of the energy sector in a way that may compel the fossil fuel industry to keep coal and oil reserves, already recognized on their balance sheet, in the ground. It would significantly impact the valuation of these organizations and the assets that could not be used would be stranded. Some investors already take this risk into consideration and manage their portfolio accordingly, either reallocating capital toward cleaner energy or through engaging with large oil and gas majors to support their energy transition. Carbon pricing would also impact the profitability of technologies related to carbon capture and storage which, despite their positive environmental impacts, have until now struggled to scale up because of high upfront costs.

Another challenge exists for pollution. Its consequences are often diffuse, appearing far down the road. Laws may be mainly national, but pollution does not know borders. Thus, there is dysfunction in the current legal and enforcement frameworks, as both the economy and environment are global while the legal and enforcement frameworks are national. As a result, the organizations responsible for pollution are not always identified and charged for those damages, while the actors suffering from the situation pay the price. Meanwhile, companies with a higher level of environmental performance, who strive to efficiently mitigate their environmental risks, may have to bear higher operating costs, at least in the short term.

The government role in addressing these market imperfections and regulating sustainability measurements and reporting is critical. Indeed, policies and regulations can help ensure that market dynamics incentivize positive outcomes for society, the planet, companies, and investors. In addition, coordinated global legal efforts and enforcement are necessary due to the nature of the issues at stake.

VI. How to Increase Chances for Positive Financial Outcomes

1. Prioritizing the Long Term

To fully reap the rewards of sustainability management, companies must consider both financial and reputational opportunities and threats in the long term. Time horizon is a key factor to consider in the decision-making processes around sustainability. Sound environmental and sustainability policies are about the long term, not about the next month's share price or the next quarterly earnings. Some sustainability professionals argue that sustainability policies should be measured not in dollars, but by the number of years in business enabled by the right initiatives.

Upfront costs are some of the greatest obstacles to implementing sustainability initiatives. As for any investment, costs directly affect financial statements, while returns typically occur in the longer term. Yet, the direct costs related to a sustainability initiative are easier to track than its benefits. Some benefits are challenging to measure and arise in the long term, such as risk mitigation or reputation gain. Companies need to overcome the measurability challenge presented by these variables and consider the long term to fully benefit from their sustainability management.

Building a strong business case for new sustainability initiatives is critical. When assessing a project, it is important to perform comprehensive sensitivity analysis to identify the fluctuating items which could affect its internal rate of return (IRR). But in some cases, it is not possible to calculate the IRR. Yet, organizations have an incentive to go beyond the analysis of the net present value while considering investing in sustainability initiatives. Indeed, it is also important to take advantage of indirect financial benefits stemming from risk mitigation or increased reputation granted by strong sustainability management. Reducing sustainability risks increase companies' likelihood of operating reliably in the long term. Thus, meeting their objectives and indirectly generating positive financial outcomes. Incorporating ESG risks is particularly critical in sectors where environmental risks and the costs of missteps are high such as the extractives industries. In addition, it is worth considering the intangible benefits that sustainability can generate on reputation when considering an initiative given their indirect impact on financial performance. This does not necessarily mean that any sustainability initiatives should be undertaken. Initiatives relevant for a business should be privileged.

Decision-making itself can be considered a moderator in the relationship between sustainability and financial performance. It can be either an obstacle or a success factor within companies. Companies have a tendency to focus on short-term benefits. This can be linked to the set timeframe during which a project needs to break even determined by company's management. It can also relate to the manager's own eagerness to see the rewards during her tenure. Short-term projects may also be preferred by employees who want projects that will show results during their occupancy rather than longer term initiatives which will drive their immediate, observable personal performance. However, neglecting long-term benefits can result in missed opportunities, and cripple a company's ability to generate cash flows in the long term (see Table 5.3). Most sustainability initiatives have to meet the same hurdle rate as any other capital expenditure project. But it may be worth accepting lower returns, if the sustainability initiatives are quite predictable. Using the same metrics as standard capital expenditure projects without differentiation for the sustainable nature of a project can be problematic because sustainability initiatives tend to break even in a longer timeline. This results in finance and executive teams prioritizing other projects, at the expense of sustainability projects.

To counter this, organizations must first acknowledge that a large part of sustainability benefits will occur over time, and some are difficult to measure monetarily. For this reason, companies should not solely consider the short-term cost-benefit analysis when selecting sustainability initiatives. They must pay particular attention to the potential long-term benefits of risk mitigation, strategic resources access and management, and

Table 5.3. The Financial Impact of Sustainability Initiatives Over Time

Short-Term Impact	Long-Term Impact
• Costs	• Savings
	• Environmentally differentiated sales
	• Reputational gains
	• Non-environmentally differentiated sales
	• Risk reduction
	• Share price

Source: Based on Simon (2015).

intangible assets such as reputation, employee commitment, and intellectual property. Understanding the impact of sustainability on intangible assets is especially crucial for companies because of the increasing contribution of intangible assets in the company's market valuation (Ocean Tomo LLC, 2020). It is also worth noting that companies can benefit from testing new technologies even if they are not profitable in themselves due to the high costs of the new technologies. Indeed, the initiative may generate long-term profits by developing employees' knowledge and skills, and prepare them to identify and seize relevant opportunities in the future when the price of the new technology drops. Testing a new technology in a small-scale project could become a source of competitiveness if the project is successful and can be scaled (Porter and Van der Linde, 1995).

2. Integrating ESG in Business Models and a Systemic Approach

There are many lessons to be learned from organizations that profit from sustainability, also known as "Harvesters" (Kiron *et al.*, 2012). The first is weighing the environmental impacts of product development and operations. For harvesters, it is also a common practice to integrate sustainability into their business model. Some now argue that adapting business models and operations to incorporate sustainability is a prerequisite to long-term financial success (Kiron *et al.*, 2012). Another is the *holistic* sustainability approach we introduced in an earlier chapter (see Chapter 3).

This means looking at the issue as a process of continuous improvement, rather than a static objective, and examining the entire product lifecycle and supply chain. These have all proven to be factors of success for these organizations. With the rise of issues like climate change, waste proliferation, and pollution, these lessons may become critical to all businesses' success.

Experts in risk management advocate for integrating sustainability by implementing risk management system standards such as ISO 14,001 (see Chapter 7). By requiring a systematic approach and integrating sustainability into the business's core operations, these standards effectively mitigate environmental risk, but also tangibly improve environmental impact and reduce reputational risk. By doing so, companies avoiding reputational damages and colossal costs which would occur in case of an accident. ISO 14,001 also has the advantage of being a leading indicator, which can offer a sense of the future, as opposed to lagging indicators based on past performance. Furthermore, it is easy to understand by investors and provides evidence that the company is taking sustainability risk seriously and is not doing some "greenwashing".

3. The Right Initiatives

By implementing environmental initiatives such as resource efficiency initiatives and by developing products that meet higher environmental performance (particularly those business-to-business sector) companies can increase their chances of success. These two types of initiatives have won praise as the most beneficial initiatives — the first for its high level of predictability, the second for a high level of profitability. Companies are recommended to perform sensitivity analysis when selecting initiatives to identify potentially fluctuating items that could skew the results.

Strong collaboration is another signature characteristic of the harvesters according to Kiron *et al.* (2012). Whether with NGOs, governments, or other stakeholders (including competitors) collaboration tends to lead to positive financial outcomes. Companies can collaborate to find solutions to tackle industry-wide problems, issues of measurement, establishing standards, etc. They can also work proactively with regulators, other stakeholders, and each other to frame regulations in a way which is less costly and might have as well a positive impact on their reputation.

In addition, fostering diversity in employee recruitment and in board have also been demonstrated as producing positive financial outcomes (McKinsey & Company, 2015).

Table 5.4 lists internal and external factors that can impact the financial performance of sustainable initiatives.

Table 5.4. Moderators at the Initiatives Level

Internal Factors	External Factors
• Company	• Country
• Business model	• Sector
• Performance and resource availability	• Profitability of initiative over time including efficiency (payback period)
• Environmental impacts	• Predictability of the initiative
• Managerial philosophy	• Upfront and maintenance costs of initiative and its technology
• Know-how	• Commodity price
• Initiative development and focus	• Regulations
• Decision-making	• Tax systems
○ Initiative assessment	
▪ Assessment of the opportunities and threats for the company over time	
▪ Short/long-term perspective	
▪ Feasibility and sensitivity analysis	
▪ Holistic approach and lifecycle examination vs. silo	
▪ Integration of risk dimension	
○ Initiative selection	
▪ Return hurdle choice	
▪ Specific treatment or not	
• Implementation and project management	
• Creativity in problem solving	
• Systematic nature of initiative	
• Integration in the business model	

"Green" products	
• Product performance	• Consumer awareness and perception
• Pricing strategy	• Demand
	• Supply chain disruption
	• Volatility risk with commodity pricing and availability

Source: Based on Simon (2015).

4. The Right Communication

Communicating around sustainability initiatives and their performance can be of make-or-break significance. Indeed, the right communication has a positive impact, but the wrong communication can do more harm than good. In the past, companies touting empty claims of sustainable initiatives would often see similar benefits as those genuinely doing so and communicating about them, and sometimes more than companies genuinely implementing sustainable initiatives and not communicating about them. Historically, the companies who have communicated most on their environmental initiatives have actually been the polluting ones. But in the mid-2000s, environmental NGOs hurled accusations of greenwashing, leading to major backlash and consumer fallout. A paradox has since emerged: the more a company claims they are greener than green, the more investors and customers are cautious. Companies need to communicate carefully to avoid the greenwashing trap. Indeed, accuracy and sincerity are paramount. They should communicate in a way that is transparent, authentic, open, honest, and self-critical, without overselling the environmental or social benefits. In addition, organizations should privilege communicating on tangible initiatives which have already been taken. The reputational benefit of sustainability management tends to be greater when companies set ambitious goals and highlight their progress toward them, as well as the areas of improvement.

Sustainable reporting, also called non-financial reporting, is a key communication tool. Sustainability reports can be done annually or quarterly to demonstrate progress against stated targets (cf. Chapter 3, Sect. IV on sustainability reporting for more details). Material sustainability topics can also be included in financial statements. Institutional investors are increasingly paying attention to those non-financial metrics as well as financial metrics, and such metrics impact their decision to hold stocks, especially for socially responsible investors. The current reporting system has two major limitations. First, it lacks standardization and there is no clear distinction between financially material sustainability matters and others which alternatively may only benefit society or the planet. Sector-specific disclosure frameworks focused on financially material sustainability issues, like the one developed by SASB, might facilitate investors' understanding of sustainability. Second, sustainable reporting mainly relies on voluntary disclosure, tainting the objectivity of information shared. Given the lack of regulations about sustainability disclosure or when they exist their excessive flexibility, companies can set their own boundaries of their sustainability disclosures, and make the call about what to include or exclude. Companies and investors can overcome this by using, or requiring companies to use, audits to check the sustainability performance disclosed by companies, similar to how financial audits are now used.

Companies should develop a compelling sustainability value-creation story for investors (Kiron *et al.*, 2017). To do so they can follow the Value Driver Model (see Figure 5.1) developed by the UN Global Compact and UNPRI (2013), which is a reporting model for companies to communicate on the value creation of their sustainability initiatives which aims to overcome the issue of measurability. The Value Driver Model recommends that companies communicate on the value created by the implementation of their sustainability initiatives, for example by highlighting the impact on revenues growth, productivity, and risk management metrics. The Value Driver Model urges companies to emphasize how sustainability impacts their strategy and business performance over the reporting following the Global Reporting Initiative framework which tends to isolate sustainability from the core business. By considering growth, productivity,

Figure 5.1.   The Value Driver Model

Source: UN Global Compact and UNPRI (2013).

and risk management metrics, the Value Driver Model (see Figure 5.1) attempts to facilitate investors' understanding of sustainability opportunities and risks by focusing on clear communication of value created.

VII. Conclusion

The financial stakes of corporate sustainability are rising and the amount of evidence suggesting their materiality to companies' financial performance and investment returns is growing. These links are observed both at the profitability level, with growing demand for sustainable products, and at the market valuation level, with more and more investors taking sustainability into consideration. Some argue that we are experiencing a new industrial revolution, wherein business model compatibility with ESG challenges will lead some companies to thrive, and some to shutter. But these positive financial outcomes tend to arise over a longer term than companies and investors are used to considering.

The standardization and the regulations of the disclosure of financially material sustainability issues could facilitate investors decision-making and the measurability of the impact of sustainability performance on financial performance.

While the relationship between sustainability performance and financial performance is not systematic and is moderated by various factors, companies may help investors better understand ESG opportunities and threats and ultimately increase their likelihood of benefiting from them. This can be done by focusing on "value-first" initiatives that target financially material sustainability issues such as the ones identified by the SASB Standards (soon to be replaced by IFRS Sustainability Disclosure Standards). And also by communicating about the value created with a focus on the impact on revenue growth, productivity, and risk management as laid out in the *Value Driver* Model.

References

Adams, C. A. (2002). "Internal organisational factors influencing corporate social and ethical reporting: Beyond current theorising", *Accounting, Auditing & Accountability Journal*, 15(2), pp. 223–250.

Amel-Zadeh, A. and Serafeim, G. (2018). "Why and how investors use ESG information: Evidence from a global survey", *Financial Analysts Journal*, 2018, 74(3), pp. 87–103. http://dx.doi.org/10.2139/ssrn.2925310.

Aupperle, K. E., Carroll, A. B., and Hatfield, J. D. (1985). "An empirical examination of the relationship between corporate social responsibility and profitability", *Academy of Management Journal*, 28(2), pp. 446–463.

Bauer, R., and Hann, D. (2010). "Corporate environmental management and credit risk", Working Paper, Maastricht University, European Centre for Corporate Engagement (ECCE).

Bebbington, J. (2001). "Sustainable development: A review of the international development business and accounting literature", *Accounting Forum*, 25(2), pp. 128–157.

Berman, S. L., Wicks, A. C., Kotha, S., and Jones, T. M. (1999). "Does stakeholder orientation matter? The relationship between stakeholder management models and firm financial performance", *The Academy of Management Journal*, 42(5), pp. 488–506.

Carbon Tracker Initiative. (2019). "The world's listed oil and gas majors must cut combined production by a third by 2040 to keep emissions within international climate targets and protect shareholder value, Carbon Tracker finds in a report today". Published on November 1, 2019. Consulted in December 2020, https://carbontracker.org/balancing-the-budget-press-release/.

Cheng, B., Ioannou, I., and Serafeim, G. (2014). "Corporate social responsibility and access to finance", *Strategic Management Journal*, 35(1), pp. 1–23. https://onlinelibrary.wiley.com/doi/abs/10.1002/smj.2131.

Christoffersen, S., Frampton, G. C., and Granitz, E. (2013). "Environmental sustainability's impact on earnings", *Journal of Business & Economics Research*, 11(7), pp. 325–333.

Copeland, T. E., Koller, T., and Murrin, J. (2000). *Valuation: Measuring and Managing the Value of Companies*, 3rd edn. Wiley, New York.

Dixon-Fowler, H. R., Slater, D. J., Johnson, J. L., Ellstrand, A. E., and Romi, A. M. (2013). "Beyond 'Does it pay to be green?' A meta-analysis of moderators of the CEP–CFP relationship", *Journal of Business Ethics*, 112, pp. 353–366.

Eccles, R., Ioannou I., and Serafeim G. (2014). "The impact of corporate sustainability on organizational processes and performance", *Management Science*, 60(11), pp 2835–2857.

Eccles, R. G., and Klimenko, S. (2019). "The investor revolution", *Harvard Business Review* (May–June 2019). pp. 106–116. https://hbr.org/2019/05/the-investor-revolution.

El Ghoul, S., Guedhami, O., Kwok, C., and Mishra, D. (2011). "Does corporate social responsibility affect the cost of capital?" *Journal of Banking and Finance*, 35(9), pp. 2388–2406. https://econpapers.repec.org/article/eeejbfina/v_3a35_3ay_3a2011_3ai_3a9_3ap_3a2388-2406.htm.

Fombrun, C., and Shanley, M. (June 1990). "What's in a name? Reputation building and corporate strategy", *Academy of Management Journal*, 33(2), pp. 233–258.

Freeman, R. (1984). *Strategic Management: A Stakeholder Perspective*, Piman, Boston, MA.

Friedman, M. (1970): "The social responsibility of business is to increase its profits", *The New York Times Magazine*, September 13.

Fulton, M., Kahn, B. M., and Sharples, C. (2012). *Sustainable Investing: Establishing Long-Term Value and Performance*, SSRN. https://papers.ssrn.com/sol3/papers.cfm?abstract_id=2222740.

Guenster, N., Bauer, R., Derwall, J., and Koedijk, K. (2011). "The economic value of corporate eco-efficiency", *European Financial Management*, 17(4), pp. 679–704.

Hart, S. L., and Ahuja, G. (1996). "Does it pay to be green? An empirical examination of the relationship between emission reduction and firm performance", *Business Strategy and the Environment*, 5(1), pp. 30–37.

Hillman, A. J., and Keim, G. D. (2001). "Shareholder value, stakeholder management, and social issues: What's the bottom line?" *Strategic Management Journal*, 22(2), pp. 125–139.

Hoepner, A. G. F., and Yu, P.-S. (March 1, 2010). "Corporate social responsibility across industries: When can who do well by doing good?", https://ssrn.com/abstract=1284703.

IMF (International Monetary Fund). (2019). "Global financial stability report", 2019, Chapter 6 Sustainable Finance. Washington DC.: IMF. https://www.imf.org/en/Publications/GFSR.

Khan, M., Serafeim, G., and Yoon, A. (2016), "Corporate sustainability: First evidence on materiality", *The Accounting Review*, 91(6), pp. 1697–1724. http://www.aaajournals.org/doi/abs/10.2308/accr-51383.

Khan, M. (October 2019). "Corporate governance, ESG, and stock returns around the world", *Financial Analysts Journal*, 75(4). https://www.tandfonline.com/doi/full/10.1080/0015198X.2019.1654299.

Kim, J. W. (2010). "Assessing the long-term financial performance of ethical companies", *Journal of Targeting, Measurement and Analysis for Marketing*, 18(3/4), pp. 199–208.

King, A., and Lenox, M. (2002). "Exploring the locus of profitable pollution reduction", *Management Science*, 48(2), pp. 289–299.

Kiron, D., Kruschwitz, N., Haanaes, K., and Von Streng Velken, I. (2012). "Sustainability nears a tipping point", *MIT Sloan Management Review*, 53(2), pp. 69–74.

Kiron, D., Unruh, G., Kruschwitz, N., Reeves, M., Rubel, H., and Meyer Zum Felde, A. (2017). "Corporate sustainability at a crossroad: Progress toward our common future in uncertain times", *MIT Sloan Management Review*, May 23, 2017, https://sloanreview.mit.edu/projects/corporate-sustainability-at-a-crossroads/.

Knoepfel, I. (2001). "Dow Jones sustainability group index: A global benchmark for corporate sustainability", *Corporate Environmental Strategy*, 8(1), pp. 6–15.

Konar, S. and Cohen, M. A. (2001). "Does the market value environmental performance?" *The Review of Economics and Statistics*, 83(2), pp. 281–289.

KPMG. (2013a). "The KPMG survey of corporate responsibility reporting 2013", https://Www.Kpmg.Com/Global/En/Issuesandinsights/Articlespublications/Corporate-Responsibility/Pages/Default.Aspx.

KPMG. (2013b). "Working with you to build long-term value: Introducing KPMG's climate change & sustainability services", pp. 6–12. http://www.Kpmg.Com/Global/En/Topics/Climate-Change-Sustainability-Services/Documents/Working-With-You.Pdf.

Kusnetz, N. (2020). "BP and Shell write-off billions in assets, citing COVID-19 and climate change", *Inside Climate News*. Published on July 2, 2020, Accessed in December, 2020, https://insideclimatenews.org/news/02072020/bp-shell-coronavirus-climate-change.

Larcker, D. F., Pomorski, L., Tayan, B., and Watts, E. M. (2022). "ESG ratings a compass without direction". Stanford Closer Look Series, August 2, 2022. https://www.gsb.stanford.edu/faculty-research/publications/esg-ratings-compass-without-direction.

Levitt, T. (September–October 1958). "The danger of social responsibility", *Harvard Business Review*, 36, pp. 38–44.

Lopez, M. V., Garcia, A., and Rodriguez, L. (2007). "Sustainable development and corporate performance: A study based on the Dow Jones sustainability index", *Journal of Business Ethics*, 75, pp. 285–300.

McKinsey & Company. (2015). "Diversity matters", February 2, 2015, https://www.insurance.ca.gov/diversity/41-ISDGBD/GBDExternal/upload/McKinseyDivmatters-201501.pdf.

Milgrom, P. and Roberts, J. (1986). "Price and advertising signals of product quality", *The Journal of Political Economy*, 94(4), p. 796.

Morgan Stanley Institute for Sustainable Investing. (March 2015). "Sustainable Reality: Understanding the Performance of Sustainable Investment Strategies".

Movassaghi, H. and Bramhandkar, A. (2012). "Sustainability strategies of leading global firms and their financial performance: A comparative case-based analysis", *Journal of Applied Business and Economics*, 13(5), pp. 21–34.

Ocean Tomo. (2020). "Intangible asset market value study", https://www.ocean-tomo.com/intangible-asset-market-value-study/.

Orlitzky, M., Schmidt, F. L., and Rynes, S. L. (2003). "Corporate social and financial performance: A meta-analysis", *Organization Studies*, 24(3), pp. 403–411.

Perrow, C. (1984). *Normal Accidents: Living with High Risk Technologies*. (Revised Edition, 1999), Princeton University Press, Princeton, NJ.

Porter, M. E., and Van Der Linde, C. (1995). "Toward a new conception of the environment-competitiveness relationship", *The Journal of Economic Perspectives* (1986–1998), 9(4), pp. 97–118.

Prahalad, C. K., and Hamel, G. (1994). "Strategy as a field of study: Why search for a new paradigm?" *Strategic Management Journal*, 15(Special Issue), pp. 5–16.

Reinhardt, F. (1999). "Market failure and the environmental policies of firms", *Journal of Industrial Ecology*, 3(1), pp. 9–21.

Rees, J. (1994). *Hostages of Each Other: The Transformation of Nuclear Safety Since Three Mile Island*. University of Chicago Press, Chicago, IL.

Robecosam, A. G. (2014). "Alpha from Sustainability", White Paper, https://www.e-education.psu.edu/ba850/sites/www.e-education.psu.edu.ba850/files/Lesson3/Alpha_from_Sustainability_06_2014.pdf.

Roberts, P. W., and Dowling, G. R. (2002). "Corporate reputation and sustained superior financial performance", *Strategic Management Journal*, 23, pp. 1077–1093.

Russo, M. V., and Fouts, P. A. (1997). "A resource-based perspective on corporate environmental performance and profitability", *Academy of Management Journal*, 40, pp. 534–559.

Sage, A. P. (1999). "Sustainable development: Issues in information, knowledge, and systems management", *Information, Knowledge and System Management*, 1(3–4), pp. 185–223.

Salzmann, O., Ionescu-Somers, A., and Steger, U. (2005). "The business case for corporate sustainability: Literature review and research options", *European Management Journal*, 23(1), pp. 27–36.

SASB (Sustainable Accounting Standards Boards). (2018). "SASB materiality map", Published in 2018, https://materiality.sasb.org/. Accessed December 2020.

Semenoval, N. and Hassel, L. G. (2008). "Industry risk moderates the relation between environmental and financial performance", Sustainable Investment Research Platform Working Papers 08-02, http://citeseerx.ist.psu.edu/viewdoc/download?doi=10.1.1.938.2643&rep=rep1&type=pdf.

Sen, S. and Bhattacharya, C. B. (2001). "Does doing good always lead to doing better? Consumer reactions to corporate social responsibility", *Journal of Marketing Research*, 38(2), pp. 225–243.

Serafeim, G. (2020). "Public sentiment and the price of corporate sustainability", *Financial Analysts Journal*, 76(2), pp. 26–46. DOI: 10.1080/0015198X.2020.1723390.

Serafeim, G., and Yoon, A. (2020). "Stock price reactions to ESG news: The role of ESG ratings and disagreement", https://papers.ssrn.com/sol3/papers.cfm?abstract_id=3765217.

Setó Pamies, D. and Angla, J. (2011). "La naturaleza de la relación entre la responsabilidad social de la empresa (RSE) y el resultado financiero".

Simon, D.-C. (2015). "How can companies increase their chances of achieving positive financial outcomes from the environmental initiatives they are implementing?" Thesis IPAG. Paris: Institut de préparation à l'administration et à la gestion (IPAG).

The Generation Foundation, UNEP FI (United Nations Environment Programme Finance Initiative) and the PRI (Principles for Responsible Investment). (2019). "Fiduciary Duty in the 21st Century", https://www.unpri.org/download?ac=9792.

Turban, D. B. and Greening, D. W. (1997). "Corporate social performance and organizational attractiveness to prospective employees", *The Academy of Management Journal*, 40(3), pp. 658–672.

UN Global Compact and UNPRI. (2013). "The value driver model: A tool for communicating the business value of sustainability", Final Version of the Interim Report Released at the UN Global Compact Leaders Summit 2013: Architects of a Better World.

University of Oxford and Arabesque Partners. (March 2015). "From the stockholder to the stakeholder: How sustainability can drive financial outperformance", https://arabesque.com/research/From_the_stockholder_to_the_stakeholder_web.pdf.

University of Oxford (2014). Smith School of Enterprise and the Environment. School of Enterprise and the Environment: "The Stranded Assets Programme",

Oxford: Oxford University https://www.smithschool.ox.ac.uk/sites/default/files/2022-04/Stranded-Assets-and-Scenarios-Discussion-Paper.pdf.

Vilanova, M., Lozano, J. M., and Arenas. D. (2009). "Exploring the nature of the relationship between CSR and competitiveness", *Journal of Business Ethics*, 87, pp. 57–69.

Waddock, S. A., and Graves, S. B. (1997). "The corporate social performance-financial performance link", *Strategic Management Journal*, 18(4), pp. 303–319.

Walley, N., and Whitehead, B. (1994). "It's not easy being green", *Harvard Business Review*, 72(3), pp. 46–52.

Whelan, T., Atz, U., Van Holt, T., and Clark, C. (2021). *ESG and Financial Performance: Uncovering the Relationship by Aggregating Evidence from 1,000 Plus Studies Published between 2015–2020*. NYU STERN Center for Sustainable Business, New York.

Chapter 6

The Financial Case for Embedding Sustainability Core into Business Strategy

Tensie Whelan

Learning Objectives

- Understand the correlation between ESG performance and operational performance
- Discuss difficulties in demonstrating causality between ESG factors and performance
- Introduce various initiatives which have attempted to tackle the above challenges
- Present the "Return on Sustainability Investment" (ROSI) model

Abstract

This chapter makes a financial case for embedding sustainability at the center of a company's business strategy. A growing number of studies are finding a strong correlation between positive ESG performance and better stock and operational performance as well as lower cost of capital.

However, it is challenging to demonstrate causality, partially because most firms do not have metrics and accounting systems in place to assess the comprehensive return on sustainability investment (ROSI). The chapter notes that most of the Fortune 500 firms have sustainability strategies and report on environmental, social, and governance (ESG) issues. Corporate managers across many industries — from manufacturing to mining, to apparel to electronics — are facing a wide range of ESG issues. These issues are highlighted by the radical transparency that social media provides, the growing expectation among millennials across the world that corporations be good citizens, and the abdication by the government of their responsibility of taking care of societal goods. The chapter presents various initiatives which have begun to tackle this problem. Some have found that cost savings, revenue enhancement, and risk reduction accompany positive ESG/sustainability performance. This chapter closely examines the methodology developed by the NYU Stern Center for Sustainable Business, along with its first case study. The chapter concludes that corporate commitments to sustainable policies and practices have outstripped their ability to track the financial impact of those practices. In some cases, establishing the financial case may not be necessary or may even be unnecessarily complex. Markets increasingly force corporate managers to increase margins by reducing costs. Companies need to be better able to demonstrate the financial case for sustainability.

I. Introduction

Imagine you are a food product company — your margins are low and you are being pressured to reduce costs so you can deliver more to shareholders. Your business is being threatened by social and environmental issues such as child labor and aging farmers in your supply chain, low farmer productivity and quality, soil and water depletion, and low water availability in the areas where your factories are located.

You believe investing in farmer sustainability and water conservation in your factories would help position you for long-term competitiveness, but the investments needed don't meet your internal hurdle rate and activist investors are threatening a takeover if you don't reduce costs. What do you do?

Corporate managers across many industries — from manufacturing to mining, to apparel to electronics — are facing a wide range of financial material environmental, social, and governance (ESG) issues. These are enhanced by the radical transparency that social media provides, the growing expectation among millennials across the world that corporations be good citizens, and the abdication by the government of their responsibility for taking care of societal goods.

Chapter 6 is organized as per the following sections:

I. Introduction
II. The Opportunity: Sustainability Improves the Bottom Line
III. The Need for a New Accounting Paradigm
IV. Making the Financial Case for Sustainability
V. NYU Stern Center for Sustainable Business Model
VI. Sustainability Drivers of Financial Performance
VII. Deforestation-Free Beef in Brazil: A Case Study
VIII. Conclusion

II. The Opportunity: Sustainability Improves the Bottom Line

In the face of these pressures, some corporate leaders are beginning to embed sustainability (ESG) core to their business strategy and discovering significant bottom-line benefits. For example, Nike embedded sustainability into its innovation process and created the $1 billion-plus Flyknit line, which is 15% lighter than its other high-performance footwear and reduces production waste by 80% (Williams, 2015). In addition, it has been demonstrated that embedding sustainability into a company's business model can bring a significant competitive advantage (Lazlo and Zhexembayeva, 2011).

In addition, a growing number of studies are finding a strong correlation between positive ESG performance and better stock and operational performance as well as lower cost of capital. For example, a University of Oxford and Arabesque study (Clark *et al.*, 2015), reviewed 200 studies assessing the relationship between ESG and corporate financial performance (CFP). Some 90% found that good ESG standards lower the cost of capital; 88% that good ESG practices result in better operational performance; and 80% that good sustainability practices result in positive stock performance. This study reinforced the similar findings of an earlier meta-analysis study, which found that companies scoring high on ESG (either composite or disaggregated) scored high on market-based CFP measures (80% of studies); higher on accounting-based CFP (85%), and effectively *all* (100%) had improved risk-based CFP measured by a lower cost of capital (Fulton *et al.*, 2012).

Boston Consulting Group released a report on five industries that undertook valuation of "total societal impact", and found that companies that demonstrated top performance on total societal impact had higher valuation multiples than their peers on downside issues (such as health and safety and environmental impact) and margin premiums. For example, the downside valuation multiple for the consumer-packaged goods industry was 11%, 12% for biopharmaceuticals, 19% for oil and gas, and 3% for retail and business banking (Beal *et al.*, 2017).

Investors are increasingly aware of the financial implications of ESG performance: many are redefining fiduciary duty to include the analysis of ESG. The Principles for Responsible Investment (PRI), which boasts 2300 members managing $90 trillion in assets https://www.unpri.org/pri/about-the-pri and the UN Financial Initiative issued a report "Fiduciary Duty in the 21st Century", which states that ESG analysis has become an investor norm, that ESG can be financially material and that policy and regulatory frameworks are changing to require the incorporation of ESG (PRI and UNEP FI, 2019).

III. The Need for a New Accounting Paradigm

Despite these positive findings, most corporations are not able to demonstrate causal relationships between sustainability and financial performance because current accounting practices do not adequately track the financial case for sustainability. In fact, accounting was designed for a time when 80 percent of a company's value was tangible assets. Today the opposite is true, with 90 percent being intangible assets (see Figure 6.1). Some sustainability-related benefits related to reputational and operational risks and employee recruitment and retention are among those intangibles.

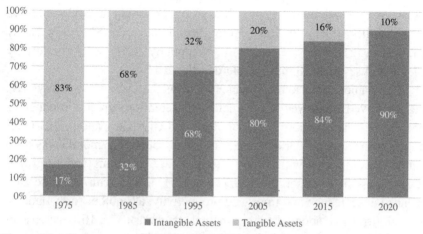

Figure 6.1. Components of S&P 500 Market Value

Source: Ocean Tomo, LLC — Intangible Asset Market Value Study 2020.

This challenge was first recognized more than 40 years ago in a study finding that financial statements capture the end result of a process chain and fail to consider management effectiveness and stakeholder influence such as "reward for virtue" and were insufficient to "objectively differentiate companies that are socially responsible from those that are not" (Parket and Eilbirt, 1975).

IV. Making the Financial Case for Sustainability

If sustainability is to be mainstreamed, its monetary value must be tracked comprehensively. The full range of costs and benefits, including intangibles such as risk mitigation and employee productivity, must be quantified and monetized to reduce uncertainty and improve corporate and investor decision-making.

Sustainability investments have grown partially because businesses have been able to obtain operational efficiencies, reduce risks (e.g. reputational and/or supply chain risk), and save money. For example, proactive environmental strategies lowered the cost of processes, inputs, and products in the oil and gas industry (Sharma and Vredenburg, 1998) and investment in pollution prevention technologies at a manufacturing plant reduced costs, improved labor productivity, and lowered throughput times

(Klassen and Whybark, 1999). Since implementing a comprehensive sustainability strategy in 2009, Hilton Worldwide reduced energy use by 14.5%, waste output by 27.6%, carbon output by 20.9%, and water use by 14.1% and saved $550 million (Hardcastle, 2016).

Companies can also reap financial returns through sustainability driving improved employee recruitment and retention, greater product or process innovation, more loyal suppliers and customers and better stakeholder management. For example, one study found that morale was 55% better in companies with strong sustainability programs and employee loyalty was 38% better (SHRM *et al.,* 2011). This can translate into reduced absenteeism and improved productivity, as another study demonstrated: firms that adopted environmental standards had a 16% increase in productivity over firms that did not (Delmas and Pekovic, 2012).

Furthermore, the downside financial impacts of ESG risks are real. Conflict over access to water in Peru, for example, resulted in the indefinite suspension of $21.5 billion worth of mining projects since 2010 (Schneider, 2016). When firms fail to engage stakeholders, increased conflict and reduced cooperation disrupts a firm's ability to operate on schedule and budget and therefore to create value (Dorobantu and Odziemkowska, 2017).

However, when companies set ESG targets and track ESG metrics, they often fail to translate their measures of ESG performance into monetary results. If a company reduces its reputational risk exposure, for example, by ensuring there is no child labor in their supply chain, they do not monetize that risk reduction. If companies cannot build a more comprehensive business case, sustainability is likely to remain an add-on activity across the business and its full value will not be realized.

A few initiatives have begun developing tools to help corporate practitioners better assess the ROI on sustainability:

- The UN Global Compact Value Driver is "a tool for establishing the relevance of sustainability to existing key business metrics" organized in three buckets: growth, productivity, and risk management. The tool aims to help companies assess the following: (1) revenue growth from sustainability-enhanced or advantaged products and services,

(2) the total cost savings plus avoidance from sustainability-related initiatives, and (3) measurable reduction in exposure to sustainability-related risks to revenue and reputation. Using the model, the UN Global Compact found that from 2009 to 2012, Pirelli Tire had reaped the following benefits: (1) Growth: increased sales of "green performance tires" approximately three times at 45% (€2.8B of €6.3B) of total revenue, (2) Productivity: new green manufacturing process made an approximate 3% contribution to operating income, and (3) Risk: sustainability-related risks declined by approximately 72% (UNGC/UNPRI, 2013).

- Project ROI Management Institute (a collaboration between IO Consulting and Babson College) is another initiative that is assessing the financial return related to sustainability in three categories: human resources; sales and reputation; and firm value, share price, and risk. Their research has found that sustainability can increase market value by up to 6%, revenue by up to 20%, and reduce employee turnover by up to 50% (Rochlin *et al.*, 2015).

- The Embankment Project, a collaboration between the Coalition for Inclusive Capitalism and Ernst & Young, has developed a "new reporting mechanism … for corporations to better measure and communicate the value they create for shareholders through their strategic attention to the broad base of their stakeholders: customers, employees, communities, government, and the environment". EY, with the help of 300 companies, developed a framework for measuring long-term value creation that focuses on talent (human capital deployment and organizational culture), innovation and consumer trends (innovation, consumer trust, consumer health, society, and environment) (contribution to the UN SDGs), and governance (Coalition for Inclusive Capitalism and EY, 2018).

- "Driving Sustainable Decisions", was a cross-sectoral group of industry, NGOs, and private sector leaders (including Antea Group, FEMSA, Kimberly Clark, and NYU Stern Center for Sustainable Business) focused on "enabling better, more sustainable business decisions", and has developed an online learning course that provides sustainability practitioners with the training and tools to develop the financial case for sustainability investments within a company. The methodology helps corporate practitioners determine how to turn intangibles (such as talent enhancement related to corporate sustainability) into monetizable returns on investment. Unilever's Sustainable Living Plan, for example, is credited with the company's position as one of the employers most searched on LinkedIn; how might Unilever assess the financial value of that? Driving Sustainable Decisions no longer exists as an organization, but its online course is still available and Alo Advisors has carried on the work.

V. NYU Stern Center for Sustainable Business Model

Complementing these efforts, the NYU Stern Center for Sustainable Business (CSB) has developed a framework and is developing a suite of tools that will help identify, quantify, and monetize the benefits of sustainable practices. Its goal is for CFOs and investors to use the CSB methodology to develop metrics that allow them to better integrate, track, and report on CFP arising from embedding ESG into business practices. Ideally, this will improve managerial decision-making on sustainability issues as well as provide more actionable information to investors. The techniques developed by the initiatives above can plug into this framework; the work aims to complement, not duplicate these efforts.

The Center for Sustainable Business model was informed first by a review of academic and corporate research to understand which factors drive positive financial performance when a company embeds material sustainability factors in their corporate strategy (Whelan and Fink, 2016). Once these benefits are operationalized for a specific company, they can be monetized through a variety of accounting methods. The framework can be applied to any sustainability initiative or industry and used to assess benefits in a value chain and at the firm level. The method can be applied retroactively to sustainability/ESG practices that have been already implemented and to practices under consideration and can project the financial benefit currently or into the future (Atz *et al.*, 2019). When companies embed sustainability, this influences a suite of mediating factors that drive financial benefits for businesses and society, which can be quantified and monetized (see Figure 6.2).

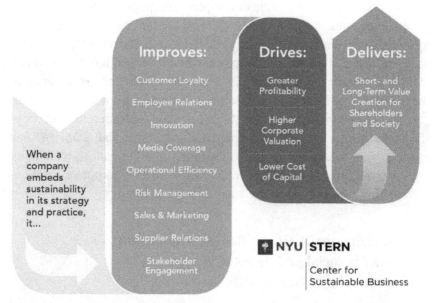

Figure 6.2. Sustainability Drivers of Financial Performance and Competitive Advantage

VI. Sustainability Drivers of Financial Performance

The Stern Center for Sustainable Business framework has four steps:

1. Identify material sustainability strategies and practices.
2. Determine the potential benefits that might drive financial and societal value from sustainability-focused practices.
3. Quantify benefits derived from the sustainability practices.
4. Derive a monetary value for the benefits.

1. Identify Material Sustainability Strategies and Practices

The adopted or potential material sustainability strategies and associated management practices are identified. Material ESG factors relevant for the company can be based on the Sustainability Accounting Standards Board (SASB), Global Reporting Initiative (GRI), the company's own assessment, and/or the sustainability practices implemented or contemplated by the company. SASB is a standard focused on material ESG factors most relevant for investors while GRI is a standard that includes issues of material interest to all stakeholders. Research has demonstrated that better financial performance is correlated with better performance on material ESG factors, while financial performance decreases if the company is focused on immaterial ESG factors (and performance even drops if the company is managing for material and immaterial factors) (Khan *et al.,* 2016). Additional research has found that the path to materiality changes over time and is dependent on factors such as corporate misalignment with societal needs (Rogers and Serafeim, 2019).

2. Determine the Potential Benefits that Might Drive Financial and Societal Value from Sustainability-Focused Practices

The benefits in Figure 6.2 include better risk management, more innovation, higher operational efficiency, greater customer loyalty, improved supplier relations, better employee relations, improved sales and marketing, better media coverage, and more value-added stakeholder engagement. Depending on the sustainability strategy, different benefit drivers will be relevant. For example, significantly reducing water consumption for a soda company should lead to lower operational and reputational risk as well as improved operational efficiency, customer loyalty, media coverage, and stakeholder engagement.

3. Quantify Benefits Derived from the Sustainability Practices

Each benefit is company-specific and has to be quantified. For example, for the soda company, reduced water consumption would lead to xx fewer units of water used, xx less energy kW to move, cool, or heat the water, xx less units of wastewater produced, while employee satisfaction may increase $xx\%$; and x positive news reports about the company's water consumption commitment may be published.

4. Derive a Monetary Value for the Benefits

Once a benefit has been quantified, it now can be monetized. When companies do monetize benefits, it is generally for additional sales or operational efficiencies because there is a tangible improvement to measure, e.g. reduced energy use = $xx per kW saved. For less tangible applications, a monetization process is needed. The accounting method to monetize the benefit may include a suite of methods and may change based on the type of benefit and available data.

To obtain this information, different functional teams within a company may be needed (e.g. finance, operations, sustainability, HR) to collect data. In cases where there are no data to monetize benefits or assumptions, estimates can be developed from the literature. An example of tangible data could be cost reduction derived from higher efficiency of input use (seeds, feed, and fertilizers) through better management. The change in actual input expenditures before and after the uptake of improved practices is calculated, while subtracting costs of the changed practices, to arrive at a net. More abstract concepts, such as talent retention, can be calculated by assessing costs associated with turnover (recruiting and training new hires), weighted by probability.

Uncertain benefits can be weighted by probability to reflect an expected net present value (NPV) and can be calculated within ranges. For the soda company example, one can value the cost savings in water, energy, and wastewater disposal, as well as estimate the monetary value of an improved employee retention rate because there is more job satisfaction, and estimate the monetary value of positive new reports (i.e. what would the coverage have cost the company to buy?).

VII. Deforestation-Free Beef in Brazil: A Case Study

Deforestation causes 10% of global GHG emissions. In the tropics, beef production is a significant driver of deforestation — due to cattle breeding and soy production as feedstock. Brazil is the world's biggest beef exporter, with nearly 20% of the world market. From 1993 to 2013, the cattle herd in the Brazilian Amazon rainforest — covering most of the country's northern region — expanded by nearly 200% to more than 60 million heads. During this period, over 300,000 km^2 of the forest was cleared, much of it for ranching.

While more than 450 companies have made deforestation-free supply chain commitments, progress remains slow, not least because there is no clear business case for the supply chain partners. NYU Stern Center for Sustainable Business partnered with A.T. Kearney, the Nature Conservancy, McDonalds, Carrefour, and other NGOs and supply chain partners, to apply its methodology to the uptake of sustainable agricultural and deforestation-free practices by ranchers, slaughterhouses, and retailers in Brazil (Whelan *et al.*, 2017).

The research demonstrated that most of the CSB-identified sustainability drivers of positive financial performance were triggered by sustainable agriculture practices, and risk mitigation was triggered by deforestation-free practices. The majority of the benefits accrued to the ranchers who were making the changes, but they accrued to upstream supply chain partners as well.

The net benefits to ranchers ranged from $18 million to $34 million (12–23% of revenues) in net present value projected over 10 years. These benefits were triggered by innovation (e.g. better practices led to higher quality beef), operational efficiencies (e.g. lower inputs led to lower costs), employee engagement (ranchers were able to recruit higher quality labor), among other factors. Some 19 sustainability benefits were identified, resulting in a 2.3× increase in productivity, nearly 7× increase in profitability, and 0–70% increase in beef rated as high quality.

For slaughterhouses and retailers, the knock-on benefits included operational and reputational risk reduction (a more stable, higher quality supplier is less likely to cause quality or quantity disruptions), price premiums for higher quality beef, and talent enhancement, among other benefits. The study projected positive benefits for slaughterhouses from $20 million to $120 million (for Marfrig up to $16.5 million and JBS up to $103.1 million), and for retailers Brazilian operations, positive benefits between $13 million and $62 million (McDonalds up to $22.2 million and Carrefour up to $39.9 million).

VIII. Conclusion

Corporate commitments to sustainable policies and practices have outstripped their ability to track the financial impact of those practices. In some cases, establishing the financial case may not be necessary or may be unnecessarily complex. However, in a world where short-termism in the markets increasingly forces corporate managers to increase margins by reducing costs, companies need to be better able to demonstrate the financial case for sustainability. The tools exist and evidence points toward significant value being created.

References

Atz, U., Tracy, V. Holt, Douglas, E., and Whelan, T. (2019). "The return on sustainability investment (ROSI): Monetizing financial benefits of sustainability actions in companies", *The Review of Business: Interdisciplinary Journal on Risk and Society*, 39(2), pp. 1–31.

Beal, D., Eccles, R., Hansell, G., Lesser, R., Unnikrishna, S., Woods, W., and Young, D. (2017). *Total Societal Impact: A New Lens for Strategy*, Boston Consulting Group, Boston, MA.

Clark, G., Fiener, A., and Viehs, M. (2015). *From the Stockholder to the Stakeholder: How Sustainability Can Drive Financial Outperformance*, University of Oxford and Arabesque.

Coalition for Inclusive Capitalism and Ernst & Young. (2018). "Embankment Project for Inclusive Capitalism", https://www.epic-value.com/#report.

Delmas, M., and Pekovic, S. (2012). "Environmental standards and labor productivity: Understanding the mechanisms that sustain sustainability", *Journal of Organizational Behavior*, 39(2), pp. 230–252.

Dorobantu, S., and Odziemkowska, K. (2017). "Valuing stakeholder governance: Property rights, community mobilization, and firm value", *Strategic Management Journal*, 38(13), pp. 2682–2703.

Fulton, M., Kahn, B. M., and Sharples, C. (2012). "Sustainable investing: Establishing long-term value and performance", *Deutsche Bank Group DB Climate Change Advisors*, https://doi.org/http://dx.doi.org/10.2139/ssrn.2222740.

Hardcastle, J. (2016). "Hilton cuts carbon output 20.9%, saves $550M", *Environment + Energy Leader*, January 7, 2016, http://www.environmental leader.com/2016/01/07/hilton-cuts-carbon-output-20-9-saves550m/.

Khan, M., Serafeim, G., and Yoon, A. (2016). "Corporate sustainability: First evidence on materiality", *The Accounting Review*, 91(6), pp. 1697–1724.

Klassen, R. D., and Whybark, D. C. (1999). "The impact of environmental technologies on manufacturing performance", *Academy of Management Journal*, 42(6), pp. 599–615, https://doi.org/10.2307/256982.

Lazlo, C., and Zhexembayeva, N. (2011). *Embedded Sustainability: The Next Big Competitive Advantage*, Stanford University Press, Stanford, CA.

Parket, I. R., and Eilbirt, H. (1975). "The practice of business social responsibility: The underlying factors", *Business Horizons*, 18(4), pp. 5–10, https://doi.org/10.1016/0007-6813(75)90019-1.

PRI and UNEP FI. (2019). "Fiduciary Duty in the 21st Century", https://www.unpri.org/fiduciary-duty/fiduciary-duty-in-the-21st-century-from-a-legal-case-to-regulatory-clarification-around-esg/5137.article.

Rochlin, S., Bliss, R., Jordan, S., and Kiser, C. Y. (2015). "Project ROI: Defining the competitive and financial advantages of corporate responsibility and sustainability", *IO Sustainability, Lewis Institute for Social Innovation at Babson College.*

Rogers, J., and Serafeim, G. (2019). "Pathways to materiality: How sustainability issues become financially material to corporations and their investors", *Harvard Business School Working Paper.*

Schneider, K. (2016). "Water-related risks strand $billions in energy, mining, and power projects", *Circle of Blue*, August 28, 2016, http://www.circleofblue.org/2016/water-climate/water-relatedrisks-strand-billions-energy-mining-power-projects/.

Sharma, S., and Vredenburg, H. (1998). "Proactive corporate environmental strategy and the development of competitively valuable…", *Strategic Management Journal*, 19(8), https://doi.org/10.1002/(SICI)1097-0266(199808)19.

SHRM, BSR, and Aurosoorya. (2011). Advancing Sustainability: HR's Role: A Research Report by the Society of Human Resource Management, BSR, and Aurosoorya. Society for Human Resource Management.

UN Global Compact and UNPRI. (2013). "The Value Driver Model: A Tool for Communicating the Business Value of Sustainability", Final Version of the Interim Report Released at the UN Global Compact Leaders Summit 2013: Architects of a Better World.

Whelan, T., and Fink, C. (2016). "The comprehensive case for sustainability", *Harvard Business Review*, https://hbr.org/2016/10/the-comprehensive-business-case-for-sustainability.

Whelan, T., Zappa, B., Zeidan, R., and Fishbein, G. (2017). "How to quantify sustainability's impact on your bottom line", *Harvard Business Review*, https://hbr.org/2017/09/how-to-quantify-sustainabilitys-impact-on-your-bottom-line.

Williams, E. F. (2015). *Green Giants: How Smart Companies Turn Sustainability into Billion-Dollar Businesses*. AMACOM.

Chapter 7

Risk Management and Sustainability

Robert Pojasek

Learning Objectives

- Propose different approaches to monitor corporate sustainability
- Understand the fundamentals of risk management
- Explore the principles, framework, and processes to implement risk management
- Describe ISO standards, their high-level structure, and ones related to sustainability
- Present the "plan-do-check-act" (PDCA) model

Abstract

This chapter proposes different approaches to monitor corporate sustainability which go beyond unstructured standalone corporate social responsibility (CSR) and sustainability programs. Historically, corporate sustainability has largely consisted in "stand-alone" sustainability programs that use publicly stated sustainability goals, independent sustainability initiatives, and sustainability reports. There has been little effort on the part of large corporations to stray from this model. The chapter focuses on companies' integration of sustainability through the lens of risk management with the support of standards and operating management systems (OMS). First, the chapter examines the foundations of risk management and a systematic method to handle sustainability risks through the International Organization for Standardization (ISO) guidelines. It then explores the principles, framework, and processes to implement a risk management practice in accordance with the ISO 31000:2018 standard. It demonstrates how to integrate all the management systems that contribute to sustainable development into a single sustainable organizational model through the high-level structure of ISO management system standards presented in this chapter. After introducing the fundamentals of ISO standards and how they function, the chapter focuses on the standards dedicated to Sustainability and CSR. The chapter presents a "plan-do-check-act" (PDCA) model which is used for the control and continuous improvement of processes and products within an organization and can be employed for corporate sustainability. The chapter concludes that a key to success is to replace old unstructured sustainability programs with a new unique structured sustainability program that works best for each organization.

I. Introduction

As sustainability and social responsibility came online in the mid-1990s, its practice was largely limited to large corporations. The practice consisted of publicly stated sustainability goals, independent sustainability initiatives, and sustainability reports. Many refer to this approach as "stand-alone sustainability". In 2014, the International Organization for Standardization (ISO) published a harmonized high-level structure (Warris and Tanger, 2012) that would be used in all new and revised management system standards. These management system standards were widely used by corporations because they helped guide the "plan-do-check-act" programs that are widely used in corporations and their supply chains. With more than 40 management systems that can be integrated and used to support the corporation and its supply chain, the time has come to make the move to standards that clarify what is necessary in a sustainable business model and to improve the operations of the corporation's facilities, the suppliers, and the large number of communities where these operations are located.

Chapter 7 is organized as per the following sections:

I. Introduction
II. Risk Management
III. Understanding Risk Management
IV. Risk Management Using ISO 31000:2018
V. Harmonized High-Level Structure
VI. The ISO Standards Involving Sustainability and CSR
VII. Conclusion

II. Risk Management

ISO has defined *risk* as "the effects of uncertainty" on the ability of the organization to meet its strategic objectives. We all recognize that the business environment has become more volatile, uncertain, complex, and ambiguous. Risk looks at these effects that create deviations from the expected — both positive and negative (i.e. opportunities and threats). It is important not to think of risk as only being negative. Uncertainty is about not having enough information related to the understanding or knowledge of an event and its consequence or likelihood. When scanning the external and internal environment for opportunities and threats, you are performing the initial components of risk analysis (Pojasek, 2017).

Other risks are identified in the planning phase of the the PDCA model that is described in what follows. There are opportunities and threats involved in how operations are managed. There are strategic risks involved in how strategy is executed to help the organization realize its strategic, operational, and tactical objectives. There are also a variety of objects associated with environmental, social, and economic activities that are characterized in the planning phase.

The naming of the opportunities and threats is crucial to effective uncertainty analysis and evaluation: meaningful names of opportunities and threats, causes or initiating events, how they might trigger an event, and the consequences that might flow from that event. Ideally, an opportunity or a threat should be identified in the following terms: (*something happens*) *leading to* (*outcomes expressed in terms of its consequences with regard to achieving the organization's objectives — positive and negative*).

The effects of uncertainty can be looked at from the perspective of threats:

- **Avoid:** Seek to remove threats to lower or eliminate uncertainty.
- **Transfer:** Allocate ownership to enable effective management of a threat, often using an insurance company for this purpose.
- **Mitigate:** Reduce the likelihood or consequence of the threat below an acceptable threshold.
- **Accept:** Recognize residual risks associated with uncertainty and devise ways to control or monitor them.

Opportunity risk response takes into consideration how to act in order to improve the likelihood and impact of an opportunity. When speaking about opportunity response options, there are four major categories of controls that can be used:

- **Exploit** identified opportunities, removing uncertainty by seeking to make the opportunity succeed.
- **Enhance** means increasing its positive likelihood or consequence to maximize the benefit of the opportunity.
- **Share** opportunities by passing ownership to a third party best able to manage the opportunity and maximize the chance of it happening.
- **Ignore** opportunities included in the baseline, adopting a reactive approach without taking explicit actions.

Risk response involves selecting one or more significant opportunities and threats, and exploiting the opportunities while avoiding the threats. In some organizations, avoiding the threats is referred to as "risk treatment". Most organizations are still focused only on threats. In other organizations, leaders do not always view opportunities as being able to offset threats.

Besides, opportunities are also risky. In order to realize the positive effect on the strategic planning, opportunities must be implemented, optimized, and their benefit must be monetized. The constraint to developing opportunities as a risk response is solely a function of an organization's experience and comfort in developing opportunities (Pojasek, 2017).

III. Understanding Risk Management

Many people struggle with the many definitions of risk. However, risk management is very easy to understand. As we know, people and the companies they work for have been managing risk for years. Historically, they have done so by purchasing insurance to cover losses. These losses occur primarily in personal situations, property, and liability. We refer to these losses as "pure risk". Examples of pure risk include the following: premature death, identity theft, and career-ending disabilities. As you can see, the outcome of pure risk is "loss" or "no loss". Insurance products include life insurance, disability insurance, as well as home-owners and automobile insurance. Companies also use insurance policies to deal with pure risks. Insurance companies are able to predict loss figures in advance and will not extend themselves in a market if they cannot make a profit.

There is also something that we refer to as "speculative risk". Unlike pure risk, speculative risks generate opportunities for gain as well as for loss. In the case of speculative risk, all potential risks need to be considered before choosing an action. When purchasing securities, you hope that they will increase their value in the stock market. However, the opportunity for a loss is always present. It was found that people and companies can manage speculative risks by hedging against them using insurance products.

This transition to what we know as risk management began after World War II. At that time, the cost of insurance became prohibitive for covering anything other than pure risk. The extent of coverage available was limited. During the 1960s, the field of corporate risk management began to grow. Contingency planning became more important to companies and home owners. There was also an emphasis on loss prevention and safety management as people moved away from risk financing for speculative risks.

In the 1970s, we began to see the willingness of larger companies to self-insure themselves along with the use of risk retention practices. Contingency plans then developed into business continuity planning and disaster recovery plans. During this time, there were considerable developments in the risk management approach adopted by occupational health and safety practitioners.

Standards of Australia began the process of creating the first national risk management standard (AS/NZS 4360:1995) which was released in 1995. With this milestone, corporate governance and listing requirements from some of the stock exchanges encouraged directors to place greater emphasis on what they called "enterprise risk management" (ERM). The first Chief Risk Officers (CROs) were appointed during this time.

During the early 2000s, financial services firms were encouraged to develop internal risk management systems and capital models. There has been a rapid growth of CRO positions in energy companies, banks, and insurance companies. Boards are now investing more time in ERM due to the enactment of the Sarbanes-Oxley Act of 2002 in the United States and similar legislation in a number of other countries. This wave of legislation required publicly traded companies to report risks to the government (e.g. US Securities and Exchange Commission).

The widespread financial crisis of 2008 called into question the contribution that risk management can make to corporate success, especially in financial institutions. There is no doubt that the application of risk management tools and techniques failed to prevent the global financial crisis. The failure to correctly apply risk management processes and procedures was likely the root cause of the failures rather than inherent defects in the risk management approach.

Today, there are two newly improved risk management standards available for use:

- **ISO 31000:2018** — an international risk management standard derived from AS/NZS 4360:2004.
- **COSO ERM:2017** — an enterprise risk management standard that was first published in 2002.

COSO ERM:2017 is an enterprise risk management standard that is based on a business model with built-in duties for the Board of Directors. ISO 31000:2018 is an organizational risk management standard that works well with other widely used ISO management system standards. It defines risk management as, "coordinated activities to direct and control an organization regarding risk". This document can be used throughout the life of the organization and can be applied to any activity, including decision-making at all levels.

IV. Risk Management Using ISO 31000:2018

This risk management approach is for use by organizations that seek to create and protect value by managing risks, making decisions, setting and achieving objectives, and improving performance. Managing risk is based on the principles, framework, and process shown in Figure 7.1. There are three elements of the ISO 31000 risk management structure:

- principles for developing a risk-aware culture in the organization;
- a framework for running the risk management program;
- a process for managing the risk assessment.

The principles are used by the organization to create a risk-aware culture. Managing risks in the internal and external contexts depends on managing the effects of uncertainty on the organization's objectives. Every organization should evaluate its existing risk management practices, evaluate any gaps, and address those gaps within the framework. The risk management process involves the systematic application of policies, procedures, and practices to the activities of communicating and consulting, establishing the context and assessing, treating, monitoring, reviewing, recording, and reporting risk.

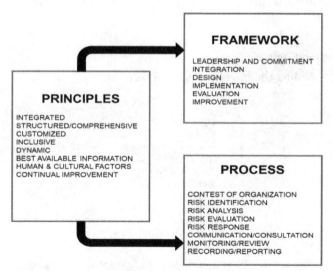

Figure 7.1. The Three Pillars of ISO 31000 Risk Management

In the following sections, risk management is used in the context and in the planning of the management system. Both the external and internal contexts need to be considered as part of identifying the risks that need to be managed.

V. Harmonized High-Level Structure

All the new and revised management system standards are printed using the harmonized high-level structure (see Figure 7.2). Items are added to this structure as required by the standard. Let's look at the basic items found in the specified high-level structure ISO, (International Organization for Standardization) and IEC (International Electrotechnical Commission), 2016).

The first three clauses provide the introductory information for each standard. Clause 1 presents the **scope** of the standard so that it is clear what is included. Clause 2 provides the referenced document(s) that is considered indispensable to the application of the standard. Not every standard provides **normative references**. Clause 3 lists some required **terms and definitions** that are found in all the standards issued with this high-level structure. There are additional terms provided that are specific to the focus of the standard.

The **context** of the organization has a minimum of four components in Clause 4:

- understanding the organization and its context
- understanding the interests of the stakeholders

1.	Scope
2.	Normative References
3.	Terms and Definitions
4.	Context of the Organization
5.	Leadership
6.	Planning
7.	Support
8.	Operation
9.	Performance Evaluation
10.	Improvement

Figure 7.2. ISO Harmonized High-Level Structure Clauses

- determining the scope of each standard
- description of the management system

Some standards have additional components in this context section. For example, ISO 19600:2014 (Compliance Management Systems — Guidelines) has additional sections on compliance obligations and identification, analysis, and evaluation of compliance risks. Other standards select the areas that are covered so that each can be described in Clause 6, on planning.

Clause 5 is focused on **leadership**. It focuses on what is expected of leaders and emphasizes that the leaders are held accountable for ensuring that the management system achieves its intended outcome(s). Each standard has a policy that is stated and described in this section. Finally, there is a statement of the organizational roles, responsibilities, and authorities for each specific standard.

Clause 6 describes the **planning** for using the standard. It begins with a section on actions to address risks and opportunities which are defined as "potential adverse effects (threats) and potential beneficial effects (opportunities)" and not only impact risks but also financial performance. The risk management in these standards is defined in ISO 31000:2009. The second section presents the objectives and the planning to achieve them. This is an important section since organizations establish strategic objectives that are derived from the mission statement. All the objectives in the organization cascade down from the top level to the lowest levels. At the lowest levels, goals are set and supported by action plans to describe how the tactical objectives will be addressed. The supervisors set goals that address the operational objectives. Finally, the operating managers set goals that help the organization meet its strategic objectives (Pojasek, 2017).

Clause 7 presents the **support** that is required in each standard. The required list is as follows:

- resources;
- competence;
- awareness;
- communication;
- documented information.

Each standard may add subsections to these support items or add additional items. The support needs to be planned within the standard and provided to support the remaining clauses.

Clause 8 presents the **operations** specific to each standard. The first item is operational planning and control. Individual standards include items such as the following:

- establishing controls and procedures;
- emergency preparedness and response;
- management of change;
- outsourced processes.

The additional operational items are specific to different standards.

Clause 9 describes how the **performance evaluation** will be conducted. The first subsection includes the following: monitoring, measurement, analysis, and evaluation. Next is the description of the internal audit function. Finally, there is a description of the management review requirements.

Finally, Clause 10 describes how the organization addresses **improvement**. Each standard must address non-conformity and corrective actions as well as how it will account for continual improvement.

This specification and ordering of information are a big deal. All the new and revised standards are incorporating this new high-level structure. It is now possible to integrate standards since most of the sections are already prescribed and the additional sections are in the same clause structure.

VI. The ISO Standards Involving Sustainability and CSR

It is important to understand the harmonized high-level structure discussed previously, as it impacts the standards related to sustainability. Since sustainability cuts across everything an organization is involved with, many ISO standards and documents involve sustainability and corporate social responsibility. In the following, we list some of these documents (see Figure 7.3). By implementing sustainability-related ISO

- ISO 9001:2015 Quality Management
- ISO 9004:2018 Managing for the Sustained Success of an Organization
- ISO 14001:2015 Environmental Management
- ISO 19011:2011 Auditing Management Systems Guidelines
- ISO 19600:2014 Compliance Management Guidelines
- ISO 22301:2012 Business Continuity Management
- ISO 22316:2017 Organizational Resilience Principles and Guidelines
- ISO 22397:2014 Public–Private Partnership Guidelines
- ISO 24000:2017 Sustainable Procurement Guidelines
- ISO 26000:2010 Social Responsibility Management Guidelines
- ISO 28000:2007 Supply Chain Security
- ISO 28001:2011 Security Management Systems for Supply Chain
- ISO 31000:2018 Risk Management Guidelines
- ISO 37101:2016 Community Sustainable Development and Resilience
- ISO 45001:2018 Occupational Health and Safety Management
- ISO 50001:2017 Energy Management
- ISO 14080:2018 Greenhouse Gas Management and Related Activities — Framework and Principles for Methodologies on Climate Actions
- ISO 21678:2020 Sustainability in Buildings and Civil Engineering Works
- ISO/TR 37150:2014 Smart Community Infrastructures
- ISO 55001:2014 Assets Management
- ISO 16813:2006 Building Environment Design — Indoor Environment
- ISO Guide 82 Sustainability
- ISO/TC 322 Sustainable Finance (in Development)
- ISO 14030 Green Debt Instruments (in Development) in four parts:
    - ISO 14030-1 Process for Green Bonds
    - ISO 14030-2 Process for Green Loans
    - ISO 14030-3 Taxonomy
    - ISO 14030-4 Verification

Figure 7.3. Some ISO Documents Involving Sustainability and CSR

standards, companies can take concrete steps to integrate sustainability in their business model and organization. It also enables a company to go beyond stand-alone sustainability which consists mainly of isolated initiatives. This latter is criticized for either not helping the business or being some sort of greenwashing, attempting to distract from the company's main activities that do not include sustainability considerations. These standards also provide evidence that a company is taking sustainability seriously. It is worth noting that achieving some of these ISO standards (e.g. ISO 14001 on Environmental Management, ISO 50001 on Energy Management, or ISO 45001 on Occupational Health & Safety Management) can be used as a key performance indicator (KPI) for sustainability-linked debt. In addition, some standards are also currently in development to cover sustainable finance, such as the ISO 14030 standard on green debt instruments.

1. Integration Platform for a Common Management System

Most of the organizations that use management systems maintain them separately from one another. Now that they are on a common platform (or can be adapted to that platform), some organizations are beginning to create integrated Operating Management Systems (OMS).

For example, the International Petroleum Industry Environmental Conservation Association (IPIECA), an international oil and gas industry association, published a guide called "Operating Management System Framework" (IPIECA, 2014). This IPIECA guide is designed to help companies define and achieve performance goals and satisfy stakeholder interests, while managing the broad range of risks (opportunities and threats) inherent in this industry. The framework applies to all kinds and sizes of operations and offers an integrated approach to the use of management systems as described above. It applies to occupational health and safety, environmental management, corporate social responsibility, process safety, quality, risk management, and security. IPIECA leaves the degree of integration and the scope of the OMS to each individual company. As a result, the OMS will differ depending on the activities, organizational structure, and management system maturity.

To compare to the ISO model above, IPIECA organizes its OMS into 10 elements:

- commitment and accountability;
- policies, standards, and objectives;
- organization, resources, and capability;
- stakeholders and customers;
- risk assessment and control;
- asset design and integrity;
- plans and procedures;
- execution of activities;

- monitoring, reporting, and learning;
- assurance, review, and improvement.

While the items are not identical, the similarity with the ISO approach discussed above is quite clear. Based on its operating activities, a company may modify these elements based on its internal and external contexts, and the opportunities and threats that come from the context. Furthermore, the elements do not aim to cover all legal, regulatory, or voluntary requirements a company may wish to address — although these are specifically addressed by the international management system standards that can be used to underpin these elements. IPIECA cautions that when developing an OMS, it should be clearly established what is expected of leaders and the workforce. Some of the elements are mandatory for the OMS users while other elements have a degree of flexibility in the implementation. When you view the OMS manuals for the major oil and gas industry, you will clearly see the differences in how the information is presented. ISO also presents "what" needs to be addressed by the management system users. However, it never instructs them "how" their clauses should be used.

The IPIECA OMS still references many of the ISO management system standards that are about to expire. If you were to consider using an OMS, you can use the updated ISO standards to update the updated management system standards. A quick review of the websites of the major oil and gas companies will demonstrate the flexibility of this approach as each company has chosen a slightly different means for using the OMS. Now, let's examine a third model for using the international management system standards.

2. PDCA Model

Many companies have selected a "plan-do-check-act" (PDCA) cycle for controlling the operations associated with their organization. When ISO started revising its management standards, it provided a PDCA model upfront in each publication. The IPIECA OMS model involves the following: leadership, risk management, continual improvement, and implementation. All the ISO management systems present information on how the information presented in the standard follows the widely used PDCA cycle. Integration of the ISO management systems is enabled by choosing how each standard and clause are embedded in the PDCA implementation instructions and specifications.

Most manufacturing organizations have a deep appreciation of the PDCA cycle that Edwards Deming made famous in the quality management field. They use PDCA to provide an iterative process that can help achieve their desired sustainability outcomes. Despite the popularity of PDCA, the method never includes the degree of rigor and specificity that one finds in the new and revised ISO management system standards.

We can begin to understand the value of PDCA by examining the ISO 14001:2015 environmental management system standard. The standard recognizes PDCA in the following ways (ISO, 2015):

- **Plan:** Establish environmental objectives and processes that are necessary to deliver results in accordance with the organization's environmental policy.
- **Do:** Implement the processes and activities as planned.
- **Check:** Monitor and measure processes against the environmental policy, including its environmental objectives and operating criteria, followed by reporting the results.
- **Act:** Take actions to continually improve.

In this way, the framework of ISO 14001:2015 provides the information to drive the PDCA processes. This can help new users to understand the importance of the systems approach needed for a viable sustainability management system. ISO has issued ISO Guide 82:2014 (ISO, 2014) to help include sustainability and social responsibility in an integrated management system. Let's take a closer look at the four elements of PDCA and see how they interact with the harmonized high-level structure of the ISO management system standards.

A. *Plan*

The planning element of the PDCA cycle is very important as it lays the foundation for the entire effort. Planning is often the step in PDCA that is left out with the haste to move forward with the implementation of the organization's process. This is the first reason why it is important to use the harmonized ISO approach to make sure that proper attention is paid to the planning effort. ISO 14001:2015 requires three discrete steps in the planning stage:

(i) Pre-planning: Pre-planning involves understanding how every organization has a unique operating context. The internal context is characterized by using a TECOP (i.e. technological, economic, cultural, organizational, and political) analysis of its internal operations (Talbot, 2011). An organization's external context is characterized using a PESTEL (i.e. political, economic, social, technological, legal, and environmental) analysis. Each analysis helps uncover the organizations uncertainties — opportunities and threats (Pojasek, 2017).

The internal and external stakeholders are the people whose faces are associated with the opportunities and threats that were identified with the context analysis. It is important to engage the stakeholders as part of the risk management effort. Planning must always take the "effects of uncertainty" (risk management) into consideration.

Now, the organization must determine the boundaries of the areas that are covered in the PDCA cycle and consider the extent of influence that it has over its activities, products, and services considering its suppliers and the community. After this has been completed, the organization can integrate its sustainability management system into its daily operating processes.

(ii) Leadership and Mandate: In the ISO management system standards, leadership is held fully accountable for the sustainability management system. Responsibility can be delegated to others. However, the effectiveness of the management system must remain with the leaders — not with the sustainability manager. The sustainability program must be compatible with the strategic direction of the organization and fully embedded in the day-to-day operations. Leaders must communicate the importance of sustainability being part of what every employee does every day. Additionally, leaders must promote continual improvement as the means to meet the organization's intended outcomes (Pojasek, 2017).

(iii) Scope of the Plan: The organization employs its risk management program to ensure that the opportunities and threats identified through its context are addressed through discrete planning actions. Sustainability aspects, impacts, and compliance obligations (i.e. codes of conduct) are identified and evaluated for significance. These actions lead to the determination of the sustainability objectives and aligning them with the organization's strategic objectives. Leaders make sure that the planning actions are implemented, and that the organization achieves its objectives in an uncertain world (i.e. with its opportunities and threats) (Pojasek, 2017).

B. *Do*

The implementation (i.e. the "do" component of PDCA) should not be started before the planning effort has been completed. In the ISO standards, operations must be conducted with the attention to many support activities. Resources include the following: human resources, natural resources, financial resources, infrastructure (i.e. buildings, equipment, HVAC, lighting, transportation, power, monitoring — measurement resources) and the environment necessary for the operation of the processes. The organization must implement and control the processes needed to meet its requirements for the provision of its products and services. All of this must be accomplished with attention to the organization's actions for environmental stewardship, social well-being, and its economic shared value with the community. Sustainability is never bolted-on in an organization — it must be built-in to be useful (Pojasek, 2017).

The type and extent of operational control will depend on the nature of the operations producing the products and/or services, the opportunities and threats, significant sustainability aspects, along with any compliance obligations. It is up to the organization to determine the extent of control that is needed within its own business processes and to direct or influence providers of services and products, and the many processes that are found in the supply chain of each organization (Pojasek, 2017).

Some of the organization's significant sustainability impacts can occur during the transport, delivery, use, end-of-life handling, or final disposal of products. The organization engages its stakeholders by providing information that can be discussed to determine if it can potentially prevent or mitigate adverse sustainability impacts during the life cycle of the products or services. Saying what you do provides a good degree of transparency for the organization. The "'do' what you say" component supports its accountability (Pojasek, 2017).

It is the responsibility of the organization to be prepared and to respond to emergency situations and to provide for the business continuity before and after disruptive events occur. Besides emergency situations, there is the constant change of the operating environment driven by innovation and learning. Proper management of change is designed to make sure that all changes are properly planned and implemented within the PDCA cycle. This activity provides a path to resilience — something that every organization needs to strive for as it operates in an uncertain world (Pojasek, 2017).

Now, it is time to shift attention to the "check" component of the PDCA cycle. It is important to remember that ISO can add a great deal of clarity, consistency, and credibility to the PDCA efforts. Many organizations are finding out that it pays to be organized in this way. It is a good way for an organization to operate for sustainable development and resilience.

C. *Check*

The "check" element is recognized as the monitoring, measurement, analysis, and evaluation of the PDCA conformance to ISO standards and leadership's expectations. What needs to be monitored and measured? What measurements will be made? When will the monitoring and measuring be performed? How will the results be analyzed and evaluated? Dutiful measurement seeks feedback from leaders regarding how sustainability expectations are being met (Pojasek, 2017).

During the check element activity, the organization will evaluate the performance and effectiveness of the PDCA process. The organization will monitor the external stakeholder interests and the degree to which they are engaged in a two-way dialogue over time. The customer's perception of the degree to which their needs and expectations have been met or exceeded is also a key part of this engagement process. A parallel examination of the internal stakeholders is also required in the check phase of the PDCA activity (Pojasek, 2017).

Organizations need to communicate relevant sustainability performance together with the effectiveness of the PDCA activity. Results should not be limited to lag indicators such as key performance indicators. Performance can be measured with lead indicators derived from available performance programs (e.g. Baldrige Performance Program). Self-evaluations and maturity matrices are another form of lead indicators that are effective in these evaluations. Leaders must review the PDCA management system on a regular basis since they are accountable for its outcomes. The extent to which the organization's strategic objectives have been effectively engaged will determine whether the organization will maintain its "social license to operate" (Pojasek, 2017).

Leaders will evaluate appropriate data and other information that arise from the monitoring and measurement methods. Stakeholders should be involved in the evaluation process. Key results are needed to address each of the following:

- performance and effectiveness of the harmonized high-level ISO management system;
- if planning has been implemented effectively;
- effectiveness of the actions taken to address the opportunities and threats;
- performance of the suppliers;
- need for improvements in the harmonized high-level ISO management system structure.

It is no longer sufficient to create a list of key performance indicators and track their trends over time. Lag indicators are only one of the measurements needed to check the PDCA comprehensively and effectively (Pojasek, 2017).

Internal audits need to be conducted at regular intervals to provide information on the performance of the PDCA process. The results of the audits need to be addressed by the leadership in the organization. Leaders should meet on a regular basis to ensure that the PDCA process is suitable, adequate, and effective (Pojasek, 2017).

D. *Act*

To most, act means to maintain and continually improve the PDCA efforts. In ISO 9004:2009, "act" is referred to as "improve, innovate, and learn". These efforts are followed by the second round of planning. PDCA is a circular logic for world-class operations. However, PDCA without the harmonized high-level structure found in all new and revised ISO management systems standards is often a banner used to make promises of continual improvement without the capability of doing so (Pojasek, 2017).

PDCA "act" should not be focused on correcting the mistakes that were made during the implementation "do" activity. Furthermore, it is not about scoring more points in the "check" process. Instead, the organization uses "act" to determine and select opportunities for improvement and implement any necessary actions to address the interests of stakeholders, including customers. Some examples of this are as follows:

- continually improving products and services to meet marketplace requirements as well as to address future interests and expectations of stakeholders;
- seeking to prevent or reduce undesirable effects over the long term;
- improving the efficiency and effectiveness of the sustainability management system.

Act is often reflective in nature. It looks back over the "do" and "check" activities to determine if there are needs or opportunities that should be addressed as part of the continual improvement that is noted. Also, remember the planning work done to determine the opportunities and threats that the organization finds among the "effects of uncertainty". Using opportunity often provides an element of innovation and learning for the organization. This will help build upon the planning in the next time through the PDCA cycle (Pojasek, 2017).

VII. Conclusion

Corporate sustainability has largely consisted in "stand-alone" sustainability programs that use publicly stated sustainability goals, independent sustainability initiatives, and sustainability reports. There has been little effort on the part of large corporations to stray from this model. At the operational levels of these corporations, the leaders are using PDCA — a model that is well known to them. The operational leaders will use the harmonized high-level structure of ISO to inform the PDCA and make it perform better. This method has its focus on operations rather than on a "sustainability" report.

First, we need to put aside those outdated concepts that we have regarding the old ways of looking at sustainability (i.e. unstructured programs). The PDCA model is widely adopted and easy to implement if not already being used. As presented in this chapter, the PDCA model works best with the harmonized high-level structure of ISO. If a business is certified to ISO standards as required by its customers, it is easy to keep the focus on PDCA. All the ISO standards have a guide for integrating the standard into PDCA programs. When customers are not requiring the use of ISO standards throughout the supply chain, the businesses can start providing some incentives to their suppliers to start building a structured sustainability program and save the cost of independent certification with the alternatives presented in all the ISO standards. This will save money yet still deliver the sustainability value throughout the supply chain.

Next, there are other items that can be added to the structured sustainability program to improve the business model described above. Greater use of the ISO 31000:2018 risk management program will help the business identify and deal with the "effects of uncertainty" — the opportunities and threats mentioned earlier in this chapter. ISO 31000:2018 should be used throughout the supply chain as a means of improving security and resilience (Pojasek, 2017).

Porter's value chain model and his shared value model are good additions to the business model. The value chain model can be used with performance excellence models (e.g. EFQM, Baldrige Performance Program, and the Australian Business Excellence Model) to create the lead indicators that are very helpful to sustainability managers — they are too focused on lag indicators. ISO 9004:2018 presents a maturity model that is used to self-assess the strengths and weaknesses of the ISO and PDCA activity and allow the sustainability manager to create a spider plot of how well the program is trending. Having a good mix of lead, lag, and maturity measurements will provide much better control over the program (Pojasek, 2017).

It is likely that organizations are using other operational excellence programs that can add more value to the integrated sustainability business model. As each organization tries the items in this chapter, they are likely to see the relevance to other improvement programs already in use. In the integrated business model, the organization can keep what is working and jettison that which is not helpful. The key to success is to replace that old unstructured sustainability program and start building a unique structured sustainability program that works best for each organization. The continual improvement efforts will benefit from this business tactic.

References

IPIECA. (2014). "Operating management system framework", IPIECA Reports, https://tinyurl.com/yaa49s37. Accessed December 30, 2017.

ISO (International Organization for Standardization) and IEC (International Electrotechnical Commission). (2016). "International organization for standardization", ISO/IEC directives, Part 1 — Consolidated ISO supplement — Procedures specific to ISO, 7th Edition, http://www.iso.org/sites/directives/ 2016/consolidated/index.xhtml. Accessed December, 2017.

ISO. (2014). "ISO guide 82: Guidelines for addressing sustainability in standards", *ISO* Website, https://www.iso.org/standard/57775.html. Accessed December 29, 2017.

ISO. (2015). "Introduction to ISO 14001", *ISO*, https://www.iso.org/files/live/ sites/isoorg/files/archive/pdf/en/introduction_to_iso_14001.pdf. Accessed December 29, 2017.

Pojasek, R. B. (2017). *Organizational Risk Management and Sustainability: A Practical Step-by-Step Guide*, CRC Press, Taylor & Francis Group, Boca Raton, Florida.

Talbot, J. (2011). "Risk... "the effect of uncertainty on objectives": 5.3.3 Internal Context. 05", http://31000risk.blogspot.com/2011/05/533-internal-context. html. Accessed December 29, 2017.

Warris, A. M., and Tanger, S. (2012). "Management makeover — New format for ISO management system standards", International Organization for Standardization, https://www.iso.org/news/2012/07/Ref1621.html. Accessed December 29, 2017.

Part II

Investment Implications

Chapter 8

Introduction to Sustainable Finance & Investing

Diane-Charlotte Simon

Learning Objectives

- Describe the sustainable finance landscape in the context of the financial system
- Understand the seven approaches to sustainable investing
- Get a sense of the relationship with financial performance
- Understand the drivers for growth and the pitfalls

Abstract

This chapter introduces Part II on Investment Implications of sustainability and other topics related to sustainable finance. The chapter begins with an introduction to finance and investing. In layman's terms, finance is defined as an instrument to support the payment of everyday expenses for individuals (personal finance), companies (corporate finance), or governments (public/government finance). From this perspective, finance provides access to things that could not otherwise be purchased with cash at hand. Personal finance can assist an individual through a student loan, a consumer loan, or a mortgage to buy a house. Corporate finance can provide a company with resources for its operations or its growth to develop new products or acquire new equipment and other companies. The financial instruments used will depend on the company's needs and the stage of its life cycle. Public/government finance can provide government resources to pay sovereign debt, country budgets (for education, social security, public health, national defense, etc.), and public servants salaries and pensions. The chapter then presents a brief history of the field of sustainable finance and describes various sustainable investment strategies ranging from risk management to mission-driven investments. It tries to bring clarity to what some call an "alphabet soup" of acronyms (MDGs, SDGs, SRIs, ESGs, etc.). The chapter notes several important challenges in sustainable finance that still need to be addressed such as the lack of a shared language and rigor in the use of terminology as well as the risk of "greenwashing" and mislabeling that fail to capture sustainability impact. The chapter concludes with a discussion on investor profiles and the relationship between sustainable investment strategies, risk, return, and impacts.

I. Introduction

Sustainable finance is one of the fastest growing areas of finance hitting new record highs year over year. The largest financial institutions from banking to asset management and asset owners are developing their capabilities and dedicating an increasing number of resources to sustainable finance driven by consumer demand but also, more recently, regulations.

The sustainable finance domain can be confusing because of the variety in its lexicon ("socially responsible investing", "responsible investing", "ethical investing", "values-based investing", "conscious investing", etc.) and the inconsistency with which terms are employed. This chapter attempts to bring clarity to the sector's terminologies, sometimes considered an "alphabet soup" due to its abundance of acronyms (SRI, ESG, etc.). In many instances these appellations point to underlying strategies to incorporate sustainability considerations while making a financing or investment decision ("ESG", "impact investing", "community investing", "best in class", etc.) that will be presented in this chapter. Unfortunately, the exercise is not straightforward as the sector still lacks standardization across geographies, and multiples approaches and definitions coexist.

This chapter is an introduction to sustainable finance and the various sustainable investment strategies. The chapter begins with an introduction to finance and investing and then articulates the need for a sustainable financial system. Readers will then be provided with a brief history of sustainable finance, which will be followed by market data about the state of sustainable finance globally. The various sustainable investment strategies ranging from risk management to mission-driven investments will then be presented. Finally, the chapter discusses investors' profile and the relationship between sustainable investment strategies, risk, return, and impacts.

Chapter 8 is organized as per the following sections:

I. Introduction
II. Introduction to Finance and Investing
III. A Needed Sustainable Financial System
IV. Sustainable Investment Definitions
V. Brief History: From SRI to ESG
VI. The Growing Sustainable Finance Sector
VII. Investment Strategies Taking into Consideration Sustainability
VIII. Risk, Return and Impact
IX. Conclusion

II. Introduction to Finance and Investing

1. What Is Finance and Why Is It So Important?

The role of finance within the economy is akin to the role of the lungs within a body. Finance is a critical mechanism that enables and facilitates the functioning of the overall economy and value creation. As a critical system, when a lung encounters a problem, it can disrupt the supply of oxygen to the entire body. In the same way, when the financial system faces issues, it can impair the functioning of the overall economy.

In layman's terms, finance is an instrument to support the payment of everyday expenses for individuals (personal finance), companies (corporate finance), or governments (public/government finance). Finance provides access to things that could not otherwise be purchased. Personal finance can assist an individual through a student loan, a consumer loan, or a mortgage to buy a house. Corporate finance can provide a company resources for its operation or its growth, to develop new products, or acquire new equipment and other companies. The financial instruments used will depend on the company's needs and stage in its life cycle. Public/government finance can provide government resources to pay sovereign debt, country budgets (for education, social security, public health, national defense, etc.) and public servants salaries and pensions.

Finance is especially critical when the individual or the organization lacks the immediate resources to handle their expenses. A college student with a part-time job may struggle to cover her tuition. A young company may not be generating revenues, or a mature company might not be able to grow "organically" because it does not have sufficient cash from its current activities. And a government might not collect sufficient taxes to pay its own debt and current budget. On these occasions, individuals, organizations, and governments can seek capital from financial institutions such as banks and investors through the capital markets.

2. What Constitutes an Investment and How Does It Relate to Finance?

Finance is often used interchangeably with investment and investment is often considered to be a subset of finance. As such, sustainable finance covers both the financing and investing activities. But if you take a closer look, these are in fact two distinct activities closely intertwined, as two sides of a coin. Indeed, the financing we have been discussing over the last few paragraphs can be referred to as an investment for the institution that initially provided the capital.

An investment is an action or process involving a dedication of resources (money, time, effort, people, etc.) with the objective of obtaining a certain outcome, intended to be of greater value. An investment is characterized by the value created between the moment when the investment was made and the moment the investment is realized. In the financial context, the realization of an investment occurs when the entity that made the original investment is either repaid for the amount provided and its remuneration, or when the financial instrument is sold to another entity.

Until then, the value of an investment may fluctuate, but will not have cash implications for the entity investing beyond some accounting implications. The assessment of the value of an asset or a company (***Valuation***) is a critical activity, which will determine the viability of an investment.

Why do individuals and institutions invest? Firstly, if they don't, inflation might decrease the value of money over time. In addition, have you ever heard the expression "putting your money to work"? In life, there are two main ways to generate revenue: being remunerated for the work you are doing either for a company or independently or by investing in financial instruments and making them work for you. The beauty of investing is that your investments can increase in value on their own over time.

Investments can be made by both individuals and financial institutions. Companies can also make investments to develop new strategies and products, but we will not cover these in this chapter. This chapter will solely focus on investments in financial instruments. Individuals can invest on their own or hire professionals to make investments for them as advisors or fund managers. Financial institutions can either invest on their own (***Asset Owners***) or manage investment for asset owners (***Asset Managers***). Asset owners include sovereign wealth funds (managing investments for government budgets), pension funds (managing investments for retirees' pensions), insurance companies (managing investments for the future insurance reimbursement), endowments (managing investments for colleges), and foundations, as well as high-net-worth and retail investors.

3. Primary Market, Secondary Market, and Liquidity

The financial system includes the capital markets which enable individuals, firms, and governments to raise funds through various financial instruments such as debt instruments, bonds, or shares, and also to trade these instruments. The capital market comprises two markets: the primary market and secondary market.

- The ***primary market*** involves a flow of cash benefiting an entity (individuals, corporations, governments) for its functioning. It is critical as it supports the financing of the production of goods and services, also called the "real economy". For companies, the primary market includes bank loans and bond issuances on the debt side and equity offerings such as Initial Public Offering (IPOs).

- The *secondary market* consists of the trading of financial instruments between buyers based on the perception of the value (or valuation) of a financial instrument (stocks, bonds, etc.) at the moment of exchange. The secondary market is influenced by the financial market's supply and demand, macro-economics trends, and technicalities. It is sometimes criticized for being disconnected from the "real economy" and companies' key performance indicators (also called *Fundamentals*).

When Company A issues a bond or stock in the capital market, this type of transaction occurs in the primary market and Company A receives cash. However, when trading that instrument, Company A receives no money. The exchange occurs between the owner of the stock and the secondary buyers of that stock.

The ease with which a financial instrument can be exchanged in the secondary market will determine its *liquidity*, which refers to how easily it can be converted into cash. Sovereign bonds, issued by governments, are the most liquid asset class in the capital markets. For this reason, they are considered to be equivalent to cash and *risk free*. They make up the benchmark on their local market to determine the premium at which a bond coupon rate will be priced. By contrast, loans and assets issued in the private markets (such as privately placed bonds, private equity, or venture capital) will have limited secondary markets as they do not trade on an exchange and thus will be considered *illiquid*.

4. Leverage, Risk and Return, and Timeframe

We will now touch on three fundamental concepts in investing:

- **Leverage**
- **Risk and Return**
- **Timeframe**

An entity's level of debt is known as *leverage*. Leverage can increase the value of an investment to a certain extent. However, too much leverage can impair the ability of a company, individual, or government to pay back its debt, putting them and any associated financial instruments at risk. The 2008 financial crisis was linked to the high leverage of individuals who were unable to repay home mortgages. It is critical to properly assess the leverage of a company when making an investment or when providing financing to ensure that the entity is able to pay back its debt.

The relationship between ***risk and return*** involves a positive correlation between the two whereby an investor expects compensation in proportion to the risk to which she is exposed. This concept is critical as it drives financial instruments pricings and investors demand and returns (see Section VIII for more details). Typically, the longer an investment (***maturity*** or ***tenor***), the higher the returns expected, given that the length of an investment increases uncertainty, which increases risk. Each type of instrument (***asset classes***) will be priced using a specific approach as they will be exposed to a similar category of risks. Investors can create investment portfolio that include various asset classes to diversify and mitigate their risks. Based on their nature, institutions have various risk appetites and thus seek different levels of return. Their risk/return profile will determine the investment strategies they can follow. For example, an investment with low risks will tend to lead to low potential returns while on the contrary an investment with high possibility of losses will tend to lead to high potential profits.

The ***timeframe*** considered for an investment to be realized greatly varies depending on the investor. This timeframe can span from a few seconds for electronic trading and robot trading, to very long-term investments that can last several decades. Sustainability tends to be particularly important for longer timeframes.

III. A Needed Sustainable Financial System

The current financial system has been threatened by colossal crises, which impacted the whole economy and is regularly criticized by numerous parties who have raise their concerns and have been thinking about solutions to address these issues. This section describes some of the most frequent criticisms, the need for a sustainable financial system, and the role that sustainable finance can play.

1. Systemic Risk

The scale of the 2008 global financial crisis was massive, as was the resulting distrust in financial institutions, from the public and policymakers. The impact of what was initially limited to a single asset class (securities backed by insolvent mortgages) in one country (USA) ended up impacting most sectors of the economy across Europe, Latin America, and other parts of the globe. The systemic risk presented by the financial sector was suddenly brought into stark relief. It has since been on the radar of regulators who developed safeguard measures to mitigate future crises and the scale of their consequences. Consecutive regulations such as Basel III or the Dodd–Frank Act in the United States, involved prudential actions requiring banks to keep more cash reserves and increase transparency and disclosure. These regulations also addressed governance concerns by implementing protection measures for whistleblowers who flag issues and require heightened internal control to identify risks early on and mitigate them if they cannot be fully avoided. In its 2014 Financial Stability Report, the International Monetary Fund (IMF) highlights the role of weak governance at financial institutions in the 2008 financial crisis as it led to excessive risk taking (IMF, 2014). Yet, governance is one of the pillars of a sustainable finance strategy called ESG which stands for Environmental, Social, and Governance factors (see Section VII.1 for more details about the ESG strategy). In its 2019 Financial Stability Report, the IMF dedicates a full chapter to Sustainable Finance stressing that some ESG issues can have a material impact on the stability of the overall financial system given their impact on companies' performance and risk profile. It highlights the role of governance failures at financial institutions and firms in past financial crises. It raises awareness around the fact that social risks and inequality may contribute to financial instability by triggering political unrest (IMF, 2019; Rajan, 2010). It flags as well that environmental risks including climate change may trigger large losses for companies, but also financial institutions and asset owners. The report emphasizes that the "integration of ESG factors into firms' business models — prompted either by regulators or by investors — may help mitigate these risks".

2. Speculation vs. Supporting the "Real Economy"

The financial markets are often criticized for being disconnected from the real economy and focusing on speculation on short-term gains. In general, this comment criticizes the speculation surrounding transactions in the secondary market whereby the actors involved have little "skin in the game" and trade very easily without bearing any consequences. However, it is important to note that the secondary market is critical as it provides the liquidity necessary for healthy financial markets. This apparent disconnect between the financial market and the real economy was striking during the coronavirus outbreak. 2020 was a record year for the debt capital markets with over $5 trillion issued globally (International Capital Market Association "ICMA") including over $2 trillion in US bonds (Securities Industry and Financial Markets Association "SIFMA") and over €1.8 trillion in European bonds (ICMA). And despite some volatility, the stock market remained strong in the middle of the crisis while countries were facing rising levels of unemployment. The records in the debt capital markets can be explained by the fact that many companies raised large amounts of money from debt in anticipation of their cash needs during the lockdown and its associated economic slowdown. In addition, the level of issuance was exacerbated given that institutional investors' abundance of liquidities as well as negative yields of European government bonds and the historically low US treasuries rates with 10-year US treasuries below the threshold of 1% yield. However, the relatively high level of the stock market despite the challenging economical backdrop is not as easy to understand. Some experts explain that the actions taken by governments to provide support to the economy were able to provide investors with sufficient confidence in the stock market. But some criticize the fact that the stock markets rely too much on projections and the growing importance of high frequency algorithmic trading, which reduce the human analysis in the decision-making and may pose some governance concerns.

But finance can create value and support the real economy, especially through the primary market. It can lead to growth and also job creation. Some question the associated inequality caused by an increase in billionaires during the past decade and concentration in wealth among fewer people (Zaouati, 2009).

3. The Potential of Sustainable Finance

As illustrated in Chapters 5 and 6, sustainability can have material financial impacts on a company's performance and properly managing sustainability is an effective way to mitigate risks. Similarly, certain sustainable finance strategies such as ESG integration (presented in greater detail in Section VII) support risk mitigation and can improve investors' long-term financial performance.

Sustainable finance also provides a blueprint that facilitate the financing of certain companies and sectors that produce positive impacts for the economy and the people. Sustainable finance can bring purpose and intention to finance and investing. In addition, it provides a complementary market-driven way to autoregulate by fostering positive externalities and deterring negative externalities. However, sustainable finance does not address all the criticisms made about the financial system. The financial system requires oversight from regulators and policymakers guided by thorough research. Policies and regulations have an irreplaceable role to play in finance, but also in economic and monetary matters.

Sustainable finance can also address some social and inequalities issues. It can be a tool to finance social changes such as promoting diversity in boards of companies, or financing companies owned by minorities.

Another major criticism coming from the sustainable finance actors flags the misalignment between the time horizon considered by some investors and companies focusing on the next quarter performance, when issues such as climate change require analysis in the scale of decades. Sustainability's impacts on businesses and investments materializes mainly in the longer term, especially when those relate to climate change. A challenge for the growth of sustainable finance relies on the fact that short-term investors might dismiss it. By contrast, long-term investors such as sovereign wealth funds or insurance companies will be more likely to integrate them in their decision-making process. These factors, alongside the fight against climate change, have been drivers accelerating the growth of sustainable finance globally.

This chapters attempts to describe the benefits that sustainable finance can generate in the financial system. Sustainable finance is based on the principles of the overall financial system and can be applied to all the different asset classes that will be discussed in further detail later in the chapter. Yet, the quality of the analysis to determine whether to make an investment or not should be of the same rigor as for any type of investment. Indeed, caution should be taken in the level of leverage of any investment and much attention should be paid during the due diligence process prior to an investment.

IV. Sustainable Investment Definitions

Assets employing sustainable strategies (see Section VII) are often qualified as "sustainable" for simplicity, but we will try to avoid this shortcut because all strategies and their implementation are not as equally effective at addressing sustainability issues (thus not equally sustainable) and may not meet the various legal definitions. Some regulations actually require that all companies and investors consider Environment, Social, and Governance risks given their importance, but this does not necessarily mean that all companies and investments under the legislation are effectively sustainable. The sector is changing fast and is not always easy to follow. New legislation is being developed and implemented around the world (especially in Europe) and is deeply transforming the sustainable finance sector with the aim to increase transparency, fight green washing, and improve standardization. All this influences the definition of what sustainable investment is.

What makes an investment sustainable? The strategy employed? The use of the investment proceeds? Recent regulations in Europe have attempted to address the complexity and the lack of standardization of the sector as well as tackle the risk of "greenwashing" by creating definitions for a set vocabulary for sustainable finance laid out in the Taxonomy (European Commission, 2020). While this is an improvement, these new regulations still need to be fully implemented, and as yet discrepancies remain across regions around the globe.

We will now introduce three main definitions of sustainable investment, and the definition of responsible investment.

1. Global Sustainable Investment Alliance (GSIA)

The Global Sustainable Investment Alliance (GSIA) definition of sustainable investment published in the 2012 Global Sustainable Investment Review (GSIR) emerged as a global standard of classification. The GSIA defines Sustainable Investment as the combination of the following:

- *investment approaches that consider environmental, social, and governance (ESG) factors in portfolio selection and management;*
- *across seven strategies (presented in Section VII)*
  - *ESG Integration*
  - *Corporate Engagement & Shareholder Action*
  - *Norms-Based Screening*
  - *Negative/Exclusionary Screening*
  - *Best-In-Class/Positive Screening*
  - *Sustainability Themed/Thematic Investing*
  - *Impact Investing and Community Investing.*

2. Sustainable Finance Disclosure Regulation (SFDR)

The landmark European Sustainable Finance Disclosure Regulation (SFDR), which entered into effect in March 2021, defines Sustainable Investment as: *"an investment in an economic activity that contributes to:*

- ***an environmental objective**, as measured, for example, by key resource efficiency indicators on the use of energy, renewable energy, raw materials, water and land, on the production of waste, and greenhouse gas emissions, or on its impact on biodiversity and the circular economy,*
- ***or an investment in an economic activity that contributes to a social objective**, in particular an investment that contributes to tackling inequality or that fosters social cohesion, social integration, and labor relations, or an investment in human capital or economically or socially disadvantaged communities,*
- ***provided that** such investments do not significantly harm any of those objectives*

- **_and_ that the investee companies follow good governance practices,** *in particular with respect to sound management structures, employee relations, remuneration of staff and tax compliance."* (European Parliament and the Council of the European Union, 2019).

3. European Sustainable Investment Forum (EUROSIF)

The European Sustainable Investment Forum (EUROSIF) defines Sustainable & Responsible Investment as follows:

- *a **long-term** oriented investment approach...that integrates **Environmental, Social & Governance (ESG)** factors ... in the **research, analysis and selection process** of securities within an investment portfolio.*
- *It combines **fundamental analysis and engagement** with an evaluation of ESG factors in order to better capture **long-term returns for investors, and to benefit society by influencing the behavior of companies*** (EUROSIF, 2021).

4. United Nations Supported Principles for Responsible Investment's (PRI) Definition of Responsible Investment

The United Nations supported Principles for Responsible Investment's (PRI) definition of Responsible Investment as a strategy and practice to incorporate ESG factors in investment decisions and active ownership (which are two sustainable investment strategies presented in Section VII). In its Fiduciary Duty in the 21st Century report, the PRI defines Responsible Investment as explicitly acknowledging the relevance of ESG factors, and of the long-term health and stability of the market as a whole. Responsible investors understand that the generation of long-term sustainable returns is dependent on well-governed social, environmental, and economic systems. Two main characteristics distinguish responsible investment from conventional approaches to investment: a longer time-frame in mind and a broader scope of analysis integrating the ESG dimensions. Responsible investors aspire to "the creation of sustainable, long-term investment returns, not just short-term returns". In addition, they need to "pay attention to the wider contextual factors, including the stability and health of economic and environmental systems and the evolving values and expectations of the societies of which they are a part" (The United Nations Global Compact, UNEP Finance Initiative, the Principles for Responsible Investment Initiative, UNEP Inquiry into the Design of a Sustainable Financial System, 2015).

V. Brief History: From SRI to ESG

The origins of sustainable finance can be traced back a long way, though it was not labeled as such. Historically, the first attempts to incorporate sustainability considerations into investment decisions started with ethical drivers. For centuries, religious beliefs led to the exclusion of investments (negative screening) in sectors considered as morally wrong including weapons, alcohol, tobacco, gambling, etc. Noteworthy examples include Jewish laws about how to invest ethically, the Quakers' prohibition from slavery business, the Methodists' investments exclusions from any business that could harm, and the application of Sharia principles in investing by the Muslim community (Townsend, 2020; Donovan, 2020).

The first major sustainable finance approach is considered to be **Socially Responsible Investing (SRI)** (Hylton, 1992; Von-Wallis and Klein, 2015). SRI is defined as the "integration of certain non-financial concerns, such as ethical, social or environmental, into the investment process" (Sandberg *et al.*, 2009). SRI puts an emphasis on the social dimension as its name suggests, and "do no harm" is its motto. SRI has been characterized by the use of screenings to exclude some sectors or companies for moral, social, or environmental concerns (negative screening). Until the 1960s, SRI was mainly employed by faith-based organizations (Alperson, 1991). The next decade's cultural changes in the United States led to the broadening of SRI topics to address the Vietnam War, racial inequality, women's rights, consumer protection, and the environment (Donovan, 2020). Some argue that the establishment of community development banks in low-income or minority communities contributed to a movement that produced the Civil Rights Act of 1964 and the Voting Rights Act of 1965 (Donovan, 2020). Notable SRI actions at the time also include the sale of Dow Chemical stocks from students' endowment funds or the creation of funds in opposition to their production of napalm to be used in Vietnam (Alperson, 1991). In 1971, Pax World Fund, the first SRI mutual fund in the US, was launched with the aim to avoid companies benefiting from the Vietnam War and weapons in general (Gittell *et al.*, 2013). In the 1980s, SRI has been critical in the ending of the apartheid regime in South Africa through considerable divestment from faith-based organizations, but also cities and pension funds in the United States. This movement put some pressure on companies' leaders who ended up reviewing some of their policies. It took also the shape of shareholder engagements initiatives (further discussed below and Chapter 11) led by organizations such as the Interfaith Center for Corporate Responsibility in the United States.

Corporate Social Responsibility (CSR) is to be distinguished from SRI as it takes a different perspective to address similar concerns for the common good. Both call for rethinking the responsibility of business and investing in Society, but CSR looks at it from a corporate point of view, while SRI considers the investor angle.

The rise of environmental issues such as climate change and pollution has increased the number of initiatives related to the environmental matters in SRI since the 1990s. Following the 1992 Earth Summit in Rio, the United Nations Environment Programme Finance Initiative (UNEP FI) was created with the intention to transform private finance to achieve sustainable development. Since its creation, UNEP FI has been engaging with governments and international organizations to develop policies encouraging sustainable finance and has published a large number of reports (accessible at the UN Environmental Program website).

After scandals such as Enron in the 2000s, a lot of emphasis has been put on governance and transparency. This led to the creation of a new wave of sustainable finance characterized by the addition of the Governance to the previous Social and Environmental factors (ESG) already covered in SRI (Fulton *et al.*, 2012). ESG has since become the most frequent strategy ahead of negative screening/SRI, to the extent that some use the terms ESG and sustainable finance interchangeably, although they are not equivalent. The ESG strategy focuses on the mitigation of sustainability-related risks while leveraging sustainability-related opportunities. The

ESG approach is more driven by financial performance than values-based sustainable investment strategies which are more driven by the intention to have a positive impact or make a difference. Impact investing and sustainability themed investing are other examples of values-based sustainable investment strategies which have recently grown significantly. Other sustainable investment strategies are discussed in more detail in Section VII. It is important to note that sustainable finance has historically been done on a voluntary basis but is now increasingly being driven by regulations in Europe, Asia, and in the USA.

We present some of the key milestones in the Sustainable Finance & Investing Timeline as follows:

- 1999 — Launch of the **Dow Jones Sustainability World Index**, the first global sustainability benchmark which gathers stocks of best ESG performances among the world's largest companies.
- 2000 — the **Global Reporting Initiative (GRI)** launched the first version of its sustainability disclosure framework which has become the most widely used.
- 2002 — Publication of **UNEP FI CEO Briefing on Climate Change**, its first major climate report exposing the relevancy of climate change to the financial services industry and the need for long-term, market-based frameworks to support its participation.
- 2003 — Establishment of the **Equator Principles** which have been adopted by financial institutions to manage environmental and social risk in project finance.
- 2006 — Launch of the **United Nations supported Principles for Responsible Investment (PRI 2022)** at the New York Stock Exchange which have since been a key driver of the sector by mobilizing institutional investors.
  The six PRI are as follows:
  - ○ "Principle 1: We will incorporate ESG issues into investment analysis and decision-making processes.
  - ○ Principle 2: We will be active owners and incorporate ESG issues into our ownership policies and practices.
  - ○ Principle 3: We will seek appropriate disclosure on ESG issues by the entities in which we invest.

- o   Principle 4: We will promote acceptance and implementation of the Principles within the investment industry.
- o   Principle 5: We will work together to enhance our effectiveness in implementing the Principles.
- o   Principle 6: We will each report on our activities and progress toward implementing the Principles".
- 2013 — NYSE Euronext joined the United Nations Sustainable Stock Exchanges (SSE) Initiative, which intends to enhance corporate transparency on ESG issues and encourage long-term investment by fostering collaboration between exchanges, investors, regulators, and companies.
- 2015 — Adoption by the heads of state of the United Nations 17 Sustainable Development Goals (SDGs) to be implemented by 2030 (UN, 2015). SDGs have since been widely adopted by corporations and financial institutions and used as reference providing categories to measure the impact of sustainable strategies, initiatives, or products.
- 2015 — The landmark Paris Agreement was reached during the COP 21. For the first time countries agreed to combat climate change and committed to limit the temperature increase to 1.5°C above pre-industrial levels (United Nations Climate Change, UNFCCC) As of 2023, 195 countries have ratified the agreement (United Nations, 2023).
- 2015 — Launch of UNEP initiative to Design a Sustainable Financial System aimed at accelerating the flow of capital dedicated to finance a sustainable, clean, and low-carbon economy. *In the wake of the global financial crisis, recognition has grown that the financial system must be not only sound and stable, but also sustainable in the way it enables the transition to a low-carbon, green economy.* Achim Steiner Executive Director, United Nations Environment Programme. United Nations Environment Programme (2015).
- 2017 — Launch of the Taskforce on Climate-related Financial Disclosure (TCFD).
- 2019 — The EU Parliament and Council agreed on the implementation of a new regulation across EU countries requiring financial institutions to integrate ESG considerations in their investment decision-making and provide adequate disclosure to investors. The

Sustainable Finance Disclosure Regulation (SFDR) was adopted in 2019 and entered into effect in March 2021. It requires financial market participants to integrate in their processes, including in their due diligence, all relevant sustainability risks that might have a relevant material negative impact on financial returns and disclose about it including in their financial annual reports.

- 2020 — Publication of the **EU Taxonomy on Sustainable Finance** recommendation to the European Commission by the EU technical expert group on sustainable finance. This report provides guidance on which economic activity can be categorized as sustainable finance provided its environmental impacts on issues such as the following:
  1. Climate change mitigation and adaptation
  2. Water and marine resources
  3. Transition to a circular economy
  4. Pollution prevention and control
  5. Biodiversity and ecosystems
- 2021 — For its 25th anniversary, UNEP FI, put together an online interactive timeline of sustainable finance (UN Environmental Program Website).

VI. The Growing Sustainable Finance Sector

The role of sustainable finance in the global financial system has become so critical that the International Monetary Fund (IMF) dedicated an entire chapter to it in its 2019 Global Financial Stability Report. The demand for sustainable financial products is growing from both institutional investors and retail clients. Among individual investors, women and values-driven millennials (Morgan Stanley Institute for Sustainable Investing, 2017, 2019) are driving the demand. Research done by Morgan Stanley Institute for Sustainable Investing in 2019 found that 85% of the general public was interested in sustainable investing and that this proportion reached 95% for Millennials. Millennials are predicted to have an growing influence over the market as the transfer of $30 trillion of assets to their benefits, increase over the next generation (Accenture, 2012). In 2019, 88% of the world 500 largest asset managers reported an increase in client interest in sustainable investing, including shareholder engagement (Willis Towers Watson and Pensions & Investments, 2020).

Sustainable finance is attracting increasing interest from asset managers (banks, financial advisors, etc.) and asset owners (pensions funds, sovereign wealth funds, foundations, college endowments, family offices, etc.). Ten years after its creation, UN supported PRI signatories represented over $59 trillion in assets worldwide in 2016 and over $120 trillion as of 2022 (PRI, 2022) equivalent to the amount managed by the world's 500 largest asset managers (Willis Towers Watson and Pensions & Investments, 2020). The amount actually dedicated to responsible investment could be as low as half of it as the PRI requires that signatories employ at least 50% of their Assets Under Management (AUM) for responsible investment since 2018.

Some of the largest asset managers such as Blackrock or Amundi have developed sustainable investment practices to answer growing client demand and leverage the opportunities they present to generate more revenues (IPE Staff, 2017). In 2015, Goldman Sachs acquired the impact investing advisor Imprint Capital to broaden its offering of ESG and Impact products. In 2016, the private equity firm TPG launched the Rise Fund, a targeted $2 billion social impact fund backed by U2 singer Bono, and Jeff Skoll (Loizos 2016). In 2017, Bain Capital, the private equity arm of the global consulting company, closed its first Double Impact fund, a $390 million fund dedicated to impact investing, up from the $250 million that was initially targeted (ImpactAlpha, 2017). In 2020, Double Impact closed its second fund at $800 million (Kreutzer 2020). Very wealthy individuals have also dedicated capital to tackle some of the world's largest problems such as Bill Gates's $2 billion Breakthrough Energy Ventures fund, which has been created to support companies that can contribute to fight climate change by significantly reducing greenhouse gas emissions from key sectors such as agriculture, buildings, electricity, manufacturing, and transportation. These examples illustrate how sustainable investing has become mainstream, showcasing the variety of sustainable investor profiles. As of 2020, 40% of the $14 trillion in alternatives industry is managed by firms committed to sustainability with more than $3 trillion of funds employing sustainable strategies since 2011 (Preqin, 2020a, 2020b). The world's 500 largest asset managers had $8.5 trillion invested in sustainable strategies in 2019, a 42.9% increase vs. the previous year (Willis Towers Watson and Pensions & Investments, 2020).

We will now discuss the sustainable investment market. One of its complexities arises from the various strategies and definitions as well as the sizing and scope, which depends heavily on claims made by the financial institutions involved, calling for some caution. This has been the approach taken by the Global Sustainable Investment Alliance (GSIA) in its biannual Global Sustainable Investment Review (GSIR), which has become a reference point for market data about the sustainable investing's market intelligence since its first GSIR publication in 2013 covering data for 2012. The GSIA is an international collaboration of regional sustainable investment organizations such as the European Sustainable Investment Forum (EUROSIF) and the United States Forum for Sustainable and Responsible Investment (US SIF). According to their research, in 2020 over $35 trillion assets globally were employing investment strategies taking into consideration sustainability (Figure 8.1). The amount of assets considering sustainable investment strategies in 2020 is close to three times more than measured in the GSIA's 2012 GSIR inaugural survey (Figure 8.1). Indeed, it increased with a 13% Compound Annual Growth Rate (CAGR) during the 2012–2020 period and with a 7% CAGR since

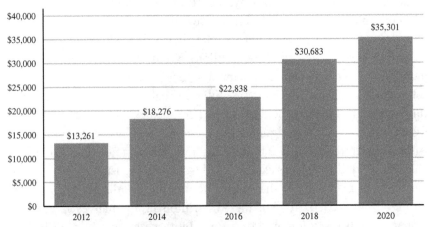

Figure 8.1.   Assets Employing Sustainable Investment Strategies 2012–2020 (in Billion USD)

Source: GSIA, GSIRs (2013, 2015, 2017, 2019, 2021).

2018. To put it into perspective, this means that in 2020 close to one-tenth of the global assets were considering sustainability in some way. And considering the regions surveyed by the GSIA study, it represents more than one out of three dollars of professionally managed assets, up from 22% in 2012 (Table 8.1).

According to the GSIA, close to half (48%) of the assets considering sustainability in 2020 came from the United States and more than a third (34%) from Europe (Figure 8.2). With more than $17 billion, the United States represented the largest sustainable investments market in the world, close to half of the global market (Table 8.2). The US market has encountered rapid growth with a 21% CAGR over the 2012–2020 period with

Table 8.1. Assets Considering Sustainability Relative to Total Managed Assets Over 2012–2020 Period (in Billion USD)

	2012 (%)	2014 (%)	2016 (%)	2018 (%)	2020 (%)
Canada	20	31	38	51	62
Europe	49	59	53	49	42
Australia New Zealand	13	17	51	63	38
United States	11	18	22	26	33
Japan	N/A	N/A	3	18	24

Source: GSIA, GSIRs (2013, 2015, 2017, 2019, 2021).

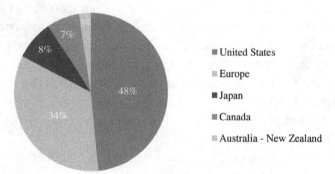

Figure 8.2. Assets Employing Sustainable Investment Strategies by Region in 2020 (in %)

Source: GSIA, 2020 GSIR (2021).

Table 8.2. Assets Considering Sustainability by Region Over 2012–2020 Period (in Billion USD)

	2012 ($)	2014 ($)	2016 ($)	2018 ($)	2020 ($)
United States	3,740	6,572	8,723	11,995	17,081
Europe	8,758	10,775	12,040	14,075	12,017
Canada	589	729	1,086	1,699	2,874
Australia — New Zealand	134	148	516	734	2,423
Japan	N/A	7	474	2,180	906
Global	13,261	18,276	22,838	30,683	35,301

Source: GSIA, GSIRs (2013, 2015, 2017, 2019, 2021).

still more room to grow. Indeed, in 2020 one out of three dollars of assets professionally managed in the US was monitoring sustainability concerns, which is still less than in Europe or Canada.

While Europe has been a pioneer and longstanding leader in sustainable finance, it has been bypassed by the United States for the first time in 2020 in terms of dollars of assets, according to the GSIA analysis. It is, however, important to note that the definition of sustainable investment has changed in Europe due to regulations (e.g. SFDR, the Corporate Sustainability Reporting Directive, the EU Taxonomy Regulation, etc.) which mandate all institutional investors to consider sustainability risk. Indeed, the GSIA highlights that negative/exclusionary screening, norms-based screening, and ESG integration have all become part of the expected practice of all financial products in the region. For this reason, one might extrapolate and consider the totality of the $28 trillion European assets as considering sustainability by necessity due to regulatory constraints, instead of the $12 trillion included in the GSIR, bringing the global market to a total of $49 trillion assets. Taking this approach, Europe may still be considered as the largest, most advanced sustainability market and is likely to remain so for the foreseeable future.

Some may be inclined to take a shortcut and call all these assets sustainable, but it would not be accurate. The following part presents the various sustainable investment strategies and demonstrates that, while qualifying all as sustainable would certainly make things simpler, they do not equally support solutions to improve our world. As discussed in the Chapter 3, some approaches to sustainability emphasize the intended impacts on society and the environment ("valueS-first") while others such as the ESG integration strategy are centered on sustainability's impacts on companies' performance and value created for the company and its shareholders ("value-first") (Krosinsky and Purdom, 2016). Considering a more stringent definition of sustainable investment, the global amount of sustainable investments could be closer to $2 trillion vs. the $35 trillion disclosed by asset owners and managers part of the regional sustainable finance association. This more conservative approach would include all the capital following sustainability-themed and impact investing strategies, but only some of the capital following ESG integration, best-in-class, and shareholder engagement and none of the investments following negative screening strategies.

Labels have been created to certify the reliability of these claims by a third party and provide a less partial opinion. "Green", "social", or "sustainable" are among the most common labels. Companies' environmental, social, and governance (ESG) performance is also rated by third parties that investors can look at when making investment decisions and monitoring their portfolio. But in some cases, the financing of sustainable activities is not labeled as such and consequently not captured in the typical market research. For instance, a large part of the financing of renewables is done as project financing, which seldom goes through a process to label and certify the financing as sustainable. According to Bloomberg New Energy Finance ("BNEF"), $920 billion was invested in energy transition in 2021 comprising $755 billion in 2021 of project financing deployed for the energy transition in addition to $165 billion financing climate-tech innovation via equity financing from public markets and private investors (BNEF, 2022). Companies, governments, and households invested $366 billion in new renewable energy capacity in 2021 (BNEF, 2022).

The OECD estimates that meeting the UN Sustainable Development Goals (SDGs) will require ~$6.3T in annual investment immediately, increasing to ~$6.9T to meet the Paris Agreement goals.

VII. Investment Strategies Taking Sustainability into Consideration

In this section, we will introduce the seven main investment strategies taking into consideration sustainability presented in the inaugural 2012 GSIR, which have since become accepted international industry terminology. These strategies can stand alone, be combined, or overlap.

1. ESG integration
2. Exclusionary screening
3. Norms-based screening
4. Best-in-class
5. Sustainability-themed
6. Shareholder engagement
7. Impact investing

The $35 trillion of assets considering sustainability in 2020 as per the GSIR report follow these seven strategies, sometimes combining several at once (Figure 8.3). Three of them comprise close to 90% of the total sustainably managed assets: ESG integration ($25 trillion), exclusionary screening ($15 trillion), and shareholder engagement ($11 trillion). See Table 8.3. Sustainability-themed ($1 trillion in 2020), ESG integration,

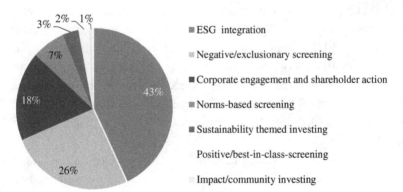

Figure 8.3. Global Assets Allocation per Sustainable Strategy in 2020
Source: GSIA, 2020 GSIR, 2021.

Table 8.3. Assets Allocation per Sustainable Strategy Across Regions 2012–2020 (in Billion USD)

	2012 ($)	2014 ($)	2016 ($)	2018 ($)	2020 ($)	2012–2020 CAGR (%)
ESG Integration	5,935	7,527	10,369	17,544	25,195	20
Negative/exclusionary screening	8,280	12,046	15,023	19,771	15,030	8
Corporate engagement and shareholder action	4,589	5,919	8,365	9,835	10,504	11
Norms-based screening	3,038	4,385	6,210	4,679	4,140	4
Sustainability themed investing	70	137	331	1,018	1,948	51
Positive/best-in-class-screening	999	890	1,030	1,842	1,384	4
Impact/community investing	86	101	248	444	352	19
Total	13,261	18,276	22,838	30,683	35,301	20

Source: GSIA, GSIRs (2013, 2015, 2017, 2019, 2021).

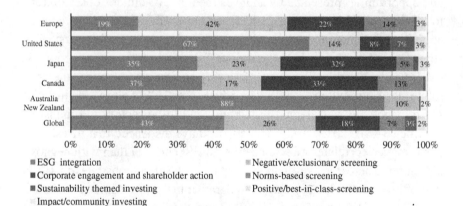

Figure 8.4. Sustainable Investment Strategies by Region in 2020 (in %)

Source: GSIA, 2020 GSIR, 2021.

and impact investing ($444 million in 2020) have encountered the highest growth with 51%, 20%, and 19% CAGR, respectively, over the 2012–2020 period (GSIA, 2021).

The popularity of sustainable strategies varies from region to region (Figure 8.4). For instance, the proportion of assets following the ESG strategy is greater in Australia, New Zealand, and the US than in the rest of the world. Negative screening is far more prominent in Europe than in other parts of the globe. It is also worth noting that assets employing shareholder engagement in the US are proportionally smaller (8%) than in other parts of the world. Ideological differences exist in the separate approaches taken in Europe and in the US, highlighting key ideological differences. The latter focuses on risk-based factors and financial materiality; the former is more likely to be driven by a values-based rationale following a "do the right thing" mantra.

1. ESG Integration

ESG integration widens the scope of traditional investing by including environmental, social, and governance elements affecting a company's financial performance through its revenues, operations, reputation, valuation, but also its cost of capital. This approach considers the financial risks and opportunities presented by an investment's ESG dimensions. Contrary to other sustainable strategies, which sometimes prioritize ethical considerations, ESG integration typically puts financial considerations first. This strategy is employed by both "traditional" investors focusing on economical drivers and "ethical" investors focusing on doing good, as per the definition used by Hylton (1992). The impacts of ESG factors on financial performance are well-demonstrated and tend to be sector- and industry-specific (SASB, 2017). Empirical studies have evidenced that investment performance correlates more closely with ESG criteria than with negative screening. The extensive financial impact of ESG demonstrates that it is part of investors' fiduciary duty to integrate it in their investment decisions (The Generation Foundation, UNEP FI and the PRI, 2019). In places like Europe, ESG integration is a regulatory requirement, as per the Regulation (EU) 2019/2088 of the European Parliament and Council published on November 27, 2019, which requires the financial services sector to publish sustainability-related disclosures.

Incorporating environmental, social, and governance factors into financial analysis influences both the selection of an investment during its due diligence and its management over the course of the holding period. ESG approaches analyze companies' corporate sustainability and assess the extent to which it is embedded into their long-term strategy and business models. ESG integration is widely used for public equities and public bonds and relies on the availability of ESG data and reporting (cf. Chapter 3). ESG integration tends to work well for large and mature companies who possess the resources to produce a lot of disclosure and data.

ESG integration has become the most frequently used sustainable strategy, representing 43% of the assets considering sustainability, with over $25 trillion in assets in 2020 according to GSIA (GSIA, 2021). These assets encountered the second fastest growth among sustainable strategies, at a 20% CAGR between 2012 and 2020. The United States alone accounts for 64% of the assets following this strategy globally, while Europe represents 16% (GSIA, 2021).

2. Screenings

The screening strategies (exclusionary screening, norms-based screening, and best-in-class screening) represented $20.5 billion in assets as of 2020, exclusionary screening being the most common (GSIA, 2021).

A. *Exclusionary Screening*

As its name suggests, exclusionary screening is considered one of the negative sustainable strategies. Also called socially responsible investing (SRI), it is the oldest sustainable investment strategy. It is often called the "do no harm" approach (Finkelman and Huntington, 2017). Negative screening excludes firms or sectors from the investment universe when their environmental, social, or governance (ESG) criteria are in conflict with an investor's values or worldview. Weapons (production and trade), tobacco, nuclear energy, pornography, gambling, alcohol, and animal testing are among the top exclusionary criteria. Screenings have also been established to align with religious principles for religious faiths like Catholicism, Islam, and Judaism. More recently, in response to climate change, the divestment movement has gained traction as an exclusionary investment, excluding companies with ownership in fossil fuel reserves. As of 2019, close to 1,000 institutional investors representing close to $10 trillion in assets under management had pledged to divest from fossil fuels (IMF, 2019).

While historically the most prevalent sustainable strategy, exclusionary screening has recently waned (see Table 8.3). Perhaps this is because it tends to not perform as well financially because you are narrowing the investible universe as more forward-looking approaches such as ESG emerge (Krosinsky *et al.*, 2012). As of 2020, it still represented one-fourth of global sustainable strategy assets with $15 trillion and has been growing at a 8% CAGR during the 2012–2020 period (see Table 8.3). Europe accounts for over half of global assets allocated to negative screening strategy; more than $4 out of every $10 dedicated to sustainable investing in Europe follow this strategy (GSIA, 2021).

B. *Norms-Based Screening*

Norms-based screening adopts business practice standards and international norms that consider ESG criteria. The three main norms of reference include those developed by the UN Global Compact, the International Labour Organization Tripartite Declaration of Principles on Multinational Enterprises and Social Policy, and the OECD Guidelines for Multinational Enterprises (EUROSIF, 2016). A company's adherence to norms or standards can impact the weight of its investments within a portfolio which will be over or underweighted accordingly (GSIA, 2017). This strategy can be easily combined with others such as exclusionary screening. Such a combination would result in the exclusion of companies with poor adherence to principles or engagement with laggard companies (EUROSIF, 2016).

Norms-based screening, mainly employed in Europe and Canada, represented 7% of global sustainable assets with over $4.1 trillion in 2020 (see Table 8.3).

C. *Best-in-Class Screening*

Best-in-class screening involves a selection of companies, projects, or sectors in an investment universe based on positive ESG performance in relation to their peers. The best-in-class approach considers only the leaders in a peer group. This approach is considered a "positive strategy" as it values high ESG-performing companies, sectors, or funds, in contrast to "negative strategies" such as exclusion or engagement. The Dow Jones Sustainability Indexes are examples of products implementing the best-in-class strategy.

Best-in-class screening represented 2% of global sustainable assets with over $1.4 trillion in 2020, coming mainly from the United States, Europe, and Japan (see Table 8.3).

3. Corporate Engagement and Shareholder Action

Engagement seeks to leverage investors' power to influence corporate behaviors. This strategy mainly applies to public stocks, but can also be employed by other asset classes. Shareholders engage with companies primarily through direct communication with their senior management and board of directors or by filing shareholder proposals and proxy voting. Engagement initiatives can take place so long as an investor is invested in a company and meets certain conditions (cf. Chapter 11 dedicated to Shareholder Engagement). This strategy is considered to be negative, as corporate engagement occurs in organizations encountering sustainability issues which require to be addressed.

Corporate Engagement and Shareholder Action is the third largest sustainable strategy with over $10.5 trillion of assets employing it, with close to half of it coming from Europe, and representing 18% of the assets applying sustainable investment strategies (see Table 8.3). The volume of assets using this strategy grew at a 11% CAGR between 2012 and 2020 (see Table 8.3).

4. Sustainability-Themed Investing

As implied by its name, the sustainability-themed investing strategy focuses on themes, sectors, or assets that are closely related to sustainable development and targets investments addressing sustainability issues such as climate change, food, water, renewable energy/clean technology, and agriculture (GSIA, 2017). Due to its focus and scope, this approach and impact investing may be considered the purest sustainable investment strategy or the backbone of sustainable investing. The most prevalent themes include the transition away from fossil fuels with clean energy,

energy efficiency, climate-related opportunities, sustainable transports, sustainable buildings, but also water management, waste management, and sustainable agriculture (EUROSIF, 2016). Green, social, and sustainable debt instruments are following this strategy (see Chapter 9).

This approach has been the fastest growing sustainable strategy over the 2012–2020 period with a 51% CAGR to reach close to $2 trillion of assets in 2020. 87% of these were from the United States and 17% from Europe. Still, this strategy remains marginal and only represents 3% of the assets considering sustainability.

5. Impact Investing

Impact-targeted investments are made "with the intention to generate positive, measurable social and environmental impact alongside a financial return" (Global Impact Investing Network (GIIN, 2020a). This strategy is often used in specific sectors such as "sustainable agriculture, renewable energy, conservation, microfinance, and affordable and accessible basic services including housing, healthcare, and education". Impact Investing tends to favor investment in companies fully embedding sustainability in their business model (see Chapter 10 on Impact Investing).

Three main characteristics differentiate this strategy from the other sustainable strategies:

- The "intentionality" to contribute to social and environmental solutions by investing.
- The use of evidence and impact data in investment design.
- The management and reporting of impact performance throughout an investment life (GIIN, 2019).

Another distinction from the other sustainable strategies relates to the fact that, while most impact investors pursue risk-adjusted market-returns, some intentionally invest for below-market-rate returns (discretionary strategies) as they privilege impacts over financial returns (GIIN, 2020a). For this reason, this strategy attracts the broadest investor base among the seven sustainable strategies, ranging from the traditional fund managers, pension funds, diversified financial institutions/banks, insurance companies, and individual investors, to NGOs and also includes development finance institutions, private foundations, religious institutions, and family offices. Many impact investors tend to be small, managing less than $100 million in impact-investing assets (GIIN, 2020a). Yet, impact investing is distinct from philanthropy in that it seeks to receive some capital back.

Impact investing is the privileged sustainable strategy for private markets (debt and equity) even though it can also be employed for public markets. Some purists argue that impact investing can only be employed in primary markets, as capital deployed in secondary markets does not affect the companies. In addition, impact investing is also the privileged sustainable strategy for early-stage to mid-sized companies.

Community investing is a subset of impact investing. Community investing consists in the dedication of capital to traditionally under-served individuals or communities or financing is provided to businesses with a clear social or environmental purpose.

Impact management and reporting are a pillar of Impact Investing. According to the GIIN (2020b) Annual Impact Investor Survey, the most frequently used frameworks are the alignment of the impacts with the UN Sustainable Development Goals (SDGs) and IRIS metrics. Yet, participants mainly expressed concerns about "impact washing", but describe also challenges to demonstrate impact results and compare results with peers. In addition, third-party impact performance review still has room for improvement.

Despite a decrease in 2020 coming from Europe, overall over the 2012–2020 period Impact Investing has been the third fastest growing sustainable investment strategy with a 19% CAGR. According to the GSIA, $352 billion of assets used an Impact investing strategy in 2020, 60% in the United States, 30% in Europe, and the remainder in Canada, Australia, and New Zealand. As of 2019, the GIIN estimates that the Impact Investing market represented $715 billion and comprises over 1,720 impact investors (GIIN, 2020b). Most of this capital was deployed in emerging markets.

VIII. Risk, Return, and Impact

1. Sustainable Investors' Risk, Return, and Impact Profiles

Investors come to sustainable finance with different objectives. The large majority of sustainable finance investors target market-rate or above-market-rate returns just like traditional investors. As a point of reference, the overall weighted average long-term rate of return on capital in the financial system is estimated to be approximately 3.4% in real terms and 5.4% in nominal terms, with average bond returns at 3%, average bank-lending returns at 5%, and average equity returns at 7% (IPCC, 2018). However, for some investors financial returns are not the primary motive driving their investment strategy. Historically, "ethical" investors have been distinguished from "traditional" investors by their willingness to pursue investments based on values irrespective of returns, while traditional investors would only do so if economically satisfactory (Hylton, 1992). Ethical investors tend to employ impact-investing strategies or negative sustainable strategies, which stems from the SRI era (e.g. exclusionary screening). In the 2020 GIIN Impact Investing Survey, while most impact investors reported seeking market returns, 33% reported seeking below-market-rate returns, among which 15% sought returns close to capital preservation. The capital invested following below-market-rate returns strategies is sometimes called "concessional capital". Blended finance, which is increasingly being used in impact investing, mixes profit capital with discretionary capital, which can partially lose its value or be given away by foundations or not-for-profit organizations. Investors targeted risk-returns. Their intended impact will influence both the asset classes included in their investment portfolio and their choice of sustainable finance strategy.

2. Sustainable Investment Strategies, Risk, Return, and Impact

Many studies have examined the financial impact of sustainability whether from the standpoint of the company (CSR) or the investor (sustainable finance, SRI, ESG, etc.). A growing amount of research suggests that companies with strong sustainability focus financially outperform comparable companies with poor sustainability performance (Eccles *et al.*, 2014; Deutsche Bank Group, 2012; Morgan Stanley Institute for Sustainable Investing, 2015; International Finance Corporation, 2020). Fulton *et al.* (2012) performed one of the most comprehensive literature reviews of the financial implications of sustainable strategies. They reviewed more than 100 academic studies, 56 research studies, 2 literature reviews, and 4 meta-analysis. They considered conjointly and separately overlapping sustainable finance terms such as CSR, SRI, and ESG. Their analysis exposed both higher accounting-based performance as well as higher market-based performance for sustainable strategies. "More recently, Whelan *et al.* (2021) reviewed more than 1,000 studies published between 2015–2020 which also found a positive relationship between sustainability and financial performance in most cases."

To fully understand the impact of investors' sustainable investment strategies on returns, it is critical to first understand the fundamental financial implications of companies' sustainability management, which illustrates superior management practices and tends to generate a competitive edge and improved financial performance (Adams, 2002; Orlitzky *et al.*, 2003). It is also important to realize that returns will depend on the asset class employed and the investment's level of risk. Yet, it has been demonstrated that strong sustainability management mitigates ESG risks (University of Oxford and Arabesque Partners, 2015).

However, not all the seven sustainable investment strategies listed in the inaugural 2012 GSIR share the same approach in tackling sustainability risks and opportunities, or the same impacts. The sustainable finance landscape includes various approaches, which emphasize different elements to produce various financial outcomes. ESG Integration demonstrates the strongest relationship with returns. Other strategies, mainly values-driven, do not necessarily translate into better financial performance; it will vary on a case-by-case basis. In the following paragraphs, we will discuss the relationship between returns and select sustainable strategies including ESG Integration, SRI strategies (including negative and norm-based screening as well as shareholder engagement), and Impact Investing. The other sustainable investment strategies will not be analyzed individually as little research has been focusing on their relationship with returns.

It is well accepted that sustainable finance can generate positive externalities (PRI, 2017; Schoenmaker, 2017; United Nations, 2016). In terms of impacts, every sustainable investment strategy can instill meaningful ethical changes and produce outsized environmental or social impacts. Yet, Impact Investing is the one which most closely focuses on establishing impact objectives and tracking their evolution. In addition, a key aspect of Impact Investing is the concept of "additionality", which refers to the duplicating effect produced by the investment which would not otherwise have taken place.

3. ESG Integration, Risks, and Returns

ESG approaches, which span from the risk management of Environmental, Social, and Governance factors to an opportunistic focus on their profitable areas, tend to be correlated with higher performance, as opposed to SRI approaches (Krosinsky *et al.*, 2012; Whelan *et al.* 2021). ESG integration can be considered to be the most pragmatic and least ideological strategy due to ESG factors' financially material impacts on companies (IMF, 2019).

ESG issues can also have material impact on firms' risk profiles (IMF, 2019). Failure to effectively manage ESG risks can lead to significant costs including fines. US banks have paid $100 billion in legal settlements for their governance failures during the 2008 financial crisis. The ten largest fines and settlements in corporate history exceed $45 billion. Global pharmaceutical firms incurred over $30 billion in fines since 1991 (University of Oxford and Arabesque Partners, 2015). Environmental incidents such as corporate liabilities related to asbestos, toxic spills in the mining industry, and chemical plant explosions can also cause dramatic costs that have led to large losses and bankruptcies (IMF, 2019). ESG-related costs and associated reputational damages can also impact a company's stock price. Following the Deepwater Horizon oil spill in the Gulf of Mexico in 2015, BP's share more than halved. Following the Brumadinho mine disaster in 2019, the Vale S.A. share price fell by close to a quarter. After being recognized as cheating on US air pollution tests for years, Volkswagen lost almost a quarter of its market value in 2015 (The Generation Foundation, UNEP FI and the PRI, 2019).

Climate change is another major ESG risk which may entail large losses for firms across sectors. It would also impact banks, insurers, financial institutions, and asset owners, amplifying systemic risks and threatening financial stability (IMF, 2019). Climate risk materializes in two main forms:

- **Physical risks** which involve damage to property, land, and infrastructure caused by severe weather, sea-level rise, fire, and other climate change-related events.
- **Transition risks** due to economic disruption during the adjustment to a lower-carbon economy that may arise from climate policy (e.g. carbon tax), technology, market sentiment changes as well as potential premature write-downs, devaluations, or conversion to liabilities of fossil fuel assets as per the stranded asset phenomenon (IMF, 2019).

Transition risks can be huge; in 2020, two major European oil companies, BP and Shell, wrote off around $40 billion in aggregate to account for stranded assets (Kusnetz, 2020). Of note, the Carbon Tracker Initiative highlighted that oil majors would need to cut the combined production by 35% from 2019 to 2040 to meet the greenhouse gas emission reduction targets set during the 2015 Paris Agreement (Carbon Tracker Initiative, 2019). In addition, the implementation of a carbon tax could deeply affect the profitability of the oil and gas sector.

The extent of ESG financial impacts is such that it has been demonstrated that it is part of investors' fiduciary duties to integrate ESG considerations in their investment decisions (The Generation Foundation, UNEP FI, and the PRI, 2019). The latter is the foundation of the European regulation on ESG disclosure (UNEP FI, 2019) which has been put in place to increase transparency and the availability of financially meaningful information, which is critical for market efficiency and for market participants to adequately price financial instruments. ESG issues can also have material impact on the stability of the financial system as a whole (IMF, 2019).

4. SRI and Returns

The link between the ideologically driven SRI (including negative and norm-based screening as well as shareholder engagement) aiming to do no harm or do good and financial performance is not as clear. Historically, there was a belief that there should be a trade-off between acting responsibly and acting profitably (Levitt, 1958; Friedman, 1970; Hylton, 1992). The noneconomic benefits derived from SRI could not possibly be cost-free in an efficient market, and ethical investors were expected to incur increased costs, higher nonsystematic risk, or lower returns. Only under the inefficient markets theory could SRI be cost-free and maximize returns (Hylton, 1992). The consequences of poor financial performance can be particularly challenging for financial institutions relying on their investments to pay for ongoing expenses such as pension funds providing resources for the elderly. Some opponents to SRI raised concerns that it could impair capital for retirement and affect Social Security while acknowledging that SRI does not present an issue for individual investors (Hylton, 1992).

5. Impact Investing and Returns

Research focusing on impact investing strategies have also demonstrated some positive financial outcomes. In the GIIN 2020 Annual Impact Investor Survey, the respondents report that "portfolio performance meets or exceeds investor expectations for both social and environmental impact and financial return, in investments spanning emerging markets, developed markets, and the market as a whole" (GIIN, 2020b).

In their 2017 research study "GIIN Perspectives: Evidence on the Financial Performance of Impact Investments", the GIIN took a closer look at the returns of the three most frequently used asset classes for impact investing by then: private equity, private debt, and real assets (Mudaliar and Bass, 2017). The analysis, which referred to the 2015 Wharton Social Impact Initiative study and a 2015 collaborative study performed by the GIIN and Cambridge Associates (one of the world's leading investment consultancies) indicated that "market-rate-seeking private equity impact investing funds can achieve returns comparable to conventional private equity funds".

In addition, a study performed in 2020 by the International Finance Corporation (IFC), (the private sector arm of the World Bank and one of the largest and longest-operating impact investors) revealed that since

1961 its impact portfolio (comprising venture capital and private equity investments), across 130 emerging markets and developing economies, outperformed the S&P 500 by 15% (Cole *et al.*, 2020). The research also indicates that "investments in larger economies have higher returns", while "returns decline as banking systems deepen and countries relax capital controls". These results show the imperfect integration of international capital markets, and "that some eligible markets do not receive sufficient investment capital".

The 2017 GIIN research also concluded that "private debt investments generally perform in line with expectations". The analysis also highlights that philanthropic organizations historically using unrecoverable grants may consider near-capital preservation strategy using high risk lending instead of grants as a funding approach enabling them to recycle their capital and by doing so increase their impact. As for real assets, which include timber, real estate, and infrastructure investment funds, the GIIN study concludes that returns of real assets investment funds employing impact-investing strategies are in line with conventional real assets funds.

6. Reflections

The relationship between sustainable finance risks and returns is not straightforward. Some economic fundamentals seem to suggest a negative correlation between sustainable finance and sustainability. Returns are determined by level of risks with higher risks commanding higher returns to compensate investors for the exposure to greater risk. Yet, many studies have evidenced that better sustainability management allows for better risk management (University of Oxford and Arabesque Partners, 2015). Does this imply that sustainable strategies should be remunerated at a lower rate, given the lower risk exposure?

Another factor driving returns is demand. Could the high demand for sustainable financial products lead to lower returns? This phenomenon, called "greenium", can already be observed in some green bonds whereby the coupon and yield are lower given the high demand from investors (Castelli, 2020; Climate Bonds Initiative, 2020; Lester, 2020; Harrison *et al.*, 2020). This may not be the most attractive strategy if an investor focuses solely on return. Yet, this will enable the issuing company to obtain cheaper debt than other counterparts, which could become a competitive advantage, translate into profitability, and increase the valuation of this company.

Conversely, divestment from heavy greenhouse gas producing companies should in theory enable greater returns for investors in these companies, while reducing companies' performance by increasing their cost of capital. These market imperfections may need to be addressed with policies such as carbon pricing or lower capital risk requirements for sustainable assets.

IX. Conclusion

Each year sustainable finance becomes more mainstream with a 13% CAGR over the 2012–2020 period globally and a growing demand coming from institutional and retail investors alike, such that it is now impossible to ignore. In some parts of the world such as Europe, ESG integration is no longer a voluntary initiative but driven by regulatory requirements. As of 2021, the UN-supported PRI signatories represented more than $120 trillion (PRI, 2021) with at least half employed for responsible investments, equivalent to half of the amount managed by the world's 500 largest asset managers (Willis Towers Watson and Pensions & Investments, 2020). According to the GSIR, $35 trillion of assets were employing sustainable strategies in 2020. As for the sustainable debt market, over $1 trillion had been issued as of 2019, including bonds and loans labeled either green, social, and sustainable or sustainability-linked (BNEF, 2019). In spite of the tremendous growth encountered in the sector, the amount invested in sustainable finance is still far from sufficient to achieve the UN SDGs or tackle the issues presented by climate change.

According to the 2018 report from the International Panel on Climate Change (IPCC), "limiting warming to 1.5°C requires a marked shift in investment patterns" both in terms of future allocation and reallocation of existing capital (De Coninck *et al.*, 2018). It would involve investing over $2.4 trillion (in 2010 dollars, excluding the impact of inflation) into the energy system annually until 2035. This is equivalent to 2.5% of the world's GDP and about 1.5% of the world's investment. Adding transportation and other infrastructure investments, the total annual incremental investments should be over 2.4% of total world investments. This implies that over $127 trillion should be invested until 2035, equal to about a third of the global financial capital. The needed capital is so colossal that it will be necessary to reallocate existing investments. Otherwise, it would have to be funded at the expense of lower consumption which could be an issue from a macro-economic perspective. But this amount should be put in perspective with the $792 trillion that could be lost if countries are not able to fulfill the greenhouse gas emission reduction targets set during the 2015 Paris Agreement (Wei *et al.*, 2020). (See Chapter 12 on Environmental Sustainability, the Energy Transition, and Climate Finance and Chapter 13 for further analysis on the Business and Financial Implications of Climate Change).

Yet, sustainable finance does not work in siloes and the systemic effects required to address global sustainability issues also depend on global political support, the social or cultural acceptability of the changes necessary, and economic considerations such as the costs involved and the capacity to mobilize investments for research and development (IPCC, 2018). ESG integration into companies' business models driven by either investors, regulators, or firms' own interest may help mitigate these risks (IMF, 2019). In addition, important challenges in sustainable finance will need to be addressed such as the lack of a shared language and rigor in the use of terminology as well as the risk of greenwashing (IMF, 2019). The availability and quality of comparable and relevant ESG data are also areas of improvement necessary to enable the further mainstreaming of sustainable finance. In addition, "failure to disclose the risks posed to business models and portfolios by climate change and other ESG risks" present important risks for investors. Policies and regulations like the Taxonomy and ESG disclosure requirement in Europe may contribute to tackle these challenges and support the sustainable growth of the sector (IMF, 2019). Moreover, the role of traditional finance instruments not necessarily labeled as sustainable but deploying capital to address or support sustainability-related topics (e.g. renewable energy financing, project finance, infrastructure capital market, etc.) should not be neglected as it is critical.

References

Accenture. (2012). "The greater wealth transfer: Capitalizing on the intergenerational shift in wealth", June 2012, p. 11.

Adams, C. A. (2002). "Internal organisational factors influencing corporate social and ethical reporting: Beyond current theorising", *Accounting, Auditing & Accountability Journal*, 15(2), pp. 223–250.

Alperson, M. (1991). "Council on economic priorities", *The Better World Investment Guide*. Prentice Hall, New York.

Bloomberg New Energy Finance (BNEF). (2019). "Sustainable debt joins the trillion-dollar club", Published on October 17, 2019, Consulted in December 2020, https://about.bnef.com/blog/sustainable-debt-joins-the-trillion-dollar-club/.

Bloomberg New Energy Finance (BNEF). (2022). "Energy transition investment trends 2022", Published on January 2022, Consulted in March 2022, https://assets.bbhub.io/professional/sites/24/Energy-Transition-Investment-Trends-Exec-Summary-2022.pdf.

Carbon Tracker Initiative. (2019) "The world's listed oil and gas majors must cut combined production by a third by 2040 to keep emissions within international climate targets and protect shareholder value, Carbon Tracker finds in a report today", Published on November 1, 2019, Consulted in December 2020, https://carbontracker.org/balancing-the-budget-press-release/.

Castelli, F. (2020). "Green bonds: ESG, sustainable or impact investments?" Published on December 11, 2020, Consulted in December 2020, https://www.cityam.com/green-bonds-esg-sustainable-or-impact-investments/.

Climate Bonds Initiative. (2020). "Green bond pricing report for Q3–Q4 2019: Spotlight on green sovereigns: Emerging Greenium: All in latest analysis of primary market performance", Published on March 31, 2020, Consulted in December 2020. https://www.climatebonds.net/2020/03/green-bond-pricing-report-q3-q4-2019-spotlight-green-sovereigns-emerging-greenium-all-latest.

Cole, S., Melecky, M., Mölders, F., and Reed, T. (2020). "Long-run returns to impact investing in emerging market and developing economies", World Bank Group Development Economics, Development Research Group Finance, Competitiveness and Innovation Global Practice & International Finance Corporation, August 2020. http://documents1.worldbank.org/curated/en/171981598466193496/pdf/Long-run-Returns-to-Impact-Investing-in-Emerging-Market-and-Developing-Economies.pdf.

De Coninck, H. *et al.* (2018). "Strengthening and implementing the global response supplementary material. In Global Warming of 1.5°C. An IPCC

Special Report on the impacts of global warming of 1.5°C above pre-industrial levels and related global greenhouse gas emission pathways, in the context of strengthening the global response to the threat of climate change", In Press, pp. 4SM: 1–82.

Deutsche Bank Group. (2012). "Sustainable investing: Establishing long-term value and performance", https://institutional.deutscheam.com/content/_media/Sustainable_Investing_2012.pdf.

Donovan, W. (2020). "The origins of socially responsible investing", The Balance Last update on April 23, 2020, Consulted in December 2020, https://www.thebalance.com/a-short-history-of-socially-responsible-investing-3025578.

Eccles, R., Ioannou, I., and Serafeim, G. (2014). "The impact of corporate sustainability on organizational processes and performance", *Management Science*, 60(11), pp. 2835–2857, https://doi.org/10.1287/mnsc.2014.

European Commission. (2020). "Taxonomy: Final report of the Technical Expert Group on Sustainable Finance", March 2020, https://ec.europa.eu/info/sites/info/files/business_economy_euro/banking_and_finance/documents/200309-sustainable-finance-teg-final-report-taxonomy_en.pdf.

European Parliament and the Council of the European Union. (2019). "Regulation (EU) 2019/2088 of the European Parliament and of the Council of 27 November 2019 on sustainability-related disclosures in the financial services sector", *Official Journal of the European Union*. https://eur-lex.europa.eu/legal-content/EN/TXT/?uri=celex%3A32019R2088.

European Sustainable Investment Forum (EUROSIF). (2016). "European SRI study 2016".

European Sustainable Investment Forum (EUROSIF). (2021). "EUROSIF report 2021: Fostering investor impact placing it at the heart of sustainable finance". https://www.forum-ng.org/de/neuigkeiten.

Finkelman, J., and Huntington, K. (2017). "Impact investing: History and opportunity", Athena Capital Advisor, January.

Friedman, M. (1970). "The social responsibility of business is to increase its profits", *The New York Times Magazine*, September 13.

Fulton, M., Kahn, B., and Sharples, C. (2012). *Sustainable Investing: Establishing Long-Term Value and Performance*, Deutsche Bank, SSRN. https://papers.ssrn.com/sol3/papers.cfm?abstract_id=2222740.

Generation Foundation, UNEP FI (United Nations Environment Programme Finance Initiative) and the PRI (Principles for Responsible Investment). (2019). "Fiduciary duty in the 21st century", https://www.unpri.org/download?ac=9792.

Gittell, R., Magnusson, M., and Merenda, M. (2013). *The Sustainable Business Case Book*, Published by Flat World Knowledge, Inc. 2013, https://saylordotorg.github.io/text_the-sustainable-business-case-book/s16-02-pax-world.html#:~:text=Pax%20World%20was%20founded%20in,not%20support%20the%20Vietnam%20War.

Global Impact Investing Network (GIIN). (2019). "Core characteristics of impact investing", Published in April 3, 2019, Consulted in December 2020, https://thegiin.org/assets/Core%20Characteristics_webfile.pdf.

Global Impact Investing Network (GIIN). (2020a). "Impact Investing: A guide to this dynamic market", Consulted in December 2020, https://thegiin.org/assets/documents/GIIN_impact_investing_guide.pdf.

Global Impact Investing Network (GIIN). (2020b). "2020 annual impact investor survey", The Global Impact Investing Network (GIIN), https://thegiin.org/assets/GIIN%20Annual%20Impact%20Investor%20Survey%202020%20Executive%20Summary.pdf.

Global Sustainable Investment Alliance (GSIA). (2013). "2012 global sustainable investment review". http://gsiareview2012.gsi-alliance.org/pubData/source/Global%20Sustainable%20Investement%20Alliance.pdf.

Global Sustainable Investment Alliance (GSIA). (2015). "2014 Global Sustainable Investment Review". https://www.gsi-alliance.org/members-resources/global-sustainable-investment-review-2014/.

Global Sustainable Investment Alliance (GSIA). (2017). "2016 global sustainable investment review". http://www.gsi-alliance.org/wp-content/uploads/2017/03/GSIR_Review2016.F.pdf.

Global Sustainable Investment Alliance (GSIA). (2019). "2018 global sustainable investment review". http://www.gsi-alliance.org/wp-content/uploads/2019/03/GSIR_Review2018.3.28.pdf.

Global Sustainable Investment Alliance (GSIA). (2021). "2020 global sustainable investment review". https://www.gsi-alliance.org/wp-content/uploads/2021/08/GSIR-20201.pdf.

Harrison, C., Partridge, C., and Tripathy A. (2020). "What's in a Greenium: An analysis of pricing methodologies and discourse in the green bond market", *The Journal of Environmental Investing*, 10(1), http://www.thejei.com/journal/. Accessed September 2, 2020.

Hylton, M. O. B. (1992). "Socially responsible investing: Doing good versus doing well in an inefficient market", *American University Law Review*, 42(1), pp. 1–52.

ImpactAlpha. (2017). "What we know about Bain Capital's $390 million Double Impact Fund", Published on July 19, 2017, Consulted in December 2020, https://impactalpha.com/what-we-know-about-bain-capitals-390-million-double-impact-fund-8dd4e0c90571/.

International Monetary Fund (IMF). (2014). "Global financial stability report", Chapter 3. Washington: IMF.

International Monetary Fund (IMF). (2019). "Global financial stability report", Chapter 6. Sustainable Finance. Washington: IMF.

International Panel on Climate Change (IPCC). (2018). "Global warming of 1.5°C." 2018. An IPCC Special Report on the impacts of global warming of 1.5°C above pre-industrial levels and related global greenhouse gas emission pathways, in the context of strengthening the global response to the threat of climate change, sustainable development, and efforts to eradicate poverty. In V. Masson-Delmotte, P. Zhai, H.-O. Pörtner, D. Roberts, J. Skea, P. R. Shukla, A. Pirani, W. Moufouma-Okia, C. Péan, R. Pidcock, S. Connors, J. B. R. Matthews, Y. Chen, X. Zhou, M. I. Gomis, E. Lonnoy, T. Maycock, M. Tignor and T. Waterfield (eds.), *Global Warming of 1.5°C: IPCC Special Report on Impacts of Global Warming of 1.5°C above Pre-industrial Levels in Context of Strengthening Response to Climate Change, Sustainable Development, and Efforts to Eradicate Poverty.* Chapter 1, p. 72, Chapter 4, pp. 373–374. Cambridge: Cambridge University Press. https://dlib.hust.edu.vn/handle/HUST/21737.

IPE Staff. (2017). "Top 400 asset managers 2017: A new, improved business?" Intelligence on European Pensions and Institutional Investment (IPE) website, Published in June, 2017, https://www.ipe.com/top-400/top-400-asset-managers-2017-blackrock-dominates-inflows/10019355.article. Accessed December, 2018.

Kreutzer, L. (2020). "Bain capital raises $800 million for second impact investing fund", *Wall Street Journal*. Updated last on November 22, 2020, https://www.wsj.com/articles/bain-capital-raises-800-million-for-second-impact-investing-fund-11606053601. Accessed December 2020.

Krosinsky, C., Robins, N., and Viederman S. (2012). "Evolutions in sustainable investing: Strategies, funds and thought leadership". New York: Wiley.

Krosinsky, C., and Purdom, S. (2016). *Sustainable Investing Revolutions in Theory and Practice.* Milton Park: Routledge.

Kusnetz, N. (2020). "BP and Shell write-off billions in assets, citing COVID-19 and climate change", Inside Climate News, Published on July 2, 2020, https://insideclimatenews.org/news/02072020/bp-shell-coronavirus-climate-change. Accessed December, 2020.

Lester, A. (2020). "Growing evidence of greenium for green bonds, says CBI", Published on April 3, 2020, https://www.environmental-finance.com/

content/news/growing-evidence-of-greenium-for-green-bonds-says-cbi. html. Accessed December, 2020.

Levitt, T. (September–October 1958). "The danger of social responsibility", *Harvard Business Review*, 36, pp. 41–50.

Loizos, C. (2016). "TPG is raising 2 billion for a social impact fund called rise", *Techcrunch* website, Published in 2016, https://techcrunch.com/2016/12/ 20/tpg-is-raising-2-billion-for-a-social-impact-fund-called-rise/. Accessed December, 2018.

Morgan Stanley Institute for Sustainable Investing. (March 2015). "Sustainable reality: Understanding the performance of sustainable investment strategies". https://www.sustainablefinance.ch/upload/cms/user/2016_06_30_sustain-ableInvestment_Performance.pdf

Morgan Stanley Institute for Sustainable Investing. (2017). "Millennials drive growth in sustainable investing", Published on August, 9, 2017, Accessed December, 2018, https://www.morganstanley.com/ideas/sustainable-socially-responsible-investing-millennials-drive-growth.

Morgan Stanley Institute for Sustainable Investing. (2019). "Sustainable signals: Individual investor interest driven by impact, conviction and choice".

Mudaliar, A., and Bass, R. (2017). "GIIN Perspectives: Evidence on the Financial Performance of Impact Investments", The Global Impact Investing Network (GIIN), Published in November 14, 2017, Consulted in December 2020.

Orlitzky, M., Schmidt, F. L., and Rynes, S. L. (2003). "Corporate social and financial performance: A meta-analysis", *Organization Studies*, 24(3), pp. 403–411.

Preqin. (2020a). "Preqin impact report: The rise of ESG in alternative assets", Published on November 16, 2020, Accessed in December, 2020.

Preqin. (2020b). "The rise of ESG in alternative assets", https://www.preqin.com/ esg/rise-of-esg#1289. Accessed December, 2020.

Principles for Responsible Investment (PRI). (2022) "2021 Annual report". https://www.unpri.org/annual-report-2021.

Rajan, R. (2010). "How inequality fueled the crisis", Project syndicate, Published July 9, 2010, Accessed in December, 2020, https://www.project-syndicate. org/commentary/how-inequality-fueled-the-crisis?barrier=accesspaylog.

Sandberg, J., Juravle, C., Hedesström, T. M., and Hamilton, I. (2009). "The heterogeneity of socially responsible investment", *Journal of Business Ethics*, 87(4), pp. 519–533.

Schoenmaker, D. (2017). *Investing for the Common Good: A Sustainable Finance Framework*, Bruegel Essay and Lecture Series, Brussels. https://core.ac.uk/ download/pdf/91633968.pdf.

Sustainable Accounting Standards Boards (c). (2017). "SASB Conceptual Framework", Published February 2017, Accessed December 2020. http://www.sasb.org/wp-content/uploads/2019/05/SASB-Conceptual-Framework.pdf?source=post_page.

Townsend, B. (2020). "From SRI to ESG: The origins of socially responsible and sustainable investing", *The Journal of ESG & Impact Investing*, 1(1). https://www.bailard.com/wp-content/uploads/2020/09/History-Socially-Responsible-Investing-and-ESG-Investing.pdf.

United Nations. (2015). "70/1. Transforming our world: The 2030 agenda for sustainable development", Resolution adopted by the general assembly on September 25, 2015, https://www.un.org/ga/search/view_doc.asp?symbol=A/RES/70/1&Lang=E.

United Nations. (2016). "The sustainable development goals report", New York.

United Nations. (2023). "United Nations Treaty Collection". Chapter XXVII Environment. 7. d Paris Agreement. https://treaties.un.org/Pages/ViewDetails.aspx?src=TREATY&mtdsg_no=XXVII-7-d&chapter=27&clang=_en.

United Nations Climate Change. "Key aspects of the Paris agreement", https://cop23.unfccc.int/most-requested/key-aspects-of-the-paris-agreement. Accessed February 2023.

United Nations Global Compact, UNEP Finance Initiative, the Principles for Responsible Investment Initiative and UNEP Inquiry. (2015). "Fiduciary duty in the 21st century", https://www.unpri.org/download?ac=1378.

UNEP FI. (2019) "EU policy makers achieve political agreement on investor disclosures and ESG", Published on March 7, 2019, Accessed December 2020.

UNEP FI. UN Environmental Program FI Website. https://www.unepfi.org/news/timeline/.

UNEP Inquiry into the Design of a Sustainable Financial System. (2015). https://wedocs.unep.org/bitstream/handle/20.500.11822/9862/-The_Financial_System_We_Need_Aligning_the_Financial_System_with_Sustainable_Development-2015The_Financial_System_We_Need_EN.pdf.pdf.

United Nations Framework Convention on Climate Change. (UNFCCC). "What is the Paris agreement?" Consulted in December 2020, https://unfccc.int/process-and-meetings/the-paris-agreement/what-is-the-paris-agreement.

University of Oxford and Arabesque Partners. (March 2015). "From the stockholder to the stakeholder: How sustainability can drive financial outperformance", https://arabesque.com/research/From_the_stockholder_to_the_stakeholder_web.pdf.

Whelan, T., Atz, U., Van Holt, T., and Clark, C. (2021). "ESG and financial performance: Uncovering the relationship by aggregating evidence from 1,000 plus studies published between 2015–2020". New York: NYU Stern Center for sustainable business.

Wei, Y. M. *et al.* (2020). "Self-preservation strategy for approaching global warming targets in the post-Paris Agreement era", *Nature Communication*, 11, p. 1624, 2020.

Willis Towers Watson and Pensions & Investments. (October 2020). "The world's largest 500 asset managers", https://www.thinkingaheadinstitute.org/research-papers/the-worlds-largest-asset-managers-2020/.

Zaouati, P. (2009). "Investir « responsable ». En quête de nouvelles valeurs pour la finance. » Paris. Ed. Lignes de Repères.

https://doi.org/10.1142/9789811240928_0009

Chapter 9

Building a Sustainable Portfolio

Diane-Charlotte Simon

Learning Objectives

- Learn about the main asset classes and their characteristics (stocks, bonds, loans, etc.)
- Understand that sustainable strategies can be employed in most asset classes
- Discover green, social, and sustainable debt instruments (bonds and loans)
- Understand sustainability-linked debt instruments (bonds and loans)
- Learn how to build a sustainable portfolio

Abstract

This chapter complements the previous chapter on sustainable finance and investing, by looking in more detail at a range of implementation strategies across the main financial instruments. The chapter begins with an introduction to the main asset classes present in the financial market (bonds, loans, equity, mutual funds, and exchange-traded-funds

(ETFs)). The chapter distinguishes between debt and equity instruments. Since their creation in 2007, more than $4 trillion of sustainable debt instruments have been issued. This estimate does not capture several sustainability-related areas that are not specifically classified as sustainable such as renewable energy financing, project finance, capital markets for infrastructure, etc. The chapter highlights the fact that it is now possible to employ investing strategies considering sustainability across nearly all financial products, which in turn makes it possible to build a sustainable portfolio. The chapter also introduces the popular Green, Social, and Sustainable bonds, and loans (sustainable debt with the *Use-of-Proceeds* approach) as well as the Sustainability-linked debt instruments (sustainable debt with the *Objectives* approach). Portfolios can be built either by investors themselves, or with the support of financial advisors. Investors can also purchase diversified pre-built portfolios like ETFs or mutual funds following sustainable investment strategies. However, while the proportion of sustainable products has dramatically increased, it still does not represent most financial assets. Strikingly, in certain regions such as Europe, considering sustainability risks is now mandatory for all financial products. The chapter concludes with an example of a climate change portfolio.

I. Introduction

In their early days, sustainable investment strategies like Socially Responsible Investment (SRI) were only applied to equities. Nowadays they can be applied to virtually all asset classes existing in the financial markets. First, this chapter introduces readers to the main asset classes (stocks, bonds, loans, etc.).

Second, it examines the application of sustainable investment strategies to each of these assets. While some strategies are more appropriate for certain asset classes, most can be applied to them all. The chapter follows with a presentation of the two types of sustainable debt instruments (bonds and loans) which have become very popular. The first follows *a Use-of-Proceeds* approach which can be applied for green, social, and sustainable purposes (i.e. Green, Social, and Sustainable bonds and loans). The second follows an *Objectives* approach whereby the pricing of the instrument is linked to the achievement of sustainability objectives (i.e. Sustainability-linked debt instruments).

Third, the chapter discusses how to build a sustainable investment portfolio and the elements to pay attention to in the process, including diversification and risk and return. The chapter touches on diversified products such as mutual funds, or Exchange Traded Funds (ETFs), employing sustainability strategies. It concludes by presenting an example of a portfolio built to address climate change.

Chapter 9 is organized as per the following sections:

I. Introduction
II. Sustainable Strategies Applied to an Investment Portfolio
III. Introduction to Asset Classes
IV. How to Build a Sustainable Investment Portfolio
V. Climate Change Portfolio Case Study
VI. Conclusion

II. Sustainable Strategies Applied to an Investment Portfolio

Sustainable strategies can be implemented in an overall investment portfolio. Sustainable investment strategies can be applied to most asset classes and financial instruments from debt instruments to equities and from the most standard products (bonds, stocks, indexes, etc.) to more sophisticated ones (venture capital, private equity, money market instruments, derivatives, etc.). They can also be used to finance companies at different stages of their life cycle: from startups (venture capital) to billion-dollar multinational companies (stocks and bonds). In addition, they can be applied to both primary markets (Initial Public Offerings (IPOs,) bond issuances, etc.) and secondary markets (trading of bonds and stocks, etc.).

We will dedicate the following paragraphs to discussing these different asset classes and how sustainable investment strategies can be applied to them (see Table 9.1).

Table 9.1.   Sustainable Products across Asset Classes

Asset Class	Breakdown	Examples
Equities	Company stocks	ESG can be adopted in traditional equities through a number of strategies. The most prominent has been negative (exclusionary) screening over the years, but it has moved to others such as engagement and positive (best-in-class) screening.
Debt Fixed Income	Traditional corporate bonds	Incorporating material ESG criteria into corporate credit analysis to better identify credit risk.
	Traditional sovereign bonds	Integrating ESG factors, together with traditional analysis that focuses on financial and macro-economic variables, to identify sovereign credit risks. PIMCO has adopted this approach since 2011 in its sovereign ratings model.
	ESG money market funds	Applying ESG factors to the investment of money market instruments. BlackRock, for example, launched an environmentally focused money market fund in April 2019.
	Green bonds	Specific bonds that are labeled green, with proceeds used for funding new and existing projects with environmental benefits.
	Social bonds	Bonds that raise funds for new and existing projects that create positive social outcomes.
	Sustainability bonds	Bonds with proceeds that are used to finance or refinance a combination of green and social projects.
	Sustainability-linked bonds	Bonds that incentivize the borrower to meet predetermined sustainability performance goals.
	Green mortgage-backed securities (MBS)	Green MBS securitize numerous mortgages that go toward financing green properties, in the case of Fannie Mae, which is the largest issuer of green MBS.
Debt Bank Loans	Green loans	Loans that have proceeds used to finance or refinance green projects, including other related and supporting expenditures such as R&D. Their size is 70–80% smaller than green bonds, but they have grown fast in 2018–19.
	Sustainability-linked loans	Loan instruments and/or contingent facilities such as guarantees or letters of credit that incentivize the borrower to meet predetermined sustainability performance goals.
Alternative Investment	Green real estate investment trusts (REIT), Private equity (PE), and venture capital (VC)	REITs with a portfolio exposure to properties that are environmentally certified. Private funds that, for example, back startups in areas such as energy, mobility, and buildings.

Source: Based on IMF (2019).

III. Introduction to Asset Classes

An organization can finance itself using either debt (e.g. loans or bonds) or equity instruments. Globally, loans make up approximately 55% of the new capital issued per year to finance organizations, while bonds represent 35% and equity 10% (IMF, 2019). The global $386 trillion of financial capital mainly comprises loans managed by banking institutions at 58% (IIF, 2017; World Bank, 2018a), bonds representing approximately 26% (SIFMA, 2017), while the remaining 16% share is made of equity (World Bank, 2018b). Each financial instrument has specificities which will be further discussed in dedicated sections following these high-level considerations. Unlike a debt provider, an equity investor has an ownership stake in a company to which she provides capital. The other fundamental differences between debt and equity instruments lie in their predictability and their priority in the order of payment, which impacts their respective risks and returns.

The balance sheet, which reflects an organization's financial condition at a point in time by listing all its assets and liabilities, also reveals an organization's capital structure by describing how it is being financed, with a mix of debt and equity. In the balance sheet, assets and liabilities (including debt) are ranked according to their level of liquidity, which represents the ease with which they can be converted to cash. Under the Generally Accepted Accounting Principles (GAAP) accounting framework used in the United States, the balance sheet lists the items starting with the most liquid (current assets and current liabilities). By contrast, under the International Financial Reporting Standards (IFRS) accounting framework, starts with the most illiquid (non-current assets, non-current liabilities, and shareholder's equity). Debt instruments can be converted to cash more easily than equity and hence are more liquid. If a company cannot meet its financial obligations by paying its debt and related costs on time, it might go into bankruptcy proceedings and need to be liquidated. The debt holders will be paid prior to the equity owners (shareholders) with the selloff of the company assets. For this reason, equity instruments are considered riskier and remunerated to an investor at a higher price than debt instruments, as per the relationship between risk and return. For debt instruments, the interest rate or coupon rate for bonds is priced based on the perceived risk as a premium on top of a benchmark considered to be risk-free (i.e. interbank exchange rate for bank and sovereign debt for bonds). Equities are priced following the Capital Asset Pricing Model (CAPM) approach.

In the next paragraphs, we will introduce debt and equity instruments and describe how sustainable strategies can be employed for each asset class. Other asset classes not discussed in this chapter include currencies, commodities, and derivatives.

1. Debt Instruments

Loans and bonds are the two main types of debt instruments. They are characterized by three elements:

- the **principal**, which is the borrowed amount by a debtor (entity borrowing the principal) from a creditor (institution providing the principal);
- the **interest rate**, which is the agreed remuneration for this borrowing that can be either fixed or variable;
- the **maturity date**, the date when the principal and any accrued interest must be paid back to the creditor by the debtor.

When one thinks about debt, the first idea that comes to mind refers to bank financing which is the historical way organizations have been financed. *Loans* are debt instruments financed by banks. But banks are not the only providers of debt. Institutional investors and retail investors can provide debt. In this case, the debt instrument will be called *bonds* and is also referred to as the main fixed income security.

In the case of a bank financing, the debtor will be referred to as a borrower and the creditors will comprise a group of banks most of the time. Banks finance a large amount of corporate debt in the world with their own balance sheet thanks to their retail customers' deposits. The interest rate will be variable and based on benchmarks such as the London Interbank Offered Rate (LIBOR), which has been the historical global benchmark since its creation in the mid-1980s. The interest rate consists in a premium applied on the benchmark based on the perceived risk of the borrower and maturity of the loan. The LIBOR represents the average cost used by banks to borrow from each other in the short term and is calculated daily by the Intercontinental Exchange (ICE). Following the LIBOR scandal involving the rigged lowering of the rate during the global financial crisis, the LIBOR was schedule to be phased out by the end of 2021 (Vaughan and Finch, 2017). The global markets are in the process of switching to other benchmarks. The Secured Overnight Financing Rate (SOFR) will become the new standard in the United States, and for dollar denominated loans. The Euro Short-Term Rate (STR) will become the new benchmark in Europe. SONIA will become the new standard in in the United Kingdom while it will be TONAR in Japan.

Over time, the role of banks has shifted from a lending business, which leverages its balance sheet, to a financial intermediary model, where hereby it connects companies to investors through the capital markets. This trend is particularly noticeable in the United States. The corporate lending business is still very important for European and Asian banks. The prevailing role of banks in financing the global economy has been decreasing since the global financial crisis, when banks were financing 80% of corporate debt as of 2008. As of 2017, banks still financed around 60% of the debt to non-financial institutions globally (Bank for International Settlements (BIS), 2019). The remaining 40% of the debt to non-financial institutions was financed by corporate bonds issued in the capital markets. Most of these bonds are publicly traded, but a smaller and a growing part is privately placed (BIS, 2019).

In the case of a bond issuance, the debtor will be referred to as an issuer. The creditors will be institutional investors. And the interest rate will be called the "coupon" and will be most likely fixed at issuance based on a benchmark plus a premium to account for the credit risk of the organization and the maturity of the bond. The United States Treasuries bonds are one of the most traded securities in the world. Their trading levels provide the reference for the pricing of US dollars bonds which represent over 40% of the total bond market (ICMA, 2020a). In some instances, bonds can also be using floating rates and use a benchmark like the LIBOR or can be inflation-indexed.

The bond market has been significantly growing over the past two decades and has benefited from the declining credits of banks to corporations. As of August 2020, the global bond market represented $128 trillion, of which 68% was issued by Sovereigns, Supranationals, and Agencies (SSA) at $88 trillion, and the remaining 32% was issued by corporations at $41 trillion (ICMA, 2020b). Out of the outstanding SSA bonds, $22 trillion is from entities located in the United States, $20 trillion, from China, $12 trillion, from Japan, and $12 trillion, from Europe. It is worth noting that outstanding US treasuries represented about 23% of the global bond market at $21 trillion. US treasuries maturities ranged from less than a year to perpetual. 70% was less than 5 years while 10% was for over 15 years. As per the corporate bonds, the United States and China made up 45% of the global market, representing $11 trillion and $7 trillion, respectively. More than half of the outstanding corporate bonds were issued by financial institutions (ICMA, 2020b). While maturities of 5-years and less represent 40% of the market, the US corporate bond market can also accommodate very long maturities with approximatively 23% of the market having maturities over 15 years.

2. Sustainable Approaches to Debt Instruments

As of the end of 2021, in excess of $4 trillion had been issued in labeled sustainable debt ("Green", "social", or "sustainable" or sustainability linked) since the first issuance in the late 2000s (BNEF, 2022a). In 2021, which was a record year, $1.6 trillion were issued in sustainable labeled debt vs. $763 billion in 2020 (BNEF, 2022a). In a little more than a decade, the sustainable debt market has hit the threshold of $1 trillion of total issuance in 2019 considering only green, social, or sustainable bonds and loans, as well as sustainability-linked bonds and loans (BNEF, 2019). This landmark milestone was announced at the International Finance Corporation (IFC), the World Bank's private sector arm that issued the first green bond in 2008. Since then, the World Bank has become one of the most frequent issuers of green bonds with over $18 billion issued through more than 115 projects in 21 currencies (World Bank, 2022). The proportion of sustainable debt issuances relative to the total volume of loans and bonds issued has significantly increased year-over-year, especially in Europe where it represents more than 20% of annual volume while it is less than 10% in the US. But, despite the tremendous growth encountered since the first green bond, sustainable bonds issued to-date still represent only about 5% of the total bonds outstanding globally (Climate Bonds Initiative, 2020).

Both bonds and loans can employ sustainable strategies. The sustainable debt market comprises two main types of approaches:

- *Use-of-Proceeds*: This approach consists in the application of funds to finance or re-finance, in part or in full, new and/or existing projects producing environmental benefits (i.e. Green Bonds and Green Loans), social benefits (i.e. Social Bonds or Social Loans), or a combination of both (i.e. Sustainable bonds). Among the different strategies described in Chapter 8, green, social, or sustainable debt instruments follow most closely the Sustainably-themed Investing strategy, while in practice this link is seldom made explicitly (Castelli, 2020).
- *Objectives*: In this case, the characteristics of the instrument, such as the coupon for bonds or the interest rate for loans, will vary depending on whether the issuer or the borrower achieves predefined Sustainability or ESG Key Performance Indicators (KPIs) (i.e. Sustainability-linked Bonds or Loans). Similarly to the approach above, while in practice the link to the strategies described in Chapter 8 is seldom made explicitly, Sustainability-linked Bonds and Loans follow most closely the ESG integration strategy.

Green bonds, which were the first labeled sustainable debt instruments, represent over 45% of the total sustainable debt market volume to date with in excess of $1.6 trillion issued as of 2021 (see Figure 9.1). They focus on the allocation of capital to projects with environmental benefits. The investors' demand for green bonds is such that discount in pricing called "greenium" is starting to be observed in public markets enabling issuers to get debt at cheaper price than traditional bonds (Climate Bond Initiative, 2020; Citi A.M., 2020). Green loans are their equivalent but using a loan instrument instead of a bond. Boosted during the COVID-19 pandemic, social bonds, which aim at producing positive social outcomes, and sustainability bonds, which target a combination of environmental and social benefits, represent, respectively, 10% and 11% of the

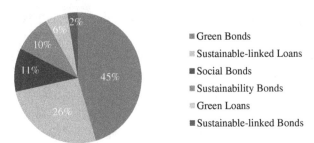

Figure 9.1. The Sustainable Debt Market Issuance Volume Over the 2008–2021 Period (in %)

Source: Author calculation based on Bloomberg and Refinitiv data.

sustainable debt market. It is worth noting that after a boost during the pandemic, the social bond market has been down.

To be labeled as green, social, or sustainable, use-of-proceeds sustainable bonds need to be aligned with the four core components of the International Capital Market Association (ICMA)'s Green Bonds Principles (GBP) and the Social Bonds Principles (SBP), which also apply to sustainability bonds. These four components are as follows:

1. **Use of Proceeds**: The first component ("Use of Proceeds") involves the application of the bond proceeds to eligible projects as per the guidelines included in the GBP for green bonds, the SBP Principles for social bonds, and the Sustainability Bond Guidelines for sustainable bonds (see Table 9.2). Eligible social projects intend to address or mitigate a specific social issue particularly for the benefits of target populations but not exclusively. Target populations include individuals living below the poverty line, excluded, marginalized and underserved communities, victims of natural disasters, people with disabilities, migrants and/or displaced persons, and undereducated and unemployed individuals (see Table 9.2).

2. **Process for Project Evaluation and Selection**: The second component ("Process for Project Evaluation and Selection") requires issuers of these instruments to clearly communicate to investors on the process to evaluate and select eligible projects.

3. **Management of Proceeds**: The third component ("Management of Proceeds") focuses on the management of the proceeds and making

Table 9.2. Eligible Projects and Categories, and Examples of Applications under the Green, Social, and Sustainable Bond ICMA Frameworks

Sustainable Bonds	
Green Bonds	Social Bonds
Renewable Energy	**Affordable Basic Infrastructure**
Energy generation and transmission	Drinking water, sewers, sanitation, transport, energy
Clean Transportation	**Access to Essential Services**
Electric, hybrid, public, rail, and related infrastructure	Health, education, training, and financial services
Energy Efficiency	**Affordable Housing**
New and refurbished buildings, energy storage, district heating, smart grids, energy efficient products	Social housing, low rent housing,
Circular Economy	**Job Creation**
Eco-efficient products and processes	SMEs financing and microfinance
Pollution Prevention and Control	**Food**
Reduction of air emissions, greenhouse gas control, soil remediation, waste prevention/reduction/recycling	Access to food, food security, medical nutrition
Natural Resources and Land	**Socioeconomic Advancement and Empowerment**
Sustainable management of agricole culture, fishery, forestry	Development of farms in developing countries, SME financing in rural areas and developing countries, progress toward gender equality
Water	
Infrastructure for clean and/or drinking water, wastewater treatment, drainage systems, flooding mitigation	
Climate Change Adaptation	
IT climate observation and early warning systems	
Biodiversity Conservation	
Protection of terrestrial and aquatic environments and life	
Green Buildings	
Buildings meeting recognized standards or certifications.	

Source: Based on (ICMA).

sure that the capital raised is effectively applied to eligible projects and managed in a manner that allows them to be tracked and distinguish from other purposes.

4. **Reporting**: The fourth component ("Reporting") requires issuers to publish an annual report on the allocation of the proceeds until they are fully deployed.

In addition, green, social, or sustainable bonds need to be certified by the third-party institutions, which are either rating agencies or consultants which are going to assess the ESG performance of those bonds and provide a rating, based on the quality of the impact.

Similar guidelines also exist for the loan market with respect to green loans with the Green Loan Principles (GLP) and social loans with the Social Loan Principles (SLP). These guidelines were established by global loan market trade associations: the Loan Market Association (LMA), Loan Syndications & Trading Association (LSTA), and Asia Pacific Loan Market Association (APLMA).

Sustainability-linked bonds and loans, which began to be issued more recently in 2019, take a different approach from Use-of-Proceeds sustainable debt instruments. In those instances, the price (i.e. the coupon or interest rate) paid by companies to investors or banks is linked to the sustainability performance of the company (ESG criteria). The better the performance, the lower the price of the financing. This mechanism is revolutionary as it internalizes some of the positive externalities discussed in the chapter on environmental economics (see Chapter 14) and incentivizes companies to improve their sustainable performance. In addition, sustainability-linked instruments can be used toward a broader scope of issuers across more sectors than Use-of-Proceeds instruments, and as such provide more diversification for investors. In addition, they are particularly relevant for hard-to-abate sectors and can help them improve their sustainability performance. On the structuring front, it is important to select material KPIs and ambitious targets for the company or sovereign issuing a sustainability-linked bond or loan. Moreover, the past performance on the KPIs as well as the performance of other companies in the same sector and region should be taken into account when determining the KPIs and targets. The ICMA website includes a useful registry of the main

KPIs by sector which are classified as "core" and "secondary". It is also worth noting that several KPIs can be chosen for an issuance. ICMA has also published the Sustainability-Linked Bond Principles (SLBP); the Sustainability-Linked Loan Principles (SLLP) is their loan market equivalent. As of the end of 2021, sustainability-linked loans were the second largest labeled sustainable debt, representing a fourth of the total market with close to $1 trillion issued (see Figure 9.1). Sustainability-linked bonds, which have been introduced more recently, represent less than 2% of the issuance volume over the 2008–2021 period (see Figure 9.1).

Getting back to the strategies presented in Chapter 8, sustainability-themed is the most commonly used strategy for debt instruments with green, social, or sustainable bonds and loans. Yet, ESG integration can also be employed to debt instruments beyond the objectives-driven sustainability-linked bonds and loans. ESG integration in fixed income is actually becoming mainstream as illustrated by the fact that credit agencies, such as Standard & Poor, Moody's, Fitch and Kroll, developed their ESG methodologies in 2019 and 2020 to integrate these criteria in the overall credit process for any debt instruments (not only sustainably labeled). The ESG analysis is considered in the attribution of credit ratings and monitored over time. Impact-investing strategies can also be employed in debt markets and mainly focused on private markets not necessarily labeled as green, social, or sustainable. Impact investments are often made in private companies. In financial brochures of financial advisors, it is common to see green bonds or social bonds listed as employing an impact investing strategy. But purists will argue that an impact strategy excludes secondary markets and is limited to primary markets whereby the funds are directly employed by the company for the qualified projects. In most cases these primary green bonds issuances will not be accessible to retail individual investors and are limited to large institutional investors.

Commercial Papers (CPs) are another type of debt which recently began employing sustainable strategies. CPs are money-market instruments which provide short duration debt (less than a year). After having issued the world's first green corporate bond in 2013, Vasakronan, Sweden's largest property company, issued the world's first green commercial paper in 2018 (Vasakronan, 2018). Since 2018, a few green CPs have been issued on the back of assets falling under the green bond principles including green real estate (Vasakronan, 2018), solar assets, portfolios of loans, and leases for electric vehicles as well as trade receivables for companies in the sectors of renewable energy, energy efficiency, clean mobility, and waste and water management. This asset class is expected to grow as it taps short-term financing needs which were not offering sustainable strategies until then.

It is worth noting that the sustainable finance debt market often does not account for the unlabeled financing of pure-play sustainable companies or projects (e.g. renewable energy sector) while some could argue that they should as it contributes to tackling some sustainability issues. As a reference, between 2010 and 2019 $200 billion of loans were used to finance renewable projects on a secured non-recourse basis (project finance) while $65 billion were issued in the project bond market (IJGlobal, 2020).

3. Equity

In parallel to debt instruments discussed above, companies can also be funded with equity. Although equity represents only about 10% of the new capital issued per year to finance organizations globally (IMF, 2019), it represents a greater proportion than bonds in the capital market. This is explained by the fact that shares' valuation evolves over time driven by company performance, the macro environment, and the secondary buyers' prices while not impacting the amount of proceeds received by the issuing company. In 2017, the median equity market capitalization represented approximately 120% of GDP in advanced economies, while the median debt capital market stood at approximately 90% of GDP (BIS, 2019). This proportion is also true in emerging countries where the capital markets are smaller. For instance, the median equity market capitalization represented approximately 60% of GDP in emerging countries that same year, while the median debt capital market represented approximately 30% of GDP.

Throughout its life cycle a company will use different financial instruments. In the early stages, start-ups at the ideation stage are typically financed either by grants, and/or by what is called "family money", which, as its names suggests, is money coming from those close to the company's founders. The period between the product development stage during which a company has no product/service ready to be sold and until a company has customers and generates revenues is a very challenging time to find capital. This phase is typically called the "Valley of Death". Traditional financial institutions such as banks typically do not finance early-stage companies, given the high risk of default. One out of ten companies will survive the first few years.

Historically, wealthy individuals have been the ones financing new ventures thanks to their financial strength and ability to take on higher levels of risks for a portion of their overall estate. They still do today. Since World War II, venture capital organizations have been institutionalizing the process and nowadays play a critical role in the financing of early-stage companies. Many early-stage investors invest either in "pure equity" or in debt instruments convertible to equity given the challenges that paying back debt can represent for organizations not generating revenues or with little predictability. Sometimes companies only pay interest on their debt before paying back the principal amount. Yet, giving away equity for a company is strategic, considering it is giving away pieces of its ownership, and that shareholders have a say in the company's strategy. Equity investors expect higher returns than debt investors provided their increased exposure to the risk of losing their investment. As a rule of thumb, the earlier the stage of the company, the higher the expected returns. Venture capital investors will typically expect to be paid back 10 times the amount they invested ("10× returns"). The realization of their investment will typically occur if the company goes public through public offerings (IPOs) or is being acquired by a larger organization.

As a company grows and generates more revenues, it gets easier to find capital, but as mentioned earlier, the early stages are challenging. As the company gets profitable, it will have more funding (term usually used for equity fund raising) and financing (term usually used for debt instruments) options. The company will be able to find cheaper sources of capital as it gets more financially stable. Bank financing will become more accessible. Similarly, debt capital market options (bonds) will get easier and cheaper as the creditworthiness of the company improves, enabling obtaining an investment grade rating by credit rating agencies. As for equity, funding could come from Private Equity firms or through equity (IPOs). After their issuance, the stocks can be sold on the secondary market to other buyers. During that transfer no direct impact will be incurred by the company. After having gone public, a company will be able to issue additional shares — these issuances are sometimes called seasoned issuances.

The expectation of the future company valuation in comparison with its current valuation will determine an investor's decision to purchase a company share. Valuation (share price) is a critical element for equities which fluctuates significantly more than for debt instruments. And there is no guarantee that the amount paid by the investor to purchase a stock will be returned, contrary to a bond where the principal invested should be paid back by the company to the investor. In the case of an equity, the investor will buy the share at a certain price at a point in time with no certainty of where that price will be in the future. The investor will do some in-depth analysis of what is called the company's fundamentals which consists of the review of the company's strategy, financial performance, and the market in which it operates, etc., and will also perform some macro-economic analysis which is independent from the company but could impact its performance.

4. Sustainable Approaches to Equity Investment

Historically, sustainable finance strategies, starting with negative screening and later on ESG integration, have been applied to equities well before debt instruments which emerged with the first green bond in 2008. In contrast to use-of-proceeds sustainable debt investments, where the proceeds can be allocated to precise isolated projects, in equity the amount invested is applied to the total company and has a more diffused use. ESG criteria will be considered both during the investment selection and due diligence, and also monitored throughout the holding of that investment. Indexes or funds can be pooled based on companies ESG performance such as the Dow Jones Sustainability Index or FTSE4good. The analysis of these criteria can be clearly related to financially material ESG topics and thus be more closely correlated with the company's financial performance than other sustainability strategies. The ESG approach has been historically a risk-driven approach, which considers the sustainability-related risks and attempts to monitor them or avoid them, but best-in-class ESG is getting more common and some research suggests links with increased financial performance.

Shareholder Engagement has historically principally been employed with equity products and led by shareholders to improve the behavior of companies through shareholder engagement initiatives usually taken by large investors or organizations representing and coordinating smaller investors (cf. Chapter 11). But the strategy is now also used for debt products, although to a lesser extent.

Impact investing is a strategy employed frequently for venture capital or private equity investments. For earlier stage companies, impact investing and sustainability-themed investing tend to be the most common sustainable strategies. A new source of capital called "blended finance" has been developed to address the needs of early-stage companies in developing countries. Blended finance mixes for-profit capital with discretionary capital, which can lose some of its value or be given away by foundations or not-for-profit organizations (GIIN, 2018). Blended finance is being used more and more in impact investing.

Equity investments can be dedicated to themes such as climate, which is one of the predominant themes in sustainable finance. According to BNEF, $165 billion was invested in climate tech in 2021. The two-thirds came from 483 public market transactions such as IPOs, secondary offerings, or Special Purpose Acquisition Company (SPAC reverse mergers while the remaining third came from 2,806 private market transactions in private equity and venture capital. Out of the $111 billion invested in public markets in 2021, more than half ($58 billion) was for the energy sector (BNEF, 2022b). Energy was also a key sector out of the $53.7 billion invested in climate technologies through venture capital and private equity, but transportation was also a large beneficiary (BNEF, 2022b). However, the additionality of these private investments was greater in newer markets such as in agriculture, food, climate, and carbon. For instance, the $3.5 billion raised in venture capital and private equity for agriculture and food startups in 2021 was greater than the amount raised for these sectors via public markets (BNEF, 2022b). This is even more true for climate and carbon startups which raised 94% of their capital from venture capital and private equity investors in 2021 (BNEF, 2022b).

This is typical of venture and private equity investments which tend to provide most of the external capital to new and growing technologies and sectors as traditional bank financing or capital market activity tend to focus on more established technologies, companies, and markets. According to Climate Tech VC, venture investments in climate tech alone raised $39.2 billion in 2021 across 605 deals by 1,400 investment firms (Purdom and Zou, 2022a, 2022b).

IV. How to Build a Sustainable Investment Portfolio

1. Fundamentals of Portfolio Management

The fundamentals of portfolio creation and management remain relevant to sustainable investment portfolios. An investment portfolio is a collection of investments. Investors build portfolios to avoid "putting all their eggs in one basket". Rather than making only one investment and bearing its specific risk, investors can increase the investments in their portfolio, diversifying characteristics such as asset class, and mitigate their overall risk. Diversification is one of the key advantages of investment portfolios. Different factors influence the specific mix of investments included in a portfolio. These include the investor's objectives and risk appetite, which determine the choice of asset classes and their respective proportion or "asset allocation". As discussed earlier, equity instruments are riskier than debt instruments and can lead to higher returns, but also greater losses. But in the long term, the return of stocks tends to be positive and outweighs the return of bonds (Tepper and Curry, 2021). A rule of thumb for retail investors is that the percentage of their investments in bonds should equal their age, and the remainder should be invested in stocks. Following this logic, a thirty-year-old person would invest 30% of their investment portfolio in bonds and 70% in stocks. The rationale behind this is that younger investors can take on more risk because they can overcome potential market hiccups, as long as they don't sell stocks when the market is at the lowest, as the stock market tends to perform well in the long term. Conversely, a seventy-year-old person close to retirement or already retired would have less risk appetite and should invest 70% of their portfolio in bonds and the remaining 30% in stocks to bring some potential upside.

2. Investment Funds and SFDR Classifications

Investors can build their own portfolio and pick and choose the financial products that best fit their strategy, even when it comes to sustainable investing strategies. They can also be assisted by financial advisors. They can also invest through asset managers, in private equity funds, or venture capital funds that employ sustainable investing strategies.

In the EU, the SFDR regulation (EU) 2019/2088 classifies funds and products as per Articles 6, 8, or 9 depending on the way sustainability is taken into account:

- Article 6: considers only sustainability risks.
- Article 8: promotes environmental or social characteristics (light green).
- Article 9: claims sustainable investment as its objective (dark green).

According to Morningstar data, as of the end of March 2022, 68.5% of funds available for sale in the EU (excluding money market funds, funds of funds, and feeder funds) were classified as Article 6, 27.9% as Article 8, and 3.6% as Article 9 (Eurosif, 2022). Article 6 products represented EUR 5 trillion or 54.7% of assets in the EU, while Article 8 products accounted for EUR 3.73 trillion (40.7%) and Article 9 products for EUR 450 billion (4.9%) (Eurosif, 2022).

3. ETFs and Mutual Funds

Investors can also benefit from built-in diversification by investing in mutual funds or in exchange-traded funds (ETFs). A mutual fund is an investment company that pools money from many investors to build diversified investment portfolios, typically comprising a mix of stocks, bonds, and short-term debt managed by professional money managers. ETFs are also diversified portfolios, but, like stocks, they can be traded intraday while mutual funds can only be purchased at the end of each trading day when net asset value (NAV) is determined. Another typical distinction is that ETFs are largely passively managed with no involvement of investment professionals. They typically track an index like the

S&P 500 whereas mutual funds are often actively managed by investment professionals, though passively-managed index mutual funds have become increasingly popular in recent years. As of 2022, ETFs accounted for more than 20% of US equity market volume and close to a third of the total dollar volume traded each day (Li, 2022). While most ETFs focus on equities, fixed income ETFs have grown from $574 billion in 2017 to $1.3 trillion in assets under management in 2022 (Li, 2022). In just that year, 45% of households owned shares in mutual funds (Statista, 2022a), and US mutual fund net assets amounted to $34 trillion (Statista, 2022b). Some mutual funds and ETFs employ sustainable investment strategies. In 2019, ETFs employing ESG integration strategies represented $8 billion in assets as fees dropped and interest in sustainable investing grew, according to Bloomberg Intelligence (Chasan, 2020). Since then, ESG-focused ETFs have significantly increased; in the US their share of total ETF national volume in 2022 was eight times that of in 2018 (Li, 2022).

V. Climate Change Portfolio Case Study

Investment portfolios are set up to produce diversification to reduce exposure to company and sector risks. They are usually composed of different classes of assets with different maturities and levels of liquidity in order to achieve objectives aligned with the risk profile of the asset owner whether it is an individual or an institution. A high-net-worth Millennial will not have the same needs and risk appetite than a soon-to-be retired middle-class person. Similarly, an insurance company will not have the same strategy as a foundation or a hedge fund. The following case study illustrates an example of a portfolio addressing climate change which lists assets that could be included. The inclusion or not of these assets as well as the proportion of each of these assets will be determined by the investor's risk profile and objectives.

The following different examples of asset classes are listed according to their maturity and liquidity:

1. Green money market instruments (such as green ABCP) on the back of loans or leases for residential solar or electric vehicles

2. ESG Indexed Mutual Funds
3. Green ETFs
4. Green bonds financing renewable energy projects
5. Stocks with best-in-class environmental performance
6. Real estate investments in energy efficient buildings
7. Private equity investments in renewable energy developers and operators
8. Venture investments in carbon capture projects
9. Project bonds backing a portfolio of renewable energy and battery storage assets — senior secured bonds issued by non-recourse special vehicle company secured by the assets, contracts, and shares.

VI. Conclusion

Since the dawn of sustainable investing, the scope of financial products which can employ sustainable strategies has significantly widened. New financial products have been created for this sole purpose; green bonds are likely the most iconic. Since their creation in 2007, more than $4 trillion of sustainable debt instruments have been issued. Sustainable strategies can now be employed across nearly all asset classes and financial products.

As a result, it is now possible to build portfolios following sustainable investment strategies and to benefit from the associated diversification while achieving a desired risk return profile. Portfolios can be built either by investors themselves, or with the support of financial advisors. Investors can also purchase diversified pre-built portfolios like ETFs or mutual funds following sustainable investment strategies. However, while the proportion of sustainable products has dramatically increased, it still doesn't represent the majority of financial assets. Strikingly, in certain regions such as Europe, considering sustainability risks is now mandatory for all financial products.

Furthermore, the role of traditional finance instruments not necessarily labeled as sustainable but deploying capital to address or support sustainability-related topics (e.g. renewable energy financing, project finance, infrastructure capital market, etc.) should not be neglected as it is critical.

References

Bank for International Settlements (BIS). (January 2019). "Committee on the global financial system". *Establishing Viable Capital Markets*, pp. 7–9. https://www.bis.org/publ/qtrpdf/r_qt1903.pdf.

Bloomberg New Energy Finance (BNEF). (2019). "Sustainable debt joins the trillion-dollar club". Published on October 17, 2019. Consulted in December 2020, https://about.bnef.com/blog/sustainable-debt-joins-the-trillion-dollar-club/.

Bloomberg New Energy Finance (BNEF). (2022a). "1H 2022 sustainable finance market outlook". Published on January 24, 2022, https://about.bnef.com/blog/1h-2022-sustainable-finance-market-outlook/.

Bloomberg New Energy Finance (BNEF). (2022b). "Energy transition investment trends 2022". Published on January 2022. Consulted in March 2022, https://assets.bbhub.io/professional/sites/24/Energy-Transition-Investment-Trends-Exec-Summary-2022.pdf.

Castelli, F. (2020). "Green bonds: ESG, sustainable or impact investments?" Published on December 11, 2020, Consulted in December 2020, https://www.cityam.com/green-bonds-esg-sustainable-or-impact-investments/.

Chasan, E. (2020). "Good business: The year ahead in sustainable finance" *Bloomberg*. Published on January 2, 2020. Consulted in December 2020, https://www.bloomberg.com/news/newsletters/2020-01-02/good-business-the-year-ahead-in-sustainable-finance.

Climate Bonds Initiative. (2020). "Green bond pricing report for Q3-Q4 2019: Spotlight on green sovereigns: Emerging greenium: All in latest analysis of primary market performance", Published on March 31, 2020, Consulted in December 2020. https://www.climatebonds.net/2020/03/green-bond-pricing-report-q3-q4-2019-spotlight-green-sovereigns-emerging-greenium-all-latest.

Eurosif. (2022). "EU Sustainable Finance & SFDR: Making the framework fit for purpose", June 2022, https://www.eurosif.org/news/eurosif-report-2022/.

Global Impact Investing Network (GIIN). (2018). "A resource for structuring blended finance vehicles". Published in October, 2018. Consulted in December 2020, https://thegiin.org/assets/upload/Blended%20Finance%20Resource%20-%20GIIN.pdf.

Institute of International Finance (IFI). (2017). "Global debt monitor", Institute of International Finance (IFI), www.iif.com/publication/global-debt-monitor/global-debt-monitorapril-2018.

IJGlobal. (2020). "Database", Consulted in December 2020, https://ijglobal.com/data/search-transactions.

International Capital Market Association (ICMA). (2020a). "International debt capital issuance volume". Data provided by Dealogic, https://www.icmagroup.org/resources/market-data/Market-Data-Dealogic/. Accessed December 2020.

International Capital Market Association (ICMA). (2020b). "Global bond markets (Secondary Markets)". Data provided by Bloomberg as of August 2020, https://www.icmagroup.org/Regulatory-Policy-and-Market-Practice/Secondary-Markets/bond-market-size/. Accessed December 2020.

International Monetary Fund (IMF). (2019). "Global financial stability report", Chapter 6 Sustainable Finance. Washington: IMF

Li, C. (2022). "ETFs rising in the turbulence". NYSE. Published March 14, 2022, Accessed in September 2022, https://www.nyse.com/data-insights/etfs-rising-in-the-turbulence.

Purdom, S. and Zou, K. (2022a). "$40B 2021 climate venture recap", Climate Tech VC. Published on January 28 2022, https://climatetechvc.substack.com/p/40b-2021-climate-venture-recap?utm_source=url.

Purdom, S. and Zou, K. (2022b). "Climate tech capital continues growth #87", Climate Tech VC. Published on January 31 2022, https://climatetechvc.substack.com/p/-climate-tech-capital-continues-growth?triedSigningIn=true.

Securities Industry and Financial Markets Association (SIFMA). (2017). "2017 Factbook", New York, NY, USA, p. 96.

Statista. (2022a). "Total net assets of mutual funds in selected countries worldwide from 2013 to 2021", https://www.statista.com/statistics/331914/total-net-assets-mutual-funds-worldwide/.

Statista. (2022b). "Share of households owning mutual funds in the United States from 1980 to 2021", https://www.statista.com/statistics/246224/mutual-funds-owned-by-american-households/.

Tepper, T. and Curry, B. (2021). "The historical performance of stocks and bonds", *Forbes*. Published on May 12, 2021, https://www.forbes.com/advisor/investing/stock-and-bond-returns/. Accessed December 2022.

Vaughan, L. and Finch, G. (2017). The Guardian. Published on January 18, 2017, https://www.theguardian.com/business/2017/jan/18/libor-scandal-the-bankers-who-fixed-the-worlds-most-important-number. Accessed December 2020.

Vasakrona. (2018). "Another world first, Vasakronan issues green commercial paper to finance green assets". Published 21 September 2018, https://vasakronan.se/pressmeddelande/another-world-first-vasakronan-issues-green-commercial-paper-to-finance-green-assets/#:~:text=Today%2C%202021%20

September%2C%20the%20company,of%20humanity%20or%20the%20 environment. Accessed December 2020.

World Bank. (2018a). Global financial development report 2017/2018: Bankers without Borders, The World Bank, Washington DC, p. 159.

World Bank. (2018b). "Market capitalization of listed domestic companies (current US$)". (2018). World Federation of Exchanges database, https://data. worldbank.org/indicator/cm.mkt.lcap.cd. Accessed December 2020.

World Bank. (2022). "Sustainable development bonds and green bonds 2021", https://issuu.com/jlim5/docs/world_bank_ibrd_impact_report_2021_web_ ready_r01?fr=sYTBhOTM4NTM3MTk.

Chapter 10

Impact Investing

James Gifford and Jerome Tagger

Learning Objectives

- Understand impact investing key concepts, opportunities, and challenges
- Understand why impact investing matters and how it is different from other strategies
- Describe the relationship between this strategy and financial performance
- Present the concept of a double/triple bottom line
- Discuss how to report on impacts

Abstract

This chapter introduces the key concepts, opportunities, and challenges of impact investing, a subset of sustainable finance characterized by the *intentionality* of an investment. Impact investing is a term coined by the Rockefeller Foundation in 2007 to describe investments that generate a social and/or environmental impact alongside a financial return. Different organizations use the term "impact investing" to describe different practices. Some investors retain a strict definition, that is, investments that themselves create impact. Other investors use the term interchangeably with sustainable and environmental, social, and corporate governance (ESG) investing. Yet others define impact investing as investing in companies whose intent is to have impactful products and services — whether or not the investor and their capital contributed to that impact. For the purposes of this chapter, impact investing is defined as an investment strategy that can deliver both financial returns and positive social and environmental outcomes — beyond what would otherwise have occurred had the investment not been made. The chapter lays out why impact investing matters and what sets it apart from other sustainable finance strategies. This type of investment considers factors beyond financial return and includes the double/triple bottom line without necessarily impairing the traditional *alpha*, as illustrated in the section on returns-on-investment. Finally, the chapter explores how to report on the impact. The chapter concludes that only a fraction of total investment made globally qualifies as impact investment. It often excludes the bulk of the development finance, renewable energy, clean tech, sustainable forestry, and the healthcare, education, and other social sectors, where the impact qualification remains inconsistent, either because of lack of intentionality or because of labeling concerns by the investors.

I. Introduction

The United Nations estimates that there is a $2.5 trillion annual funding gap that must be covered in order to achieve the 2030 Sustainable Development Goals (SDGs) — in developing countries alone (Wilson, 2016).

There are different ways investors are contributing to closing this gap — whether intentionally or not — although taken together these efforts are not even close to rising to the challenge: assets channeled into this agenda by the world's 200 or so self-identified impact investors amount to $502 billion (Mudaliar *et al.*, 2017), a fraction of what is required. Adding in close to a quarter billion of US dollars annual investment into renewable energy — largely by investors who don't identify as impact investors, the gap is still large. In addition, the actual impacts of mainstream business (and therefore the related contribution of run-of-the-mill equity and debt) remains poorly understood, particularly for themes where, unlike with clean energy and decarbonization, there is no obvious link between sectors, geographies, and impacts (UNEP FI, 2018).

In theory, there is no shortage of capital that could address the world's biggest problems. The private wealth market alone, which stood at $250 trillion in 2015 (UBS, 2017), is still barely investing in impact strategies. According to the Campden Wealth UBS Global Family Office survey, 25% of family offices undertake impact investing, with 71% of them allocating no more than 10% of their capital (UBS, 2019).

The potential, however, is significant: when surveyed, investors state their clear intention to invest impactfully. At the same time, they will often say that they are not sure how to go about it.

So: what is impact investing? This chapter is an introduction to the key concepts, opportunities, and challenges of impact investing.

For all the hype, readers should bear in mind that capital is not the only lever to address global issues and meet the SDGs. Public policy, businesses, NGOs, and cross-sector partnerships are critical levers as well.

Chapter 10 is organized as per the following sections:

I. Introduction
II. What Is Impact Investing?
III. Does Intention Matter?
IV. Do Impact Investments Sacrifice Financial Returns?
V. Additionality: The Secret Ingredient in Impact Investing
VI. Impact Measurement
VII. Conclusion

II. What Is Impact Investing?

1. Definitions

Impact investing is a term coined by the Rockefeller Foundation in 2007 to describe investments that generate a social and/or environmental impact alongside a financial return. In the decade since it emerged, impact investing has been transitioning from a niche, often philanthropy-related activity, into a visible part of many mainstream portfolios (The Rockefeller Foundation, n.d.). It is gaining significant traction, underpinned by the shifting attitudes toward sustainability and increased awareness of how investments can be mobilized to solve the world's most critical issues as outlined in the United Nations SDGs.

The Global Impact Investing Network (GIIN) provides a widely accepted definition of impact investing as "investments made with the intention to generate positive, measurable social and environmental impact alongside a financial return". This definition features "intentionality" as central to impact investing: that is, the desire on the part of the investor to deliver environmental or social impacts alongside financial returns. The definition also stresses the importance of impact measurement as a hallmark of the practice.

That said, different organizations use the term "impact investing" to describe different practices. Some investors retain a strict definition, that is, investments that themselves create impact because of the additional capital brought by the investor (or in other ways, so long as the investor is the change agent). Other investors use the term interchangeably with sustainable and environmental, social, and corporate governance (ESG) investing, while still others define impact investments as investing into companies that have impactful products and services — whether or not the investor and their capital contributed to that impact (Impact Management Project, 2018).

For the purposes of this chapter, impact investing will be defined as an investment strategy that can deliver both financial returns and positive social and environmental outcomes — beyond what would otherwise have occurred had the investment not been made. In practice, it involves investing into companies and organizations in ways that can deliver concrete positive impacts that are measurable, verifiable, and where there is a clear link between the investment, the investee company's outputs, and the benefits it delivers on the ground to populations or the environment. The authors of this chapter consider that impact investing also includes active ownership activities (e.g. shareholder engagement (see Chapter 11), capacity building by the investors, and participation in governance) that enhance the enterprise's positive impacts beyond business as usual. In addition, impact investors increasingly expect their investments to meet minimum ESG standards, co-opting long-standing responsible investment practices, to ensure that negative impacts are addressed or mitigated, alongside the delivery of positive impacts.

Ultimately, if there is anything differentiating about impact investing, it is that it exists to solve problems. This guides our thinking as we further navigate its theoretical and practical aspects here.

We list in the following some articles in ImpactAlpha referring to examples of impact investing initiatives:

- Global Goals give impact investors a model for collective action (ImpactAlpha, August 29, 2018).
- What we know about KKR's $1 billion Global Impact Fund (ImpactAlpha, April 30, 2018).
- New York State pension fund to energy cos: How will you adapt to low-carbon future? (ImpactAlpha, April 11, 2018).
- Foundations collaborate on catalytic financing to accelerate climate action (ImpactAlpha, August 29, 2018).
- Sustainable Ocean Fund raises $37.5 million for "life underwater" (ImpactAlpha, July 9, 2018).
- Nigeria's Piggybank raises $1.1 million to help West Africans save (ImpactAlpha, June 25, 2018).

2. What Sets Impact Investing Apart from Other Sustainable Finance Strategies?

There is a critical distinction between impact investing on the one hand and the broader sustainable/ESG investing space on the other. The latter often involves simply buying stocks and bonds in sustainable or impactful companies in liquid, secondary markets. With these approaches, the causal link between investments and impacts on the company (and the company's impacts on the world) is largely severed, starting with the fact that there is no provision of new capital (there may be cases where liquid markets are inefficient, or companies rely on shareholders to raise fresh capital, but in general, most of the ESG funds operate in highly liquid, secondary markets where they do not directly contribute to the company's sources of capital). With impact investing, investment capital is applied directly to a company's or project's balance sheet, allowing the enterprise to expand and produce more impactful goods or services. This is most clearly demonstrated in asset classes such as private equity, private debt, venture capital, and unlisted real assets. Once a company is trading on a highly liquid stock market, simply buying shares from another shareholder is unlikely to result in any additional impact.

In that context, the clearest mechanism for impact in public equities however is shareholder engagement, where shareholders use their power and influence to directly encourage companies to improve aspects of their sustainability performance (this is increasingly being practiced in bond investment as is done by Hermes International). Shareholder engagement — also known as "active ownership" — is a mainstay of ESG investing. It has a decades-long track record of impact (US SIF). It entails private and public approaches (letters, meetings) and very public ones, such as filing of shareholder resolutions at company annual general meetings demanding change. Where shareholder engagement is successful, and the companies improve an aspect of their ESG or sustainability performance, these improvements can map directly onto the SDGs, and can form the clearest pathway to impact within public equities. While fund managers with robust shareholder engagement activities have a clear intention to have a positive impact on the companies they engage with, few of them consider themselves impact investors. However, shareholder engagement that can demonstrate clear, attributable outcomes is perhaps the only effective impact investing strategy in liquid markets.

III. Does Intention Matter?

As noted earlier, the GIIN defines impact investing as "investments made with the intention to generate positive, measurable social and environmental impact alongside a financial return" (GIIN). Investor motivation is core to impact investing, but whether an investment is intentionally impactful is not always simple to determine.

An argument for the focus on intentionality is that most investments have positive impacts such as job creation, and without an intention to create impact, the impacts will be accidental and there is no evidence that they will be considered alongside financial considerations in the strategy. Like philanthropy, the purpose of impact investing is to solve problems that need to be addressed, and without an intention, these problems are unlikely to be solved as quickly or effectively.

However, we must explore intentionality at both the investor level and the enterprise level to understand its nuances and assess its importance. An impact investor, whose mission it is to create a positive impact, could finance, for example, a wind farm that may displace a considerable amount of coal-fired electricity, a strategy that appears to be highly impactful. However, what if it is the case that the developers of the wind farm themselves have no intention to contribute to climate solutions and are in the wind business only for the money? What about an impact investor that invests in mainstream frontier market private equity fund managers (who themselves have no explicit impact lens)? What about a mainstream investor — without any consideration of the positive climate impacts — financing a wind farm built by a developer who is highly committed to addressing the climate challenge? Consider also a scenario where multiple investors take part in the financing of an emerging market's small and medium enterprise (SME) fund, with some categorizing the investment as "impact", and others not, based on their own subjective intention. These are ambiguous but very real scenarios that the market confronts every day. Whether they fall under the definition of intentionality requires judgment. Ultimately, what matters is that some entity in the investment chain is keeping the focus on delivering impact, whether they are investors or investees. Indeed in 2019, the International Finance Corporation (IFC) produced the Operating Principles for Impact Management, a set of guidelines defining the key elements required to deliver impact within the investment. They state that "many impact investors also find opportunities to achieve impact by investing in commercial enterprises that may not, themselves, have the intent to achieve impact. For this reason, the definition of impact investing rests on the investor's intent to have impact, not on the intent of the investee enterprise" (IFC, 2018).

Another rationale for the intentionality requirement is that businesses have many dimensions of impact, and if an investor or company manager has clear intention, he or she will seek out positive impact wherever it can be found. The commitment to generating environmental and social outcomes beyond what any similar business or investor would bother doing can be a major source of additional impact. For example, a manager of a solar panel manufacturer who is committed to impacting more broadly would ensure that the company also performs well on many other areas of environmental, social, or impact-oriented performance, such as pollution, workers' welfare, human rights, etc. It may strive to have additional impact, through facilitating microfinance loans to its workers. Intentionality is, in this context, an insurance policy that the people in charge have the right attitude, and that the company will be as impactful as possible, not only relating to its products and services but also relating to the production and sourcing processes. A commitment to impact can also result in the managers of enterprises being considerably more proactive in pushing businesses to further enhance their impact over time. For example, an emerging market healthcare company with a commitment to the UN SDGs may intentionally be more proactive in exploring business models that serve the base of the pyramid.

Impact investors, particularly in developing countries, can also have additional impact through putting pressure on non-impact fund managers and enterprises to live up to high ESG standards. Investors with an intention to create impact are more likely to encourage consideration of these issues when sitting on company boards, include sustainability issues in investment agreements, and monitor companies' ESG and impact metrics — all of which can result in additional impact that may not have otherwise been realized. Certain impact investors will also be concerned about who they might exit to and will be more likely to sell to like-minded investors.

Investors with the intention to generate impact will also be more proactive in addressing systemic issues that may be preventing an issue from being solved. Examples could include investors building coalitions to address a collective action problem around climate change or rainforest destruction, or engaging with policymakers to price in an externality through tax or introduce regulation that would address a problem that the market alone is unable to address.

While intentionality is important and must form part of a formal definition, it is not a prerequisite for creating impact, and in some situations, may not be required in order to solve problems that can be solved through mobilizing mainstream, non-impact, focused investors. This can often happen when a business achieves adequate scale and profitability and is well-funded by mainstream markets.

Finally, there is the pragmatic — and fair — criticism of intentionality that there simply is not enough "intentional" capital to address the global investment gap in funding for the SDGs, which, according to the UN agency charged with calculating this, requires an additional \$2.5 trillion per year (UNCTAD, 2014). It can be argued that the only way to solve these big challenges is to mobilize mainstream capital at scale, regardless of whether this capital or the enterprises it invests in can demonstrate intentionality.

IV. Do Impact Investments Sacrifice Financial Returns?

There are no definitive conclusions regarding the financial returns from impact investing — in large part because it is such a heterogeneous set of activities. One of the most advanced efforts to assess the returns of the impact investing sector is The Impact Investing Benchmark, undertaken by the GIIN and Cambridge Associates (Matthews *et al.*, 2015). This benchmark was limited to funds seeking social impact only (excluding environmental technologies, forestry, renewable energy, etc.). It also excluded many mainstream healthcare and biotech companies which were not sufficiently "intentional". It found returns to be highly variable, with some funds underperforming traditional comparator funds in certain sectors and regions, and others outperforming. Given the limited set of funds that are covered by this benchmark, the wide range of definitions of the impact investing universe, the tremendous regional and sector diversity, and the recent entry into the space by large, mainstream, institutional-grade fund managers, it is too early to generalize about returns. The industry has also matured considerably, and the past performance of funds that were operating before 2010 would not be a good indicator of the future of these sectors.

It is more interesting to look at returns from the perspective of investor expectations. Indeed, the return investors should expect depends on the impact strategy adopted — in particular, whether it is actually seeking commercial returns or not — as well as usual factors such as manager skill, and the macro, sector, and regional trends, etc. While below-market strategies — those that do not seek fully commercial returns for a given level of risk — play a critical role in solving some of the more intractable problems such as getting capital to small businesses in remote rural areas of developing countries, the fastest growing part of the industry is the market-rate return segment that seeks equivalent, or ideally better, returns than traditional strategies. Each year the GIIN publishes its annual investor survey which articulates its expectations and results. According to the 2019 GIIN Annual Impact Investing Survey, "About two-thirds of respondents principally target market-rate returns (66%)" (Mudaliar *et al.*, 2019). Return expectations also vary according to geography, sector, instrument, and stage of business.

V. Additionality: The Secret Ingredient in Impact Investing

Additionality is the notion that an intervention has an additional effect when compared to a baseline. In other words, the question becomes: is there more impact *because* of the investment? This concept was core to the Kyoto Protocol on Climate Change, in that projects would only get credit for reducing emissions, and thereby be counted in a country's (or company's) reduction targets, if those projects were *additional to what would have happened anyway*. The trajectory of emissions was projected based on "business as usual" scenarios, and then countries, funders, and companies would get credits — either in the voluntary or mandatory carbon markets — for projects that reduced emissions in a way that wouldn't have happened if not for their intervention.

Paul Brest from Stanford argues that "for an investment or non-monetary activity to have an impact, it must provide additionality — that is, it must increase the quantity or quality of the enterprise's social outcomes beyond what would otherwise have occurred" (Brest and Born, 2013). While additionality is not contained in the GIIN definition of impact investing, in part because it is challenging to quantify, it is also arguable that without it, there is simply no impact to measure. Practitioners remain divided on the centrality of the additionality to impact investing.

In order to determine whether there is additionality in an investment, it is important to consider where there is potential to contribute to impact in the investment chain:

1. Impact of the enterprise on the world — the enterprise impact.
2. Impact of the investors (typically fund managers) on the enterprise — the investor impact.

The enterprise impact is the layer that receives the most attention. Reporting frameworks such as the Impact Reporting Investment Standards (IRIS) tend to focus on the enterprise level measuring metrics such as the number of "Client Households: Provided New Access (to water)". While there is still considerable debate about what can be measured, there is a lot of momentum on this topic, with indicators constantly being improved. Interestingly, this momentum is also visible within listed equities (and large companies) where an additional layer of metrics relating to the company's impact is being added to "traditional" ESG metrics. These impact indicators typically focus on products and services, and the degree to which the companies are contributing to solving the world's problems. These metrics are increasingly framed in terms of contribution to the UN SDGs. There are now several listed equity funds using impact metrics for stock selection. These funds refer to themselves as "impact funds". However, while it may be true that they are indeed investing in impactful companies, there is no assertion from these funds that they are responsible for the impact, and therefore they would not fulfil the requirements of the definition used by many impact investors.

Which leads us to explore the impact of direct investors on investees. Even if the enterprise itself is impactful, it is important to assess the extent to which the investor contributed to that impact. For example, merely purchasing shares in an impactful company on a liquid and relatively efficient stock market does not lower the cost of capital of the company, affect the share price, or otherwise have any material effect on the company. When markets are relatively efficient and liquid, investment (or divestment) has little impact. Of course, if a large proportion of the market invested in an impactful stock at the same time, it would drive up stock price and lower the cost of capital. However, this is not a common occurrence and most companies in liquid "impact funds" are being priced in the same way as any other stock, and are unaffected by the choices of their "impact" investors. Their purpose, however, is to provide exposure to impactful companies that are solving problems, and many of these companies are in fast-growing sectors and may well be good investments.

That said, in some situations, investments into (or divestments out of) companies can have an impact. Starting with divestment, it is possible to have a negative impact on a company through divestment if that decision is accompanied by a public announcement of that divestment, and the investor is legitimate and credible in the eyes of the company or the market. An example of this is when the "Rockefeller Brothers Fund divested from fossil fuels with the announcement making it to the front page of major newspapers" (Schwartz, 2014).

Another potential mechanism for impact in public equities is investment in the less liquid and less efficient end of the market, namely microcap and frontier market stocks, or stocks trading on small exchanges. Investment into these companies by respected investors would likely send strong signals to other investors that the company is a good investment, allowing the companies to access cheaper capital.

As discussed above, the clearest and most common mechanism for impact in public equities is shareholder engagement — the use of shareholder power to directly influence a company to improve some aspect of its sustainability performance.

It could be argued that an investor should only consider themselves an impact investor if they, themselves, are creating impact through one or more of these mechanisms. Investors who are simply "buying in" or aligning to impact that would have happened anyway will have a harder time claiming this role (or no desire to do so). While there is nothing wrong with aligning your investments with the most impactful companies, investors should be clear as to whether they are actually driving impact, or simply aligning with impact, as there is an opportunity cost. Some investors genuinely want to drive impact and it is important that the fund management industry differentiates between these two strategies.

Private markets face their own challenges when it comes to additionality. Prima facie, capital invested via private markets (private equity, private debt, venture capital, infrastructure, unlisted real estate) directly expands the balance sheet of a company, allowing it to increase the quantity or quality of whatever impactful activity it is undertaking. Traditionally, impact investing was typically considered something you do in private markets, where there is a direct link between the provision of capital and the activity of the enterprise.

It is possible, however, for companies to be efficiently priced, even in private markets. Consider a highly profitable, well-known Silicon Valley startup which is already producing strong cash flows and is able to choose from a dozen potential private equity investors, their selection being made on the basis of whom they would like to work with. It is likely that if one investor decided not to invest, another one would. In a situation such as this, there is an argument that there is no additionality of capital, given that the enterprise would have raised the same amount at similar terms from any number of other investors. A counterargument is that in private markets there is indeed a sloping demand curve for capital, even with high profile deals: the more the investors seeking to jump on board, the higher the valuation the company can attain. The greatest potential for impact through capital allocation is in markets where capital is scarce, and where deals may not go ahead at all but for the investment.

Even when there is no additionality arising from the allocation of capital, public and private markets investors can achieve additionality through active ownership during the investment period. A good example of this type of additionality in private markets is demonstrated by development finance institutions (DFIs), such as the IFC, which impose strict ESG performance standards on companies they invest in or lend to, resulting in significant improvements in performance on a range of metrics. They also offer technical expertise to help companies improve their ESG performance. While the DFIs tend not to frame these ESG improvements in terms of "impact", it is clear that the delta between where the company was before the DFI investment and where it is some years later is a demonstrable "impact" and should be considered so. Similarly, some mainstream private equity firms are now launching impact funds, which tend to focus on the thematic impact of the enterprises themselves (renewable energy, education, healthcare, etc.), and also have ESG teams that encourage higher ESG standards within investee companies.

Finally, there is the possibility that a particular private equity firm can grow impactful companies faster than the counterfactual (for example, passive family office capital). Large PE firms such as The Rise Fund have dozens of staff working in "business building" who offer consultation to the portfolio companies in all aspects of their business. They argue that they can grow businesses faster than otherwise would have happened, and this is one of their key value adds. To the extent that this is true, these firms can argue that they provide additionality through expanding impact-ful businesses faster than the counterfactual, even if the original capital was not additional and the company would have secured it at similar terms from other investors.

VI. Impact Measurement

Impact measurement is an important and continually debated component of the practice of impact investing. The GIIN added impact measurement to its definition of impact investing in 2014, 5 years after it developed its first definition.

The most established and widely used repository for impact metrics is Impact Reporting Investment Standards (IRIS), developed by the GIIN in a multi-stakeholder process. IRIS+ (the new version, updated and streamlined in 2019) seeks to catalog impact metrics at the enterprise level across sectors and provide a standardized set of metrics. Given the diversity of sectors, approaches, and impacts, IRIS offers different sets of metrics for different industries, such as agriculture, education, environment, financial services, and health. It creates a common language and allows — where appropriate — a comparison of standard indicators across different enterprises.

IRIS has been in development for over a decade and has thousands of enterprises and investors using its indicators. But more recently, there has been interest in a higher level of analysis than enterprise metrics in order to facilitate a more holistic process for investors and companies to manage impact.

The Impact Management Project was convened in 2017 as "a global network of standard-setting organisations to coordinate impact measure-ment and management principles, frameworks, disclosure standards and benchmarking initiatives that, taken all together, provide clarity for any-one looking to measure, manage and report their impact" (Impact Management Project, 2018).

One of the key contributions of the Impact Management Project is a framework for evaluating impact of enterprises (see Figure 10.1).

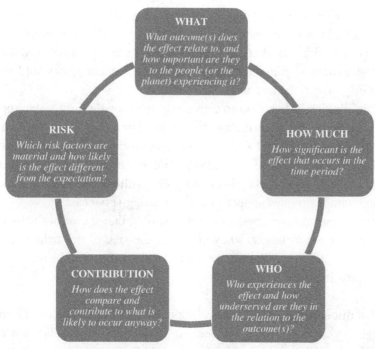

Figure 10.1. Impact of Enterprises

Source: Impact Management Project (2018).

Added together, analysis of these dimensions provides an additional framework for evaluating the impacts — *ex-ante* and *ex-post* — of enterprises receiving impact investments. How might these dimensions be used to analyze investments?

- What? This asks whether the enterprise is seeking to achieve a more or less important impact. Is the healthcare company seeking a cure for malaria or for minor ailments?
- How much? This seeks to differentiate between those enterprises that could go to scale (an education technology company with millions of potential students) and those that affect a limited number of people (a small network of private schools operating in one country).
- Who? This question asks whether the beneficiaries (people or the environment) are indeed under-served, and in real need of the services

being offered. Many people may think any educational institution is by definition an impact investment. However, if the enterprise only serves wealthy children (e.g. a high-fee private school network that is inaccessible to middle- and lower-income students), it would score poorly on this dimension.

- Contribution? This seeks to capture the additionality of the enterprise. Is the enterprise contributing to positive impacts in ways that would not occur regardless? For example, a microfinance institution that is first to a market could provide more additional impact than an institution that enters a market that is saturated with microfinance providers, and whose services simply displace existing services.
- Risk? Impact investments not only involve the risk of not achieving financial return targets, they also face the risk of not achieving the impact targets. There are also risks associated with ESG externalities.

Practitioners have begun to operationalize these dimensions of impact through developing ratings and seeking to quantify them. They are now integrated in IRIS+. The Impact Management Project is also working with leading organizations through a structured network to help streamline approaches to impact measurement and drive adoption of the five dimensions.

Between the high-level analysis of the Impact Management Project dimensions and the catalog of IRIS metrics at the enterprise level, there are also a number of for-profit frameworks and "middleware" that facilitate the process of impact management. The B Impact Assessment Platform from B-Analytics scores enterprises and fund managers based on a range of bottom-up indicators. Typically, it would use IRIS metrics to perform these assessments. There are now thousands of enterprises and funds using this platform. There are also a number of reporting frameworks, such as the Global Reporting Initiative, that provide additional reporting guidelines for enterprises and fund managers on sustainability and impact performance.

Another important contribution of the Impact Management Project is to clearly separate investor impact from investee (enterprise) impact and recognize that investors have different motivations, such as simply avoiding harm, benefiting stakeholders of the companies (e.g. responsible business), or contributing to solutions to the world's problems (what we could typically consider impact investing). While much of the focus remains on building an impact management process around the impact of the investee enterprises, there is now a recognition that investor impact (i.e. through, for example, providing additional capital that wouldn't have been provided otherwise, active ownership activities, or other indirect impacts) has a separate set of factors to manage and, if possible, measure.

Quantifying these investor dimensions is not easy. However, like the five dimensions of impact at the enterprise level mentioned above, it is possible to evaluate investor contribution at a high level by assessing the capital allocation impact, the active ownership impact, and the indirect impacts (see Figure 10.2).

Another interesting development in impact measurement is the attempt to place a monetary value on all impacts, so the total "value" of various impacts can be compared — building on the Social Return on Investment (SROI) methodologies of previous decades. This involves using social and environmental valuation methodologies that have been developed over the last decades across many areas of development and putting a dollar value on the positive impact. For example, *carbon emissions abated* can be translated easily into dollar figures, given a modeled or actual cost of carbon. Social valuation can be more difficult, but there have been efforts to put a dollar value on additional years in school in developing countries or additional years of productive life offered to people from health interventions. TPG Rise is one fund manager using this "Impact Multiple of Money" concept, co-developed with Bridgespan and now being implemented by TPG spin-off Y-analytics. Each investment must meet both a financial hurdle and an impact hurdle as defined by the dollar value of the expected impact (Addy *et al.*, 2019). Separately, for mainstream business, a recent Harvard Business School initiative has developed impact-weighted accounts, which are line items on a financial statement, such as an income statement or a balance sheet, which are added to supplement the statement of financial health and performance by reflecting a company's positive and negative impacts on employees, customers, the environment, and the broader society. Working off its own

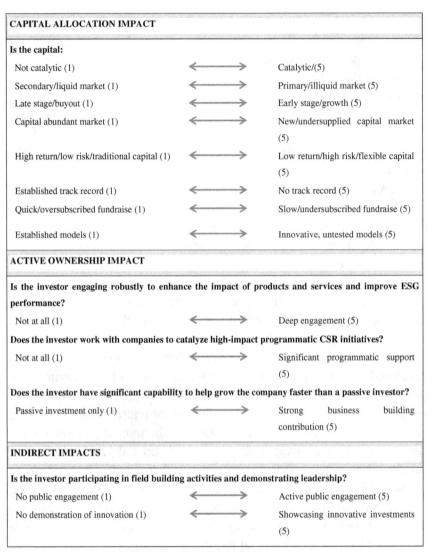

Figure 10.2.	Investor Contribution

theory of impact which seeks to support the development of impact-based business models in mainstream business, UNEP FI's Positive Impact Initiative proposes its own tools, including an Impact Radar, model frameworks, and tools for impact analysis and management, conceived to identify, assess, and monitor corporate impact, with a view to determining companies' existing impact as well as impact potential. While very few impact investors are relying on these valuation methodologies to compare impact across different sectors, these approaches are likely to become more widely used and robust over time.

There is an expectation that increased standardization and clarity around impact will drive investment and help scale impact investing. However, this takes time. It is also unlikely that lack of metrics and measurement is the greatest obstacle to scaling impact investing. Our experience suggests that developing impact investing strategies that fit into existing mainstream investment strategies and appeal to non-impact investors will deliver the greatest capital into the space.

VII. Conclusion

The impact investment industry is growing strongly. The annual survey conducted by the GIIN found that assets under management in impact strategies were recently in excess of $500M (Mudaliar and Dithrich, 2019). In 2019, there were in excess of 400 funds listed in Impactbase, the fund database of the GIIN. However, this figure is only a fraction of the actual investment made globally that could qualify as impact investment, as it excludes the bulk of the development finance, renewable energy, clean tech, sustainable forestry, healthcare, and education sectors, where the impact qualification remains inconsistent, either because of lack of intentionality or because of labeling concerns by the investors.

Large, mainstream private equity firms such as TPG, Partners Group, and KKR have launched impact funds, and wealth managers such as Credit Suisse, UBS, and Goldman Sachs are putting considerable resources into driving this agenda within their client bases. Impact-oriented megatrends around decarbonization, affordable housing, and emerging market healthcare are capturing large volumes of capital.

The momentum around the UN Sustainable Development Goals is further increasing the interest in impact investing. Both institutional and private investors are expressing their intention to invest in the solutions to the world's problems. The next decade is sure to see a dramatic increase in the volume of capital that is explicitly seeking a positive impact in the world.

As the industry scales, it is essential that impact investing further refines its approaches to impact measurement and additionality, in particular, around the impact of investors themselves, and not just the impact of enterprises.

Investment professionals and aspiring practitioners can use the tools and concepts presented in this chapter to assess products, build product strategies, and more importantly, contribute to achieving the impacts.

References

Addy, C., Chorengel, M., Collins, M., and Etzel, M. (2019). "Calculating the value of impact investing", *Harvard Business Review*, https://hbr.org/2019/01/calculating-the-value-of-impact-investing.

Brest, P. and Born, K. (2013). "Unpacking the impact in impact investing", *Stanford Social Innovation Review*, https://www.hermes-investment.com/sg/products/strategy-page/hermes-sdg-engagement-high-yield-credit-fund/.

GIIN (Global Impact Investing Network). Website "Impact-investing", https://thegiin.org/impact-investing/.

GIIN. (Global Impact Investing Network). Website "What you need to know about impact investing", https://thegiin.org/impact-investing/nee.

IFC. (2018). "Guide to investing for impact: Operating principles for impact management". Washington, D.C: IFC.

ImpactAlfa. Webite https//impactalpha.com/.

Impact Management Project (IMP). (2018). https://impactfrontiers.org/norms/.

Matthews, J., Sternlicht, D., Bouri, A., Mudaliar, A., and Schiff, H. (2015). "The impact investing benchmark 2015", The Cambridge Associates and the Global Impact Investing Network.

Mudaliar, A., Bass, R., Dithrich, H., and Nova, N. (2019). "2019 annual impact investor survey", *Global Impact Investing Network*, https://thegiin.org/research/publication/impinv-survey-2019.

Mudaliar, A. and Dithrich, H. (2019). "Sizing the impact investing market", *Global Impact Investing Network*, https://thegiin.org/research/publication/impinv-market-size.

Mudaliar, A., *et al.* (May 2017). "2017 Annual impact investor survey", *The Global Impact Investing Network*.

Schwartz, S. (2014). "Rockefellers, heirs to an oil fortune, will divest charity of fossil fuels", *The New York Times*, September 21, https://www.nytimes.com/2014/09/22/us/heirs-to-an-oil-fortune-join-the-divestment-drive.html.

The Rockefeller Foundation. (n.d.). "Innovative finance & impact investing", https://www.rockefellerfoundation.org/our-work/initiatives/innovative-finance/.

UBS. (January 2017). "Mobilizing private wealth for public good", UBS Wealth Management Chief Investment Office whitepaper.

UBS (2019). https://www.ubs.com/global/en/wealth-management/uhnw/global-family-office-report/global-family-office-report-2019/_jcr_content/mainpar/toplevelgrid_1271688915/col2/innergrid/xcol2/actionbutton.1323713949. file/bGluay9wYXRoPS9jb250ZW50L2RhbS9hc3NldHMvd20vZ2xvYmF sL3VobncvZG9jL2dsb2JhbC1mYW1pbHktb2ZmaWNlLXJlcG9ydC0yM DE5LXNwcmVmaZHMucGRm/global-family-office-report-2019-spreads.pdf.

United Nations Conference on Trade and Development. "The Rise in the Sustainable Fund Market" Geneva: UNCTAD. https://unctad.org/system/files/official-document/diae2021d1_en.pdf.

UNEP FI. (2018). "Rethinking impact to finance the SDGs". UN Position Paper. New York: UNEP https://www.unepfi.org/wordpress/wp-content/uploads/2018/11/Rethinking-Impact-to-Finance-the-SDGs.pdf.

US SIF. https://www.ussif.org/trends.

Wilson, G. E. R. (2016). "There's a $2.5 trillion development investment gap. Blended finance could plug it", *World Economic Forum*, 18 July, www.weforum.org/agenda/2016/07/blended-finance-sustainable-development-goals/.

Chapter 11

Shareholder Engagement

James Gifford and Robert L. Berridge

Learning Objectives

- Define shareholder engagement
- Understand the origins of shareholder engagement
- Understand primary strategies of shareholder engagement
- Explore a few of the main tools in shareholder engagement

Abstract

This chapter focuses on shareholder engagement, a subset of sustainable finance dedicated to the unique role that investors can play in influencing a company's strategy in areas of sustainability. Pension funds, mutual funds, foundations, wealth managers, insurance companies, and other institutional investors control most of the capital invested in listed equities globally. Shareholder engagement by US and European pension funds on environmental and social issues is increasing rapidly. The chapter describes a broadening of the mainstream shareholder engagement agenda, from traditional governance and strategic financial issues, to include environmental and social drivers. This is potentially one of the most profound shifts in institutional investment seen over many years and may significantly increase the role of investors in moving

287

the corporate sector, and ultimately society, toward a more sustainable future. While traditional shareholder activists focus exclusively on the financial performance of individual firms, ESG engagement can also address economywide and systemic sustainability issues. The chapter traces the origins of shareholder engagement and explores its primary strategies and tools. It raises the critical question of whether shareholder engagement works. One convenient mechanism (primarily relevant in the US) that indicates whether shareholder activism has been effective in changing corporate behavior is the number of resolutions withdrawn after successful negotiation in advance of going to a vote. The chapter concludes by emphasizing that although shareholder engagement may not be the highest profile strategy within the sustainable investing space, given recent evidence of its efficacy, its scalability, and its potential for delivering financial returns, its importance should be elevated in the future.

I. Introduction

Institutional investors are increasingly engaging in dialog with companies and voting their shares on a broad range of environmental, social, and corporate governance (ESG) issues, and increasingly, on the positive impact that companies could generate in terms of delivering the UN Sustainable Development Goals (SDGs). This includes not only investors that consider themselves sustainable or impact investors but also mainstream investors. As of 2020, the UN-backed Principles for Responsible Investment (PRI), which contain commitments to active ownership on ESG issues in Principle 2, had over 3000 signatories, representing more than $100 trillion in assets under management. Principle 2 of the PRI contains a commitment to actively engage with investee companies on ESG issues (through approaches that can include dialog, proxy voting, and filing shareholder proposals) and this commitment forms part of the annual PRI Reporting and Assessment process (UNPRI).

Pension funds, mutual funds, foundations, wealth managers, insurance companies, and other institutional investors control the majority of capital invested into listed equities globally. Shareholder engagement by US and European pension funds on environmental and social issues is increasing rapidly. The broadening of the mainstream shareholder engagement agenda, from traditional governance and strategic financial issues, to include environmental and social drivers, is potentially one of the most profound shifts in institutional investment seen over many years and may significantly increase the role of investors in moving the corporate sector, and ultimately society, toward a more sustainable future. Added to this is the new focus on the SDGs and companies' and investors' roles in proactively contributing to their achievement. If a large proportion of shareholder capital is managed with an active ownership philosophy around ESG and impact, resulting in significant effort applied to shareholder engagement, the improvements in corporate ESG performance and the implications for the sustainability of our society and good governance will be dramatic. If, as argued by many, this can also enhance the financial performance of the funds and the economy as a whole, then it will go a long way toward aligning the incentives of the corporate world more closely with those of society, particularly over the long term.

Chapter 11 is organized as per the following sections:

I. Introduction
II. Shareholder Evolution
III. The Origins of Shareholder Engagement
IV. Shareholder Engagement vs. Sustainable Investing
V. Shareholder Engagement vs. Shareholder Activism
VI. The Evolution of Shareholder Engagement
VII. Why Investors Pursue Shareholder Engagement Strategies
VIII. The Evolution of Shareholder Engagement Toolkit
IX. Shareholder Engagement Results
X. Conclusion

II. Shareholder Evolution

At the beginning of the last century, corporations were predominantly owned and controlled by wealthy individuals. In the 1930s, Berle and Means in their famous work *The Modern Corporation and Private Property* (Berle and Means, 1932) wrote of the separation of ownership and management of corporations, advancing the idea that dispersion of ownership of corporations would undermine the power and influence of owners over managers and posing the question whether managers would begin to act in their own interests at the expense of the interests of the owners. The shift toward "managerial capitalism" was driven in part by the uptake of classic portfolio theory, which encouraged diversification to the point that most shareholders held only small stakes in companies. This led to a more diffuse shareholder base and less incentive for individual shareholders to incur costs to monitor corporate managers and, if concerns are identified, to seek to change them (Admati *et al.*, 1994).

However, toward the end of the 20th century, shareholders began to assert themselves, reacting to the increasing agency costs being incurred, due to relatively unaccountable managers. This rise of active ownership by institutional investors occurred for a number of reasons. Perhaps most importantly, there have been numerous examples of ESG crises, scandals, and poor governance, and investors have seen opportunities to improve corporate performance. This has contributed not only to growth in ESG shareholder activism but also to demand for ESG investment products, which in 2020 accounted for 33% of assets under management in the US (UNPRI). Meanwhile, institutional investors now have larger stakes in companies than ever before, and their increasing size makes divestment (exit) less attractive than active ownership (voice). They have also increasingly implemented ESG strategies across the board, with ESG requirements commonplace in requests for proposals to the fund management industry.

The larger the stake (or combined stake if shareholders work together), the greater the investment reward to the shareholder from its monitoring activities, resulting in more of the benefits being captured by those shareholders undertaking the monitoring and engagement activities. Added to this, the greater the proportion of the market controlled by institutional investors with the resources and motivation to collaborate, the greater their combined ability to seek and achieve changes in corporate behavior (and to pool the costs of doing so).

III. The Origins of Shareholder Engagement

The growth of institutional investment resulted in it becoming more difficult for large shareholders to do the "Wall Street Walk" and divest from companies in which they had lost confidence. Divestment was perceived to be less attractive for these large shareholders, in part because it would be difficult to divest their shares without depressing the share price and incurring losses themselves in the process (Sethi, 2005). To sell a large block of shares would most often require a similarly large institution as a buyer (or a very gradual divestment over time). In addition, many institutional investors use low-fee indexed approaches for a large proportion of their assets for a range of reasons, and this strategy, by definition, precludes divestment of poor ESG performers (though this is now changing with a plethora of new products, such as carbon-optimized and other ESG-focused exchange-traded and index funds). If a large proportion of a portfolio is indexed, therefore, the obvious tool for improving ESG performance is shareholder engagement.

Additionally, there is considerable pressure on fund managers and trustees alike to match benchmarks based on the index. The pressure not to underperform typically exceeds the pressure to outperform. This encourages fund managers to keep their portfolios tracking the index fairly closely, and they end up holding predominantly the same portfolio as the index, further discouraging divestment as a solution to underperforming companies (Waygood, 2004).

A major boost was given to the cause of shareholder monitoring of corporate behavior in the early 2000s because of the spectacular collapses of Enron, Worldcom, and Tyco in the US, and HIH and others in Australia, and then later by environmental catastrophes such as the BP Deepwater Horizon accident. While it is arguable whether increased shareholder monitoring could have prevented environmental and social damage or fraud of the scale perpetrated in some of these cases, it is likely that because of these cases, investors have a far greater recognition of their responsibilities as owners and a greater willingness to invest in shareholder engagement activities.

IV. Shareholder Engagement vs. Sustainable Investing

A parallel movement also grew over the last decades of the 20th century which has as its goal the alignment of people's investments with their values. Socially responsible investment (SRI) — now more commonly known simply as "sustainable investing" — has a number of objectives:

- To provide vehicles for investments, in a way that is consistent with the investors' values.
- To make a difference (deliver social and environmental returns).
- To make a profit (deliver financial returns).

There are a number of different approaches to sustainable investing. One of the earliest forms was based on the principle of not profiting from unethical activities and was practiced by the Quakers in the 17th century (Kinder and Domini, 1997). This is often referred to as negative screening and involves avoiding or divesting the shares of companies that have poor corporate sustainability performance. The term "SRI" is often associated with negative screening because that was the predominant strategy when SRI investing began, but SRI is now often synonymous with ESG because both terms describe the full range of sustainable investing strategies.

"Positive screening" or "best-in-class" involves actively investing in companies which are rated highly in terms of sustainability performance. Examples might include investments in environmental technology or health-related companies which have a positive environmental or social impact or the best companies in each sector in the case of "best-in-class" approaches. These investments are most often equity investments on mainstream stock exchanges. Some of these thematic solutions focusing on companies whose products and services contribute directly to solving the SDGs are now being called "impact-aligned" funds.

Since the launch of the PRI in 2006, the concept of ESG integration has gained considerable momentum and is now recognized by many as an important part of any fundamental stock selection process. It is the idea that environmental, social, and corporate governance (ESG) issues can be material to investment returns and should therefore be integrated into mainstream investment processes in systematic ways. It is argued that many of these ESG issues are the drivers of long-term value, and they are simply being ignored by traditional investment analysts. As the "space" around analysis of companies' financial information becomes crowded, fund managers that take on this approach see ESG issues as a way to outperform, based on their greater understanding of the long-term strategic value drivers of firms, sectors, and the economy. This strategy is encapsulated in Al Gore's fund management firm, Generation Investment Management, which states: "Our approach to active investment management is based on an investment process that fully integrates sustainability analysis into our decision-making and is focused on long-term performance" (Generation Investment Management, 2017).

Impact investing is a newer form of sustainable investing which focuses on that subset of the spectrum that delivers measurable and verifiable impact and is primarily conducted in private markets, such as private equity/debt, venture capital, infrastructure, and unlisted real estate. There are also a small number of liquid strategies that have been set up explicitly to deliver measurable SDG outcomes through shareholder engagement and activism, and these can also be considered impact funds.

Shareholder engagement (also called shareholder activism or advocacy) on sustainability issues has become the other major strand of sustainable investing and the subject of this chapter. It has a rich history, particularly in the US. SRI shareholder activists (more recently the field is more commonly referred to as sustainability-focused or ESG engagement) have for many decades attempted to use their shareholder rights to press companies to improve environmental and social performance. ESG engagement differs from traditional, mainstream shareholder engagement in terms of the issues campaigned upon and the motivation for seeking changes in corporate behavior. Traditional activism often seeks board positions, removal of the CEO, short-/medium-term boosts in share prices or major changes in company strategy. ESG engagers seek improvements in corporate sustainability, and most often back up these calls with arguments around better managing risk and leveraging ESG opportunities. While sometimes moral or values-based arguments can be used, the great majority of engagement on sustainability focuses on the business case.

V. Shareholder Engagement vs. Shareholder Activism

While traditional shareholder activists focus exclusively on the financial performance of individual firms, ESG engagement can also address economywide and systemic sustainability issues. A good example is the engagement of the oil majors around climate change. When ExxonMobil works to prevent enactment of public policies needed to address climate change, the result could be damage to the global economy and, theoretically, a reduction in long-term returns for widely diversified investors. Investors engaging with Exxon are working not only to improve its long-term performance by pushing it more quickly into a transition to a cleaner energy provider but also to seek to protect the performance of the rest of their portfolio that could suffer damage from climate change. Here, we see a powerful alignment between the interest of passive (index) investors (who are widely diversified and often can't sell, for example, ExxonMobil shares) and the interests of society at large and the global economy.

VI. The Evolution of Shareholder Engagement

Public pension fund engagement on social issues began in earnest during the Apartheid era, with the pressure put on companies by US public pension funds in the 1980s to adopt the Sullivan Principles and later to divest from South Africa completely. This work originated in the early 1970s by religious investors affiliated with the Interfaith Center on Corporate Responsibility. Then in the 1990s, investors took up the cause of the Ceres Principles (formerly named the "Valdez Principles") followed by the pressure for the systematic disclosure of environmental and social performance, using frameworks such as the Global Reporting Initiative (Kasemir *et al.*, 2001). Climate change has, over the past decade, risen up the investor agenda with the signing of the Paris Agreement and the maturing of a number of investor collaborations, such as the Asia Investor Group on Climate Change (AIGCC), Carbon Disclosure Project (CDP), the Ceres Investor Network on Climate Risk & Sustainability (North America) (Ceres.org), the Investor Group on Climate Change (Australia and New Zealand) (IGCC), and the Institutional Investors Group on Climate Change (Europe). Shareholder proposals relating to climate change issues routinely garner over 35% support and in 2017 began to be endorsed by some of the world's largest fund managers, such as Blackrock, for the first time. BlackRock voted for climate change shareholder proposals at ExxonMobil and Occidental Petroleum during the 2017 proxy season (both proposals received majority votes). These were the first climate change proposals supported by BlackRock despite several years of corporate engagement on the topic using tools such as annual letters to portfolio companies from CEO Larry Fink that requested management of climate risk in addition to other ESG issues.

VII. Why Investors Pursue Shareholder Engagement Strategies

There are many reasons why institutional investors seek improvements in the environmental and social performance of investee companies. Overwhelmingly, institutional investors claim to engage on ESG issues in order to increase the value (or reduce risks) of the companies with which they engage, resulting in increased returns to their portfolios (at lower risk) over the longer term. A few large institutions have explicit ethical mandates (mostly government reserve funds, reflecting their governments' policies such as the Norwegian Government Pension Fund (Ministry of Finance Norway, 2007) and the New Zealand Superannuation Fund (New Zealand Superannuation Fund, 2007)) which allow investment decision-making based on non-financial factors. However, most large investors with policies to engage on a broad range of ESG issues justify their activities on the basis that these issues are connected with material risks or opportunities that may affect the portfolio, particularly over the longer term. This view is best summed up by the preamble of the PRI (UNPRI), drafted by leading pension funds and reflecting the motivation for their consideration of these issues. Between 2006 and 2020, these principles were adopted by more than 3000 mainstream institutions representing in excess of $100 trillion in assets under management. They state as follows:

> "As institutional investors, we have a duty to act in the best long-term interests of our beneficiaries. In this fiduciary role, we believe that environmental, social, and corporate governance (ESG) issues can affect the performance of investment portfolios (to varying degrees across companies, sectors, regions, asset classes, and through time). We also recognize that applying these Principles may better align investors with broader objectives of society".

In Principle 2, signatories commit to being "active owners and incorporate ESG issues into our ownership policies and practices". These principles encapsulate the most widely held view of the rationale for shareholder engagement today.

While improving financial performance is the ostensible rationale put forward by most investors, there is evidence that the pressure on investors to take on these approaches does not necessarily come from clients or beneficiaries of the fund. Forces helping to drive pension fund consideration of ESG issues in their ownership practices include public reputation, the need to secure more detailed information on companies for various ESG processes, and pressure from NGOs (McLaren, 2002). In addition, US State pension funds are often headed by elected officials, some of who are motivated by opportunities to simultaneously boost long-term investment returns and protect the public interest. For example, reducing greenhouse gas (GHG) emissions frequently achieves both goals, and many shareholder proposals ask companies to set GHG reduction goals.

An extension of this idea is the more general argument that pension and superannuation funds should represent the broader interests of their beneficiaries, including the enhancement of beneficiaries' environmental and social welfare. Under this rationale, it makes no sense that pension funds deliver returns to their members while at the same time harming the world into which their members will retire. Interestingly, as the number of members of pension funds increases, it could be argued that the interests of beneficiaries converge with those of the community in which the fund operates and therefore should reflect the democratic wishes of that society. This is even more the case given the shift from defining benefit to defining contribution plan, i.e. the capital is increasingly owned by the members themselves and should reflect their aspirations for the world into which they will retire.

Turning to the financial rationale, a common argument for investors to seek improvements in corporate sustainability performance is that strong performers make more money (or are less risky investments), and, if investors can seek and achieve improvements in CSP among the companies in their portfolio, they too will share in those increased profits. A 2015 meta-study of more than 2000 studies found that a large majority of studies report a positive relationship between CSP and financial performance (Friede *et al.*, 2015).

VIII. The Evolution of Shareholder Engagement Toolkit

Shareholders have a range of tools with which to influence corporate behavior.

The first step shareholders often take when issues of concern are identified is to initiate a dialog with the target company, starting with a letter expressing concerns about an issue. This is often followed up with face-to-face or telephone meetings with company representatives, often over a period of months or years. These company dialogs are opportunities for shareholders to raise issues of concern in a private and non-confrontational atmosphere. Investors use these meetings to better understand the issue of concern from the company's perspective and to explain further the case for the improvement they are calling for.

Beyond dialog, shareholders can use their formal shareholder rights to send a message of disapproval to company management. There are many examples of investors voting against the company's own shareholder proposals, such as endorsement of the remuneration report, based on an ESG issue that the investor deems problematic.

There are also numerous shareholder resolutions filed every year at company meetings, many of which do not have the support of management. Shareholders can also support other shareholders' resolutions in order to amplify the signal sent to management. In the US, UK, and Australia, there are mechanisms for the filing of shareholder resolutions at company meetings. In the UK and Australia, these tend to be used as a last resort, but, in the US, they are often used to attract the attention of management as the first or second step in having a dialog (many US investors send letters to initiate dialog and then file a proposal, if necessary, based on the company's response or lack thereof).

A shareholder resolution is often considered by ESG-focused investors to be somewhat successful if it gains more than about 25% of the vote. This figure is considered high enough that boards and management take notice and feel additional pressure to engage in dialog with the filer(s). In addition, in the US, once a proposal reaches 25%, it meets the highest

SEC threshold to be refiled in future years. Recently, ESG shareholder proposals are garnering higher votes, for example, resolutions broadly related to climate change and sustainability reporting averaged a record 30.8% (combined) during the 2020 season, and the small subset of climate proposals related to setting greenhouse gas reduction goals averaged about 45% in 2020 (Ceres).

Indeed, the purpose of shareholder proposals is not to gain 50% — the proposals are nearly always "non-binding", so a majority vote does not technically force companies to take any action — but rather to call sufficient attention to the issue so that the company is willing to engage in dialog about it so that an agreement can be reached and the resolution can be withdrawn by the filer in return for a commitment by the company. This is often referred to as a successfully negotiated withdrawal. Many filers of ESG resolutions, particularly those related to climate change, have successfully negotiated withdrawal rates well over 30% each year. During the 2020 proxy season, Ceres tracked 141 climate-related resolutions (broadly defined and including requests for sustainability reports) that resulted in 57 corporate commitments in return for withdrawals. This is the most important impact of shareholder proposals — changes in corporate practices.

However, votes remain important when corporations are reluctant to make the changes requested by the proposal. Investors who file a resolution can use a range of approaches to help build their case and increase the vote in favor. Since approaches and rules vary by country, we will describe the options used for companies headquartered in the US. Some investors do nothing more than file a proposal with a US company and wait for the vote, letting the proposal speak for itself. Others draft a memo making the business case for why other shareholders should vote "for" the proposal. In the US, a primary audience for these memos are the proxy advisory firms ISS, Glass Lewis, and Egan-Jones. If each of these firms recommends a "for" vote to their clients, the vote in favor will increase by 15–25%. An additional step a filer can take is to issue an "exempt proxy solicitation" for posting on the US SEC's EDGAR database. This document is often a shorter version of the memo sent to the proxy advisory firms and uses a special format required for posting to the SEC database. Once posted on EDGAR, the memo appears alongside all the official disclosure documents the SEC requires of companies, such as annual financial reports. In addition, the solicitation may also appear on the company's website if the company automatically posts all documents that appear on its EDGAR pages.

Filing proposals, engaging in dialogue with companies, and building support for a "yes" vote all require staff time on the part of investors. In addition, if a company formally requests an SEC opinion about whether the proposal violated SEC rules, investors may incur legal expenses defending their right to have it appear on the ballot. While many pension funds do not operate their own engagement teams, an increasing proportion do have specialists whose job it is to engage with companies and make voting decisions. Pension funds without these internal capabilities will either instruct their fund managers to engage and vote on their behalf or outsource their engagement to an unbundled engagement service provider to do so, whether or not they are connected to the management of the funds. These unbundled engagement services operate in Europe and Australia, but not yet in the US, where public pension funds have a more hands-on approach to company engagement. The largest asset managers have traditionally not been active in engaging companies on behalf of their clients, at least on environmental and social issues. This is changing fast as large asset managers in the US, such as State Street and BlackRock, are adding staff to in-house engagement teams driven by issues perceived as financially material such as climate change.

ESG research used for shareholder engagement activities can be generated in-house or purchased from ESG data providers, which collectively have a well-developed set of research services available for purchase covering many markets around the world (although ESG data for companies headquartered in emerging markets is less well developed).

Wherever a fund manager operates in a competitive market, there is marketing potential in using engagement capabilities to gain more clients. Due to the importance of the PRI and widespread adoption of Principle 2 on Active Ownership, engagement capability is now considered almost mandatory for large asset managers in Europe and the US. Even so, some of the largest US fund managers are only recently coming on board when it comes to voting in support of issues such as climate change. For example, it was not until 2017 when American Funds, BlackRock, Fidelity, and

Vanguard voted for the first time ever in favor of any climate proposals (Ceres).

There are many different ways in which shareholder engagement can be undertaken, with a range of cost implications. It would be relatively inexpensive (on a per engagement basis) for an investor to co-file shareholder proposals led by others or to call for the adoption of existing standards or codes of conduct across a range of companies, as well as write letters and hold conference calls with key companies to encourage adoption. However, it is more expensive to undertake engagement and public shareholder campaigns on cutting-edge issues that require untested, customized shareholder proposals and high-level, company-specific expertise, knowledge, and research.

There are also numerous collaborative investor initiatives, the goals of which are to leverage the combined influence of shareholders to seek corporate change, thereby reducing the costs and enhancing the effectiveness of engagement. These include long-running groups such as the Investor Group on Climate Change, the Ceres Investor Network on Climate Risk & Sustainability, the UN Principles for Responsible Investment Collaboration Platform, and more recent collaborations such as Climate Action 100+ and the Investor Alliance for Human Rights (launched in 2017 by the Interfaith Center on Corporate Responsibility).

IX. Shareholder Engagement Results

A critical question is whether shareholder engagement actually works. One convenient mechanism (primarily relevant in the US) that indicates whether shareholder activism has been effective in changing corporate behavior is, as previously mentioned, the number of resolutions withdrawn after successful negotiation in advance of going to a vote. The withdrawal of shareholder proposals by the proponents can be an indication that the proponents were sufficiently satisfied with the company's response that they agreed to withdraw it. Data provided by ISS reveal that less than half of all submitted shareholder proposals actually go to a vote. Out of the 11,706 proposals that the ISS database tracked between 2004 and 2017, only 5,342 proposals (46%) went to a shareholder vote. The SEC permitted companies to omit 1,741 proposals (15%). The remaining proposals were withdrawn after mutually agreeable outcomes with companies or otherwise did not go to a vote. Ceres has documented an impressive 344 corporate commitments related to climate change (broadly defined) by US companies in response to shareholder proposals during the six proxy seasons ending with 2018 (Ceres).

Once it is established that shareholders can have an impact on corporate behavior, the next step is to determine whether these changes led to any financial impact on the company. Any financial benefits arising from activism on corporate environmental and social performance would depend on whether

- there is a link between environmental/social issues and financial performance;
- shareholder activities can add value by pressuring management to address those risks and opportunities;
- the shareholder activity costs less to conduct than the value it adds.

There have been a number of studies that have explored these questions. Dimson *et al.* (2015) have perhaps conducted the most comprehensive study, reviewing over 2,100 engagements across 613 companies between 1999 and 2009. They find outperformance associated with those companies which were the targets of engagement, with the greatest outperformance coming from engagements focused on corporate governance and climate change. Hoepner *et al.* (2018) find that shareholder engagement on ESG issues results in reduced downside risk and, again, is most impactful when addressing governance and environmental policies.

X. Conclusion

With the rise of impact investing and the focus on the SDGs, it is essential that investors who wish to contribute to improving the state of the world recognize that in highly liquid, relatively efficient markets, shareholder engagement is the primary tool for delivering impact and should form a core part of their sustainable and impact investing strategy. The good news is that the industry is delivering, with more engagement happening than ever before, and this engagement appears to result in positive financial outperformance. Engagement is not the highest-profile strategy within the sustainable investing space, but given the evidence of its efficacy, its scalability, and its potential for delivering financial returns, it is reasonable to argue that it should become so.

References

Admati, A. R., Pfleiderer, P., and Zechner, J. (1994). "Large shareholder activism, risk sharing, and financial market equilibrium", *The Journal of Political Economy,* 104(6), pp. 1097–1130.

Berle, A. J., and Means, G. C. (1932). *The Modern Corporation and Private Property*, Macmillan, New York.

Dimson, E., Karaka, O., and Li, X. (2015). "Active ownership", *Review of Financial Studies (RFS)*, 28(12), pp. 3225–3268. SSRN: https://ssrn.com/abstract=2154724 or http://dx.doi.org/10.2139/ssrn.2154724.

Friede, G., Busch, T., and Bassen, A. (2015). "ESG and financial performance: Aggregated evidence from more than 2000 empirical studies", *Journal of Sustainable Finance & Investment*, 5(4), pp. 210–233.

Generation Investment Management. (2017). "Generation investment philosophy", Accessed on October 30, 2017, https://www.generationim.com/generation-philosophy/.

Hoepner, A., Oikonomou, I., Sautner, Z., Starks, L., and Zhou, X. (2018). "ESG shareholder engagement and downside risk", AFA 2018 paper. SSRN: https://ssrn.com/abstract=2874252; http://dx.doi.org/10.2139/ssrn.2874252.

Kasemir, B., Suess, A., and Zehnder, A. J. B. (2001). "The next unseen revolution: Pension fund investment and sustainability", *Environment*, 43(9), pp. 8–19.

Kinder, P. D., and Domini, A. L. (1997). "Social screening: Paradigms old and new", *Journal of Investing*, 6(4), pp. 12–19.

McLaren, D. (2002). "Engagement practices in socially responsible investment: Competing paradigms of governance and the emergence of standards", MBA Thesis, University of Cambridge.

Sethi, S. P. (2005). "Investing in socially responsible companies is a must for public pension funds — Because there is no better alternative", *Journal of Business Ethics*, 56(2), pp. 99–129.

Waygood, S. (2004). "NGOs and equity investment: A critical assessment of the practices of UK NGOs in using the capital market as a campaign device", PhD Thesis, University of Surrey.

Part III

Environmental Implications

https://doi.org/10.1142/9789811240928_0012

Chapter 12

Environmentally Sustainable Businesses, Energy Transition, and Climate Finance

Diane-Charlotte Simon

Learning Objectives

- Learn the definition of sustainable activities according to the EU Taxonomy
- Discover the concept of "circular economy"
- Understand climate change mitigation and adaptation strategies
- Learn about the main greenhouse gasses (GHG)
- Learn the concepts of the "energy transition" and "net-zero" targets
- Understand the importance of climate finance and financing of the energy transition

Abstract

This chapter introduces Part III on Environmental Implications of sustainability. It discusses how environmental sustainability has become a critical matter for stakeholders, and also provides a unique opportunity for businesses to enter a potentially lucrative and high impact area of the economy. While presenting risks for businesses and investors, environmental sustainability also presents an opportunity amounting to trillions of dollars for those developing and scaling successful solutions. The chapter highlights how, in the past few decades, there have been increased stakeholder expectations for corporate environmental responsibility, which has transformed the business landscape. Consumers, investors, NGOs, and regulators are now pressing companies to account for their environmental impact. The chapter introduces the European Union (EU) Taxonomy for sustainable activities. It presents the concept of a *circular economy* which aims to reduce waste and improve product design to optimize recycling. It explores climate change mitigation for companies, touching on greenhouse gases, net-zero targets, the energy transition, and the critical importance of carbon removal solutions. It then covers adaptation strategies. The chapter concludes by calling attention to the need to develop and scale economically viable carbon capture technologies. It emphasizes that, while necessary, the energy transition alone may not be sufficient to tackle climate change given the long lifespan of carbon dioxide in the atmosphere. Carbon capture and transformation technologies following the *circular economy* model, such as mineral carbonation, are particularly promising as they would transform carbon dioxide, a threat, into a valuable resource.

I. Introduction

The recent focus on environmental sustainability provides a unique opportunity for businesses to enter a potentially lucrative and high impact area of the economy. First, this chapter begins by bringing to light the societal trends signaling the growing importance of the environment. Second, the chapter presents the definition of sustainable activities according to the European Union's Taxonomy for sustainable activities as a point of reference coming from a regulator. According to this definition, environmentally sustainable businesses foster the transition to a circular economy, and attempt to mitigate and adapt to climate change. For this reason, the chapter then presents the concept of circular economy, which is based on the logic that waste can be valuable and transformed in order to reduce pollution and the amount of waste. The chapter then explores climate change mitigation and adaptation for companies. This involves an introduction to the main greenhouse gases, net-zero targets, the Energy Transition, and the critical importance of carbon removal solutions. The chapter concludes with an introduction to climate finance, which finances climate change mitigation and adaptation with a particular focus on the financing of the energy transition.

Chapter 12 is organized as per the following sections:

I. Introduction
II. The Rise of Environmental Considerations
III. The European Union Taxonomy for Sustainable Activities
IV. The Circular Economy
V. Climate Change for Businesses: Net Zero, Energy Transition, etc.
VI. Climate Finance & Financing the Energy Transition
VII. Conclusion

II. The Rise of Environmental Considerations

The last few decades have seen higher stakeholder expectations for corporate environmental responsibility, which has transformed the business landscape. Consumers, investors, NGOs, and regulators are now pressing companies to account for their environmental impact (Hoffman, 1999; King and Lenox, 2000). The development of information and communications technologies have empowered stakeholders to make their voices heard through social media, putting companies' reputations on the line. The pressure on organizations to reduce their ecological footprints has never been so high (Christoffersen *et al.*, 2013).

Climate change is increasingly at the center of the public's attention and more and more citizens, consumers, and shareholders are requesting more accountability from governments and businesses alike. In 2014, the People's Climate March initiated by Avaaz and 350.org mobilized 675,000 people worldwide. In 2019, that amount rose to 6 million fueled by the release of additional research by scientists from the Intergovernmental Panel on Climate Change (IPCC) which concluded that greenhouse gas (GHG) emissions must entirely disappear by 2100, and by the *Fridays for Future* movement led by the young Greta Thunberg which began organizing global school strikes in 2018 (Haynes, 2019). In the US, another youth-led movement, the Sunrise Movement, introduced a Green New Deal in the political agenda calling for a clean economy and the spread of renewable energy which can be credited for the 2022 Inflation Reduction Act which became the largest US climate bill with $369 billion dedicated to clean energy and greenhouse gas reduction. Legal action has also spiked; the United Nations Environmetal Program (UNEP) reports that as of 2020, 1,550 climate change cases were filed in 38 countries, close to double those reported in 2017 (UNEP, 2020a). Some of these suits claim corporate liability and responsibility for climate harms and request greater climate disclosures and an end to corporate greenwashing. The call to act on climate change can also be heard from the business world. In December 2019, 631 institutional investors with $37 trillion in assets urged governments to step up efforts to tackle the climate crisis and reach the goals of the Paris Agreement (Ceres, 2019). CEOs are now aware of the threats presented by climate change and environmental damage as illustrated in PWC's 23rd Annual Global CEO Survey in which it was listed among the top 15 issues for 2020. Perhaps the most striking moment was when the CEO of Blackrock, the world's largest asset manager, opened up the climate change discussion in its annual Letter to CEOs by outlining the risks and opportunities for investment and how they would impact the firm's decision-making (Fink, 2020, 2021).

III. The European Union Taxonomy for Sustainable Activities

The European Union (EU) established the Taxonomy Regulation (EU) 2020/852 in order to facilitate the transition to a sustainable, low-carbon, resilient, and resource-efficient economy. Other objectives included to protect against greenwashing, foster sustainable finance, and direct investments toward sustainable projects and activities. The Taxonomy Regulation, which entered into force on 12 July 2020, is a classification system defining economic activities that can be considered environmentally sustainable by meeting the three following technical screening criteria:

1. The activities make a substantive contribution to one of six environmental objectives:
    (a) Climate Change Mitigation
    (b) Climate Change Adaptation

    (c) The Sustainable Use and Protection of Water and Marine Resources

    (d) The Transition to a Circular Economy

    (e) Pollution Prevention and Control

    (f) The Protection and Restoration of Biodiversity and Ecosystems.

2. They do no significant harm (DNSH) to the other five environmental objectives.

3. They meet minimum safeguards such as the OECD Guidelines on Multinational Enterprises and the UN Guiding Principles on Business and Human Rights.

In May 2021, the European Commission agreed on a first Delegated Act which contained detailed technical screening criteria focused on climate mitigation and adaptation. In March 2022, the Commission adopted a Complementary Climate Delegated Act which includes under certain conditions nuclear and gas in the list of economic activities covered by the EU taxonomy. The inclusion of gas was justified by its role as a transition fuel (in replacement to coal). However, the Complementary Climate Delegated Act has received some important pushback from the general public who considers it as greenwashing and environmental groups have started legal actions to remove the classification of gas as a sustainable activity.

The EU Taxonomy Compass available on the European Commission website lists the activities that qualify as sustainable as well as the criteria which justified this qualification.

Even though this classification system only applies to Europe, it is a good reference point to understand what can be considered as a sustainable activity.

IV. The Circular Economy

The circular economy concept emphasizes the value of waste as a resource and attempts to address its issues along with those of finite resource management and, to a lesser extent, pollution. To reach environmental sustainability, companies need to tailor their business models and operations to circular economy principles. The essence of these principles is captured in

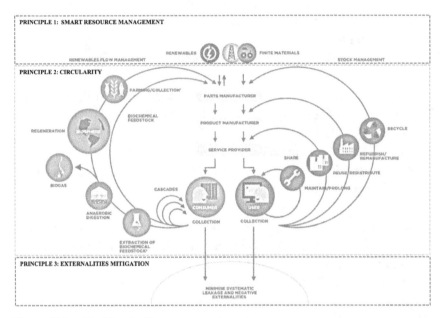

Figure 12.1. The Circular Economy

Notes: (1) Hunting and fishing.

(2) Can take both post-harvest and post-consumer waste as an input.

Source: Based on the Ellen MacArthur Foundation's Circular Economy System Diagram (2019).

the famous quote from French chemist Lavoisier on the foundation of physics: "Nothing is lost, nothing is created, ***everything is transformed***". The circular economy examines the environmental impacts of a given product during its entire life cycle, from development to recycling, from supply chain to the product's use. The framework applies a closed-loop model whereby all waste is the feedstock of something else and nothing is wasted (see Figure 12.1). It envisions a systemic approach that shifts away from a linear economy in order to build long-term resilience and generate business and economic opportunities, while also benefiting society and the environment (Ellen MacArthur Foundation, 2017).

The circular economy comprises three main principles:

- **Principle 1: Smart Resource Management** — Preserve and enhance natural capital by controlling finite stocks and balancing renewable resource flows.

- **Principle 2: Circularity** — Optimize resource yields by circulating products, components, and materials in use at the highest level possible at all times in both technical and biological cycles.
- **Principle 3: Externalities Mitigation** — Foster system effectiveness by revealing negative externalities and designing around them.

The "cradle-to-cradle approach", developed by architect William McDonough and chemist Michael Braungart, is one of the foundational schools of thought on the circular economy (McDonough and Braungart 2008). McDonough and Braungart describe this approach as "an integration of design and science that provides enduring benefits for society from safe materials, water, and energy in circular economies and eliminates the concept of waste". They believe that "everything is a resource for something else" and that "everything can be designed to be disassembled and safely returned to the soil as biological nutrients, or re-utilized as high-quality materials for new products as technical nutrients without contamination". Establishing these fundamental assertions, McDonough and Braungart provide the core working principles for the Impact Economy discussed later in the chapter.

The circular economy distinguishes two types of cycles based on the product's material: biological and technical. Biological cycles can be implemented for food and natural materials. Used feedstock can be fed back into the system through processes like composting and anaerobic digestion. Living systems such as soil can thus be regenerated and reused as a resource. Technical cycles apply to products, components, and materials which can be recovered or restored through reuse, repair, remanufacture, or recycling (Ellen MacArthur Foundation, 2017).

V. Climate Change for Businesses: Net Zero, Energy Transition, etc.

Our planet now stands face-to-face with the reality of climate change. We are witnessing the increase and intensification of extreme weather events, sea-level rise, and water shortages, which will likely lead to mass migrations, disease, and biodiversity loss (see Chapter 2). In order to reach the objectives of the Paris Agreement and significantly reduce the risks and impacts of climate change, the global target is to hold the increase in the global average temperature to well below 2°C above pre-industrial levels and to pursue efforts to limit the temperature increase to 1.5°C above pre-industrial levels. In October 2018, the Intergovernmental Panel on Climate Change (IPCC), the reference organization for climate change science, reported that we are nearing a tipping point for mitigating the effects of climate change, and avoiding this cliff edge requires a drastic transformation of our society over the next decade. The report calls for radical and rapid changes in all aspects of our lives to prevent a global temperature increase exceeding 1.5°C above pre-industrial levels, which would trigger uncontrollable catastrophic events. The science behind these forecasts is abundant, well-documented, and easily accessible in our digital era. Climate change is perhaps the greatest sustainability issue, but it is not the only one. Waste profusion, pollution, clean water access, diversity, and inequalities all pose sustainability challenges.

All this may seem outside the purview of business. But like everything on this planet, businesses and the economy rely on natural resources and the environment to operate and thrive. Neither is immune to environmental risks. A study published by the US government states that without "substantial and sustained global mitigation and regional adaptation efforts", climate change will cause considerable damage to the US economy, with hundreds of billions of dollars in annual losses projected by the end of the century (USGCRP, 2018).

The period from the late 1800s to the early 2000s saw a rise in average global temperature of 1.06°C (33.9 Fahrenheit) due to human activity and is on a path to 2.7°C by the end of the century, (IPCC, 2021). This is well beyond the 1.5°C-above-pre-industrial-levels threshold expected to trigger uncontrollable disastrous events, according to the IPCC's 2018 report. Their 2021 report asserts that climate change has already affected every region across the globe, with the increase in frequency and strength of extreme weather conditions leading to drought, fires, flooding, and overall destruction which impacts citizens and businesses alike. Climate change impacts most sectors with different levels of severity (Cho, 2019). The heat alone can impact human health, the overall productivity of employees, companies' ability to operate, and even disrupts transportation and supply chains. To overcome record heatwaves in the summer of 2022,

China had to close factories across the country. Some worried that the consequences on its supply chain could be worse than COVID-19 lockdowns (Daniel, 2022). Agriculture is considered to be the most vulnerable sector as temperature, water availability, pest, and fires impact crop yields. Ocean acidification is also impacting marine biodiversity and fish stock (Frommel *et al.*, 2011). Infrastructure and physical assets are at risk from flooding and extreme weather events.

Companies can serve the environment *and themselves* by adopting both mitigation and adaptation strategies. Effectively addressing climate change requires mitigation strategies to limit additional warming with sustained reductions in GHG. This will involve major shifts in the energy sector away from fossil fuels, the main contributors to GHG (UNEP, 2020b), reconfiguring industrial processes to reduce GHG emissions, or even changing business models (e.g. the food industry developing plant-based protein options like Beyond Meat). But mitigation initiatives alone are insufficient; businesses will need initiatives to adapt as well. We will examine both.

1. Mitigation

Mitigation approaches attempt to prevent further warming by drastically reducing the atmospheric concentration of greenhouses gases. Mitigation requires changing the way we produce energy but also the way we live, consume, and travel. Before delving into the two main mitigation strategies which involve "The Energy Transition" and the development of effective carbon removal solutions, we will explore the main greenhouse gases, companies' carbon footprints, and net-zero targets.

A. *Greenhouse Gases*

CO_2 has been the main driver of global warming to date, so its reduction is a critical angle for mitigation. It is important to simultaneously take another angle with four super climate pollutants: methane, black carbon, hydrofluorocarbons, and tropospheric ozone. When we stop emitting these pollutants, 90% of the warming they cause will stop within a decade, whereas 25–40% of CO_2 has remained in the atmosphere for 500 years

(Miller *et al.*, 2021). Slashing these emissions will reduce warming *faster* than with CO_2.

To take a closer look at the main greenhouse gases:

- **Carbon Dioxide (CO_2)** is the primary cause of global warming. The bulk of CO_2 emissions come from fossil fuel combustion in transportation (cars, trucks, buses, ships, airplanes, etc.), electricity production (mostly coal and gas-fired power plants), and heating for commercial and residential buildings. Emissions also come from deforestation and industrial processes such as cement production (see Table 12.1). CO_2 is also produced in smaller quantities from natural sources (e.g. the ocean, volcanoes, wildfires, and decomposing vegetation) which are

Table 12.1. Major GHG, Impact, and Sources

Greenhouse Gas	Global Warming Potential (GWP)	Atmospheric Lifetime (years)	Major Sources
Carbon Dioxide (CO_2)	1	Up to 500	• Fossil fuel combustion • Deforestation • Cement production
Methane (CH_4)	28–36	12	• Fossil fuel production and transportation • Agriculture • Landfills
Black Carbon (BC)	460–1,500	Up to 2 weeks	• Combustion of fossil fuels, wood and other fuels
Hydrofluorocarbon (HFC)	12,400	15	• Refrigerants
Nitrous Oxide (N_2O)	265–298	121	• Fertilizer • Fossil fuel and biomass combustion • Industrial processes
Nitrogen Trifluoride (NF_3)	16,100	500	• Semiconductor manufacturing
Sulfur Hexafluoride (SF_6)	23,500	3,200	• Electric transmission

Source: Based on the IPCC Fifth Assessment Report 2014, EPA 2022, The Center for Climate and Energy Solutions and the Climate and Cleanair Coalition 2021.

offset by "sinks" such as photosynthesis by plants, absorption into oceans, and soil creation.

- **Methane (CH_4)** is the secondary cause of global warming. CH_4 warms the planet at a greater rate than CO_2 by a factor of 28–36 but stays in the atmosphere for a shorter amount of time (around 12 years), making it a unique lever to limit additional warming (see Table 12.1). Methane is emitted mostly from fossil fuel production and transportation (leaks from oil and gas wells, pipelines, power plants, refineries, gas liquefaction plants, petrochemical plants, etc.), agriculture (manure pits and cow belches), and landfills. Methane is also released from frozen permafrost during Arctic melting.
- **Black Carbon (BC)** or soot remains in the atmosphere only a few weeks, so its reduction may also rapidly reduce warming. Black Carbon is produced by the incomplete combustion of fossil fuels, biofuels, and biomass which occurs naturally and through human activities. Diesel engines, cook stoves, wood burning, and forest fires are the primary sources of soot. Black carbon is particularly important in developing countries (The Center for Climate and Energy Solutions (C2ES), 2010).
- **Hydrofluorocarbons (HFC)** are another short-lived GHG (15 years in the atmosphere). HFC come mostly from our air-conditioners and refrigerators, but also from insulating foams and aerosol propellants. HFCs are man-made and have only been emitted since the early 1990s. The current amount of HFCs in the atmosphere is small, but their potential for warming is greater than CO_2 by a factor of 12,000 and they are one of the fastest-growing GHGs due to the increasing demand for refrigeration and air-conditioning in developing countries.
- **Tropospheric Ozone (O_3)** is a harmful type of ozone at ground level, not to be confused with the helpful ozone higher in the stratosphere, which shields the Earth from the sun's dangerous radiation. Tropospheric Ozone is formed when sunlight interacts with hydrocarbons and nitrogen oxides, which are emitted by fueled vehicles, factories, power plants, and refineries. (UCAR, 2014).

As illustrated in Table 12.2, the historic 5% reduction in GHG in 2020 due to the COVID-19 related lockdowns was just a blip. Global GHG

Table 12.2. Global GHG Emissions and Sector Contribution

	2012	2013	2014	2015	2016	2017	2018	2019	2020	2021
Total Global GHG (in Million metric tons of CO_2 equivalent)	47,246	47,843	48,231	48,136	48,264	48,960	49,898	50,263	47,935	51,340
Year-on-Year Variation	2%	1%	1%	0%	0%	1%	2%	1%	–5%	7%
				Sector Contribution to Total GHG						
Electricity, Gas, Steam, and Air Conditioning	28%	28%	28%	28%	28%	28%	28%	27%	27%	27%
Manufacturing	19%	19%	19%	18%	18%	18%	19%	19%	19%	20%
Agriculture, Forestry, and Fishing	13%	13%	13%	13%	13%	13%	13%	13%	13%	13%
Households	10%	11%	11%	11%	11%	11%	11%	11%	11%	11%
Water, Waste, and Remediation	6%	6%	6%	6%	6%	6%	6%	6%	6%	7%
Transportation and Storage	6%	6%	6%	6%	6%	6%	7%	7%	6%	6%
Construction	6%	6%	6%	6%	6%	6%	6%	6%	6%	6%
Mining	6%	6%	6%	6%	5%	5%	5%	6%	6%	5%
Other Services Industries	5%	5%	5%	6%	6%	6%	6%	6%	6%	5%

Source: Based on data from 2022 IMF Climate Change Dashboard.

emissions were back to pre-pandemic levels in 2021 and rose to new record highs with emissions increasing across sectors (Bhanumati *et al.*, 2022). In retrospect, given the massive disruption to the global economy linked to COVID-19, seeing that only 5% of GHG decreased in 2020 gives a hint to the scale of the efforts which need to be undertaken to tackle climate change. Considering the current annual GHG emissions, we have less than a decade to drastically slow global warming before we risk hitting irreversible tipping points that will trigger catastrophic climate change (Miller *et al.*, 2021).

Electricity, Gas, Steam, and Air Conditioning is the sector producing most GHG at 27% in 2021 (see Table 12.2 based on the GHG Protocol (2013). It is followed by Manufacturing at 20% and Agriculture, Forestry, and Fishing at 13% in 2021 (see Table 12.2). Combined, these three sectors contributed 60% of the overall GHG in 2021. As a result, these sectors' mitigation efforts should be targeted with greater scrutiny.

Now that we know the main greenhouse gases, let's explore companies' carbon footprints and net-zero targets.

B. *Companies' Carbon Footprint*

Measuring greenhouse gases emissions and their overall levels in the atmosphere is critical to managing them and assessing the efficiency of mitigation initiatives. It is also important to understand GHG's origin to be able to effectively reduce them. A 2017 research paper from CDP, a leading environmental disclosure not-for-profit, found that 100 companies in the fossil fuel industry were responsible for 70% of global emissions since 1988 (Griffin, 2017).

While companies have historically been voluntarily reporting on their GHG emissions, investors and regulators are increasingly requiring it. In 2022, investors managing $130 trillion in assets have contacted more than 10,000 companies to disclose their environmental performance data including their GHG emissions to CDP (Jessop, 2022).

In 1998, the World Resources Institute (WRI) and the World Business Council for Sustainable Development (WBCSD) launched the Greenhouse Gas Protocol (see Figure 12.2), which has become the most commonly used standard for measuring and reporting emissions.

To be exhaustive, a company's GHG reduction policy needs to address both direct emissions and indirect emissions across its value chain. These fall into three categories of emission scopes, as defined by the Greenhouse Gas Protocol (see Figure 12.2):

- Scope 1 includes direct emissions from owned or controlled sources.
- Scope 2 includes indirect emissions from the purchased electricity, steam, heating, and cooling systems.
- Scope 3 covers the remaining indirect emissions in a company's value chain.

In 2017, the Financial Stability Board created the Task Force on Climate-related Financial Disclosures (TCFD) chaired by Michael R. Bloomberg. The TCFD recommends disclosures going beyond GHG emissions to include considerations on governance, strategy, risk management, as well as metrics and targets to facilitate the assessment of climate-related risks and opportunities for companies and their investors.

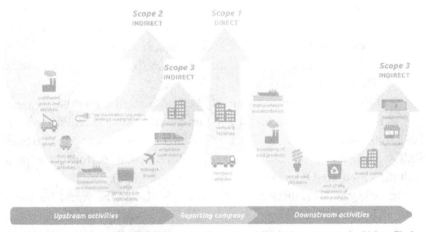

Figure 12.2. Overview of GHG Protocol Scopes and Emissions across the Value Chain

Source: Based on the GHG Protocol (2013), "Corporate Value Chain (Scope 3) Standard".

C. *Net-Zero Targets*

More and more companies and financial institutions are making commitments to "net-zero". This means reducing their greenhouse gas emissions, and offsetting emissions that they can't reduce. Striving for net-zero targets can be considered a mitigation strategy.

Net-zero targets are an improvement, but some argue they are far from sufficient. Indeed, some label this strategy as greenwashing, criticizing these organizations for relying too much on offsets with unproven impact and without sufficiently adjusting their business models to reduce their emissions. Others argue that the commitments made are targeting deadlines in a too distant future.

D. *The Energy Transition*

The Energy Transition refers to the transition away from fossil fuels such as coal, oil, and gas toward less carbon-intensive sources of energy like renewable energy, nuclear energy, or green hydrogen which can be made with renewable energy through a process called electrolysis. Fossil fuels (e.g. coal and gas) are mainly used for electricity generation, in the transportation sector (e.g. cars, truck, airplanes, shipping, etc.), and in industrial processes.

The Energy Transition is already underway. While in 2010, renewable energy (onshore and offshore wind, solar PV, hydro) contributed to 20% of the global electricity generation mix, this amount increased to 28% in 2020 according to the International Energy Association (IEA), (IEA, 2021). This shift has been enabled by the sharp decrease in the cost of renewables whose Leveraged Cost of Electricity (LCOE) is now cheaper than fossil fuels in most parts of the globe. Yet, to reach a net-zero greenhouse gas emissions scenario, the contribution of renewables to electricity generation must rise to 88% by 2050 (IEA, 2021). In terms of built energy capacity, this involves the increase of renewables capacity by almost tenfold from that of 2020 to reach 27 TW by 2050 and the massive expansion of the use of battery storage to reach 3 TW by 2050, which would involve a 19% CAGR from the 17 GW installed in 2020 (IEA, 2021). This represents a huge opportunity in the growing clean energy market, comprising renewables, battery storage, fuels cells, and electrolyzers, to produce green hydrogen, which is forecasted to be worth a cumulative $27 trillion by 2050 (IEA, 2021). Close to half of this market is expected from the Asia Pacific region (IEA, 2021). It is also important to remember that as of 2020 close to one out of ten people still lived without electricity in the world, mostly in developing countries and in Africa (IEA, 2021). This situation could benefit from the energy transition, especially from distributed generation and microgrid solutions including small-scale solar projects and storage, that would leapfrog lack of infrastructure.

However, energy transition does not affect the energy sector only. It actually impacts many sectors including the following (see Section VI for more details about these sectors and investments targeting the energy transition):

1. **Energy** (e.g. renewable energy, nuclear power, energy storage, hydrogen)
2. **Transportation & Mobility** (e.g. electric vehicles)
3. **Heating & Buildings** (e.g. heat pumps)
4. **Industry & Materials** (see circular economy concept above)
5. **Agriculture & Food**
6. **Climate Solutions & Carbon Capture**

While the energy transition is necessary to address climate change, it poses some challenges that still need to be addressed and new technologies need to be developed and deployed as quickly as possible. The transition is not simple nor is it straightforward. Key challenges include:

- The **intermittency of renewable energy sources**. Renewable energy is produced only when the sun shines or when the wind blows, and these moments don't always align with moments of consumer need. Power assets that are functionable day and night, or "baseload assets", are important for the electricity grid. Hydro power, nuclear energy, and gas-fired power plants are all considered baseload assets. Battery storage offers a solution to tackle energy intermittency. However, most storage batteries to date only allow to store energy for shorter periods than needed by consumers. Developing longer-term storage solutions will be key for a smooth energy transition, without damaging the electric grid or threatening consumer access to cheap, reliable energy.

- **The role of gas**. Gas produces less GHG than coal and oil, and it has been steadily replacing coal over the last decade, proving to be a crucial element in reducing global carbon emissions. For this reason, gas is considered a "transition fuel". Moreover, carbon efficient gas assets remain important in the electricity mix to address the intermittency of renewable assets, while battery storage with longer lasting capacities are developed.
- **Mismatch between renewable electricity production and electricity demand**. The volume of electricity produced during certain times of the day (when the sun shines and the wind blows) can be so important that it drives electricity prices negative. On the other hand, when the electricity demand peaks, typically when people get back home after work, solar energy is not available as the sun goes down. This can lead to hikes in price. Storage solutions can address these problems as they arise.
- **Sectors hard to electrify**. While many economic sectors can be electrified and operated without fossil fuels (e.g. electric vehicles), other sectors are more challenging to electrify such as the cement, iron, steel, and chemical sectors because of their high-temperature heat requirements. Hydrogen may become a useful solution for these industries.

Companies in the energy and electricity sector have key roles to play in the fight against climate change but are also uniquely vulnerable to macro shifts brought on by climate change mitigation. Oil majors and companies in the coal sector face considerable transition risks stemming from changing consumer tastes as well as regulatory changes such as the potential implementation of a carbon tax. Furthermore, some fossil fuel reserves recognized on companies' balance sheets may become inaccessible and face the "stranded assets" risk, impacting both companies and their investors, which may in turn lead to systemic risk which would impact the entire economy. Pre-empting this, some companies have transitioned away from coal entirely. Others are focusing on developing their activity in renewable energy either by in-house growth or through acquisitions.

E. *Carbon Removal Solutions*

Given the amount of time some GHGs remain in the atmosphere, limiting further warming requires **carbon removal solutions**, in addition to energy transition. Different approaches exist. Nature-based solutions include afforestation, reforestation, restoration of coastal and marine habitats as well as measures to enhance naturally occurring processes such as increasing carbon content in soil (IEA, 2020). Carbon capture and sequestration/storage solutions "CCS", which have been more widely developed and tested, are implemented during power generation and industrial processes to capture and store up to 100% of CO_2 emissions generated (Gonzales *et al.*, 2020). According to the Global CCS Institute 2020 Report, 26 commercial CCS facilities were operating globally as of 2020 and 37 were in various stages of development and construction. Direct air capture with carbon storage (DACCS) technologies extract CO_2 directly from the atmosphere (IEA, 2020). As of 2021, 27 carbon capture facilities were in operation, 5 under construction, 66 in advanced development, and 97 in early stage according to the International Energy Agency (IEA, 2021).

Carbon capture and storage (CCS) is a chemical approach to carbon dioxide removal involving anthropogenic activities that seek to remove CO_2 from the atmosphere and durably store it in geological, terrestrial, or ocean reservoirs, or in products (IPPC 2021 AR6). CSS differs from approaches enhancing biological or geochemical carbon sinks on land in vegetation, soils, or geological formations (such as afforestation, soil carbon sequestration, bioenergy with carbon capture and storage or wet land restoration) or in the oceans (such as ocean fertilization or ocean alkalinization) (IPCC 2021). The development and implementation of carbon removal solutions at scale could play a pivotal role in limiting climate warming. Carbon capture and transformation technologies following the circular economy model, such as the mineral carbonation, are particularly promising as they would transform carbon dioxide, a threat, into a valuable resource which can be used as a feedstock. Mineral carbonation is a process resulting in the creation of solid carbonates from the reaction of CO_2 with metal oxide bearing materials such as calcium and magnesium. Mineral carbonation can be observed in nature as the process of rock weathering by rainwater which stores the excessive CO_2 in the atmosphere in rocks. Geologists believe that this process, which took place for over millions of years, reduced the amount of CO_2 present in the atmosphere to levels that enable life to survive today.

At this stage, however, these are not as developed as renewable energies which, even without financial assistance, are more economical than fossil fuel in most parts of the globe (IRENA, 2019). More viable solutions must be developed, tested, and implemented at a large scale. Policy support or a carbon price could help to improve profitability, but for now, carbon capture solutions generally remain expensive and do not make economic sense (IPCC, 2005).

2. Adaptation

Adaptation strategies reduce the negative impact of warming and extreme weather events already upon us. They include:

- reconsidering building construction along coastlines to manage rise in sea levels;
- improving water drainage and storage with stormwater systems in areas prone to flooding;
- adapting city infrastructure and buildings to reduce heat by using clear colored roofs or green roofs, which also help to deal with rainwater;
- using fire resistant materials to build homes in fire-prone areas
- ecosystem-based adaptation such as
  - reforestation to combat desertification
  - rehabilitating wetlands to reduce flooding
  - water and land management practices
  - restoring coastal ecosystems such as coral reefs, mangrove forests, dune systems, and salt marshes to reduce the impact of tropical storms.

Adaptation strategies become more and more critical as the effects of climate change become more and more present.

VI. Climate Finance & Financing the Energy Transition

While it is ironically not always labeled as "sustainable" or "green", financing climate change mitigation and adaptation (***climate finance***) and the transition away from fossil fuels is core to the concept of sustainability. The low-carbon energy transition fits within the sustainability theme strategy discussed earlier and, provided its critical role in the fight against climate change, we argue that it can exist as a subset of sustainable finance on its own.

2021 was a record year for the energy transition, with $920 billion invested globally (see Table 12.3) according to Bloomberg's Energy Transition Investment Trends 2022 report (Bloomberg New Energy Finance (BNEF, 2022). This is progress, but the capital deployed in 2021 is still insufficient to get us on track for net-zero emissions by 2050, a requirement for 1.75 °C of warming (BNEF, 2022). To reach that goal, Energy Transition finance must scale and accelerate **to a yearly average of $2.1 trillion between 2022 and 2025 and then double to $4.2 trillion annually over the 2026–2030 period**, according to Bloomberg New Energy Outlook 2021 (BNEF, 2022).

1. Subsector Analysis

More than half of all 2021 Energy Transition investments were directed to the energy sector and particularly renewable energy (see Table 12.3).

Table 12.3. Energy Transition Investments by Subsectors and Stage (in Billion USD)

Sector	Technology Status		Total	%
	Advanced	Early-Stage		
Energy	409	68.5	**477.5**	52%
Transportation & Mobility	273	67.4	**340.4**	37%
Heating & Buildings	53	1.4	**54.4**	6%
Industry & Materials	17.7	9.1	**26.8**	3%
Agriculture & Food	0	14.9	**14.9**	2%
Carbon & Climate	2.3	3.8	**6.1**	1%
Total	**755**	**165.1**	**920.1**	**100%**

Source: Estimates based on BNEF (2022).

Transportation & Mobility was the second largest subsector at 37% and encountered the fastest growth (see Table 12.3). Other subsectors included Heating & Buildings, Industry & Materials, Agriculture & Food as well as Carbon & Climate. Provided that these sectors contributed to close to 90% of 2019 global greenhouse gases emissions in aggregate (see Figure 13.2 in Chapter 13), investments reducing emissions in these sectors are crucial to address global warming.

A. *Energy*

Unsurprisingly, energy attracted more than half of Energy Transition investments and was the largest subsector for both advanced and early-stage climate-tech technologies with $409 billion and $68.5 billion, respectively (see Table 12.3). Most investments in the sector targeted the financing of renewable energy equipment but also software and systems, such as virtual power plants and distributed energy resource management systems, especially for climate tech.

- **Renewable energy** encompasses sources of electricity such as wind (onshore and offshore), solar, hydro power, and geothermal. Renewable energy was the largest contributor to Energy Transition financing in 2021 (BNEF, 2022). $366 billion was deployed across utility-scale, commercial, and industrial projects as well as small-scale residential projects (mainly solar) benefiting households directly (BNEF, 2022). This represented a 6.5% increase since the previous year.
- **Nuclear power** has historically been excluded from the scope of sustainable investments because of nuclear waste, but it has recently gained popularity due to its low carbon profile. Nuclear is also more reliable than renewables, which generate electricity intermittently only when the sun is shining or the wind is blowing. $31 billion was deployed in 2021 to finance the construction of new reactors and major refurbishments (BNEF, 2022).
- **Energy storage** solutions have become critical with the increased penetration of renewables in the energy mix provided the intermittency of renewable electricity generation. Indeed, when the demand for electricity is high, typically at the end of the day when people

come back home from work, the sun is not shining anymore and if there are not enough alternative sources of electricity to meet the demand, electricity price increases. This phenomenon is accentuated with the retirement of fossil fuel assets such as coal plants or gas-fired power plants driven by greenhouse gas emissions reduction goal to limit the negative effects of climate change.

- ○ Most of the installed energy storage capacity to date utilizes hydroelectricity from pumped hydro plants. However, there are many technologies able to store energy, such as stationary battery storage projects, which are a growing asset class and can be built on a standalone basis or coupled with other power generating assets (typically solar plants).

- ○ Close to $10 billion was deployed for lithium-ion batteries in 2021. The capital dedicated to this asset class is projected to continue growing provided their critical role in addressing BNEF forecasts that by 2030 the installed capacity of battery storage will represent 20x that of 2020, which was 17 GW/34 GWh, to reach in excess of 350 GW/1,000 GWh (BNEF, 2021). This means that batteries would be able to store up to 34 GWh (power capacity) to discharge up to 350 GW (energy capacity) by 2030. BNEF estimates that it will require investments in excess of $262 billion (BNEF, 2021).

- **Hydrogen** is currently attracting a lot of attention; it is a technology with great potential for transitioning sectors that cannot be electrified. Investments in hydrogen typically include electrolyzer projects, fuel cell vehicles, and hydrogen refueling infrastructure. Hydrogen is still at an early stage and attracted only $2 billion in 2021. This amount is expected to grow significantly over the next decade.

B. *Transportation & Mobility*

Transportation was the fastest-growing sector in 2021 and the second largest for both advanced and early-stage climate-tech technologies with $273 billion and $67.4 billion, respectively (see Table 12.3). Most investments were directed to electrified transportation including electric vehicles (EVs) such as electric cars as well as buses and their associated charging infrastructure. Other subsets financed for early-stage companies comprised e-scooters, electric airplanes, fuel cells, and mobility tech such as ride-sharing or route efficiency.

C. *Heating & Buildings*

With $53 billion deployed in 2021, most of the investments in the Heating & Buildings subsector were directed toward electrified heat such as residential heat pumps. The remaining investments went to early-stage low-carbon buildings of companies related to insulation, energy efficiency systems, or waste heat reuse, which raised $1.4 billion in 2021.

D. *Industry & Materials*

Approximately $18 billion were invested in climate-conscious industry and sustainable materials in 2021. Themes falling under this sector include circular economy, recycling, innovative materials as well as biochemicals and process electrification.

E. *Agriculture & Food*

Agriculture and Food was the fourth largest sector attracting $14.9 billion in early-stage climate tech. Agriculture technologies and subsegments include alternatives such as meats, indoor farming, vertical farming, increasing crop yields, decreasing food waste, and precision agriculture.

F. *Climate & Carbon*

Climate and carbon startups raised $3.8 billion in 2021. A large number of companies financed in this sector were software startups. Subsegments include satellite imagery, carbon accounting, weather forecasting, climate modeling, and carbon offsetting.

2. Expansion of Existing Technologies vs. Climate Tech Innovation

Out of the close to $1 trillion 2021 energy transition investments, $165 billion (18%) focused on equity investments in **new climate-tech**

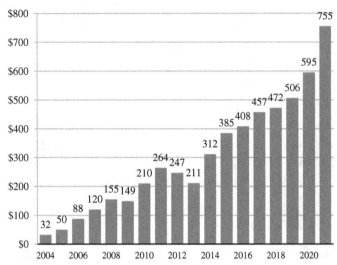

Figure 12.3. Global Investment in the Deployment of Existing Energy Transition Technologies

Source: BNEF (2022).

innovation while over 80% was used to deploy **existing technologies** largely through specific power and infrastructure projects (see Figure 12.3). 2021 investments in the deployment of existing climate solutions reached $755 billion, up from $595 billion in 2020, representing a 27% year-over-year increase (see Figure 12.3).

In 2021, renewable energy and electrified transport combined made up 96% of the amount dedicated to deploy existing technologies, with renewable energy making up close to half of it and electrified transport, 35% (BNEF, 2022). The remaining $24 billion invested were dedicated to hydrogen, storage, sustainable materials, and carbon capture (BNEF, 2022). Despite its critical importance to limit the warming provided the long lifespan of CO_2 in the atmosphere, CCS was the only subsector to experience decrease in investment in 2021 to reach $2.3 billion (BNEF, 2022).

Investment climbed to new records in all regions of the globe in 2021. With close to half of the global capital deployed to existing energy transition technologies, the Asia Pacific (APAC) region attracted investments the most at $368 billion while recording the highest growth at 38% driven

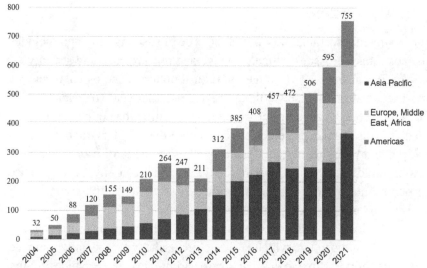

Figure 12.4. Global Investment in Energy Transition by Region
Source: BNEF (2022).

by electrified transport which more than doubled year-over-year (see Figure 12.4). Europe, Middle East, Africa (EMEA) comprised the second region attracting 31% of the global capital deployed to existing energy transition technologies, including $154 billion out of European Union member states (BNEF, 2022). The remaining 20% came from the Americas which lagged behind (BNEF, 2022). Considering the two main subsectors, it is worthwhile to note that while investments in electrified transport grew in the three regions, renewable investments grew only out of the APAC region and remained flat in EMEA and the Americas.

At the country level, China was by far the country attracting most energy transition investments in 2021, recording $266 billion invested, a 60% increase from the previous year. This represents more than twice the capital invested by the US which took the second rank with $114 billion, increasing its 2020 level by 17%. Germany, the United Kingdom, and France were part of the top 5 with $47 billion, $31 billion, and $27 billion invested, respectively. Other members of the top 10 included Japan, India, South Korea, Brazil, and Spain all exceeding $10 billion in energy transition investments.

VII. Conclusion

Environmental sustainability lies at the core of sustainability and includes its most pressing issues: climate change and resource use and scarcity.

Each year since 1970, humanity's consumption of ecological resources has exceeded that which Earth can regenerate that year (biocapacity). In 2022, our ecological footprint would have required the equivalent of 1.75 planets. This chapter presented the concept of the circular economy which has potential to mitigate this issue as well as the issue of waste. For businesses, building organizations around the circular economy is a way to use resources more efficiently and ensure access to input materials sustainably which can both produce positive financial impacts.

It is critical to reduce as fast as possible the amount of greenhouse gases in the atmosphere which causes climate change, especially methane due to its short lifetime in comparison to carbon dioxide, to avoid reaching the tipping point that would trigger irreversible snow ball effects. While this chapter highlights the massive opportunity presented by the energy transition away from fossil fuels, this transition will impact most sectors including transportation and must occur as fast as possible to keep global warming from reaching an irremediable tipping point. There must be a pragmatic transition to maintain reliable access to energy which will vary from region to region based on their energy mix. It will require the phasing out of the most polluting energy sources such as coal plants, while preserving gas-fired plants in the short-to-medium term and nuclear facilities in complement to the addition of renewable energy sources and batteries. While 2021 was a record year for the financing of the energy transition, also called climate finance, with $920 billion invested globally, it is still insufficient to get us on track for net-zero emissions by 2050, which would require between two-to-four times more reduction per year (BNEF, 2022).

Further, the chapter calls attention to the need to develop and scale economically viable carbon capture technologies, as, while necessary, the energy transition alone may not be sufficient to tackle climate change provided the long lifespan of carbon dioxide in the atmosphere. Carbon capture and transformation technologies following the circular economy model, such as the mineral carbonation, are particularly promising as they would transform carbon dioxide, a threat, into a valuable resource.

References

Bhanumati, P., de Haan, M., and Tebrake, J. M. (2022). "Greenhouse emissions rise to record, erasing drop during pandemic", *IMF*, Published on June 30, 2022, Accessed September 2022.

Bloomberg New Energy Finance (BNEF). (2021). "Global energy storage market set to hit one Terawatt-Hour by 2030", Published on November 15, 2021, Consulted in August 2022, https://about.bnef.com/blog/global-energy-storage-market-set-to-hit-one-terawatt-hour-by-2030/.

Bloomberg New Energy Finance (BNEF). (2022). "Energy transition investment trends 2022", Published on January 2022, Consulted in March 2022, https://assets.bbhub.io/professional/sites/24/Energy-Transition-Investment-Trends-Exec-Summary-2022.pdf.

Ceres (2019). "Record 631 institutional investors managing more than $37 trillion in assets urge governments to step up ambition to tackle global climate crisis", https://www.ceres.org/news-center/press-releases/record-631-institutional-investors-managing-more-37-trillion-assets-urge.

Center for Climate and Energy Solutions (C2ES). (August 2021). "Main greenhouse gases", https://www.c2es.org/content/main-greenhouse-gases/.

Christoffersen, S., Frampton, G. C., and Granitz, E. (July 2013). "Environmental sustainability's impact on earnings", *Journal of Business & Economics Research*, 11(7), pp. 325–333.

Cho, R. (2019). "How Climate Change Impacts the Economy". Columbia Climate School. https://news.climate.columbia.edu/2019/06/20/climate-change-economy-impacts/. Accessed March 2023.

Climate and Cleanair Coalition. (2021). "Black carbon", Consulted in August 2021, https://www.ccacoalition.org/en/slcps/black-carbon.

Daniel, W. (2022). "China just ran into something that could be even more devastating for its supply chains than COVID-19 lockdowns: A record heat wave". Published on August 20, 2022, https://fortune.com/2022/08/20/china-heatwave-supply-chain-covid-lockdowns/. Accessed March 2023.

Ellen MacArthur Foundation. (2017). Consulted December 21, 2020, https://www.ellenmacarthurfoundation.org/circular-economy/concept.

EPA. (2022). "Sources of Greenhouse Gas Emissions". Last Updated on August 5, 2022. https://www.epa.gov/ghgemissions/sources-greenhouse-gas-emissions. Accessed March 2023.

European Union's Website. "EU taxonomy for sustainable activities", https://finance.ec.europa.eu/sustainable-finance/tools-and-standards/eu-taxonomy-sustainable-activities_en. Accessed October 2022.

Fink, L. (2020). "Larry Fink's 2020 letter to CEOs — A fundamental reshaping of finance", https://www.blackrock.com/corporate/investor-relations/2020-larry-fink-ceo-letter.

Fink, L. (2021). "Larry Fink's 2021 letter to CEOs", https://www.blackrock.com/corporate/investor-relations/larry-fink-ceo-letter.

Frommel, A., Maneja, R., Lowe, D. *et al.* (2011). "Severe tissue damage in Atlantic cod larvae under increasing ocean acidification". *Nature Climate Change*, 42–46. https://www.nature.com/articles/nclimate1324.

GHG Protocol. (2013). "Corporate value chain (Scope 3) standard", Greenhouse Gas Protocol. pp. 7, https://ghgprotocol.org/sites/default/files/standards/Corporate-Value-Chain-Accounting-Reporing-Standard_041613_2.pdf.

Global CCS Institute. (2020). "Global Status of CCS 2020". https://www.globalccsinstitute.com/previous-reports/.

Gonzales, V., Krupnick, A. and Dunlap, L. (2020). "Carbon capture and storage 101". Resources for the Future. https://www.rff.org/publications/explainers/carbon-capture-and-storage-101/.

Griffin, P. (2017). "The carbon majors database: CDP carbon majors report 2017", https://cdn.cdp.net/cdp-production/cms/reports/documents/000/002/327/original/Carbon-Majors-Report-2017.pdf?1501833772.

Haynes, S. (2019). "Students from 1,600 cities just walked out of school to protest climate change. It could be Greta Thunberg's biggest strike yet", *Time*, 24 May, Published on 23 July 2019, Consulted in March 2021.

Hoffman, A. (1999). "Institutional evolution and change: Environmentalism and the U.S. chemical industry", *Academy of Management Journal*, 42, pp. 351–371.

Intergovernmental Panel on Climate Change (IPCC). (2005). "Special report on carbon dioxide capture and storage", https://www.ipcc.ch/site/assets/uploads/2018/03/srccs_wholereport-1.pdf.

Intergovernmental Panel on Climate Change (IPCC). (2021). "Climate change 2021 the physical science basis", http://www.Ipcc.Ch/Report/Ar5/.

International Energy Agency (IEA). (2020). "Direct air capture", https://www.iea.org/reports/direct-air-capture.

International Energy Agency (IEA). (2021). "World Energy Outlook".

International Monetary Fund (IMF). (2022). Climate change indicators dashboard. Annual Greenhouse Gas (GHG) Air Emissions Accounts. Accessed in October 2022.

International Renewable Energy Agency (IRENA). (2019). "Renewable power generation costs in 2018", https://www.irena.org/-/media/Files/IRENA/Agency/Publication/2019/May/IRENA/Renewable-Power-Generations-Costs-

in-2018.pdf?la=en&hash=99683CDDBC40A729A5F51C20DA7B6C297F7
94C5D.

IPCC. (2014). "Climate change 2014: Synthesis report." Contribution of Working
Groups I, II and III to the Fifth Assessment Report of the Intergovernmental
Panel on Climate Change. Core Writing Team, R. K. Pachauri and L. A.
Meyer (eds.). IPCC, Geneva, Switzerland, 151 pp.

Jessop, S. (2022). "Investors push 10,000 companies to disclose environmental
data to CDP", *Reuters*, Published on March 14, 2022, Consulted in
September 2022, https://www.reuters.com/business/sustainable-business/
investors-push-10000-companies-disclose-environmental-data-cdp-2022-
03-14/.

King, A., and Lenox, M. (2000). "Industry self-regulation without sanctions: The
chemical industry's responsible care program", *Academy of Management
Journal*, 43(4), pp. 698–716.

McDonough, W., and Braungart, M. (2008). *Cradle to Cradle: Remaking the Way
We Make Things*, North Point Press, New York, 2002.

Miller, A., Zaelke, D., and Andersen, S. O. (2021). *Cut Super Climate Pollutants
Now!*, Resetting Our Future. ChangeMaker Books, Washington, D.C.

PWC. (2019). "23rd Annual global CEO survey — Navigating the rising tide of
uncertainty", www.ceosurvey.pwc.

UCAR Center for Science Education. (2014). "Ozone in the troposphere",
Consulted in October 2021, https://scied.ucar.edu/learning-zone/air-quality/
ozone-troposphere.

UNEP. (2020a). "Global climate litigation report 2020 status review", https://
wedocs.unep.org/bitstream/handle/20.500.11822/34818/GCLR.
pdf?sequence=1&isAllowed=y.

UNEP. (2020b). "Emissions gap report 2020", https://www.unep.org/emissions-
gap-report-2020.

USGCRP. (2018). *Impacts, Risks, and Adaptation in the United States: Fourth
National Climate Assessment, Volume II*, D. R. Reidmiller, C. W. Avery,
D. R. Easterling, K. E. Kunkel, K. L. M. Lewis, T. K. Maycock and B. C.
Stewart (eds.), U.S. Global Change Research Program, Washington, DC,
USA, 1515 pp, DOI: 10.7930/NCA4.2018.

Chapter 13

Business and Financial Implications of Climate Change

Alan S. Miller

Learning Objectives

- Understand the implications of climate change for business and investment
- Discuss clean energy businesses, and climate-resilient infrastructure and transport
- Describe how climate change has created challenges for businesses and investors
- Distinguish between short-term returns and medium- to long-term impact
- Explore several disclosure initiatives, regulators, and regulatory initiatives
- Discover methods and products to identify, evaluate, and mitigate climate risks

---

Abstract

This chapter draws attention to the fact that, as temperatures and sea levels rise and extreme weather events become more frequent and intense, climate change has begun to impact businesses and investments in increasingly diverse ways. Science is also making it possible to attribute these events to climate change and to predict the timing and severity of future events with greater precision and confidence. The magnitude of financial impacts from climate extremes is already becoming significant and much larger damages are on the way. Based on this background, the chapter introduces readers to the many implications of climate change for business and investment, ranging from the direct physical impacts of higher temperatures, sea-level rise, and more intense storms to more indirect risks and opportunities resulting from climate policies, litigation, and good and bad reputational benefits/damages. The chapter highlights new business opportunities for clean energy, climate-resilient infrastructure, and new means of transport requiring investments in the many trillions of dollars but cautions that the transformation of the global energy system is an enormous challenge that will not be accomplished quickly. The chapter underlines that corporate management must internalize an understanding of climate risks and opportunities to make timely decisions; waiting until after its impacts are realized or certain will often cost much more and limit the range of options. Investors and the financial community, particularly those with long-term obligations and perspectives like pension funds and insurance companies, are beginning to appreciate climate risks and demand greater transparency from their investments, potentially impacting risk calculations among companies. The chapter concludes that the tools to develop business-specific climate change strategies are improving rapidly and becoming widely available.

I. Introduction

Climate change refers to the change in weather patterns and events resulting from an increase in global average temperatures — global warming. Scientists generally prefer the term climate change as it encompasses the broad range of effects from an increase in average global temperatures, to changes in rainfall patterns, sea-level rise, and changes in the chemistry of the oceans.

Human activity, through the production of greenhouse gases (GHG) such as carbon dioxide (CO_2), methane (CH_4), and nitrous oxide (N_2O), is the main cause of climate change according to the Intergovernmental

Panel on Climate Change (IPCC), the UN-supported group of scientists with expertise in climate change.

The 1992 United Nations Framework Convention on Climate Change (UNFCCC), which entered into force on March 21st, 1994, aims at preventing the dangerous human interference with the climate system and binds member states to act in the interests of human safety. The 197 countries that have ratified the Convention, called Parties to the Convention, reunite every year during the Conference of the Parties (COP). The Landmark Paris Agreement was negotiated by 196 parties during COP21 in 2015 and entered in effect on November 4th, 2016. For the first time, a binding agreement brought countries together to take actions in order to limit global warming to well below 2 °C, and ideally 1.5 °C, since preindustrial levels and adapt to its effects. Another highlight of the COP21 conference was the acknowledgment of the important role of the private sector to find solutions to address climate change and contribute toward financing the considerable investments needed.

National commitments announced as of end 2021 fall considerably short of meeting the goals announced in Paris (UN Climate Change News, 2022). The Russian invasion of Ukraine in 2022 resulting in a reduction in oil and gas supply and increasing energy costs has also created new demands to increase fossil fuel production despite conflict with climate goals (Economist, 2022). The July 2022 decision by the European Union Parliament to classify natural gas (along with nuclear power) as a green investment exemplifies this development (Rouhala, 2022).

While climate change is often discussed in terms of impact decades hence, many businesses and investors are already beginning to feel these effects. An IPCC report in 2021 concluded that climate change is already affecting every region on Earth, in multiple ways, and that these impacts will increase with additional warming (IPCC, 2021). These impacts materialize in a number of ways: natural disasters leaving damages in the billions of dollars; adaptive measures such as raising buildings and roads against sea levels rise (also leading to multi-billion-dollar expenditures); and climate policies at the international, national, and local levels. They also lead lawsuits against companies for their contributions to climate change. But mitigating and adapting to climate change also represent billions of dollars in business and investment opportunities.

In this chapter, we will first expose the Climate problematique. We will then highlight the factors driving the new climate reality for business and the implications of climate change for business and investment. Following a discussion on climate risks, the critical role of climate-related financial disclosures, and climate risk analysis providers, we will focus on the market opportunities associated with climate mitigation and adaptation while acknowledging the need to support changing consumer preferences. Finally, we will conclude the chapter with investors' initiatives and their roles.

Chapter 13 is organized as per the following sections:

   I. Introduction
  II. The Climate Problematique
 III. Factors Driving the New Climate Reality for Business
  IV. Climate Change Implications for Business and Investment
   V. Climate Risks and the Critical Role of Climate-Related Financial Disclosures
  VI. Importance of Climate Risk Analysis Providers — An Emerging Industry
 VII. Market Opportunity Associated with Climate Mitigation and Adaptation
VIII. Behavioral Issues: Changing Consumer Preferences and Demands to Support a Climate-Friendly Economy
  IX. Investors' Initiatives and their Role
   X. Conclusion

II. The Climate Problematique

The warming of the land, atmosphere, and oceans due to emissions of heat-trapping gases was first put forward more than 100 years ago by the Swedish Nobel Laureate Svante Arrhenius, who described the "hot house" theory of the atmosphere in his 1908 book *Worlds in the Making*. Arrhenius calculated that the surface of the Earth was about 30 °C warmer due to the presence of carbon dioxide, which both traps heat in wavelengths radiated from land and adds to water vapor, which further adds to warming. He also recognized the likelihood of further warming due to the increase of carbon dioxide release from combustion of fossil fuels, which he thought was likely to be beneficial (NASA Earth Observatory, 2000). Naturally occurring GHGs have enabled life on Earth as without them our planet would be too cold (EIA Website).

But since the industrial revolution, as a result of many human activities that rely heavily on combustion of fossil fuels, the amount of these gases has dramatically increased and new kinds of GHGs appeared. Since 1850, CO_2 emissions were multiplied by more than 180 times while CO_2 concentration in the atmosphere increased by more than to 40% (see Figure 13.1). Scientists have come to the conclusion that this negatively affects the Earth's climate (see (EIA Website).

The first recognition that the buildup of carbon dioxide and subsequent warming might be a serious problem came much later, in the 1960s and 1970s. As a history of the issue published by the *New York Times* observed, "Nearly everything we understand about global warming was understood in 1979. Nor was the basic science especially complicated. It could be reduced to a simple axiom: the more carbon dioxide in the atmosphere, the warmer the planet" (Rich, 2018).

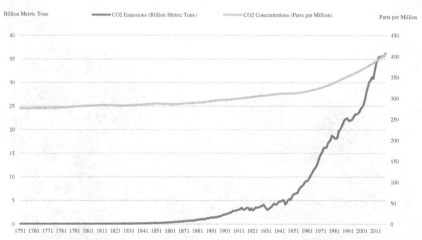

Figure 13.1. World CO_2 Emissions from Fossil Fuel Combustion and Global Atmospheric Concentrations CO_2 (1751–2018)

Source: Oak Ridge National Laboratory, Carbon Dioxide Information Analysis Center, Scripps Institute of Oceanography CO_2 program, and the US Energy Information Administration, International Energy Statistics, accessed December 7, 2020 (AIE Website).

Historically, in aggregate the two main sources of man-induced carbon dioxide have been:

- The burning of fossil fuels (coal, oil, and gas), which has contributed to two-thirds of the CO_2 emissions since the beginning of the Industrial Revolution.
- Deforestation, mainly the conversion of forests to agricultural land (pastures, croplands, etc.).

Oceans and lands are removing approximately half of the CO_2 emissions, but half of it remains in the atmosphere, leading to global warming and other climate imbalances.

While CO_2 represents close to 75% of global GHG emissions (see Figure 13.2), it is also important to address emissions from other GHGs such as hydrofluorocarbons (HFCs), black carbon, methane, and tropospheric ozone because they can reduce the warming faster as they will fall out of the atmosphere much faster than CO_2 when we stop emitting them. Burning coal also emits heat-reflecting sulfates — an offsetting source of cooling. While these particles fall out of the atmosphere quickly, the

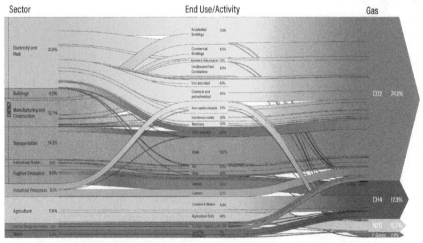

Figure 13.2.   Global GHG Emissions by Sector, End Use, and Gas in 2019

Source: Climate Watch 2022 based on raw data from IEA (2021), GHG Emissions from Fuel Combustions modified by the World Resources Institute.

resultant absence of their cooling effect is that it will take at least a decade before closing coal power plants slows the rate of warming. Consequently, the best (and some would argue only) way to meet the Paris climate goals in the near term is by aggressive efforts to reduce these short-lived climate pollutants (Miller *et al.*, 2021).

The production and use of energy contribute to close to three-fourths of the global GHG emissions (an estimate based on comparing GHGs over 100 years, as the share is lower when compared over shorter time frames (EPA website)). Representing close to a third of the global GHG emissions, electricity and heat generation are the largest GHG-emitting sectors globally (see Figure 13.2). These are followed by transportation, manufacturing and construction, and agriculture (see Figure 13.2).

The seriousness of climate change and the impacts it has already caused were emphatically described in several recent reports by the IPCC. A review of climate impacts published in 2022 included the following summary (IPCC, 2022): "Human-induced climate change is causing dangerous and widespread disruption in nature and affecting the lives of billions of people around the world, despite efforts to reduce the risks. People and ecosystems least able to cope are being hardest hit". One of the lead authors said "This report is a dire warning about the consequences of inaction. It shows that climate change is a grave and mounting threat to our well-being and a healthy planet. Our actions today will shape how people adapt and nature responds to increasing climate risks". The report describes many consequences of climate change beyond extreme heat, including more intense rainfall events but also drought, widespread coastal flooding, major losses in biodiversity, reduction in agricultural productivity, and mass migration from areas no longer able to support human life.

To Go Further

- Watch the short video "Climate 101" With Bill Nye on the Climate Reality Project Website which explains the scientific fundamentals of climate change.
- Visit the Global Carbon Atlas Website. You may watch the Carbon Story which describes the evolution of the man-made carbon

emissions ranging from prehistoric time to current time and also includes projections according to different scenarios. You may also explore their maps and see the carbon emissions by country and leverage the data available on the website.

- Visit the NASA Website for further scientific background on climate change.
- Visit the EPA website for more information on GHGs.
- Visit the IPCC website which gathers the most prominent research on climate change including reports released in 2021 and 2022.

There is a fundamental requirement for global cooperation for any effective response to climate change. The need for an international agreement to address the problem was discussed seriously as early as 1979, at the first World Climate Conference. As the historian Yuval Harari has written, "When it comes to climate, countries are not just sovereign. They are at the mercy of actions taken by people on the other side of the planet" (Harari, 2018). China and the United States are the two largest emitters of greenhouse gases, but even so are responsible for less than half of current emissions. Many other countries will need to be engaged to limit warming, and many more to address the consequences of sea-level rise, severe storms, and droughts resulting in mass migration. There is arguably no precedent for this degree of cooperation among nations from all parts of the globe, from diverse cultures and political traditions.

As of 2019, over two-thirds of global GHG emissions came from only 10 emitters (considering the European Union (EU) made up of 27 countries as an entity) which also account for 75% of the world's GDP and more than half of the global population (see Figure 13.3). China, the United States, India, and the EU made up the top 4 (in order) contributing 63% of global GHG emissions in aggregate and 26%, 13%, 7%, and 7%, respectively (Climate Watch Website).

The United States was the largest CO_2 emitter per capita globally in 2018, followed by Russia, South Korea, and Iran (see Figure 13.4).

An international agreement, the UN Framework Convention on Climate Change, was signed in 1992, and since then multiple efforts to create some global approach to the problem largely failed until the Paris

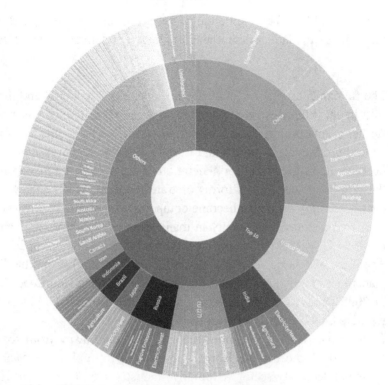

Figure 13.3. GHG Emissions by Country and Sector in 2019

Source: Climate Watch. 2022. Washington, DC: World Resources Institute.

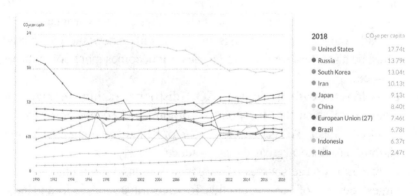

Figure 13.4. CO$_2$ Emissions by Capita in 2018

Source: Climate Watch Website

Agreement in 2015. The challenge in reaching an agreement and its limited impact to date reflect the complexity and magnitude of the issue:

- The fundamental role of fossil fuels in the global economy and their role in the lifestyles of affluent populations. This reality has been further dramatized by the war in Ukraine and policies to increase fossil fuel production in the US and Europe. In many countries coal had become the primary fuel for generation of electricity, and petroleum, the dominant fuel for all forms of transportation. While renewable energy technologies have become competitive or even less expensive than coal-generated electricity in many parts of the world, replacing fossil fuels will take time and massive investment (Marchese, 2022). There are also issues of social disruption and backlash from the displacement of existing workers. In the US, a Supreme Court decision in 2022 has also raised questions about the government's power to regulate GHG emissions (Mecklin, 2022).
- In addition, while many industries can transition away from fossil fuels through the use of electricity generated from clean renewable sources (electricity sector, automotive industry, etc.) other industries (e.g. steel, cement, aviation, etc.) encounter more challenges. These industries need a lot of energy or heat to function and are sometimes qualified as "molecule-based". These industries can't leverage the cheap renewable energies. Some believe that green hydrogen, which is made out of the electrolysis of water with renewable electricity, could be a solution for these industries if it becomes more competitive in price.
- Emissions of carbon dioxide (CO_2) distribute rapidly through the atmosphere, such that the point of origin is of no relevance to the eventual impact. The economic growth of China and other developing nations has done a great deal to reduce poverty but has also made more nations large sources of carbon emissions. China has been the largest emitter of carbon dioxide for more than a decade and now emits more than the US and the European Union combined.
- Once emitted, carbon dioxide has an atmospheric lifetime measured in centuries. Reducing its concentration can therefore be

accomplished only very gradually and through significant reductions in global emissions. Thus, while global emissions of CO_2 declined 5% in 2020 due to COVID-19 impacts on economic activity, atmospheric concentrations did not. The longer the world waits to act, the more serious the threat and the more rapid the reductions must be to stay within any desired temperature limit.

- Many of the countries and populations most at risk from climate change are among the world's poorest and least able to prepare or adapt. Many of the same countries are also already among the least attractive for private investment. Equity is an additional economic issue to be addressed.

- The ecosystem is also at great risk from climate change, with threatened extinction of many species and a significant reduction in biodiversity. While difficult to quantify in economic terms, there is increasing scientific evidence that these trends will have substantial human consequences (Radford, 2017; Shankman *et al.,* 2019).

- While almost all the nations of the world signed the 2015 Paris Agreement pledging to do what they could to reduce emissions, the total sum of what has been agreed to date will not keep warming within 2°C — the stated goal of the Agreement to avoid very serious adverse consequences. (You can follow the commitments of the Nationally Determined Contributions (NDC) for each country that was party to the Paris Agreement and how they evolve overtime on the Climate Watch Website.

Discussion of climate change has unfortunately become a very partisan issue in the United States, with views largely defined by political affiliations. At one extreme there are climate deniers, or as some prefer to be described, "skeptics". Their simple response to the National Climate Assessment description of the economic risks of climate change to the US economy is "I don't believe it". At the opposite extreme are proposals to operate the entire US electricity system on renewable energy technologies within a decade and mandate dramatic changes in lifestyles to achieve climate goals. In between lie many complicated and difficult choices. What can be done for coal mining regions and workers lacking the skills for an energy transition? Should carbon capture and removal strategies be given the major support needed to become part of a climate strategy? Should nuclear power and other non-fossil energy sources other than solar and wind be supported? Can electrification of transportation be accomplished consistent with decarbonizing the electricity system?

Given all the characteristics described above, it should not be surprising that finding effective solutions is proving to be difficult. Major changes in economies are required that threaten substantial vested interests. The costs are apparent today, while at least until very recently the dangers have seemed to be some distance in the future — presenting a cognitive challenge (Wallace-Wells, 2019). Not all the technologies required are proven, commercial, and cost-effective. And the time for making the necessary transitions is a closing window as warned by the 2018 IPCC Special Report which calls for a rapid reduction in greenhouse gas emissions to avoid major and largely irreversible impacts of climate change. Evidence of a closing window of time is increasing rapidly; a report by the World Meteorological Organization (WMO) in 2022 concluded that there is a 50:50 chance of the average global temperature reaching 1.5 °C above pre-industrial levels in the next five years (UN News, 2022).

In response to this increasingly challenging reality, interest has been growing in two strategies rarely taken seriously in the past, removal of carbon dioxide from the atmosphere through technologies for direct air capture and geoengineering, cooling of the atmosphere through the injection of heat reflecting aerosols. An environmental way to capture carbon is by expanding tree cover but doing so on a large scale with lasting results is complicated both by human activity (deforestation of the Amazon for cattle grazing) and the effects of climate change (heat and drought adding to the risks of wildfires). Technologies are being developed for direct air capture but so far are at an early stage and very expensive (IEA, 2021). Sulfate aerosol injection emulates the effects of volcanic eruptions and could be done for a very limited cost but is opposed by many scientists who fear the likelihood of unintended consequences (Kaufman, 2019).

Not surprisingly, as discussed in the following section, attention is increasingly turning to understanding climate risks and identifying strategies to prepare for the impacts that now seem likely or even inevitable.

III. Factors Driving the New Climate Reality for Business

The business response to climate change has until recently been characterized by a lack of urgency due to the perception that any severe impacts will not occur for some decades in the future, by which time solutions may be found. This perception was shattered by multiple publications of the Intergovernmental Panel on Climate Change (IPCC), the international body created to produce consensus reports on the status of climate science. The first of these was a *Special Report on Global Warming of 1.5°C* (IPCC, 2018). A principal conclusion of the report is that we are *already* seeing the consequences of 1°C of global warming through more extreme weather, rising sea levels, and diminishing Arctic Sea ice. The IPCC report goes beyond summarizing the science to urge immediate and aggressive efforts to limit emissions of greenhouse gases to avoid irreversible impacts such as the loss of entire ecosystems, while noting that achieving this goal would require "rapid and far-reaching" transitions in land, energy, industry, buildings, transport, and cities. Even more dire conclusions were included in the IPCC reports released in 2021 (IPCC, 2021) and 2022 (IPCC, 2022).

Yet, another major review of climate science, the *Fourth National Climate Assessment* by an inter-agency task force of the US government, the US Global Change Research Program, was released in November 2018 and echoes the IPCC conclusion that climate change is already occurring (US GCRP, 2017).[1] The report states that it is "extremely likely" human activities are the dominant cause of warming in the past century, and further points to "documented changes in surface, atmospheric, and oceanic temperatures; melting glaciers; diminishing snow cover; shrinking sea ice; rising sea levels; ocean acidification; and increasing atmospheric water vapor".

The IPCC Reports also makes clear that improving climate science now makes it much easier to attribute some — but not all — extreme

---

[1] The 2018 release was the second volume of the report and focuses on the impacts of climate change. The first volume focusing on the science of climate change was published in 2017.

weather events to climate change. Until relatively recently, scientists could only generally describe likely associations but not make the case for any specific weather event. This is important for business planning purposes and has been changing with research (Lindsey, 2016). A recent review of "attribution science" by the National Academy of Sciences (NAS) concluded that "in many cases, it is now often possible to make and defend quantitative statements about the extent to which human-induced climate change (or another causal factor, such as a specific mode of natural variability) has influenced either the magnitude or the probability of occurrence of specific types of events or event classes. The science behind such statements has advanced a great deal in recent years and is still evolving rapidly" (Harvey, C., 2022).

A recent example of this evolving science is an analysis of the role climate change had in the unusually intense rainfall and subsequent flooding caused in 2017 by Hurricane Harvey. A combination of the observational record and state-of-the-art climate modeling allowed researchers to conclude that "global warming made the precipitation about 15% (8–19%) more intense, or equivalently made such an event three (1.5–5) times more likely" (Oldenborgh, 2017).

But how feasible is it to say that a hurricane, flood, or other specific extreme weather event is due to climate change? Advances in climate science are making it increasingly possible to attribute extreme weather events to climate change, most often as an increase in the probability that such events will occur — e.g., an event that had historically been considered as a 1 in 100-year event may now be expected to occur once in 20 years. Or expressed another way, the likelihood of a specific event may be 20% more due to climate change.

We now turn to consider the implications of these developments for business and financial planning and strategy and describe some of the actions already being taken by corporate leaders.

IV. Climate Change Implications for Business and Investment

But what does it mean for business and investment?

Consider the following:

- In 2017, losses due to weather-related natural disasters exceeded US $300 billion and losses have been in a similar range in subsequent years. In the US, losses incurred by property and casualty insurers exceeded premium revenue. Hurricane Maria in September 2017 led to power outages for much of the island of Puerto Rico lasting months, leading to the departure of tens of thousands of residents, and reducing the economy by 8%.
- Allegations that downed power lines contributed to deadly wildfires in California in 2017 and 2018 resulted in claims for billions of dollars, forcing the utility PG&E to file for bankruptcy. Bankruptcy proceedings resulted in a corporate contribution of $13.5 billion to a trust fund for payment of damages and reorganizing the company with a new board of directors (Eavis and Penn, 2019; Penn, 2020).
- Almost half of a $400 million general obligation bond approved by Miami, Florida, voters in November 2017 was for measures that address flooding due to sea-level rise. The adjoining city of Miami Beach has a locally financed $500 million program to raise more than 100 miles of roads, install dozens of pumps, build higher sea walls and revamp drainage systems.
- Union of Concerned Scientists (UCS) analysis in 2018 using Zillow data found more than 150,000 existing homes and commercial properties, worth $63 billion, potentially at risk from repeated flooding in the coming 15 years.
- Large oil companies are facing a growing number of lawsuits alleging liability for their contribution to greenhouse gas emissions. The first such lawsuit brought by a state, Rhode Island, was filed July 2, 2018. A suit brought by the state of New York against Exxon Mobil alleging the company misled shareholders by understating climate risks was dismissed, but a similar suit has been brought by the state of Massachusetts alleging violation of consumer protection laws (Schwartz, 2019). The number of climate-related lawsuits globally doubled between 2015 and 2022 (Kaminski, 2022).
- Companies producing important foodstuffs are reporting significant risks to the costs and quality of their products, including such staples

as wheat, corn, coffee, and rice. Fisheries are also at risk from changes in marine ecosystems. Higher value products such as wine are also already being affected.

- Many less obvious examples indicate the endless ways climate change may impact the economic activity such as water shortages limiting operation of power plants; heat extremes and flooding limiting aviation; restrictions on outdoor construction workers during heat extremes; and river barge traffic constrained by low water levels — all of which have already occurred.
- In addition to impacts on climate vulnerable businesses, financial analysts are beginning to highlight the potential for more *systemic risks* — the potential for economic recessions or worse as a consequence of the aggregate losses across geographies and economies.

In the following two sections we will take a look at two specific industries (aviation and hotel) and how they are affected by climate change.

1. Operational Risks to Airlines

Airlines might be thought to be among the industries less at risk from climate change — after all their operations are primarily in the air and above ground level climate. In actuality, they are being affected in multiple ways — almost all adversely — by heat, storms, and floods. Airplanes cannot fly when temperatures are too high due to the lower lift provided by hotter, thinner air; on a particularly hot day in Phoenix in 2017 more than 50 flights had to be canceled or rerouted. Reducing weight can help, but that means fewer passengers and cargo and reduced revenue. More flights may need to be concentrated during cooler night time hours, a conflict with noise regulations in many places. More frequent and intense thunderstorms can also impact flight routes and risks. Airport runways in coastal areas may need to be raised or protected by sea walls — investments already being made in Singapore and Hong Kong (*Economic Times*, 2018).

Air travel is also at risk from criticism of its carbon intensity, which has been termed "flight shaming". This issue was highlighted by climate activist Greta Thunberg's decision to travel to New York by a zero-emission sailboat in 2019. In the Netherlands, environmental groups are suing the airline KLM alleging it breaches consumer laws against misleading advertising. "KLM has … stuck by the false message that it is on the path to more sustainable flying", one of the environmental campaigners said. "There is no way it can do this while planning continuous air traffic growth …" (Reuters, 2022).

As an executive in an airline, what options might you consider in response to climate change-related challenges? Could you imagine some changes that position your company to gain relative to competitors? What types of actions could your company implement individually, and what types in cooperation with other airlines and airplane manufacturers? What support might you seek from the government?

Some factors to consider are as follows:

- Airlines are buyers, not designers of equipment; however, they do influence equipment manufacturers through their purchase decisions and some have become actively engaged in supporting development of alternative fuels. Electric planes have become feasible for short flights and at least one major airline has announced plans to use one in 2026 (Garay, 2022).
- Some public funding to support the development of more climate-friendly airplanes may be justified based on the benefits of reducing travel delays and improving the transportation system.
- Some improvements can be made over time within capital improvement budgets, such as raising runways.
- Airport locations may also need to be reconsidered; some coastal locations may simply be too expensive to maintain.

2. Coastal Resort Hotel Chain Response to Nuisance Flooding

Resort hotels in low-lying coastal areas continue to be built in many parts of the world (Hotel Business, 2018). Such properties continue to be popular investments (Blackstone, 2017). This is true even in areas already prone to tidal flooding such as Virginia Beach on the Chesapeake Bay (Hotel Management, 2018; Hall, 2018).

Assume you are hired as a climate advisor to a major hotel chain. What information would you seek as the basis for evaluating the risks to properties in coastal areas? What expertise might be available to support your assessment? In properties in flood-prone areas, what measures would you propose to mitigate risks and how would you justify the necessary investment?

Some factors to consider are as follows:

- Specialized firms with the ability to project coastal flooding (Dahlberg, 2017; Coastal Risk (website)) may be worth employing.
- Insurance products may be available and worthwhile; some insurance companies also offer detailed risk management support (Takeuchi, 2017; Deloitte (website)).
- Collaboration with local officials may be essential to explore risks associated with access roads, power reliability, and other public services at risk during extreme weather events.

V. Climate Risks and the Critical Role of Climate-Related Financial Disclosures

A key assumption with respect to the effective functioning of markets is the availability of information necessary for investors to evaluate potential risks and returns. This has been a challenge for climate change risks as there has been little guidance on when and in what manner climate change-related business risks should be disclosed by companies. In 2010, the Securities and Exchange Commission, which regulates reporting and disclosure by publicly traded companies in the United States, issued guidance recognizing that climate change could be a "material" risk and thus a subject for annual reports. However, SEC staff recognize the limitations of existing disclosure requirements and the information provided has been criticized as inadequate by many investors. For example, companies report climate-related disclosures in varying formats and specificity, making it difficult to compare and analyze related disclosures across company filings. Disclosures are often made using generic language, spread across different sections of reports, and lack quantitative metrics (GAO, 2018).

Beginning in 2012, the Sustainability Accounting Standards Board (SASB) undertook a process of analysis and consultations on climate risks from an accounting perspective resulting in a 2016 publication in which the systemic risk presented by climate risks across sectors is highlighted and assessed to result in $27.5 trillion impacted, or 93% of US equities by market capitalization. These impacts materialize under three forms: through **physical effects** linked to increase in frequency and scale of environmental extreme weather events (e.g. fires, floods, hurricanes etc.); market changes related to a **transition to a low-carbon resilient economy** leading to changes in technologies, consumer demand, and supply chains; and expected **climate regulation** (SASB, 2016).

The issue of climate risk disclosure was also highlighted in a 2015 speech by Mark Carney, then the Governor of the Bank of England, who termed the inability of investors to look past short-term returns and to recognize long-term, irreversible threats the "tragedy of the horizon". In his speech, he warns that by the time climate risks become evident, the impacts on the financial system, and not simply individual investors, could be devastating.[2] The SASB report and Carney's speech led to the creation of a Task Force on Climate-Related Financial Disclosures (TFCD Websites) under the auspices of the G20 Financial Stability Board. The Task Force comprised representatives from leading financial institutions, insurers, and institutional investors, and was chaired by former New York City Mayor Michael Bloomberg. The Task Force issued its initial report in June 2017, outlining guidance and recommendations for voluntary climate-related financial disclosures in four thematic areas: governance, strategy, risk management, and metrics and targets.

One innovative feature of the report is a focus on the value of scenario analysis, a tool for companies to consider, in a structured way, potential future conditions that differ from business-as-usual and to evaluate how business strategies might perform under those circumstances (TCFD Scenario Analysis Website). The Task Force explains that scenario analysis is important as a means of facilitating consistent comparisons of companies and

---

[2]Carney was appointed UN Special Envoy on Climate Action and Finance in December 2019. https://www.un.org/press/en/2019/sga1927.doc.htm.

- is based on hypothetical constructs, not forecasts, predictions, or sensitivity analyses,
- comprises assumptions that describe a path of development leading to a particular outcome,
- should challenge conventional wisdom about the future, and
- provides the basis to explore alternatives that may significantly alter the basis for "business-as-usual" assumptions.

Annual "Status Reports" issued by the Task Force in 2018, 2019, 2020, and 2021 reviewed business implementation of the disclosure recommendations. The absence of consistent scenarios is a major problem, as without them investors are unable to make meaningful comparisons of companies within a sector. However, enough good examples were found to conclude that "it is both possible and practicable for companies to disclose certain baseline climate-related information today" (TCFD, 2018). Disclosure has steadily increased since the 2017 report; the 2020 report found that nearly 60% of the world's 100 largest public companies support the TCFD, report in line with the TCFD recommendations, or both. On the other hand, only 1 in 15 companies analyze and disclose the impact of climate change on business and strategy, the most useful information for financial decision-making (TCFD, 2020). Reporting continued to increase in 2020 but still reflected significant limitations as only one in three companies reviewed disclosed climate-related information aligned with the TCFD recommendations (TCFD, 2021).

Among the contributions of the TCFD was the categorization and definition of climate risks as either *transition risks or physical risks* from the impacts of climate change. The former include changes in policy such as the adoption of carbon taxes; changes in technology such as the introduction of renewable market risks due to changes in supply and demand for products and services; reputational risks tied to changing consumer preferences; and liability risks resulting from lawsuits against companies for damages resulting from climate change. Reference was made early in this chapter to the growing number of lawsuits brought by state and local governments against oil companies for climate change damages and suits based on misleading shareholders and consumers (Grandoni, 2018; Wang, 2018). These suits have so far had limited success, while suits against the utility PG&E resulted in bankruptcy and reorganization of the company. A database maintained by the Sabin Center for Climate Change Law at Columbia University provides updated descriptions of the hundreds of such cases brought in the United States and a growing number in other countries (Sabin Center website).

While voluntary, the TCFD recommendations have been endorsed by many financial regulatory agencies, investors, and companies and are widely seen as an indicator of future directions in markets. The Financial Stability Board (FSB) publishes recommendations for supervisory and regulatory approaches to climate-related risks and calls for continued progress on disclosures (FSB, 2022). More recently, regulations requiring companies and financial institutions to disclose their climate-related risk are being adopted in many parts of the world as indicated in what follows. Such disclosure also is at least a partial response to the Tragedy of the Horizon, insofar as investors are made aware that climate risks are real and rapidly approaching.

One issue attracting increasing attention is the lack of consistent definitions and meaning for climate goals announced by companies. Terms such as "net zero" and "climate neutral" have been criticized by diverse sources for relying too much on unproven carbon removal and avoiding current efforts by adopting distant future dates (Galey, 2022). The Federal Trade Commission (FTC) has authority to penalize companies for false advertising including claims considered to be "greenwashing". Environmental groups petitioned the agency to use its authority to penalize Chevron alleging the oil company overstates its commitment to renewable energy and efforts to reduce GHG emissions (Volcovici, 2021).

1. New York State Department of Financial Services (October 2020)

For the first time, an American state or federal regulator set a holistic set of expectations for managing the financial risks from climate change for banking organizations and the insurance industry. This guidance expects that these institutions start developing their approach to climate-related financial risk disclosure and consider engaging with the Task Force on Climate-related Financial Disclosures' framework and other established initiatives when doing so. For financially regulated organizations, it requires that they integrate the financial risks from climate change into their governance frameworks, risk management processes, and business strategies. A board member, a committee of the board, as well as a senior management function should be designated as accountable for the organization's assessment and management of the financial risks from climate change. An enterprise-wide risk assessment needs to be implemented to evaluate climate change and its impacts on risk factors including credit risk, market risk, liquidity risk, operational risk, reputational risk, and strategy risk (NYS Department of Financial Services Website, 2020)

2. European Central Bank (ECB) to Conduct Climate-Related Stress Tests of Lenders (November 2020)

The ECB has asked banks to study the climate-related risks that may affect their financial performance. The resultant bank disclosures and plans would then be subject to a stress test in 2022 (Comfort, 2020).

3. United Kingdom Requirements for Climate Risk Disclosure by 2025 (November 2020)

The UK Treasury announced in November 2020 that new TCFD-aligned disclosure regulations will be mandatory and would require compliance by 2025. The rules cover a significant portion of the economy, including listed commercial companies, UK-registered large private companies, banks, building societies, insurance companies, UK-authorized asset managers, life insurers, pension schemes regulated by the Financial Conduct Authority, and occupational pension schemes (Elliott, 2020).

4. Federal Reserve Recognizes Climate Risks to the Stability of the Financial System

In its November 2020 semiannual report on financial stability, the Federal Reserve for the first time made reference to the risks of climate change. The Fed indicated its intent to deepen its understanding of climate risk issues and called on banks to do the same, without mandating action — as of now (Guida, 2020).

5. Climate Risk Disclosure Act of 2019

A bill on climate change was presented in October 2020 to the Congress. It would broaden the disclosure requirement of the Securities and Exchange Commission (SEC) for the issuer of securities to annually disclose climate change-related risks posed to the issuer, as well as their strategies and actions to mitigate these risks. Issuers would have to disclose on (1) their direct and indirect greenhouse-gas emissions, (2) their fossil fuel-related assets, and (3) establish standards regarding the social cost of carbon USA 2019.

6. SEC Proposes Rules to Enhance and Standardize Climate Risk Disclosure

In response to growing concerns that climate risk disclosure by publicly traded companies has been inconsistent and sometimes even misleading, the SEC in March 2022 proposed requirements to make such reporting more transparent and meaningful for investors (SEC, 2022). The proposed rules would add substantially to the level of detail and clarity required in corporate climate reporting, including GHG emissions including downstream emissions by its consumers when "material". Also of significance, reporting would need to discuss how any identified climate-related risks have affected or are likely to affect the registrant's strategy, business model, and outlook. The proposal generated many comments both positive and negative, but particularly from companies concerned whether compliance could be burdensome and expensive (Corb *et al.*, 2022).

VI. Importance of Climate Risk Analysis Providers — An Emerging Industry

A key requirement for meaningful assessment of climate risk is the analytical tools and data required to evaluate climate-related risks in terms that are meaningful for investment decision-making. Climate science and global climate models have been developed to predict long-term, global changes given assumptions about emissions of carbon dioxide and other greenhouse gases — climate scenarios that are in turn based on assumptions about projected changes in population, economic activity, technology, and lifestyle. Projections of climate change are often made for 2100, far beyond the time horizon of even institutional investors (Recall the climate reports for Chevron and ExxonMobil go "only" to 2030/2040.). Climate forecasts become more difficult when applied to shorter time frames and more limited geographic areas, and model results sometimes differ. Scientists also have more confidence when predicting the likelihood of hotter days but less confidence when asked to predict the likelihood of more frequent and intense hurricanes. Predictions of changes in precipitation can be made with greater confidence for some regions than others; in some locations, climate models produce conflicting results and judgments must be made about which are most reliable (World Bank, 2015). Methods have been developed for regional and localized forecasting, but as a generalization, natural variability will remain a source of significant uncertainty until about 2030, after which human activity is expected to be the increasingly dominant influence on changing weather (USGCRP, 2017).

The increasing awareness of climate risks and opportunities has led to the growing demand for services that can offer such analysis (Smart, 2020). A UK-based NGO, CDP (originally the Carbon Disclosure Project), solicits climate risk information from major companies and, based on responses received, issues rankings (Carbon Disclosure Project Website. A Silicon Valley startup, Jupiter, with $10 million in venture capital, a high-powered management, and climate scientists from leading research institutions, reportedly has "developed tools to help customers plan for hazards two hours to 50 years into the future all the way down to the street or even building level" and not only to predict precipitation and temperature changes "but also simulate their interactions with the built environment and the surrounding landscape" (Samenow, 2018).

Climate risk screening tools have also been developed for use by international financial institutions (World Bank, 2018a), for lenders to infrastructure projects (Acclimatise, 2018), and for homeowners and buyers concerned about flooding risks (Dahlberg, 2017; Coastal Risk

Consulting Website). A climate risk analysis company, Four Twenty Seven, joined a real estate technology and information company, GeoPhy, to create a data product that provides granular projections of the impacts of climate change on real estate investment trusts (REITs) (Starkman, 2018). Services initially developed by pure play organizations have recently started to be acquired by larger organizations, attesting to the growth and attractiveness of the sector. Rating agencies have recently realized the importance of climate risks and have both internally developed methodologies and acquired climate risk companies, such as Four Twenty Seven by Moody's, Trucost and The Climate Service by S&P, and Acclimatise by Aon. Mainstream providers of business analysis such as Bloomberg and MSCI are also now offering climate risk analysis tools (Bloomberg Analysis Brochure and MSCI Climate Solutions). However, there are concerns that the climate modeling that underlies these tools is not transparent and may in some cases require assumptions that go beyond the limits of scientific knowledge (Fiedler *et al.*, 2021).

VII. Market Opportunities Associated with Climate Mitigation and Adaptation

Studies of climate risk often note opportunities as well as risks from climate change, e.g., "progressively higher temperatures may make some existing or new tourist destinations served by transportation and sports and recreational infrastructure more attractive, offering increased revenue potential" (Acclimatise, 2018). Being prepared when your competitors are not can also be a source of significant competitive advantage. For example, at the recommendation of their insurance company, a juice company starting operations in Florida installed backup generators and strengthened its roof in anticipation of hurricane-force winds. Shortly thereafter, storms knocked out most of their competitors' operations making their products highly profitable (Takeuchi, 2017).

In addition, climate policies can have important impact on business and investors. For example, many state and local governments in the United States are adopting ambitious targets for being "carbon free" in the source of their power, viz, the substitution of renewable energy for fossil fuels. Some jurisdictions such as California have gone much further and adopted cap-and-trade regulations on large emitters.

Many climate-related challenges may also result in opportunities for new products and services. For example, climate change may make predicting wind speed more difficult, an issue for developers of wind power projects. In response, some insurance companies are now offering insurance to cover the risk of low power production in years when wind speed is below average (Swiss Re, 2017). Other more basic products can protect effectively against flooding (waterproof barriers) and hurricane-force winds (stronger roofing materials, using thicker boards to protect windows) (Takeuchi, 2017). Many homes survived the intense 2018 wildfires in California because their owners had removed neighboring brush, sprayed water on their roofs, and adopted other similar modest measures (Kaplan and Sellers, 2018).

The Morgan Stanley Institute for Sustainable Investing engaged the Economist Intelligence Unit to survey climate mitigation opportunities in 20 countries and five sectors (Morgan Stanley Institute for Sustainable Investing, 2017). Their report is in the form of an index providing country specific insights into factors most appealing for investment such as technological adoption, innovation capacity, and financial risk. The index assesses demand for climate change mitigation across five sectors — energy, agriculture, the built environment, transport, and industry. In each sector, demand is linked with innovation capacity, rates of technological adoption, and financial risk as a further measure of investment opportunities. The initial product evaluated 20 potentially high opportunity markets to represent markets with different levels of economic development in various regions, and to encompass markets where interesting developments are occurring. The overriding conclusion of their analysis is that "there are vast opportunities for private capital to invest in climate change solutions, and attractive profits to be made by doing so".

Climate change is increasingly being seen as an enormous investment opportunity as well as a source of financial risk. Renewable energy technologies and associated providers have been among the early beneficiaries, but investors are increasingly seeking out a wider range of opportunities for both products and services that enhance resilience (e.g., fire retardant materials for housing; flood control barriers and gates; more efficient water management) as well as more efficient equipment for air conditioning and less carbon intensive food products like plant-based alternatives to meat (Gray, 2019).

Development institutions have also helped identify climate-related investment opportunities in emerging markets (World Bank, 2010). While many of the products and services are similar to those suitable for developed countries, the fact that new infrastructure will constitute a much greater share of economic growth reduces some stranded asset concerns but offers different opportunities and challenges. For example, the International Finance Corporation, the private sector arm of the World Bank, reviewed the investment opportunities associated with climate change mitigation and adaptation in a 2017 study, *Creating Markets for Climate Business* (IFC, 2017). Based on a detailed look at 21 large emerging market economies, the report concludes that the projects and measures required to achieve the Paris Agreement goals will require over $23 trillion in investment potential between now and 2030. This estimate was in turn based on insights from analysis of seven sectors:

1. **Grid-tied renewables:** The report identified $6 trillion in new investment potential in wind and solar power up to 2040, half in the Asia-Pacific region. The trend in this sector is already well underway with almost $280 billion invested in 2016, twice the amount invested in fossil-fuel power projects. A 2018 assessment of energy market trends projects $11.5 trillion being invested globally in new power generation capacity between 2018 and 2050, with $8.4 trillion of that going to wind and solar; "by 2050, wind and solar technology will provide almost 50% of total electricity globally" (BNEF, 2018). Solar and wind installations have continued their rapid growth in 2021 and 2022 despite higher material and transportation costs as fossil energy costs rose even faster. However, the IEA has expressed concerns that this growth will plateau in 2023 in the absence of stronger policies (IEA, 2022).

2. **Off-grid solar and storage:** Investment in emerging market energy storage is set to grow from $2.5 billion to $23 billion in 2025 and

provide 89 million people in the developing world with at least one solar light. According to the World Bank, off-grid solar energy and storage are critical to meeting international goals for universal electricity access. Current trends include both good and bad news: nearly 1 billion people in Sub-Saharan Africa are expected to gain electricity access by 2040, but over 500 million people will still be without it (World Bank, 2017).

3. **Climate-smart agriculture:** Agriculture is a $5 trillion industry, responsible for about a third of global GHG emissions. Climate-smart agriculture will require major investments to improve the efficiency of production (especially water use) and reduction in food waste (currently over a third of all food grown).

4. **Green buildings:** A focus on energy-efficient buildings is a feature of most national climate plans prepared in response to the Paris Climate Agreement and justifies $300 billion in investment per year. Investment to improve the energy efficiency of buildings is typically cost-effective (the investment is recouped through reduced energy costs). Supportive regulatory policies and technical assistance will be needed in addition to finance.

5. **Transport and logistics:** IFC projects investment in transport infrastructure will grow to $900 billion per year by 2025, while doubling vehicle efficiency and enabling fuel switching could save $8 trillion cumulatively by 2050. Other climate measures evaluated include a switch to electric vehicles and the implementation of bus rapid transit systems.

6. **Climate-smart water infrastructure:** Changes in precipitation will lead to droughts in some areas and flooding in others, making water management increasingly important. At the same time private investment in water management has been growing and now exceeds $5 billion per year. The global market for water recycling technologies is $23 billion and also growing. Technologies for desalination are also improving and will be critical in many coastal areas.

7. **Climate-smart urban waste management:** Methane emissions from municipal solid waste management contribute 5% of global greenhouse-gas emissions and will have much greater impact if measured over the next two decades. The global waste market is expected to

reach $2 trillion by 2020, while waste recovery and recycling exceed $250 billion.

A key point in the IFC analysis is the importance of the enabling environment for investment — countries need to remove barriers and adopt supportive policies if the potential investment is to come about, particularly in regulated sectors like power and buildings. National climate policies, a requirement of the 2015 Paris Climate Agreement, have become a focus for efforts to create more climate-friendly business environments (Ge and Levin, 2018). The adoption of climate policies by state and local governments is also accelerating. Examples include restrictions on new natural gas hookups and adoption of heat action plans in dozens of US cities (Nature Editorial, 2021).

Some of the sectors discussed previously as subject to the greatest risk (Acclimatise, 2018) are the same as those IFC identified as having the greatest investment potential. This is not coincidental. Electric utilities are a prime example. On the one hand, they are major investors in grid-tied renewable energy projects, which can reduce regulatory risks associated with use of fossil fuels and operational impacts associated with higher temperatures, which can both reduce the efficiency of thermal power generation and increase peak demand. On the other hand, profits from investment opportunities will not offset predicted global economic losses due to climate change. According to one recent study costing out the effects of climate change for a range of scenarios, costs are roughly 1.2% of GDP per 1 °C on average but distributed very unequally resulting in large income transfers northward and westward (Hsiang *et al.*, 2017).

The prospect of new products and services in response to climate change was part of the motivation behind the creation of a climate resilience investment fund, the Climate Resilience and Adaptation Finance & Technology Transfer Facility (CRAFT), the plan is for CRAFT to invest in 10–20 companies, located in both developed and developing countries, which have proven technologies and solutions for climate resilience and are expected to be profitable. Potential businesses include weather analytics, catastrophe risk modeling services, and drought resilient seed companies (The Lab, 2017).

VIII. Behavioral Issues: Changing Consumer Preferences and Demands to Support a Climate-Friendly Economy

Would you pay more for a product that was more environmentally friendly if you had the choice of getting cheaper alternatives without these attributes? Would you be able to stop or reduce doing things that you enjoy doing like eating meat or traveling to contribute to tackle climate change? Would you say no to modern comforts such as air conditioning?

Many of the changes in products and lifestyle required to address climate change can only be accomplished with public support. While governments and utility companies are the primary agents deciding on the source of fuel for generating electricity, consumers will have to be engaged and convinced in the process of making buildings more energy efficient and accepting electric cars as a replacement for gasoline (ESMAP, 2020). The use of air conditioning is growing rapidly and if unchecked, will require significant increases in power production, an understandable response to rising temperatures and increasing income in poor tropical countries. Personal decisions about when and how to use cooling equipment will be very influential (IEA, 2018). Reducing meat consumption, by some estimates responsible for about a third of total global warming through emissions from livestock and deforestation, may be an even more personal and potentially difficult transition (Carrington, 2018b). On the other hand, growing awareness of the health and environmental dangers of meat-intensive diets is leading to development and marketing of substitutes, a demonstration of market response.

Some behavioral changes may be encouraged by government incentives. For example, carbon taxes could increase the relative price of meat and contribute to reduced consumption, much as small taxes on plastic bags have had some success reducing their use. Exxon may be rare among fossil fuel companies financially supporting advocacy for carbon taxes, but many large companies are using carbon prices in their analysis of financial return and evaluating options for alternative climate policies. Some risks may also be reflected in rising insurance costs, a trend evident in coastal areas subject to flooding due to storms and sea-level rise. Regulations such as building codes that require use of fire-resistant materials can also be effective. Ultimately, however, public understanding and support will be required. Companies can contribute to this education process through their product development and marketing but ultimately cannot be too far ahead to remain in business.

IX. Investors' Initiatives and their Role

A focus on socially responsible investing has a long history. For example, the UN Principles for Responsible Investing (PRI), initiated in 2005, began with work by a 20-person investor group drawn from institutions in 12 countries, supported by a 70-person group of experts from the investment industry, intergovernmental organizations, and civil society. The Principles now have more than 3,000 signatories. One product of the PRI is a guide explaining the importance and relevance of climate change in the context of the investment process and to outline how asset owners might incorporate this into responsible investment policies, investment processes, and stewardship practices (PRI website).

The influence of the PRI and other initiatives on mainstream investment has been gradual but increasingly evident in recent years. For example, the New World Capital Group issued reports on "The Rise of Environmental Business Markets" and "The Rise of Environmental Infrastructure Markets" in 2014. Both, the fund managers reported, offered "opportunities for impactful investing that can deliver strong economic returns while benefiting society in important ways". Noting painful memories of unsuccessful forays into cleantech investing, investors were encouraged to approach environmental business opportunities somewhat cautiously.

One expression of the growing support for climate-related financial risk disclosure has been recent investor statements and shareholder resolutions asking for reports on the potential impacts of climate change on company business. Some of the largest institutional investors have issued reports recognizing the need to consider the implications of climate change. For example, BlackRock, the largest institutional investor with over $7 trillion in assets, issued a climate report in 2016 stating "[A]ll asset owners can — and should — take advantage of a growing array of climate-related investment tools and strategies to manage risk, to seek excess returns, or improve their market exposure". In January 2020, in his annual letter to CEOs of the world's largest companies, BlackRock CEO Larry Fink went further, warning that the fund would begin to exit certain investments that "present a high sustainability-related risk", such as those in coal producers (Sorkin, 2020).

Investors have also begun to express opposition to corporate projects and activities on the basis of climate risks. In 2018, for example, institutional investors with $2.5 trillion in assets sent a public letter to oil and gas companies urging that they not engage in drilling in the Arctic National Wildlife Refuge. "We strongly urge banks and oil and gas companies to honor their fiduciary duty to investors and refuse to engage in drilling in the Arctic Refuge", they wrote. "We, as investors, encourage expanding support for the wide range of clean energy solutions and sustainable industries in Alaska, instead of helping to destroy this natural wonder".

Investors have also begun to express opposition to corporate projects and activities on the basis of climate risks. In 2018, for example, institutional investors with $2.5 trillion in assets sent a public letter to oil and gas companies urging that they not engage in drilling in the Arctic National Wildlife Refuge. "Any oil company or bank that supports drilling in the Arctic National Wildlife Refuge faces enormous reputational risk and public backlash", they wrote. "Their brands would be associated with destroying pristine wilderness, contributing to the climate crisis, and trampling on human rights". (Moffit, 2018). A focus on taking climate change into account by investors was a major theme at the 2020 World Economic Forum, a frequent indication of trends in global strategy and finance (Sullivan, 2020).

Many companies have responded to this pressure from investors by releasing climate-related financial risk reports. Chevron voluntarily produced its first climate report in 2017 and a second more analytical report, "Climate Change Resilience: A Framework for Decision Making", in 2018 (Chevron, 2018). The report follows the scenario-modeling approach recommended by the TCFD and considers physical risks (e.g., "to protect the facilities against possible storm surges, we spent $120 million on raising a dike at our Pascagoula, Mississippi, refinery"), litigation risks ("The claims are factually and legally without merit"), and concludes that while the share of oil and gas in the global energy mix may decline, consumption of oil and gas will not decline for at least the next two decades — even if climate policy "increasingly attempts to limit fossil fuel use and reduce GHG emissions".

Chevron justified their belief that oil demand will not decline for at least two decades by several trends: energy transitions are lengthy due to the long time periods required to turn over the energy-consuming capital stock; over the next decade more than 40% of the global population may achieve income levels triggering rapid growth in energy demand; and over 40% of oil consumption is for agriculture and petrochemical applications (and thus not affected by shifts in transportation). While acknowledging technological changes such as electric vehicles and battery storage could accelerate the timing of "peak oil", the report concludes that for this to happen in the next two decades "would represent a historic and unprecedented revolution". In 2020, the International Energy Agency (IEA) did a series of scenarios describing energy futures. One is based on policies currently in place while others are designed to achieve the Paris goals and the target of "net-zero" carbon emissions by 2050. Based on policies currently in place, oil demand would "flatten" in the 2030s while meeting the Paris goals and net-zero targets would require more rapid reductions (IEA, 2020).

Some companies that did not initially prepare climate risk assessments are being forced to do so by shareholder resolutions. In 2017, such resolutions were passed for ExxonMobil, Occidental Petroleum, and PPL (Pennsylvania's largest utility). The resolutions were approved in part due to support from large investment firms, including BlackRock, the world's largest (Lavelle, 2017). While a reflection of increasing investor awareness and concern, the value of such reporting may also be questioned based on the report ExxonMobil prepared, "2018 Energy and Carbon Summary: Positioning for a Lower-Carbon Energy Future". While recognizing that the Paris Agreement might require cutting oil use by 20% by 2040, the company concludes based on logic similar to that of Chevron that use of its products will continue rising until peaking in 2040 (Cushman, 2018).

Perhaps in an effort to show more acceptance of climate risk concerns, in October 2018, Exxon announced it was giving $1 million to

CarbonDividends, a non-profit advocacy organization, to support a carbon tax and dividend plan (Mufson, 2018). The proposal, developed by a group that includes two former Reagan Administration officials, would initially tax fossil fuels as a function of their carbon content at a rate of $40 per ton, with revenue returned to taxpayers through some rebate mechanism. While significant politically, the financial commitment was modest by most measures — about the amount the company spends on capital investment every 20 minutes. In addition, the proposal includes provision for ending potential tort liability for damages caused by oil company contributions to climate change. Reflecting some shareholder dissatisfaction, Exxon was forced to accept three new board members bringing more climate activist perspectives in a landmark vote in June 2021 (Phillips, 2021).

One of the oil majors, BP, announced a radical shift in corporate strategy in 2020. The company declared it would halt oil and gas exploration in new countries, slash oil and gas production by 40%, and boost capital spending on low-carbon energy tenfold, as well as becoming net-zero in its carbon emissions by 2050. Oil and gas production will decline by 2030, with asset sales achieving a 40% reduction by the same year (Mufson, 2020).

Divestment, or selling of shares to express a social concern, has become another form of pressure for some institutional investors in response to climate change. The most frequent targets are fossil fuel companies. While initially mostly an action by socially conscious philanthropies and universities, several very large pension funds, including those for New York State and New York City, have announced they would cease new investments in fossil-fuel related companies and seek to "decarbonize" their portfolios (McKibben, 2017). Some pension funds have also expressed their concerns to energy and mining companies, asking that they not engage in lobbying against climate policies (Holder, 2023). A group of long-term investors has organized to promote climate action as Climate Action 100+. The initiative aims to use the collective financial clout of its members to push companies to improve governance on climate change, curb emissions, and strengthen climate-related financial disclosures — a strategy that requires continuing ownership of shares in the companies being criticized.

In 2018, the $1 trillion sovereign wealth fund in Norway announced it would formally review its fossil fuel-related investments, focusing first on electricity producers and thereafter oil and gas companies, while the much smaller national investment fund of Ireland ($8 billion) passed legislation that requires selling all its investments in coal, oil, gas, and peat "as soon as is practicable" (Carrington, 2018a). In 2015, the UK Environment Agency Pension Fund set "decarbonization" goals for reducing carbon emissions associated with its portfolio and announced in 2018 that they had been achieved (Environmental Finance, 2018). While the equity value of the coal and oil industries have been adversely affected by several factors in recent years, climate change concerns are among the reasons ExxonMobil and other energy majors are no longer nearly as significant businesses as they were a decade ago.

Institutional investors, including pension funds, insurance companies, and sovereign wealth funds, collectively manage over $80 trillion in assets in OECD countries alone and consequently have enormous influence on markets and risk assessments (Ang and Copeland, 2018; Schmukler, 2015). While all have significant assets under management, their investment strategies and risk tolerance vary reflecting differences in ownership (public versus private), regulatory oversight, and management philosophy.

Pension funds are among the institutional investors with the most reason to consider the impact of climate change on their portfolios. "These risks are particularly relevant to public pension funds, which have long-running, predefined obligations to beneficiaries and need to sustain growth over longer time horizons" (Binsted *et al.*, 2017). In an effort to evaluate how climate change might impact the financial performance of pension funds, Mercer Associates, a financial advisory firm, worked with 16 investors to evaluate the financial impact of four scenarios for lower and greater rates of warming and physical impacts. The study shows the following: (1) climate change has an impact on financial performance in all four scenarios; (2) sector risks are most meaningful over the 10 year period from 2015 to 2025; (3) asset class impacts can be meaningful but vary by scenario; and (4) a scenario consistent with the Paris Agreement need not reduce diversified portfolio returns out to 2050 (Mercer Associates, 2015).

Public pension funds are overseen by governments and consequently subject to legislative direction. Public policy is responding to the issue as reflected in recent government actions and high-level international discussions (OECD, 2018). The Maryland Pension Risk Mitigation Act of 2018 requires an annual risk assessment that includes climate risk and that considers relevant recent studies or reports and recommends best practices. California also announced requirements for state pension funds to consider climate risks in 2020 (Sims, 2020).

The French Law on Energy Transition and Green Growth passed in August 2015 requires major institutional investors and asset management companies to explain how they take environmental, social, and governance (ESG) criteria into account in their risk management and investment policies, including climate change.

X. Conclusion

The business and financial communities are becoming increasingly aware of the need to include climate change as a consideration in strategies. Some sectors, including energy and agriculture, are particularly at risk, as are some locations, particularly low-lying coastal areas. The analytical tools to predict and evaluate such risks are becoming more sophisticated and available but localized, short-term forecasts remain challenging. Pension funds and other long-term asset holders are also becoming aware of their exposure to climate risks due to their need to plan decades into the future. Public policy including legislation to require consideration of climate risks and reduction of greenhouse gas emissions is also becoming a significant issue for business planning.

The release of the IPCC *Special Report on Global Warming of 1.5 °C* has brought new urgency to the need for companies and investors to consider climate risks and opportunities. As the issues vary considerably by geography, sector, and business model, there are no silver bullet solutions applicable to business in general — beyond the need to be as informed as possible. However, some strategies do have broad applicability. The first is to understand climate risks with as much specificity as possible, utilizing the steadily improving state of climate science and increasing availability of tools for analyzing financial risks and options specific to business type and location — products that were not available even a few years ago. Such assessments can facilitate the type of risk disclosure recommended by the TCFD and that are under active consideration by the SEC and are likely to be expected or even required by investors and asset owners.

Second, businesses need to expect and plan for a new generation of climate policies. More than 100 countries have announced "net-zero" emission targets in some form (Gronewold, 2020). While differing in date and detail, the intent to use government powers to reduce carbon emissions is increasingly clear. While the United States was an exception to this trend, with the election of President Biden, who has announced climate change action will be a priority in his US Administration, support for coordinated international climate policy is certain to grow. State and local governments have also been increasingly active in adopting climate policies (C2es website; Astor, 2022). California, the fifth largest economy in the world, has an aggressive climate action plan including a cap-and-trade program and a commitment to 100% carbon-free power by 2045 and an 80% reduction in GHG emissions relative to 1990 by 2050. As of September 2020, 23 states and the District of Columbia have adopted greenhouse gas reduction targets. Many US cities have become active in formulating clean energy and climate policies, some including commitments to go carbon free (US Mayors website). State and local governments have a significant role in regulating utilities; revising and enforcing building codes; transportation planning; water management; and other significant sources of greenhouse gas emissions and climate resilience. International companies also need to consider policies in other countries; publicly traded companies and large institutional investors and asset managers in France are now required to report on the impacts of both physical and "transition" risks from climate change to their operations and investments.

A more short-term agenda is behind a coalition of large power consuming companies, including many from the internet and IT sectors, who have organized as the Renewable Energy Buyers Alliance. By aggregating their collective buying power, these companies have been able to invest in 60 GW of wind and solar power — roughly equal to the total installed capacity of solar systems in the US today (REBA website). A few companies have gone further and taken advocacy positions supporting or opposing environmental candidates, although perhaps based on the belief that their products are primarily oriented to "green" consumers (Gelles, 2018).

Philanthropies could be a source of funding for financing risks associated with early stage, innovative technologies. Collectively, charitable investors had $600 billion in assets under management in 2015 and under US law are allowed "program-related investments" in ventures related to the missions of the charity. This opportunity has historically been little utilized but could help accelerate development of climate-related technologies (Burger *et al.*, 2018).

Why are international financial institutions like the World Bank seen as important facilitators for attracting private investment in climate projects in developing countries? Because of their access to concessional finance and ability to take greater risks, the World Bank and other international financial institutions are being seen as key facilitators enabling private sector investment in climate projects in developing countries. Climate-related investments in developing countries are particularly important, as much of the growth in carbon emissions is expected to come from these countries, particularly China and India (IEA, 2017). Many developing countries, including small island states and very poor nations responsible for a small fraction of global greenhouse gas emissions, are also among the most vulnerable (ND-Gain website). However, investment in developing countries is often seen as bringing greater risks. Development finance institutions (DFIs) such as the World Bank are increasingly active in facilitating climate-related private sector investments and have made ambitious commitments to increasing such support in coming years (Multilateral Development Banks, 2018). These institutions have the resources and financial flexibility needed to negotiate government guarantees and to do greater due diligence than commercial lenders. Private investors with potential interest in supporting climate-related projects in developing countries have called on the DFIs to use their greater risk tolerance and capital more effectively to attract private finance, arguing that this could go a long way to meet development goals. For their part, the DFIs have agreed on a set of enhanced principles on the operational use of blended (concessional) finance in private sector operations toward increasing the impact of donor funds (DFI Working Group on Blended Concessional Finance for Private Sector Projects, 2018).

In addition to their role as enablers of private investment, the Multilateral Development Banks (MDBs) also sometimes have taken on a more active role in promoting climate solutions. For example, in September 2018 the World Bank announced it would loan $1 billion for battery storage projects, solicit an additional $1 billion in donor support, and with these resources leverage $3 billion more in private co-financing. Battery storage was chosen for support because of its potential for facilitating greater reliance on solar and wind power, both intermittent sources of energy. In making the announcement, the bank noted that industry players could engage in several ways: bids on procurement packages; partnering with the bank's private sector arm, the IFC, to develop private sector projects; and submitting expressions of interest for contracts (World Bank, 2018b). The International Finance Corporation, the private sector arm of the World Bank group, has a portfolio of early-stage investments in sustainable cooling, another technology critical for a climate-friendly future (TechEmerge Website).

The 2018 and subsequent reports of the IPCC make a strong case that the impacts of climate change due to human activity are now demonstrable and almost certain to become much more serious in the coming decades. While if energy efficiency and non-fossil energy sources were implemented very aggressively globally, the rate of warming could be slowed and more time made available for enhancing resilience and adaptation, the political will to do so seems lacking. Opposition from short-term "losers", particularly powerful fossil fuel industries, is also a reality in the United States and many other countries. In the short term, those companies that effectively anticipate and prepare for climate risks and opportunities are likely to be more successful than their less proactive competitors. However, there is a possibility over the next 10–25 years that overall losses will be much greater than any gains, as the cumulative impact of individual damages could overwhelm the financial and economic system. This systemic risk has come to be recognized by financial regulators and some business leaders, who may be able to push public policy in directions more consistent with risk management (Grippa *et al.*, 2019).

Yet, some promising developments are taking place every day with the increasing public awareness and various actors taking steps to tackle the issues. Tackling climate change will require the collaboration of civil society, its representatives, and the private sector to identify pathways to a sustainable future that are (i) technically feasible, (ii) economically realistic, (iii) politically acceptable, and (iv) achievable without the necessity for very disruptive change in lifestyles and social customs.

References

Acclimatise. (2018). Navigating a new climate, Part 2: Physical risks and opportunities (report prepared for the UNEP Finance Initiative), https://www.unepfi.org/wordpress/wp-content/uploads/2018/07/NAVIGATING-A-NEW-CLIMATE.pdf.

Ang and Copeland. (2018). Integrating climate change-related factors in institutional investment background paper for the 36th Round Table on Sustainable Development 8–9 February 2018, https://www.oecd.org/sd-roundtable/papersandpublications/Integrating%20Climate%20Change-related%20Factors%20in%20Institutional%20Investment.pdf.

Astor, M. (2022). "As federal climate-fighting tools taken away, cities and states step up", *New York Times*, July 7, 2022, https://www.nytimes.com/2022/07/01/climate/climate-policies-cities-states-local.html.

Binsted *et al.*, (2017). Climate Change Risk and the Maryland State Retirement and Pension System, Matthew Binsted1, Nathan Hultman1, Wes L. Hanson1, Alan Miller2, Travis St. Clair3 October 2017, https://spp.umd.edu/sites/default/files/2021-02/Climate%2BChange%2BRisk%2Band%2Bthe%2BMD%2BSRPS.pdf.

Blackstone (press release). (2017). "Blackstone acquires hotel investment partners in Spain", October 17, 2017, https://www.blackstone.com/media/press-releases/article/blackstone-acquires-hotel-investment-partners-in-spain.

Bloomberg Analysis Brochure. https://data.bloomberglp.com/professional/sites/10/Climate-related-Analysis-Brochure.pdf.

Bloomberg NEF (BNEF). (2018). "New energy outlook 2018", https://about.bnef.com/new-energy-outlook/.

Burger, S., Murray, F., Kearney, S., and Ma, L. (2018). "The investment gap that threatens the planet", *Stanford Social Innovation Review*, https://d2l8rne3sx3c3l.cloudfront.net/wp-content/uploads/2017/12/Winter_2018_the_investment_gap_that_threatens_the_planet.pdf?x57461.

C2es (Center for Climate and Energy Solutions). "State climate policy maps", https://www.c2es.org/content/state-climate-policy/.

Carrington, D. (2018a). "Ireland becomes first country to divest from fossil fuels", *The Guardian*, July 12, https://www.theguardian.com/environment/2018/jul/12/ireland-becomes-worlds-first-country-to-divest-from-fossil-fuels.

Carrington, D. (2018b). "Huge reduction in meat-eating 'essential' to avoid climate breakdown", *The Guardian*, October 10, https://www.theguardian.com/environment/2018/oct/10/huge-reduction-in-meat-eating-essential-to-avoid-climate-breakdown.

Carbon Disclosure Project Website. https://www.cdp.net/en.

Chevron. (2018). "Climate change resilience: A framework for decision making", https://www.chevron.com/-/media/shared-media/documents/climate-change-resilience.pdf.

Climate Reality Project Website, https://www.climaterealityproject.org/climate-101.

Climate Watch Website, https://www.climatewatchdata.org.

Comfort, N. (2020). "Central bank to test lenders' climate risk", *ClimateWire*, November 30, https://www.eenews.net/climatewire/2020/11/30/stories/1063719397?utm_campaign=edition&utm_medium=email&utm_source=eenews%3Aclimatewire.

Coastal Risk Consulting Website, https://riskfootprint.com/corp-home/.

Corb, L. *et al.* (2022). "Understanding the SEC's climate risk disclosure rule", *McKinsey*, June 3, https://www.mckinsey.com/business-functions/strategy-and-corporate-finance/our-insights/understanding-the-secs-proposed-climate-risk-disclosure-rule.

Cushman. (2018). "Exxon Reports on Climate Risk and Sees almost None," *Inside Climate News*, February 5, https://insideclimatenews.org/news/05022018/exxon-climate-risk-report-oil-reserves-paris-climate-goals-electric-vehicles/.

Dahlberg, N. (2017). "How sea-rise ready is your home or business? Startup offers the lowdown", *Miami Herald*, August 6, https://www.miamiherald.com/news/business/technology/article165783672.html.

Deloitte. "How insurance companies can prepare for risk from climate change", https://www2.deloitte.com/us/en/pages/financial-services/articles/insurance-companies-climate-change-risk.html.

"DFI Working Group on Blended Concessional Finance for Private Sector Projects", *Joint Report, October 2018 Update*, https://www.adb.org/sites/default/files/institutional-document/457741/dfi-blended-concessional-fiance-report.pdf.

Eavis, P. and Penn, I. (2019). "The struggle to control PG&E", *New York Times (NY Times)*, February 13, 2019, https://www.nytimes.com/2019/02/13/business/energy-environment/pge-wildfire-bankruptcy-control.html.

Economic Times. (October 1, 2018). "Airports taking action against rising seas, storms, as climate change," https://economictimes.indiatimes.com/news/international/business/sunk-costs-airports-taking-action-against-rising-seas-storms-as-climate-changes/articleshow/66025416.cms?from=mdr.

Economist. (2022). "Why the War in Ukraine is driving up Europe's use of coal — And it's price", https://www.economist.com/the-economist-explains/2022/05/09/why-the-war-in-ukraine-is-driving-up-europes-use-of-coal-and-its-price.

EIA Website. US Energy Information Administration. "Energy and the environment explained: Greenhouse gases and the climate." Accessed March 2023, https://www.eia.gov/energyexplained/energy-and-the-environment/greenhouse-gases-and-the-climate.php

Elliott, L. (2020). "UK to make climate risk reports mandatory for large companies", *The Guardian*, November 9, 2020, https://www.theguardian.com/environment/2020/nov/09/uk-to-make-climate-risk-reports-mandatory-for-large-companies.

Environmental Finance. (July 25 2018). "Environment agency pension fund smashes 2020 decarbonisation goal". https://www.environmental-finance.com/content/news/environment-agency-pension-fund-smashes-2020-decarbonisation-goal.html.

EPA (Environmental Protection Agency). "Understanding global warming potentials", https://www.epa.gov/ghgemissions/understanding-global-warming-potentials; https://www.epa.gov/ghgemissions/overview-greenhouse-gases.

ESMAP (Energy Sector Management Assistance Program). (2020). *Integrating Behavior Change in Energy Efficiency Programs in Developing Countries: A Practitioner's Guide*. ESMAP Knowledge Series; No. 029/20. IGO, https://openknowledge.worldbank.org/handle/10986/34788.

Fiedler, T. *et al.* (February 2021). "Business risk and the emergence of climate analytics", *Nature Climate Change*, DOI: 10.1038/s41558-020-00984-6.

FSB (October 13 2022). https://www.fsb.org/2022/10/fsb-publishes-recommendations-for-supervisory-and-regulatory-approaches-to-climate-related-risks-and-calls-for-continued-progress-on-disclosures/.

Galey, P. (2022). "Net-zero promises from major corporations fall short, climate groups say", *NBC News*, February 12, https://www.nbcnews.com/science/environment/net-zero-promises-major-corporations-fall-short-climate-groups-say-rcna14460.

GAO (General Accounting Office). (2018). "Climate Related Risks: SEC Has Taken Steps to Clarify Disclosure Requirements", https://www.gao.gov/assets/700/690197.pdf.

Garay, E. (2022). "Electric planes are coming sooner than you think", *AFAR*, March 3, https://www.afar.com/magazine/electric-planes-are-coming-sooner-than-you-think.

Ge, M. and Levin, K. (2018). "INSIDER: What's changing as countries turn INDCs into NDCs? 5 early insights", *World Resources Institute Blog*, April 18, https://www.wri.org/blog/2018/04/insider-whats-changing-countries-turn-indcs-ndcs-5-early-insights.

Gelles, D. (2018). "Patagonia vs. Trump", *New York Times*, May 5, 2018, https://www.nytimes.com/2018/05/05/business/patagonia-trump-bears-ears.html.

Global Carbon Atlas Website, http://www.globalcarbonatlas.org/; http://www.globalcarbonatlas.org/en/content/project-overview?q=outreach.

Grandoni, D. (2018). "The energy 202: Why New York's new climate lawsuit against ExxonMobil is different", *Washington Post*, October 25, https://www.washingtonpost.com/news/powerpost/paloma/the-energy-202/2018/10/25/the-energy-202-why-new-york-s-new-climate-lawsuit-against-exxonmobil-is-different/5bd0ed2f1b326b559037d2ed/?utm_term=.44a5259fec03.

Gray, T. (2019). "Climate change funds try to profit from a warming world", *NY Times*, April 12, https://www.nytimes.com/2019/04/12/business/climate-change-funds-profit-global-warming.html.

Grippa, P., Schmittmann, J., and Suntheim, F. (2019). "Climate Change and Financial Risk", https://www.imf.org/en/Publications/fandd/issues/2019/12/climate-change-central-banks-and-financial-risk-grippa.

Gronewold, N. (2020). "More nations aim for net zero by 2050", *ClimateWire*, November 30, https://www.eenews.net/climatewire/2020/11/30/stories/1063719299?utm_campaign=edition&utm_medium=email&utm_source=eenews%3Aclimatewire.

Guida, V. (2020). "Fed formally calls out climate change as stability risk", *Politico*, November 10, https://www.politico.com/news/2020/11/10/fed-climate-change-risk-435685.

Hall, B. (July 26 2018). "After days of severe flooding in Virginia Beach, many wonder if it's the new normal", https://www.wavy.com/news/local-news/virginia-beach/after-days-of-flooding-in-virginia-beach-many-wonder-if-it-s-the-new-normal/1324772478.

Harari, Y. (2018). *21 Lessons for the 21st Century.* Spiegel & Grau, New York.

Harvey, C. (2022). "Attribution science linking warming to disasters is rapidly advancing", *Scientific American*, June 3, https://www.scientificamerican.

com/article/attribution-science-linking-warming-to-disasters-is-rapidly-advancing/.

Holder, D. (2023). "Investors push mining companies to adopt better sustainability standards," *Wall St Journal*, Jan 25, https://www.wsj.com/articles/investors-push-mining-companies-to-adopt-better-sustainability-standards-11674644471.

Hotel Business. (June 22 2018). "Across the globe, new build beach resorts to watch", https://www.hotelbusiness.com/across-the-globe-new-build-beach-resorts-to-watch/.

Hotel Management. (May 16 2018). "Virginia beach resort hotel & conference center sold for $19 million", https://www.hotelmanagement.net/transactions/virginia-beach-resort-hotel-conference-center-sold-for-19-million.

Hsiang, S. *et al.* (June 30 2017). "Estimating economic damage from climate change in the United States", *Science*, 356, pp. 1362–1369, http://science.sciencemag.org/content/356/6345/1362.

IEA (International Energy Agency). (2017). "World energy outlook 2017", https://www.iea.org/weo2017/.

IEA. (2018). "The future of cooling", https://www.iea.org/reports/the-future-of-cooling.

IEA. (2020). "World energy outlook 2020", https://www.iea.org/reports/world-energy-outlook-2020.

IEA. (2021). "Direct air capture", https://www.iea.org/reports/direct-air-capture.

IEA. (2022). "Renewable energy market update — May 2022", https://www.iea.org/reports/renewable-energy-market-update-may-2022.

IFC. (2017). "Creating Markets for Climate Business", *Report*. IFC, Washington DC.

IPCC (Intergovernmental Panel on Climate Change). (2018). "Special report on global warming of 1.5°C: An IPCC special report on the impacts of global warming of 1.5°C above pre-industrial levels and related global greenhouse gas emission pathways, in the context of strengthening the global response to the threat of climate change, sustainable development, and efforts to eradicate poverty", http://www.ipcc.ch/report/sr15/.

IPCC. (2021). "Climate change 2021: The physical science basis", https://www.ipcc.ch/report/sixth-assessment-report-working-group-i/.

IPCC (2022). "Sixth assessment report: Impacts, adaptation, and vulnerability", https://www.ipcc.ch/report/ar6/wg2/resources/press/press-release/.

Kaminski, I. (2022). "Fossil fuel industry faces surge in climate lawsuits", *The Guardian*, June 30, https://www.theguardian.com/environment/2022/jun/30/fossil-fuel-industry-surge-climate-lawsuits.

Kaplan, S. and Sellers, F. (2018). "How they survived: Owners of the few homes left standing around Paradise, Calif., took critical steps to ward off wildfires", *Washington Post*, November 30, https://www.washingtonpost.com/national/how-they-survived-owners-of-the-few-homes-left-standing-around-paradise-calif-took-critical-steps-to-ward-off-wildfires/2018/11/30/db323782-f34b-11e8-80d0-f7e1948d55f4_story.html?utm_term=.68b9e5a49319.

Kaufman, R. (2019). "The risks, rewards, and possible ramifications of geoengineering earth's climate", *Smithsonian*, March 11, https://www.smithsonianmag.com/science-nature/risks-rewards-possible-ramifications-geoengineering-earths-climate-180971666/.

Lavelle, M. (2017). "Exxon shareholders approve climate resolution: 62% vote for disclosure", *Inside Climate News*, May 31, https://insideclimatenews.org/news/31052017/exxon-shareholder-climate-change-disclosure-resolution-approved/.

Lindsey, R. (December 15 2016). "Extreme event attribution: The climate versus weather blame Game", https://www.climate.gov/news-features/understanding-climate/extreme-event-attribution-climate-versus-weather-blame-game.

Marchese, D. (2022). "This eminent climate scientist says climate activists need to get real", *New York Times*, April 22, https://www.nytimes.com/interactive/2022/04/25/magazine/vaclav-smil-interview.html.

Maryland Pension Risk Mitigation Act of 2018, http://mgaleg.maryland.gov/2018RS/Chapters_noln/CH_769_hb0993e.pdf.

McKibben, B. (2017). "The movement to divest from fossil fuels gains momentum", *New Yorker*, December 21, https://www.newyorker.com/news/daily-comment/the-movement-to-divest-from-fossil-fuels-gains-momentum.

Mecklin, J. (2022). "Good, bad, ugly, relieved: Reactions to the Supreme Court decision on the EPA and climate change", *Bulletin of the Atomic Scientists*, July 1, https://thebulletin.org/2022/07/good-bad-ugly-relieved-reactions-to-the-supreme-court-decision-on-the-epa-and-climate-change/?utm_source=Newsletter&utm_medium=Email&utm_campaign=MondayNewsletter07042022&utm_content=ClimateChange_EPASupremeCourt_07012022#post-heading.

Mercer Associates. (2015). *Investing in a Time of Climate Change*, https://www.mercer.com/our-thinking/wealth/investing-in-a-time-of-climate-change.html (summary online, full report available on request).

Meyer, R. (2018). "Will Washington State voters make history on climate change?" *The Atlantic*, August 15, https://www.theatlantic.com/science/archive/2018/08/washington-state-carbon-tax/567523/.

Miller, A., Zaelke, D., and Andersen, S. (2021). *Cut Super Climate Pollutants Now!* St Alresford, England: Changemakers Books.

Moffit, L. (2018). Industry take note: Drilling in the Arctic refuge is bad business (Sierra Club blog, May 2018), https://www.sierraclub.org/articles/2018/05/industry-take-note-drilling-arctic-refuge-bad-business.

Morgan Stanley Institute for Sustainable Investing. (2017). "The climate change mitigation opportunities index 2017", https://www.morganstanley.com/content/dam/msdotcom/ideas/climate-change-mitigation-index/MorganStanley_EIU-ClimateChangeIndex_Report.pdf.

MSCI Climate Solutions. https://www.msci.com/our-solutions/esg-investing/climate-solutions.

Mufson, S. (2018). "ExxonMobil gives $1 million to promote a carbon tax and dividend plan", *Washington Post*, October 9, https://www.washingtonpost.com/energy-environment/2018/10/09/exxonmobil-gives-million-promote-carbon-tax-and-dividend-plan/?utm_term=.59bc45fa1b04.

Mufson, S. (2020). "BP built its business on oil and gas. Now climate change is taking it apart", *Washington Post*, August 4, 2020, https://www.washingtonpost.com/climate-environment/2020/08/04/bp-built-its-business-oil-gas-now-climate-change-is-taking-it-apart/.

Multilateral Development Banks (2018) MDBs including African Development Bank (AfDB), Asian Development Bank (ADB), European Bank for Reconstruction and Development (EBRD), European Investment Bank (EIB), Inter-American Development Bank (IDB), World Bank Group). Joint Report of Multilateral Development Banks' Climate Finance, http://www.greengrowthknowledge.org/resource/2017-joint-report-multilateral-development-banks-climate-finance.

NASA Earth Observatory. (January 18, 2000). "Svante Arrhenius", https://earthobservatory.nasa.gov/features/Arrhenius/arrhenius_2.php.

NASA Website. https://climate.nasa.gov/.

Nature Editorial. (2021). "Cities must protect people from extreme heat", *Nature*, July 14, https://www.nature.com/articles/d41586-021-01903-1.

ND-GAIN (Notre Dame Global Adaptation Initiative). https://gain.nd.edu/our-work/country-index/.

NYS Department of Financial Services Website (2020). https://www.dfs.ny.gov/reports_and_publications/press_releases/pr202010291.

Oldenborgh, G. (2017). "Attribution of extreme rainfall from Hurricane Harvey, August 2017", *Environmental Research Letters,* 12(12), http://iopscience.iop.org/article/10.1088/1748-9326/aa9ef2.

Organization for Economic Cooperation and Development (OECD). (2018). "Integrating Climate Change-related Factors in Institutional Investment Background Paper for the 36th Round Table on Sustainable Development

8–9 February 2018", G. Ang, and H. Copeland, https://www.oecd.org/sd-roundtable/papersandpublications/Integrating%20Climate%20Change-related%20Factors%20in%20Institutional%20Investment.pdf.

Penn, I. (2020). "PG&E, troubled California utility, emerges from bankruptcy", *NY Times*, July 28, https://www.nytimes.com/2020/07/01/business/energy-environment/pge-bankruptcy-ends.html.

Phillips, M. (2021). "Exxon's board defeat signals the rise of social-good activists", *NY Times*, June 9, https://www.nytimes.com/2021/06/09/business/exxon-mobil-engine-no1-activist.html.

Principles for Responsible Investment (PRI). (2020). "An introduction to responsible investment: Climate change for asset owners", https://www.unpri.org/an-introduction-to-responsible-investment/an-introduction-to-responsible-investment-climate-change-for-asset-owners/5981.article.

Radford, T. (2017) "Warmer climate raises extinction risk", *Climate News Network*, June 9, https://climatenewsnetwork.net/warmer-climate-raises-species-extinction-risk/.

Renewable Energy Buyers Alliance (REBA), https://rebuyers.org/.

Reuters. (July 7, 2022). "Dutch Airline KLM Sued by environmental groups over alleged 'Greenwashing' Ads", Repost in the *Insurance Journal*, https://www.insurancejournal.com/news/international/2022/07/07/674938.htm?print.

Rich, N. (2018). "Losing earth: The decade we almost stopped climate change", *NY Times*, August 1, https://www.nytimes.com/interactive/2018/08/01/magazine/climate-change-losing-earth.html.

Rouhala, E. and Aries, Q. (2022). "Amid energy crisis, EU says gas, nuclear can sometimes be green", *Washington Post*, July 6, https://www.washingtonpost.com/world/2022/07/06/eu-parliament-nuclear-gas-green/.

Sabin Center for Climate Change Law. "Climate change litigation databases", http://climatecasechart.com/.

Samenow, J. (2018). "Climate change could put businesses underwater. Start-up firm Jupiter aims to come to the rescue", *Washington Post*, February 12, https://www.washingtonpost.com/news/capital-weather-gang/wp/2018/02/12/climate-change-could-put-businesses-underwater-start-up-firm-jupiter-aims-to-come-to-the-rescue/?utm_term=.d7c862512485.

Schmukler, S. (2015). "Institutional investors: From myth to reality", World Bank Policy Research Talk, June 1, http://pubdocs.worldbank.org/en/31971148173 6949205/Sergio-Schmukler-PRT-Institutional-Investors-1June2015.pdf.

Schwartz, J. (2019). "New York loses climate change fraud case against Exxon mobil", *NY Times*, December 10, https://www.nytimes.com/2019/12/10/climate/exxon-climate-lawsuit-new-york.html.

SEC (Securities and Exchange Commission). (March 21, 2022). "SEC proposes rules to enhance and standardize climate-related disclosures for investors", https://www.sec.gov/news/press-release/2022-46.

Shankman, S., Gustin, G., and Cushman, J. (2019). "Humanity faces a biodiversity crisis. Climate change makes it worse", *Inside Climate News*, May 6, https://insideclimatenews.org/news/05052019/climate-change-biodiversity-united-nations-species-extinction-agriculture-food-forests.

Sims, D. (September 25, 2020). "California's climate investment framework funds the future", https://www.nrdc.org/experts/douglass-sims/californias-climate-investment-framework-funds-safer-cle.

Smart, L, (July 21, 2020). "Understanding and navigating climate risk at the asset level", https://www.spglobal.com/marketintelligence/en/news-insights/research/understanding-and-navigating-climate-risk-at-the-asset-level?utm_medium=email&utm_source=ecobusiness&utm_campaign=Climate%20Analytics%20Case%20Study-MI-P-AD-CRTA-ESG-ESG-GL-200716&utm_content=ecobusniess#.

Sorkin, A. (2020). "BlackRock C.E.O. Larry Fink: Climate crisis will reshape finance", *NY Times*, February 24, 2020, https://www.nytimes.com/2020/01/14/business/dealbook/larry-fink-blackrock-climate-change.html.

Starkman, K. (2018). "Report: Climate risk, real estate, and the bottom line", *Four Twenty Seven Blog*, October 11, http://427mt.com/2018/10/11/climate-risk-real-estate-investment-trusts/.

Sullivan, P. (2020). "A call for investors to put their money toward a green future", *NY Times*, January 24, https://www.nytimes.com/2020/01/24/business/green-investments-climate-change.html.

Sustainable Accounting Standard Board (SASB). (2016). "Technical bulletin 2016-01," Climate Risk, https://drive.google.com/file/d/0BxCWvv1wxY35ajljQ0xsSHZMZk0/view.

Swiss Re. (2017). "Hedging Wind risk: New study shows big benefits to the wind industry" (press release), https://corporatesolutions.swissre.com/insights/knowledge/hedging_wind_risk_new_study.html.

Takeuchi, H. (2017). "To test for climate disasters: Break, burn, and throw stuff", *NY Times*, December 11, https://www.nytimes.com/2017/12/11/climate/test-climate-disasters-risk.html.

TCFD (Task Force on Climate Related Financial Disclosures). (June 2017). "Final report and recommendations", https://www.fsb-tcfd.org/.

TCFD (Task Force on Climate Related Financial Disclosures). (2018). "2018 status report", https://www.fsb-tcfd.org/publications/tcfd-2018-status-report/.

TCFD (Task Force on Climate Related Financial Disclosures). (2020). "2020 status report", https://www.fsb.org/2020/10/2020-status-report-task-force-on-climate-related-financial-disclosures/.

TCFD (Task Force on Climate Related Financial Disclosures). (2021). "2021 status report", https://www.fsb.org/2021/10/2021-status-report-task-force-on-climate-related-financial-disclosures/.

TCFD (Task Force on Climate Related Financial Disclosures) Scenario Analysis Website. https://www.tcfdhub.org/scenario-analysis/.

TechEmerge (IFC). "Sustainable Cooling", https://www.techemerge.org/our-focus/sustainable-cooling/.

The Lab. (2017). "Climate resilience and adaptation technology transfer facility", https://www.climatefinancelab.org/project/climate-resilience-adaptation-financetransfer-facility-craft/.

UN Climate Change News. (2022). "Climate commitments not on track to meet Paris agreement goals as NDC synthesis report published", https://unfccc.int/news/climate-commitments-not-on-track-to-meet-paris-agreement-goals-as-ndc-synthesis-report-is-published.

UN News. (May 9, 2022). "Climate: World getting 'measurably closer' to 1.5-degree threshold", https://news.un.org/en/story/2022/05/1117842.

USA. Bill H.R.3623. Climate Risk Disclosure Act 2019. https://www.congress.gov/bill/116th-congress/house-bill/3623.

US Global Change Research Program (USGCRP). (2017). *Climate Science Special Report: Fourth National Climate Assessment*, DOI: 10.7930/J0J964J6.

US Mayors. "Cities with city-wide renewable energy goals", http://www.usmayors.org/wp-content/uploads/2018/01/Cities-with-city-wide-renewable-energy-goals.pdf.

Volcovici, V. (2021). "Green groups file FTC complaint against Chevron over climate claims", *Reuters*, March 16, 2021, https://www.reuters.com/article/us-usa-ftc-greenwashing/green-groups-file-ftc-complaint-against-chevron-over-climate-claims-idUSKBN2B82D7.

Wallace-Wells, D. (2019). "Time to panic", *NY Times*, February 16, https://www.nytimes.com/2019/02/16/opinion/sunday/fear-panic-climate-change-warming.html.

Wang, U. (2018). "New York Attorney general files suit against Exxon for climate fraud", *Climate Liability News*, October 24, https://www.climateliabilitynews.org/2018/10/24/new-york-attorney-general-exxon-climate-fraud/.

World Bank. (2010). *World Development Report 2010: Development and Climate Change*, A World Bank Policy Research Report, World Bank, Washington, D.C.

World Bank (press release). (April 27, 2015). "Africa: Benefits of adapting Africa's infrastructure to climate change outweigh the costs", http://www.worldbank.org/en/news/press-release/2015/04/27/benefits-of-adapting-africas-infrastructure-to-climate-change-outweigh-the-costs.

World Bank. (2017). "State of electricity access report", http://documents.worldbank.org/curated/en/285651494340762694/pdf/114841-ESM-PUBLIC-P148200-32p-FINALSEAROverviewWEB.pdf.

World Bank. (2018a). "Climate and disaster risk screening tools — Agriculture projects", https://climatescreeningtools.worldbank.org/agr/agriculture-welcome.

World Bank. (October 15, 2018b). "Accelerating battery storage for development", https://www.worldbank.org/en/topic/energy/brief/battery-storage-program-brief.

Part IV

Policy Implications

Chapter 14

Market Imperfections: Internalizing the Externalities

Ingmar Schumacher

Learning Objectives

- Understand the concept of market imperfections and externalities
- Describe how market prices rarely factor in market imperfections and externalities
- Review how this affects consumer behavior, producers, and government intervention
- Understand what each market actor can do to address externalities

Abstract

This chapter introduces Part IV on Policy Implications of sustainability. It introduces the concept of market imperfections and externalities. It reviews the theoretical economic background and some empirical evidence on the concept of *externalities* which is key to understanding market imperfections related to sustainability issues (one entity pays while others get the benefit or bear the burden). It highlights the fact that market prices rarely factor in these externalities and that actors producing negative externalities do not always pay for them and that other actors bear the negative consequences (i.e., end up paying for them). The chapter highlights the trend that consumers, producers, and governments are starting to take production and market externalities much more seriously. Consumers more and more buy only products that are labeled organic, as they know that these products contain fewer pesticides that harm them and those that produce these products. Producers and investors understand that corporate social responsibility is not simply a buzzword that attracts consumers but that it does provide a value-added for the company. Employees are more motivated to work if they feel that they are needed and welcomed, and supply chains work more efficiently if every company down the chain gets a fair share. Products produced by motivated employees and manufactured with high-quality materials tend to last longer and are more appealing to consumers. Governments are understanding that they need to be careful in the way they introduce new policies, and they are starting to introduce these in a more subtle way. Some environmentally harmful industries, energy sources, technologies, or processes may become obsolete. The chapter concludes that although corporate social responsibility is the right way, it needs to be supplemented with more consumers who are less price-oriented, and it needs to be induced by governments that understand that maximizing the pie also requires dealing with these externalities.

I. Introduction

Population growth, economic expansion, and an increasing use of natural resources have all given rise to questions about the sustainability of the development path humanity is pursuing (Dasgupta and Ehrlich, 2013). The key problems underlying the pressures on sustainability are market failures that lead to a misallocation of resources. This chapter studies the source of these failures and what can be done about them.

Markets tend to work well if the market participants have sufficient information to make the best choices for themselves if no one holds market power, if there are no distortions such as transaction costs, and when there are no external effects on others. Under these circumstances, no government intervention is necessary, unless the purpose is redistribution.

However, if one of these requirements is not fulfilled, then markets may lead to a misallocation of resources. The outcome will be an inefficient market with losses to society that could be avoided if these misallocations were to be corrected. In other words, there are obstacles that prevent free markets from working well, or efficiently, but there are also solutions on hand that require intervention.

One of the main requirements for markets to lead to efficient outcomes is the absence of external effects. In reality, however, almost every production decision, every consumption decision, and thus every market transaction induces an external effect on others (Buchanan and Stubblebine, 1962). An external effect arises if a person is impacted by someone else's choice or activity without receiving adequate compensation. These external effects can appear in the form of both costs and benefits. This chapter focuses on externalities that largely turn out to be costs to society. For example, if a firm's production pollutes a river which then in turn kills the fish inside the river and the costs of this side effect are not included in the price of the firm's product, then we speak of an external effect, or simply an externality.

Example: Great Pacific Garbage Patch (Day *et al.*, 1988; Moore, 2003). The Great Pacific Garbage Patch was hypothesized by several researchers already in 1988 and finally spotted by Captain Charles Moore in 1997. It is the biggest known marine trash vortex in the world, covering an area three times the size of France. The garbage in this trash vortex consists mostly of plastic, which is not biodegradable but instead breaks down into smaller pieces, called microplastics. Recent studies have shown that these microplastics can now be found in our drinking water, and even remote mountain lakes (Free *et al.*, 2014). We have little scientific knowledge as to how microplastics affect ecosystems or mankind, but preliminary results for marine life suggest strongly negative impacts (Gall and Thompson, 2015).

This chapter discusses why externalities are the key to understanding the obstacles to sustainability, how market actors are involved in creating externalities, and what can be done about them.

Chapter 14 is organized as per the following sections:

I. Introduction
II. Externalities
III. The Economic Actors
IV. Conclusion

II. Externalities

Traditionally, free-market economists relied on Adam Smith who argued that markets are self-correcting (Smith 1776). He called this the *"invisible hand"*. The argument was that there exists an invisible hand that brings buyers and sellers together and coordinates prices and quantities in the markets. Even though everyone acts in their own self-interest when buying or selling a product, this was also supposed to bring about the highest benefit to society. This worldview is still the predominant view in the free market economies across the world, especially in the United States.

However, it very quickly becomes apparent that this invisible hand neglects the indirect impacts on others that are not part of these market transactions. Thus, if an upstream firm which pollutes a river during the production process does not compensate those affected by this pollution, and then sells the product to its customers, then the price of the product clearly does not include the costs of this pollution. This is called an external effect, or in short an *externality* (Buchanan and Stubblebine, 1962).

This externality has two consequences. Firstly, it leads to a lower-than-optimal price. Thus a higher quantity of the product will be sold on the market than is good for society as a whole. Economists call this an inefficient outcome. It is inefficient because it leads to overconsumption due to the low price and hence more resources will be devoted to a product that only benefits a subset of the population and harms another. These resources may be put to better use somewhere else. Furthermore, the overproduction of the harmful product leads to a too high level of harm imposed upon the third party compared to what would be ideal from the society's point of view.

Secondly, it hurts an individual who is not part of this market exchange. If property rights were well-defined and enforceable and there was no cost to bargaining, then the individual could charge the polluter the costs of this externality. Economists call this *internalizing the externality*. For example, if the river that a firm is polluting were to belong to an individual, then the fact that the individual has a property right over the river would allow this individual to charge the firm the costs of this pollution. The problem, obviously, is that property rights are not everywhere well-defined. Who has a property right over the air that we breathe? Who has a property right over the oceans or the water in the rivers? This is the reason why many externalities continue to persist even though they are harmful to third parties.

> **Example:** Cuyahoga river on fire (Stradling and Stradling, 2008). The Cuyahoga river in Cleveland, USA, was among the most polluted rivers of the United States, owing to one of Cleveland's largest accumulation of industries along its banks. The pollution was so severe that it was devoid of fish in the highly polluted parts. Even worse, it was so polluted that it had caught fire at least 13 times. This finally spurred the public's concern in 1969 and, as a result, major environmental laws and regulations were introduced in the USA. These laws and regulations, such as the resulting Clean Water Act or the Environmental Protection Agency, defined property rights over the river. As a result, the Cuyahoga river tends to have sufficient water quality to again carry fish and even be classified as bathing water.

Assume now that someone would have to pay for the clean-up costs and these costs would be reflected in the market price. In this case, the new market price that now internalizes the externality would be higher. This new price would then be made up of the previous price (adjusted upwards for a potential decrease in demand) plus the costs of the externality. There are three issues associated with this. Firstly, what is the correct price? Secondly, who pays for the externality? Thirdly, who are the parties that are interested in internalizing the externalities and what are their means to achieving this?

1. The Correct Price?

When faced with a market that is subject to an externality, there are essentially two prices, the market price at which the product is traded, but also the social price which includes the costs of the externality to society. While it is indeed the invisible hand that guides the market to a price at which consumers and producers want to trade, the much harder question concerns the correct social price that internalizes the externality. Think of climate change. Our carbon emissions today will increase the stock of carbon with a delay of up to 70 years and thus our emissions today will have the strongest impact on the climate of the next two generations (Rogelj *et al.*, 2011). Most of us will not be around any longer to feel the impact of the externality that we impose today upon the future. So, who is going to represent the interests of the future generations? How do we even know that they will hold the same preferences as we do? What if they developed technologies that allowed them to fully adapt to the climatic changes? It is no surprise that the world has, as of now, been unable to settle upon a unique price to internalize this externality.

Example: United Nations Framework Convention on Climate Change (UNFCCC) meetings and their problems to settle upon a carbon price (Friman and Hjerpe, 2015). Since 1995, the United Nations has held annual conferences where world leaders come together to discuss climate change and find means to achieve international collaboration on this problem. While it is clear that a price on carbon is the most efficient solution to tackle climate change, the main problem is that countries do not agree on their respective responsibilities. Poorer countries tend to feel that they should be allowed to increase their carbon emissions in order to achieve similar wealth levels as developed countries, while developed countries, especially the USA, tend to argue that a price on emissions hurts the local economy too much.

One of the reasons for a lack of consensus is that there is no wide-spread agreement about the correct price for carbon. This correct price for carbon should reflect carbon's negative impact on society, and therefore is mostly referred to as the social cost of carbon. Economists such as Nobel Laureate William Nordhaus have spent significant efforts to try to calculate this social cost. Estimates average around 54\$ per ton of CO_2 with a significant uncertainty from −13\$ to 2,387\$ per ton of CO_2 (Wang *et al.*, 2019).

A reason for this large uncertainty surrounding the estimate of the social cost of carbon is that in order to calculate its value, we must know the impacts of climate change on ecosystems and humankind from adding a ton of CO_2 into the atmosphere. Not only that, we also must know how these impacts change over time and furthermore how these costs should be valued over time.

While the valuation of these impacts at a specific point in time is an entirely empirical question, it is also an ethical question and subject of great controversy. The valuation of these costs over time is being accomplished by what is called the social discount rate. If future generations are expected to be richer than current generations, then their welfare will receive a lower valuation (i.e. be discounted) compared to the welfare of the current generation. This is a positive parameter, in the sense that empirical evidence can aid us in finding its level. Another component of the social discount rate is the rate of pure time preference, which measures how much we discount future generations simply because their welfare is in the distant future. This is essentially a normative issue and subject to great controversy.

Another question concerns the price of nature. To value an externality, we need to know how valuable nature is for sustainability. There is a large literature on ecosystem services that attempts to quantify, through various methods, the value of ecosystems (Daily, 1997). In general, something becomes more valuable the less there is of it, and the more useful it turns out to be. While trees can re-grow, it is also clear that a species that has become extinct cannot. How valuable are species and ecosystems? For example, the Bramble Cay melomys, a rodent that lived on an island at the Great Barrier Reef, is widely believed to be the first mammal that was pushed to extinction due to human-induced climate change (Gynther *et al.*, 2016). While it can be argued that the extinction of this particular mammal is not an issue for mankind, the same cannot be said about the Great Barrier Reef (van der Linden and Hanson, 2007). Our limited understanding of how ecosystems form and interact is also not very helpful to assess which animals or plants are necessary to sustain ecosystems.

Hence, we face significant uncertainty about the correct price, if any, that we should attach to nature.

Adding to this uncertainty is the question of sustainability. Sometimes people argue that there is substitutability between nature and human-made capital (Pezzey, 1992; Neumayer, 2003; Withagen, 2009). This is called *weak sustainability*. It is argued that most of nature is not essential for mankind and it is not an issue for us if we transform large parts of the rainforest into grazing areas or expand cities into nature resorts. The price of nature in this case would be somewhat limited and mostly include the harvesting costs of the trees, the mining costs of the materials, or the cost of land for our urban expansions. In fact, starting with the industrial revolution, much of the economic growth has been achieved on the back of nature by transforming nature into man-made capital.

Other times people argue that there is very limited, if any, substitutability between nature and human-made capital (Pezzey, 1992; Neumayer, 2003; Withagen, 2009). This paradigm is called *strong sustainability* and is very closely aligned with the precautionary principle (Arrow and Fisher, 1974). The argument goes that, if we are not entirely sure as to what is important for us or if some changes are irreversible, then we ought to prefer to keep the option of not making the wrong decisions. In other words, we should err on the side of precaution. This becomes even more relevant for the case of *tipping points*. A tipping point occurs if a small impact induces a large structural change in an ecosystem and this ecosystem tips into a bad and potentially irreversible state. The problem obviously is that we are mostly unaware of tipping points until it is too late.

Example: Collapse of the Atlantic thermohaline circulation (Lenton *et al.*, 2008). The thermohaline circulation is an ocean circulation working like a conveyer belt transporting warmer water across the Atlantic. A sufficient sea level rise, caused by climate change, is expected to shut down this conveyer belt. In case of a collapse, a substantial long-lasting cooling over the North Atlantic, Europe, and North America would be the consequence (Rahmstorf and Ganopolski, 1999), with potentially drastic consequences for agricultural production and living conditions.

In reality, the true degree of substitutability lies most likely somewhere between the weak and strong paradigm. When there is still a large degree of nature around us, then substituting some of this for man-made capital comes at a low cost. This would correspond to the case of weak sustainability. When very little of nature is left, or once pollution has reached a high level, then any potential further substitution could be disastrous. As a result, strong sustainability should be expected in case we are close to tipping points. We should therefore see an increasing price of nature that corresponds to its increasing scarcity (Hotelling, 1931), and when we are close to tipping points, then this price will rise to such a level that further extraction is too costly (Schumacher, 2011).

2. Who Pays for the Externality?

In addition to understanding as to what the correct price of an externality is, it is also not entirely clear as to who should pay for the externality. Imagine a company that develops a new product to produce electricity. Imagine further that this product is more expensive than that of a dirty competitor. Imagine electricity produced from wind energy versus coal. The more wind turbines are bought, the lower will be the production costs in the future and the less CO_2 will be emitted in the atmosphere. There are two ways to deal with this positive externality from wind energy and the negative one from coal. On the one hand, we have the market-driven approach that tends to rely on market dynamics and market participants such as consumers or financiers to auto-regulate the market. On the other hand, we have the public intervention approach that would lead to the use of market interventions to deal with these externalities. In some cases, one approach might be more appropriate than the other. For example, if property rights are not well-defined, then it is very often the government that steps in and imposes fines or regulations upon the polluter. In other cases, the choice may be determined by ideological or political views as well as ethical underpinnings.

In this respect, a widely accepted rule is the so-called *Polluter-pays principle*. It suggests that whoever creates an externality should also be charged for this externality. However, from an economist's perspective, to induce efficiency, it does not matter who pays for the externality, whether it be the producer or the consumer. The only concern, in order to maximize society's pie, is to internalize the externality.

Nevertheless, when asked about who should pay for an externality like pollution, the public nearly exclusively pushes for the polluter-pays principle. This is reflected in the fact that the European Union and the United States have included this principle in their environmental laws, while the OECD has strongly suggested to include it in its environmental policy guidelines. The underlying reason is an ethical one, not one based on efficiency. When asked why they push for the polluter-pays principle, then people argue it is a question of responsibility. Those responsible for a problem should also be the ones to deal with it. This has been called the Kindergarten rule of sustainability (Brock and Taylor, 2005), named after the observation that children in the kindergarten are taught that whatever mess they make they must also clean up.

There are, however, quite a few circumstances under which the polluter-pays principle is difficult to be implemented. For example, who is to be held accountable if there are non-point source emissions and it is difficult to assess who pollutes and is responsible for what amount? Think of pesticide and herbicide use or sewage water in a river. How can one assess as to how much of the pesticides in the water are due to which farmer? As another more concrete example, think of the Great Pacific Garbage Patch. Who is responsible for this? Who can be made accountable? How can one impose the polluter-pays principle in this case and especially retrospectively?

Also, think of the nuclear industry. A large-scale meltdown in one nuclear plant will affect several countries and significant numbers of ecosystems and individuals. No nuclear company has the kind of money necessary to cover these costs, and no insurance company would be able to adequately insure a disaster of that size. In this case and the cases above, it is clear that it is very difficult to implement the polluter-pays principle.

III. The Economic Actors

Each transaction in the market involves several actors. The businesses, which are the suppliers of products; those who demand the products, namely, the consumers; and the governments that undertake regulatory interventions. A somewhat neglected but important additional actor is civil society. The way in which these actors participate in market transactions differs widely and any changes induced by one actor subsequently leads to reactions by the other actors. In order to understand the role that each actor plays, we shall analyze these separately.

1. The Businesses

The businesses themselves and the way they interact in the market are crucial for sustainability. A business can be run solely with shareholders' profits in mind, or it can be organized in a more socially responsible way. The key to understanding that the socially responsible way is (generally) not yielding the highest profits for a company is to see that a socially responsible company takes more into account in its production decisions than its own interests. A company that provides a fair wage or makes its packaging more environmentally friendly will incur higher costs. If it cannot fully transfer these higher costs onto the consumers, then naturally it will incur smaller profits.

Which business model is chosen then depends on the owners of the businesses, the managers' visions, the type of business, and the market structure itself (Osterwalder and Pigneur, 2010). It is fair to say that the predominant business model is based on a profit-maximizing maxim. After all, most shareholders tend to invest their money in the company that yields them the highest returns. The way a company finances itself, and the financial institutions providing capital, will significantly impact its ability to adapt its business models.

In the case where the managers are also the owners, the managers obviously have much more freedom to choose the business model. Prominent examples here are Patagonia, Lego, or IKEA. These companies are still predominantly privately owned and thus have more liberty to (potentially) forgo some profit in preference of a more socially responsible approach. In contrast to these, other companies shift their production sites to regions with fewer regulations to exploit relatively lower production costs. For example, many companies from developed countries have outsourced a large proportion of their businesses to the developing countries to exploit the lack of labor unions, or to produce under weaker environmental regulations.

> **Example:** Patagonia (Lindgreen *et al.*, 2009). This outdoor company is still predominantly owned by its founders, Yvon and Malinda Chouinard, and is only one of a few outdoor clothing companies that take sustainability seriously by including environmental targets, codes of conduct, and labor rights (Simon, 2013). Patagonia donates annually 1% of its sales to grassroots environmental groups. In contrast to companies such as Nike that produced in the Rana Plaza factory which collapsed and killed over 1000 workers, Patagonia also produces partly in Bangladesh, but it subjects its production sites to even higher standards than the agreement on fire and building safety that was drawn up in the aftermath of the factory collapse.

However, it is not only the ownership that matters but also the type of business that the companies are in. For example, Monsanto Bayer, a global producer of herbicides and pesticides, is widely viewed as one of the least socially responsible companies. Similar things can be said about those in the business of non-renewable resources such as oil-producing companies. Yet, it can be argued that these companies simply supply what is demanded. Thus, who is the polluter — the one who produces a product that induces potentially significant externalities, or the consumer, the one that uses it? With whom lies the responsibility?

The market structure is one of the critical stumbling blocks to introducing a corporate sustainable approach to one's business (Varian, 2014). At one end is the *monopoly market*. In this case, the monopolist is the main, if not sole, producer of a product and owns a market share of more than 40%. Hence, it can set the price and quantities on the market, while the other very small firms have little influence on the actual outcomes. In this case, as the monopolist is virtually free to decide over the product and the market, the ownership is crucial for whether or not the monopolist wants to minimize the externalities that (s)he imposes upon society.

In contrast, at the opposite end of the spectrum, we have markets which are *perfectly competitive*. A perfectly competitive market is characterized by a large set of small companies that produce essentially identical products that are indistinguishable from each other. No company alone has an impact on the product's price. The price will, due to competition, drop to a level where no company makes any profit. Since, as we argued above, a socially responsible business model does not come for free, a company in a perfectly competitive market that wants to produce more socially responsibly than before would also face higher costs. If it wants to cover those costs by setting the price of its product higher than that of the competitors, then no consumer will buy that product as the products are indistinguishable. A perfectly competitive market makes it thus extremely difficult to implement a socially responsible business model.

2. The Consumers

Consumers are nowhere alike. They have different attitudes, cultures, and demands. They prefer different products, have different living standards, and various needs and desires. Furthermore, they change their demands over time. While, for example, years ago the car was a major status symbol, inhabitants of larger cities in Europe are moving away from this social conformity and are starting to rely more on public transport. Until the mid-50s households in the Western world were predominantly characterized by several generations living together and they had a larger number of children. Today's households tend to consist of singles or couples with one or two children. This, naturally, has an impact on the demands, businesses, and market structures.

However, the biggest change that we have recently seen is the move toward a socially responsible consumer. Awareness created by fast-spreading news via the internet and social media as well as much larger freedom of choice have given consumers the option to take more into account in their consumption choices than simply the product itself. The previously dominating approach *Not In My BackYard* is starting to be replaced by an approach that not only includes one's own backyard but also that of others. There is evidence that consumers prefer those products that have been produced with a socially responsible business model, and this also shows in company profits to some extent (Margolis *et al.*, 2009; Saeidi *et al.*, 2015).

One of the reasons why consumers become more socially responsible actors in the marketplace is the emergence, or manifestation, of social norms that target sustainable behavior (Schumacher, 2015). We observe a cultural change where status quo products are no longer those that show a consumer's wealth, but those that reveal how socially responsible the consumer is. This new culture is driven by social norms that are spreading and evolving through society, fostered by tacit government interventions that nudge individuals to make a more socially responsible choice (Thaler and Sunstein, 2009).

Social media and the quick spreading of good and bad news have also had an effect on the *codes of conduct* that many companies follow when outsourcing their labor. After the Rana Plaza garment factory incident in 2013, most companies that had outsourced their labor to Bangladesh started to adopt more stringent building and safety requirements. Companies that did not, like Walmart, are in the lower third of the Harris Poll reputation ranking, while those that did, such as Nike, can be found in the upper third. Adopting voluntary codes of conduct seems to have a positive influence on a company's reputation (Wright and Rwabizambuga, 2006), showing that consumers are willing to support socially responsible corporate efforts.

One of the big market failures that hinder efficient market outcomes is informational asymmetry. If consumers are unaware of the actual quality of the products, for example, if they cannot differentiate between organic and non-organic production due to a lack of labeling, then they also cannot choose according to their best interests. In this respect, certification in the form of, e.g. ecolabels, fair-trade labels, or other labels related to various indicators of corporate social responsibility has allowed consumers to also trust what businesses advertise and thus reduce the information gap between consumers and producers. Additionally, labels allowed businesses to distinguish themselves from their close competitors, gain reputation, and increase customer loyalty. Survey results have shown that ecolabels nowadays play an important role for 50% of the European consumers. In addition to labels, another important means to reduce asymmetric information are disclosures such as voluntary company disclosures, which are introduced by managers who feel it is important for their company to be recognized for their social efforts. These disclosures may also be driven by civil society organizations (such as the Global Reporting Initiative or the Integrated Reporting) or by regulations (such as the European Directive 2014/95/EU on disclosure of non-financial sustainability-related information, or the Management Discussion and Analysis in the SEC filing in the United States). To further the development of these disclosures, there are also initiatives such as the Taskforce on Climate-related Financial Disclosures (TCFD) whose aim is to develop recommendations for voluntary financial disclosures that are relevant for climate issues.

Example: Ecolabel the Flower. The EU Ecolabel "The Flower" was introduced in 1992 by the European Commission. It is a voluntary label that companies can apply for if their product is more environmentally friendly than those of their competitors and if their product fulfills certain criteria. In the first 10 years after its establishment, this label awarded 237 licenses overall. Now it awards on average 2000 licenses per year. Hence, companies are understanding that there is a high demand for environmentally friendly products and are, thus, in the process of reforming their productions in order to reach the standards necessary for this label.

3. The Governments

Often enough property rights are not sufficiently well-defined and sometimes businesses use these opportunities to reduce their costs by avoiding dealing with the externalities that they produce. The only actor that then has the power to act upon this is the government. Governments try to internalize these externalities via appropriate tools. While the government has a multitude of possible approaches to intervene in the markets (such as the provision of information, mandates, direct funding, public production, and nudging), the two main methods used are regulation and taxation. There are obvious advantages and disadvantages to these.

Regulations tend to be used when there are known hazardous thresholds to pollution levels. For example, the European Union has set environmental quality standards for most pollutants through the Industrial Emissions Directive, the Water Framework Directive, and the Surface

Water Directive. Japan has heavily relied on the Best Available Technology regulation, which requires other products in the same market to apply the same environmental technology as the product with the best environmental technology. The European Union has, for example, introduced this Best Available Technology regulation for the case of products containing mercury.

However, from an economic perspective, regulation is often considered inefficient and inferior to subsidies or taxes (market-based instruments). When a government puts a regulation in place, then the cost of adhering to the regulation for low pollution levels is zero, while it is infinity above this threshold. Consider, for example, an ambient threshold on air pollution, say on PM2.5, a pollutant that arises through combustion. Throughout some summers, when PM2.5 levels were elevated, several European cities did not allow cars to any longer enter cities. While this is the fairest way to deal with the problem, a more efficient way would be to charge fees that are related to the level of pollution. This would yield what economists call a *double dividend*. The first advantage is that it will not be a zero-one, reactive policy, implying that decisions are taken only when thresholds are already crossed. Instead, the increasing cost of entering the city when pollution levels are rising will give the opportunity to enter to those that have a high benefit from entering the city, while it will deter those that only rely on the car as it is the easiest means of transport. The second advantage is that the money received through the fees can be used to clean the air, improve public transport, or be used for other governmental expenses.

The main problem that most governments face when evaluating the costs and benefits of an environmental policy is the impact on international competition. If one imposes tighter environmental regulations on the home companies, then their costs of production will be higher than those of their international competitors who produce in countries with less stringent environmental regulations. Similarly, a country that imposes strict labor regulations with respect to working time and working conditions will have higher labor costs compared to a country that does not protect its labor force to the same extent. If a company from a country with tight regulations has to compete with a company from a country with lax regulations, then it is clear that the company facing lax regulations can bring its product on the market more cheaply and hence will reap most of the market share. This problem leads to so-called pollution havens, whereby companies relocate to countries with laxer environmental regulations. As an example, a significant share of old US batteries is now recycled in Mexico after the USA introduced stricter regulations that made the recycling of batteries more demanding and thus more expensive.

The other issue that governments need to be made aware of when intervening in markets is whether these interventions also have the support of the wider public. While a government may feel that an intervention is necessary, a less-informed public may believe otherwise. For example, the yellow vest movement in France in 2019 blocked the introduction of a carbon tax. Also, local norms may prevent the introduction of interventions. While the United Kingdom is again reducing the speed limit on highways in order to decrease carbon emissions, this kind of policy would be unthinkable in the car-dominant German society. A recent means to influence market participants without restricting their actions is what has been called nudging (Thaler and Sunstein, 2009). This form of government intervention leaves individuals the choice to act however they want but provides incentives or information so that they may make the more socially responsible choice.

One should also not neglect the widespread view that government intervention can be badly implemented and lead to additional unanticipated distortions. A prominent example is that companies that are run by governments tend to make fewer profits and be less efficient than those run in a free market system. Other examples relate to the printing of money or increasing of government debt, which may help to resolve a current problem while introducing future costs. Clearly, any large-scale intervention into the economy, such as a carbon tax that is high enough to actually induce changes in the public's behavior, will also lead to further distortions and changes that not only impact a single market itself but have potential repercussions for the whole economy.

4. Other Actors

One aspect that tends to be neglected when it comes to the public is its role in what is known as civil society. Fridays for Future schools strikes for climate initiated by Greta Thunberg, NGOs such as the Climate Accountability Institute, as well as social media platforms help to spread information through society at a hitherto unimaginable speed. They make markets more transparent and thereby inform consumers about the products that fit their preferences. In various cases this has induced changes in social norms that lead to more sustainable outcomes. For example, a significant share of the more expensive but organic products not only get bought as they contain fewer pesticides than their non-organic counterparts, but also because they strain local ecosystems much less and are healthier for agricultural workers (Schumacher, 2010). Clearly, consumers nowadays not only buy organic products because these are healthier alternatives, but also because civil society is enforcing social norms that induce consumers to internalize some production externalities.

We should also mention that both higher education levels across the world and a significant shift of countries to the service society have allowed more individuals to become researchers and scientists, which through the expansion of the digital networks helps to transmit more research results throughout the planet. The increase in research output helps us to gain more understanding as to how ecosystems work (Biggs *et al.*, 2015), how they are connected (Grunewald and Bastian, 2015), how and when it is profitable for companies to be more socially responsible (McWilliams and Siegel, 2001), and how and when government interventions are useful and effective (Winston, 2007).

A final point concerns the increasing role of investors and shareholders who are starting to take a more holistic approach to investing which encompasses sustainability considerations. This is especially the case for long-term investors such as pension funds or insurance companies. This change in mentality, coupled with the increasing market of green bonds and ESG products, is providing credit to companies that are in the progress of transforming their products into more sustainable ones. Nowadays, shareholders and investors understand that value-added or shareholder value and corporate socially responsible production are not orthogonal (Smith and Colgate, 2007), but that a more sustainable production can increase a company's profits, too (Crane *et al.*, 2019).

IV. Conclusion

We are clearly living through a period where both science and social media are changing our understanding of how our production, consumption, and investment decisions affect us and others. This greater awareness adds a layer of conscience to our market decisions that previously were mostly driven by motives related to personal profit. This layer of conscience speaks to our moral self and the increasing amount of information about the products that we sell, buy, or invest in does not allow us anymore to ignore that voice.

Consumers more and more buy only products that are labeled organic, as they know that these products contain fewer pesticides that harm them and those that produce these products. They buy products that are labeled fair, in order to help poor workers in developing countries get a fairer share. Furthermore, as more and more individuals are moving into apartments in cities, they are starting to be more conscious about what they need and buy fewer products that have a lower use value.

Producers and investors understand that corporate social responsibility is not simply a buzzword that attracts consumers but that it does provide a value-added for the company. Employees are more motivated to work if they feel that they are needed and welcomed, and supply chains work more efficiently if every company down the chain gets a fair share. Products produced by motivated employees and manufactured with high-quality materials tend to last longer and are more appealing to consumers, which leads to greater customer loyalty and this by itself creates a value-added for the company. On the converse, companies that do not take part in this movement toward a more responsible production may quickly get name-shamed and potentially must face a civil society that, in one way or another, punishes them for this.

Governments are understanding that they need to be careful in the way they introduce new policies, and they are starting to introduce these in a more subtle way. A whole field of nudging has developed, where nearly every government has its own nudge unit that tries to find ways in which market participants can be influenced to make the "right" choices without coercing them through regulation or other hard constraints.

In short, we are currently in a transition period where fast-spreading information changes our habits in the marketplace and no market participant can afford to ignore this any longer.

In this chapter, it is argued that companies, consumers, and governments are starting to take production and market externalities much more seriously and there are efforts from every market participant to internalize these externalities in one way or another. While consumers can push producers to adopt a more socially responsible business model, it is also true that some markets are more challenging to change. Furthermore, some environmentally harmful industries, energy sources, technologies, or processes may become obsolete.

Thus, the role of governments is to understand when a certain market structure, for example, perfect competition or international competition, hinders the introduction of a corporate socially responsible business model. In this case, the tools to internalize the externalities may need to vary, and a thorough Cost–Benefit Analysis is indispensable (Tietenberg and Lewis, 2016).

It goes without saying that internalizing the externalities comes, at least quite often, at a significant price. Even more problematic is that regulators often do not have a good understanding of what the correct price actually is. Hence, there is an immediate need for businesses, consumers, and governments to carefully work together with the incentive to internalize the externalities. Corporate social responsibility is the right way, but it needs to be supplemented with more consumers that buy in a less price-oriented way, and it needs to be induced by governments that understand that maximizing the pie also requires dealing with these externalities.

References

Arrow, K. J. and Fisher, A. C. (1974). "Environmental preservation, uncertainty, and irreversibility", *Classic Papers in Natural Resource Economics*, Palgrave Macmillan, London pp. 76–84.

Biggs, R., Schlüter, M., and Schoon, M. L. (eds.). (2015). *Principles for Building Resilience: Sustaining Ecosystem Services in Social-ecological Systems*, Cambridge University Press, Cambridge.

Brock, W. A. and Taylor, M. S. (2005). "Economic growth and the environment: A review of theory and empirics", in *Handbook of Economic Growth*, vol. 1, Elsevier, Amsterdam, pp. 1749–1821.

Buchanan, J. M. and Stubblebine, W. C. (1962). "Externality", *Classic Papers in Natural Resource Economics*, Palgrave Macmillan, London, pp. 138–154.

Crane, A., Matten, D. and Spence, L. (eds.). (2019). *Corporate Social Responsibility: Readings and Cases in a Global Context*, Routledge, Milton Park, UK.

Daily, G. (ed.). (1997). *Nature's Services: Societal Dependence on Natural Ecosystems*, 1st edn., Island Press, Washington, DC.

Dasgupta, P. S. and Ehrlich, P. R. (2013). "Pervasive externalities at the population, consumption, and environment nexus", *Science,* 340(6130), pp. 324–328.

Day, R. H., Shaw, D. G., and Ignell, S. E. (1988). "Quantitative distribution and characteristics of neustonic plastic in the North Pacific Ocean, Final Report to US Department of Commerce, National Marine Fisheries Service, Auke Bay Laboratory", Auke Bay, Alaska, US.

Free, C. M., *et al.* (2014). "High-levels of microplastic pollution in a large, remote, mountain lake", *Marine Pollution Bulletin,* 85(1), pp. 156–163.

Friman, M. and Hjerpe, M. (2015). "Agreement, significance, and understandings of historical responsibility in climate change negotiations", *Climate Policy,* 15(3), pp. 302–320.

Gall, S. C. and Thompson, R. C. (2015). "The impact of debris on marine life", *Marine Pollution Bulletin,* 92(1–2), pp. 170–179.

Grunewald, K. and Bastian, O. (eds.). (2015). *Ecosystem Services–Concept, Methods and Case Studies*, Springer, Berlin.

Gynther, I., Waller, N., and Leung, L. K.-P. (2016). Confirmation of the extinction of the Bramble Cay melomys Melomys rubicola on Bramble Cay, Torres Strait: Results and conclusions from a comprehensive survey in August–September 2014, Queensland Government.

Hotelling, H. (1931). "The economics of exhaustible resources", *Journal of Political Economy,* 39(2), pp. 137–175.

Lenton, T. M., *et al.* (2008). "Tipping elements in the Earth's climate system", *Proceedings of the National Academy of Sciences*, 105(6), pp. 1786–1793.

Lindgreen, A., Swaen, V., and Johnston, W. J. (2009). "Corporate social responsibility: An empirical investigation of US organizations", *Journal of Business Ethics,* 85(2), pp. 303–323.

Margolis, J. D., Elfenbein, H. A., and Walsh, J. P. (2009). "Does it pay to be good… and does it matter? A meta-analysis of the relationship between corporate social and financial performance". SSRN Papers. https://papers.ssrn.com/sol3/papers.cfm?abstract_id=1866371

McWilliams, A. and Siegel, D. (2001). "Corporate social responsibility: A theory of the firm perspective", *Academy of Management Review*, 26(1), pp. 117–127.

Moore, C. (2003). "Trashed", *Natural History*, 112(9), pp. 46–51.

Neumayer, E. (2003). *Weak versus Strong Sustainability: Exploring the Limits of Two Opposing Paradigms*, Edward Elgar Publishing, Northampton, Massachusetts.

Osterwalder, A. and Pigneur, Y. (2010). *Business Model Generation: A Handbook for Visionaries, Game Changers, and Challengers*, John Wiley & Sons, Hoboken, NJ.

Pezzey, J. (1992). "Sustainability: An interdisciplinary guide", *Environmental Values*, pp. 321–362.

Rahmstorf, S. and Ganopolski, A. (1999). "Long-term global warming scenarios computed with an efficient coupled climate model", *Climatic Change*, 43(2), pp. 353–367.

Rogelj, J., *et al.* (2011). "Emission pathways consistent with a 2°C global temperature limit", *Nature Climate Change*, 1(8), p. 413.

Saeidi, S. P., Sofian, S., Saeidi, P., Saeidi, S. P., and Saaeidi, S. A. (2015). "How does corporate social responsibility contribute to firm financial performance? The mediating role of competitive advantage, reputation, and customer satisfaction", *Journal of Business Research*, 68(2), pp. 341–350.

Schumacher, I. (2010). "Ecolabeling, consumers' preferences and taxation", *Ecological Economics*, 69(11), pp. 2202–2212.

Schumacher, I. (2011). "When should we stop extracting nonrenewable resources?" *Macroeconomic Dynamics*, 15(4), pp. 495–512.

Schumacher, I. (2015). "The endogenous formation of an environmental culture", *European Economic Review*, 76, pp. 200–221.

Simon, B. (2013). "A path for Patagonia", *Corporate Knights* (Summer).

Smith, A. (1776). *An Inquiry into the Nature and Causes of the Wealth of Nations*, W. Strahan and T. Cadell, London.

Smith, J. B. and Colgate, M. (2007). "Customer value creation: A practical framework", *Journal of Marketing Theory and Practice*, 15(1), pp. 7–23.

Stradling, D. and Stradling, R. (2008). "Perceptions of the burning river: Deindustrialization and Cleveland's Cuyahoga River", *Environmental History*, 13(3), pp. 515–535.

Thaler, R. H. and Sunstein, C. R. (2009). *Nudge: Improving Decisions about Health, Wealth, and Happiness*, Penguin, London.

Tietenberg, T. H. and Lewis, L. (2016). *Environmental and Natural Resource Economics*, Routledge, Milton Park, UK.

van der Linden, P. J., and Hanson, C. E. (2007). *Climate Change 2007: Impacts, Adaptation and Vulnerability*, in M. Parry, O. Canziani and J. Palutikof (eds.), vol. 4, Cambridge University Press, Cambridge.

Varian, H. R. (2014). *Intermediate Microeconomics: A Modern Approach: Ninth International Student Edition*, WW Norton & Company, New York.

Wang, P., Deng, X., Zhou, H., and Yu, S. (2019). "Estimates of the social cost of carbon: A review based on meta-analysis", *Journal of Cleaner Production*, 209, pp. 1494–1507.

Winston, C. (2007). *Government Failure versus Market Failure: Microeconomics Policy Research and Government Performance*, Brookings Institution Press, Washington DC.

Withagen, C. (2009). "Weak and strong sustainability", *Principles of Sustainable Development-Volume III*, Free University and Tinbergen Institute, Amsterdam, p. 186.

Wright, C. and Rwabizambuga, A. (2006). "Institutional pressures, corporate reputation, and voluntary codes of conduct: An examination of the equator principles", *Business and Society Review,* 111(1), pp. 89–117.

Chapter 15

Environmental Policies, Laws, and Regulations

Karl Boyd Brooks and Diane-Charlotte Simon

Learning Objectives

- Understand why governments regulate actions that affect the environment
- Perceive the difference between environmental policy, law, and regulation
- Understand the concepts of jurisdiction, hierarchy of law, and enforcement
- Discover the main policy instruments and when they best apply
- Understand how regulations can contribute to sustainable prosperity

Abstract

This chapter introduces the history and basics of environmental policies, laws, and regulations. It explains why governments regulate actions that affect the environment. While policies outline the intention to act on a topic to achieve certain objectives, they do not carry legal force. Environmental law therefore includes a combination of rulemaking, interpretation, and enforcement. The chapter expands on the concept that rulemaking and law enforcement can take place at different levels which can be driven by geographical scope (international, multi-country, country, state, etc.) or by subject matter (e.g. agricultural, industrial, etc.). It stresses that a hierarchy of laws exists and determines which law has ultimate control or primacy. Given the complexity of environmental issues and the range of adverse impacts, the reader is reminded of the importance of understanding what laws govern and identifying which one has primacy, especially if there is a conflict of laws whereby different laws coexist but are contradictory. The chapter also stresses the importance of understanding in which jurisdiction a law applies and determining which court or institution has the power, right, or authority to interpret and apply the law. The chapter also reviews the forces that shape regulations. Unlike most other types of law that shape business and finance — contract law, labor law, and corporate law, etc. — environmental law arouses intense political passions and commands vibrant (though not always accurate) news coverage. The chapter describes how the rules governing air, water, or land pollution typically include not only a mix of considerations of science, technical feasibility, and economics, but also both explicit and hidden political agendas. The chapter concludes by presenting the main tools of economic regulations ranging from traditional command-and-control approaches to market-based instruments that policymakers can employ.

I. Introduction

Traditionally, the government has been the primary actor seeking to address market imperfections and externalities discussed in the previous chapter. Nowadays, the private sector is playing an increasingly important role in addressing sustainability issues, but when the market fails to internalize externalities and companies' voluntary initiatives are insufficient, regulation becomes necessary. "Environmental law is a foundation for environmental sustainability and the full realization of its objectives is ever more urgent vis-à-vis growing environmental pressures" (United Nations 2022a).

Environmental laws can have important consequences for the private sector as they can impact either positively (e.g. tax incentives) or negatively (e.g. tax, fines) the profitability of an industry, a product, or an investment. Investors and enterprise managers can profit (literally as well as metaphorically) by understanding — and working within — modern environmental law. Regulation can benefit innovative companies and investors and inspire or constrain them to take sustainability seriously.

This chapter is an introduction to environmental policies, laws, and regulations. It begins by providing the justification behind the regulation of the environment. This chapter then presents the fundamentals of law-making and enforcement which can take place at different levels either geographic (international, multi-country, national, state, etc.) or based on subject matter. It also introduces the concept of hierarchy of laws. We then explore the forces that shape regulation. The chapter closes by presenting the main policy instruments that policymakers can employ, the policy-makers' toolkit. In the environmental realm, policies have mainly taken the shape of command-and-control approaches, which consist in the implementation of standards. But other approaches are increasingly used as well, such as market-based instruments (e.g. tax incentives, subsidies, etc.) or hybrid tools mixing both (e.g. information disclosure). The characteristics of an environmental issue and the goal of a policymaker will influence the choice of a regulatory instrument.

Chapter 15 is organized as per the following sections:

I. Introduction
II. Why Governments Regulate Actions that Affect the Environment
III. The Fundamentals of Environmental Law
IV. The Policymakers' Toolkit
V. Conclusion

II. Why Governments Regulate Actions that Affect the Environment

People use and alter the natural environment to survive. We must eat, so we turn the soil. We shrink from the cold, so we cut trees and forge metal. As securing prosperity diminished the brute imperative to survive, people also began altering nature to amass wealth and power. Our ideas and tools have so enabled us to disorder the natural world that imposing restraints became a public duty. Individual actions, multiplied as populations grow, threaten the larger community's very ability to exist, let alone to prosper. Governments, at all levels, must regulate human interactions with nature to secure their societies' continuation.

Humans have made rules about using the natural world for as long as there have been human beings, and rules. In the United States, Native Americans devised sophisticated understandings to regulate fisheries, berrying sites, and hunting grounds. Some of the most poignant — and pregnant — misunderstandings between the original inhabitants and European immigrants arose from fundamental differences about rights to and responsibilities for natural resources. Euro-Americans themselves soon had to restrain individual actions to safeguard larger communities' capacity to survive. Among the oldest American laws are seventeenth-century ordinances to prevent polluting water sources, over-cutting wood lots, and heedless deer harvesting.

III. The Fundamentals of Environmental Law

1. Principles of Rulemaking, Interpretation, Enforcement

To protect the environment, policies and laws can be used. Both are inter-related but different. While policies outline the intention to act on a topic to achieve certain objectives, they do not carry legal force. Policies can, however, inspire new laws which *can* be enforced. For this reason, laws are considered to "have more teeth".

Rulemaking and law enforcement can take place at different levels, which can be driven by geographical scope (international, multi-country, country, state, etc.) or by subject matter (e.g. agricultural, industrial, etc.). A hierarchy of laws exists and determines which law has ultimate control or primacy. When looking at a case or an issue it is important to understand what laws apply and identify which one has primacy, especially if there is a conflict of laws whereby different laws coexist but are contradictory. It is also important to understand in which jurisdiction a law applies and determine which court or institution has the power, right, or authority to interpret and apply the law (Legal Dictionary, 2015).

Regulating to protect environmental quality sounds straightforward: an entity with authority over a domain or jurisdiction decides to control an action that affects a natural system. That decision produces a rule which can be named differently based on the entity which created it.

To resolve uncertainty about the rule's meaning, a public tribunal (usually, but not always, a court) supplies a binding interpretation. Environmental regulations, like all public rules, carry consequences. That's what distinguishes governmental from private actions: compliance with rules generate benefits, but disregard of the rule triggers public punishments enforced by deprivations of liberty (imprisonment) and/or property (monetary fines and/or loss of opportunities). One strength of environmental regulation is its capacity to afford interested parties' multiple opportunities to make their arguments. Courts do require the challenger to show the rule will injure them.

This simplistic outline works, of course, only on the law teacher's whiteboard. Law safeguarding the natural environment works like a complex, dynamic machine, operated by multiple control levers that generate fluid outcomes. Still, non-lawyers responsible for investing and/or managing should grasp these essentials.

A. *In the United States*

In the US, laws can be enacted by the legislative body at every level of government — local, state and federal. A "statute" is enacted by a representative legislative body, like Congress, while a "regulation" is issued by an executive body, charged with carrying out statutes, like the Environmental Protection Agency (EPA). Once a law is passed, its implementation will be specified in a regulation by a governmental agency with responsibility, or jurisdiction, over the domain.

There are several federal agencies responsible for the implementation and enforcement of US federal environmental law (Tanaka *et al.*, 2021), as follows:

- **Environmental Protection Agency (EPA)** is the most renowned federal environmental agency which implements and enforces most of the federal environmental statutes. The EPA is in charge of the country's air, water, waste, and chemical safety and shares responsibility with states and other federal agencies under certain federal environmental laws.

- **Department of Justice (DOJ)** through its Environment and Natural Resources Division can be involved in litigation arising under the federal environmental laws.
- **Department of the Interior** administers environmental laws involving public lands, mining, minerals, natural resources, wildlife, and plant conservation. The sub-agencies include the following:
  ○ Bureau of Land Management
  ○ US Fish and Wildlife Service (FWS)
  ○ Bureau of Ocean Energy Management
  ○ Bureau of Safety and Environmental Enforcement
  ○ Office of Surface Mining Reclamation and Enforcement
- **Army Corps of Engineers** is responsible for the disposal of material in waters as well as activities and structures in navigable waters under the Rivers and Harbors Act.
- **National Marine Fisheries Service** is a sub-agency within the Department of Commerce which is responsible for the conservation and management of marine resources.
- **Pipeline and Hazardous Materials Safety Administration** is a sub-agency of the US Department of Transportation which is responsible for the transportation of hazardous materials, including oil and gas.

American environmental law, in its current form, originated in post-World War II public concerns about the quality and safety of the water we drink and the air we breathe. Key federal statutes, enacted in the early 1970s, aim to protect human health and environmental quality by controlling water and air pollutants through state-issued permits to discharging facilities. This federal/state partnership established a basic model for environmental regulation. Other pollutants have since been handled primarily by the federal government. Complex environmental threats pose scientific, legal, and technical challenges in the twenty-first century. Traditional regulatory models will likely have to be adapted to handle these emerging issues.

The Clean Water and Clean Air Acts, both nearing their sixth decade, establish a national commitment to use government power to safeguard public health. Each statute built on previous federal laws; and each borrowed from, and improved on, earlier state and local regulatory efforts. Congress, in the early 1970s, determined that national standards were essential to protect natural systems that spanned political boundaries. Congress also acknowledged both the long record of state action to control water and air pollution and the political need to conciliate powerful economic interests that preferred to deal with state governments. Federal standard-setting, therefore, relies on state permitting for implementation. Fundamental constitutional tradition assigns local (and, to some extent, state) governments primacy for managing private lands. Despite the obvious connection between land uses and pollution (factory siting, suburban building, intensive agriculture), a bipartisan commitment, reinforced by judicial precedent, has limited federal environmental regulation of land quality to specific instances: abandoned waste sites and waste disposal.

Federal environmental laws enacted after the keystone Clean Air and Water Acts have typically assigned primary regulatory duties to the federal government. The Environmental Protection Agency (EPA) has the crucial jobs of handling threats from chemical use and misuse, chemical waste disposal, and emerging technologies at the genetic and molecular levels. Often, though, the agency must work in tandem with other federal regulatory agencies, such as the Food and Drug Administration and the Department of Agriculture.

With respect to enforcement (Tanaka *et al.*, 2021):

- Most federal and state environmental laws authorize regulators to pursue administrative, civil, and/or criminal enforcement actions, or issue orders to compel compliance with environmental laws.
- Many federal environmental laws also allow individuals to initiate enforcement actions against alleged violators of environmental laws.

In August 2022, President Joe Biden signed the Inflation Reduction Act, which aims to cut the US 2005 greenhouse gas emission levels by 40% by 2030. This legislation is the largest climate legislation in US history and is expected to generate 10 times more climate impact than any other single piece of legislation ever enacted in the US (Regan, 2022). While the bill involves close to $370 billion of investments in climate, clean energy, and environmental solutions by 2030, the law could cut the social costs of climate change by up to $1.9 trillion by 2050 (Vahlsing, 2022). The law involves various measures and tools mainly market-based, including a new fee on methane emissions, tax credits for carbon capture projects, renewable energy projects, and electric vehicles, as well as grants and loans benefiting various clean technologies and nuclear energy (Sidley Austin LLP, 2022).

B. *In the European Union*

In Europe, the European Union is competent in all areas of environment policy as per Articles 11 and 191–193 of the Treaty on the Functioning of the European Union (Kurrer, 2021). But the EU's scope for action is limited by the principle of subsidiarity as Member States also have competence with respect to environmental law (Pavy, 2022). The EU has legal personality, is in itself a source of law, and is able to enter into international agreements (Kurrer, 2021). EU law has direct or indirect effect on the laws of its Member States and becomes part of the legal system of each Member State (Fact Sheets on the European Union, 2022). Typically, the European Commission proposes new laws, which are adopted by the Parliament and Council of the European Union. The Member States then implement them, while the European Commission ensures that the laws are properly applied. The EU legal order is divided into primary legislation (the Treaties and general legal principles), secondary legislation (based on the Treaties), and supplementary law. Primary legislation is at the top of the hierarchy and is followed by secondary legislation (Fact Sheets on the European Union, 2022). Of note, international agreements concluded by the EU are subordinate to primary legislation and secondary legislation is valid only if it is consistent with the acts and agreements which have precedence over it (Fact Sheets on the European Union, 2022).

EU environment policy began following the first UN conference on the environment when the European Council held in Paris in 1972 declared the "need for a community environment policy flanking economic expansion, and called for an action programme" (Kurrer, 2021).

The first legal basis for a common environment policy is the Single European Act of 1987, which introduced a new Environment Title in order to preserve "the quality of the environment, protecting human health, and ensuring rational use of natural resources" (Kurrer, 2021). The European Environment Agency was created in 1990 to support the development, implementation, and evaluation of environment policy and to inform the general public on the matter (Kurrer, 2021). Landmark treaties which laid the ground to EU environmental policies include:

- **the Treaty of Maastricht in 1993,** which made the environment an official EU policy area;
- **the Treaty of Amsterdam in 1999,** which established the duty to integrate environmental protection into all EU sectoral policies with a view to promoting sustainable development;
- **the Treaty of Lisbon in 2009,** which established the fight against climate change and sustainable development as goals.

Today, hundreds of environmental directives, regulations, and decisions are in force in the EU (Kurrer, 2021). Legislative proposals and goals are displayed in Environment Action Programmes (Kurrer, 2021). As for the enforcement of EU environmental law, Member States are required to implement criminal sanctions for the most serious environmental offences, such as the illegal emission or discharge of substances, trade in wildlife, trade in ozone-depleting substances, and shipment or dumping of waste (Kurrer, 2021).

In 2019, the European Commission launched the *European Green Deal,* which is a package of policy initiatives for reaching its goal of climate neutrality by 2050 to deliver on its commitments under the 2015 Paris Agreement (European Council of the European Union, 2022). The strategy is cross-sectorial and spans across the climate, the environment, energy, transport, industry, agriculture, and sustainable finance. It also aims to reduce net greenhouse gas emissions by at least 55% by 2030, compared to 1990 levels (European Council of the European Union, 2022). The overall European Green Deal is forecast to cost in excess of $600 billion, which is expected to translate in economic growth and job creation while mitigating some of the costs resulting from climate change.

The European Green Deal includes the following initiatives (European Council of the European Union, 2022):

- European climate law — which was approved by the Council in May 2021 and turned the EU's ambition of achieving climate neutrality by 2050 into a legal obligation
- Fit for 55 legal package
- EU strategy on adaptation to climate change
- EU biodiversity strategy for 2030
- Farm-to-fork strategy
- European industrial strategy
- Circular economy action plan
- Batteries and waste batteries
- A just transition
- Clean, affordable, and secure energy
- EU chemicals strategy for sustainability
- Sustainable and smart mobility
- Forest strategy and deforestation-free imports
- Sustainable Finance — the Commission has pledged to mobilize at least €1 trillion in sustainable investments over the next decade.

C. *International Environmental Law*

As for international environmental law, it regulates the behavior of states and international organizations with respect to the environment. The first time environmental issues were placed at the forefront of international concerns was during the 1972 United Nations Conference on the Environment in Stockholm when UN Member States declared that people have the right to "an environment of a quality that permits a life of dignity and well-being" and called for concrete action and the recognition of this right (United Nations, 2022b). The United Nations Environment Programme (UNEP) was created to promote the development and implementation of international environmental law.

Since the 1972 Stockholm Conference, countries have become parties to treaties (see Table 15.1) which form the core of international

Table 15.1.   Global Environmental Agreements

Theme	Representative Global Environmental Agreements	Number of State Parties	Opened for Signature	Entered into Force
Global Atmosphere	Montreal Protocol	197	1985	1988
	UN Framework Convention on Climate Change	195	1992	1994
	Kyoto Protocol	192	1997	2005
	Paris Agreement	166	2015	2016
Wildlife and Biodiversity	Convention on Biological Diversity	193	1992	1993
	Convention on International Trade in Endangered Species (CITES)	178	1973	1987
	Convention on Migratory Species	120	1979	1983
	Convention to Combat Desertification	195	1994	1996
	UNESCO World Heritage Convention	190	1972	1975
Oceans	Law of the Sea Convention	166	1982	1994
	Straddling Fish Stocks Agreement	88	1995	2001
Chemicals	Basel Convention on Hazardous Wastes	181	1989	1992
	Rotterdam Convention on Prior Informed Consent Procedure (PIC)	154	1998	2004

Source: Based on Hunter (2021).

environmental law (Hunter, 2021). Noteworthy treaties include the adoption of the Montreal Protocol, which entered into force in 1988 and successfully curbed the use of chemicals leading to ozone depletion, and the 2015 Paris Agreement on Climate Change, which is the first legally binding international agreement to combat climate change and adapt to its effects.

These international environmental treaties can be grouped into four main themes (Hunter, 2021):

- The protection of the global atmosphere, including preventing climate change and ozone depletion.
- The conservation of wildlife and biological diversity.
- Oceans and marine environment.
- Chemicals, wastes, and other hazardous substances.

On July 28, 2022, the United Nations General Assembly (UNGA) adopted a historic resolution recognizing the right to live in a clean, healthy, and sustainable environment as a universal human right (International Institute for Sustainable Development, 2022). While the resolution is not legally binding, the "UNGA calls upon States, international organizations, businesses, and other stakeholders to "scale up efforts" to ensure a clean, healthy, and sustainable environment for all" (International Institute for Sustainable Development, 2022).

2. The Forces That Shape Regulation

A. *The Politics of Environmental Laws*

Environmental regulation engages every interested individual, not just those with formal lawmaking power and certainly not just those trained in law, engineering, or science.

Unlike most other types of law that shape business and finance — contracts, labor, corporate — environmental law arouses intense political passions and commands vibrant (though not always accurate) news coverage. Multiple interests including industrial lobbies or local communities conduct ferocious debates. These forces shape the rules which evolve over time. Fundamental legal principles and institutions, however, restrain the pace and amplitude of environmental law change, so both lawyers and their clients can plan with some confidence for the future.

An example will illustrate: Suppose a civic group organizes a non-profit association to fight a proposed expansion of a local solid-waste disposal site. They lobby elected officials to amend applicable laws. They hire expert engineers to persuade their professional colleagues in government to abandon or modify the plan. They retain legal counsel to threaten a lawsuit intended, if successful, to prompt the government to redesign the site, or to seek a new location. Countervailing interests can intervene at every stage: new elections can oust representatives; new administrative managers can reject predecessors' plans; adverse court judgments can stimulate both appeals to higher courts and parallel efforts to change the laws on which the case was decided.

Unpredictable in this example is the final outcome. What is predictable is that, in our democratic society with its tradition of civic engagement, "the law" structuring this environmental decision will generally reflect the preferences of actors with the most political power. Power may come from numbers at the polls. It may flow from deeper pockets. It may reflect superior expertise. And it may also embody popular respect for established traditions, such as a judge's ruling. Operating effectively within this environmental law system subject to competing forces requires accepting a level of uncertainty, identifying the most salient decisional factors, and appreciating how deeply politics permeates environmental law because people care passionately about both their lives and livelihoods.

B. *Political Influence on Regulation*

Whether made to control air, water, or land pollution, rules typically mix considerations of science, technical feasibility, and economics. But sometimes they are also driven by political agendas. In the US, generalized public approval of government action to protect the environment conceals a deep vein of popular resistance to regulation. Opinion polls over nearly two decades have shown that federal environmental regulation generates the deepest partisan splits whereby some republicans disagree with the principle that laws must constrain liberty to ensure security and opportunity. This may be surprising as the EPA was created by President Nixon, a republican, in 1970 and for some time environmental regulations enjoyed bipartisan support (Uhlmann, 2020). Some argue that control rules can undermine prosperity, interfere with managerial prerogatives, and confiscate private property. Other critics denounce unconstitutional federal interference with state and local responsibilities. Things are very different in other parts of the globe. In Europe, for example, there seems to be a directionality in environmental regulation, with politics influencing the pace, rather than generating full swings.

IV. The Policymakers' Toolkit

To attempt to transform consumption, production, or even investment habits to be more respectful of the environment, policymakers can use two broad types of instruments:

- **Command-and-control** policies, which are the traditional regulatory approaches that set specific standards.
- **Market-based** policies also called economic incentives that rely on market forces to amend producer, consumer, or investor behavior.

The choice of a policy approach and characteristics depends on many factors including the nature of the environmental problem, the type of market failure being addressed, and the goals of policymakers. These policy tools can be employed for any domain but will be created and enforced by competent actors (regulatory agencies, enforcement bodies, tribunal, etc.) in the specific area. For example, the EPA will be competent to regulate companies' production, while the United States Securities and Exchange Commission (SEC) will be responsible for investment and investors' behavior. In this chapter, we will focus on the tools used by the environmental agencies such as the EPA in the US.

Regulations can be either uniform, following a "one size fist all" approach, or progressive, following an approach proportional to the wealth (e.g. individual's income tax). For companies, it implies that the parameters to meet as per the regulation may vary according to their size. Progressive policies are tailored to enable companies to meet certain criteria in a way that they can afford and to avoid penalizing smaller organizations with a burden that could lead them out of business.

1. Command-and-Control Policies

"Command-and-control policy refers to environmental policy that relies on regulation (permission, prohibition, standard setting, and enforcement) as opposed to financial incentives, that is, economic instruments of cost internalization" (OECD, 2001).

Pollution of the air or water is legal — if the facility has a license to pollute, or a "permit". Just as broad statutes require detailed rules for implementation, so, too, do detailed implementation rules require transla-tion into site- and pollutant-specific legal documents. Permits are an ancient legal form. Environmental law's pioneers borrowed them as the principal tool aiming first to limit and then to reduce and then ultimately to eliminate air and water pollutants. Permits entitle the permittee to emit stated amounts or types of pollutants. Permits require compliance; viola-tions can, in some instances, trigger harsh financial penalties or even imprisonment for responsible officials of the permittee.

Traditional environmental regulatory approaches comprise two main types of standard settings:

- **Technology or design** standard, which commands the use of specific control technologies or production processes that companies must use to meet a standard. This sometimes involves the ban or phase out of a product or pollutant in companies' production processes such as with chlorofluorocarbons (CFCs) and certain pesticides.
- **Performance-based** standard, also requires that companies meet a standard while giving more flexibility enabling companies to choose the method to meet that standard (National Center for Environmental Economics in the EPA, 2001).

While command-and-control policies are critical tools to address environmental problems, they are criticized for the cost burden they put on companies that provide competitive advantage to less regulated juris-dictions which are able to provide products at a lower cost to customers. In addition, some policymakers argue that such policies limit companies' actions to meet the regulated level. But in some cases, they are the most appropriate option; for example, when a risk is too high and requires a prohibition of a pollutant or there issues for which market-based mechanisms may trigger equity concerns (National Center for Environmental Economics in the EPA, 2001).

2. Market-Based Policies

Market-based approaches, which are an alternative to command-and-control approaches, are becoming increasingly popular. They have been used for issues such as climate change. Market-based policies are creating economic incentives encouraging the private sector to reduce its negative environmental impacts and incorporate environmental considerations into production, consumption decisions, and innovation to develop the least costly method of pollution abatement (National Center for Environmental Economics in the EPA, 2001).

This approach functions as long as it makes financial sense, so it cannot replace command-and-control, but complements it. In addition, in some cases it may pose some equity concerns. For example, EPA warns that emissions trading programs may create pollution hot-spots concentrating pollution in economically disadvantaged areas.

In the following paragraphs, we will discuss some main types of economic incentives:

- taxes and fees
- subsidies
- tax–subsidy combinations
- trading programs.

A. *Taxes and Fees*

Taxes and fees are widely used to reduce pollution and waste (e.g. pollution taxes, solid-waste disposal fees, wastewater discharge fees, water user fees, etc.). They act as a deterrent for companies and consumers; they are the "stick". The carbon tax follows this approach to fight climate change and is supported by numerous economists and policymakers globally. The main limitation of these tools is that even though they penalize polluters, the resulting amount of pollution reduction cannot be guaranteed (National Center for Environmental Economics in the EPA, 2004).

B. *Subsidies*

Subsidies function in the opposite way from taxes and fees. They reward environmentally friendly behaviors and activities with financial government support such as favorable tax treatment, low-interest loans, grants, and procurement mandates. Grants and low-interest loans have been employed to foster solutions to environmental issues such as recycling, land conservation, erosion control, or brownfield development after contamination from a hazardous substance. Investment Tax Credit for renewable energy is an example of a tax incentive. In addition, by incentivizing companies and individuals to benefit from them, subsidies can support the development of new markets and products that are more environmentally friendly (National Center for Environmental Economics in the EPA, 2004).

C. *Tax–Subsidy Combinations*

In some cases, taxes and subsidies are combined to maximize the incentives. One familiar example of a Tax–Subsidy incentive is the deposit-refund system which is used to foster recycling. Most of us have come across its application for beverage containers whereby a tax is applied on the selling price of a beverage, but the consumer can receive a refund by recycling the container. Such deposit–refund systems are common with lead-acid batteries, beery keys, propane containers, pesticide containers, or car parts (EPA, 2021).

D. *Trading Programs*

Trading programs provide firms with the flexibility to either cut their own emissions or purchase more leeway from other firms that have done so. Two types of trading programs exist and are presented here: credit systems and capped allowance systems (cap-and-trade). The US Acid Rain program is a cap-and-trade system which successfully lowered sulfur dioxide emissions for electric utilities, and at little cost. Other success stories include voluntary carbon trading programs like the Chicago Climate Exchange or the nutrients trading program, struck between agricultural producers and polluters, to prevent excessive dumping of pesticides and fertilizers into bodies of water (EPA, 2021).

- **Credit Systems** are rate-based trading systems enabling companies to earn credits by reducing their pollutant release below a specified rate (e.g. pollutant emission level per car). This approach is criticized for being "uncapped" as it does not set a limit on the maximum permissible level of pollution within a specified area.
- **Capped Allowance Systems** or **"cap-and-trade"** systems set a cap on the maximum permissible emissions for a regulated area and set up a marketplace of "allowances" to release pollution. The allowances to release pollution are distributed to companies, which can either reduce their pollution release or purchase allowances from other firms that have reduced their pollution below their required level. One of the advantages of cap-and-trade measures is that they have high predictability on the magnitude of environmental improvement that will be achieved.

3. Hybrid Policies

Another set of regulatory instruments combines certain aspects of command-and-control and market-based incentives. They are becoming increasingly popular in practice as they preserve the predictability enabled by standards while allowing companies the flexibility to pursue the most cost-effective method to reach them. In the following paragraphs, we will explore a few key hybrid approaches:

- information disclosure
- combining standards and pricing approaches
- liability rules.

A. *Information Disclosure*

Information disclosure programs are put in place to improve market transparency and efficiency. They can be mandatory or voluntary. Disclosure encourages responsible behavior by requiring the dissemination of environmental impacts data such as pollution levels or production processes but also labor standards to the public, investors, and government agencies. They influence business owners, employees, shareholders, and customers (National Center for Environmental Economics in the EPA, 2001).

Labels are a common form of voluntary reporting which guarantees that certain environmental objectives are met. Typically, a non-profit organization or government agency will set environmental or sustainability standards for a type of product to meet. If a company meets these standards, they are allowed to place the label's seal on their product, often earning a competitive edge with consumers. You will likely catch sight of ecolabels in any grocery store or appliance store (National Center for Environmental Economics in the EPA, 2001).

B. *Combining Standards and Pricing Approaches*

On the one hand, by setting up hard limits, pollution standards effectively prevent damages to health or the environment, but this often involves large costs to companies. On the other hand, emissions taxes succeed in mitigating these costs by instead requiring companies to pay a tax on emissions, but leave the door open to limitless pollution. A "safety-valve" approach combines both standards and pricing mechanisms to limit both costs and pollution. This type of approach leads all polluters to be subject to the same emissions standards while being charged for any emissions in excess. This hybrid policy offers not only both flexibility for polluters but also assurances for human health and the environment as it provides protection against excessive levels of pollution. However, it can lead polluting firms to prefer paying fees as a right to pollute instead of implementing concrete changes in their operations to avoid the pollution (EPA 2021).

C. *Liability Rules*

Liability rules are often targeting producers of emissions or waste that are clearly hazardous to public health. They are designed to hold them accountable for proper management of waste and emissions, cleanup and remediation costs, and financial damages for victims of environmental incidents. In the US, there exist two major liability-based laws: the Oil

Pollution Act of 1990 and the Comprehensive Environment Response, Compensation, and Liability Act (CERCLA) of 1980.

4. Voluntary Actions

Companies can also employ non-regulatory approaches based on voluntary initiatives to mitigate environmental hazards and improve emissions controls. These initiatives are not intended to replace or circumvent regulation, but to complement it. Some of these voluntary programs urge polluters to go beyond the mandates of existing regulation. Others seek to preemptively improve environmental conditions in areas currently unregulated but likely to be regulated in the future, such as pollution of non-point source water or greenhouse gas emissions.

The purposes of voluntary actions are widespread, offering benefits to different players. For policymakers, they can help promote better production and consumption practices, and can also serve as a test drive for potential policies and regulations. For businesses, the benefits are perhaps even greater. Joining voluntary programs can improve a company's image and social appeal. In exchange for participation, programs may also offer free technical or logistical assistance. Because these programs are often designed as a pilot test of regulation, being involved can help prepare the company for a quick transition to a formal law, possibly limiting future enforcement costs, monitoring, and litigation (National Center for Environmental Economics in the EPA, 2001).

5. Selecting a Policy Instrument

We have examined the array of policies ranging from traditional command-and-control tools to market-based tools and hybrids. So how does the regulating body choose the most appropriate one? This decision rests on many factors, a few of which we will explore in the following paragraphs:

- type of market failure
- nature of the environmental issue

- assessment of costs and benefits
- market competitiveness concerns
- monitoring and enforcement
- policymakers' goals

A. *The Type of Market Failure*

Market-based and hybrid tools can address different types of market failures. Market-based or hybrid instruments that incorporate the costs of environmental externalities are suitable when firms, consumers, or investors fail to consider the impact of their production, consumption, or investment decisions. Information disclosure or labeling are relevant when parties make poor decisions on investment options, abatement technologies available, or the associated risks because of a lack of information as it will help private and public sector decision-makers address environmental issues (EPA, 2021).

B. *The Nature of the Environmental Issue*

The selection of a policy depends on the nature and gravity of the environmental problem to address. Whether a pollutant persists and tends to accumulate over time (a stock pollutant) or tends to dissipate quickly (a flow pollutant) will impact the choice of regulatory instrument. For instance, stock pollutants are better addressed with direct regulation imposing strict limits provided their long-term negative impacts or their detrimental health effects at small doses. Flow pollutants can be handled differently including with various market and hybrid policies. If a pollutant can be limited at a level not close to zero, then a trading program or a standard-and-pricing approach could be appropriate options.

The location and the way an environmental issue spreads are other elements to consider. Environmental issues that flow from a point source, which originates and manifests at identifiable and specific locations, are far easier to control than scattered non-point sources.

Trading programs or standard-and-pricing policies are relevant when pollution levels are not uniform across geographies. Market instruments are easier to implement to stationary sources of pollution but can also be employed for the mobile sources of pollution such as vehicles. In addition, environmental issues can evolve based on the time of the day or the season, and policies should be targeted accordingly. For example, the health impacts related to vehicle traffic occur mainly during rush hours and as such the cost of public transportation can be reduced during these peak hours to limit the pollution linked to traffic congestions (National Center for Environmental Economics in the EPA, 2004).

C. *Assessment of Costs and Benefits*

For policymakers, the choice between quantity-based instruments (such as marketable permits) or price-based instruments (taxes or fees) often rests on the degree of uncertainty of the effects of pollution control.

If, for instance, there is uncertainty around abatement costs and policymakers aim to prevent imposing high fees on polluters because of regulation, this can be done using a price instrument. And if there is greater uncertainty around the benefits of controlling pollution and policymakers may seek to protect the environment, a quantity instrument would be the effective choice.

D. *Market Competitiveness*

Market competitiveness is another element to consider prior to choosing a policy instrument. Market power can lead to a type of market failure, driving output lower and prices higher than those found in a competitive market. In sectors in which some companies benefit from a certain degree of market power, a combination of market-based instruments often works better than a single instrument involving the reduction of output which could further accentuate market inefficiencies. In addition, depending on how well cost burdens are differentiated, certain market-based instruments may trigger a shift in market structure favoring established firms, putting up barriers of entry, and giving these firms some control over price. This can be prevented through permit systems which allocate permits for new firms.

E. *Monitoring and Enforcement Issues*

There are situations when non-point sources of pollution exist, there are many small polluters, and emissions need to be estimated. This complicates government monitoring. In these circumstances, attempts to tax polluters are often met with widespread noncompliance and evasion, and command-and-control measures are accompanied with costly enforcement. Market-oriented instruments leaving the burden of proving compliance on regulated entities such as information disclosure, deposit-refund systems, and subsidies can be appropriate tools in these situations. Firms are typically better equipped to monitor and report their own environmental impacts and can generally do so at a lower cost even though some third-party audit might be necessary.

F. *The Policymakers' Goals*

Naturally, the instrument chosen to regulate the environment must suit the goals of policymakers and will depend on the extent they will seek fixed outcomes or enable markets to influence them. The selection of policy instrument will have its own set of equity and distributional implications for costs and benefits (see Table 15.2).

V. Conclusion

While environmental law and regulation impose real costs on most governments and businesses, economic analyses document the enormous monetary benefits enjoyed from healthier air, cleaner water, and safer waste management. Evidence shows that reduction in air pollution saves lives, prevents lost-time work and school hours, and secures more solid prosperity by shaving medical expenses. The billions invested by governments in environmental initiatives have saved countless lives and secured investments.

Regulatory instruments play an important role in securing environmental sustainability. These instruments need to build on a coherent underlying policy framework that addresses some of the known market

Table 15.2.   Uses of Economic Incentives

Incentive	Examples	Pros and Cons
Pollution Charges and Taxes	• Emission charges • Effluent charges • Solid waste charges • Sewage charges	**Pros:** • Stimulates new technologies • Useful when damage per unit of pollution varies little with the quantity of pollution **Cons:** • Potentially large distributional effects • Typically requires monitoring data
Input or Output Taxes and Charges	• Leaded gasoline tax • Carbon tax • Fertilizer tax • Pesticide tax • Virgin material tax • Water user charges	**Pros:** • Administratively simple • Does not require monitoring data • Raises revenues • Effective when sources are numerous and damage per unit of pollution varies little with the quantity of pollution **Cons:** • Often weak link to pollution
Subsidies	• Municipal sewage plants • Land use by farmers Industrial pollution	**Pros:** • Politically popular • Targets specific activities **Cons:** • Financial impact on government budgets
Deposit-refund Systems	• Lead-acid batteries • Beverage containers • Automobile bodies	**Pros:** • Deters littering • Stimulates recycling **Cons:** • Potentially high transaction costs • Product must be reusable or recyclable
Marketable Permits	• Emissions • Effluents • Fisheries access	**Pros:** • Provides limits to pollution • Effective when damage per unit of pollution varies with the amount of pollution • Provides stimulus to technological change

Table 15.2. *(Continued)*

Incentive	Examples	Pros and Cons
		Cons: • Potentially high transaction costs • Requires variation in marginal control costs
Reporting Requirements	• Proposition 65 • SARA Title III	**Pros:** • Flexible • Low cost **Cons:** • Impacts may be hard to predict • Applicable only when damage per unit of pollution does not depend on the quantity of pollution
Liability	• Natural resource damage assessment • Nuisance	**Pros:** • Provides strong incentive **Cons:** • Assessment and litigation costs can be high • Burden of proof large
Voluntary Programs	• Project XL • 33/50 • Energy Star	**Pros:** • Low cost • Flexible **Cons:** • Uncertain participation

Source: National Center for Environmental Economics in the EPA (2001, 2004).

imperfections related to the environment described in Chapter 14 that competitive markets are unlikely to solve. The chapter presents some of the main economic policy options, ranging from traditional command-and-control approaches to market-based instruments that policymakers can employ.

References

EPA. (2021). "Economic incentives". Consulted in February 2021, https://www.epa.gov/environmental-economics/economic-incentives.

European Council of the European Union. (2022). "European green deal", Last reviewed on June 29 2022, https://www.consilium.europa.eu/en/policies/green-deal. Accessed September 2022.

Fact Sheets on the European Union. (2022). "Sources and scope of European Union law", https://www.europarl.europa.eu/factsheets/en/sheet/6/sources-and-scope-of-european-union-law. Accessed September 2022.

Hunter, D. (2021). "International environmental law", *Insights on Law and Society*, 19(1), Article 1. Published on January 5, 2021, https://www.americanbar.org/groups/public_education/publications/insights-on-law-and-society/volume-19/insights-vol--19---issue-1/international-environmental-law/.

International Institute for Sustainable Development. (2022). "UNGA recognizes human right to clean, healthy, and sustainable environment". Published on August 3 2022, https://sdg.iisd.org/news/unga-recognizes-human-right-to-clean-healthy-and-sustainable-environment/. Accessed September 2022.

Kurrer, C. (2021). "Environment policy: General principles and basic framework", Fact Sheets on the European Union. Published in October 2021, https://www.europarl.europa.eu/factsheets/en/sheet/71/environment-policy-general-principles-and-basic-framework. Accessed September 2022.

Legal Dictionary. (2015). "Jurisdiction", https://legaldictionary.net/jurisdiction/. Accessed September 2022.

National Center for Environmental Economics in the EPA. (2001). "The United States experience with economic incentives for protecting the environment". Published in January 2001, https://www.epa.gov/sites/production/files/2017-08/documents/ee-0216b-13.pdf. Accessed January 2022.

National Center for Environmental Economics in the EPA. (2004). "International experiences with economic incentives for protecting the environment". Published in November 2004, https://www.epa.gov/sites/production/files/2017-08/documents/ee-0487-01.pdf. Accessed in January 2022.

OECD. (2001). "Command — and — control policy", https://stats.oecd.org/glossary/detail.asp?ID=383. Accessed September 2022.

Pavy. E. (2022). "The principle of subsidiarity", Fact sheets on the European Union. Published in May 2022, https://www.europarl.europa.eu/factsheets/en/sheet/7/the-principle-of-subsidiarity. Accessed September 2022.

Regan, M. (2022). "The inflation reduction act: A big deal for people and the planet". Published on August 26 2022, https://www.epa.gov/perspectives/inflation-reduction-act-big-deal-people-and-planet. Accessed September 2022.

Sidley Austin, LLP. (2022). "Inflation reduction act: Comprehensive summary of energy and environment titles", https://www.sidley.com/-/media/update-pdfs/2022/08/inflation-reduction-act_comprehensive-summary-of-energy-and-environment-titles.pdf.

Tanaka, P., *et al.* (2021). "Environmental law and practice in the United States: Overview", https://content.next.westlaw.com/0-503-4622?__lrTS=20210 205132930881&transitionType=Default&contextData=(sc.Default)&first Page=true.

Uhlmann, D. M. (2020). "Back to the future: Creating a Bipartisan environmental movement for the 21st Century", *Environmental Law Reporter*, 50(10) pp. 10800–10807.

United Nations. (2022a). "Environmental law", https://www.un.org/ruleoflaw/thematic-areas/land-property-environment/environmental-law/. Accessed September 2022.

United Nations. (2022b). "United nations conference on the human environment, 5–16 June 1972, Stockholm", https://www.un.org/en/conferences/environment/stockholm1972. Accessed September 2022.

United Nations Africa Renewal. (2022). "UN general assembly declares access to clean and healthy environment a universal human right". Published on July 28 2022, https://www.un.org/africarenewal/magazine/july-2022/un-general-assembly-declares-access-clean-and-healthy-environment-universal-human. Accessed September 2022.

Vahlsing, C. (2022). "New OMB analysis: The inflation reduction act will significantly cut the social costs of climate change". Published on August 23 2022, https://www.whitehouse.gov/omb/briefing-room/2022/08/23/new-omb-analysis-the-inflation-reduction-act-will-significantly-cut-the-social-costs-of-climate-change/. Accessed September 2022.

Chapter 16

Climate Change Adaptation, the Role of the State, and Fiscality

Peter S. Heller

Learning Objectives

- Review the challenges presented by climate change
- Understand the difference between climate change mitigation and adaptation
- Discuss adaptation policies
- Present approaches to quantify the costs related to climate change
- Introduce the principles of government finance and fiscal policy
- Highlight challenges presented by climate changes for government finance

Abstract

This chapter summarizes some of the main fiscal challenges to sustainability arising out of the use of fossil fuels as a predominant source of energy and related environmental damage from climate change. The chapter argues that countries need to be actively engaged

439

in considering the fiscal and macro-economic implications of the climate change hazards they will confront. The phenomenon of climate change poses significant challenges for analysts seeking to assess a government's long-run financial condition. Looking forward, climate change hazards are likely to increasingly threaten multiple aspects of a country's environment. Governments will necessarily be challenged to support private sector agents in adapting to these hazards. While for most countries, the effects of climate change are an exogenous policy threat, considerable uncertainty exists as to the nature and magnitude of the adaptation burdens that will be faced, in part because the trajectory of climate change that will be experienced will to some extent depend on whether global mitigation efforts succeed. The chapter emphasizes that most developing and many emerging market countries will face serious limits in their fiscal capacity to confront these adaptation challenges. The chapter highlights differences in the two main approaches for addressing climate change: *mitigation*, which focuses on reducing greenhouse emissions; and *adaptation*, which focuses on reducing the vulnerability of economic agents to the negative effects of climate change. Existing development strategies now tend to silo the challenge of climate change, only adding to the prospective burdens that will be experienced. The chapter highlights recent initiatives by the International Monetary Fund (IMF) to strengthen its economic policy surveillance in support of member countries' climate change adaptation policies (complementing its support for aggressive mitigation efforts). The chapter concludes that to wait for a decade on this issue until we are clearer on the success of mitigation efforts is to delay policy development and implementation on adaptation that could reduce serious economic and social losses looking forward.

I. Introduction

What are the long-term macro-economic policy challenges presented by climate change?

It is now widely recognized that climate change will cause social and economic harm in coming decades to most countries of the world and that the financial position of some governments may be adversely affected. Such harms are already in the pipeline from the climate change already built in from past emissions. The success or failure of current global efforts at mitigation will determine how much more harm will arise from future emissions.

Before going further, it is important to understand the difference between the two approaches to responding to climate change:

- *Mitigation*, which focuses on reducing greenhouse emissions to prevent additional warming (by transitioning away from fossil fuels, using renewable energy, developing carbon capture technologies, etc.). Policy efforts have focused on three principal mitigation instruments: the levy of a substantial carbon tax to sharply raise the price of carbon and encourage economic agents to shift away from carbon sources of energy; the use of emission trading regimes that effectively achieve the same ultimate effects as a carbon tax; and regulatory regimes that seek to curtail the emissions associated with the various sources of energy production (e.g. limits on gas mileage, requirements for sequestration of carbon emissions in coal-fired plants, etc.).
- *Adaptation*, which focuses on reducing the vulnerability of economic agents to the negative effects of climate change (such as wildfires, food insecurity, increased intensity and frequency of extreme weather events, impact of a rising sea level on cities and coastal real estate). Adaptation efforts also extend to the response of a country to the impact of climate-engendered natural disasters.

This chapter focuses on the challenge of assessing the fiscal risks on public finances associated with adaptation, particularly for the many countries where climate change hazards are felt. This is not meant to downplay the importance of global mitigation efforts to reduce climate change. Indeed, the chapter fully supports the aggressive mitigation efforts discussed at the 2015 Paris and 2021 Glasgow Intergovernmental Panel on Climate Change (IPCC) conferences as all scientific evidence points to the irreparable damage and harm that will arise from a rise in average global temperatures above 1.5°C (Wallace-Wells, 2019; Sengupta and Cai, 2019; Crausbay and Ramirez, 2018; DeFries *et al.*, 2019; Lu and Flavelle, 2019; Nicholls *et al.*, 2011). Such efforts will be critical to minimize the risks and damages that this chapter cautions about.

Section II exposes the enormous complexity of the issues that will be posed by climate change over the next several decades. This includes the uncertainty of what climate change trajectory can be anticipated, both as a consequence of what global mitigation efforts eventuate looking forward and the numerous geological, biological, and meteorological interaction effects that will further influence the trajectory. It will also discuss what hazards are likely in the context of different potential trajectories, given the specifics of a country's location, its physical characteristics, and its social and economic dimensions. In addition, it will touch on what are the vulnerabilities of a country's population in the context of its current social and economic development path.

Section III offers some thoughts on what kinds of methodologies could support analysis of the costs of adaptation to climate change hazards. It will emphasize the role that scenario analysis can play, especially if such scenarios can draw on the increasingly rich experience of the insurance and reinsurance industries in addressing climate change risks. But there is much more that countries can now do to begin adapting to the climate change hazards that will threaten in the future.

Section IV suggests a number of initiatives that countries and the international community could undertake to respond to the adaptation challenge. These ideas build on the significant work and insights of the Global Commission on Adaptation (GCA, 2019), the IPCC, and various elements of the insurance and reinsurance industry.

Section V provides an introduction to government finance. This chapter highlights that climate change will pose substantial financial risks for many countries. Compared to many other contingent liabilities (e.g. for public sector pensions) which are recognized as negatively affecting a country's budget, climate change poses unusually difficult and complex challenges for any assessment of a country's financial position. Indeed, this chapter argues that the scope of existing fiscal policy assessments are too narrow and short term for the threats arising from climate change and that one must seek methodologies that facilitate longer-term policy analyses. The challenge for a government is not only to estimate the extent and magnitude of the risks affecting its balance sheet under different scenarios but also to grapple with the multiple dimensions of the challenges that climate change will pose. What economic and social policies can be pursued to manage the risks that are entailed? What budgetary and fiscal tools can be used to achieve maximum leverage to support the efforts of the private sector agents who will undoubtedly bear much of the burden from the effects of climate change?

Finally, Section VI examines the International Monetary Fund's (IMF) recent efforts to integrate the climate change risks associated with large natural disasters into its assessment of a country's fiscal policy. It also highlights the Fund's increasingly supportive role in highlighting climate change issues in its annual surveillance discussions of economic policy with member countries.

Chapter 16 is organized as per the following sections:

I. Introduction
II. Grappling with the Uncertainties and Challenges Posed by Climate Change
III. Quantifying the Costs of Climate Risks
IV. Addressing Climate Change Adaptation
V. Climate Change and Government Finance
VI. How has the IMF's Perspective on Fiscal Policy Been Shaped by its Concerns for Climate Change?
VII. Conclusion

II. Grappling with the Uncertainties and Challenges Posed by Climate Change

1. Intertemporal Dimensions

Climate change is an ongoing phenomenon that has largely been the consequence of past CO_2 and methane emissions of industrial and emerging market countries. Even if all new CO_2 emissions and methane discharges were to suddenly disappear, climate change has already been cooked into the terrestrial environment and will continue to happen looking into the long-term future. These will have multidimensional effects on all aspects of society for most countries of the world. But regrettably all the adverse determinants of climate change — the subject of mitigation policy initiatives — are still occurring, whether from CO_2

emissions, methane discharges, deforestation, or from the interplay of existing climate change effects with multiple geophysical, ecological, and biological forces.

Thus, the adverse effects of climate change are likely to worsen over time. How much will they worsen will depend in part on how successful mitigation policies will prove to be, over what specific time periods such policies will have an impact, and also as a function of factors that are simply too difficult to assess. These include the various interaction effects of climate change on other key geophysical determinants such as the speed of the melting of the polar ice caps and the Greenland Ice sheet, changes in oceanic circulation patterns, and the capacity of the ocean to absorb increasing carbon dioxide levels. Other examples encompass the extent to which the ongoing melting of the permafrost will release highly charged methane into the atmosphere and how the changing composition of soil will interact with bacteria and other species. Also, interactive with mitigation initiatives is the pace of development of countries, their growth in population and per capita income as well as the energy intensity of likely consumption patterns.

In the scientific or adaptation modeling literature, all these uncertainties are typically distilled to alternative scenarios on the likely change in global temperatures. These are typically expressed as follows:

1. **Business-as-usual**: greenhouse gas (GHG) emissions proceeding as in the recent past without significant progress in reducing emissions.
2. **Moderate mitigation efforts**: Policies that represent substantial improvement but which still fall short of limiting global warming to 2°C above pre-industrial levels.
3. **Aggressive mitigation policies**: Policies that succeed in holding the change in the average global temperature to below 2°C above pre-industrial levels, as per the legally binding Paris Agreement adopted on 12 December 2015 by 196 Parties at COP 21 in Paris and entered into force on 4 November 2016.

How aggressive these policies need to be remains uncertain, particularly after the contentious discussions in November 2021 at the UN Climate Change Conference in Glasgow (Center for Climate Energy

Solutions, 2021). The needed policy effort will depend on many uncertain feedback effects that scientists are still trying to understand. Indeed, depending on the nature of tipping points, some desired outcomes may prove impossible to realize, particularly if the pace of the required mitigation efforts is itself a critical variable. Some argue that substantial up-front efforts will be needed to avoid the effect of such tipping points.

With the possible exception of those countries whose mitigation policy efforts really matter in terms of the success of global mitigation efforts, most countries in the world face the reality that the trajectory of climate change that will be encountered is highly uncertain. Indeed, this truth is also relevant for the major emitters as well, since their efforts may be offset by failure in the efforts of other countries. Pragmatically, most countries would not err in their approach if they at least took account of the least desirable possible outcome, viz., the business-as-usual scenario (though even this adverse scenario may prove optimistic). We now realize that the speed of climate change has been consistently underestimated in the last two decades and that the climate change effects that were assumed to be 20–30 years in the future are now already being observed with unexpected frequency and damage.

The intertemporal dimensions of climate change are manifested in the fact that the experience of climate change hazards will change over time, and typically this means they will most likely worsen. The world of tomorrow will not be the world of today, and that may increasingly be the norm. Policies of adaptation today may succeed only for a while, but it may be necessary to pursue further adaptation efforts in some spheres. For some countries, "adaptation" can be of an existential nature given that coastal borders may shrink dramatically and coastal cities may be swamped by a rise in sea level or be vulnerable to storm surges. Areas normally available for a certain kind of agriculture may no longer be viable, and areas fit for habitation may require new approaches to ensure their viability (Lu and Flavelle, 2019; Nicholls *et al.*, 2011). For economists used to discount benefits, the marginal calculations may need to be supplemented with consideration of the nature of "future states" for different regions. "Ceteris Paribus" — i.e. holding other variables constant — may be a questionable assumption as one looks forward in time.

2. Multiple Hazards

For any country, climate change will be associated with multiple hazards. A recent model by Mora *et al.* (2018) illustrates this fact.[1] The model allows an analyst to place a cursor on any position on a map of the globe in order to be informed about the relative importance of multiple potential hazards of climate change, with positive or negative effect, at any point in time between now and 2095 and under the three scenarios described above.

Such hazards include such risks as fire, drought, ocean change, freshwater deficits, precipitation, storms, heat waves, warming, deforestation, floods, and sea level rise. Each of these hazards could have significant and substantial economic consequences in the case of a particular country. Some hazards might take the form of discrete events or disasters that result in damage or a substantial loss of different kinds of public infrastructure, homes, and schools. The productivity of individual economic sectors (in agriculture, forestry, etc.) may be impaired with losses in the production of a wide range of services over time. Government or the private sector might attempt to insure some physical assets against such risks when they are perceived as infrequent or randomly distributed.

Other hazards might be of a different kind, affecting the economic viability of specific areas of production and, if possible, necessitating adaptation to alternative technologies or alternative product lines. Others might affect the viability of places of habitation, necessitating large-scale migration out of previously inhabited regions. Sea level rise, salinization of previously arable land, or excessive heat waves may force such movements.

Complexity in the frequency or the timing of the occurrence of such hazards is likely to prove analytically problematic. For many hazards, such as the exposure of coastal areas to serious storm damage from winds or storm surges, residents of a region may increasingly recognize their potential exposure to these risks and their increased frequency relative to the past. In contrast, many kinds of hazards will not have been previously

---

[1] Another recent model from Stanford's Natural Capital Project (see Chaplin-Kramer, 2019) allows one to pinpoint where people are most likely to lose vital benefits as ecosystems degrade.

encountered, reflecting new and unanticipated meteorological patterns. As an example, the recent fires afflicting many parts of Australia and the Western states of the United States suggest an intensification and increased frequency of risks not previously encountered (Webb and Xu, 2018). The untimely and intense precipitation that affected the US Midwest in 2019 is another illustration, with dramatic flooding in areas not heretofore affected, disrupting normal patterns of agricultural planting, followed by subsequent periods of rain or dryness that disrupted the harvesting of what crops had previously been able to be planted (Schwartz, 2019).

With the mindset of an insurance analyst, the policymaker would then need to consider, for any region within his or her country, the nature of that region's "exposure" to such hazards and the "vulnerability" associated with that exposure. For an economist, drawing on the dry meaning of an insurance optic, "exposure" would mean both what populations would be most at risk from that hazard as well as what economic, social, and cultural assets might be affected by such hazards. The tableau of such exposures, the populations affected, the specific assets potentially at risk, and the economic sectors involved can become large and important.

The policy challenges then become a function of the nature of the vulnerability. What are the economic, social, political, and cultural losses that emerge if the hazard were to occur in a serious way? As indicated above, the model may indicate that the hazards of climate change for the region of a country may be minor in the next decade or so, but then become much more quantitatively serious looking out over several decades. It is important to note the uncertainty as to which trajectory we are dealing with. Even more difficult to grapple with are the interaction effects from the occurrence of these potential multiple hazards in a given region and their follow-up consequences for other parts of a country not directly impacted. Some may prove highly existential, rendering a region uninhabitable or largely unviable, either as a place to live or as a productive environment.

What becomes clear as one gets into the weeds of considering the consequences of such hazards for different regions of a country is that the challenge of understanding and taking stock becomes overwhelming. The only analytically viable approach to reaching such an understanding would take the form of scenario analyses that can highlight hypothetical but nevertheless detailed alternative cases. Specifically, such scenarios would constitute stories about what could potentially occur and what the consequences would be for different population groups, economic sectors, and important assets. Imagine that certain regions are no longer viable places for habitation, and that one may have to contemplate significant resettlement of populations to less exposed regions of a country, to major urban centers (Van Vuuren *et al.*, 2011) or even to other countries. This is certainly a potentially relevant scenario to consider for the many coastal regions and small island states of the world now predicted to be susceptible to major flooding as a consequence of sea-level rise. Equally, imagine the consequences of a significant glacial melt in some countries with heavy flooding.

3. The Systemic Risk for the Global Economy and Finance

With climate change, countries are potentially confronting forces which will continue shaping and changing the environment where people live, work, produce, consume, and raise families. Climate change will progressively have a negative impact on the environment, on the existence of many species, and on the viability of many aspects of economic and social life.

Several central banks have recently moved toward stress testing the financial sector for the implications of climate change. This has been reflected by their participation (with financial system supervisors) in the Network for Greening of the Financial System (NGFS). In this context, prudential regulators increasingly seek to assess the risks posed by climate change, both from the impact of climate hazards as well as from the transitional risks to sectors particularly affected by climate change mitigation efforts. In 2018, the Dutch Central Bank, DNB, conducted a stress test to account for transition risks for its financial sector. The Bank of England included climate change scenarios in its 2019 stress tests for UK insurance companies and for the entire financial sector, including banks, in 2020. The European Central Bank, the Bank of Canada as well as the French financial regulator have signaled similar steps and voices of support have come from members of the US Federal Reserve Board, which joined the

NGFS in 2020.[2] The systemic risks of the impact of climate change could be disruptive and lead to large financial losses across entire sectors and spread across countries (IMF, 2019a, 2019b, 2019c, 2019d).

Such initiatives provoke the obvious question as to whether the balance sheet of governments should be subject to comparable stress tests. Further work should be done to assess the threats posed by climate change to a country or government through its asset portfolio (including financial assets), its economy, and its infrastructure. This will also impact sovereign risks and the cost at which countries access capital on the financial markets.

4. Climate Risk Insurance

The perspective of the insurance industry from such types of risk analysis is particularly insightful. For an insurance analyst considering the insurance of physical infrastructure or housing, it is possible to consider multiple scenarios of different hazards and to assess what premium might need to be charged to make insurance a profitable possibility. But as noted in a recent chapter commissioned by the GCA:

> "There is evidence of increasing use of multi-year contracts for physical assets, particularly catastrophe bonds, which typically have a 3- to 5-year duration. However, multi-year contracts of sufficient duration to cover a climate adaptation window of, say 10 years, would be challenging to implement under a regulatory framework that also demands solvency for insurers. Specifically, to ensure they could pay claims against

---

[2] The Bank of England's 2021 Biennial Exploratory Scenario (BES) (2019) argues that the largest banks and insurers will need to test the resilience of their current business models to the physical and transition risks from their exposure to climate-related risks and to assess the "scale of adjustment that will need to be taken in coming decades for the [financial] system to remain resilient". The BES will require multiple scenarios that embody the risks that might arise *over a 30-year* modeling horizon from less successful mitigation initiatives than had been envisaged in the Paris Accord, including the least desirable "business-as-usual", no-policy-action scenario where "the Paris Agreement target is not met and more severe physical risks crystallize as a result". Also, see Vermeulen (2018), Howcroft and Jones (2019), Molico (2019), Reuters (2019), Federal Reserve Bank of San Francisco (2019), and Flavelle (2019a).

a long-term and uncertain risk future, insurers would need larger capital reserves. These would need to be built into pricing that would make the cost of premiums prohibitive." (Jarzabkowski *et al.*, 2019; and Audley *et al.* (2019)

5. The Role of Government in Adaptation

What should the government's role be in adapting to climate change? Many analysts have argued that the government's principal responsibility is to clarify for its citizens the potential consequences of the climate change that is likely to occur, with the hope that market forces will penalize (or favor) those sectors and regions likely to be most adversely (or positively) affected (Heller, 2003). A more active government role could also be contemplated as is the case in the USA (United States Congress, 2019). This could to include:

1. Addressing the vulnerability of physical infrastructure assets offering significant externalities;
2. Anticipating the need for physical infrastructure in regions likely to be the focus of increased internal migration by population groups;
3. Providing a social safety net for those population groups most adversely affected by the increased non-viability of a region for habitation or for continued economic involvement;
4. Encouraging regulatory regimes that limit those investments most exposed to recognized risks or in regions likely to be most adversely affected;
5. Subsidizing insurance products in situations where the private insurance industry is unwilling to cover the risks of many hazards, while avoiding the enabling of a moral hazard that incentivizes the private sector to undervalue the extent of the risks that such hazards may engender; and
6. Responding to the significant hits to the economy (particularly in small developing states) not only when caused by natural disasters but also when affected by geopolitical shocks (e.g. as globally experienced in the aftermath of Russia's invasion of Ukraine).

This kind of perspective on the role of government might seek to limit the extent to which potential losses are borne on a government's balance sheet. Yet, it would appear equally irresponsible for governments to avoid serious consideration of the scenarios that could emerge from climate change or to propose policies or investments that essentially pretend that these hazards will not occur and that the world of tomorrow is just a logical continuity of the world of the recent past. If it is likely that many regions or sectors may become largely nonviable, this should be reflected in both budgetary priorities and in the regulatory and policy signals conveyed to a population.

6. Interactions with the Public Policy Agenda

Recognizing the nature of the climate change phenomenon is important in clarifying the nature of the challenges facing a traditional economic policymaker. Specifically, one has to recognize that there are forces working against the success of many of the policies that might traditionally be seen as promoting economic growth and improved living standards. One of the more serious consequences of entertaining consideration of the risks of climate change for a country is that the vulnerability is magnified by the size of the assets or of the population at risk. Particularly in Sub-Saharan Africa, the Middle East, and parts of South Asia, the high rates of current fertility easily portend the doubling or quadrupling of populations that, in the present size, are already challenging for the local environment, e.g. in the availability of freshwater, in the capacity of regions to feed themselves, and in terms of the investments required to maintain per capita income at current levels. Policymakers that are unwilling to confront the challenge of high fertility and the consequent dangers posed by climate change risks in a higher population environment are inviting increased vulnerability.[3]

---

[3] Some gender specialists would argue the absence of women at high levels of political leadership invites a pro-fertility mindset that overrides those groups in society that bear the highest cost from high fertility.

III. Quantifying the Costs of Climate Risks

The above discussions underscore the difficulty and complexity involved in making quantitative estimates of the potential financial burdens on the public sector associated with the effects of climate change or in responding to the welfare impact on populations whose lives will be severely disrupted by the impact of natural disasters and environmental change. Both the uncertainty of what climate change trajectories to assume and the range and complexity of the climate change hazards that will arise suggest the difficulty of any such exercise. Attempting to come up with a single estimate that accounts for long-term climate risks is likely to be a fool's game.

But there are ways to approach quantification of climate change hazards that may be worth considering, particularly if associated with the use of scenario analysis and taking account of what may be learned from the experience of recent developments in the insurance and reinsurance industries.

1. The Role of Scenario Analysis

In the absence of hard numbers on the financial burden that might arise from the effects of climate change, assessing the fiscal implications will require a different approach than normally used. Specifically, it calls for the periodic use of scenario analyses based on recently developed models on the likely effects of climate change. As noted above, there now are models able to provide much greater specificity on the range and magnitude of climate hazards that could be faced by individual countries (and indeed even specific within-country regions), looking forward at least 75 years and under alternative scenarios on the trajectory of climate change.

Such models provide a sufficient basis to construct economic and social scenarios for individual countries that can explore the likely economic and social ramifications of such climate change hazards looking forward. Such scenarios (or stories) can be elaborated to also reflect the manifold uncertainties on how climate change effects may be manifested — witness even today the unpredictability of droughts, excessive precipitation, flooding, and fires that are afflicting many countries, developed and undeveloped. Most important, such scenarios could be designed to also incorporate the non-climate change factors that will influence the likely economic and social impacts that will be felt. This relates to the expected growth of population in many countries; the projected growth in the economy; and the sensitivity of particular sectors to climate effects. For many countries, the scale of the adverse effects will be much larger as a consequence of any failure to contain or adapt to these forces.

Scenario analyses also afford the possibility of introducing a quantitative dimension in assessing climate change hazards. While one is not likely to be able to offer a quantitative equivalent to the existing empirical macro-economic models, country analysts could seek at least to estimate the financial consequences of specific climate change hazards or multiple hazards specific to a region as they might eventuate under different plausible scenarios. With such estimates, one would at least be in the position to roughly assess the tradeoff between alternative non-climate-related investments (e.g. an education project) as opposed to having the financial capacity to address a climate change hazard. One would also be able to assign a probabilistic measure as to the likelihood of a climate change-induced hazard occurring.

Current experience in many countries of the world with forms of adaptation, resilience building, reconsideration of the economic viability of a region, and social safety net burdens is now providing a useful bounty of data, both financial and experiential, on the challenges, the costs, and the issues that arise in adaptation. The GCA and the IPCC are increasingly proving valuable resources in providing such data. If scenario analyses for an individual country's exposure to future climate hazard risks suggest a mirroring of the experiences that are already being encountered by other countries, this should allow for a richer estimate of the likely costs that a society will bear. It would further illuminate government policy decisions on what the government's role should be (IPCC 2022).

2. Leveraging the Insurance Industry Experience

The analytic challenge can be readily presented. One wants to look forward several decades and scenario analysis provides a good starting point for characterizing a picture of how the economy and society may be affected by climate change hazards under alternative potential climate trajectories, given the uncertainty on the effectiveness of global mitigation efforts. That picture can potentially identify the types of economic and social harm that may arise, but not necessarily the full quantitative consequences of that harm. It also leaves unanswered the question of what the government's own risk exposure is likely to be, or in other words, how much will the government need to rely on the private sector (and possibly, for some countries, external donors) to bear the costs and burdens of adaptation or to respond to the costs of a natural disaster. Government policymakers are likely to be the best judges of what role the government can play, but only when tempered by their having some sense of the financial implications of different potential roles for the government and the affordability of such roles. But the question remains, how to estimate the overall financial consequences of the multiplicity of climate hazards that might be encountered?

One potential source of guidance could potentially come from the experience of the insurance and reinsurance industries. Already, the industry is encountering manifestations of climate change hazards in a number of spheres, whether fires, typhoon winds, storm surges, drought, excessive precipitation, coastal inundation, etc., in the case of individual countries. In some cases, the nature of the experience may appear similar to the types of climate risks being projected for a given country or a region in the context of future climate change.

As such, the insurance industry has an ever-improving understanding of what the costs of such hazards might be as well as an acute understanding of what premium needs to be charged to a government seeking to insure against such hazards looking forward, with the caveat that this may encompass a time profile rarely exceeding 10 years. Obviously, such premia also reflect the state of development (in terms of infrastructure) of the countries exposed to climate risks, thus qualifying the task of applying the data from one country to another country of very different socio-economic characteristics. In principle, such cost estimates for premia could be used to assess the up-front cost to a country's government seeking insurance payments in the context of the occurrence of climate change hazards. The use of such estimates might overstate the costs that one might anticipate from a story that only emerges in a long-term scenario analysis. One might also need to discount the costs substantially, since it is a phenomenon that might only happen in several decades (though Nicholas Stern's recommendations (Stern, 2007) for using a zero-discount rate could modify this argument).

However, arguing against this point is the recognition by many in the reinsurance industry that a *retrospective* perspective on the risks may understate the financial burdens that the insurance industry may encounter in the future (a point of contention in the case of the fires experienced a few years ago in California). Some assignment of probabilities would equally be needed for hazards whose timing is uncertain.

Such estimates of financial cost could also prove valuable in a number of ways. First, it would allow a clearer understanding of the potential tradeoffs faced by a government in deciding on other elements of budget and development policy. If one can assign a measure of the budgetary cost to provide adequate insurance in the event of hazards, one can weigh that cost against the value to be realized from other expenditures. Second, a government policymaker would be able to judge whether a government has sufficient resources to afford a particular role in climate change adaptation. If perceived as too costly, it suggests that a government must pursue a different strategy in facilitating private sector adaptation. It might mean that a government might need to fall back on a social safety net role rather than some more aggressive form of adaptation such as strengthening the resilience of infrastructure or the rebuilding of an area.

IV. Addressing Climate Change Adaptation

This section offers some ideas on how countries should approach the challenge of adaptation to the risks and consequences of climate change. Particularly for the many developing countries likely to be in the bull's eye of uncertain adverse climate change events in coming decades, it is questionable whether policy guidance should ignore the potential consequences of a business-as-usual outcome.

1. Overcome Institutional Silos

The most recent work on adaptation emphasizes that the macro-financial challenge is only one part of a comprehensive strategy to confront the risks that climate change will pose. Such risks will touch on broader societal issues and on the productivity of different sectors. And it is not only a challenge at the aggregate macro level but also one faced by different levels of government.

Thus, to be effective, the government's challenge in facilitating adaptation to climate change over the long term is to avoid a "siloed" effort, viz., one that is restricted to a single environment-tasked agency. The recent work of the GCA clearly underscores the necessity of a government-wide effort. Surveying the response to the IPCC's efforts in the early 2000s to foster individual government reporting on adaptation efforts, the oft-times lack of frequency and limited depth of country reports suggests the lack of penetration of the issue into the day-to-day work of government ministries, whose functions will need to be adapted to respond to the challenges that climate-related hazards will pose.

The GCA has underscored that assessments need to be made as to whether climate change risk issues are explicit elements of the operational policy framework and analytical capacity of different sectoral ministries. While IMF surveillance discussions with a country can emphasize the importance of the adaptation issue (see IMF, 2022a), the IMF might work with countries seeking its financial assistance to set targets for achieving progress in the institutional integration of climate change adaptation into sectoral programs, with climate change experts integrated into sectoral ministries. It can also support central government efforts to assist lower levels of government that are particularly exposed to climate-related hazards.[4]

2. Global Coordination and Action

Reliance on the financial experience of the reinsurance industry is also providing some sense of the costs being borne as a consequence of the

---

[4]IMF technical assistance efforts can also be marshaled to assist governments in the implementation of such efforts. This has proven a key element of the IMF's response in the past and the IMF has demonstrated its ability to ramp up its own capacity and that of global experts around the world. The challenge is to draw on the already substantial capacity and experience in many countries at the state and local levels in order to aggressively assist countries that have less experience on adaptation issues.

lack of success from current mitigation efforts. The costs being borne in Australia from wildfires can only modestly be attributed to inadequate mitigation efforts, given the global nature of climate change. Nevertheless, such costs begin to highlight the losses that are already being borne by an inadequate mitigation strategy by the largest emitting countries. Rising reinsurance premia illustrate what successful mitigation forestalls in costs. As the more recent forest fires in the Far West of the United States illustrate, failure of mitigation efforts bears on the major emitting countries as well as all others, and it illustrates why even the major emitting nations have a stake in encouraging all countries to pursue mitigation strategies. Global cooperation to mitigate climate change will reduce the overall costs related to adaptation.

3. Collaboration with the Scientific Community

Policymakers and economists working on surveillance in particular regions need to be able to understand better what current science suggests are the signals on the pace of climate change and the factors influencing the occurrence of climate change hazards. Clearly, much of this is distilled by the periodic reports of the IPCC. Nevertheless, fiscal policymakers should be actively interacting with the IPCC and with other agencies to absorb what can be gleaned by the intensified monitoring of scientists of biosphere and geophysical signals.

For the nonscientist, one becomes quickly aware of the complexity of the factors influencing these issues. They involve issues relating to: clouds, the chemical quality of the seas; the stability of ice sheets in West Antarctica and Wilkes Basin of East Antarctica; the vulnerability of boreal forests in the subarctic; the state of melting of the permafrost in the Arctic and Greenland; the role, extent, and impact of coral bleaching; the extent of forest loss observed in the Amazon; the evidence of any further slow-down in the AMOC (Atlantic Meridional Overturning Circulation) with effects on the Amazon, the East Asian Monsoon, the West African Monsoon; any signals of the breakup of stratocumulus clouds above 1,200 parts per million of carbon dioxide. One quickly becomes aware also of the concept of interacting drivers; fire and climate feedbacks as interacting tipping mechanisms; similarly the concept of cascading effects.

4. Scenario Analysis by Multilateral Institutions

In the early 2000s, the IMF and the World Bank put together teams to support countries as they produced poverty reduction strategy chapters in connection with the Heavily Indebted Poor Countries and Multilateral Debt Relief Initiative. A recent IMF initiative for six pilot countries during 2018–2020 (specifically, the Climate Change Policy Assessments for Belize, Grenada, Micronesia, Seychelles, St. Lucia, and Tonga), in coordination with the World Bank, examined the impact of climate change. This approach can be built upon to include the elaboration of alternative scenarios on the long-term effects of climate change for individual countries under alternative climate change trajectories. A country's own experts would be integral and essential to the formulation of these scenarios. Ideally, the scenarios could be publicly available as part of the published background documents for IMF surveillance. The challenge in producing the scenarios would involve an initial up-front investment such that updating would be necessary only every 5–7 years, largely to reflect the extent to which global estimates of the climate change trajectory are felt to have changed substantively or to the extent that more precise views of the specific hazards likely to be encountered have become available.

The objective of such exercises would be to achieve the following:

1. Engage with country authorities in a dialogue on the implications of the scenarios, both in terms of development strategies and in the likely role that governments would play, whether in terms of preventive structural resilience efforts, more extensive restructuring of regions or sectors, reconsideration of current sectoral development strategies, and/or potential social prevention efforts that a government might need to finance.
2. Clarify for fiscal surveillance, the magnitude of the financial burdens that might be borne by a government, the extent of the challenge this would imply for its ability to finance its budget, and to enhance its policy dialogue on how to approach these challenges.
3. Depending on a government's views on its role in the adaptation, resilience, and potentially the restructuring process, draw on available data from the insurance and reinsurance industries on the cost of

insurance against major climate hazards of different kinds, thus allowing some specification on the potential fiscal burden that might arise.

4. Clarify for the international community the magnitude of the financial
    resource challenges to be confronted by individual countries, particu-
    larly those with limited financial resources.
5. Clarify transparently to the citizens of individual countries the magni-
    tude of the challenges that climate change will pose, the extent to
    which private sector agents will be forced to respond, and to clarify
    the government's political accountability in responding (or not
    responding) to the challenge.
6. Provide a template for dialogue in subsequent annual surveillance
    discussions on how the government is managing its adaptation
    efforts.

Such scenario models could facilitate active consultation by the IMF
and other agencies with government policymakers on what the consequences bode for a country looking forward. Any policymaker with a
capacity for a retrospective view recognizes two or three decades is not
that long a period and that what might seem like "long-term" phenomena
will start happening sooner rather than later.

Active risk management approaches need to be high on the agenda,
again recognizing that a long-run optic needs to be embedded in short-
term policy thinking. Climate change adaptation will also raise to the fore
issues that require further discussion in the context of surveillance. These
could include an opportunity to integrate the potential challenges and
consequences of current development policies and raise questions in a
surveillance context. These include understanding better the relative roles
of public and private sector agents in adaptation and clarifying the spheres
of responsibility of government.

As noted above, scenario analysis can be a starting point for a quantitative reassessment of available long-term financial resources for a government. It can also clarify whether active engagement with the reinsurance
community or access to bonds might address short-term financial needs.
It also provides a vehicle to assign probabilities to the likelihood of climate change events occurring. The analysis can also further underscore
the importance of industrial and larger emerging market economies

meeting their promises to provide financial support to the many low-income countries that face severe climate threats.

Assessment will be needed from multilateral partners such as the World Bank and regional development banks, as to whether climate change risks are being embedded into the perspective revealed by a country or region's development plans. Does the development plan suggest a "business-as-usual" approach to assessing priorities or does it integrate the most recent estimates of what might be the impact from different climate change hazards? What policies can facilitate increased resilience? Or does the nature of the climate risk suggest the need for a reconsideration of the underlying rationale for an economic sector or region or the viability of a region for habitation?

It should be noted that a scenario exercise could complement and be the basis for expanding existing IMF efforts to support stress testing of debt sustainability assessments in response to large natural disasters as well as other issues of climate change adaptation faced by member countries. The recent IMF policy paper on fostering resilience to natural disasters (IMF, 2019c) highlights recent assessments for the Bahamas and Jamaica of "scenario-based stress test[s] analyzing the macro-economic impact of a severe hurricane in the former and a massive natural disaster in the latter". It notes that the "IMF has recently joined the Network for Greening the Financial System (NGFS) and is collaborating with its members to develop an analytical framework for assessing climate-related risks".

5. Marshaling Global Transparency

The international community has recognized the role that global transparency on the state of country policy efforts can play. One observes the Millennium Development Goals and more recently the United Nations Sustainable Development Goals, not to mention other efforts to shine a light on country performance (Doing Business Indicators, indices of Corruption, etc.). The Paris Accords have enabled monitoring of country mitigation efforts.

The IMF's recent initiative to embed adaptation issues into its surveillance (IMF, 2022a) could serve to facilitate the development of indicators that could shine a light on the relative performance of countries on these issues, ranking countries on the various aspects of how countries are dealing with climate change adaptation. One could envisage indicators characterizing the transparency of a country's own stated assessments of climate change risks; the institutional capacity of a country to respond to these risks; and the vulnerability of a country to different climate change risks. The global community already faces a challenge in how to work with countries that are downplaying or ignoring the issue of climate change adaptation, or who are counting on the international community to assume a major financing role. While the latter will necessarily be the case for many countries, given their lack of financial resources, the challenge will be to avoid the moral hazard that such dependence can give rise to, or the temptation to use global financing as a source of financial mismanagement.

6. Assessing and Monitoring the Private Sector Vulnerabilities to Climate Change

One important recent development emerging from the NGFS is the initiative to prepare "NGFS transition scenarios and guidelines on scenario-based climate risk analysis" (see NGFS Website). Several central banks already undertook assessments of the potential vulnerability of banks and financial institutions to climate change. Systemic risks may arise if the perceptions of financial markets suddenly change as to whether the impact of climate change could be disruptive and lead to large financial losses across entire sectors and spread across countries. In addition, the physical risks related to natural disasters would trigger insurance losses and non-performing loans.

Financial markets are only beginning to integrate climate change effects into companies' valuations or into their credit quality assessments. Credit rating agencies have made progress on the integration of climate change risks in their analyses of companies and governments alike. But this is still at an early stage and comparing organizations' performance in the proper context can be challenging. In addition, some major improvements could be made if regulations were implemented to require companies and financial institutions to disclose their exposure to climate risks and their strategies to mitigate them. This would improve transparency and market efficiency. The IMF's Global Financial Stability Report has already begun to address this issue in the 2019 edition (IMF, 2019a), including a chapter on sustainability.

7. Build-Up an International Training Dedicated to Climate Change Adaptation

At the international level, one would want to see major universities developing Masters' level programs focused on training civil servants to understand the technical issues that will arise in structural government programs to incorporate adaptation issues. Analogous to the expansion of global health programs in Schools of Public Health in the last two decades, a similar effort is needed to establish Masters' Programs in University Schools of Public Policy, Education, Public Health, Public Resource Management, and Agriculture. This would appear an appropriate challenge for major eleemosynary institutions (e.g. Gates, Ford, Rockefeller, etc.) focused on climate change-related issues.

V. Climate Change and Government Finance

1. Introduction to Government Finance

Government needs financing to operate and finance its budget (for education, social security, public health, national defense, etc.), public servants' salaries and pensions, and to pay back ("service") its accumulated debt. Most of this capital comes from fiscal policies which govern how a state can receive taxes, but many governments and public entities can also raise money on the capital market. As with companies, it is necessary to appraise a government's balance sheet not only in the short term, but also over the long term. The concept of "fiscal space" captures whether a government has the financial room to undertake new policy initiatives — such room may be created by increased taxation, cutbacks in inessential expenditures, or additional borrowing. The latter option is typically constrained by whether capital markets are willing to increase lending to a government without concerns as to its ability to repay at the prevailing sovereign interest rate.

For policy analysts assessing a government's fiscal position, two important foci are the magnitude of a government's debt ratio in GDP and its likely sustainability looking forward. More broadly, assessments of fiscal sustainability judge whether, looking into the future, a government will be able to finance its explicit public debt obligations as well as other implicit liabilities (e.g. associated with pensions and other social insurance promises).

In the last few years in the context of the COVID-19 pandemic and the Russian invasion of Ukraine, debt ratios have risen to worrisome levels, not only in some advanced economies but even more so in many emerging market and low-income countries. Debt sustainability has become a concern, raising issues of whether governments can service their debts, and whether the resulting burden will imply a tax ratio that will prove politically damaging.

Managing for fiscal sustainability is further complicated by other economic policy issues, e.g. a depreciating exchange rate or changes in commodity prices for a country's principal exports. The well-recognized myopia of politicians further complicates the issue, as policy commitments are often made without regard to their longer-term tail of anticipated budgetary costs (e.g. with regard to pensions and medical insurance). In addition, the change in the demographic picture, with the unanticipated drop in fertility in many countries, gives rise to a broader concern for the fiscal sustainability of a government's finances. The challenge of rising public debt levels has also provoked concerns in both multilateral lending institutions and capital markets as to whether governments will be constrained in their capacity to finance new investments. Rising debt shares could provoke an increase in the sovereign debt premium, further tightening the debt sustainability noose.

The question is then often posed as to whether a government has the "fiscal space" to finance expanded budgetary investments and policy initiatives (Heller, 2005). For countries already burdened by high levels of public debt and facing challenges in issuing domestic debt by monetary financing or raising capital on international capital markets, the creation of additional fiscal space requires either increasing taxes or cutbacks in existing public expenditure programs. For countries with access to capital markets, the amount of available fiscal space was seen as constrained by whatever debt ratio was seen to precipitate a significant adverse change in the sovereign debt premium.

With the incorporation of the fiscal space concept into IMF surveillance, a pre-COVID-19, pre-Ukraine study by the IMF (IMF, 2018) suggested that there were many industrial and emerging market countries still having fiscal space, with levels of public debt significantly below the threshold that markets would deem as too high. Even at that time, one could argue that these measures of fiscal space were overestimates in that they did not capture the contingent risk from known off-balance sheet liabilities (notably from pension and other social insurance risks, e.g. particularly in terms of medical insurance).

In the current global environment, it is likely that many low-income countries and some emerging market countries possess little or no traditional fiscal space. For these countries, expanded public sector budgets principally depend on the support that might be obtained from foreign assistance or from significant subsidies from multilateral lenders. Recent developments in the conjunctural environment for fiscal policy, notably the efforts to curb inflationary pressures through tightened monetary policy, have also added to these concerns. In sum, current perspectives on fiscal sustainability and fiscal space underscore that long-run fiscal challenges could further limit the financing possible for climate-tasked policy initiatives, whether of a short- or long-run nature.

2. The Challenge of Climate Adaptation on Government Finance

Recognizing the uncertainties associated with climate change, scenario analysis will not in itself provide clarity as to how countries should balance the policy tradeoffs in allocating scarce fiscal resources for adaptation relative to other urgent policy challenges. One cannot ignore that in political economy terms, climate change hazards that may only gradually worsen over the next several decades may seem dwarfed for politicians faced with other difficult budgetary challenges in the context of limited fiscal space. Poverty challenges for those alive today need to be weighed against reducing poverty and economic disruption for future generations. Investments in infrastructure may have a higher rate of return relative to the returns from a reduction in longer-term losses from climate change hazards.

For almost all countries, the adaptation challenges posed by climate change hazards suggest that the availability of fiscal space over the longer term may be much tighter than previously assumed. For countries with sound fiscal positions, their budgets will find it possible to facilitate private sector efforts to adapt to climate change hazards and to provide social welfare support to an increasing share of the population unable to cope with the effects of climate change hazards. However, for the many countries whose fiscal space is today already severely constrained or nonexistent, adding adaptation to the policy agenda will obviously be difficult without external financial support (Jubilee Debt Campaign, 2020).

Presumably, one would find that the extent of government involvement may be linked to whether fiscal space is available domestically or provided only by external resource transfers from donors.

Looking forward beyond the short term, where does this leave us in considering the concepts of fiscal space and fiscal sustainability? Perhaps the key answer is that taking account of climate issues requires a broader optic on fiscal space, one that requires different methodological approaches. While the fiscal space concept may continue to be relevant for managing day-to-day fiscal policy, for longer-term fiscal policy, climate change looms as an important qualifying consideration. Some countries, with highly diversified and developed economies and geographic locations that suggest manageable consequences from climate change hazards, may find only a limited need to revise their approach to the management of fiscal policy, even while addressing significant climate change hazards and playing a role in assisting countries more adversely affected.

For others, those that have much less developed and diversified economies or whose geographic locations suggest much more consequential adverse effects from climate change on their environment, much more serious reconsideration of their approach to fiscal and development policy may be required. Otherwise, there would be a danger in treating available fiscal space for public sector investment as not threatened by the risks posed by climate hazards. Even in the short term, the longer-term environmental challenges may not be easy to ignore. As a simple example, a seemingly meritorious investment in roads or infrastructure in a coastal area may prove to be a "white elephant" looking forward not that many years, with offshoots reflected in private investment that will equally be at risk looking forward.

Applying a negative filter associated with potential climate risks would be a necessary clarifying task. An important facet of the analysis would be to actively assign more probabilistic assessments to the likelihood of these climate hazards occurring. Over time, one would expect that the science of climate change modeling will provide greater certitude on the probabilities that one might encounter. The need to draw on the experience of countries already encountering climate change hazards will prove a necessary corrective in considering potential financial challenges faced by governments.

Moreover, for some countries, the issue of fiscal space, or of fiscal sustainability, may be transcended by the concept of political, social, and environmental sustainability. Some countries may find their viability eroded or endangered by the loss of territory associated with coastal flooding. Some may find that important economic sectors, particularly in agriculture, will no longer be viable, unless innovations in research and development can offset the risks from climate-induced effects on insect vectors, increased salinization, or soil depreciation. Urban areas, already expected to rapidly grow, may expand as a consequence of climate-induced population movements.

Thinking ahead as to how to respond to such potential risks needs to be broached. Countries will need to begin developing much greater institutional capacity in many government agencies to consider and respond to these risks. In such countries, even the role of government may need to be reconsidered. Particularly for those countries with highly limited fiscal space, governments will need to consider where their efforts should be focused in terms of climate change adaptation. For many, the elaboration of a much more resilient social safety net capacity may be the highest priority, since governments are not likely to have the financial capacity to participate in significant adaptation efforts in many sectors beyond providing some technical assistance and expertise.

3. Introducing the Long Run into Government Finance

While the focus is normally on the short-to-medium term, issues of fiscal sustainability and long-term growth are also part of government and multilateral agencies' implicit welfare function. Yet, the treatment of long-run issues by macroeconomists has been fairly limited (Heller, 2003). We have argued above that the concept of fiscal space continues to be relevant when thinking about the short-to-medium term, even when one seeks to embed some types of long-term implicit or explicit obligations of the government such as those associated with potential social insurance liabilities. Actuarial estimates of potential shortfalls in pension funding can be made, reflecting reasonably solid demographic projections. Weaknesses in the funding of medical insurance plans need to take into account links between demographic projections, epidemiological data on the incidence of illness, and recent experience on medical cost trends and treatment patterns.

Still, climate change epitomizes the issue of a long-run policy challenge that affects the picture in a number of ways:

- First, the insurance and reinsurance sectors, by offering private sector resources to address the consequences of natural disasters, may now be providing an additional way to expand future fiscal space (the Caribbean regional initiative is illustrative of this approach), though at the cost of insurance premia in the short run. The key challenge that parametric insurance and other reinsurance policies will confront in a climate-afflicted world is the extent to which many risks may prove more frequent or more correlated than heretofore.
- Second, some mitigation initiatives, in particular, the levying of a carbon tax, could actually create fiscal space by the revenues mobilized (though most proposals involve offsetting reductions in other types of taxation or increased expenditure for other purposes).
- Third, while both mitigation policy initiatives and the burdens of adaptation to climate change hazards involve behavioral changes by private sector agents, it is now recognized that governments are likely to be involved in financing some of these efforts. Adaptation efforts, particularly disaster relief and the rebuilding of infrastructure damaged by climate events, could result in future fiscal costs that would add implicit charges on available fiscal space. However, the incorporation of climate change issues, particularly with regards to adaptation, will involve, particularly looking forward, much more substantial

charges on a country's economy, raising questions as to the role that governments will be able to play in supporting adaptation efforts.

VI. How has the IMF's Perspective on Fiscal Policy Been Shaped by Its Concerns for Climate Change?

The last few years have seen an important evolution in the extent to which climate change is perceived by the IMF as an issue influencing fiscal policy. Two important developments can be identified. First, in the last several years, the IMF has recognized the heightened immediate challenge faced by a number of small developing states arising from the higher probability of climate-related natural disasters. Second, more recently, the IMF has begun to recognize that climate change concerns cannot be ignored in considering the appropriateness of a country's short- to medium-term fiscal policy position.

1. Integration of Natural Disasters into a Country's Financial Policy Strategy

An important factor precipitating the IMF's increasing concern with the effects of climate change arose from its experience with several small developing states dramatically affected by hurricanes. The economic consequences of these events highlighted both the increasing frequency of such natural disasters relative to historic trends and the potential size of their economic and social impact on small states heavily reliant on a narrow economic base. Over the course of the last decade, the IMF, in concert with the World Bank, focused on the need to build resilience in the face of the prospect of such potentially cataclysmic events. Working with these countries (particularly Dominica and Grenada), the Fund outlined a three-pillar approach that involved the following:

1. Investments in structural resilience to limit the impact of natural disasters;
2. building financial resilience to create fiscal buffers and using pre-arranged financial instruments to protect fiscal sustainability and manage recovery costs; and

3. the creation of post-disaster (and social) resilience requiring contingency planning to ensure a speedy response to a disaster.

Briefly summarizing this approach, *structural resilience* is seen as a preventive approach involving investment in both hard policy measures (physical infrastructure) and softmeasures (establishing early warning systems, customizing building codes, and zoning rules). It recognizes that in the absence of a comprehensive strategy to build resilience, investment in adaptation is often poorly coordinated if not sufficiently prioritized and takes a back seat to other urgent social and development needs. It notes that underinvestment in structural resilience reflects a short term bias in policymaking, tight fiscal constraints, and limits on borrowing capacity due to elevated debt levels or poor credit worthiness and limited concessional financing.

While the *financial resilience* pillar is implicitly linked to the concepts of fiscal sustainability and fiscal space, it also includes considerations of the multi-level risk management approaches emphasized by the World Bank. It is the principal pillar that one might associate with a Ministry of Finance's role in adaptation. The concept of self-insurance entails the provision of fiscal buffers". While the focus is largely on contingency reserves, the buildup of financial assets implies a reduction of net debt on a government's balance sheet and thus the creation of fiscal space, whether at the national, state, or local government level. It is an acknowledgment of the negative implicit financial burden associated with a government's role in adaptation, or more specifically in its reconstruction and rebuilding role in the aftermath of disasters arising from climate events.

An important element of the financial resilience pillar involves the transference of risk through insurance and other risk-sharing mechanisms. The principal modalities available include *explicit insurance* (often backed by reinsurance by the insurance provider) and *parametric insurance* modalities whereby a government pays a premium to insurers that issue catastrophe bonds that make payments to a government when a specified qualifying event occurs that meets the trigger conditions necessary to activate a payout. Both mechanisms may be viewed as alternative modalities by which a government's fiscal space can be augmented, at least over the medium term. This nevertheless carries the contingent risk that reliance on these approaches can imply larger longer-term risks than reliance on alternative approaches to adaptation, including some which are associated with the first pillar.

Both approaches have been used in recent years by some island economies in the Caribbean to facilitate a regional sharing of the risks associated with a hurricane disaster striking an individual island economy. Two obvious costs are associated with these approaches. First, the premiums may be costly. Conceptually, they are analogous to debt service outlays that reduce expenditures available for other types of public goods and services and public investment. Second, as profit-making institutions, insurers rarely provide these policies for periods in excess of five years.

A final source of financial resilience may derive from pre-arranged credit lines with international financial institutions or from the expectation that humanitarian assistance would be provided in the wake of a natural disaster.

The third pillar relates to the *provision of post-disaster relief*. In most low-income countries, this would involve a discretionary budgetary response to emergencies. More developed low-income and emerging market countries may have more systemic social protection approaches involving social safety nets or explicit types of insurance.

2. Integration of Issues of Climate Change into the IMF's Surveillance Process

The IMF's evolution in expanding its approach to financial and economic policy surveillance to address the multiple effects of climate change on the economy was further motivated by the increasing evidence of climate change-induced events affecting all regions of the globe. Increasingly it became clear that the template of a disaster resilience strategy had to be expanded to address the much larger and more complex challenges that countries will face over time, requiring both adaptation and potentially important issues of economic and social restructuring. Looking forward, climate change risks can cause systemic environmental changes, affecting many different aspects of an economy or the social-economic environment of particular regions, in effect comparable to "a train wreck in slow motion". Obviously, the Fund also recognized that mitigation initiatives would also be critical if there is to be any chance of limiting the extent and severity of the climate change that can be envisioned.

The most palpable evidence of the change in the IMF's attitude toward climate change can be found in its new guidelines to its staff on the conduct of the IMF's annual surveillance review of its member economies. These reviews, historically focused on the short and at best the medium term, now are expected to consider those effects of climate change on a country's economy that are likely to be of a "macro critical nature".

The 2022 guidelines (IMF, 2022a) represent a significant scaling up in the Fund's attention to issues of climate change, in the context of its annual surveillance of a member's economy. With regard to adaptation policy, the guidelines suggest that where climate change impacts are "macro critical", even when occurring beyond a 3 to 5-year medium-term framework, the IMF staff are expected to discuss issues of adaptation policy. The relevant guideline suggests:

"[the need for an] assessment of exposure to climate risk and the possible impact that the materialization of such risks would have; ... discuss[ing] policies to strengthen resilience to climate change and identify...corresponding financing gaps... Staff reports would discuss options to cover such gaps, including re-prioritizing expenditures..., strengthening revenue collection, and accessing more financing. The discussion would be anchored by the DSA [debt sustainability assessment] and factor in issues such as policy implementation capacity, ...as well as placing adaptation in the country's overall development context... The discussions would also explore how to enhance financial resilience, including through fiscal buffers and possibly insurance and contingency finance... In some cases, an Article IV may need to cover the potential impact of climate change on financial stability and elaborate on issues such as migration and the corresponding economic cost".

The Guidelines were also associated with policy notes expanding on the Fund's perspective on the economic principles for integrating adaptation to climate change into fiscal policy (IMF, 2022b), the macro fiscal implications of adaptation (IMF, 2022c), the planning and mainstreaming of adaptation in fiscal policy (IMF, 2022d)

Importantly, the Guidelines also extend to discussions in the surveillance process of mitigation policy and the management of the implications from the global transition to a low-carbon economy. The former would be particularly relevant for the countries seen as responsible for a significant share of the greenhouse gas emissions such as the United States or China. The latter would focus on the economic policy challenges faced by fossil fuel exporters and industrial sectors that would be negatively affected by the transition away from a global reliance on fossil fuels.

It should be readily apparent that the issues confronting the IMF in incorporating climate change into surveillance will be complex and difficult, and that the issues faced will significantly differ according to whether a given member country's principal focus will be on its role in engendering global greenhouse emissions; whether its role will derive from the nature of its industrial base as opposed to the role of its consumption in engendering such emissions; and/or whether it will principally be affected by climate change-induced hazards. Over time, the challenges will only mount according to the success or failure of global efforts to limit the degree of climate change and from the complexity of how such change will unfold. In this chapter, the focus is on several concerns that will need to be considered as the IMF addresses the adaptation issues that will confront macro fiscal policy.

First, the IMF's new strategy underscores that a finance ministry of a country exposed to climate change-induced effects will need to judge how much financial resilience will be required. How much of a contingency fund, or lower net debt target is appropriate, given a country's long-term exposure to climate change hazards? How much of a tradeoff should be sought in reliance on a financial buffer rather than in a continuous upgrading of insurance coverage? Will the size of the requisite buffer change over time as a function of how much the anticipated trajectory of climate change itself evolves over time? How much account should be taken of what we know will be the buildup of climate change forces over time, the increased likelihood of different kinds of climate hazards, and the systemic structural shifts that could occur (including the non-viability of sectors and the complexity in the way in which "disasters" can occur)?

Second, as with most issues in budgetary policy, devolvement of decision-making to other government agencies is required for estimating what projects and programs will be necessary, particularly in relation to the first pillar-type projects. As often happens in other spheres of public policy, "silos" will develop in relation to climate change planning (Tett, 2016). The key responsible agencies, particularly those dealing with the environment, are often not integrated with other key actors that would play a role in thinking and acting on issues of climate change adaptation. Moreover, much adaptation is necessarily the responsibility of lower levels of government, often ones with only limited fiscal autonomy.

Third, particularly for climate risks, any adaptation strategy, particularly one that involves insurance, may entail "moral hazard" challenges. Integration of thinking about climate change risks across government agencies cannot thus be separated from other aspects of development policy and investment which may easily "assume away" climate risks because of the assumption that insurance, fiscal buffers, or external donors will "deal with adaptation in the event of a disaster". Another way to consider this issue is to examine how and whether climate change adaptation issues influence (if at all), how most development policies are thought about, and specific projects and programs are formulated. The problem of "silos" is too normal and common to be ignored for this type of issue.

Fourth, the IMF's approach in relation to disaster resilience has been grounded on "a comprehensive forward-looking diagnostic of the country's vulnerability to natural disasters". Much of the IMF's discussion in that context has related to the type of physical disasters that have occurred in coastal countries that have suffered extreme storm, wind, and sea damage from hurricanes and tsunamis. Yet the challenge of adaptation to the impacts of climate change will be much broader and complex than the response that may be appropriate in the case of responding to a large "natural disaster" and the way in which their economic and social impact is felt. The IMF's approach, while an important step forward, still may be considered as too much of a ratification of a "business-as-usual" development strategy. This chapter argues that the path of climate change requires a rethinking of this strategy, one that is broadened and strengthened to take account of the dramatic effects that climate change can have on many countries.

Finally, much of the focus in the IMF's approach relates to the strengthening of the "resilience" of infrastructure and economic systems in response to the likely effects of climate change. Such resilience will be at the heart of lending under the IMF's recently established "Resilience and Sustainability Facility" (in March 2022). But the IMF still needs to clarify the meaning of "resilience". Several dictionary definitions of resilience include: (i) "the power or ability to return to the original form, position, etc., after being bent, compressed, or stretched; elasticity"; (ii) "the capability of a strained body to recover its size and shape after deformation caused especially by compressive stress"; (iii) an ability to recover from or adjust easily to misfortune or change. For many countries, all three definitions seem deficient as a basis for a strategy for adaptation, raising questions as to whether resilience should be the principal or only focus for climate change adaptation.

Specifically, the effects of climate change may be such that many aspects of a country's current economic strategy may no longer be viable. A return to the previous approach may not be possible or desirable. Rather than "snapping back" to restore an economic structure as the requirement for achieving resilience, a government might wish to foster the realization of changes in a local economy that safeguards the social cohesion of an affected population group in a way that allows it to meet its needs (or at least restore much of its previous welfare).

Moreover, for many countries, the current development strategy may be such as to render the consequences of climate change much more damaging than would be the case if the current strategy were to be significantly altered. The most obvious illustration relates to countries that would be seriously afflicted by climate change in the next several decades and where their fertility rates will double or triple the population that will be adversely affected. The urgency of addressing high fertility thus may be a critical component of an adaptation strategy. Resilience is not even relevant in these cases as a strategy.

In sum, the IMF's expansion of its surveillance effort will substantially exceed the challenge of achieving greater resilience to large natural disasters in small developing states. That approach, while eminently sensible, will prove insufficient and reflective of a continued short-run optic. This is made clear when recent IMF policy notes on adaptation (IMF, 2022b, 2022c, 2022d) are examined. This is particularly the case as one considers these hazards as they will be posed looking further into the future and taking account of the uncertainties associated with how effective the global mitigation efforts will be. This underscores the relevance of our argument for the value of scenario-based analyses that take account of the complexity of these uncertain issues.

VII. Conclusion

The impact of climate change will be large and societal in its scope. As well recognized in the work of the IPCC from its inception, and more recently in the extremely important work of the GCA, adaptation will require action and institutional capacity at many levels of government and in many different sectors of policy. In most low-income and many emerging market countries, the challenges of adaptation will be confronted by constrained circumstances in terms of available resources. They may have only limited options in terms of their capacity to create fiscal measures or access capital via the capital markets. And in many cases, they will have to address the fact that their development policies need to be seen through the optic of climate change effects. Some policies that may have seemed optimal in a world without climate change may now prove disadvantageous as the forces of climate change strike.

There is little doubt that meeting the challenge of climate change mitigation must be a dominant policy priority for the group of countries largely responsible for most carbon emissions in the next several decades. Successful action by these countries, particularly in the next decade may also serve to motivate mitigation efforts by those developing and emerging market countries whose development programs are likely to generate substantial emissions. But for the other countries in the rest of the world, their long-run economic and social prospects will be heavily determined by the climate hazards that result from such global mitigation efforts.

Virtually all countries in the world are faced with the uncertainty as to the nature of the climate change adaptation that will be required in this century. This chapter has highlighted the uncertainties and difficulties that policymakers will face in grappling with this challenge. Their efforts are rendered even more difficult because of the longer-term character of the climate change phenomenon and here we are not talking about the 22nd century but of a near future that will shape the lives of many alive today and of their children and grandchildren.

Nevertheless, policy decisions relating to current needs and current budgets must be made, and there are legitimate policy tradeoffs that must be made. The rate of return to spending on current policy priorities may indeed be analyzed as higher than the gains from adapting to challenges of the 2040s and beyond. Weighing the relative benefits to those currently alive and voting rather than to those of the future has always been difficult, but that does not mean that myopic biases are, in welfare terms, appropriate.

Finally, climate change is a phenomenon whose occurrence will be exogenously experienced by almost all countries of the world, most of whom will be forced to monitor the evidence and signals as to how the determinants of climate change are being manifested. Even the five or six countries of the world whose mitigation efforts will determine the pace of climate change, will have to adapt to its consequences since they too will have to live with the uncertainty of the policy efforts of others.

Alternative scenario analysis techniques are likely to be more useful in a policy context to highlight and illuminate the potential financial challenges that may need to be built into long-run financial policy frameworks. Such scenario analyses would allow at least for some quantification of the specific financial cost of particular climate change hazards, particularly if enriched from the recent experience of insurance and reinsurance industries in dealing with climate change effects.

Climate change will be a defining challenge of this century that will profoundly affect the fiscal and macro-economic policy capacity of governments. In assisting finance ministries to address the budgetary challenges that climate change will entail, the IMF is the premier institution whose relationship with these ministries can facilitate their efforts. Recent developments in the IMF's approach to surveillance give hope that its work will help countries confront the challenge of adapting to the effects of climate change.

To wait for a decade on this issue until we are clearer on the success of mitigation efforts is to delay policy development and implementation on adaptation that could reduce serious economic and social losses looking forward. Building up capacity for policy implementation, particularly in many low-income countries, is not an overnight proposition. The next decade will also be critical in furthering a dialogue with countries on what the scientific signals suggest about the likely climate change trajectory and the role that many potential tipping points might play in characterizing the critical risks.

References

Audley, K. *et al.* (August 2019). "Emerging risks in insurance: Climate change", *Milliman White Chapter*. CEP Council on Economic Policies. https://www.cepweb.org/wp-content/uploads/2020/01/CEP-Scenarios-for-Fiscal-Space.pdf.

Bank of England. (December 2019). "The 2021 Biennial exploratory scenario on the financial risks from climate change", Discussion Chapter.

Center for Climate and Energy Solutions. (November 2021). *Outcomes of the UN Climate Change Conference in Glasgow*. UN Climate Change Website. https://unfccc.int/process-and-meetings/conferences/glasgow-climate-change-conference-october-november-2021/outcomes-of-the-glasgow-climate-change-conference.

Chaplin-Kramer, R. (2019). "Global modeling of nature's contributions to people", *Science Magazine*, October 11, 2019.

Crausbay, S. D. and Ramirez, A. R. (2018). "Defining ecological drought for the twenty-first century", *Bulletin of the American Meteorological Society*, 98(12), pp. 2543–2550.

DeFries, R. *et al.* (September 2019). *The Missing Economic Risks in Assessments of Climate Change Impacts*, Grantham Institute of Climate Change and the Environment, The Earth Institute, Columbia University, Potsdam Institute of Climate Impact Research.

Federal Reserve Bank of San Francisco. (2019). "Strategies to address climate change risk in low and moderate-income communities", *Community Development Innovation Review*, 14(1), https://www.frbsf.org/community-development/files/CDIR_vol_14_issue_1_.pdf.

Flavelle, C. (October 17, 2019a). "Bank regulators present a dire warning of financial risks from climate change", *New York Times*.

Furman, J. and Summers, L. (March/April 2019). "Who's afraid of budget deficits? How Washington should end its debt obsession", *Foreign Affairs*, 98(2), pp. 82–88.

GCA. (September 2019). "Adapt now: A global call for leadership on climate resilience", Global Commission on Adaptation.

Heller, P. S. (2003). *Who Will Pay? Confronting Aging Societies, Climate Change and other Long-Term Fiscal Challenges*, International Monetary Fund, Washington DC.

Heller, P. S. (March 2005) "Understanding fiscal space", *Policy Development Paper 05/4*, International Monetary Fund.

Howcroft, E. and Jones, M. (2019). "ECB considers putting climate change risks in future bank stress tests", *Reuters*, November 14.

International Monetary Fund (IMF). (June 2018). "Assessing fiscal space: An update and stocktaking". Washington, D.C.: IMF.

International Monetary Fund (IMF). (October 2019a). "Sustainable finance", Chapter 6, *Global Financial Stability Report*. Washington, D.C.: IMF.

International Monetary Fund (IMF). (May 2019b). *Fiscal Policies for Paris Climate Strategies: From Principle to Practice*, *IMF Policy Chapter*. Washington, D.C.: IMF.

International Monetary Fund (IMF). (June 2019c). *Building Resilience in Developing Countries Vulnerable to Large Natural Disasters*, *IMF Policy Chapter*. Washington, D.C.: IMF.

International Monetary Fund (IMF). (December 2019d). "The economics of climate", *Finance and Development*. Washington, D.C.: IMF.

International Monetary Fund (IMF). (October 2020). "How to mitigate climate change", *World Economic Outlook*. Washington, D.C.: IMF.

International Monetary Fund (IMF). (2022a). *Guidance Note for Surveillance under Article IV Consultations*. Washington, D.C.: IMF.

International Monetary Fund (IMF). (2022b). "Economic principles for integrating adaptation to climate change into fiscal policy", *IMF Staff Climate Note 2022/001*. Washington, D.C.: IMF.

International Monetary Fund (IMF). (2022c). "Macro-fiscal implications of adaptation to climate change", *IMF Staff Climate Note 2022/002*. Washington, D.C.: IMF.

International Monetary Fund (IMF). (2022d). "Planning and mainstreaming adaptation to climate change in fiscal policy", *IMF Staff Climate Note 2022/003*. Washington, D.C.: IMF.

Intergovernmental Panel on Climate Change (IPCC). (2022). *Summary for Policymakers*, Cambridge: Cambridge University Press.

Jarzabkowski, P., Chalkias, K., Clarke, D., Iyahen, E., Stadtmueller, D., and Zwick, A. (2019). *Insurance for Climate Adaptation: Opportunities and Limitations*, Rotterdam and Washington DC.

Jubilee Debt Campaign. (2020). *The Growing Global South Debt Crisis and Cuts in Public Spending*. Website summary. https://jubileedebt.org.uk/

wp-content/uploads/2020/01/The-growing-global-South-debt-crisis-and-cuts-in-public-spending_01.20.pdf.

Lu, D. and Flavelle, C. (2019). "Rising seas will erase more cities by 2050, new research shows", *New York Times*, October 29.

Molico, M. (2019). "Researching the economic impacts of climate change: Implications for monetary policy and financial stability", *Bank of Canada*, November 19.

Mora, C., Spirandelli, D., Franklin, E. C. *et al.* (2018). "Broad threat to humanity from cumulative climate hazards intensified by greenhouse gas emissions", *Nature Climate Change*, 8, pp. 1062–1071.

NGFS Website. Network for greening of the financial system. https://www.ngfs.net.

Nicholls, R. J. *et al.* (2011). "Sea-level rise and its possible impacts given a 'beyond 4°C world' in the twenty-first century", *Philosophical Transactions of the Royal Society*, 369, pp. 161–181.

Reuters. (November 21 2019). "France to stress test banks, insurers' climate risks next year". London: Reuters https://www.reuters.com/article/us-france-climate-finance/france-to-stress-test-banks-insurers-climate-risks-next-year-idUSKBN1Y30CS.

Schwartz, J. (2019). "A wet year causes farm woes far beyond the floodplains", *New York Times*, November 21.

Sengupta, S. and Cai, W. (2019). "A quarter of humanity faces looming water crises, study says", *New York Times*, August 6.

Stern, L. N. (2007). *The Economics of Climate Change: The Stern Review*, Cambridge University Press, Cambridge.

Tett, G. (2016). *The Silo Effect: The Peril of Expertise and the Promise of Breaking Down Barriers*, Simon & Schuster, New York.

United States Congress. (2019). "H. Res. 109: Recognizing the duty of the federal government to create a green new deal", February 7. https://www.congress.gov/bill/116th-congress/house-resolution/109/text.

Van Vuuren, D. P. *et al.* (December 2011). "The use of scenarios as the basis for combined assessment of climate change mitigation and adaptation", *Global Environmental Change*, 21(2), pp. 575–591.

Vermeulen, R. *et al.* (2018). "An energy transition risk stress test for the financial system of the Netherlands", *DNB Occasional Studies* (No. 1607), Netherlands Central Bank, Research Department.

Wallace-Wells, D. (2019). *The Uninhabitable Earth: Life after Warming*, New York, Tim Duggan Books.

Webb, C. and Xu, E. (2018). "The California wildfire conundrum", *Milliman.com Insight*.

Chapter 17

Macro-economic Implications of Sustainability

Alexander S. Preker and Susan C. Hulton

Learning Objectives

- Define what is meant by macro-economic factors
- Review the difference between non-renewable and renewable resources in this context
- Understand the impact of mitigation and adaptation on these factors
- Highlight physical and transition risks and related macro-economic linkages
- Describe relevance of sustainable use of resources for macro-economic performance
- Identify hidden threats to macro-economic performance

Abstract

This chapter demonstrates strong links between the sustainable use of non-renewable and renewable resources, and macro-economic performance. The chapter goes beyond earlier discussion of factors that contribute to climate change and the narrow focus on the fossil fuel industry to include

481

consideration of a broader range of non-renewable and renewable resources that are an integral part of a sustainable environment. The chapter describes both physical and transition risks. And it highlights relevant linkages that exist between mitigation and/or adaptation strategies and macro-economic performance in terms of gross domestic product (GDP), national wealth, economic growth, inflation, stagnation, deflation, consumer spending, borrowing, employment, unemployment, monetary policy, and fiscal policy. The review indicates that well-planned and well-executed sustainability policies and action plans can confer significant macro-economic benefits. At the same time, it reveals that overzealous and poorly executed mitigation strategies as well as failure to pursue adaptation in the meantime can damage industrial performance and lead to significant negative macro-economic outcomes in terms of slowing growth, damaging supply chains, contributing to inflation, increasing unemployment, and reducing sectoral competitiveness. The chapter warns about the potentially damaging effect of expanding the environmental (E) sustainability agenda to the social (S) and governance (G) spheres. And it raises doubts about the use of industrial policy to achieve durable industrial transformation. The chapter presents cautionary remarks about several hidden threats to macro-economic performance from overambitious, poorly designed, and badly executed sustainability policies. These threats include pitfalls associated with lack of realism, mission creep in corporate governance, single-issue capture, hidden political agendas, greenwashing, whitewashing, and loss of competitiveness. The chapter concludes that if these threats are addressed effectively, "doing business" in this area could possibly provide an attractive commercial opportunity for businesses and investors, while at the same time it might advance the sustainability agenda and contribute to macro-economic performance.

I. Introduction

This book provides a unique introductory text to the business and investment implications of one of the most pressing issues of our times — the sustainable management of the Earth's precious resources and reducing the harmful effects of their careless use. Other chapters in the book focus extensively on environmental factors, with a particular emphasis on links between climate change and the fossil fuel industry (Bressler, 2023). In this chapter, the topic is broadened to include the macro-economic implications of the sustainable management of a broader range of non-renewable and renewable resources. The chapter reviews the complex linkages between policies aimed at addressing the many challenges to the sustainable use of both non-renewable and renewable natural resources — through mitigation and adaptation — and macro-economic outcomes. It highlights the importance of protecting macro-economic stability and financial sector factors that are needed to ensure a successful transition from the current neglect to a more sustainable business environment for the future (Hassani and Bahini, 2022).

For readers who are new to the topic of macro-economics or to considering the macro-economic implications of sustainability, the next section will define a few concepts and terms that will be used throughout the chapter.

Chapter 17 is organized as per the following sections:

I. Introduction
II. Definitions
III. Conceptual framework
   ○ macro-economic framework
   ○ mitigation and its macro-economic implications
   ○ adaptation and its macro-economic implications
IV. Linkages between macro-economic risks and sustainability
V. Hidden threats to macro-economic performance
VI. Conclusion

II. Definitions

The macro-economic factors that are the focus of this chapter include concepts and terms that are different from the micro-economic aspects that were discussed in earlier chapters. Macro-economic concepts (Kharit, 2021) include such terms as gross domestic product (GDP), gross national product (GNP), national wealth, economic growth, inflation, stagnation, deflation, consumer spending, borrowing, employment, unemployment, monetary policy, fiscal policy (Rasure, 2022), and financial sector performance (Boyle, 2022). This list is not exhaustive. Chapter 3 of the recent International Monetary Fund publication *World Economic*

Outlook: A Long and Difficult Ascent provides a good primer on some of the basic concepts behind these terms as applied to the environmental and sustainability topics (IMF, 2020).

In this chapter, the concepts of mitigation and adaptation that have been used extensively in discussions on climate change and the fossil fuel industry will be applied to a full range of topics related to non-renewable and renewable resources. Non-renewable resources will refer to land, water, air, minerals, and energy sources including, but not limited to, fossil fuels that do not regenerate over time (Chen, 2022a). All countries have finite reserves of these resources that will eventually be depleted over time through extraction and use. Non-renewable resources are also sometimes referred to as natural resources (Lioudis, 2022). Renewable resources will refer to animals, birds, fish, forests, agriculture products, and other living organisms that can be sustained almost indefinitely if allowed to reproduce more rapidly than they are depleted. Renewable resources also include alternative energy sources like wind turbines, solar panels, hydroelectric power from dams and waves, and biomass. Most renewable resources will also be depleted eventually if efforts are not made to manage them properly (Banton, 2022). Both non-renewable and renewable resources play a critical role in the economy, in social development, and in security (Ruckstuhl, 2009; Scognamillo *et al.*, 2016).

Mitigation as used in this chapter refers to policies and actions that avoid or reduce the risk of shortages developing in any of these resources and limiting spill-over effects like waste, pollution (soil, water, and air), and other undesirable effects such as climate change. Adaptation refers to the process of adjusting to and preparing the economy and society to deal with past, existing, and future resource shortages and addressing the resulting waste, pollution, and other undesirable effects such as climate change.

The depletion of non-renewable resources and the failure to generate or regenerate renewable resources in a timely way have been associated by several authors with significant macro-economic risks (IMF, 2020; Feyen *et al.*, 2019). At the same time, a rapid and forced transition from reliance on one resource category to another, if not carefully executed, can also cause significant macro-economic instability and stress.

Take, for example, the recent disruption in global trade and economic activities associated with the COVID-19 pandemic and the war in Ukraine.

This experience underscores that a sudden restriction in trade and supply chains of the products made from any of these categories of resources can lead to devastating damage to Governments' balance sheets, financial institutions, profitability of firms, labor markets, employment, and household incomes. Economic growth, fiscal revenue and expenditure, debt sustainability, investments, and the evaluation of financial assets are all impacted in a very negative way by sudden disruptions that affect macro-economic stability and growth. This, in turn, can have a "boomerang" effect on the very objectives of policies and actions that promote a transition toward a more sustainable resource use by weakening resilience to resource shortages in any of these areas.

III. Conceptual Framework

The conceptual framework used in this chapter to discuss the macro-economic implications of the sustainable use of non-renewable and renewable resources adapts an approach that has been used extensively with policies and actions aimed at limiting the impact of the fossil fuel industry on global warming and air pollution. It includes a consideration of the macro-economic framework, and mitigation and adaptation strategies.

A. Macro-economic Framework

Sustainability risks associated with a continuation of the unsustainable use of both non-renewable and renewable resources, and with the transition to their more sustainable use, both have macro-economic impacts. The interaction between macro-economic factors and sustainability risks can create either virtuous or vicious cycles. Mitigation and adaptation strategies may themselves cause macro-economic imbalances that undermine the objectives of the transition from unsustainable to more sustainable use. In many cases, the transformation magnifies the macro-economic implications during the transition period. In other cases, macro-economic instability can reduce the scope for successful mitigation and adaptation in terms of funding and political support. See Figure 17.1 for the Interaction between Macro-Economic/Financial Factors and Sustainability.

Figure 17.1. Interaction between Macro-Economic/Financial Factors and Sustainability

Source: Adapted from Feyen *et al.*, 2019.

A World Bank Policy Research Working Paper (Feyen *et al.*, 2019) grouped these sustainability risks into two categories: physical risks and transition risks. These are discussed in turn below.

Physical risks are associated with both the use of non-renewable resources and the by-products resulting from their use. Much has been written about the damage caused by fossil fuels and other sources of carbon footprint, like agriculture and husbandry, because of their effects on global warming. The macro-economic sector implications of climatic events such as hurricanes, cyclones, flooding, heat waves, and droughts are significant. Although this topic has dominated the public conversation on mitigation and adaptation in recent years, it is just the tip of the iceberg. In 2021, the total value of all natural resources was estimated to be in the hundreds of trillions of dollars. Many of the issues not related directly to fossil fuels are ignored almost completely. The total estimated value of the main natural resources held by each of the top 10 countries as of 2021 is summarized in Figure 17.2.

As noted above, physical risks are associated with both the exploitation and use of these resources and damage from their use (e.g. waste and pollution). It is estimated that 140,000 new chemicals and pesticides have been introduced into the environment since 1950, and many of these have

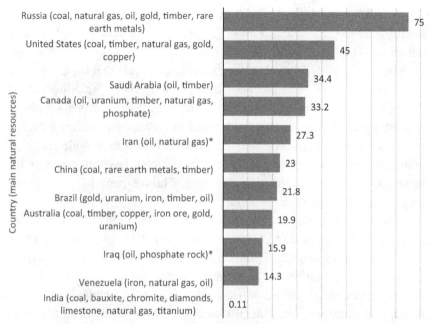

Figure 17.2. Total Value of Natural Resources in Top 10 Countries (in Billion USD, 2021)

Source: Adapted from Garside, 2022.

become widely disseminated in the environment (Landrigan and Goldman, 2011; Prüss-Ustün *et al.*, 2011). Yet, most resource rich countries are highly dependent on a limited number of export products. Any change in supply and demand affects prices, profitability, and business viability. If any of their non-renewable or renewable natural resources are lost, it is extremely difficult for them to "reinvent" themselves by developing other areas of productivity (see Figure 17.2).

As discussed in "Elements of a Greener Economy" by *Bloomberg Business Week* in a special issue on *Shocks to the System*, the "dirty secret of the shift to a lower carbon economy is that it will be really dirty" (Deaux and Teoldi, 2022). Creating the industries that will underpin the transition to a greener economy requires digging up vast amounts of minerals. For example, batteries to store solar, wind, water, and other sources of electrical power require lanthanide and silicone. New electrical grids require millions of tons of copper. A wide range of rare minerals go into making magnets. Electrical sensors require vast amounts of rhodium and palladium. The list goes on.

Mining for such minerals tears up the countryside and the associated pollution causes climate change, loss of biodiversity, acidification of oceans, desertification, and depletion of the world's fresh water supply. It destabilizes the Earth's ecological balance and endangers the sustainability of all life forms (McMichael, 2017). Pollution from a wide range of industrial emissions, not only exhaust from vehicles, has increased rapidly throughout the world in the past 100 years. Children, animals, and plants are particularly vulnerable to pollution.

Pollution significantly affects growth, trade, inflation, labor markets, fiscal balance, and the financial sector. In 2015, the main report of the Lancet Commission on Pollution and Health (Landrigan *et al.*, 2017) estimated that pollution is the largest environmental cause of disease and premature death in the world today. It is responsible for an estimated 9 million premature deaths annually (16% of all deaths worldwide), which is three times more than the deaths annually from AIDS, tuberculosis, and malaria combined and 15 times more than from all wars and violence.

Young children playing in lead-contaminated soil and water contaminated from batteries and other sources often have brain damage, learning disabilities, and lower labor productivity with devastating economic consequences (Heckman's Curve, 2022; Bae and Burton, 2020). Pollution results in an annual loss of 268 million disability-adjusted life-years (DALYs).

The supplementary appendix of the Lancet Commission on Pollution and Health estimated the annual macro-economic cost of pollution at 6.2% or more of global GDP. Pollution therefore has significant negative effects on both macro-economic and fiscal indicators (Preker *et al.*, 2016). Depending on the model used, annual expenditures on health care range from $240 billion (lower bound) to $630 billion (upper bound) or approximately three to nine percent of global spending on health care in 2013 (the reference year for the analysis). Money spent on avoidable healthcare removes resources from productive activities that would contribute to economic growth.

Dependencies of industries on natural capital

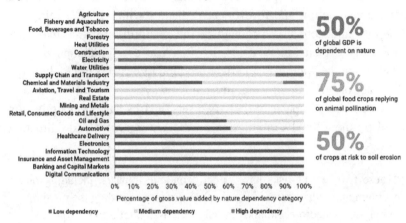

Figure 17.3. Role of Biodiversity in Providing Critical Resource for Industries
Source: MSCI, 2023.

Loss of biodiversity can also significantly affect macro-economic performance. A variety of living species are declining at an alarming rate, predominantly from human encroachment on their natural habitat and overharvesting, less so from greenhouse gases and climate change (MSCI, 2023). Such loss of biodiversity not only reduces nature's ability to absorb greenhouse gases — forests, wetlands, and oceans annually absorb 5.6 gigatons of carbon — it also poses a material threat to economic performance. Figure 17.3 shows the role of biodiversity in other industries.

Transition risks are associated with the move toward a more sustainable use of resources. They are particularly acute if there are abrupt shifts in technology and consumer preferences from one area to another either due to deliberate policy interventions or because of naturally occurring shifts in market circumstances. Such risks may be associated with mitigating measures intended to address a specific natural resource challenge or they may be associated with adaptation measures (when mitigating measures are either not enough or will take too long to come into effect).

For example, incentives introduced through sudden massive public subsidies or disincentives introduced through regulatory restrictions may change the underlying market context before the needed transformative infrastructure has developed. This can cause major shifts in the private sector's consumption and investment decisions which do not reflect the real supply and demand. Although in the medium-term this may meet ideologically driven policy goals, it often causes significant structural changes along the way that can affect productivity, costs, and global competitiveness of the economy etc. in negative ways.

The economic impacts of these two sets of risks have been aptly summarized by the Global Commission on the Environment and Climate as follows:

"These two sets of risks have direct economic impacts, including on economic growth, increased levels of uncertainty regarding the medium to long-term macro-economic outlook, increased public and private sector financing needs, structural changes to the economy, and the distribution of wealth and income. While physical risks reduce the productivity of all types of capital (human, physical, natural, social...) and thus impact economic growth, the impact of transition risks on economic growth is less clear cut. On the one hand, adaptation and mitigation measures create significant financing needs that may crowd-out public and private investment, but on the other, could also provide new growth impulses towards a green economy". (The New Climate Economy, 2018, as quoted in Feyen *et al.*, 2019).

Some authors have suggested that over-reach in using subsidies and regulations can lead to lower economic growth, unsustainable fiscal load, and disruption in financial markets (USA, 2022c; and USA, 2022d). Because of interdependence, disruption in one area can result in a serious negative impact not just on the specific area in question but on the balance sheets of all sectors — public, financial, corporate, and households. As has already been observed, weaknesses in the balance sheets of businesses reduce their willingness and ability to adopt needed transition strategies for mitigation and adaptation. All these factors erode investor confidence and have a profound negative medium- to long-term impact on capital investment and the financial flows that are needed for vibrant business growth and productivity (Hallegatte *et al.*, 2012).

Figure 17.4 summarizes resource risks and related macro-economic linkages.

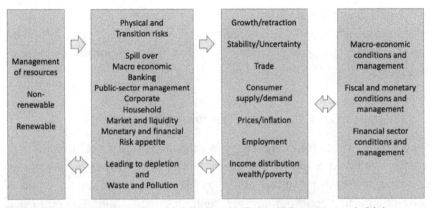

Figure 17.4. Physical and Transition Risks with Related Macro-economic Linkages
Source: Adapted from Feyen *et al.* (2019).

Although climate change and its associated impact on overall global warming is the most prominent among today's discussion about sustainability, it is useful to remember that the use of fossil fuels is merely one example of the complex interaction between the management of a non-renewable natural resource and macro-economic stability. A similar approach can be applied to any of the non-renewable natural resources (e.g. land, water, air, minerals, etc.) as well as to renewable resources (e.g. animals, birds, fish, forests, agriculture, other plants, and alternative energy like wind, solar, waves, etc.)

During the COVID-19 lockdown in 2020/21 and the war in Ukraine in 2022/23, there was good evidence of how asset values, higher production costs associated with supply chain problems, and labor shortages created a toxic economic environment, especially when combined with sharp increases in energy prices. These events had a significant destabilizing macro-economic impact globally. Yet, both the threat of a pandemic and the vulnerability of oil and gas supplies to political factors had been warned about and repeatedly ignored by policymakers. In the case of a pandemic, the US had developed Federal Interagency Operational Plans (January 2017) and a Pandemic Crisis Action Plan Version 2 (January 2018). Neither, however, was operationalized. From its inception, the construction of the Nord Stream 2 gas pipeline between Russia and Germany triggered controversy about the vulnerability of European oil and gas dependency on Russia. These are examples of transition risks which were anticipated but ignored. Others were simply not identified in time to take corrective measures before serious macro-economic repercussions.

B. Mitigation and Its Macro-economic Implications

As noted above, mitigation as used in this chapter refers to policies and actions that avoid or reduce the risk of shortages developing in any of the resources and limiting spill-over effects like waste, pollution (soil, water, and air), and other undesirable effects such as climate change. Governments can use a range of public sector instruments (regulatory and financial) to redirect the focus of the private sector and markets toward activities that policymakers think would lead to a more sustainable use of such resources.

An often-overlooked aspect of mitigation, however, is the costs and benefits of the measures used to mitigate the depletion of a specific non-renewable resource or improve the sustainability of a renewable resource. For example, the shift to renewable energy sources like solar panels and wind turbines have significant implications for the depletion of the materials that are used for the solar panels and the resulting polluting by-products. Many lower- and middle-income countries are graveyards for broken solar panels, batteries, and other pollutants that are not recycled.

C. Adaptation and Its Macro-economic implications

Although many recognize that mitigation is not enough, very little serious attention or financial resources are devoted to adaptation, such as disaster preparedness and restructuring coast-lines, or developing alternative technologies, improved waste management, sewage water treatment, etc.

Yet, all countries that depend on non-renewable and renewable resources will one day — sooner or later — face a depletion of their non-renewable resources and difficulties renewing in a timely fashion those that can be replenished. Adaptation as used in this chapter refers to the process of adjusting to and preparing the economy and society to deal with past, existing, and future shortages of resources and addressing the resulting waste, pollution, and other undesirable effects from their use, such as climate change. It is not a question of "if" but "when".

With population growth and industrialization, demand simply outstrips supply of potable water in the foreseeable future. A mitigation strategy would be not to use potable water for agricultural and industrial needs. An adaptation strategy would be to increase capacity for wastewater treatment and desalination. Ignoring such inevitability creates significant macro-economic risks.

IV. Linkages between Macro-economic Risks and Sustainability

At least nine areas of interaction have been identified between macroeconomic factors and the sustainable use of both non-renewable and renewable resources. Associated physical and transition risks for each of these nine areas are summarized in Table 17.1.

A detailed discussion of each of these linkages is beyond the scope of this chapter. But a few key points are worth highlighting to demonstrate the macro-economic implications of some illustrative mitigation and adaptation strategies. They include economic linkages, fiscal linkages, monetary linkages, financial sector linkages, banking sector linkages, institutional investor linkages, and insurance sector linkages.

Economic Linkages. There is large uncertainty and disagreement on the economic costs of mitigating policies for dealing more effectively with non-renewable and renewable natural resources. In most cases, the data and economic tools needed to estimate the economic cost of poor resource management vs the cost of mitigation measures on GDP are simply not available. In general, however, there is probably a gross underestimation of the impact on economic growth, discount levels, productivity, employment, distributional impacts, migration, conflicts, and damage from both the unsustainable use of the resource in question and mitigating policies designed to address the problem. The focus on aggregate GDP losses fails to consider important distributional aspects as global estimates do not capture well what happens in low- and middle-income countries where most of the world's population and the poor live. Another shortcoming is

Table 17.1.   Linkages between Macro-economic Risks and Sustainability

---

Spill-over risks (from the external environment outside the specific sector, country, or region)

Description
- Exposure to external shocks through trade and financial channels
- Exchange rate market pressures
- Buffers against external shocks (i.e. level of international reserves)

Physical risks
- Global commodity prices related to any of the non-renewable and renewable resources
- Cross-border trade

Transition risks
- Global commodity prices of any of the non-renewable and renewable resources
- Availability of capital flows for any of the non-renewable and renewable resources

Macro-economic risks

Description
- Macro-economic risk and sovereign credit performance
- Macro-economic outlook
- Market perception of sovereign risk

Physical risks
- Productivity and economic growth outlook, due to impacts on health and labor productivity, population displacement, and destruction of infrastructure and assets
- Inflation dynamics due to shortages of any of the non-renewable and renewable resources
- Productivity and economic growth outlook for any of the non-renewable and renewable resources

Transition risks
- Inflation dynamics due to shortages of any of the non-renewable and renewable resources
- Sovereign creditworthiness of the non-renewable and renewable resources

Banking risks

Description
- Banks' exposure to the corporate, household, and public sectors
- Bank risk indicators (leverage, asset quality, currency, and maturity mismatches)
- Banks' buffers against shocks

Physical risks
- Damages to financial infrastructure
- Collateral damages
- Loan defaults

Table 17.1.   *(Continued)*

Transition risks
- Valuation of exposed non-renewable and renewable resource assets
- Demand for sector specific equity investment or loans

Public sector risks

Description
- Public debt level
- Fiscal position

Physical risks
- Acute financing needs and debt sustainability issues

Transition risks
- Expenditure related to climate adaptation and mitigation policies
- Revenue potential from carbon taxes

Corporate sector risks

Description
- Corporate debt level
- Maturity mismatch
- Profitability and stock market returns

Physical risks
- Collateral damages
- Lower demand

Transition risks
- Viability of exposed non-renewable and renewable resource business models and assets
- Transition costs

Household risks

Description
- Household debt
- Unemployment
- Property price growth
- Stock market returns

Physical risks
- Employment
- Damages of household assets

Transition risks
- Impact on labor productivity and employment associated with structural shifts toward a low-carbon economy

(Continued)

Table 17.1.   (*Continued*)

Market and liquidity risks

Description
• Market and bank funding and liquidity conditions

Physical risks
• Re-pricing of financial assets
• Financial market volatility

Transition risks
• Sudden re-evaluation of resource-intensive assets and industries

Monetary and financial risks

Description
• Monetary policy stance
• Availability of bank credit

Physical risks
• Acute need for monetary stimulus
• Ability of banks to lend counter-cyclically

Transition risks
• Finance demands from core non-renewable or renewable resource sectors
• Increased economic volatility and uncertainty regarding banks' balance sheets exposure to non-renewable or renewable resource assets

Risk appetite

Description
• Market prices of sovereign bonds and equities
• Volatility of market prices
• Portfolio and Foreign Direct Investment (FDI) flows

Physical risks
• Investor risk aversion

Transition risks
• Risk aversion toward non-renewable or renewable resource assets and industries
• Higher demand for non-renewable or renewable resource assets

Source: Adapted from Feyen *et al.* (2019).

that such estimates typically do not include money, finance, and banking. Yet, understanding the financial sector is crucial for understanding economic cycles.

Fiscal Linkages. As seen in the previous chapter on fiscal implications, the physical impacts of climate change generate significant revenue and expenditure pressures. Similar risks to the public balance sheets exist in relation to all the non-renewable and renewable resources. For example, physical risks have a direct impact on fiscal revenue by hurting the revenue base, on public expenditure for outlays on disaster relief and reconstruction, and on the net-income of state-owned enterprises (SOEs) if their activities are impacted by severe resource shortages or surpluses. Changes in relative prices and availability of resources can be expected to have a large impact on a country's growth trajectory, and subsequently on the country's debt sustainability, borrowing space, and borrowing costs.

Monetary linkages. Non-renewable and renewable resource challenges (shortages and surpluses) create additional challenges for a country's monetary policy because they add significant volatility and uncertainty to the economic outlook. Mitigating policies can create temporary and permanent supply-side shocks to the economy, affecting both output and prices. Monetary policy instruments that may be used to address these issues include credit spreads, precautionary savings, and real interest rates manipulation. All this causes financial instability, which in turn may cause inflation, which may have been the original target of the monetary policy. Dealing with the gas and oil crisis during the war in Ukraine is a very good example of this challenge.

Financial sector linkages. Disruption in resource availability, whether from production to trade to distribution to sale, is now well recognized as a major source of risk to the financial sector. For example, over 50 central banks and supervisory agencies have come together to form the Network for the Greening of the Financial System (NGFS) aiming to manage climate change risks and support the transition to a low-carbon economy (NGFS Website). However, similar collaborative action by banks and supervisory agencies has not happened to address other natural resource constraints (non-renewable or renewable). There are deep uncertainties and data gaps regarding the impact and timing of both physical risks and transition risks on the financial sector, as well as their interactions with the broader economy. Resource-related risks are often grossly underpriced because they are beyond investor horizons, or are not adequately measured and disclosed. As a result, both social and environmental externalities are often grossly underestimated with the real cost of paying for the future externalities being hidden from investors and beneficiaries like pensioners.

Banking sector linkages. The physical impacts of resource shortages can lead to increased operational, credit, market, and liquidity risks for banks. The limited empirical literature provides some evidence for the materiality of the impact of physical risks on banks. Trade barriers and supply chain problems, as seen in 2022, can trigger losses due to higher defaults and lower collateral valuations — particularly if uninsured. Liquidity could also tighten, due to lower savings and higher withdrawals, as demand for cash surges. Supply shocks can also damage payment systems and bank branches. Banks are facing risks from loan and investment exposures to natural resource intensive sectors. Providing finance for shunned industries and assets also exposes banks to reputational risks, in the face of changing public opinion.

Institutional investor linkages. Institutional investors — such as pension funds and life insurance companies — will be disproportionately affected by natural resource disruptions given their much longer-term investment horizons. In addition, investment strategies of institutional investors in natural resources must be designed to manage long-term risks. These risks are often not transparently reported to either investors or beneficiaries of large funds such as pension funds. Without transparency in costing medium to long-term contingent liabilities, it is impossible for institutional investors and beneficiaries like pensioners to assess risk to both private funds and sovereign funds from mispricing and effective management of risks.

Insurance sector linkages. Non-renewable and renewable resource challenges also have implications for insurance companies on both sides of the balance sheet: as investors and as underwriters. As investors, insurance companies face largely similar physical and transition risks as other asset managers. In line with institutional investors, insurers may also be disproportionally affected due to the long-term nature of their equity and infrastructure investments. As underwriters, pricing risks may arise from changing risk profiles to insured assets. For example, climate-change trends may affect the size of segments in the insurance market (e.g. some risks may become hard to insure) but may also offer opportunities for innovative insurance offerings. Moreover, sudden supply shocks in a natural resource may increase the complexity of catastrophe models, making it harder to make valid predictions about expected and unexpected losses and increasing the uncertainty in estimates. Finally, insurance companies may be affected by increased liability risks due to negligent policies. Changing risk profiles of insured assets and property, as well as changing mortality and demographics, can lead to distress or failure of insurance companies.

V. Hidden Threats to Macro-Economic Performance

As seen in this chapter, the transition from the unsustainable use of non-renewable and renewable resources to a more sustainable consumption and disposal of these products has serious macro-economic sector implications that go far beyond the specific resource in question. It impacts every aspect of the economy and welfare of people living in a country, including national wealth (gross domestic product/output (GDP/GNP), economic growth, inflation/stagnation/deflation, consumer spending, borrowing, employment/unemployment, monetary policy, fiscal policy, and the financial sector.

This section of the chapter provides a few cautionary remarks about some of the pitfalls for policy makers, businesses, and investors arising from overambitious, poorly designed, and badly executed industrial policies applied to sustainability (see the Afterword for a detailed discussion on the history and pitfalls of industrial policy (Carnegie, 2016)).

The ensuing section considers the following topics:

- lack of realism
- mission creep in corporate governance
- single-issue capture
- hidden political agendas
- greenwashing
- whitewashing
- loss of competitiveness

A. Lack of Realism

Realistic targets need to be set that allow adequate time for organic growth in mitigation and adaptation strategies. This cannot happen under artificial regulatory frameworks, threats of sanctions, and unsustainable financial carrots and sticks. From years of experience in the development area, it may be seen that most high-level development targets are not implementable during the proposed time framework. Two notable high-level initiatives that set ambitious but unrealistic targets are the *WHO Health for all by the year 2000* and the *UN Millennium Development Goals (MDGs) 2015*. The *UN Sustainable Development Goals (SDGs) 2030* and *Net Zero 2050* are at high risk of falling into the same trap of setting laudable but unrealistic targets.

The UN itself admits that although progress has been made, in general, action to meet the SDGs falls far short in both the speed and scale required to meet the ambitious targets set for the Goals by 2030. In the preamble to *The Sustainable Development Goals Report 2022*, António Guterres, Secretary-General of the United Nations, warned "We must rise higher to rescue the Sustainable Development Goals — and stay true to our promise of a world of peace, dignity and prosperity on a healthy planet" (UN, 2022a).

Avoiding this trap is particularly important because missing targets causes serious damage to the credibility of and commitment to a movement. Less ambitious but achievable goals are much more likely to sustain such credibility and commitment.

B. Mission Creep in Corporate Governance

Corporate governance refers to the set of resolutions, policies, rules, practices, processes, and controls by which large firms are directed and controlled (Chen, 2022b). The basic principles of corporate governance include accountability, transparency, fairness, responsibility, and risk management. Historically, corporate governance has focused on balancing the interests of a company's many stakeholders, such as shareholders, senior executives, customers, suppliers, and financiers, and ensuring compliance with government regulations and tax laws. Different countries have approached this in various ways, with three dominant models: the Anglo-American Model, the Continental Model, and the Japanese Model.

The Shareholder Model, the principal Anglo-American model, gives the board of directors and shareholders maximum control in running a company in a transparent way that maximizes shareholder interests while minimizing the risk to shareholder value (usually measured in return on investment). The focus is on fiduciary responsibility and meeting share-holders' expectations for return on investment. Supporters contend this model is the best strategy for corporate governance because maximizing economic returns will ensure the survival of the company.

Motivated originally by decades-old social movements and environ-mental concerns, the original UN Millennium Development Goals (MDGs) expanded over time into the UN Sustainable Development Goals, which have a much broader scope. The sustainability movement has fallen into a similar trap of mission creep which promotes an ever-expanding range of international goals. Started as an effort to secure a more sustainable use of non-renewable and renewable resources, under the E (environment) component of ESG, mission creep led to a broaden-ing of this agenda to include the S (social) and G (governance) compo-nents of ESG.

Under the ESG sustainability movement, new rules have been added to corporate governance which stretch far beyond financial optimization. They call for more attention to human capital, the gender pay-gap, gen-der diversity, and a wide range of other progressive social and gover-nance issues that go far beyond the traditional role of companies in maximizing shareholder interest and accountability (in terms of returns on investment). The result is effectively to require a "double bottom line", measuring not just financial performance (the conventional bottom line) but also performance in meeting certain social criteria (the second bottom line). This concept has been expanded recently to a "triple bot-tom line", which includes a measure for cost-benefit analysis and life-cycle cost analysis.

Increasingly, for example, some asset managers are voting against investing in companies whose boards do not meet gender, diversity, or some other progressive criteria, even when those companies provide high monetary returns on investments.

C. Single-Issue Capture

Single-issue capture is the flip side of mission creep. While, on the one hand, the current trends in the field of sustainability have been to ever broaden the sustainable development goals to include almost every sector of the economy, on the other hand, there is an unbalanced focus on social advocacy, political action, and reducing funding aimed at the fossil fuels industry and achieving date-specific emission targets (e.g. carbon neutral energy emissions by 2050).

Given the limited bandwidth of many governments, "single-issue capture" runs the risk of starving other areas of attention and funding. As an example, global warming and the fossil industry dominated the UN General Assembly meeting on the SDGs in 2021; the 26th Conference of the Parties (COP26) to the United Nations Convention on Climate Change in Glasgow in 2021; and the COP27 meeting in Sharm El-Sheikh, Egypt in 2022. They are also anticipated to dominate the COP28 meeting in Dubai in 2023.

As mentioned earlier, other key aspects of sustainability, such as pollution prevention and reduction, or concerns for biodiversity, are mostly crowded-out of the agenda. The Lancet Commission on Pollution and Health noted that many countries, especially high-income and some upper-middle-income countries have developed robust, cost-effective, and politically viable pollution-control strategies based on law, policy, science, and technology. The Commission expressed the view that pollution-control strategies that have proven to be successful are ready to be "taken off-the-shelf, brought to global scale, and applied in cities and countries at every level of income" (Landrigan *et al.*, 2017).

Likewise, at the recent 15th Conference of the Parties (COP15) to the United Nations Convention on Biological Diversity (CBD) in Montreal (December 7–19, 2022), it was noted that "despite on-going efforts, biodiversity is deteriorating worldwide, and this decline is projected to worsen with business-as-usual scenarios" (UN, 2022b). This agenda is not only about saving the natural habitat of plants and animals. A significant amount of carbon dioxide from a wider range of sources is absorbed by natural ecosystems. Critics note that "lofty promises" about diversity have been "made and broken" many times. They claim that many of the "so-called carbon-offset schemes that involve firms paying money to, say plant a forest, are dubious and opaque — and belong to the realm of con-artists and scams rather than science" (*Economist*, 2022).

Yet, the recent failed $2.2 trillion "Build Back Better Act" proposal by the 117th US Congress, the $1.2 trillion Infrastructure Investment and Jobs Act (H.R.3684, 2017), and the $737 billion Inflation Reduction Act of 2022 focused mostly on fossil fuels and climate change. Issues such as pollution and biodiversity were given scant attention and few resources compared to the alternate energy agenda. Similar trends are observed in other OECD countries and developing countries. Likewise, the foreign aid budgets of the European Commission, the US Agency for International Development, and other bilateral development agencies neglect non-fossil fuel-related pollution. No major foundation has made pollution prevention its priority even though the macro-economic sector impact has been shown to be major (Landrigan *et al.*, 2018). The story about weak action to support biodiversity is similar.

D. Hidden Political Agendas

The focus on ESG (Environmental, Social, and Governance) has gained a lot of momentum recently among asset managers and other financial institutions because it has been shown to be lucrative to these money managers. It is easy for them to re-brand something as ESG-friendly or "compliant" and then charge higher fees for products like index funds. This has grown in tandem with progressive social movements and progressive investing movements, which believe that worker pension funds, foundation endowments, etc. should serve social or environmental objectives without legislative approval or approval from workers or pensioners that are investing in such funds.

Getting a specific issue onto a company's Board Agenda is in many cases difficult if not impossible. In recent years, ESG activists have successfully pressured boards to adopt environmental and social issues that normally they would not focus on by collecting proxy ballots to cast votes that support their agenda ahead of annual meetings. According to Bloomberg (Dwyer and Gillen, 2022a), in the first half of 2022 alone, 272 such measures made it onto proxy ballots compared with 158 during all of 2021. This is one of many ways that controversial progressive social advocacy issues, that may not be directly related to a company's core business interests, have suddenly become an important agenda item during annual meetings of some larger corporations. Most shareholders are not aware of this process or issues that may impact on the bottom line of their investments.

As of 2022, broadly described ESG investing accounted for $17 trillion of investments and is growing rapidly. This is much larger than the Exchange-Traded Funds (ETFs) labeled as ESG-focused. This means that mutual funds, pension funds, and all manner of investment vehicles that involve almost all gainfully employed citizens are affected by ESG ratings (Shay, 2021). Two firms are doing the bulk of the screening for ESG: MSCI and Morningstar. MSCI Inc. (formerly Morgan Stanley Capital International and MSCI Barra) is an American finance company headquartered in New York City which serves as a global provider of equity, fixed income, hedge fund stock market indexes, multi-asset portfolio analysis tools, and ESG products. Morningstar Sustainalytics is a leading independent ESG and corporate governance research, ratings, and analytics firm that supports investors around the world with the development and implementation of responsible investment strategies.

The power of these two companies to direct where this huge sum of money goes is massive. Being flagged as non-ESG compliant means that the $17 trillion investment pool will exclude a particular firm, which amounts to a *de facto* boycott. Such decisions are taken behind closed doors and there is no due process for challenging the decisions. As people are becoming more aware of the various ESG criteria and the coercive techniques used to enforce business and investor compliance, there is a growing backlash against what is perceived to be a 21st century Orwellian parody, with "big brother" watching every aspect of peoples' lives and day-to-day business behavior of companies. Some see this as heavy-handed intrusions by government regulators, large investment firms and social media activists (Orwell, 1949).

Laurence D. Fink, the CEO of BlackRock, the world's largest asset manager and a leader in sustainable investing, has urged corporate leaders to embrace the ESGs, not only the environmental concerns (E), but also a range of social issues (S) such as diversity and significant changes in corporate governance (G). But many others disagree. "Right-wing officials are attacking BlackRock for overstepping. Those on the left say the world's biggest asset manager is not doing enough" (Goldstein and Farrell, 2022). Millions of Americans rely on life-time savings for support during their retirement. It has been estimated that it takes $1 million to generate around 40,000 in retirement income. Retirees are demanding full transparency in how their life savings are being managed. They do not appreciate decisions being taken without their consent by asset managers or corporate boards that have been hijacked by social activists who did not toil for years to build up life-time savings (WSJ, 2022). Now groups like Bluebell Capital Partners, a $250 million hedge fund, and others are demanding Fink step down. They do not consider "Blackrock Investment Stewardship ... to be in the best interest of our clients" (NYT, 2022, December 7). On the other hand, at the same time progressive left-wing groups are calling the ESGs a whitewash and "sham" (Taparia, 2022).

Others are joining in this backlash. State Legislatures, Attorney Generals, and Treasurers in some states are now beginning to look at the legality of using pension funds and more broadly other taxpayer dollars to promote these environmental, social, and corporate governance objectives that have not been formally approved by legislatures and are seen to have little to do with the mandate of the funds to ensure maximum economic benefits to their shareholders.

In August 2022, Arizona Treasurer Kimberly Yee, for example, issued an update to her office's investment policy statement, prohibiting the consideration of non-pecuniary factors, including ESG ratings, to guide state treasury investment decisions (Arizona State Treasurer's Office, 2022).

On September 1, 2021, the Texas Legislature passed "Act (S.B. No. 13) relating to state contracts with and investments in certain companies" which prevents Texas from investing in environmental, social, and governance (ESG) financial products that boycott specific Texas companies (Texas, 2021). Following months of study, on August 31, 2022, the spokesman for Texas Comptroller Glenn Hegar said that "Elected and appointed public officials have a duty to act in the best interests of the people they serve ... Politicizing state pension funds, restricting access to investments, and impacting the financial returns of retirees is not consistent with that duty." The counterargument adduced in support of ESG investing is that ESG compliant companies *are* competitive and produce the same rate-of-return as non-ESG-compliant companies.

As a result of the Texas legislation, several financial firms whose investment guidelines support the ESGs have been prohibited from doing business with the State of Texas. The companies include: BNP Paribas SA, a French international banking group; Swiss-based Credit Suisse Group AG and UBS Group AG; Danske Bank A/S, a Danish multinational banking and financial services corporation; London-based Jupiter Fund Management PLC, a fund management group; Nordea Bank ABP, a European financial services group based in Finland; Schroders PLC, a British multinational asset management company; and Swedish banks Svenska Handelsbanken AB and Swedbank AB. The funds within larger companies aimed at sustainable investing, such as Goldman Sachs's "Paris-aligned Climate US Large Cap Equity ETF" and JP Morgan's "US Sustainable Leaders Fund", may also be targeted by such exclusions in the future.

Texas Act (S.B. No. 13) contends that there could be serious damage to macro-economic objectives, fiscal balance, and financial sector confidence if social agendas were forced onto commercial entities through the "back door" without transparent public discourse and legislative approval. Critics, however, have argued that millions of dollars would be lost in additional borrowing costs if the range of financial institutions that would be available to cities and municipalities were restricted by the legislation (Garrett and Ivanov, 2022). This is an ongoing dispute.

To avoid further erosion in trust, to improve transparency, and to protect investors, shareholders, pensioners, and other beneficiaries in the capital markets, there are now proposals to transfer the responsibility of the corporate rating agencies to the Securities and Exchange Commission. This is to address the concern that many of the larger funds trade in public equities and may be violating securities regulations by adding criteria that are not based on methods that are formally accepted as part of stock valuations. Critics, however, warn that this could cause additional problems by transforming the SEC into the "Securities and Environment Commission" (Peirce, 2022).

E. Greenwashing

The field of sustainability has progressed from being a "cottage industry" to being "big business" with massive international conglomerates. Not surprisingly, when there is big money on the table, corruption and abuse quickly emerge.

"Greenwashing", also known as "green sheen", is a play on the term "whitewashing" (Coen *et al.*, 2022; Quinson, 2023). It is part of process of providing misleading information or conveying a false impression about how a company, product, or business practice is being environmentally friendly. In essence, it is an unsubstantiated claim to deceive consumers, businesses, government and investor ESG oversight bodies into believing that an individual or a company is compliant with regulations or guidelines on the sustainable use of non-renewable and renewable resources. It is a form of "scamming" in the sustainability domain that has many benefits for the scammer and risks for the scammed. Even large, committed firms like Blackrock have been under attack for what critics call a "sham" (Taparia, 2022).

Some examples of Greenwashing include the following:

- The hotel industry has devised one of the most blatant examples of greenwashing by placing notices in hotel rooms asking guests to reuse their towels to save the environment. In reality, the real motive is to lower laundry costs.
- When a package with a plastic object is labeled "recyclable", it is not clear whether the package or the object is recyclable. In either case, the label is deceptive if any part of the package or its contents, other than minor components, cannot be recycled.
- An item is labeled "50% more recycled content than before" although the manufacturer only increased the recycled content from 2% to 3%. Once again, the message conveys the false impression that a rug, for example, contains a significant amount of recycled fiber.
- A trash bag is labeled "recyclable" even though such bags are unlikely to be separated from other trash at the landfill or incinerator. Once again, the claim is deceptive because it gives the false impression of an environmental benefit whereas in reality no such benefit exists.

- Energy companies that are among the world's biggest carbon emitters, have recently attempted to greenwash themselves as champions of the environment, by renaming, rebranding, and/or repackaging themselves.

The rewards for engaging in such greenwashing practices are enormous and the punishments for not doing so are harsh. On the one hand, in almost every sector today there are large sums of money at stake for companies and investors as well as large fines for violators of regulations. Moreover, companies can be shamed and driven into bankruptcy through social media and other channels of consumer pressure if they do not tout such symbolic compliance. On the other hand, companies that are successful in creating an environmentally friendly "image" through supposed more natural, healthier, free of chemicals, recyclable, or less wasteful use of non-renewable and renewable resources get an informal "stamp of approval" by social media outlets. In short, scammers gain access to the carrots while avoiding the sticks.

Lack of compliance carries enormous consequences for companies that do not "play the game". Conversely, those companies that seriously try to comply with sustainability guidelines, have higher production costs. This affects their profitability compared with companies that "game the system".

It is easy to see how businesses that are built on a false basis of "greenwashing" are distorting in terms of trade, access to capital, prices, volatility, etc., especially in the corporate, banking, and finance sectors.

F. Whitewashing

Almost 80% of African Americans live in heavily polluted communities, which include landfills, hazardous waste sites, and other industrial facilities, industrial ground pollution, water pollution, and air pollution. But such issues are often swept off the agenda in efforts to pursue more elitist complex climate goals. Craig Bennett, CEO of Friends of the Earth, has called the environmental movement a "white, middle-class ghetto" (Bowden, 2015). While the ESG and Corporate Social Responsibility (CSR) movements are pressing for diversity goals in investing, the leadership and staffing of many of the environmental organizations, agencies, and foundations are less diverse than companies in the private sector.

For example, people of color comprise 36 percent of the US general population and 29 percent of the workforce in science and engineering. Yet, in one recent report on diversity in the environmental movement, they do not exceed 16 percent of the staff of the organizations surveyed. Although for decades environmental organizations have stressed the value of diversity, the diversity composition has not broken the 16 percent "green ceiling". The failure of environmental organizations and agencies to recruit and retain people of color comes at a high cost because they are the group that are most exposed to many of the pollution-related environmental hazards that have largely dropped off the policy map today. In one survey, none of the largest budget environmental organizations had a president, vice president, or assistant/associate director who was a person of color (Green 2.0, 2020).

G. Loss of Competitiveness

During policy reforms, governments often use a combination of carrots (grants, loans, debt relief, tax incentives, etc.) and sticks (fines, taxes, etc.) to incentivize and enforce compliance with their official industrial policy goals. In essence, "industrial policy" or "industrial strategy" is any intervention by governments that encourages the growth or strengthening of the economy in general or that causes a shift from one industry to another, by deliberate interventions that affect supply, demand, price equilibrium, or the competitive environment of the industries in question (see *Afterword* in this book for a more detailed discussion about the pitfalls of industrial policy).

A recent OECD review shows that aggressive policies in the renewable energy area can have a negative impact on competitiveness and lead to "statistically significant adverse effects on trade, employment, plant location and productivity in the short run, particularly in pollution- and energy-intensive sectors" (Dechezleprêtre and Sato, 2017, 2018). See Table 17.2 for links between competition, macro-economic performance, and sustainability.

Table 17.2. Effects of Competition on Macro-economic Performance and Sustainability

First-order effect	Second-order effect	Third Order Effect			
Cost impacts	Firm response	Economic outcomes	Technology outcomes	International outcomes	Environmental outcomes
Changes in relative costs	Production volume	Profitability	Product innovation	Trade flows	Pollution level and intensity
	Product prices	Employment	Process innovation	Investment location	Pollution liability
	Product investment	Market share	Input saving technology	Foreign direct investment	
	Investment in abatement		Total factor productivity		

Source: Dechezleprêtre and Sato (2017).

There are several ways that the implementation of environmental policies can have an anticompetitive effect: (a) the formation of cartels that use their market power to extract uncompetitive prices from consumers and prevent other companies from competing in the market; (b) below-market pricing made possible by subsidies and ability to hide the true price of negative externalities; (c) market distortions created by subsidies, taxes, and the transaction costs of regulatory compliance; and (d) consumer ignorance.

Cartels. When businesses, unions, and governments collude in this way, under various forms of "public–private partnerships", it often leads to private cartels that can be damaging to consumers both in terms of availability of supply and prices. "Only the coercive powers of the state can guarantee the survival of a privately organized cartel" (DiLorenzo, 1990). Initially, consumers may benefit from subsidized lower prices. But eventually, if those subsidies become a structural part of the public budget and/ or the cartel abuses its market power, customers end up paying the price through taxes and uncompetitive prices.

There are multiple recent examples that cartel behavior is real and a threat to well-functioning competitive markets. Solar panel makers supported by the Chinese government are one of many examples of a massive cartel. They have in the past faced anti-trust lawsuits (Dobrik, 2013). The Hungarian Government recently fined several solar panel firms for cartel behavior (Hungary, 2022). The windmill industry and other areas of the renewable energy industry are equally plagued by cartels and anti-trust lawsuits (Vinson & Elkins, 2022). The emergence of such cartels in the green energy space is probably inevitable, especially in industries that have a quasi-monopoly like those that provide rare minerals like lithium (Rapier, 2022).

Externalities. The oil, gas, and coal industries have long been accused of not pricing externalities (costs not fully reflected in the price of the goods or services themselves), such as waste, pollution, and recycling costs. The same is true for most green industries like wind turbines, windfarms, solar panels, and wave energy generation. These products have large and costly externalities themselves, including the costs of their hidden social (S) and governance (G) aspects that are buried and hidden from consumers and investors through subsidies, tax credits, and access to discounted capital.

For example, copper is essential for solar power and windfarms promoted to partially replace fossil fuels with clean energy needed for electricity in transport, industry, and residential and commercial buildings. Bloomberg estimates that global demand for copper will rise by 50 percent by 2040. Chile is the biggest producer of copper with 27 percent of worldwide production. It is also a major producer of lithium needed to produce the batteries used in electric vehicles as well as consumer electronics. Although the new draft constitution put forward in 2022 was touted to be "a model of environmental reform" by having a lot of references to "protecting the planet", it would have made it riskier and harder to develop new projects needed for the "green economy" and would have done little in practical terms to deal with the cost of environmental impact of the pollution created by the extractive industry.

By weakening many mining rights, such as property rights to water, the mining industry would be forced to shift to desalination plants of their own. This would add significantly to the production costs of the extractive industry which have not been transparently costed. These additional production costs would have a significant impact on Chile's competitiveness in the global copper and lithium industries which would affect its exports of raw materials, one of the main pillars of the economy (Jobet, 2022). And the desalination process itself has serious ecological effects because the salt from the process is returned to the sea, thereby changing the seawater salt concentration around the desalination plants.

Market Distortions. All stimulus through incentives or suppression through disincentives are distorting and time limited. They prevent the businesses from becoming truly competitive and foster business models that are not fully sustainable without this external support. There is extensive evidence from the field of development aid that programs that are set up with or depend on such government support crowd out other initiatives and are usually not sustainable in the medium term. This affects the real pricing and competitiveness of many of the mitigation and adaptation activities that are part of the "green economy" and has major macroeconomic sector implications.

The current heavy reliance on industrial policy to achieve a restructuring of industries involved in many areas of sustainability, like the energy sector or other areas of renewable and non-renewable resources, is likely to fail in the medium to long term, unless underpinned by viable and competitive markets. A critical part of transforming the economy to more sustainable use of non-renewable and renewable resources will depend on the success of businesses to generate real income from sales in an open and competitive marketplace. They cannot depend indefinitely on market-distorting government subsidies, and a favorable regulatory framework.

Consumer Ignorance. According to Bloomberg Intelligence and Morningstar Inc., over the past 10 years, $2.5 trillion dollars have been allocated to sustainable investment funds. Many of these funds are now part of a new class of Exchange-Traded Funds (ETFs) that focus on the ESGs and the environment. In 2022, only 3 percent of the 166 US-listed ESG stock funds had a positive rate of return compared with 9 percent for overall exchange-traded stock funds (Dwyer and Gillen, 2022b). ESG stock funds and ETFs are only a small part of the $17 trillion of investments in sectors that have an environmental impact. This means that the managers of mutual funds, pension funds, and a range of other investment vehicles are taking decisions on behalf of those whose funds they manage.

Consumers and investors alike are at risk of being fooled by false promises (Dwyer and Gillen, 2022c). There is recent evidence that the non-competitive decisions related to ESG investing have over the medium-term hurt returns on investment for shareholders, or at best had no impact at all on returns. Some recent studies also seem to indicate that many broad based ESG investments are failing to achieve their promised environmental, social and governance impact. And divestiture from fossil fuel companies does not seem to have a significant impact on that industry in the short to medium-term. (Keeley, 2022). The scope for poor macro-economic performance and even malfeasance is enormous. There is a "squeeze on 'greenium' as ESG bond investors demand more value" (Stubbington, 2021).

"The ESG model — as an investment strategy and a driver of change — is still up for debate. Vanguard Group researchers found no significant difference in returns between ESG and non-ESG funds over a 15-year period. Companies in ESG funds had worse compliance on labor and environmental rules than companies in non-ESG funds, a study from researchers at the London School of Economics and Political Science and Columbia University concluded" (Au-Yeung, 2022).

A strong case can be made for improving the performance of competitive markets that address a range of sustainability issues without mission creep into social and political agendas. This means letting entrepreneurs and investors find focused and viable business solutions that are market-based and do not depend on distorting industrial policies, subsidies, and regulations. The latter add costs to doing business and investing that often outweigh their benefits. It means greater price transparency so that consumers, businesses, and investors can make informed choices. And it also means strengthening anti-trust legislation and enforcement to improve the competitive marketplace, while countering trends toward the formation of cartels and other threats to competition.

If the above threats — lack realism, mission creep in corporate governance, single-issue capture, hidden political agendas, greenwashing, whitewashing, and loss of competitiveness — are addressed effectively, "doing business" in this area could possibly provide an attractive commercial opportunity for businesses and investors, while at the same time it might advance the sustainability agenda and contribute to macroeconomic performance.

V. Conclusion

This chapter demonstrates strong links between the sustainable use of non-renewable and renewable resources, and macro-economic performance. The chapter describes relevant linkages that exist between mitigation and/or adaptation strategies and macro-economic performance in terms of gross domestic product (GDP), national wealth, economic growth, inflation, stagnation, deflation, consumer spending, borrowing, employment, unemployment, monetary policy, and fiscal policy. The chapter goes beyond the earlier discussion of factors that contribute to climate change and the narrow focus on the fossil fuel industry to include consideration of a broader range of non-renewable and renewable resources that are an integral part of a sustainable environment.

The review indicates that well-planned and well-executed sustainability policies and action plans can confer significant macro-economic benefits. At the same time, it reveals that overzealous and poorly executed mitigation strategies as well as failure to pursue adaptation in the meantime can damage industrial performance and lead to significant negative macro-economic outcomes in terms of slowing growth, damaging supply chains, contributing to inflation, increasing unemployment, and reducing sectoral competitiveness.

The chapter warns about the potentially damaging effect of expanding the environmental (E) sustainability agenda to the social (S) and governance (G) spheres. And it raises doubts about the use of industrial policy to achieve durable industrial transformation. The chapter also provides a cautionary reference to several hidden threats to macroeconomic performance from overambitious, poorly designed, and badly executed sustainability policies. These threats include pitfalls associated with lack of realism, mission creep in corporate governance, single-issue capture, hidden political agendas, greenwashing, whitewashing, and loss of competitiveness.

Businesses and financial institutions must be "financially sustainable" to survive. When corporate boards are captured by interests that do not safeguard their "bottom line", they can go bankrupt. When that happens to large businesses and large financial institutions, it can have a devastating impact not only on the business and financial institutions themselves but also on the overall economy, pensioners and working-class families who lose their jobs.

The chapter concludes that if these risks are addressed effectively, "doing business" in this area could provide an attractive commercial opportunity for businesses and investors, while at the same time it might advance the sustainability agenda and contribute to macro-economic performance. To achieve this objective, the chapter makes a strong case for improving the performance of competitive markets that address a range of sustainability issues without mission creep into social and political agendas. This means letting entrepreneurs and investors find focused and viable business solutions that are market-based and do not depend on distorting industrial policies, subsidies, and regulations. The latter add costs to doing business and investing that often outweigh their benefits. It means greater price transparency so that consumers, businesses, and investors can make informed choices. And it also means strengthening anti-trust legislation and enforcement to improve the competitive marketplace while countering trends toward the formation of cartels and other threats to competition.

References

Arizona State Treasurer's Office (Press Release). (August 30, 2022). "Arizona Treasurer Kimberly Yee announced newly adopted investment policy statement that protects taxpayer dollars from ESG policies", https://www.aztreasury.gov/_files/ugd/88330d_56370345dc9048e7ae16509d7058fb0a.pdf.

Au-Yeung, A. (November 12, 2022). *This Former BlackRock Executive says ESG Investment Model is Broken*, New York: Wall Street Journal, https://www.wsj.com/articles/this-former-blackrock-executive-says-esg-investment-model-is-broken-11668230290.

Bae, D. and Burton, T. (April 2020). "New evidence of the Heckman curve", *Journal of Economic Surveys*, 34(2), pp. 241–261, https://onlinelibrary.wiley.com/doi/abs/10.1111/joes.12353.

Banton, C. (2022) "What is a renewable resource?" https://www.investopedia.com/terms/r/renewable/resource.asp.

Bowden, T. (2015). "Green movement must escape its 'white middle-class ghetto' says friends of the earth chief Craig Bennett". *The Independent*, July, https://www.independent.co.uk/climate-change/news/green-movement-must-escape-its-white-middleclass-ghetto-says-friends-of-the-earth-chief-craig-bennett-10366564.html.

Boyle, M. J. (2022). "Financial sector", https://www.investopedia.com/terms/f/financial_sector.asp.

Bressler, R. D. (2023). "Chapter 2: Science and Challenges of Sustainability", in *Sustainability: Business and Investment Implications*, World Scientific Publishing, New Jersey/London/Singapore.

Carnegie. (2016). "Industrial policy: A guide for the perplexed", https://carnegieendowment.org/2016/02/01/industrial-policy-guide-for-perplexed-pub-62660.

Chen, J. (2022a). "Nonrenewable resources definition", https://www.investopedia.com/terms/n/nonrenewableresource.asp.

Chen, J. (2022b). "What is corporate governance", https://www.investopedia.com/terms/c/corporategovernance.asp.

Coen, D., Herman, K., and Pegram, T. (2022). "Are corporate climate efforts genuine? An empirical analysis of the climate 'talk–walk' hypothesis", *Business Strategy and the Environment*, https://onlinelibrary.wiley.com/doi/10.1002/bse.3063.

Deaux, J. and Teoldi, F. (November 7, 2022). "Elements of a Greener Economy", in *Shocks to the System*, Bloomberg Business Week, New York, NY.

Dechezleprêtre, A. and Sato, M. (2017). "The impacts of environmental regulations on competitiveness", *Review of Environmental Economics and Policy*, 11(2), pp. 173–195, https://www.journals.uchicago.edu/doi/full/10.1093/reep/rex013.

Dechezleprêtre, A. and Sato, M. (2018). *Issue Paper Green Policies and Firms' Competitiveness*, OECD, Paris, https://www.oecd.org/greengrowth/GGSD_2018_Competitiveness%20Issue%20Paper_WEB.pdf.

DiLorenzo, T. (1990), "The Genesis of Industrial Policy", *Foundation for Economic Education,* https://fee.org/articles/the-genesis-of-industrial-policy/.

Dobrik, A. (2013). "Chinese solar panel makers face US$950 million cartel lawsuit", *Global Competitive Review*, https://globalcompetitionreview.com/article/chinese-solar-panel-makers-face-us950-million-cartel-lawsuit.

Dwyer, P. and Gillen, D. (2022a). "The battle of the proxy ballots", *Bloomberg Businessweek*, September 5, Special Section Finance.

Dwyer, P. and Gillen, D. (2022b). "The ESG crown is slipping", *Bloomberg Businessweek*, September 5, Special Section Finance.

Dwyer, P. and Gillen, D. (2022c). "Targeting 'Woke' wall street", *Bloomberg Businessweek*, September 5, Special Section Finance.

Economist. (2022). "Climate change and biodiversity: The laws of nature", *Economist*, December.

Feyen, E., Utz, R., Huertas, I. Z., Bogdan, E., and Moon, J. (2019). "Macro-financial aspects of climate change", *Policy Research Working Paper 9109*, Washington DC, https://openknowledge.worldbank.org/handle/10986/33193.

Garrett, D. and Ivanov, I. (2022). "Gas, guns, and governments: Financial costs of anti-ESG", Elsevier SSRN Website, https://papers.ssrn.com/sol3/papers.cfm?abstract_id=4123366.

Garside, M. (2022). "Leading countries worldwide based on natural resource value as of 2021", https://www.statista.com/statistics/748223/leading-countries-based-on-natural-resource-value/.

Goldstein, M. and Farrell, M. (2022). "BlackRock's pitch for socially conscious investing antagonizes all sides", *New York Times*, December 23, https://www.nytimes.com/2022/12/23/business/blackrock-esg-investing.html?referringSource=articleShare.

Green 2.0. (2020). https://diversegreen.org/research/the-challenge/. Accessed August 29 2022.

Hassani, B.K. and Bahini, Y. (2022). "Relationships between ESG Disclosure and Economic Growth: A Critical Review". *J. Risk Financial Manag.* 15(11), 538, https://doi.org/10.3390/jrfm15110538.

Heckman's Curve. (2022). https://heckmanequation.org/resource/the-heckman-curve/. Last accessed August 29 2022.

Hallegatte, S., Shah, A., Lempert, R., Brown, C., and Gill, S. (September 2012). "Investment decision making under deep uncertainty — Application to climate change", *World Bank Policy Research Working Paper 6193*, https://openknowledge.worldbank.org/handle/10986/12028.

Hungary. (2022). "The GVH fines solar battery producers for cartel activity", *Hungary Competition Authority*, https://www.gvh.hu/en/press_room/press_releases/press_releases_2019/the_gvh_fines_solar_battery/producers/for/cartel/a.

IMF. (2020). *World Economic Outlook: A Long and Difficult Ascent*, IMF, Washington DC, Chapter 3, https://www.imf.org/en/Publications/WEO/Issues/2020/09/30/world-economic-outlook-october-2020.

Jobet, J. C. (2022). "Chile's draft constitution would stop the country becoming a green powerhouse, says Juan Carlos Jobet", *Economist*, Chile's Energy Minister 2019–2022 and Mining Minister, 2020–2022.

Keeley, T. (2022). *Sustainable: Moving Beyond ESG to Impact Investing*, Columbia Business School, New York.

Kharit, K. (2021). "Macro environment", https://www.investopedia.com/terms/m/macro-environment.asp.

Landrigan, P. J. and Goldman, L. R. (2011). Children's vulnerability to toxic chemicals: A challenge and opportunity to strengthen health and environmental policy, *Health Affairs (Millwood)*, 30(5), pp. 842–850, https://pubmed.ncbi.nlm.nih.gov/21543423/.

Landrigan, P. J., Fuller, R., Acosta, N. J. R., Adeyi, O., Arnold, R., Basu, N., *et al.* (February 3, 2017). "The lancet commission on pollution and health", *Lancet*, 391(10119), pp. 462–512, https://pubmed.ncbi.nlm.nih.gov/29056410/; https://www.thelancet.com/journals/lancet/article/PIIS0140-6736(17)32345-0/fulltext.

Landrigan, P. J., Fuller, R., Hu, H., Caravanos, J., Cropper, M. L., Hanrahan, D., Sandilya, K., Chiles, T. C., Kumar, P., and Suk, W. A. (2018). "Pollution and global health — An agenda for prevention", *Environmental Health Perspectives*, 126(8), https://ehp.niehs.nih.gov/doi/full/10.1289/EHP3141.

Lioudis, N. (2022). "Commodities trading: An overview", https://www.investopedia.com/investing/commodities-trading-overview/.

McMichael, A. J. (2017). *Climate Change and the Health of Nations: Famines, Fevers, and the Fate of Populations*, Oxford University Press, London.

MSCI. (2023). "Biodiversity: The new frontiers of sustainable finance", https://www.msci.com/our-solutions/climate-investing/biodiversity-sustainable-finance?creative=641174233586&keyword=biodiversity, https://www.msci.com/documents/1296102/35426413/MSCI+Biodiversity-crb-en.pdf.

NGFS Website. "Network for greening of the financial system", https://www.ngfs.net.

NYT. (2022). "An activist investor takes on BlackRock over ESG", *New York Times*, December 7, https://www.nytimes.com/2022/12/07/business/dealbook/blackrock-esg-activist-bluebell.html?referringSource=articleShare.

Orwell, G (1949). *Nineteen Eighty Four*, Secker & Warburg, London.

Peirce, H. M. (March 21, 2022). SEC commissioner statement "We are not the securities and environment commission — At least not yet", https://www.sec.gov/news/statement/peirce-climate-disclosure-20220321.

Preker, A. S., Adeyi, O. O., Lapetra, G. M., Simon, D. C., and Keuffel, E. (September–October 2016). "Health care expenditures associated with pollution: Exploratory methods and findings", *Annals of Global Health*, 82(5), pp. 711–721, https://www.researchgate.net/publication/314714545/Health/Care/Expenditures/Associated/With_Pollution_Exploratory_Methods_and_Findings.

Prüss-Ustün, A., Vickers, C., Haefliger, P., and Bertollini, R. (2011). Knowns and unknowns on burden of disease due to chemicals: A systematic review. *Environmental Health*, 10(9), https://ehp.niehs.nih.gov/doi/full/10.1289/EHP3141.

Quinson, T. (2023). "What's the legal definition of greenwashing?", *Bloomberg* https://www.bloomberg.com/news/articles/2023-01-11/what-s-the-legal-definition-of-greenwashing-green-insight#xj4y7vzkg.

Rapier, R. (2022). "Is a lithium cartel inevitable?" *Forbes*, January 20, https://www.forbes.com/sites/rrapier/2022/01/20/is-a-lithium-cartel-inevitable/?sh=40d0e31a1b0b.

Rasure, E. (2022) "Fiscal capacity", https://www.investopedia.com/terms/f/fiscalcapacity.asp.

Ruckstuhl, S. (2009). "Renewable natural resources: Practical lessons for conflict-sensitive development", *Working Paper*, World Bank, Washington, DC. https://openknowledge.worldbank.org/handle/10986/28150.

Scognamillo, A., Mele, G., and Sensini, L. (2016). "Nonrenewable resources, income inequality and per capita GDP: An empirical analysis", *Working Paper*, World Bank, Washington, D.C. https://openknowledge.worldbank.org/handle/10986/25147.

Shay, S. A. (2021). "A smear by name", Op. Eds., *Jewish Link*, November 4, https://jewishlink.news/features/46931-a-smear-by-any-name.

Stubbington, T. (2021). "Squeeze on 'greenium' as ESG bond investors demand more value". *Financial Times*, October 11, https://www.ft.com/content/ecbed322-1709-4ed6-9f7f-d974f6e181da.

Taparia, H. (2022). "One of the hottest trends in the world of investing is a sham", *New York Times*, https://www.nytimes.com/2022/09/29/opinion/esg-investing-responsibility.html?smid=nytcore-ios-share&referringSource=articleShare.

Texas. (2021). SB 13, https://capitol.texas.gov/tlodocs/87R/billtext/pdf/SB00013F.pdf.

The New Climate Economy. (2018). "Unlocking the inclusive growth story of the 21st Century 2018 report of the global commission on the economy and climate, new climate economy", https://newclimateeconomy.report/2018/.

UN. (2022a). *The Sustainable Development Goals Report 2022*, United Nations, New York, Preamble, https://unstats.un.org/sdgs/report/2022/.

UN. (2022b). "UN biodiversity conference", Home page, https://www.unep.org/events/conference/un-biodiversity-conference-cop-15. Accessed January 1 2022.

USA. (2022a). Bill H.R.3684 2017, *Infrastructure Investment and Jobs Act*, https://www.congress.gov/bill/117th-congress/house-bill/3684.

USA. (2022b). Bill H.R.5376 2017, *Inflation Reduction Act*, https://www.congress.gov/bill/117th-congress/house-bill/5376.

USA. (April 4, 2022c). "Climate-related macro-economic risks and opportunities", *White Paper*, Council of Economic Advisors, Office of Management and Budget.

USA. (April 2022d). "Climate risk exposure: An assessment of the federal government's financial and risk to climate change", *White Paper*, Council of Economic Advisors, Office of Management and Budget.

Vinson & Elkins. (2022). "Antitrust issues in renewable energy", *V&E Anti-Trust Update*, June 20, https://www.velaw.com/insights/antitrust-issues-in-renewable-energy/.

WSJ. (2022). "Here is what a 1 million retirement looks like in America", *Wall Street Journal*, December 27, https://www.wsj.com/articles/heres-what-a-1-million-retirement-looks-like-in-america-11671890735.

Afterword

Pitfalls of Industrial Policy

Alexander S. Preker and Susan C. Hulton

Learning Objectives

- Define what is meant by industrial policy
- Review past experiences in using industrial policy, both strengths and weaknesses
- Describe the recent use of industrial policy to advance the sustainability agenda
- Identify the pitfalls of using industrial policy in structural transformation

---

Abstract

The Afterword provides a minority opinion, among the authors that contributed to this book, on the use of industrial policy as a public policy tool for influencing businesses and investors to engage in the sustainable use of non-renewable and renewable resources. The section defines "industrial policy" or "industrial strategy" as any intervention by governments that encourages the growth or strengthening of the economy in general or that causes a shift from one industry to another, by deliberate policies that influence supply, demand, price equilibrium, or the competitive environment of those industries. The section describes how industrial policies are often used to achieve economic objectives such as growth, competitiveness, and strengthening a particular sector. They can also be used to achieve political, security, ideological, and social objectives through sanctions, trade embargos, and import or export restrictions that favor a specific sector (agriculture, steel, fossil fuels, alternative energy, etc.). The section also describes how industrial policy has had some notable successes in the past when used in large public infrastructure and civic works projects. But it distorts markets, often leads to poor economic outcomes, and rewards companies for their lobbying skills rather than maximizing economic value and return on investment for shareholders. It has had mixed results when used for strategic purposes like sanctions, trade barriers, and other areas where the negative economic impact on the countries imposing such measures can be significant. Examples are provided of spectacular failures in industrial policy when used for restructuring manufacturing industries and when used for the purpose of social engineering. The Afterword concludes that, given the checkered history and lack of broad consensus on the use of industrial policy in the manufacturing sectors, the increased reliance on such policy interventions in many areas of sustainability, like the energy sector and other areas, carries significant medium- and long-term risks. Some of these risks can be mitigated by fostering truly competitive businesses and investment opportunities that have high financial performance on their own without being reliant on subsidies, tax credits or distorting legislation for their survival. The guiding principle for any policy intervention – regulatory intervention, government funding, or public production – should always be *primum non nocere* (first, do no harm).

I. Historical Context

The term "industrial policy" or "industrial strategy" can be defined as any intervention by governments that encourages the growth or strengthening of the economy in general or that causes a shift from one industry to another, by changing supply, demand, price equilibrium, or the competitive environment (Rodrik, 2004). Sometimes, as in the case of policies to contain the use of fossil fuels, it is also used to achieve structural change and suppress a specific sector of the economy in favor of alternative sources of energy.

Government intervention in the economy in the form of industrial policy is not new. Its origins are deeply rooted in the past and it has been an ongoing topic of controversy among policymakers, political scientists, and economists for millennia (Dadush, 2016). Although it had its heyday in the past, it fell out of favor during contemporary times, especially after the 1980s and the collapse of the Soviet Union (Siripurapu and Berman, 2022). It has had a recent revival, however, with the erosion in commitment to globalization, increased protectionism, economic sanctions (Iran and Russia), trade wars (China) and specific goal-oriented social policies such as promoting sustainability and combating climate change.

Industrial policy has had a mixed legacy (Neely, 1993). Looking back, the Egyptian Pharaohs built granaries and intervened in the agricultural sector. The Greeks built a naval fleet to promote trade in wine, olives, metalwork, and pottery. The Romans built public infrastructure such as roads, bridges, and aqueducts throughout their empire. To encourage these efforts, the Egyptians, Greeks, and Romans all relied on subsidizing their export industries and import/substitution/industrialization (build-at-home) sectors. Funding came from crushing domestic taxes and territorial expansion was used to pillage the wealth of other countries. They suppressed individual entrepreneurship in favor of economic activities that served the state. Despite temporary success in achieving imperial policy goals, all ended with uncontrollable inflation, economic collapse, and popular revolt (Bartlett, 1994).

More contemporary industrial policy included the mercantilism which became the dominant school of economic thought in Europe throughout the Renaissance and early modern period (from the 15th to the 18th centuries). Countries like France, Italy, Netherlands, Portugal, Spain, and Great Britain relied on imperialist territorial expansion and colonialism to achieve an artificial current account surplus, accumulating monetary reserves. They did this by maximizing exports of their own goods, importing goods at greatly discounted rates from their colonies, and imposing crushing taxes on their overseas subjects (Johnson, 1974).

In 1791, just two years after the American Constitution was adopted, Alexander Hamilton, a politician, lawyer, and economist, best known as one of the Founding Fathers of the United States and the nation's first Treasury Secretary, wrote his *Report on the Subject of Manufactures*.

Presented to the US Congress on December 5, 1791, the report called for direct policy intervention in support of the fledgling US manufacturing sector through a combination of tariffs and subsidies, regulations, and other government intervention. Motivated by protecting the growing American economy based on major exports such as cotton, tobacco, and native sod, Hamilton sought to create an economic system for expanding trade. In light of his approach, Alexander Hamilton is widely considered to be the first major proponent of industrial policy in the United States. His ideas found expression in what became known as the "American System" – a combination of tariffs, a national bank, and infrastructure development – which was prominent in the early nineteenth century (Clay, 1832).

Hamilton's position was challenged at the time by leading opponents of government intervention in the economy, such as Thomas Jefferson and James Madison. They strongly opposed subsidies to selective industries. The last quarter of the 18th century had seen a significant confluence of events. Best known as the date of the American Declaration of Independence, 1776 was also the date that Adam Smith, sometimes called the founding father of capitalism, published his seminal work *An Inquiry into the Nature and Causes of the Wealth of Nations* (Smith, 1776). Smith, a Scottish moral philosopher and political economist, wrote *The Wealth of Nations* during the British industrial revolution. He described the emerging capitalist system of the industrial revolution that upended the mercantilist system which assumed that wealth was fixed and finite. The central thesis of *The Wealth of Nations* was that a free market with an "invisible hand", free from government interference, would lead to the best economic outcomes. Smith's work was well known to the American founding fathers. His political economy extolling reason, enlightened self-interest, free trade, agriculture and rural life, and America's long-term prospects appealed to Jefferson and Madison, both members of Virginia's planter aristocracy. Though much of it also appealed to Hamilton, it was diametrically opposed to the "hands-on" Hamiltonian approach.

This set the scene to continue the centuries old battle between those who advocated a free and open market and those who saw significant advantages to government intervention in the market. Many intellectuals and politicians have lined up on either side of this divide. Notably, free market advocates like Milton Friedman sided with Adam Smith, arguing against government interference (Friedman, 1999), with John Maynard Keynes (Bartlett, 1985), siding with Hamilton, and arguing for government intervention and an active industrial policy.

The "American System" became popular again during the period between the First and Second World Wars during the Great Depression when President Franklin D. Roosevelt presented his New Deal. This constituted a range of programs of the 1930s that sought to regulate wages and prices across several industries. The massive government-directed World War II reconstruction and mobilization that followed was a more radical example. Many countries, including Germany, Japan, South Korea, and most Latin American countries, have implemented aggressive industrial policies with varying degrees of success and failure, often accompanied by heavy taxation and slow growth.

By the late 1970s, 1980s, and 1990s, heavy-handed industrial policy that relied on subsidies, regulations, and other government interventions had fallen out of favor. By that time, it was clear that the Marxist–Leninist system of a centrally planned economy, also known as a command economy, under which governments make all economic decisions regarding the production and distribution of goods, especially in the manufacturing sectors, had failed. It had caused enormous economic damage and led the countries that pursued these policies to fall decades behind in innovation and technological development.

To critics, the collapse of the Soviet Union in 1990 was seen as stark proof that this approach did not work. The command-and-control communist economic model failed to produce innovation. And it led to a gross misallocation of resources and low economic growth (World Bank, 1994; Barr, 1994, 2005). Bureaucrats are not good in business (World Bank, 1995). State owned enterprises are a load on the public budget and usually do worse than the private sector. Efforts to repair the damage are still ongoing decades and trillions of dollars later (World Bank, 1996, 1997, 2002). Although the damage done may be difficult if not impossible to repair (Zubok, 2021), populists in many developing countries continue to flirt with this approach.

As a result, during the 1990s and early 2000s, there was a return to a belief in competitive markets under what was coined the "Washington

Consensus". The main elements of the Washington Consensus include policies focused on "maintaining fiscal discipline, reordering public spending priorities (from subsidies to health and education expenditures), reforming tax policy, allowing the market to determine interest rates, maintaining a competitive exchange rate, liberalizing trade, permitting inward foreign investment, privatizing state enterprises, deregulating barriers to entry and exit, and securing property rights" (Irwin and Ward, 2021). Today the Washington Consensus has become the cornerstone of a fiscal and macro-economic policy needed for growth that has stood the test of time better than populist economic policies (Irwin, 2020).

II. 21st Century Revival

Recent policy interventions to reduce reliance on fossil fuels to address climate concerns and improve management and investment in the sustainable use of non-renewable and renewable resources can be seen as a 21st century return to industrial policy (Economist, 2022a, 2022b). One recent such example is the industrial policy that targets climate change adopted under the Inflation Reduction Act of 2022. This omnibus legislation has some aspects of industrial policy applied to much needed upgrading of infrastructure, like the earlier policies of FDR, but it also includes a variety of direct government intervention in several manufacturing sectors which historically has not had good outcomes.

To supporters, such government policies are seen as an essential strategic tool to stimulate growth, promote competitiveness, and strengthen a sector such as the alternative energy sector (Dadush, 2016; Cimoli *et al.*, 2009).

However, more recently, during the war in Ukraine and economic interventions during the COVID-19 pandemic in 2020–2022, imposing policies on industrial sectors caused significant macro-economic disruption in the countries using them (economic shut down, price distortions in the energy sector and massive supply chain disruptions, etc.). When businesses, unions, and governments collude in price fixing and industrial output in one area, this often leads to private cartels that are notoriously unstable. Both subsidies and industrial policies are unsustainable over time. This once again casts doubt on the undue reliance on industrial policy in restructuring the energy sector.

II. Conclusion

As discussed in the Preface, over the past few decades, the world has witnessed significant improvements in economic development that meet a wide range of human needs. Ensuring that such development takes place in a "sustainable" way is the central focus of this book. These trends have created a business environment and investment climate in which there is strong consumer demand for sustainable solutions and new technological solutions that meet that demand.

But controversy abounds. There are differing and conflicting opinions and ideologies, and often a paucity of evidence on how best to address the many topics related to sustainability. There is a broad consensus on the "why" – importance of addressing the challenges of sustainable development (ranging from a measured concern to extreme depictions of systemic collapse). There is less consensus on the "what" – prioritization of the issues (ranging from a focus on a number of pressing concerns to a central focus on the fossil fuel industry and global warming). There is even less consensus on the "how" – the approaches used (ranging from market-driven solutions to more interventionist industrial policies, coercive rating agencies, and capture of corporate boards by social activists). There is little agreement on the "when" – starting-point and timeframe (ranging from gradual transformation to an immediate "call to arms"). And there is a lack of consensus on the "to what effect" – does it make any difference (ranging from a focus on clear measurable results to "leaps of faith").

This Afterword provides a minority opinion on the use of industrial policy as a tool for influencing business and investor engagement in the energy transition, and the use of other non-renewable and renewable resources. It defines "industrial policy" or "industrial strategy" as any intervention by governments that causes a shift from one industry to another, by deliberate policies that affect supply, demand, price equilibrium, or the competitive environment of those industries. Although industrial policy may have had some notable successes in large public infrastructure and civic works projects, in the manufacturing sectors, it distorts markets and often rewards companies for their lobbying skills rather than maximizing economic performance of businesses and return on investment for shareholders.

At first glance, industrial policies that introduce new regulations, subsidies and other environmentally friendly policies provide an opportunity for companies that are skilled at taking advantage of such conditions. The opportunities include profits from sectors that also have a potential positive social impact. Smart managers understand that a company's financial success also depends on the interdependence between development, nature, and society. If this additional information is considered when making investment and resource allocation decisions it can result in short-term profitability of the company.

Unfortunately, as seen in this Afterword, even well-meaning industrial policies when applied to the manufacturing sectors often drift beyond their commercial goals. Companies are encouraged and even forced to include a wide range of social, political and governance objectives (double and triple bottom lines) that have little to do with the commercial success of the company or investor. Well-meaning industrial policies that cause major disruption in the competitive marketplace usually go well beyond the social contract approved by voters during elections. Coercive rating agencies that blacklist companies, and the capture of corporate boards by social activists usually go beyond the authorizing environment bestowed on them by their private shareholders.

These factors pose a significant threat to market equilibrium in the manufacturing settings. They cannot capture the much more granular conditions of the competitive marketplace or broad fiscal and macroeconomic trends. The past two years have been brutal for both businesses and investors, with months of forced closure due to the global pandemic, supply chain disruptions, distorting subsidies, and inflation. Both the 2008 and the 2023 banking crises underscore just how vulnerable businesses and investors are. Yet, existing industrial policy on the energy transition was not adjusted accordingly.

Corporations that are forced by industrial policies or pressured by rating agencies and special interest groups to spend an undue amount of time and money on activities that are unrelated to their core commercial interests, risk compromising their "bottom line" and going bankrupt. When that happens to large businesses and large financial institutions, it can have a devastating impact not only on the business and financial institutions themselves, but also on the overall economy, pensioners, and working-class families who lose their jobs. Even experienced businesses and investors are vulnerable when they operate in a highly regulated and politically charged area of the economy like manufacturers engaged in the energy transition.

Even businesses and investors that may benefit initially from favorable industrial policies are often left vulnerable when there are sudden shifts in policy or changes in the perception of their activities. After spending millions and sometimes even billions of dollars to adapt their business and investment strategies, companies can be burdened by politically motivated requirements, like adding a "made in America" condition for favorable regulatory or financial treatment. This can change a lucrative business that depends on subsidies for its profit margin into a failure.

Given the checkered history and lack of broad consensus on the use of industrial policy in the manufacturing sectors, the increased reliance on such policy interventions in many areas of sustainability, like the energy sector and other areas, carries significant medium- and long-term risks. To survive and have any impact at all, businesses, and investors much first and foremost be financially "sustainable" themselves. They can partially protect themselves against the negative effects of industrial policy, shifts in the criteria used by rating agencies, and the vagaries of social activists by focusing on being truly competitive even without favorable legislation, subsidies, and tax credits. Government intervention should always be based on the principle *primum non nocere* (first, do no harm).

References

Barr, N. (1994). *Labor Markets and Social Policy in Central and Eastern Europe: The Transition and Beyond*, World Bank, Washington, D.C.

Barr, N. (2005). *Labor Markets and Social Policy in Central and Eastern Europe: The Accession and Beyond*, World Bank, Washington, D.C.

Bartlett, B. (1985). "America's new ideology: 'Industrial policy'", *The American Journal of Economics and Social Policy*, 44(1), pp. 1–7.

Bartlett, B. (1994). "How excessive government killed ancient Rome", *Cato Journal*, 14(2), pp. 287–303.

Cimoli, M., Dosi, G., and Stiglitz, J. E. (eds.) (2009). *Industrial Policy and Development: The Political Economy of Capabilities Accumulation,* Oxford University Press, *Oxford,* https://academic.oup.com/book/32519/chapter-abstract/270240035?redirectedFrom=fulltext.

Clay, H. (1832). "In defense of the American system", *Classic Senate Speeches,* February 2, 3, and 6, https://www.senate.gov/artandhistory/history/common/generic/Speeches_ClayAmericanSystem.htm.

Dadush, U. (2016). "Industrial policy: A guide for the perplexed", *Policy Brief Carnegie,* https://carnegieendowment.org/2016/02/01/industrial-policy-guide-for-perplexed-pub-62660.

Economist. (2022a). "The new industrial policy: Many countries are seeing a revival of industrial policy", *Special Report,* January 2022, https://www.economist.com/special-report/2022/01/10/many-countries-are-seeing-a-revival-of-industrial-policy.

Economist. (2022b). "A law meant to boost America's security becomes industrial policy", *Economist,* June.

Friedman, M. (1999). "Milton Friedman on business suicide", *Policy Forum,* March/April, https://www.cato.org/policy-report/march/april-1999/policy-forum-milton-friedman-business-suicide.

Irwin, D. A. (2020). "The Washington Consensus stands test of time better than populist policies", Peterson Institute for International Economics, Washington, https://www.piie.com/blogs/realtime-economic-issues-watch/washington-consensus-stands-test-time-better-populist-policies.

Irwin, D. A. and Ward, O. (2021). "What is the Washington Consensus?" *Peterson Institute for International Economics,* Washington, https://www.piie.com/blogs/realtime-economic-issues-watch/what-washington-consensus.

Johnson, H. G. (1974). "Mercantilism: Past, present and future", *The Manchester School,* March, 42, pp. 1–17.

Neely, M. C. (1993). "The pitfalls of industrial policy", *Federal Reserve Bank,* April 1, https://www.stlouisfed.org/publications/regional-economist/april-1993/the-pitfalls-of-industrial-policy.

Rodrik, D. (2004). "Industrial Policy for the Twenty-First Century", *Industrial Policy for the 21st Century,* UNIDO.

Siripurapu, A. and Berman, N. (2022). "Is industrial policy making a comeback", *Policy Brief,* Council of Foreign Relations, New York, https://www.cfr.org/backgrounder/industrial-policy-making-comeback.

Smith, A. (1776). *An Inquiry into the Nature and Causes of the Wealth of Nations,* W. Strahan and T. Cadell, London.

World Bank. (1994). *World Development Report 1994: Infrastructure for Development,* A World Bank Policy Research Report, World Bank, Washington, D.C.

World Bank. (1995). *Bureaucrats in Business. The Economics and Politics of Government Ownership,* A World Bank Policy Research Report, World Bank, Washington, D.C.

World Bank. (1996). *From Plan to Market. World Development Report 1996,* World Bank, Washington, D.C.

World Bank. (1997). *The State in a Changing World. World Development Report 1997,* World Bank, Washington, D.C.

World Bank. (2002). *Building Institutions for Markets. World Development Report 2002,* World Bank, Washington, D.C.

Zubok, V. M. (2021). *Collapse: The Fall of the Soviet Union,* Yale University Press, Yale, https://yalebooks.yale.edu/book/9780300268171/collapse/.

Glossary A

Sustainability Terms

S. C. Hulton & D-C. Simon

The following glossary provides an alphabetical list of specialized definitions for sustainability terms. The list includes both terms used in this book and other terms that the reader may find useful when reading some of the references that are cited in the book.

Sustainability is an evolving field. Many terms related to sustainability are therefore used in different ways by different chapter authors and will vary from source to source. The definitions used in this glossary are all from major accepted sources. The sources used for this glossary and their associated online links are found at the end in the Reference list. These and other specific sources may be consulted if the reader wants to look up the definition of sustainability terms not found in this glossary.

Adaptation refers to an adjustment in natural or human systems in response to actual or expected climatic stimuli or their effects, which moderates harm or exploits beneficial opportunities. UNFCCC

Agenda for Sustainable Development 2030 is a UN resolution of September 2015 adopting a plan of action for people, planet and prosperity in a new global development framework anchored in 17 Sustainable Development Goals. See also *Sustainable Development Goals (SDGs)*. IPCC

Air Pollution refers to the degradation of air quality with negative effects on human health or the natural or built environment due to the introduction, by natural processes or human activity, into the atmosphere of substances (gases, aerosols) which have a direct (primary pollutants) or indirect (secondary pollutants) harmful effect. IPCC

Biodiversity refers to the wide-ranging variety of life forms that inhabit a particular Habitat or ecosystem. Biodiversity or a lack thereof can have important implications for the health of the world's ecosystems. Book of Jargon

Biomass Fuels or Biofuels are fuels produced from dry organic matter or combustible oils produced by plants. These fuels are considered renewable as long as the vegetation producing them is maintained or replanted, such as firewood, alcohol fermented from sugar, and combustible oils extracted from soybeans. Their use in place of fossil fuels cuts greenhouse gas emissions because the plants that are the fuel sources capture carbon dioxide from the atmosphere. UNFCCC

Blended Finance is the strategic use of development finance for the mobilization of additional finance towards sustainable development in developing countries. It attracts commercial capital towards projects that contribute to sustainable development, while providing financial returns to investors. This innovative approach helps enlarge the total amount of resources available to developing countries, complementing their own investments and Official development assistance (ODA) inflows to fill their SDG financing gap, and support the implementation of the Paris Agreement. OECD DAC

Bloomberg ESG Disclosure Scores are metrics that measure how well a company is implementing ESG programs. The metrics help investors determine which companies are reflecting their sustainability commitments in their business operations. Book of Jargon

Brundtland Commission Report (also called "Our Common Future") is the report issued in 1987 by the World Commission on Environment and

Development, chaired by Norwegian Prime Minister Gro Harlem Brundtland. This report communicated the relationship between poverty around the world and the natural environment. It is also credited with establishing a viable definition of *Sustainable Development*. According to the Brundtland Commission Report, Sustainable Development is the process of meeting the needs of today without jeopardizing the needs of future generations. In this preeminent work, Brundtland laid the foundation for the *Sustainable Development Goals*. Book of Jargon

Carbon Capture, Utilization and Storage (CCUS). Carbon Capture Storage (CCS) is a set of technologies aimed at capturing, transporting, and permanently storing CO_2 that would be otherwise emitted into the atmosphere. CCS can be applied on industrial installations, such as cement or steel plants, and in power plants. Carbon capture and utilization (CCU) technologies allow captured carbon to be reused, increasing its circularity, and potentially reducing its emissions to the atmosphere. IPCC

Carbon Footprint refers to the total amount of *GHG Emissions* in carbon dioxide equivalent that individuals or entities directly or indirectly cause. A carbon dioxide equivalent or CO2 equivalent is a metric measure used to compare the emissions from various greenhouse gases based on their global-warming potential (GWP), by converting amounts of other gases to the equivalent amount of carbon dioxide with the same global warming potential. Book of Jargon and IPCC

Carbon Neutrality refers to having a net zero *Carbon Footprint*, or in other words, balancing the amount of *GHG Emissions* released into the atmosphere with an equivalent amount of carbon removal, or simply eliminating carbon Emissions altogether. Reaching carbon neutrality by mid-21st century is essential to limit global warming. Book of Jargon and IPCC

Carbon Offsetting is a mechanism used to compensate the emissions of an organization or territory by purchasing carbon offsets also called carbon credits which are tradable "rights" or certificates linked to activities that lower the amount of GHG in the atmosphere through either emissions reduction, avoidance, or sequestration. One carbon credit equates to one metric ton of reduced, avoided, or sequestered carbon equivalent by the project financed through this mechanism. A downside of carbon offsets is that they may involve carbon leakage which decreases the GHG reduction initially anticipated. IPCC

Carbon Sequestration refers to a biochemical process by which atmospheric carbon is absorbed by living organisms, including trees, soil micro-organisms, and crops, and involving the storage of carbon in soils, with the potential to reduce atmospheric carbon dioxide levels. OECD Glossary

Carbon Tax refers to a form of carbon pricing, whereby a fee is imposed on the production, distribution, or use of *Fossil Fuels* based on how much carbon such processes emit. The primary purpose of carbon taxation is to reduce *Greenhouse Gas Emissions* and encourage alternative energy uses. Book of Jargon

Circular Economy refers to an economic framework aimed at eliminating waste. The framework calls for keeping resources in use for as long as possible, to extract the maximum value from them, then recovering and regenerating products at the end of each service life. Implementing a Circular Economy can result in a more competitive economy, as it addresses Climate Change, decreases the amount of waste, drives productivity, allows for growth, and offers a solution to potential resource scarcity. Book of Jargon

Climate Change refers to long-term shifts in global temperatures and weather patterns that can be identified (e.g., by using statistical tests) by changes in the mean and/or the variability of its properties and that persists for an extended period, typically decades or longer. These shifts may come naturally through variations in the solar cycle and volcanic eruptions. But since the 1800s, human activities have been the primary driver of climate change, mainly due to the burning of fossil fuels such as coal, oil and gas which emit greenhouse gases that trap heat from the sun and raise temperatures. IPCC and UN

Conference of the Parties (COP) is the supreme body of UN conventions, such as the United Nations Framework Convention on Climate Change (UNFCCC), comprising parties with a right to vote that have ratified or acceded to the convention concerned. The COP is the decision-making body responsible for monitoring and reviewing the implementation of the United Nations Framework Convention on Climate Change. It brings together the 199 Parties (198 States and the European Union) that have ratified the Framework Convention. The COP has met annually since 1995. See also the United Nations Framework Convention on Climate Change (UNFCCC). IPCC

Convention on Biological Diversity (CBD) is a multilateral treaty with three main goals: the conservation of biological diversity; the sustainable use of its components; and the fair and equitable sharing of the benefits arising out of the utilization of genetic resources. Signed by 150 government leaders at the 1992 Rio Earth Summit, the Convention has been ratified by 196 states. UN

Corporate Governance refers to the framework of rules and practices in a corporation that determine corporate direction and performance. Typically, the board of directors' relationship with other primary participants, including shareholders and management, is critical. Book of Jargon

Corporate Social Responsibility (CSR) refers to the practices put in place by a corporation to manage the social, environmental, and economic effects of its operations while promoting sustainability. Some aspects may be required by law, such as the requirement of banks to protect people's private information, while other aspects are voluntary. Book of Jargon

Corporate Sustainability refers to an approach to conducting business that creates sustainable, long-term shareholder, employee, consumer, and societal value by pursuing responsible environmental, social, and economic (or governance) strategies.

There are three pillars of a corporate sustainability strategy: the environmental, the socially responsible, and the economic. They are referred to as pillars because, together, they support sustainable goals. Investopedia

Decarbonization is the process by which countries, individuals or other entities aim to reduce or eliminate GHG emissions. It typically refers to a reduction of the carbon emissions associated with electricity, industry, and transport. IPCC

Emissions refers to the production and discharge of gases and other pollutants by processes and activities. Emissions often refers to *Greenhouse Gases*, such as carbon dioxide and methane, but it can include other pollutants, such as effluent. Book of Jargon

Environmental, Social, and Governance (ESG) refers to the three factors that are considered by an increasing number of businesses, investors, and other stakeholders (alongside more traditional factors) in a variety of decision-making processes (e.g., the undertaking of ESG due diligence as part of an investment, the preparation of ESG-related disclosures by a company, or the preparation of a report by ESG Research Providers). Examples of ESG considerations include a company's sustainability policies (including *Greenhouse Gas* emissions), approach to supply chains and ensuring supply chain resilience, labor policies, and governance issues (such as board diversity, reporting systems and processes and good *Corporate Governance*). A number of organizations establish ESG principles and/or standards that companies can use to guide their ESG-related actions and reporting (e.g., *Principles for Responsible Investment* and *Sustainable Development Goals*). Book of Jargon

Ethical Investing refers to the practice of integrating ethical considerations into the investment decision-making process. This practice is less clearly tied to analysis of a company's risks and prospects and more overtly related to the personal values of the investor. Some investors may choose to eliminate certain industries entirely from their portfolio (negative screening) and/or to over-allocate to industries that meet an investor's ethical principles (positive screening). Book of Jargon

Externality is a concept in economics referring to a cost paid, or a benefit received by a party that was not involved in the production of that cost or benefit. An Externality can be positive or negative, and can affect a person, an organization, or a society (e.g., factory pollution is a negative Externality that affects society by increasing healthcare costs). Externalities are sometimes referred to as "spillovers." Book of Jargon

Fossil Fuels include coal, oil, and natural gas. They are natural fuels formed from the fossilized remains of once living organisms. They are the world's No. 1 source of energy. The burning of fossil fuels is a primary contributor to the emission of pollution and *Greenhouse Gases*. Book of Jargon

Global Warming refers to the increase in the temperature of the atmosphere near the Earth's surface and in the troposphere, which can contribute to changes in global climate patterns. Global warming can occur from a variety of causes, both natural and human induced. In common usage, "global warming" often refers to the warming that can occur as a result of increased emissions of greenhouse gases from human activities. US EPA

Green Bond is the flagship form of activity-based Sustainable Finance in which a bond financing is expressly linked to business activities with green attributes. Green Bonds are generally characterized by their disclosure of the eligible projects the bond proceeds will be allocated to and the level of reporting that will be provided, with minimal or no changes to the definitive debt documents. Book of Jargon

Greenhouse gases (GHGs) refer to such atmospheric gases as carbon dioxide, methane, nitrous oxide, ozone, and hydrofluorocarbons occurring both naturally and resulting from human production and consumption activities. They trap heat from the sun on the surface of the earth by absorbing infrared radiation, contributing to the greenhouse effect (*global warming*). Each GHG has a Global Warming Potential (GWP) which is a factor referring to its heat-trapping ability relative to that of CO_2. Because GHGs vary in their ability to trap heat in the atmosphere, some are more harmful to the climate than others. For example, methane is 25 times more potent than CO_2, so methane has a GWP of 25. OECD and Book of Jargon

Greenhouse Gas Protocol (GHGP) is an international accounting and management tool for government and business leaders to quantify, manage, and better understand GHG Emissions.

The GHGP categorizes greenhouse gasses into three scopes based on the source. Scope 1 refers to the direct emissions from an organization's operations from owned or controlled sources, including company vehicles and buildings. Scope 2 accounts for indirect emissions from purchased electricity, heating, and cooling. Scope 3 comprises all other indirect emissions in a company's value chain, including both upstream (e.g., supply chain) and downstream emissions. Book of Jargon

Greenhouse Gas Protocol is an international accounting and management tool for government and business leaders to quantify, manage, and better understand GHG Emissions. Book of Jargon

Greenwashing is the practice of overstating the environmental benefits of a product, service, or idea. Book of Jargon

Impact Investing is a *Sustainable Investment* strategy characterized by investments made with the intention to generate positive, measurable social and environmental impact alongside a financial return. Impact investments can be made in both emerging and developed markets and target a range of returns from below market to market rate, depending on investors' strategic goals. GIIN

Intergovernmental Panel on Climate Change (IPCC) is the United Nations body for assessing the science related to climate change. Established by the World Meteorological Society and the United Nations Environment Programme in 1988, the IPCC's mandate is "to provide the world with a clear scientific view on the current state of knowledge in climate change and its potential environmental and socio-economic impacts." The unique authority of this UN climate body lies in the breadth and depth of its climate assessment reports. Experts from around the world synthesize the latest scientific findings on the impacts of and the potential responses to climate change with the IPCC's comprehensive Assessment Reports released every five to seven years. IPCC

Kyoto Protocol is a legally binding international treaty linked to the United Nations Framework Convention on Climate Change (UNFCCC). It effectively operationalizes the UNFCCC by committing industrialized countries and economies in transition to limit and reduce greenhouse gases (GHG) emissions in accordance with agreed individual targets. The Kyoto Protocol applies t9 seven greenhouse gases: Carbon dioxide (CO_2), Methane (CH_4), Nitrous oxide (N_2O), Hydrofluorocarbons (HFCs), Perfluorocarbons (PFCs), Sulphur hexafluoride (SF_6), and Nitrogen trifluoride (NF_3). The Kyoto Protocol was adopted in December 1997 in Kyoto, Japan, at the Third Session of the Conference of the Parties (COP3) to the UNFCCC. The Protocol entered into force on 16 February 2005 and as of April 2023 had 192 Parties (191 States and the European Union). IPCC

Materiality refers to the significance of a matter in relation to a set of financial or performance information. If a matter is material to the set of information, then it is likely to be of significance to a user of that information. OECD Glossary

Materiality Assessment refers to a method of identifying ESG issues within a business that could affect the business and be important to the business' stakeholders. A Materiality Assessment is used to inform company metrics and to identify the information that might be appropriate for reporting to investors and other stakeholders. Subjects that are material might include issues that reflect the economic, environmental, and social impact of the business. Book of Jargon

Materiality Map is a tool which compares sustainability issues that are disclosed across industries and sectors. See *Sustainability Accounting Standards Board (SASB).* Book of Jargon

Millennium Development Goals (MDGs) were a set of eight timebound and measurable goals for: eradicating extreme poverty and hunger; combating disease; achieving universal primary education; promoting gender equality; reducing child mortality; improving maternal health; ensuring environmental sustainability; and promoting global partnerships for development. These goals were agreed at the UN Millennium Summit in 2000 together with an action plan to reach the goals by 2015. IPCC

Mitigation, in the context of climate change, refers to a human intervention to reduce the sources or enhance the "sinks" of greenhouse gases. Examples include using fossil fuels more efficiently for industrial processes or electricity generation, switching to solar energy or wind power, improving the insulation of buildings, and expanding forests and other "sinks" to remove greater amounts of carbon dioxide from the atmosphere. UNFCCC

Nationally Determined Contributions (NDCs). A term used under the *United Nations Framework Convention on Climate Change* (UNFCCC) whereby a country that has joined the Paris Agreement outlines its plans for reducing its emissions. IPCC

Net Zero CO$_2$ Emissions. Net zero carbon dioxide (CO2) emissions are achieved when anthropogenic CO2 emissions are balanced globally by anthropogenic CO2 removals over a specified period. Net zero CO2 emissions are also referred to as carbon neutrality. IPCC

Non-renewable Natural Resources are exhaustible natural resources, such as mineral resources, that cannot be regenerated after exploitation. OECD Glossary

Paris Agreement is a legally binding international treaty on climate change. It was adopted by 196 Parties at COP 21 in Paris, on 12 December 2015 and entered into force on 4 November 2016. Its goal is to limit global warming to well below 2, preferably to 1.5 degrees Celsius, compared to pre-industrial levels. To achieve this long-term temperature goal, countries aim to reach global peaking of greenhouse gas emissions as soon as possible to achieve a climate neutral world by mid-century. The Paris Agreement is a landmark in the multilateral climate change process because, for the first time, a binding agreement brings all nations into a common cause to undertake ambitious efforts to combat climate change and adapt to its effects. UNFCCC

Precautionary Principle is a guiding philosophy in considering the implementation of new technologies and practices across a range of sciences, particularly environmental sciences. The Precautionary Principle incorporates four supporting tenets: (i) taking preventive action when facing uncertainty, (ii) shifting the burden of proof of the efficacy of an activity or a technology to the proponents of that activity or technology, (iii) exploring a range of alternatives to potentially harmful actions, and (iv) increasing public participation in the decision-making process. Book of Jargon

Principles for Responsible Investment (PRI) is an independent investor initiative in partnership with the United Nations Environment Programme (UNEP) Finance Initiative and the UN Global Compact which promotes responsible investment. The PRI has developed a signatory program for financial institutions which requires them to commit to a set of six principles. The principles are as follows: (i) incorporate ESG issues into investment analysis and decision-making, (ii) incorporate ESG principles into ownership and management practices, (iii) seek appropriate disclosure on ESG issues by the subjects of the investment, (iv) promote the PRI within the investment industry, (v) collaborate to optimize effectiveness in implementing the PRI, and (vi) report progress on implementing the PRI. The launch of the PRI in 2006 is a remarkable milestone for the incorporation of sustainability considerations by the financial industry and the PRI signatory initiative has been crucial to the mainstreaming of sustainable finance. As of 2022, there were 4,902 signatories to the PRI representing $121.3 trillion in assets under management. PRI

Renewable Energy generally refers to electricity supplied from renewable energy sources, such as wind and solar power, geothermal, hydropower, and various forms of biomass. These energy sources are considered renewable sources because they are continuously replenished on the Earth. US EPA

Renewable Natural Resources are natural resources that, after exploitation, can return to their previous stock levels by natural processes of growth or replenishment. Conditionally renewable resources are those whose exploitation eventually reaches a level beyond which regeneration will become impossible. Such is the case, for example, with the clear-cutting of tropical forests. OECD Glossary

Responsible Investment involves considering environmental, social and governance (ESG) issues when making investment decisions and influencing companies or assets (known as active ownership or stewardship). It complements traditional financial analysis and portfolio construction techniques. Responsible investors can have different objectives. Some focus exclusively on financial returns and consider ESG issues that could impact these. Others aim to generate financial returns and to achieve positive outcomes for people and the planet, while avoiding negative ones. PRI

Shareholder Advocacy is advocacy that attempts to use stock ownership to promote change in a publicly traded company. Shareholder Advocacy can take the form of creating a dialogue between shareholders and the company or filing a shareholder resolution to encourage certain corporate behavior. Book of Jargon

Shareholder Engagement refers to all the ways that shareholders can influence the companies in their investment portfolios. Three main techniques are proxy voting, shareholder dialogue and shareholder proposals. Through these techniques and others, shareholders can exercise their rights and privileges and have an impact on corporate policy. Book of Jargon

Social Bond or Social Impact Bond is a form of activity-based *Sustainable Finance* in which the financing is linked to business activities with social benefits. Although there are no definitive criteria for what constitutes a social benefit, Social Bond projects typically aim to promote infrastructure development, access to essential services, employment generation, food security, and socioeconomic advancement or empowerment to advance the prospects of target populations. See also *Green Bond* and *Sustainability Bond*. Book of Jargon

Socially Responsible Investing (SRI) refers to investing in companies and funds that have a positive social impact. Strategies for SRI include Negative Screening of disfavored industries, *Shareholder Advocacy*, and sustainability-themed investing, such as investing in *Green Bonds*. Book of Jargon

Sustainability: A dynamic process that guarantees the persistence of natural and human systems in an equitable manner. IPCC

Sustainability Accounting Standards Board (SASB) is an independent standards board whose mission is to establish industry-specific disclosure standards across ESG topics and facilitate communication between companies and investors on these issues. Book of Jargon

Sustainability Bond is a bond issued to finance a mix of green and social projects, as described in the Sustainability Bond Guidelines. The Sustainability Bond Guidelines (SBG) of the International Capital Market Association confirm the relevance of the Principles in this context and facilitate the application of their guidance on transparency and disclosure to the sustainability bond market. See also *Green Bond* and *Social Bond*. Book of Jargon**

Sustainable Development refers to development that meets the needs of the present without jeopardizing the needs of future generations (see also *Brundtland Commission Report, 1987*) and balances social, economic, and environmental concerns. IPCC

Sustainable Development Goals (SDGs) are the 17 global goals for development for all countries established by the United Nations in 2015 through a participatory process and elaborated in the *2030 Agenda for Sustainable Development*. These include ending poverty and hunger; ensuring health and well-being, education, gender equality, clean water and energy, and decent work; building and ensuring resilient and sustainable infrastructure, cities, and consumption; reducing inequalities; protecting land and water ecosystems; promoting peace, justice, and partnerships; and taking urgent action on climate change. See also *Sustainable Development*. IPCC

Sustainable Finance refers to financial services that integrate ESG factors into financial products or investment decisions, such as *Green Bonds* and *Sustainability-Linked Bonds*. (See Chapter 9) Book of Jargon

Sustainable Investing is an investing philosophy wherein an investor takes a company's environmental, social, and corporate governance (ESG) factors into account. This allows investment dollars to be used as a tool to promote positive societal impact and corporate responsibility without sacrificing long-term financial returns. Strategies for investing sustainably include avoiding companies that conflict with ESG principles and seeking out industries that are inherently more sustainable. There are a wide variety of investments that can be considered "sustainable" based on the environmental, social, and corporate governance (ESG) framework. Industries that promote good environmental practices, via more renewable energy sources or by combating air and water pollution, are perhaps the first things that come to mind for most people. However, sustainable investing can also include investing in companies that support human rights initiatives, more ethical and inclusive corporate culture, and a wide range of other social criterial. Investopedia (*Note*: This term currently does not have a single definition globally agreed upon. See Chapter 8 for a detailed discussion).

Triple Bottom Line (TBL) is a business concept that posits firms should commit to measuring their social and environmental impact—in addition to their financial performance—rather than solely focusing on generating profit, or the standard "bottom line." The TBL is also used to refer to an accounting framework that incorporates three dimensions of performance: social, environmental, and financial. This differs from traditional reporting frameworks as it includes ecological (or environmental) and social measures that can be difficult to assign appropriate means of measurement. The TBL dimensions are also commonly called the three Ps: people, planet, and profits. Book of Jargon

United Nations Environment Programme Finance Initiative (UNEP FI) is a partnership between UNEP and the global financial sector to mobilize private sector finance for sustainable development. UNEP FI works with more than 450 banks, insurers, and investors and over 100 supporting institutions – to help create a financial sector that serves people and planet while delivering positive impacts. UNEP FI was launched in 1992 in the wake of the Rio Earth Summit. UN

United Nations Framework Convention on Climate Change (UNFCCC). The UNFCCC was adopted in May 1992 and opened for signature at the 1992 Earth Summit in Rio de Janeiro. It entered into force in March 1994 and as of April 2023 had 199 Parties (198 States and the European Union). The Convention's ultimate objective is the 'stabilization of greenhouse gas concentrations in the atmosphere at a level that would prevent dangerous anthropogenic interference with the climate system.' The provisions of the Convention are pursued and implemented by two treaties: the *Kyoto Protocol* and the *Paris Agreement.* See also Kyoto Protocol and Paris Agreement. IPCC

United Nations Global Compact (UNGC) is the world's largest corporate sustainability initiative. It is a call to companies to align strategies and operations with universal principles on human rights, labor, environment, and anti-corruption, and to take actions that advance societal goals. UN

References

Global Impact Investing Network (GIIN). Impact Investing, https://thegiin.org/impact-investing/.

IPCC, 2018: Annex I: Glossary, in Matthews, J.B.R. (ed.), Global Warming of 1.5°C. An IPCC Special Report on the impacts of global warming of 1.5°C above pre-industrial levels and related global greenhouse gas emission pathways, in the context of strengthening the global response to the threat of climate change, sustainable development, and efforts to eradicate poverty, https://www.ipcc.ch/site/assets/uploads/sites/2/2022/06/SR15_AnnexI.pdf.

Latham & Watkins LLP. Glossary of ESG Slang and Terminology. "Book of Jargon: Environmental, Social & Governance", https://www.lw.com/en/book-of-jargon/boj-environmental-social-governance.

OECD Development Assistance Committee (DAC) Sustainable Development Blended Finance Principles, https://www.oecd.org/dac/financing-sustainable-development/blended-finance-principles.

OECD Glossary of Statistical Terms, https://stats.oecd.org/glossary/index.htm.

Principles for Responsible Investment (PRI), "About the PRI" https://www.unpri.org/about-us/about-the-pri; "What is responsible investment?", https://www.unpri.org/introductory-guides-to-responsible-investment/what-is-responsible-investment/4780.article.

UNFCCC Glossary of climate change acronyms and terms, https://unfccc.int/process-and-meetings/the-convention/glossary-of-climate-change-acronyms-and-terms.

United Nations (UN). UN website, https://www.un.org/; "Biological Diversity Convention", https://www.un.org/en/observances/biological-diversity-day/convention; "What is Climate Change?", https://www.un.org/en/climatechange/what-is-climate-change.

United States Environmental Protection Agency (EPA). Terminology Services, https://sor.epa.gov/sor_internet/registry/termreg/searchandretrieve/termsandacronyms/search.do.

Glossary B

Business and Investment Terms

A. S. Preker & S. C. Hulton

The following glossary provides an alphabetical list of standard definitions for business and investment terms. The list includes both technical terms used in this book and other terms that the reader may find useful when reading some of the references that are cited in the book.

All the terms provided in this glossary are direct quotes from either the IMF or Investopedia websites. Online links to these two sources are provided in the Reference list at the end of this Glossary. These and many other standard sources may be consulted if the reader wants to look up the definition of business and investment terms not found in this glossary.

Adverse Selection refers generally to a situation in which sellers have information that buyers do not have, or vice versa, about some aspect of product quality. In other words, it is a case where asymmetric information is exploited. Asymmetric information, also called information failure, happens when one party to a transaction has greater material knowledge than the other party. Typically, the more knowledgeable party is the seller. Symmetric information is when both parties have equal knowledge. In the case of insurance, adverse selection is the tendency of those in dangerous jobs or high-risk lifestyles to purchase products like life insurance. In these cases, it is the buyer who actually has more knowledge (i.e., about their health). To fight adverse selection, insurance companies reduce

549

exposure to large claims by limiting coverage or raising premiums. Investopedia

Acquisition refers to an action when one company purchases most or all of another company's shares to gain control of that company. Purchasing more than 50% of a target firm's stock and other assets allow the acquirer to make decisions about the newly acquired assets without the approval of the company's other shareholders. Acquisitions, which are very common in business, may occur with the target company's approval, or in spite of its disapproval. With approval, there is often a no-shop clause during the process. We mostly hear about acquisitions of large well-known companies because these huge and significant deals tend to dominate the news. In reality, mergers and acquisitions (M&A) occur more regularly between small- to medium-size firms than between large companies. Investopedia

Angel Investor (also known as a private investor, seed investor or angel funder) refers to a high-net-worth individual who provides financial backing for small startups or entrepreneurs, typically in exchange for ownership equity in the company. Often, angel investors are found among an entrepreneur's family and friends. The funds that angel investors provide may be a one-time investment to help the business get off the ground or an ongoing injection to support and carry the company through its difficult early stages. Investopedia

Annuity refers to an insurance contract issued and distributed by financial institutions with the intention of paying out invested funds in a fixed income stream in the future. Investors invest in or purchase annuities with monthly premiums or lump-sum payments. The holding institution issues a stream of payments in the future for a specified period of time or for the remainder of the annuitant's life. Annuities are mainly used for retirement purposes and help individuals address the risk of outliving their savings. Investopedia

Asset refers to a resource with economic value that an individual, corporation, or country owns or controls with the expectation that it will provide a future benefit. Assets are reported on a company's balance sheet.

They're classified as current, fixed, financial, and intangible. They are bought or created to increase a firm's value or benefit the firm's operations. An asset can be thought of as something that, in the future, can generate cash flow, reduce expenses, or improve sales, regardless of whether it's manufacturing equipment or a patent. Investopedia

Asset Management refers to the practice of increasing total wealth over time by acquiring, maintaining, and trading investments that have the potential to grow in value. Asset management professionals perform this service for others. They may also be called portfolio managers or financial advisors. Many work independently while others work for an investment bank or other financial institution. Investopedia

Balanced Scorecard (BSC) refers to a strategic management performance metric used to identify and improve various internal business functions and their resulting external outcomes. Used to measure and provide feedback to organizations, balanced scorecards are common among companies in the United States, the United Kingdom, Japan, and Europe. Data collection is crucial to providing quantitative results as managers and executives gather and interpret the information. Company personnel can use this information to make better decisions for the future of their organizations. Investopedia

Bond refers to a fixed-income instrument that represents a loan made by an investor to a borrower (typically corporate or governmental). A bond could be thought of as an I.O.U. ("I owe you") between the lender and borrower that includes the details of the loan and its payments. Bonds are used by companies, municipalities, states, and sovereign governments to finance projects and operations. Owners of bonds are debtholders, or creditors, of the issuer. Bond details include the end date when the principal of the loan is due to be paid to the bond owner and usually include the terms for variable or fixed interest payments made by the borrower. Investopedia

Budget refers to an estimation of revenue and expenses over a specified future period of time and is usually compiled and re-evaluated on a periodic basis. Budgets can be made for any entity that wants to spend money, including governments and businesses, along with people and households at any income level. To manage your monthly expenses, prepare for life's unpredictable events, and be able to afford big-ticket items without going into debt, budgeting is important. Keeping track of how much you earn and spend doesn't have to be drudgery, doesn't require you to be good at math, and doesn't mean you can't buy the things you want. It just means that you'll know where your money goes, and you'll have greater control over your finances. Investopedia

Business Cycles refer to fluctuations found in the aggregate economic activity of a nation — a cycle that consists of expansions occurring at about the same time in many economic activities, followed by similarly general contractions (recessions). This sequence of changes is recurrent but not periodic. The business cycle is an example of an economic cycle. Investopedia

Business Model refers to a company's plan for making a profit. It identifies the products or services the business plans to sell, its identified target market, and any anticipated expenses. Business models are important for both new and established businesses. They help new, developing companies attract investment, recruit talent, and motivate management and staff. Established businesses should regularly update their business model or they'll fail to anticipate trends and challenges ahead. Business models also help investors evaluate companies that interest them and employees understand the future of a company they may aspire to join. Investopedia

Capital is a broad term that can describe anything that confers value or benefit to its owners, such as a factory and its machinery, intellectual property like patents, or the financial assets of a business or an individual. While money itself may be construed as capital, capital is more often associated with cash that is being put to work for productive or investment purposes. In general, capital is a critical component of running a business from day to day and financing its future growth. Business capital may derive from the operations of the business or be raised from debt or equity financing. When budgeting, businesses of all kinds typically focus on three types of capital: working capital, equity capital, and debt capital. A business in the financial industry identifies trading capital as a fourth component. Investopedia

Capitalism is an economic system in which private individuals or businesses own capital goods. At the same time, business owners (capitalists) employ workers (labor) who only receive wages; labor does not own the means of production but only uses them on behalf of the owners of capital. The production of goods and services under capitalism is based on supply and demand in the general market—known as a market economy—rather than through central planning—known as a planned economy or command economy. The purest form of capitalism is free market or laissez-faire capitalism. Here, private individuals are unrestrained. They may determine where to invest, what to produce or sell, and at which prices to exchange goods and services. The laissez-faire marketplace operates without checks or controls. Today, most countries practice a mixed capitalist system that includes some degree of government regulation of business and ownership of select industries. Investopedia

Collateral refers to a valuable asset that a borrower pledges as security for a loan. When a homebuyer obtains a mortgage, the home serves as the collateral for the loan. For a car loan, the vehicle is the collateral. A business that obtains financing from a bank may pledge valuable equipment or real estate owned by the business as collateral for the loan. A loan that is secured by collateral comes with a lower interest rate than an unsecured loan. In the event of a default, the lender can seize the collateral and sell it to recoup the loss. Investopedia

Command Economy (also called to as a "planned" economy) refers to a key aspect of a political system in which a central governmental authority dictates the levels of production that are permissible and the prices that may be charged for goods and services. Most industries are publicly owned. The main alternative to a command economy is a free market system in which demand dictates production and prices. The command economy is a component of a communist political system, while a free market system exists in capitalist societies. Investopedia

Demand refers to an economic concept that relates to a consumer's desire to purchase goods and services and willingness to pay a specific price for them. An increase in the price of a good or service tends to decrease the quantity demanded. Likewise, a decrease in the price of a good or service will increase the quantity demanded. Demand is a concept that consumers and businesses are very familiar with because it makes sense and occurs naturally in the course of practically any day. For example, shoppers with an eye on products that they want will buy more when the products' prices are low. When something happens to raise the prices, such as a change of season, shoppers buy fewer or perhaps none at all. Generally speaking, there is market demand and aggregate demand. Market demand is the total quantity demanded by all consumers in a market for a given good. Aggregate demand is the total demand for all goods and services in an economy. Multiple stocking strategies are often required to handle demand. Investopedia

Diversification is a risk management strategy that mixes a wide variety of investments within a portfolio. A diversified portfolio contains a mix of distinct asset types and investment vehicles in an attempt at limiting exposure to any single asset or risk. The rationale behind this technique is that a portfolio constructed of different kinds of assets will, on average, yield higher long-term returns and lower the risk of any individual holding or security. Investopedia

Dividend refers to the distribution of a company's earnings to its shareholders and is determined by the company's board of directors. Dividends are often distributed quarterly and may be paid out as cash or in the form of reinvestment in additional stock. The dividend yield is the dividend per share and is expressed as dividend/price as a percentage of a company's share price, such as 2.5%. Common shareholders of dividend-paying companies are eligible to receive a distribution as long as they own the stock before the ex-dividend date. Investopedia

Economic Growth refers to an increase in the production of economic goods and services in one period of time compared with a previous period. It can be measured in nominal or real (adjusted to remove inflation) terms.

Traditionally, aggregate economic growth is measured in terms of gross national product (GNP) or gross domestic product (GDP), although alternative metrics are sometimes used. Investopedia

Economics refers to a social science that focuses on the production, distribution, and consumption of goods and services, and analyzes the choices that individuals, businesses, governments, and nations make to allocate resources. Investopedia

Entrepreneur refers to an individual who creates a new business, bearing most of the risks and enjoying most of the rewards. The process of setting up a business is known as entrepreneurship. The entrepreneur is commonly seen as an innovator, a source of new ideas, goods, services, and business/or procedures. Entrepreneurs play a key role in any economy, using the skills and initiative necessary to anticipate needs and bring good new ideas to market. Entrepreneurship that proves to be successful in taking on the risks of creating a startup is rewarded with profits, fame, and continued growth opportunities. Entrepreneurship that fails results in losses and less prevalence in the markets for those involved. Investopedia

Equity, also referred to as shareholders' equity (or owners' equity for privately held companies), represents the amount of money that would be returned to a company's shareholders if all of the assets were liquidated and all of the company's debt was paid off in the case of liquidation. In the case of acquisition, it is the value of company sales minus any liabilities owed by the company not transferred with the sale. In addition, shareholder equity can represent the book value of a company. Equity can sometimes be offered as payment-in-kind. It also represents the pro-rata ownership of a company's shares. Equity can be found on a company's balance sheet and is one of the most common pieces of data employed by analysts to assess a company's financial health. Investopedia

Externality refers to a cost or benefit caused by a producer that is not financially incurred or received by that producer. An externality can be both positive or negative and can stem from either the production or consumption of a good or service. The costs and benefits can be both private—to an individual or an organization—or social, meaning it can affect society as a whole. Investopedia

Fiduciary refers to a person or organization that acts on behalf of another person or persons, putting their clients' interests ahead of their own, with a duty to preserve good faith and trust. Being a fiduciary thus requires being bound both legally and ethically to act in the other's best interests. A fiduciary may be responsible for the general well-being of another (e.g., a child's legal guardian), but the task often involves finances—for example, managing the assets of another person or a group of people. Money managers, financial advisors, bankers, insurance agents, accountants, executors, board members, and corporate officers all have fiduciary responsibility. Investopedia

Finance refers to the management, creation, and study of money and investments. It involves the use of credit and debt, securities, and investment to finance current projects using future income flows. Because of this temporal aspect, finance is closely linked to the time value of money, interest rates, and other related topics. Finance can be broadly divided into three categories: Public Finance, Corporate Finance and Personal Finance. There are many other specific categories, such as behavioral finance, which seeks to identify the cognitive (e.g., emotional, social, and psychological) reasons behind financial decisions. Investopedia

Financial institution (FI) refers to a company engaged in the business of dealing with financial and monetary transactions such as deposits, loans, investments, and currency exchange. Financial institutions encompass a broad range of business operations within the financial services sector including banks, trust companies, insurance companies, brokerage firms, and investment dealers. Virtually everyone living in a developed economy has an ongoing or at least periodic need for the services of financial institutions. Investopedia

Fiscal Policy refers to the use of government spending and tax policies to influence economic conditions, especially macro-economic conditions. These include aggregate demand for goods and services, employment, inflation, and economic growth. During a recession, the government may lower tax rates or increase spending to encourage demand and spur economic activity. Conversely, to combat inflation, it may raise rates or cut spending to cool down the economy. Fiscal policy is often contrasted with monetary policy, which is enacted by central bankers and not elected government officials. Investopedia

Globalization refers to the spread of the flow of financial products, goods, technology, information, and jobs across national borders and cultures. In economic terms, it describes an interdependence of nations around the globe fostered through free trade. Investopedia

Government bond is a debt security issued by a government to support government spending and obligations. Government bonds can pay periodic interest payments called coupon payments. Government bonds issued by national governments are often considered low-risk investments since the issuing government backs them. Government bonds issued by a federal government may also be known as sovereign debt. Investopedia

Gross domestic product (GDP) is the total monetary or market value of all the finished goods and services produced within a country's borders in a specific time period. As a broad measure of overall domestic production, it functions as a comprehensive scorecard of a given country's economic health. Though GDP is typically calculated on an annual basis, it is sometimes calculated on a quarterly basis as well. In the U.S., for example, the government releases an annualized GDP estimate for each fiscal quarter and also for the calendar year. The individual data sets included in this report are given in real terms, so the data is adjusted for price changes and is, therefore, net of inflation. Investopedia

Gross national product (GNP) is an estimate of the total value of all the final products and services turned out in a given period by the means of production owned by a country's residents. GNP is commonly calculated by taking the sum of personal consumption expenditures, private domestic investment, government expenditure, net exports, and any income earned by residents from overseas investments, then subtracting income earned by foreign residents. Net exports represent the difference between what a country exports minus any imports of goods and services. GNP is related to another important economic measure called gross domestic (GDP), which takes into account all output produced within a country's borders regardless of who owns the means of production. GNP starts with GDP, adds residents' investment income from overseas investments, and subtracts foreign residents' investment income earned within a country. Investopedia

Hedge fund is a limited partnership of private investors whose money is managed by professional fund managers who use a wide range of strategies, including leverage or trading of non-traditional assets, to earn above-average investment returns. Hedge fund investment is often considered a risky alternative investment choice and usually requires a high minimum investment or net worth, often targeting wealthy clients. Investopedia

Holding Company is a business entity—usually a corporation or limited liability company (LLC). Typically, a holding company doesn't manufacture anything, sell any products or services, or conduct any other business operations. Rather, holding companies hold the controlling stock in other companies. Although a holding company owns the assets of other companies, it often maintains only oversight capacities. So while it may oversee the company's management decisions, it does not actively participate in running a business's day-to-day operations of these subsidiaries. A holding company is also sometimes called an "umbrella" or parent company. Investopedia

Hyperinflation is a term to describe rapid, excessive, and out-of-control general price increases in an economy. While inflation measures the pace of rising prices for goods and services, hyperinflation is rapidly rising inflation, typically measuring more than 50% per month. Although hyperinflation is a rare event for developed economies, it has occurred many times throughout history in countries such as China, Germany, Russia, Hungary, and Georgia. Investopedia

Index Fund is a type of mutual fund or exchange-traded fund (ETF) with a portfolio constructed to match or track the components of a financial market index, such as the Standard & Poor's 500 Index (S&P 500). An index mutual fund is said to provide broad market exposure, low operating expenses, and low portfolio turnover. These funds follow their benchmark index regardless of the state of the markets. Index funds are generally considered ideal core portfolio holdings for retirement accounts, such as individual retirement accounts (IRAs) and 401(k) accounts. Legendary investor Warren Buffett has recommended index funds as a haven for savings for the later years of life. Rather than picking out individual stocks for investment, he has said, it makes more sense for the average investor to buy all of the S&P 500 companies at the low cost that an index fund offers. Investopedia

Industrial Policy refers to government efforts to shape the economy by targeting specific industries, firms, or economic activities. This is achieved through a range of tools such as subsidies, tax incentives, infrastructure development, protective regulations, and research and development support. When implementing industrial policy as part of their growth strategy, countries are often faced with competing objectives, such as securing sustainable economic growth, maintaining financial and fiscal stability, and establishing "national champions." Although the use of industrial policy to establish national champions has been successful in some cases, it remains controversial. Economists worry that picking winners and losers can lead to market distortions and inefficient allocation of resources. Despite the concerns, the revival of industrial policy shows no signs of slowing down. IMF

Industrial Revolution was a period of major mechanization and innovation that began in Great Britain during the mid-18th century and early 19th century and later spread throughout much of the world. The British Industrial Revolution was dominated by the exploitation of coal and iron. The American Industrial Revolution, sometimes referred to as the Second Industrial Revolution, began in the 1870s and continued through World War II. The era saw the mechanization of agriculture and manufacturing and the introduction of new modes of transportation including steamships, the automobile, and airplanes. Investopedia

Inflation is a rise in prices, which can be translated as the decline of purchasing power over time. The rate at which purchasing power drops can be reflected in the average price increase of a basket of selected goods and services over some period of time. The rise in prices, which is often expressed as a percentage, means that a unit of currency effectively buys less than it did in prior periods. Inflation can be contrasted with deflation, which occurs when prices decline and purchasing power increases. Investopedia

Interest Rate is the amount a lender charges a borrower and is a percentage of the principal—the amount loaned. The interest rate on a loan is typically noted on an annual basis known as the annual percentage rate (APR). An interest rate can also apply to the amount earned at a bank or credit union from a savings account or certificate of deposit (CD). Annual percentage yield (APY) refers to the interest earned on these deposit accounts. Investopedia

Joint Venture (JV) is a business arrangement in which two or more parties agree to pool their resources for the purpose of accomplishing a specific task. This task can be a new project or any other business activity. Each of the participants in a JV is responsible for profit, losses, and costs associated with it. However, the venture is its own entity, separate from the participants' other business interests. Investopedia

Junk Bonds are bonds that carry a higher risk of default than most bonds issued by corporations and governments. A bond is a debt or promise to pay investors interest payments along with the return of invested principal in exchange for buying the bond. Junk bonds represent bonds issued by companies that are financially struggling and have a high risk of defaulting or not paying their interest payments or repaying the principal to investors. Junk bonds are also called high-yield bonds since the higher yield is needed to help offset any risk of default. Investopedia

Keynesian economics is a macro-economic theory of total spending in the economy and its effects on output, employment, and inflation. It was developed by British economist John Maynard Keynes during the 1930s in an attempt to understand the Great Depression. The central belief of Keynesian economics is that government intervention can stabilize the economy. Keynes' theory was the first to sharply separate the study of economic behavior and individual incentives from the study of broad aggregate variables and constructs. Based on his theory, Keynes advocated for increased government expenditures and lower taxes to stimulate demand and pull the global economy out of the Depression. Subsequently, Keynesian economics was used to refer to the concept that optimal economic performance could be achieved—and economic slumps could be prevented—by influencing aggregate demand through economic intervention by the government. Keynesian economists believe that such intervention can achieve full employment and price stability. Investopedia

Laissez-faire is an economic theory from the 18th century that opposed any government intervention in business affairs. The driving principle behind laissez-faire, a French term that translates to "leave alone" (literally, "let you do"), is that the less the government is involved in the economy, the better off business will be, and by extension, society as a whole. Laissez-faire economics is a key part of free-market capitalism. Investopedia

Law of Demand is one of the most fundamental concepts in economics. It works with the law of supply to explain how market economies allocate resources and determine the prices of goods and services that we observe in everyday transactions. The law of demand states that the quantity purchased varies inversely with price. In other words, the higher the price, the lower the quantity demanded. This occurs because of diminishing marginal utility. That is, consumers use the first units of an economic good they purchase to serve their most urgent needs first, then they use each additional unit of the good to serve successively lower-valued ends. Investopedia

Law of Supply is the microeconomic law that states that, all other factors being equal, as the price of a good or service increases, the quantity of goods or services that suppliers offer will increase, and vice versa. The law of supply says that as the price of an item goes up, suppliers will attempt to maximize their profits by increasing the number of items for sale. Investopedia

Liability is something a person or company owes, usually a sum of money. Liabilities are settled over time through the transfer of economic benefits including money, goods, or services. Recorded on the right side of the balance sheet, liabilities include loans, accounts payable, mortgages, deferred revenues, bonds, warranties, and accrued expenses. Liabilities can be contrasted with assets. Liabilities refer to things that you owe or have borrowed; assets are things that you own or are owed. Investopedia

Liquidity refers to the efficiency or ease with which an asset or security can be converted into ready cash without affecting its market price. The most liquid asset of all is cash itself. Investopedia

Macro-economics is a branch of economics that studies how an overall economy—the markets, businesses, consumers, and governments—behave. Macro-economics examines economy-wide phenomena such as inflation, price levels, rate of economic growth, national income, gross domestic product (GDP), and changes in unemployment. Some of the key questions addressed by macro-economics include: What causes unemployment? What causes inflation? What creates or stimulates economic growth? Macro-economics attempts to measure how well an economy is performing, understand what forces drive it, and project how performance can improve. Investopedia

Mercantilism was an economic system of trade that spanned the 16th century to the 18th century. Mercantilism was based on the principle that the world's wealth was static, and consequently, governments had to regulate trade to build their wealth and national power. Many European nations attempted to accumulate the largest possible share of that wealth by maximizing their exports and limiting their imports via tariffs. Investopedia

Microeconomics is the social science that studies the implications of incentives and decisions, specifically about how those affect the utilization and distribution of resources. Microeconomics shows how and why different goods have different values, how individuals and businesses conduct and benefit from efficient production and exchange, and how individuals best coordinate and cooperate with one another. Generally speaking, microeconomics provides a more complete and detailed understanding than macro-economics Investopedia

Milton Friedman was a U.S. economist and Nobel laureate known as the most influential advocate of free-market capitalism and monetarism in the 20th century. At the beginning of his career in the 1950s and 1960s, Friedman's strong advocacy of monetary policy over fiscal policy and free markets over government intervention was considered radical by the established macro-economics community, which was dominated by the Keynesian position that fiscal policy—government spending and tax policies to influence the economy—is more important than monetary policy—control of the overall supply of money available to banks, consumers, and businesses—and that an interventionist government could moderate recessions by using fiscal policy to prop up aggregate demand, spur consumption, and reduce unemployment. Investopedia

Mixed Economic system is a system that combines aspects of both capitalism and socialism. A mixed economic system protects private property and allows a level of economic freedom in the use of capital, but also allows for governments to interfere in economic activities in order to achieve social aims. According to neoclassical theory, mixed economies are less efficient than pure free markets, but proponents of government interventions argue that the base conditions required for efficiency in free markets, such as equal information and rational market participants, cannot be achieved in practical application. Investopedia

Monetary Policy is a set of tools used by a nation's central bank to control the overall money supply and promote economic growth and employ strategies such as revising interest rates and changing bank reserve requirements. In the United States, the Federal Reserve Bank implements monetary policy through a dual mandate to achieve maximum employment while keeping inflation in check. Investopedia

Neoliberalism is a policy model that encompasses both politics and economics. It favors private enterprise and seeks to transfer the control of economic factors from the government to the private sector. Many neoliberal policies concern the efficient functioning of free market capitalism and focus on limiting government spending, government regulation, and public ownership. Neoliberalism is often associated with the leadership of Margaret Thatcher, the prime minister of the U.K. from 1979 to 1990 (and leader of the Conservative Party from 1975 to 1990) and Ronald Reagan, the 40th president of the U.S. from 1981 to 1989. More recently, neoliberalism has been associated with policies of austerity and attempts to cut government spending on social programs. Investopedia

Not-for-Profit organizations do not earn profits for their owners. All of the money earned by or donated to a not-for-profit organization is used in pursuing the organization's objectives and keeping it running; income is not distributed to the group's members, directors, or officers. Typically, organizations in the nonprofit sector are tax-exempt charities or other types of public service organizations; as such, they are not required to pay most taxes. Some well-known nonprofit organizations include the American Red Cross, the United Way, and The Salvation Army. There are also nonprofit corporations known as nonstock corporations, which are usually formed for such purposes as clubs, rescue squads, and religious and charitable organizations. Investopedia

Opportunity Costs represent the potential benefits that an individual, investor, or business misses out on when choosing one alternative over another. Because opportunity costs are unseen by definition, they can be easily overlooked. Understanding the potential missed opportunities when a business or individual chooses one investment over another allows for better decision making. Investopedia

Perfect Competition refers to a theoretical market structure. Although perfect competition rarely occurs in real-world markets, it provides a useful model for explaining how supply and demand affect prices and behavior in a market economy. Under perfect competition, there are many buyers and sellers, and prices reflect supply and demand. Companies earn just enough profit to stay in business and no more. If they were to earn excess profits, other companies would enter the market and drive profits down. Investopedia

Profit describes the financial benefit realized when revenue generated from a business activity exceeds the expenses, costs, and taxes involved in sustaining the activity in question. Any profits earned funnel back to business owners, who choose to either pocket the cash, distribute it to shareholders as dividends, or reinvest it back into the business. Investopedia

Rate of Return (RoR) is the net gain or loss of an investment over a specified time period, expressed as a percentage of the investment's initial cost. When calculating the rate of return, you are determining the percentage change from the beginning of the period until the end. Investopedia

Security refers to a fungible, negotiable financial instrument that holds some type of monetary value. A security can represent ownership in a corporation in the form of stock, a creditor relationship with a governmental body or a corporation represented by owning that entity's bond; or rights to ownership as represented by an option. Investopedia

Stock, also known as equity, is a security that represents the ownership of a fraction of the issuing corporation. Units of stock are called "shares" which entitles the owner to a proportion of the corporation's assets and profits equal to how much stock they own. Stocks are bought and sold predominantly on stock exchanges and are the foundation of many individual investors' portfolios. Stock trades have to conform to government regulations meant to protect investors from fraudulent practices. Investopedia

Subsidiary is a company that belongs to another company, which is usually referred to as the parent company or the holding company. The parent holds a controlling interest in the subsidiary company, meaning it has or controls more than half of its stock. In cases where a subsidiary is 100% owned by another firm, the subsidiary is referred to as a wholly owned subsidiary. Subsidiaries become very important when discussing a reverse triangle mortgage. Investopedia

Sustainable Investing is an investing philosophy wherein an investor takes a company's environmental, social, and corporate governance (ESG) factors into account. This allows investment dollars to be used as a tool to promote positive societal impact and corporate responsibility without sacrificing long-term financial returns. Strategies for investing sustainably include avoiding companies that conflict with ESG principles and seeking out industries that are inherently more sustainable. Following the environmental, social, and corporate governance (ESG) framework, there are a wide variety of investments that can be considered "sustainable." Industries that promote good environmental practices, via more renewable energy sources or by combating air and water pollution, are perhaps the first things that come to mind for most people. However, sustainable investing can also include investing in companies that support human rights initiatives, more ethical and inclusive corporate culture and a wide range of other social criterial. Investopedia (This term currently does not have a single agreed definitions. See Chapter 8 for a more detailed discussion).

Transaction is a completed agreement between a buyer and a seller to exchange goods, services, or financial assets in return for money. The term is also commonly used in corporate accounting. In business bookkeeping, this plain definition can get tricky. A transaction may be recorded by a company earlier or later depending on whether it uses accrual accounting or cash accounting. Investopedia

Triple Bottom Line (TBL) maintains that companies should commit to focusing as much on social and environmental concerns as they do on profits. TBL theory posits that instead of one bottom line, there should be three: profit, people, and the planet. A TBL seeks to gauge a corporation's level of commitment to corporate social responsibility and its impact on the environment over time. In 1994, John Elkington—the famed British management consultant and sustainability guru—coined the phrase "triple bottom line" as his way of measuring performance in corporate America. The idea was that a company can be managed in a way that not only makes money but which also improves people's lives and the well-being of the planet. Investopedia

Trustee is a person or firm that holds and administers property or assets for the benefit of a third party. A trustee may be appointed for various purposes, such as in the case of bankruptcy, certain types of retirement plans or pensions, or to manage assets for someone. Trustees are required to make decisions in the beneficiary's best interests and have a fiduciary responsibility to them, meaning they act in the best interests of the beneficiaries to manage their assets. Investopedia

Unicorn refers to a privately held startup company with a value of over $1 billion. It is commonly used in the venture capital industry. The term was first popularized by venture capitalist Aileen Lee. Unicorns are very rare and require innovation. Because of their sheer size, unicorn investors tend to be private investors or venture capitalists, which means they are out of the reach of retail investors. Although it isn't necessary, many unicorns work their way to going public. Investopedia

Valuation is the analytical process of determining the current (or projected) worth of an asset or a company. There are many techniques used for doing a valuation. An analyst placing a value on a company looks at the business's management, the composition of its capital structure, the prospect of future earnings, and the market value of its assets, among other metrics. Fundamental analysis is often employed in valuation, although several other methods may be employed such as the capital asset pricing model (CAPM) or the dividend discount model (DDM). Investopedia

Value Investing is an investment strategy that involves picking stocks that appear to be trading for less than their intrinsic or book value. Value investors actively ferret out stocks they think the stock market is underestimating. They believe the market overreacts to good and bad news, resulting in stock price movements that do not correspond to a company's long-term fundamentals. The overreaction offers an opportunity to profit by buying stocks at discounted prices—on sale. Investopedia

Venture Capital (VC) is a form of private equity and a type of financing that investors provide to startup companies and small businesses that are believed to have long-term growth potential. Venture capital generally comes from well-off investors, investment banks, and any other financial institutions. However, it does not always take a monetary form; it can also be provided in the form of technical or managerial expertise. Venture capital is typically allocated to small companies with exceptional growth potential, or to companies that have grown quickly and appear poised to continue to expand. Though it can be risky for investors who put up funds, the potential for above-average returns is an attractive payoff. For new companies or ventures that have a limited operating history (under two years), venture capital is increasingly becoming a popular—even essential—source for raising money, especially if they lack access to capital markets, bank loans, or other debt instruments. The main downside is that the investors usually get equity in the company, and, thus, a say in company decisions. Investopedia

Warrants are a derivative that give the right, but not the obligation, to buy or sell a security—most commonly an equity—at a certain price before expiration. The price at which the underlying security can be bought or sold is referred to as the exercise price or strike price. An American warrant can be exercised at any time on or before the expiration date, while European warrants can only be exercised on the expiration date. Warrants that give the right to buy a security are known as call warrants; those that give the right to sell a security are known as put warrants. Investopedia

Yield refers to the earnings generated and realized on an investment over a particular period of time. It's expressed as a percentage based on the invested amount, current market value, or face value of the security. Yield includes the interest earned or dividends received from holding a particular security. Depending on the valuation (fixed vs. fluctuating) of the security, yields may be classified as known or anticipated. Investopedia

References

IMF, https://www.imf.org/en/Publications/fandd/issues/Series/Analytical-Series/industrial-policy-and-the-growth-strategy-trilemma-ruchir-agarwal.

Investopedia, https://www.investopedia.com/terms/.

Index

A

accelerator(s), 90–91, 93–94, 107–108

acquisition, 90, 257, 321, 550

activists, 156, 288, 293, 350, 368, 503–504, 527–528

adaptation, 4, 60, 88, 212, 306, 309, 313, 324, 338, 361, 439–477, 482–483, 485, 489, 492–493, 500, 514, 533

additionality, 228, 257, 274–278, 280, 284

adverse selection, 549–550

Agenda for Sustainable Development 2030, 533

agile engineering, 92

agriculture, 6, 11, 14, 17–19, 25, 95, 115, 166, 213, 223–224, 257, 278, 313–317, 327, 341, 360, 362, 367, 370, 417, 445–446, 462, 466, 484, 486, 491, 522, 524, 559

air pollution, 22–23, 120, 133, 228, 402, 417, 433, 485, 508

American System, 524–525

angel investor, 75, 90, 550

annuity, 550

anthropocene, 12

anti-trust, 511, 513, 515

asset, 3, 5–6, 8, 12, 60, 76, 101, 114–115, 119–120, 128–129, 131–132, 142, 158, 196, 199–200, 202, 205, 213–216, 219, 221–225, 229–232, 242–246, 253–254, 259–261, 266, 269, 288, 291, 299, 308, 320–321, 356–357, 365, 368, 370–371, 447, 449, 469, 485, 501, 503, 505, 544, 550–551

asset management, 196, 370, 506, 551

asset manager, 67, 199, 212–213, 232, 259, 299, 308, 356, 371, 501, 503–505, 598

asset owner, 8, 120, 196, 199, 202, 213, 217, 229, 260, 365, 371

authorizing environment, 528

B

balanced scorecard, 551

banking risks, 494–495

banking sector linkages, 493, 498

bankrupt, 5, 119, 228, 349, 355, 508, 515, 528, 567

B Corporation ("B Corp"), 105–106

behavioral issues, 338, 364–365

best-in-class, 206, 217–219, 221–223, 244, 257, 261, 292

biocapacity, 330

biodiversity, 4, 9, 13, 24–25, 29, 62, 123, 212, 311, 313, 345, 421, 489, 502

biological resources, 311, 322

biomass fuels/biofuels, 315, 534

B-Lab, 66, 106

black carbon (BC), 313–315, 340

blacklist, 528

blended finance, 105, 226, 257, 534

Bloomberg ESG Disclosure Scores, 534

bonds, 3, 6, 199–200, 203, 221, 241–256, 258, 261, 269–270, 404, 459, 469, 513

boomerang effect, 485

borrowing, 246, 467, 482–483, 497, 499, 506, 514

bottom line, 7, 50, 61, 65, 76, 83–84, 96, 99, 157–158, 266, 501, 504, 515, 528

Brundtland Commission Report, 534–535

budget, 61, 160, 198–199, 351, 442–443, 455, 462–465, 503, 509–510, 551–552

buildings, 10, 17, 186, 224, 251, 261, 320, 323, 327, 337, 347, 362–364

business(es), 1–30, 41–76, 81–109, 113–147, 155–167, 171–191, 195–233, 241–261, 265–284, 287–302, 305–330, 335–374, 387–406, 411–435, 439–477, 481–515, 521–529

business cycles, 552

business model, 6, 10, 30, 45, 49, 63, 72, 84, 87, 93, 98, 121–122, 128, 132, 138, 142–143, 147, 162, 172, 181, 190–191, 224, 233, 282, 319, 370, 397, 399, 406, 449, 552

Business Model Canvas, 92–93

C

call to arms, 527

cap-and-trade, 360, 371, 427–428

capital, 4, 7–8, 45–46, 70, 75, 83, 90, 94, 104–105, 114, 124, 128, 130, 141, 157, 161, 198–200, 203, 211, 213, 217, 225–226, 230–233, 242–243, 245–247, 250, 252, 254–255, 257–259, 267, 269–270, 275–278, 282–283, 288–289, 310, 324, 351, 360, 365, 368, 372, 394–395, 449, 462–463, 475, 490, 501, 506, 511, 552–553

capitalism, 4, 67, 85, 96, 290, 524, 553, 561, 563–564

capital structure (for a company), 567

capped allowance systems, 427–428

capture of corporate boards, 527–528

carbon capture and storage (CCS), 123, 139, 322, 328, 535

carbon capture, utilization and storage (CCUS), 535

carbon dioxide (CO_2), 13–15, 17–18, 23, 139, 306, 314. 322, 330, 336, 338–340, 344, 346, 358, 444, 457, 502, 534–536, 538–539, 541–542

carbon footprint, 313, 317–318, 486, 535

carbon neutrality, 535
carbon offsetting, 327, 534–535
carbon removal solutions, 306, 313, 322–323
carbon sequestration, 322, 535
carbon tax, 8, 18, 53, 120–121, 229, 321, 364, 403, 426, 441, 467
cartels, 510–511, 513, 515, 526
catastrophe bonds, 449, 469
central banks, 448, 461, 497, 563
charity, 44, 70, 372, 564
circular economy, 6, 122, 206, 212, 251, 305–307, 309–311, 320, 322, 327, 330, 420, 536
climate adaptation, 449, 464–466, 495
climate change, 3–5, 7–9, 13–18, 20, 23–26, 29, 44, 56, 60, 62, 72–73, 83, 96, 98, 109, 115, 120, 131–132, 139, 143, 202, 204, 209–213, 221, 223, 229, 232–233, 242–243, 260–261, 272, 274, 294, 298–301, 305–308, 311–324, 326, 330, 335–374, 392–394, 418–422, 426, 439–477, 482, 484, 488–493, 496–498, 502, 513–514, 523, 526, 536–537, 540–542, 546
climate change adaptation, 4, 251, 308, 439–477
climate change mitigation, 212, 305–308, 321, 324, 360–361, 439–440, 448, 475
Climate Disclosure Standard Board (CDSB), 55
climate finance, 3, 233, 305–330
climate mitigation, 23, 309, 338, 359–363
climate problematic, 338–346

climate-related stress tests, 356
climate risk, 8, 120, 229, 295, 335–336, 338, 341, 346, 349, 352–359, 366–370, 373, 452–455, 460–461, 466, 471, 473
climate risk analysis providers, 338, 357–359
climate risk insurance, 449
climate tech, 46, 217, 257, 288, 325–327
coercive rating agencies, 527–528
collateral, 498, 533
command-and-control, 412–413, 424–426
command economy, 525, 553
commercial interests, 528
communist economic model, 525
company life cycle, 198, 243, 254
company stages, 257
competitive markets, 8, 299, 398–399, 432, 435, 510, 512–513, 515, 525
concessionary capital, 70, 226
conference of the parties (COP), 211, 337, 444, 502, 537, 542
conscious capitalism, 43, 68–69
consumer(s), 2, 6, 42, 46, 49–50, 53, 61, 63, 66, 73, 82, 99, 101–102, 104, 109, 115, 120, 124–126, 144–145, 161, 196, 198, 208, 306–307, 320–321, 338, 349, 351, 353–354, 357, 364–365, 372, 387–388, 392, 395–400, 404–406, 424, 426–427, 429, 431, 482–483, 489, 499, 507–508, 510–515, 527, 537, 554, 561–563
consumer ignorance, 510, 512
consumer spending, 482–483, 499

contamination, 311, 427
contingency planning, 175, 469
convention on biological diversity
    (CBD), 502, 537
corporate financial performance
    (CFP), 116, 157–158, 162
corporate governance, 50, 62, 176,
    301, 482, 500–501, 505, 513–514,
    537
corporate sector risks, 495
corporate social responsibility (CSR),
    5, 42–43, 46, 55, 63–71, 75, 116,
    172–173, 180–182, 209, 226–227,
    388, 400, 405–406, 508, 537, 566
corporate sustainability, 2–3, 5,
    42–44, 49–50, 55–56, 59–72,
    74–75, 113–147, 162, 171, 189,
    216, 220, 292–293, 296, 537, 547
corporate sustainability reporting
    directive (CSRD), 55, 216
corporations, 45–50, 58, 64–65, 67,
    73, 82, 93, 106, 108, 131, 156–158,
    161, 172, 190, 199, 211, 248, 289,
    298, 464, 504, 506, 528, 537, 550,
    558, 560, 564–566
COVID, 5, 27–28, 249, 313, 315,
    317, 345, 463–464, 484, 491, 526
cradle-to-cradle approach, 311

D
debt, 5, 47–48, 61, 90, 124, 181–182,
    196, 198–201, 203, 224–225,
    230–232, 241–259, 261, 266, 269,
    276, 293, 403, 458, 460, 462–465,
    469–472, 485, 495, 497, 509, 539,
    551–553, 555–557, 560, 568
debt instruments, 182, 199, 224,
    241–243, 245–256, 258, 261, 568
decarbonization, 267, 283, 369, 538

deflation, 482–483, 499, 514, 560
demand, 17, 46, 49, 58, 66, 74, 82,
    84, 100–102, 104, 109, 122,
    124–126, 131, 147, 196, 200,
    212–213, 231–232, 249, 290, 321,
    325–326, 338, 353–354, 358,
    363–365, 367, 391, 399, 487, 490,
    498, 505, 509, 522, 527, 553–554
development, 4, 7–10, 12, 25, 30, 44,
    51, 59, 61, 64, 70, 72–75, 81–82,
    84–85, 87–88, 91–95, 98–100,
    102–105, 107–109, 121, 123,
    125–126, 128, 142, 175, 181, 208,
    225, 233, 251, 255, 266, 278,
    281–283, 307, 310, 313, 322, 337,
    348, 351, 354, 360–361, 364–365,
    372, 374, 388, 401, 419–420, 427,
    440, 442, 444, 452, 454–455,
    458–461, 464–466, 468–469, 471,
    473–476, 484, 500, 503–504, 512,
    524–525, 527–528, 533–534, 542,
    544–545, 559
directive(s), 56, 419
distorting legislation, 522
diversification, 125, 134, 243, 252,
    258–259, 261, 290, 554
diversity washing, 508
divestment, 120, 209, 221, 232,
    275–276, 290–291, 368
dividend, 368, 554
doing business, 45, 68, 82, 482, 506,
    513–515
do no significant harm (DNSH), 309
double materiality, 41–42, 51–55
dynamic materiality, 51, 53

E
eco-entrepreneurship, 97
ecological footprint, 307, 330

economic actors, 53, 390, 396–404

economic growth, 11, 65, 73, 98, 344, 361, 394, 419, 451, 482–483, 485, 488, 490, 493–494, 499, 514, 525, 554–555, 557, 559, 562–563

economic impact, 27, 65, 490, 522

economic linkages, 493

economics, 4, 6, 10, 15, 26–27, 52–53, 65, 70, 73, 84–85, 98–99, 120, 173, 185, 203–204, 208, 215, 229, 231, 233, 308, 310, 321, 345, 350, 358, 361, 363, 373, 388, 396–404, 419, 425–426, 435, 440–443, 446, 448, 450, 452–454, 463–464, 468, 470–472, 474, 476, 481–515, 523–528, 555

economic sanctions, 523

ecosystems, 25, 65, 69, 72, 82, 84, 98, 102–103, 107, 109, 212, 323, 341, 345, 347, 350, 389, 393–394, 396, 404, 446, 502, 534, 545

emissions, 14–18, 23, 26, 44–45, 72–73, 123, 132, 165, 206, 233, 274, 296, 313–314, 317–319, 324, 330, 338–347, 349, 357–358, 362, 367–368, 370–382, 392, 396, 403, 418–419, 426–427, 429–430, 433, 441, 444, 472, 475, 488, 502, 538

employment, 44, 82, 99, 482–483, 485, 493, 495, 499, 509, 514, 544, 556, 561, 564

energy storage, 17, 251, 320, 325–326, 361

energy transition, 3, 7, 139, 217, 233, 305–330, 345, 367, 527–528

enforcement, 59, 139–140, 411–422, 424–425, 430–431, 433, 513, 515

enterprise risk management (ERM), 176

entrepreneur, 84–85, 88, 90, 92, 94–95, 108, 555

entrepreneurship, 3, 47, 81–109, 523, 555

entrepreneurship life cycle, 88, 90, 94

entrepreneurship stages, 88–90

environmental entrepreneurs, 95

environmental protection agency (EPA), 341–342, 391, 415, 417, 423–432, 539, 543

environmental, social and governance (ESG), 2, 5, 7, 13, 41–43, 46, 50–51, 53, 55, 57–70, 74–76, 100–101, 113–120, 123–124, 126–133, 135–136, 138, 141–143, 147, 155–158, 160, 162–164, 196–197, 202, 206–213, 216–222, 226–229, 232–233, 244, 249, 252–253, 256–257, 260–261, 266, 268–270, 272, 275, 277, 280, 282, 288–293, 295–299, 301, 370, 404, 501, 503–508, 512–513, 534, 538, 541, 543–546, 566

equator principles, 210

equity, 6, 46–48, 90, 104–105, 131, 200, 213, 217, 221, 225–226, 230–231, 241–246, 254–261, 266, 269–271, 275–277, 283, 288, 292–293, 327, 345, 353, 369, 426, 433, 495–496, 498, 504, 506, 550, 552–553, 555, 565, 568

equivalent entrepreneur, not found

ESG data, 42–43, 53, 57–59, 76, 127, 221, 233, 299

ESG integration, 204, 206, 216–221, 227–229, 232–233, 249, 253, 256, 260, 292

ethical investing, 196, 538

European financial reporting advisory group (EFRAG), 55

European green deal, 419–420

EU taxonomy on sustainable finance, 212

exchange-traded funds (ETFs), 3, 242–243, 259–261, 291, 504, 506, 512, 559

exclusionary screening, 206, 216, 218–219, 221–222, 226, 244

explicit insurance, 469

externalities, 3–4, 18, 23, 30, 61, 138–139, 204, 228, 252, 272, 280, 311, 385–406, 412, 431, 450, 497–498, 510–511, 538–539, 555

F

fiduciary, 50–51, 116, 120, 134, 158, 207, 220, 295, 556

finance, 44, 70, 74–75, 92, 105, 124, 130, 134, 141, 165, 196–201, 203–204, 209–211, 225–226, 233, 242–246, 249, 254–255, 257, 261, 266, 271, 283, 307, 325, 362, 366, 372, 397, 412, 422, 439, 442, 448–449, 458, 462–463, 471–472, 476, 496, 498, 504, 508, 534, 536, 545, 547, 551–552, 556

financial flows, 490

financial institution, 2–3, 5, 8, 51, 61, 75, 136, 196, 198–199, 202, 210–211, 214, 229–230, 247–248, 255, 319, 353, 355, 358, 372, 397, 461, 485, 503, 506, 515, 529, 543, 556

financial materiality, 2, 7, 42, 51–54, 60, 113, 116, 135, 220

financial resilience, 468–472

financial risks, 220, 355–356, 360, 365–366, 370, 442, 496

financial sector linkages, 493, 497

fiscal, 5, 119, 439–477, 483, 485, 488, 490, 493, 495–497, 499, 506, 514, 526, 528, 556–557, 559

fiscal discipline, 526

fiscal linkages, 493, 496

fiscal policy, 3, 439, 442–443, 464–465, 468–475, 482–483, 499, 514, 553, 556–557

food, 4, 10–11, 16, 25, 60, 70, 83, 125, 136, 156, 223, 251, 257, 313, 320, 324–325, 327, 349, 361–362

foreign investment, 526

fossil fuel industry, 8, 139, 317, 482, 484–485, 514, 527

fossil fuels, 7–8, 10, 14, 18, 22–23, 119–120, 139, 221, 223, 229, 276, 313–315, 317, 319, 321, 323–324, 326, 330, 337–340, 344, 357, 361, 363–364, 367–369, 373, 441, 472, 482, 484–486, 491, 502–503, 511, 513–514, 522, 526–527, 534, 536, 539, 542

free market, 389–390, 403, 524, 553, 561, 563–564

Friedman, Milton, 63, 66, 525, 563

G

global environmental agreements, 421

globalization, 27, 523, 557

global reporting initiative (GRI), 52, 54–55, 58, 65–66, 146, 163–164, 210, 280, 294, 401

global trade, 484

global warming, 7, 23, 313, 317, 330, 337, 348, 370, 444, 485–486, 491, 502, 527, 539 government(s), 4, 18, 23, 50, 56, 61, 66, 68, 70, 75, 90, 93, 95, 99, 108, 120, 125, 136, 139–140, 143, 156–157, 161, 176, 197–201, 203, 209, 217, 295, 307–308, 312, 347, 351, 354, 359, 363–364, 370–372, 387–388, 395, 397, 400–406, 411–412, 415–417, 423, 427, 429, 433–434, 439–440, 442, 446, 449–451, 453–456, 458–459, 461–463, 465–469, 472–476, 485, 492, 500, 502, 504, 507, 509–510, 512, 522–527, 529, 537, 540, 551–553, 555–557, 559–561, 563–565

government bond, 203, 557

government finance, 197–198, 439, 442–443, 462–468

government intervention, 387–388, 400, 403–404, 523–526, 529, 561, 563

grants, 70, 90, 105, 231, 254, 418, 427, 509

great depression, 525, 561

Great Pacific Garbage Patch, 389, 396

green bonds, 3, 181, 231, 244, 248–251, 253, 256, 261, 404, 539, 544–546

green bonds principles (GBP), 250

green buildings, 62, 251, 362

greenhouse gases (GHG), 14, 18, 23–24, 24, 44, 72, 121, 139, 165, 206, 213, 229, 232–233, 251, 296, 298, 305–308, 313–319, 321–322, 325–326, 330, 336, 339–344, 346–347, 349, 355, 357–358, 362, 367, 370–372, 417, 419, 430, 444, 472, 489, 534–536, 538–542, 547

greenhouse gas protocol (GHGP), 318, 540, 549

green loan principles (GLP), 252

green loans, 181, 244, 249–250, 252

greenwashing, 6–7, 48, 71, 73–74, 76, 143, 145, 181, 196, 205, 233, 308–309, 319, 355, 499, 507–508, 513–514, 540

greenwashing, whitewashing, 6–7, 48, 71, 73–74, 76, 143, 145, 181, 196, 205, 233, 308–309, 319, 355, 482, 499, 507–509, 513–514, 540

gross domestic product (GDP), 15, 23, 82, 232, 254, 342, 363, 463, 482–483, 488, 493, 499, 514, 555, 557–558, 562

gross national product (GNP), 483, 555, 557–558

H

hands on, 299, 524

hazard(s), 28, 134, 136, 358, 430, 440–442, 445–461, 464–467, 472, 474–476, 509

heating, 14, 251, 314, 318, 320, 324–325, 327, 540

hedge fund, 260, 504–505, 558

hidden political agendas, 482, 499, 503–506, 513–514

hidden threats, 4, 481, 483, 499–514

hierarchy of laws, 411–414

holding company, 558

household income, 485

household risks, 495

human-made capital, 394

human right(s), 55, 57, 65, 71, 272, 300, 309, 366, 422, 546–547, 566

hydrofluorocarbons (HFC), 313–315, 340, 539, 541

hydrogen, 7, 319–321, 326, 328, 344
hyperinflation, 558

I

IFRS accounting standards, 54
IFRS sustainability disclosure
    standards, 54, 117, 134, 136, 147
impact, 2–5, 7–8, 12, 14–15, 17,
    21–22, 24–25, 27, 41–44, 46,
    48–49, 51–53, 55, 58, 60, 65–67,
    70–76, 81, 83, 93–94, 96, 98,
    100–107, 109, 113–136, 138–139,
    142–147, 156, 158, 160, 167, 174,
    179–180, 186–187, 196–197,
    201–202, 204, 206, 210–213,
    217–220, 222–232, 245, 252–254,
    256–257
impact economy, 41–43, 72–75, 81,
    83, 98, 109, 311
impact entrepreneurs, 83, 96
impact investing, 3, 7, 46, 70, 101,
    104–105, 196, 206, 210, 213,
    217–219, 223–228, 230–231, 253,
    257, 265–284, 293, 301, 540
impact materiality, 42, 51–53
impact measurement, 267–268,
    278–284
incentives, 17, 23, 74–75, 122, 124,
    133, 135, 140, 190, 289–290, 364,
    403, 406, 412–413, 424–428,
    434–435, 489, 509, 512, 559, 561,
    563
index fund, 291, 503, 559
industrial policy, 4, 482, 499, 509,
    512, 514, 521–529, 559
industrial revolution, 10–12, 339,
    394, 524, 559–560
industrial strategy, 420, 509, 522, 527

industry, 6, 14, 17–18, 22, 45, 55, 89,
    101, 115–117, 119, 121–123, 125,
    128–129, 132–133, 135–136, 141,
    156–159, 161–162, 182–183,
    210–211, 213, 218, 228, 273–274,
    276, 278, 283–284, 290, 301, 313,
    317, 320–321, 325, 327, 344, 347,
    350, 355, 357–360, 362, 365–366,
    369, 373, 388, 391, 396, 406, 413,
    419, 442, 449–450, 452–456, 458,
    476, 487, 489, 496, 498, 502, 507,
    509, 511–513, 522–525, 527, 538,
    541, 543–546, 553, 559, 566–567
Inflation Reduction Act, 308, 417,
    503, 526
inflation, stagnation, 45, 199, 232,
    482–483, 488, 494, 497, 499, 514,
    523, 528, 554, 557–558, 560–562,
    564
information disclosure, 413, 428–
    429, 431, 433
instability, 202, 484–485, 497
institutional entrepreneurs, 96
institutional entrepreneurship, 97
institutional investor linkages, 493,
    498
insurance sector linkages, 493, 498
intangible assets, 76, 119, 128–129,
    131–132, 142, 158–159
integrated finance, *see also* blended
    finance
intentionality, 98, 224, 268, 270–273,
    283
interest rate, 245–247, 249, 252, 462,
    497, 526, 553, 556, 560, 563
Intergovernmental Panel on Climate
    Change (IPCC), 16, 27, 73, 226,
    232–233, 307, 312, 322–323, 337,

341–342, 347, 373, 441–442, 453, 456–457, 475, 533–538, 540–542, 545–547

International Integrated Reporting Council (IIRC), 55

International Monetary Fund (IMF), 27, 118–120, 202, 212, 221, 228–229, 233, 245, 254, 443, 449, 456, 456, 458–460, 462, 464, 468–476, 483–484, 549, 559

International Organization for Standardization (ISO) standards, 171–173, 180–190

International Sustainability Standards Board (ISSB), 54–55

intrapreneurs, 83

investment tax credit (ITC), 427

investors (in the context of climate change), 109

invisible hand, 390, 392, 524

IPAT equation, 21–22

J

joint venture, 560

Jumpstart Our Business Start-ups (JOBS) Act, 104–105, 503

junk bonds, 560

K

Keynesian, 561

Kindergarten rule of sustainability, 396

Kyoto Protocol, 274, 541, 547

L

lack of realism, 499–500, 514

laissez-faire, 553, 561

large enterprises, 45

law(s), 4, 47–50, 106, 116, 139, 208, 349, 351, 372, 391, 396, 411–435, 500, 502, 537, 561–562

lawmaking, 413, 422

law of demand, 561

law of supply, 562

lean start-up, 92–93

leaps of faith, 527

leverage, 74, 96, 200–201, 205, 213, 223, 247, 300, 342, 344, 373, 443, 494, 558

liability, 48–49, 119, 217, 349, 368, 429–430, 435, 562

liberalizing trade, 526

limited liability companies (LLCs), 48–49, 105–106, 142, 159, 558

linkages, 481–483, 490–491, 493–499, 514

liquidity, 199–200, 203, 245, 260, 356, 496, 498, 562

liquidity risks, 356, 496, 498

loans, 90, 105, 198, 200, 232, 241, 244–250, 252–254, 260, 272, 373, 418, 427, 461, 494–495, 498, 509, 551, 553, 556, 560, 562, 568

lobby(ies), 422–423

logistics, 362

loss of competitiveness, 482, 499, 509–510, 513–514

M

macro-economic, 4, 200, 233, 256, 453, 460, 476, 481–515, 526, 528, 556, 561–563

macro-economic performance, 482–483, 489, 499–514

macro-economic risks, 483–484, 493–499

man-made capital, 394–395
marginal utility, 26, 561
marine resources, 212, 309, 416
market(s)
market-based instruments, 402, 413,
    432, 435
market distortions, 510, 512, 559
market failure, 388, 400, 424,
    430–432
market imperfections, 3, 140, 232,
    387–406, 412
market price, 391, 496, 562
market risks, 134, 354
materiality, 2–3, 7, 42–43, 51–52,
    54–55, 58–60, 114, 116, 133,
    135–137, 147, 167, 220, 498, 541
materiality assessment, 541
materiality map, 136–137, 541
materials, 95, 206, 311, 320, 322–
    325, 327–328, 330, 360–361, 365,
    388, 394, 405, 416, 492, 512
maturity, 44, 88–89, 135, 182, 188,
    190–191, 201, 247, 260, 494
maturity date, 246
mercantilism, 523, 562
methane (CH_4), 313–315, 330, 340,
    362, 418, 443–444, 538–539, 541
microeconomics, 562–563
Millennium Development Goals
    (MDGs), 11, 29, 460, 500–501,
    541
minimum viable product (MVP), 92
minority opinion, 527
misallocation of resources, 388–389,
    525
mission creep, 482, 499–502,
    513–515
mitigation, 23, 60, 140–141, 156,
    166, 204, 251, 306–309, 311,
313–324, 338, 359–363, 370,
    443–445, 448–449, 454, 457, 460,
    467, 470, 475–476, 482–486, 490,
    492–493, 500, 512, 514, 542
mixed economic, 563
mobility, 244, 254, 320, 324–327m
    450
monetary
    linkages, 493, 497
    policy, and, 464, 482–483,
        496–497, 499, 514, 557,
        563–564
    risks, 496
Montreal Protocol, 421
moral hazard, 450, 461, 473
multilateral institutions, 458–460
mutual funds, 242–243, 259–261,
    288, 504, 513

N
Nationally Determined Contributions
    (NDCs), 345, 542
national wealth, 482–483, 514
natural disasters, 250, 337, 349, 443,
    450, 452, 460–461, 468–470, 474
natural resources, 60, 96, 138–139,
    186, 250, 312, 412, 415, 483–484,
    486–487, 491, 493, 498, 542–543
nature, 6, 16, 25, 47, 49, 59, 116,
    123, 127, 139–141, 166, 186, 189,
    201, 322, 341, 363, 393–395,
    413–414, 424, 430–432, 440, 445,
    447, 451, 454, 457, 460, 464,
    471–472, 475, 498, 524, 528
neoliberalism, 564
net asset value (NAV), 259
net zero, 306–307, 311–313, 317,
    319, 324, 330, 355, 367–368, 371,
    500, 542

net zero CO_2 emissions, 542
new deal, 20, 307, 525
nitrous oxide (N_2O), 314, 326, 539, 541
Non-Financial Reporting Directive (NFRD), 51, 55–56, 145
non-renewable natural resources, 491, 542
non-renewable resources, 398, 484, 486, 512
norms-based screening, 216, 218–219, 221–222
not-for-profit organizations, 226, 257, 564
nuclear power, 23, 320, 325, 337, 346

O

objectives approach (for sustainable finance instruments), 242
omnibus legislation, 526
open market, 524
operating management systems (OMS), 142, 182
opportunity costs, 276, 564
outcomes, 6, 83, 114, 118, 126–127, 138, 140–147, 173, 184–185, 188, 227, 230, 244, 266, 268, 270–271, 274, 301, 389, 398, 400, 404, 415, 433, 445, 482–483, 510, 514, 522, 524, 526, 544, 551

P

parametric insurance, 467, 469
Paris Agreement, 121, 211, 217, 229, 233, 294, 308, 311, 337, 345, 361, 367, 369, 419, 421, 444, 449, 534, 542, 547
partnerships, 30, 47–48, 108, 267, 510, 541, 546

perfect competition, 406, 564–565
permit, 425, 432
Philanthropic Enterprise Act, 106
philanthropist, 70
philanthropy, 65, 69–71, 225, 267, 270
physical risk, 120, 229, 354, 366, 449, 461, 486, 494–498
plan-do-check-act (PDCA) model, 172, 183
planet, people and profit, 66
point source (of pollution), 431
policy(ies), 3–4, 6–8, 23, 26, 50, 66, 75, 86, 98, 103, 105, 120, 131, 140, 158, 175, 179, 184, 204, 209–210, 222, 229, 232–233, 267, 272, 295, 301, 318, 323, 336–337, 354, 361–365, 367–368, 370–371, 373, 396, 402–403, 405, 411–435, 440–445, 447, 451, 453, 455–456, 458–460, 462–464, 467–476, 482–485, 489–490, 493, 497, 499, 502, 505, 509–510, 512–514, 521–529
policymakers, 8, 30, 73, 109, 202, 204, 412–413, 424–433, 435, 447, 451, 454–455, 457, 459, 475, 491–492, 523
political agenda, 7, 307
polluter-pays principle, 395–396
pollution, 4, 22–23, 71, 120, 122, 125, 133, 139, 143, 159, 195–197, 209, 212, 228, 272, 306, 309, 312, 390–391, 402–403, 412, 417, 423, 426–435, 484–485, 488, 492–493, 502–503, 508–511, 534, 539, 566
populist, 526
poverty, 4, 10–11, 25–27, 29–30, 65, 250, 344, 458, 464

precautionary principle, 394, 543
price of nature, 393–395
primary market, 199–200, 203
primum non nocere, 522, 529
principal, 246, 255–256, 347, 425,
    441, 450, 463, 469, 472, 474, 501,
    551, 560
Principles for Responsible Investment
    (PRI), 46, 158, 207–208, 288, 300,
    543
privatization, 526
privatizing, 526
profit, 63, 65, 67–68, 95, 105–106,
    127, 135, 142, 175, 292, 397, 399,
    405, 529, 552, 565
profitability, 2–3, 5, 68, 114, 116–
    128, 130, 138–139, 143–144, 147,
    166, 229, 232, 272, 323, 413, 485,
    487, 495, 508, 528
property rights, 390–391, 395, 401,
    511, 526
protectionism, 523
Public Benefit Corporations (PBCs),
    49, 105
public finance, 441, 556
public intervention, 395
public-private partnerships, 30, 510
public sector risks, 495

R
rate of return, 123, 140, 226, 464,
    476, 506, 512, 565
regulation(s), 2–4, 18, 23, 50, 53, 56,
    59, 61, 73–76, 104–107, 118, 120,
    123, 125, 132, 135, 140, 146–147,
    196, 202, 204–207, 210–212, 216,
    229, 233, 259, 272, 308, 350, 353,
    355–356, 360, 364, 391, 395, 397,
    401–403, 405, 411–435, 461, 490,
    500, 506–508, 513, 515

renewable energy, 7, 17, 60, 95, 122,
    206, 217, 223–224, 233, 242, 254,
    261, 266, 273, 277, 283, 306,
    319–321, 324–325, 328, 330,
    344–345, 355, 359–360, 363, 371,
    418, 427, 441, 492, 509, 511, 543,
    546, 566
renewable natural resources, 483,
    487, 491, 493, 543–544
renewable resources, 398, 482–486,
    491–494, 497, 499, 501, 507–508,
    512, 514, 526–527, 543
renewables, 217, 319, 325, 361
resilience, 2, 10, 187, 190, 310, 360,
    363, 371, 373, 449, 453, 455, 458,
    460, 468–474, 485
responsible investment, 46, 100, 158,
    205, 207–208, 210, 213–214, 232,
    242, 268, 288, 292, 300, 365, 504,
    538, 543
return on sustainability investment
    (ROSI), 156
risk and return, 200–201, 243, 245
risk appetite, 201, 258, 260
risk management, 3, 6, 50–51, 89, 99,
    119, 121, 130, 143, 146–147, 160,
    164, 171–191, 196–197, 228, 231,
    352, 370, 373, 459, 469, 554, 700
rule(s), 255, 258, 395–396, 415
rulemaking, 414–422

S
scenario analysis, 353, 442, 452–453,
    458–460, 464, 476
scenario analysis (in the context of
    climate risks), 452–453
Scope 1 (in context of Greenhouse
    Gas Protocol), 318, 540
Scope 2 (in context of Greenhouse
    Gas Protocol), 318, 540

Scope 3 (in context of Greenhouse Gas Protocol), 318, 540

secondary market, 199–200, 203, 225, 243, 253, 256, 269

Securities and Exchange Commission (SEC), 104, 176, 352, 357, 424, 506

security, 11, 175, 182, 202, 246, 423, 484, 506, 522, 565

SFDR Regulation (EU) 2019/2088259

shareholder activism, 288–290, 293–294, 300

shareholder advocacy, 544, 546

shareholder engagement, 3, 7, 48, 209, 213, 217–218, 220, 223, 227, 229, 257, 268, 270, 276, 287–302, 544

shareholder resolutions, 50, 270, 297, 365, 367

single-issue capture, 482, 499, 502–503, 513–514

single materiality, 42

small and medium-size enterprises (SMEs), 44–45, 82

Smith, Adam, 390, 524–525

social bonds, 249–250, 253

Social Bonds Principles (SBP), 250

social cost of carbon, 18, 357, 392–393

social entrepreneurs, 70, 85–86, 94–95, 97, 103, 109

social entrepreneurship, 70, 85, 94, 97, 103, 109

social impact bond, 544

socialism, 563

social loan principles (SLP), 252

social loans, 249, 252

socially responsible investing (SRI), 7, 116, 196, 208, 221, 365, 545

social price, 392

solar (power), 361, 371, 511, 543

sole proprietorships, 47–48

spill-over effect, 484, 492

spill over risks, 494

stakeholder theory, 43, 49, 63, 66–68, 70, 75

standards, 4, 11, 54–55, 59, 63, 106, 117, 121, 125, 134–136, 143, 147, 157, 160, 163, 172, 176, 178–187, 189–190, 222, 268, 272, 275, 277–278, 300, 353, 357, 398–399, 401, 413, 417, 424, 428–429, 451, 538, 541, 545

start-up, 48, 254

state enterprises, 526

statute, 415–417, 425

stock, 48, 56, 121, 127, 130–134, 157, 176, 200, 203, 209–210, 223, 242–243, 258–259, 275–276, 292, 313, 367, 392, 431, 504, 543, 559, 565

storage (energy), 17, 320, 325–326, 361

stranded assets, 8, 18, 119, 121, 229, 321

stress testing, 448, 460

strong sustainability, 114–115, 132, 141, 160, 226–227, 394–395

structural resilience, 458, 468–469

structural transformation, 521

subsidiary, 418, 565–566

subsidies, 402, 413, 426–427, 433–434, 464, 489–490, 510–513, 515, 522, 524–526, 528–529

surveillance process, 470–475

sustainability, 1–30, 41–78, 81–109, 113–147, 155–167, 171–191, 195–233, 241–261, 265–284, 287–302, 305–330, 335–374,

387–406, 411–435, 439–477,
  481–515, 521–529
Sustainability Accounting Standards
  Board (SASB), 55, 117, 135, 353,
  545
sustainability bond, 249–250, 545
sustainability data, 53, 57
sustainability disclosure framework,
  42–43, 54–55, 210
sustainability impacts, 3, 42, 51, 146,
  186–187, 204, 217
sustainability-linked bond principles
  (SLBP), 253
sustainability-linked bonds, 248–249,
  252–253, 546
sustainability-linked loan principles
  (SLLP)
sustainability-linked loans, 253
sustainability reporting, 53–59, 65,
  145, 216, 298
sustainability-themed, 217–218,
  223–224, 257, 545
sustainable activities, 217, 306–309
sustainable bonds or loans, 242,
  248–249, 253
sustainable business, 6, 42–43, 46,
  69, 71–72, 76, 156–157, 161–163,
  166, 172, 305–330, 483
sustainable development, 4–5, 10,
  12–29, 61, 82–84, 94–97, 102, 104,
  108–109, 172, 187, 209, 211, 217,
  223, 266, 283, 288, 317, 336, 419,
  422, 527, 534
sustainable development goals
  (SDGs), 10, 13, 29–30, 57, 61, 83,
  98–99, 211, 217, 225, 288, 460,
  500–502, 535
sustainable entrepreneurs, 96–97,
  107–109

sustainable entrepreneurship, 96–97,
  108–109
sustainable finance, 2–3, 5–6, 53, 58,
  74, 100, 116, 182, 195–233, 254,
  256–257, 266, 269–270, 308, 324,
  419–420, 544, 546
Sustainable Finance Disclosure
  Regulation (SFDR), 206–207, 212
sustainable investing, 3, 6–7, 42, 48,
  53, 60, 70, 101, 117, 124, 130, 197,
  205–208, 210, 212–217, 219, 221,
  223, 225–228, 242–243, 258–261,
  289, 291–293, 302, 305, 360, 420,
  504, 506, 512, 540, 546, 566
system, 13, 68, 72–73, 76, 96, 122,
  133, 139, 145, 172, 176, 178–179,
  182–185, 188–189, 197, 199,
  201–205, 208, 211–212, 226, 229,
  232, 308–311, 337, 345–346, 351,
  353, 356, 373, 403, 415, 418, 423,
  427, 448–449, 460, 487, 497,
  524–525, 553, 563
systemic risk, 136, 202, 321, 353,
  373, 448–449

T
tariffs, 524, 562
Task Force on Climate-Related
  Financial Disclosures (TCFD),
  318, 353, 355
taxes, 18, 47–48, 106, 198, 354, 364,
  402, 426–427, 429, 432, 462–463,
  509–510, 523, 561, 564–565
tenor, 201
territorial expansion, 523
The Wealth of Nations, 524
timeframe or time horizon (for an
  investment), 5, 141, 200–201, 207,
  527

tipping point(s), 7, 312, 317, 330, 394–395, 445, 477

trading programs, 426–428, 431

transaction, 18, 200, 203, 257, 388–390, 396, 510, 566

transition risk, 8, 120–121, 229, 321, 354, 371, 448–449, 482, 486, 489–498

transition strategies, 490

transportation or transport, 5–7, 14, 17, 25, 115, 122, 186, 213, 233, 257, 312, 314–315, 319–320, 325–327, 330, 344, 346, 351, 356, 361, 367, 371, 416, 432, 560

triple bottom line, 65, 83–84, 87, 96, 266, 501, 528, 546, 566–567

tropospheric ozone (O3), 313, 315, 340

trustee, 291, 567

U

uncertainty, 16, 134, 159, 173–174, 177, 185, 189–190, 201, 358, 392–394, 415, 423, 432, 440, 442, 447, 452, 454, 475–476, 490, 493, 497, 499, 543

unemployment, 203, 482–483, 499, 514, 562–563

UN Framework Convention on Climate Change, 342, 421

Unicorns, 45–46, 567

United Nations Environment Programme (UNEP), 84, 209, 211, 406, 420, 540, 543, 547

United Nations Environment Programme Finance Initiative (UNEPFI), 209, 547

United Nations Framework Convention on Climate Change (UNFCCC), 211, 337, 392, 537, 541–542, 547

United Nations General Assembly (UNGA), 422

United Nations Global Compact (UNGC), 547

United Nations supported Principles for Responsible Investment (PRI), 46, 207–208, 210

United Nations Sustainable Stock Exchanges (SSE), 211

unsustainable, 10, 485, 490, 493, 499–500, 526

Use-of-Proceeds approach (for sustainable finance instruments), 242

V

valley of death, 75, 87, 89, 255

valuation, 3, 5, 8, 114, 119, 121, 128, 131–132, 139, 142, 147, 158, 173, 179–180, 187–188, 199–200, 229, 232, 250, 254, 256, 277, 281, 283, 393, 416, 461, 485, 498, 506, 567–568

value-driven, 7, 60

value driver model, 146–147

value-first, 2, 42, 60, 117, 134, 147, 217

value investing, 567–568

Value Reporting Foundation, 55

valueS-driven, 7, 60–61, 63, 72, 212, 227

valueS-first, 2, 43, 60, 117, 133–134, 217

venture capital, 7, 45, 75, 90, 200, 231, 243, 255, 257, 259, 276, 293, 568

voluntary actions, 430

W
warrants, 59, 127, 568
Washington Consensus, 526
waste, 6, 83, 98, 122, 124, 136, 143,
   157, 160, 164–165, 206, 224, 251,
   254, 306, 309–312, 325, 327, 330,
   362–363, 416–417, 419–420, 422,
   426, 429, 484, 486, 492–493, 508,
   511, 536
water, 4, 13, 18–21, 25, 65, 83, 95,
   135–136, 138, 156, 160, 164–165,
   206, 212, 223–224, 254, 275, 309,
   311–313, 323, 338, 347, 350,
   360–362, 371, 389, 391, 394, 396,
   401–402, 412, 414, 416–417, 423,
   425–426, 428, 430, 433, 484,
   487–488, 491–493, 508, 545–546,
   566
weak sustainability, 394–395
wind (power), 360, 373
World Bank, 26, 230, 248, 361–362,
   372–373, 458, 460, 468–469, 486

Y
yield, 14–15, 85, 119, 123, 133, 203,
   231, 311, 313, 397, 402, 568

World Scientific Series in Health Investment and Financing

(Continued from page ii)

Forthcoming

Financing Universal Access to Healthcare: A Comparative Review of Incremental Health Insurance Reforms in the OECD
 Alexander S. Preker

Capital Finance in the Health Industry: A User Manual for Investors and Companies
 Alexander S. Preker and Les Funtleyder

Handbook on Health System Financing and Organization
 Dov Chernichovsky

How Health Aid Meets the Challenge of Mixed Health Systems: Reluctant Partners
 April Harding

Printed in the USA
CPSIA information can be obtained
at www.ICGtesting.com
JSHW011403271123
52336JS00001B/1